Iron Age Communities
in Britain

Iron Age Communities in Britain

An account of England, Scotland and Wales from the seventh century BC until the Roman conquest

Barry Cunliffe

Professor of European Archaeology in the University of Oxford

Book Club Associates London

This edition published 1975 by
Book Club Associates
by arrangement with
Routledge & Kegan Paul Ltd.
Printed in Great Britain by
Redwood Burn Limited, Trowbridge & Esher

Who the first inhabitants of Britain were,
whether natives or immigrants, remains obscure;
one must remember we are dealing with barbarians.

Tacitus, *Agricola*, 2

Contents

Plates

Text figures

Introduction

When, in 1969, I mentioned to my colleague Leo Rivet that I was thinking of writing a book on the British Iron Age, he said that it could not be done. Now that I have finished the work, I am inclined to agree with him. To write a complete account of the period *is* impossible. Thought on the subject is changing rapidly; established dictums which have found worldwide support for decades are being overthrown; and new ways are developing for looking at familiar material. While the actual body of data increases only gradually, the new questions now being asked of it are enlarging our understanding dramatically. Indeed, some might consider it to be too early to write a book such as this, but since it will *always* be too early a beginning must be made sometime.

The most difficult problem to be faced in producing a work of this kind lies in selecting and balancing the material. Three types of selection have been made here. First, Ireland has been omitted, partly through problems of space and partly because I have no first-hand familiarity of the sites and material. Second, I have attempted to limit comment on the vast mass of interpretive writing which befogs the actual data and much of which is now redundant, always preferring to begin with the factual material and build up to a synthesis. It is surprisingly difficult to distinguish fact from interpretation in many examples of the earlier publication of primary material. The third type of selection is liable to be more open to criticism – that is the actual choice of which evidence to include and which to leave out. Any such choice is likely to be biased by personal interests. I can only hope that I have given a balanced review of the material and have done justice to most of the major issues and problems.

The arrangement of the book falls into two parts. Chapters 2 to 9 deal with Britain from a chronological and regional standpoint, underlining minor points of difference from one area or period to another, while chapters 10 to 16 are concerned with the broader mechanisms at work which tend to slur over the minor differences. The problems of constructing theoretical models are referred to in the historical chapter 1 and again finally in chapter 17. Such an approach, while necessitating some repetition, has the advantage of allowing the threads to be more loosely spread out for examination. The fabric of which they form a part is, and should remain, loosely knit.

To be of any lasting value, a work of this kind should be thoroughly illustrated and referenced and periodically revised. The publishers have encouraged the first and will, I hope, subsequently request the second. One slightly novel procedure has been adopted with regard to the referencing of sites. To include references in the text would be unnecessarily cumbersome, particularly when several locations are mentioned in a single line. Instead, a list of principal sites is provided in appendix C, in which the major published sources are given. Similarly, with radiocarbon dates, the nature of the sample, the laboratory number and other details are all given in a separate appendix (B). The illustration of a large quantity of pottery referred to in the main text has also been relegated to an appendix (A).

Finally, I would like to thank the large number of individuals and institutions who have helped during the preparation of this work and in particular those museum staffs who have allowed me to work through their reserve collections, making the occasion as comfortable as possible. Several bodies have been kind enough to supply photographs from which the plates have been reproduced, and one need hardly emphasise the enormous debt of gratitude to those authors whose illustrations have been re-drawn for the text figures, an undertaking in which I was considerably aided by the Carto-graphic Unit of the Department of Geography, University of Southampton, who undertook to add the lettering and scales. Lastly, I would like to thank Frances Cunliffe and Denise Brenchley for translating the manuscript of this book into a typescript, and to Jane Holdsworth for her help and advice in all aspects of the work during the last stages of preparation.

Southampton,   BARRY CUNLIFFE
31 December 1971

Chapter 1

The Development of Iron Age Studies

It is not proposed in this chapter to indulge in an extensive and somewhat incestuous examination of the growth of Iron Age studies in Britain simply for the sake of conventional completeness, nor for the specious exercise of holding up to ridicule the views of previous generations who have written on the subject. But some idea of how patterns of thought have developed to their present state is essential, not only because the models of the past have necessarily influenced the interpretations, and indeed the gathering, of the facts, but also because current views may tend to overreact against established dogma.

That an 'Iron Age' existed at all was suggested by the Danish archaeologist, C. J. Thomsen in a book published in 1836, but it was not until G. Ramsauer's excavation at Hallstatt between 1846 and 1862, and the discoveries made at La Tène in 1858, that any permanent chronological divisions could be made. Then followed several schemes: C. Schumacher divided the Hallstatt material into four groups: A (1000–800 BC), B (800–700), C (700–600) and D (600–500); while G. O. A. Montelius, working on French discoveries, propounded three periods for the La Tène epoch: I (400–250 BC), II (250–150 BC) and III (150–1 BC). Subsequently P. Reinecke, J. Déchelette, R. Viollier and others evolved finer and differing classifications influenced by new material and by regional considerations. It was against this background that the British finds came to be interpreted.

The first half of the nineteenth century saw the gradual amassing in museums and private collections of quantities of Iron Age finds, usually tools, weapons and art objects, brought together by casual discovery and by the pilferings of the early barrow diggers like the Rev. E. W. Stilling-fleet, who managed to excavate between 100 and 200 barrows of the Arras culture between 1815 and 1817. Barrow-sacking in high Victorian style continued to produce Iron Age finds from east Yorkshire throughout the century, ending with the carefully observed researches of J. R. Mortimer, published between 1895 and 1911. But outside Yorkshire the British Iron Age was not susceptible to this type of acquisitive excavation, and the bulk of the finds continued to be made by accident. The emphasis of the early collectors was naturally enough upon the works of art. In 1857, the year before the discovery at La Tène, J. Thurnham listed objects of 'Late British Art' and even six years later, when Sir Wollaston Franks illustrated a series of La Tène objects at the British Museum, he was forced to refer to them as 'Late Keltic' for want of a more precise terminology. With the development of the continental Hallstatt and La Tène classifications after 1872, however, British archaeologists were provided with a simple system with which to compare their own material; thus gradually the European nomenclature gained acceptance.

In the second half of the nineteenth century, excavations began on occupation sites and hillforts in an attempt to understand the people and their way of life. This was a marked advance on the somewhat sterile art-historical approach. Between 1857 and 1858 the first large-scale excavation of a settlement site was undertaken at Standlake in Oxfordshire by Stephen Stone, in advance of gravel-working. Altogether 134 pits were exposed, and were duly reported to the Society of Antiquaries. Ten years after the Standlake excavation, a similar area of Iron Age settlement was cleared at Highfield, Fisherton, near Salisbury. At both sites it was naturally the more obvious features such as pits and gullies that were examined, but quantities of occupation rubbish were recovered and gradually the nature of Iron Age peasant settlement began to force itself on the attention of an archaeological world hitherto blinded by the quality of a few art objects.

The next major advances were made by General A. H. L. F. Pitt-Rivers. Following a meticulously recorded but relatively small-scale excavation at the Caburn, Sussex, in 1877–8 during which he had sectioned the ramparts as well as clearing out pits, he finally turned his attention to his Cranbourne Chase estates, where between 1880 and 1890 he totally excavated the two settlements of Woodcuts and Rotherley Down, and partially examined the hillfort at Winklebury (Pitt-Rivers, 1887; 1888). His work was of an exceptionally high standard and was published in a detailed manner never before achieved. It emphasised two things above all: the value of considering the commonly occurring debris of occupation as the principal means by which people and their lives could be reconstructed, and the importance of large-scale regional studies.

The last decade of the nineteenth century saw the unremitting development of these two principles. In Devon the Dartmoor Exploration Committee was set up in 1894, and within the first ten years of its existence had examined twenty sites and excavated nearly 150 hut circles, under the direction of S. Baring-Gould. At the turn of the century Baring-Gould extended his interests into south-west Wales with the excavations of the hillforts of St David's Head and Moel Trigarn. Other hillforts were now receiving attention: excavations at Worlebury in Somerset were published in 1902 at the same time as the first adequate consideration of Bigbury in Kent.

Pitt-Rivers's dictum of large-scale excavation was extended into Somerset by his assistant H. St George Gray who, in conjunction with A. Bulleid, began the famous excavations at the so-called Glastonbury Lake Village in 1892, work which was to continue until 1907 and was finally published in 1911 and 1917. Nor were regional studies neglected: in Wiltshire Benjamin Cunnington and his wife Maud undertook annually, an impressive series of excavations: Oliver's Camp (published 1908), Oare (1909), Knap Hill (1911), Casterley Camp (1913) and

Lidbury (1917), but the most famous of all was their work at All Canning Cross between 1911 and 1922, finally published in 1923. A two-year season at Hengistbury Head started in 1911 (Bushe-Fox, 1915); excavations began on the Somerset village of Meare under the direction of Bulleid and Gray in 1910, and between 1908 and 1912 the cave of Wookey Hole was carefully examined (Balch, 1914).

After the First World War, discoveries continued to be made and reported in increasing numbers: Hallstatt style pottery from Eastbourne, excavations at Abington Pigotts in Cambridgeshire, Park Brow in Sussex and Fifield Bavant in Wiltshire, all in 1924, and excavations at Swallowcliffe Down and Figsbury in Wiltshire in 1925. Thus by the year of the publication of the British Museum's *Guide to the Antiquities of the Early Iron Age* (R. A. Smith, 1925), a vast mass of material – common artefacts – had been amassed to redress the balance of the collectors' pieces, and it is much to the credit of Reginald Smith, the *Guide*'s compiler and a Deputy Keeper of the Museum, that so much was said of these common things. Iron Age communities were at last being considered in all their aspects.

With the rapid increase in the bulk of the potential evidence, classifications and interpretation developed in parallel. The turning point was undoubtedly the discovery in 1890 of the Belgic cemetery at Aylesford and its publication in the same year by A. J. (later Sir Arthur) Evans. The report was an outstanding contribution to Iron Age studies: in it Evans characterised the Aylesford people, showing their differences from the inhabitants of the rest of Britain, and tracing their immediate origins to northern France and ultimately back through the Marnian culture to the Illyro-Italic cultures of the fifth century. After a masterly consideration of the metalwork, he concluded that the Aylesford cemetery dated to after 150 BC and went on to link the Aylesford culture to the statement by Caesar that the coastal parts of Britain had been settled by Belgic invaders. In spite of a somewhat cursory treatment of the archaeological evidence by T. Rice Holmes in his famous work *Ancient Britain and the Invasions of Julius Caesar* (1907), Evans's conclusions were widely accepted and further consolidated by Reginald Smith's publication of the rich Belgic grave groups from Welwyn in 1912. Some geographical precision was given to the distribution of the Aylesford culture by Sir Cyril Fox in his *Archaeology of the Cambridge Region* (1923), but he retained reservations about their exact identity. New discoveries of a major cemetery at Swarling, Kent, in 1921 and its subsequent publication by J. P. Bushe-Fox in 1925, however, firmly established the Aylesford–Swarling culture as an intrusive element but refined Evans's dating, showing that there was nothing with the burials earlier than 75 BC.

With the demonstrable reality of a Belgic invasion and the growing awareness of the intrusive nature of the Arras culture represented in the La Tène style barrow cemeteries of Yorkshire, a climate of opinion arose in the first two decades of the twentieth century which considered invasion to be the principal, and sometimes the sole, cause of change. Such views were well rooted in the ideology of Victorian imperialism and, after all, nineteenth century colonial history could produce many striking parallels. In 1912 J. Abercromby suggested that the so-called Deverel–Rimbury urns were introduced into Britain from the Lausitz culture area of central Europe between 700 and 650 BC, and ten years later O. G. S. Crawford developed the invasion theory further by suggesting that the immigrants were Goidelic Celts, but arriving a century or so earlier, bringing with them weapon-types which characterised the Late Bronze Age. H. Peake elaborated the idea still further in *The Bronze Age and the Celtic World* (1922) in which, arguing principally from the evidence of the swords, he proposed three invasions: the first about 1200; the second about 900, bringing much of the Deverel–Rimbury assemblage; and the third about 300 BC, representing the intrusion of the Brythonic Celts, after iron and elements of the La Tène culture had already arrived as the result of trade.

Whilst the Abercromby–Crawford–Peake invasion hypothesis was evolving, discoveries were made at Hengistbury Head and All Cannings Cross of assemblages containing furrowed haematite-coated bowls and coarse finger-impressed wares. The continental Hallstatt analogies were at once evident. Moreover, the association at All Cannings Cross of haematite pottery, finger-impressed wares like Deverel–Rimbury types, and bronze implements suggested to some that the All Cannings Cross community represented an intrusive population, which Peake readily ascribed to his second invasion. Maud Cunnington summed up the situation in the following words (1923):

A big movement of people northwards on the continent, whether the incentive was search for better farming land, or mere love of adventure, was bound sooner or later to make itself felt in Britain. This invasion is not likely to have come about as a single incursion but ... by a long continued series of small incursions and colonisation.

So by 1925 linguistics, implement typology, settlement archaeology and historical parallels were in broad agreement: a complex of Late Bronze to Early Iron Age invasions led to the All Cannings Cross style of culture before the middle of the first millennium; an incursion from the Marne gave rise to the Yorkshire barrow culture in the third century; and colonisation by the Belgae absorbed the south-east of Britain in the first century.

The discoveries of the next five years were, however, to complicate the issue. Several new hillforts were being excavated, including Ham Hill, Somerset (1925–7); Chun, Cornwall (published 1927); the Caburn, Sussex (published 1927); Bury Hill, Glos (published 1929); the Trundle, Sussex (published 1929 and 1931); and St Catherine's Hill, Hants (excavated 1925–8 and published 1930). New groups of finds from occupation sites at Findon Park, Sussex, and Scarborough, Yorks, were published in 1928, while in the previous year Fox's paper on La Tène I fibulae had appeared. In this atmosphere of rapid new discovery Christopher Hawkes produced three important papers: the first, entitled 'The earliest Iron Age culture of Britain', appeared in the St Catherine's Hill report (Hawkes, Myres & Stevens, 1930); the second, 'Hill forts', was published in *Antiquity* for March 1931; while the third, written with Gerald Dunning and called 'The Belgae of Gaul and Britain', appeared in the *Archaeological Journal* in the same year. These three papers totally altered the direction of thought on the Iron Age and paved the way for the next three decades of constructive study. Taking account of all the evidence at the time available, a new scheme was proposed as a logical development of the invasion hypothesis bandied about somewhat loosely in the previous twenty years. Hawkes visualised a massive series of migratory movements among the Celts in central and northern Europe, beginning in the seventh century or before. 'It reached its height in the sixth century, when those groups who crossed over to Britain became our principal Early Iron Age immigrants.' Other Celts in the Late Hallstatt stage of culture who were displaced from France also migrated to Britain.

Thus was completed our widespread agglomeration of Late Hallstatt immigrant groups, predominantly Celtic in blood, but inevitably including other racial elements out of the melting pot of contemporary Europe. Fusing here and there with the Late Bronze Age peoples, they established Iron Age civilisation all over the south and south east of Britain . . . The main block of their area remained in their undisturbed tenure till the first century B.C., and their civilisation, though essentially of Hallstatt character, soon began to absorb influence from the La Tène culture across the Channel. Thus it really requires a name of its own: here we shall be content to call it 'Iron Age A', and the succeeding immigrant cultures 'Iron Age B' and 'C'. The former, in the south west and north east, merely bit into its fringes; it was only the latter, brought by the Belgae, that superseded it in its real home, and in some districts, notably east Sussex, it was never superseded at all till the Roman conquest (Hawkes, 1931, 64).

Hawkes, then, visualised a complex folk movement impinging in stages on south-east Britain in the sixth century, giving rise to his Iron Age A culture. Life was at times troubled and great hillforts had to be built, 'for as there was no doubt constant tribal bickering, warfare must always have been liable to spring from the background into the foreground of existence' (ibid., 76). Early in the fourth century a new invasion took place: La Tène peoples from Spain, the Atlantic seaboard and Brittany thrust their way into Cornwall (an idea put forward by E. T. Leeds in 1927, following his excavation at Chun Castle) and spread into Devon, Somerset, Dorset and the Cotswolds, 'absorbing or driving out such Iron Age A people as they found, and superseding their settlements' (ibid., 77). These were the Iron Age B people: Spanish La Tène I fibulae, distinctive decorated pottery and historical contacts connected with the tin trade could be

quoted in support of this view. In this country the south-western Iron Age B immigrants built great multivallate earthworks and lived in the Somerset lake villages, making highly ornamented pottery. The northern counterpart to the south-western B invasions came in the third century with the incursion of a band of immigrants from Gaul, spreading from Yorkshire to the Cambridge region. These northern Iron Age B peoples eventually linked up with the south-western invaders by means of the Jurassic zone, encircling the A people of the south-east.

The third major series of invasions, giving rise to Iron Age C, began in about 75 BC with the influx of Belgic tribesmen from northern Gaul initially into Kent and the Thames valley (Evans, 1890), spreading subsequently into Essex, the Fens and the Cherwell valley. Later, soon after Caesar's expedition, a second Belgic invasion – refugees from the Roman advance – took place further west (Bushe-Fox 1925) and spread from the Hampshire harbours into Huntingdonshire, Berkshire and Wiltshire, and probably west Wessex, with subsequent extensions into Dorset and some parts of Somerset.

This précis of the original ABC system has been laid out in some detail because the scheme was to serve as the basis of Iron Age studies in Britain for more than thirty years. The scheme was not revolutionary; it took over the main elements of the earlier historical model with a few additions. Its importance lay in its breakaway from the stranglehold of continental terminology and in its elegant simplicity. British Iron Age studies had at last come of age.

The restatement did not pass unchallenged: in 1932 Maud Cunnington (1932c) threw doubt upon the whole concept of a second Belgic invasion. She considered that the change to beadrimmed wheel-made pottery did not herald an incursion of new people, but merely a technological advance brought about by the introduction of the potter's wheel. Hawkes replied to her criticisms (Hawkes and Dunning, 1932) and the second Belgic invasion stayed.

The theorising and consolidation of 1930 and 1931 focused British archaeological activity firmly upon the problems of the Iron Age. Many relationships were hazy and some parts of the country were virtually unstudied. It was natural in such a climate that many excavators should decide to concentrate their energies upon Iron

Age sites. In the next decade the results were impressive. The publication of hillfort excavations came thick and fast. When Hawkes was writing in 1931 he could list only thirty-seven where the defences had been sectioned; in less than ten years the number had more than doubled.[1]

Not all the activity centred upon defended sites. Meon Hill, Kimmeridge, Twyford Down, Chysauster, Horsted Keynes and Little Woodbury – all open settlements – were excavated; old collections of material from Hunsbury and Spettisbury were published; a number of specific articles were written on metal objects, including the Llyn Fawr hoard and groups of swan's neck and ring-headed pins from various parts of the country (Dunning, 1934) and in 1933 Leeds published his book *Celtic Ornament*, summarising the main elements of British Iron Age art. Attempts were also made to collate the new material on a regional basis in articles like E. C. Curwen's 'The Iron Age in Sussex' (1939) and R. R. Clarke's 'The Iron Age in Norfolk and Suffolk' (1939). Finally, attention was being paid to Belgic settlement sites and their relationship to Roman urbanisation in the large and important excavations at Camulodunum and Verulamium, both of which began in 1930.

It is hardly surprising that such phenomenal activity and the vast increase in material available for study should demand the modification of the ABC system, put forward when relatively little data were to hand. The large-scale excavations at Maiden Castle forced the issue. In the first interim report (1935) R. E. M. (later Sir Mortimer) Wheeler proposed a threefold division of Iron Age A: A1 (600–400 BC) was typified by

the classic All Cannings Cross haematite-coated assemblage; A2 (400–200) was marked by derivatives of the sharp-shouldered situla types; while AB (200–early first century AD) showed a hybridisation of A2 and B ceramic forms. The next year the date of 200 was modified to 100, with the hint that the incoming cultural elements constituting the B assemblage may have been dislodged from Gaul by the invasions of the Cimbri and Teutones. The new subdivisions were widely accepted in southern Britain although Myres (1937, 26–7), writing of the pottery from Mount Farm, Dorchester, Oxon., found the system difficult to apply in the Oxford region. Curwen, in his *Archaeology of Sussex* (1937, 2nd ed. 1954), using the improved nomenclature to describe the finds from the South Downs and the Weald, proposed a further category, called ABC, which ran broadly parallel to La Tène III and showed an overlap in styles between the AB wares and Belgic C elements.

Iron Age B was similarly subdivided, but on a regional rather than a chronological basis. In the third interim report on Maiden Castle, Wheeler referred to 'that composite culture which, in Britain, has been named Early Iron Age B' (1937, 274). In the south-west, he suggested, there were in fact three groups: a *Cornish group* extending up the Bristol Channel to the Cotswolds at Bredon Hill, a *Glastonbury group* originating from refugee landings in the Lyme Bay and Exe valley region, and a *Wessex hillfort group* founded by a relatively few newcomers, 'since their culture . . . only slowly and incompletely modified the established A2 culture. But they were determined and masterful, and their influence upon the military aspect of Maiden Castle was immediate and drastic' (ibid., 275). He was referring to the remodelling of the defences in glacis style. In the definitive publication (Wheeler, 1943, 56), it was finally suggested that the immigrants were Venetic refugees ousted by Caesar's Gaulish campaigns.

The excavations at Bredon Hill, Glos, in 1935–7 refocused attention on the stamped wares of the south-west. Leeds (1927) had put forward the view that stamped ware was introduced by way of the Atlantic seaways, probably from Iberia, while in 1936 Donovan and Dunning had drawn attention to the rather different group of this general type found in the Cotswolds. Petrological examination implied contact with

---

[1] Hembury (published 1930–5), Cissbury, Salmonsbury and Chastleton (1931), Hollingbury Camp, Lydney and Chisbury (1932), Llanmelin, Thundersbarrow, Yarnbury and Chisenbury Trendle (1933), Little Solisbury (1935), Maiden Castle, Bickerton (1934, 1935), Bigbury and Buckland Rings (1936), Harrow Hill and the Breiddin (1937), Bredon Hill (1938), Quarley, Castle Hill (Newhaven), the Caburn, Oldbury, the Knave, Highdown, Castle Hill (Almondbury) and Sudbrook (1939), Balksbury, Gurnard's Head, Poundbury, Bury Hill and Cherbury (1940). Several other important excavations carried out during the decade were published later: Chalbury, excavated 1939 (1943); Pen Dinas, excavated 1933–7 (1963); Castle Ditch (Eddisbury), excavated 1935–8 (1950); Ffridd Faldwyn, excavated 1937–9 (1942). Other equally important excavations have never been fully published.

Cornwall. (More recent work (Peacock, 1968) has, however, disproved the Cornish connections). At Bredon Mrs T. C. Hencken was able to define two pottery styles: linear tooled wares, which she called Iron Age A (more strictly, the parallels were with the AB wares only then being defined in the south), and duck-stamped wares. The former she considered to be the product of the native population, the latter an importation by immigrants coming from the Breton area *c.* 100–50 BC by way of the Bristol Channel. It was on the basis of this evidence that Wheeler proposed his 'Cornish group'.

The complexities of Iron Age B were further developed by the work of J. B. Ward-Perkins (1938; 1939) and Hawkes (1939a) in their discussion of material from south-eastern Britain. Describing pottery from Crayford, Ward-Perkins drew together a group of similar highly decorated vessels distributed principally in Sussex, Kent and Essex, calling them *South-eastern B* in contrast to the decorated pottery of the Glastonbury group. As to its origins, he concluded: '. . . it does seem more probable that . . . the pottery of the Crayford type represents an intrusive element, than that it was evolved spontaneously from the preceding culture. The source of this intrusive element can hardly as yet be defined' (1938, 156). A year later Hawkes published his considerations of the Caburn pottery (1939a) and in it stated firmly his belief that the south-eastern B wares were introduced by intrusive people, who were probably displaced from Armorica by Caesar in the middle of the first century. Following the excavations at Oldbury, Ward-Perkins defined another group – the *Wealden culture* – typified by plain vessels with foot-rings, which he concluded was earlier than south-eastern B and had spread to the Weald from Sussex (1938, 152–5; 1944, 146).

At the same time Hawkes's work on the pottery and finds from various of the Sussex sites (1939a) and from Worth in Kent (1940a) led him to the view that:

About 250 B.C. an incursion of Iron Age B Celtic peoples from the continent, after first forcing all the South Downs peoples to defend themselves by building hillforts, was successful in establishing a new domination in the Cissbury region of central Sussex, depopulating the Brighton region and leaving the Caburn I folk as an isolated group of Iron Age A culture in East Sussex (1939a, 241).

The invasion was by 'Marnians' from northern Gaul and for the resulting hybrid he adopted Curwen's term 'AB' (after Wheeler, 1935). 'But,' he warns, 'the A-B-C terminology is no more than a set of symbols for use while we are feeling our way towards the correct identification of culture-groups defined in factual terms of time and space. Now that such culture-groups are beginning to acquire definition of that order, we ought not to hesitate to give them regional names to which, according to established archaeological usage, they are thereby entitled' (1939a, 238–9). He goes on to suggest that 'Iron Age AB' in Sussex includes the *Wealden culture* in the north-west and the *Cissbury culture* in the central area.

By 1940, then, the southern British Iron Age was still thought of in terms of the three basic cultural groups suggested ten years earlier: Iron Age A, approximately equivalent to the continental Hallstatt culture, Iron Age B, running parallel to La Tène I and II, and Iron Age C, reflecting La Tène III. But an unprecedented spate of excavation had so complicated the picture that each of the three broad divisions was now thought to be the result of multiple incursions of invaders, who could be recognised and defined by their pottery types.

In northern Britain the pace of Iron Age research was more leisurely. After the pioneer work of John Williams on vitrified forts (1777), D. Christison's survey of hillforts (1898) and R. Munro's publication of his work on crannogs (1882), little advance was made until V. Gordon Childe began a series of hillfort excavations: Earn's Heugh (Childe & Forde, 1932), Castle Law Fort (1933) and Finavon (1935b) followed by Rahoy (Childe & Thorneycroft, 1938), where he carried out experiments into the nature of vitrification, and Kaimes hillfort (1941). It was in 1935 that he published his celebrated *Prehistory of Scotland*, in which for the first time he arranged the Scottish Iron Age against the general background of British and European development, defining a native continuum represented by the continued occupation of the hilltop towns and crannogs, upon which two major intrusive elements impinged. In the east he recognised an *Abernethy complex* consisting of the vitrified forts and a scatter of La Tène artefacts, while in the west and north lay the *castle complex* of brochs, duns and wheelhouses with their associations of bone artefacts similar in form to those from south-west Britain. To Childe, then, the more distinctive characteristics of the Scottish Iron Age were introduced from the south of Britain during the latter part of the first millennium.

The next decade in the south saw little change in established views and the publication of comparatively little new material. Regional surveys were being undertaken in Oxfordshire (Bradford, 1942a) and the Isle of Purbeck (Calkin, 1949), and W. J. Varley (1950b) produced a lengthy consideration of the hillforts of the Welsh Marches, in which he suggested the diffusion of the hillforts architecture from a 'primary area of contour hillforts' in Hampshire, Wiltshire and Sussex into Dorset, Surrey, the Welsh borderland, north Wales and the Midlands, taking place some time before 100 BC. About 100 BC or soon after he proposed a second diffusion, this time from the south-west peninsula into the Bristol Channel area and west Wales. Other notable contributions of the period concentrated on non-ceramic material. D. F. Allen published his definitive account of 'The Belgic dynasties of Britain and their coins' in 1944: Fox described the metalwork of the Llyn Cerrig hoard in a monograph published in 1946; and A. S. Henshall examined the problems of textiles and weaving in an article which appeared in 1950.

Although it is true that there was more diversification of interest, hillfort excavation continued, at Blewburton Hill (sporadically), Highdown, High Rocks, Breedon-on-the-Hill and elsewhere. In her publication of the last-named site, Dr K. M. Kenyon appended an analysis of the pottery of the area, defining a *Trent valley* regional group which was culturally Iron Age A but so dissimilar to that from sites further to the south that she suggested an invasion 'at a late date from a backward area of the Low Countries' in the first century BC into the central Midlands, 'an area apparently hitherto unoccupied by Iron Age people. Here they developed a fairly widespread, but crude and unprogressive culture, which may have lasted until the Roman conquest' (1950, 67). In 1952 she extended her study of the earliest Iron Age material in an important article, 'The chronology of Iron Age A', setting out broad ideas on a number of regional 'A' groups and calling for a complete redating. In Sussex she discussed the idea of a Marnian invasion, concluding: 'It is therefore suggested that in the South Downs area, as in Wessex, Iron Age A lasted down, without any supervening AB or Cissbury culture, until the first century BC' (Kenyon, 1952, 58). The article was essentially an attempt to bring the existing ABC framework into line with new discoveries. The essentials of the invasion hypotheses remained unchallenged.

The nineteen-fifties saw increased interest in hillfort excavation. Sutton Walls and several neighbouring sites were examined between 1948 and 1951, Hod Hill between 1951 and 1958. Excavations at Blewburton Hill continued to be published in 1947, 1953 and 1959, and Little Solisbury in 1957 and 1962; more limited programmes were undertaken at Blackbury, Devon (published 1955), St Mawgan, Cornwall (1957), Wandlebury, Cambs (1957), Poston, Herefordshire (1958), etc. Several papers on the regional groupings of hillforts were now published. Dr M. A. Cotton discussed Cornish cliff castles (1959), Gloucestershire hillforts (1961a), Wealden forts (1961b) and Berkshire forts (1962), while Lady Fox considered the south-western multiple-enclosure forts (1953 and 1961b). Regional variations in style and function were now being emphasised.

Large-scale examination of settlement sites was becoming more widespread, no doubt encouraged by the impressive results of G. Bersu's excavation of Little Woodbury (1940). The work at Kestor on Dartmoor (1954), Bodrifty, Cornwall (1957), Itford Hill, Sussex (1957) and Staple Howe, Yorks (1963) marked an important advance in our understanding of social structures and economy. There was an increase too in the number of articles on Iron Age metalwork, culminating in a detailed study of art and technology in Sir Cyril Fox's *Pattern and Purpose* (1958).

The reviving interest in the problems of subsistence economy and class structure, which these developments encouraged, was reflected in more studies biased towards understanding the economic basis, an approach which received an added stimulus from J. G. D. Clark's *Prehistoric Europe, the Economic Basis* (1952). Since before the war, many of the better excavation reports had contained brief summaries of the faunal and floral remains, and sometimes of the mollusca which served as an indication of environmental conditions, but no attempts were made to synthesise or assess the data statistically until H. Helbaek produced a valuable account of the early crops in southern Britain (1953). Even now, adequate studies of animal bones are sadly lacking. The nature of arable farming in the south has, however, received attention from E. S. Applebaum in his studies of field systems near Sidbury (1955), from Lady Fox, writing of farms and fields on Dartmoor (1955), and from H. C. Bowen in several important papers including *Ancient Fields* (1961), and more recently 'The Celtic background' (1969). The work has not yet been extended in detail to other environments.

Tribal organisation and political structure were also examined in several articles, beginning with a general survey of the tribes of southern Britain (Radford, 1955). D. F. Allen's work on coinage has subsequently extended the picture still further with 'The origins of coinage in Britain: a reappraisal' (1961a), 'A study of the Dobunnic coinage' (1961b), an article and maps issued with the Ordnance Survey's *Map of southern Britain in the Iron Age* (1962), *The coins of the Coritani* (1963), 'The chronology of Durotrigian coinage' (1968b), 'The coins of the Iceni' (1970) and 'British potin coins: a review' (1971); together these papers provide an essential historical basis for the first centuries BC and AD.

The post-war period in northern Britain was highly productive for Iron Age studies. In the east of Scotland, extending down to Northumberland and Durham, extensive field-work was undertaken leading to the publication of important regional surveys (Jobey, 1962a, 1965, 1966a, 1966b, 1971; and RCHM(S) *Stirlingshire*, 1963, *Roxburghshire*, 1956, *Selkirkshire*, 1957, *Peeblesshire*, 1967), while in parallel a programme of excavation was carried out to examine the range and development of the smaller fortified settlements. Between 1950 and 1970 about twenty settlements had been excavated.[1] As a result, it was now realised that homesteads and hamlets, defended first by palisades and later by earthworks, were densely distributed over much of the area and that they must have had a considerable ancestry. Paucity of material culture, however, prevented firm dating until the first radiocarbon dates became available (MacKie, 1969), showing that their origins lay in the sixth century or earlier.

The west and north of Scotland, the area of brochs, wheelhouses and duns, was also intensively studied, beginning with two papers by Sir Lindsey Scott (1947 and 1948) in which he put forward the view of colonisation from the southwest. New evidence from the excavations at Jarlshof (1956) and Clickhimin (1968) led to a more extensive reassessment. In 1964 A. Young published her survey of brochs and duns, and in the following year E. MacKie's important and detailed consideration entitled 'The origin and development of the broch and wheelhouse building cultures of the Scottish Iron Age' appeared (1965a). He rejected the idea of late colonists bringing broch architecture with them, and instead suggested a local development arising from hillfort traditions. The material culture, he felt, was however derived from the south. Regional differences brought out by these two areas of study were formalised by Stuart Piggott (1956) when he proposed four major regions in Scotland: Atlantic, Solway–Clyde, Tyne–Forth and north-eastern.

In southern Britain the advances made to general Iron Age theory in the immediate post-war period were considerable. Some modifications had been made to the ABC classifications like those proposed by Kenyon and noted above. Kenyon (1954) had also introduced the term *Bristol Channel B* for both the linear pottery and the duck-stamped wares, which she regarded as co-intrusive into the Severn region, while J. W. Brailsford (1958a) distinguished the Iron Age C *Durotrigian culture* of Dorset from the Iron Age C Belgic cultures further east. In addition to the cultural-historical ABC scheme of description and classification, archaeologists were now developing other, broader approaches based on the classic definitions of 'culture' and upon systems of trading, subsistence economy and political organisation.

In this atmosphere of change, the Council for British Archaeology held a conference entitled 'The Problems of the Iron Age in Southern Britain' in December 1958, which was subsequently published in 1961 (ed. S. S. Frere). The central paper at the conference, 'The ABC

---

[1] Including Hownam Rings (1950), Bonchester Hill (1952), Castle Law (1954), Huckhoe (1959), Harchope (1962), West Brandon (1962), Alnham (1966) and Burradon (1970).

of the British Iron Age', was given by Hawkes. In this he restated the ABC model in a more advanced form, enlarging upon ideas which he had previously placed in outline form before the International Congress at Madrid in 1954 (Hawkes, 1956). Taking note of the increasing desire for regional definition, he divided Britain south of the Tyne into five provinces, subdivided into thirty regions. This formed the horizontal structure of a grid, the vertical element being provided by a fixed series of periods further divided into phases and sub-phases. Within the three-dimensional framework thus formed, the cultural material, still described in ABC terms, could be supported. To avoid confusion with the regional and chronological numbering schemes, Hawkes proposed that the cultural letters should be prefixed with an ordinal number; thus 'A1' now became 'First A'. Regional differences could be brought out by adding a geographical prefix such as 'eastern First A' or 'southern First A'. 'The whole array of determinable cultures, lastly, like the hanks of an embroiderer's coloured wools or silks, has to be stitched on to the net of absolute time, which our frame of Periods and Phases holds stretched between its bars' (Hawkes, 1959). He followed his summary of the new method of classification with a short historical outline demonstrating the way in which the existing material could neatly be fitted into the classificatory structure.

The newly formulated scheme, first published in *Antiquity* in 1959, was generally adopted: T. C. M. Brewster (1963) used it to describe the Yorkshire material published in his report on Staple Howe; Cotton (1961a) based her consideration of the Cotswold finds and sites firmly on the new scheme, and when in October 1961 a second CBA conference was held on the problems of the Iron Age in northern Britain, Piggott projected the classification to Scotland (S. Piggott, 1966). The most extended treatment of the Iron Age in terms of the restated ABC was provided by Frere in the introductory chapters of *Britannia* (1967).

But in other circles some disquiet was becoming manifest. In 1960 F. R. Hodson offered a number of theoretical criticisms based upon the fear that the rigidity of the framework would obscure the true pattern of Iron Age cultures. 'Might it not, after all, be both simpler and more objective', he asked, 'to define cultural groups in

the accepted way, by starting with type-sites and type-fossils . . . Cultural boundaries could then be defined by the distribution of type-fossils and not by fixed "provinces" or "regions", and a different pattern for the British Iron Age might emerge' (1960, 140). Hodson was in fact making a plea, much as Hawkes had done in 1939 (p. 6 above), for the introduction of a classic 'cultural' model of the type formalised by Childe. A few years later he provided an outline for testing this approach (1964), in which he proposed an indigenous *Woodbury culture* developing in the seventh century out of native traditions divisible only in terms of regional pottery styles. Upon this was imposed a possible group of Hallstatt adventurers, the La Tène I and II *Arras culture* of Yorkshire and the La Tène III *Aylesford–Swarling culture* centred upon Kent, Hertfordshire and Essex. Both the Arras culture and the Aylesford–Swarling culture were at this time receiving detailed study as the subjects of doctoral theses subsequently published as *The La Tène Cultures of Eastern Yorkshire* (Stead, 1965) and 'The Aylesford–Swarling culture: the problem of the Belgae reconsidered' (Birchall, 1965). Later MacKie extended the general concept of broadly defined cultures to Scotland by defining three substantially indigenous groups: the *broch culture*, the *Abernethy culture* and the *Hownam culture* (1969).

Chronological divisions were more difficult to define but Hodson recognised three horizons indicated by the presence of imported metalwork, which could be used to distinguish three periods. The first, or *earliest pre-Roman Iron Age* phase, began with the appearance of Hallstatt C types; the second, or *earlier pre-Roman Iron Age*, was marked by the introduction of La Tène I types; the third, or *late pre-Roman Iron Age*, began only after La Tène III contacts were under way. More recently the production of radiocarbon dates is beginning to offer an independent method of calibration which is proving particularly important in placing the early northern British material in its correct perspective (MacKie, 1969).

The cultural model emphasised two things: the indigenous nature of much of the material and the completely false emphasis which had been placed on changes of pottery styles. Much of the earlier writing reads as though the Iron Age consisted only of animated ceramics endowed with all the qualities of living creatures, with evolutionary properties appropriate to the theories of Lysenko. Hodson showed the weaknesses of such a syndrome by systematically destroying the basis of the 'Marnian invasion' theory (Hodson, 1962) while the more recent work of D. P. S. Peacock (1968 and 1969) has demonstrated with some clarity that the differing pottery styles of the south-west and the west Midlands are more the result of commercial production centres than of cultural determinates. As a consequence of his work, much of the complex reasoning surrounding Bristol Channel B (or western Second and Third B) can now be swept away and many thousands of words of intricate discussion rendered obsolete.

The lessening of emphasis on the cataclysmic nature of culture change in the Iron Age and the realisation that a broad cultural continuum existed, firmly rooted in the second millennium, has encouraged an examination of sites relating to the centuries spanning the conventional change-over from Late Bronze Age to Early Iron Age – sites such as Ivinghoe, Eldon's Seat and the Breiddin – and is now beginning to demand a reassessment of the nature and relevance of bronze metallurgy to Iron Age studies.

The cultural model, as described by Hodson, has therefore gone some way towards loosening the joints of Iron Age studies and creating a climate in which the differing approaches to the material, already under way, could develop; but even in the present state of research it is becoming clear that the definition of cultures in the traditional sense is no longer sufficient. Iron Age communities were too intimately in contact. Their patterns of economy, their styles of pottery and their spheres of trading all constitute overlapping systems which require individual treatment and definition. In such an approach might lie a more productive understanding of the people and their lives, before the first century BC when the threads of recognisable history appear. Whether or not it will be possible to reconstruct a history before 100 BC is a problem to be returned to in the final chapter.

The Background

A detailed assessment of the period conventionally called the 'Late Bronze Age' – broadly from the beginning of the first millennium until the seventh century BC – is a subject more appropriate to another volume in this series. But before we can begin to define the social, economic and technical changes which began in the eighth century and became intensified during the seventh, it is necessary to sketch in something of the indigenous background, if only to emphasise the strong element of continuity which underlies the social and economic history of the country throughout the first millennium.

SETTLEMENT AND ECONOMY IN SOUTH-EASTERN BRITAIN

Settlements belonging to the period 1300–700 BC are tolerably well known on the chalklands of southern Britain, where more than two dozen individual sites have been recorded and at least half of them subjected to excavations of differing thoroughness (Fig. 2:1). Taken together, the evidence allows certain generalisations to be made. The basic structural unit appears to be an enclosure, frequently of sub-rectangular form, defined in various ways by combinations of banks, ditches and palisades. At Shearplace Hill, Dorset (Fig. 2:2), the settlement area is enclosed by a U-shaped ditch 8–10 ft (*c.* 3 m) wide, with an internal bank in which may once have been bedded a palisade or perhaps a thorn hedge. At Cock Hill, Sussex, on the other hand, the bank and palisade are external to a 6 ft (2 m) wide ditch. Another variant appears at New Barn Down, Sussex (Fig. 2:2), and at Thorney Down,

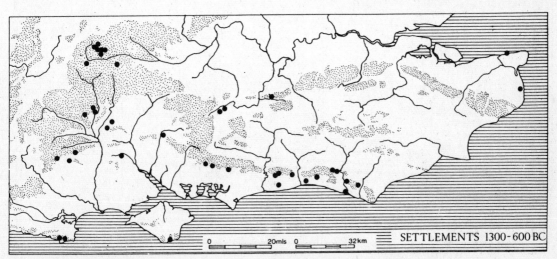

2:1 Major settlements in southern Britain: Middle Bronze Age to Early Iron Age (sources: various)

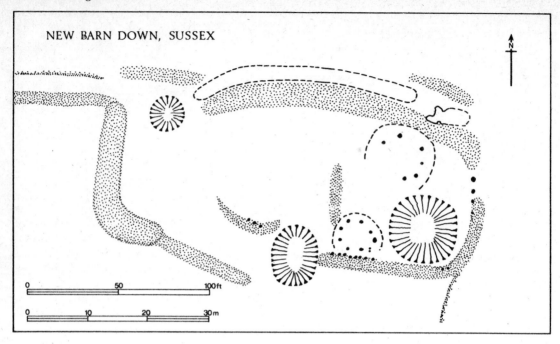

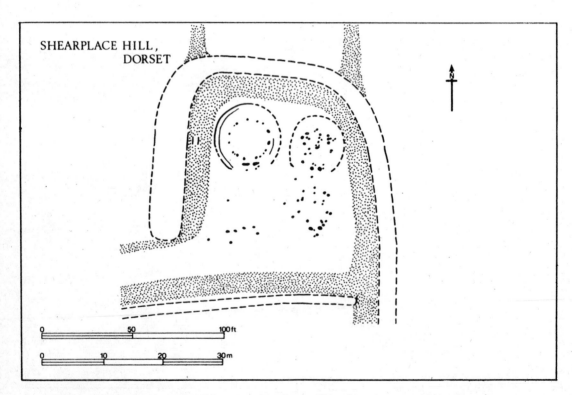

2:2   Homesteads in southern Britain, second to first millennium (sources: *New Barn Down*, Curwen, 1934b; *Shearplace Hill*, Rhatz & ApSimon, 1962)

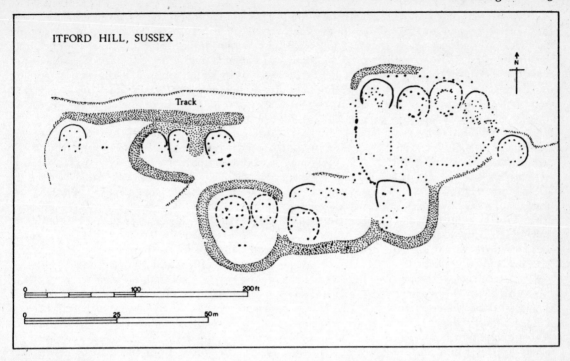

ITFORD HILL, SUSSEX

Track

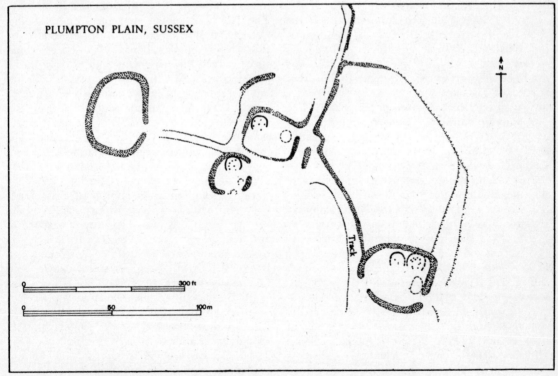

PLUMPTON PLAIN, SUSSEX

Track

2:3 Nucleated settlements of *c.* 1000 BC in Sussex (sources: *Itford Hill*, Burstow & Holleyman, 1957; *Plumpton Plain*, Holleyman & Curwen, 1935)

Wilts, where one side only is ditched, the other three being defined by banks, which at New Barn Down supported a close-set palisade. In all these examples, internal settings of posts show that the earthworks enclosed circular huts, usually 20–25 ft (6·0 – 7·5 m) in diameter. There were at least two at New Barn Down, two or three at Shearplace Hill, five or more at Cock Hill, and probably as many as nine at Thorney Down. Not all, of course, need have been in use at one time, since replacement and rebuilding were probably the general rule. The plan is clear at Shearplace Hill, however, where two definite houses and a possible third, enclosing a working area, seem to constitute a single contemporary unit, which would have been ideally suited to a social group of family or extended family size. The unenclosed settlement at Chalton, Hants, was of similar size, with one large hut, a smaller hut with a central hearth for cooking and two un-roofed working areas. Here a tentative assessment of grain-production, based on the capacities of the storage pits, supported the idea of a single family unit and indicated a total arable in the order of 16 acres (6·5 hectares).

While single-enclosure habitations of the types mentioned above are relatively common on the chalklands, at some sites nucleation appears to exist. Admittedly, the question must to some extent be left open since it is difficult to show that all structural elements of these supposedly nucleated settlements were contemporary. The possibility remains that the overall pattern is caused by a gradual shift in location of a single enclosure within a defined and limited territory. Archaeological methods cannot at present distinguish such subtlety. But if the overall plans of sites such as Plumpton Plain A and Itford Hill, in Sussex (Fig. 2:3), do reflect a total contemporary settlement area, then settlement of hamlet or small village size must be postulated. Strictly, two variants of nucleation can be defined. The first, of Plumpton Plain A type, consists of four sub-rectangular enclosures defined by banks, spread out along a street over a distance of about 700 ft (213 m). Three of them have been partially excavated and each has proved to contain at least one hut. The second class, typified by Itford Hill, is a denser form of nucleation in which a complex of about six enclosures lying adjacent to each other forms an elongated area some 420 by 150 ft (128 by 46 m). Here, fortunately, extensive excavation under modern conditions has allowed much of the plan to be recovered, suggesting distinctions in both size of house-type and function, which might imply social differentiation as well as specialisation in working area. The main palisaded enclosure contained a single large hut about 22 ft (7 m) in diameter, provided with a porch, together with three smaller huts. The three adjacent palisaded enclosures contained one or two huts each. Further to the west, along a hollowed approach road, were two apparently unenclosed huts with a small banked enclosure between, probably for cooking. Three other more isolated huts were excavated, bringing the total to at least thirteen structures. It is tempting to interpret the overall plan in terms of a central establishment for a patriarch around which about six other family units have clustered, giving rise to a substantial hamlet.

A second type of enclosure exists in the same general area as the enclosed settlements, belonging to a broadly similar period. These enclosures (Fig. 2:4), invariably ditched with a bank on the inner side, differ from the settlements in that they are without trace of extensive habitation. The two well-known examples, South Lodge Camp and Martin Down Camp, excavated by Pitt-Rivers on Cranbourne Chase, are both strongly rectilinear in form; South Lodge Camp possesses a single entrance while Martin Down has two entrances and an apparently undefended length along the north side which may originally have been closed with hurdles or some temporary structure leaving no archaeological trace. The interiors of both sites were substantially cleared, showing that apart from a few undated pits they were barren of structures. Clearly, then, they were not for permanent habitation, although a scatter of Middle to Late Bronze Age artefacts implies use at this period, if only of a sporadic and temporary nature. Less certainty attaches to the contemporary Wiltshire enclosures on Boscombe Down East, Preshute Down and Ogbourne Down. At Boscombe Down East limited excavation only was undertaken, but sufficient to show that the enclosed quarter-acre (0·1 hectares) was largely without occupation, although a scatter of pottery was found outside. The ditch clearly related to a linear 'ranchboundary' of the type to be described later (pp. 177–9), which formed its southern side. The northern entrance was provided with a pair of double

SOUTH LODGE, DORSET

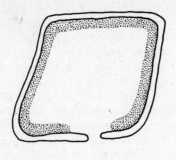

MARTIN DOWN, HANTS

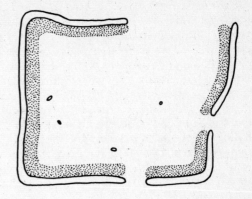

BOSCOMBE DOWN EAST, WILTS

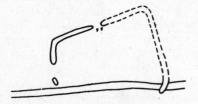

HARROW HILL, SUSSEX

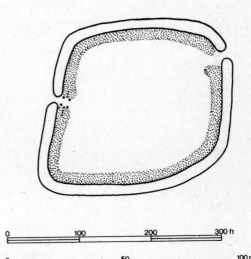

PRESHUTE DOWN, WILTS

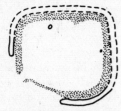

2:4 Ditched enclosures in southern Britain, second to first millennium (sources: *South Lodge and Martin Down*, Pitt-Rivers, 1898; *Boscombe Down East*, Stone, 1936; *Preshute Down*, C.M. Piggott, 1942; *Harrow Hill*, Holleyman, 1937)

(recut?) post-holes, presumably defining the position of a gate, a little over 3 ft (1 m) wide, set back to be on line with the inner bank. This suggests that the bank may have formed a bedding for a continuous palisade, the holes for which have not penetrated the solid chalk. The same may well have been the case with the South Lodge Camp and Martin Down Camp enclosures, but the possibility is not susceptible of proof. The enclosures from Preshute Down and

Ogbourne Down in north Wiltshire are even less well known, but they do not differ significantly from those just described.

On the Sussex downs this type of earthwork would appear to be rare, possibly because of accidents of survival rather than actual absence. The one excavated site that may well belong to the class is Harrow Hill, where limited excavation examined a sub-rectangular enclosure defined by a shallow bank; into this had apparently been set a close-spaced palisade of timbers, the holes for which penetrated the natural chalk. At the one entrance excavated, two pairs of gate-posts 7 ft (2 m) apart flanked an entrance passage. Excavation inside, though limited, produced a few indeterminate sherds of uncertain date together with parts of more than fifty cow skulls, a remarkable discovery which will be referred to again later (p. 17). It will be seen, therefore, that in size and structure Harrow Hill fits well with the Wiltshire enclosures, but its dating evidence is far less clear and the possibility remains that it may not have been constructed until the sixth or fifth century. It is nevertheless within the tradition of the Late Bronze Age sites.

Before considering the economic pattern to which these settlements and enclosures belong, something must be said of their date. Radio-carbon dates are available for Shearplace Hill, 1180 ± 180 (1274 BC); Chalton 1243 ± 69 (1339 BC) and Itford Hill 1000 ± 35 (1089 BC).[1] The Shearplace Hill date confirms the view, based on the ceramic evidence, that the settlement originated in what is conventionally known as the Middle Bronze Age. Similarly, the Chalton assessment, together with two of the stratified bronze objects found in the main hut – a low-flanged palstave and a conical fitting – again imply late second millennium occupation. The Itford Hill date is consistent with this. The dating of the other Late Bronze Age sites is based on less firm evidence but it is clear that the Deverel–Rimbury style of economy continued into the eighth century. At Plumpton Plain an analysis of the surfaces of the whetstones suggested the sharpening of iron tools which, if true, can hardly allow the site to be dated much before the eighth century. Similarly, at Boscombe Down East what was claimed to be iron slag was found in the primary silt of the ditch.[2]

Besides pottery, the surviving material culture of these Middle to Late Bronze Age settlements is sparse. Awls and needles of bone and scrapers of flint point to leather-working on a large scale. Cylindrical loom-weights of clay, clay spindle whorls and a single example of a bone weaving

comb from Shearplace Hill show that wool was being spun and woven, and numbers of frag-mentary querns of saddle type underline the significance of grain-production to the economy. Bronze tools and weapons are relatively rare, no doubt because of their value, but awls were found at Chalton, Martin Down and South Lodge Camp; socketed spears occur at Thorney Down, South Lodge and New Barn Down; knives of various kinds are known from Chalton, New Barn Down and Plumpton Plain, where a ferrule and a fragment of winged axe were also found. The early settlement at Chalton produced a palstave. Razors from South Lodge Camp and Martin Down Camp, ribbed bracelets from Thorney Down and South Lodge Camp and a conical bronze mounting from Chalton show that bronze was also used for less utilitarian purposes. While it is fair to suppose that many of the above types could have been current after 1000 BC, the palstave, conical mounting and ribbed bracelets all derive ultimately from 'orna-ment horizon' hoards of the thirteenth to eleventh centuries BC and must indicate a second millennium origin for the sites on which they occur. In contrast, the winged axe and socketed knife from Plumpton Plain and the collection of objects from Highdown Hill, near Worthing, are firmly in the Late Bronze Age tradition of metal-work, dating perhaps to as late as the eighth or seventh century.

The presence of saddle querns and grain storage pits on many of the settlement sites (both cultural traits can be traced back into the Neo-lithic period) underlines the fact that the basis of the subsistence economy was corn-growing. Analysis of carbonised grains and grain im-pressions on pottery provides a general picture of the Late Bronze Age grain-production, with barley predominating – amounting to about 80 per cent of the total output compared to emmer wheat. Of the total barley crop some 70 per cent was of the hulled variety – a type suitable for winter sowing. A large quantity of carbonised grain found in one of the pits at Itford Hill proved to be almost entirely of hulled barley of both the nodding bere variety (*Hordeum tetra-stichum*) and the erect form (*Hordeum hexastichum*); only five grains of emmer wheat were recorded in the entire sample, but careful analysis allowed the seeds of fourteen different weeds of cultiva-tion to be isolated, including false cleavers,

---

[1] For an explanation of the citation and for further details see appendix B.

[2] The sample, however, cannot now be traced and should be viewed with some reserve.

barren broom, black bindweed, opium poppy and many others. These broad figures for the Late Bronze Age must be seen against a gradually increasing amount of hulled barley at the expense of naked, and of wheat gaining in importance over both types of barley, as improved farming methods, including a greater reliance on winter-sown crops, gradually came into use towards the beginning of the first millennium.

Several of the settlements referred to in the foregoing pages are intimately connected with field systems defined by banks – known as lynchets – created largely as the result of plough-ing on a slope, a process which allows soil to accumulate at the lower boundaries of the ploughed area. These banks were often increased in height by flints and rubble picked off the fields during cultivation. Since the light ard available at the time would only have broken the soil and not turned a furrow, as in the case of a plough provided with a mould-board, it is generally assumed that each field was ploughed in two directions to break the soil sufficiently for sowing. Archaeological traces of cross-ploughing are well attested in Bronze Age contexts in this country and abroad. Such a treatment would result in a patchwork of small, squarish fields, many hundreds of acres of which are known. It is often very difficult to distinguish between fields of Bronze Age, Iron Age or Roman date, but one of the Ogbourne Down enclosures evidently post-dates the initial use of a group of fields, while at Itford Hill, New Barn Down, Martin Down Camp and Plumpton Plain A, the trackways leading to the settlements are closely related to field systems, which may therefore be con-temporary.

While the preparation of crops must have accounted for much of the communities' efforts, the tending of flocks and herds can have been of no less importance. Each of the excavated sites has produced abundant evidence of oxen, sheep and goats, with lesser numbers of pigs, horses, dogs and deer usually present. Where samples are large enough and adequate quantitative records have been kept, oxen are found to pre-dominate. This applies particularly to the en-closures at Martin Down Camp, South Lodge Camp and Harrow Hill. At the last-named site between fifty and a hundred cows' skulls were discovered in relatively limited excavations, with hardly a trace of a limb bone. If the density is

even throughout the enclosure it is estimated that more than a thousand animals may be repre-sented there. Interpretation is difficult: it may be that some form of ritual deposit is indicated; alternatively, the enclosure could have been used for slaughtering surplus stock at certain times during the year, the worthless parts of the carcasses, including the heads, being discarded before the rest was carried off. Such economy of effort would not be surprising.

In the relatively simple type of subsistence economy in operation during the Late Bronze Age in south-east Britain, there would have been a close inter-reliance between the arable and pastoral sides of farming, particularly the use of cattle to manure fields while gleaning from the stubble after the harvest. During the growing seasons the flocks and herds would no doubt have been turned loose on the open downland to forage for themselves. All the time that settle-ments were few, the system would have worked well, but with increased pressure on land con-sequent upon a rapidly growing population, more formal methods of land-division would have been required, leading eventually to the construction of ditched boundaries – the so-called 'ranch boundaries', cross-ridge dykes and spur dykes – many of which originated in the Late Bronze Age and continued to be constructed throughout the first millennium BC. These structures will be discussed in more detail in a later chapter (pp. 177–9).

THE SOUTH-WEST PENINSULA

Another area to have received detailed study is the south-west peninsula, particularly Dartmoor, Exmoor and Penwith. Of these regions, the settlement history of Dartmoor is the most informative, not least because of the attention which it has recently received from soil scientists and palaeontologists, enabling regional ecologi-cal variations to be mapped in relation to the contemporary settlement patterns (Fig. 2:5), (Simmons, 1970). It is now clear that in the Late Bronze Age the high moorland areas above the 1,400 ft (427 m) contour were already covered with a blanket bog in excess of 2 ft (0·6 m) in depth. Below this and down to approximately the 800 ft (243 m) contour, the limit of the thick forest, lay a densely settled area of open grassland or heathland interspersed with relict woodland.

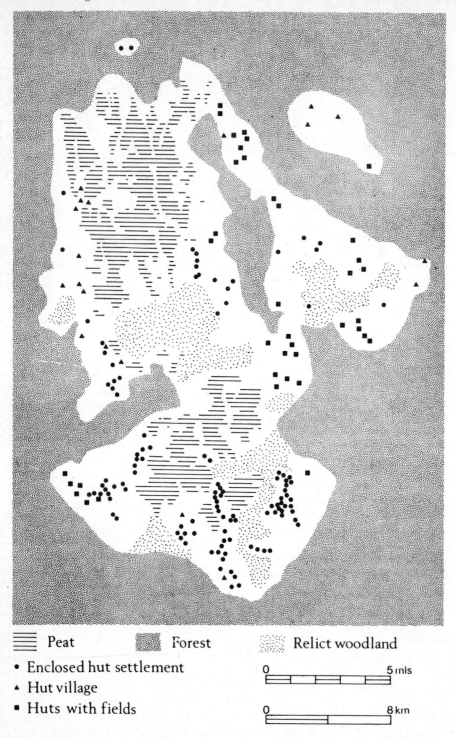

≣≣≣ Peat	▓ Forest	⠂⠂ Relict woodland

• Enclosed hut settlement

▲ Hut village

■ Huts with fields

0   5 mls

0   8 km

2:5   The ecology and settlement pattern on Dartmoor, late second to early first millennium (source: Simmons, 1970)

The open areas originated in the coalescence of clearings which began at the beginning of the third millennium or even a few centuries earlier. Once the forest cover had been removed, continuous grazing and the leaching effect of heavy rainfall prevented forest regeneration.

Three types of settlement have been defined, each showing some preference for different climatic environments. The first, the pastoral enclosures, are concentrated on the south side of the moor, usually on south-facing slopes above river valleys close to a water supply (Fig. 2:6). These settlements typically have substantial enclosure walls inside which lie scattered huts, usually in sufficient numbers to be considered as villages. While it is not impossible that small-scale cultivation was carried out within the enclosed area – and indeed at Rider's Rings there are several small walled garden plots – evidence of agricultural activity on a large scale is lacking. Some of these villages show signs of growth. At Legis Tor a sequence of walls can be traced, demonstrating that the enclosed area was greatly increased in three successive stages, but whether this is related to a growth in the size of the population is impossible to say.

The second type of Dartmoor settlement is the unenclosed village, where the clusters of circular huts are linked together by low stone walls, creating multi-angular enclosures which could well have served as both cultivation plots and paddocks for stock at different times of the year. Sometimes these villages reach considerable proportions – sixty-eight huts are recorded at Stanton Down (Fig. 2:7) but not all are so strictly nucleated: at Rough Tor on Bodmin Moor, for example, huts and their attached enclosures spread for about half a mile (0·8 km) along a track, but here we may well be dealing with a linear development representing settlement shift over a considerable period of time. Enclosed villages are not particularly numerous; with rare exceptions, they concentrate on the climatically wetter western fringes of Dartmoor, usually within easy reach of streams.

The third type of settlement is the isolated farm or group of farms found in intimate association with rectangular stone-walled fields (Fig. 2:8). Several such settlements are known in their entirety, showing that the arable area is hardly likely to have produced sufficient food for the occupants – only an acre (0·4 hectares) for the single-hut farm at Rippon Tor and 2·2 acres (0·8 hectares) for the three huts at Blissmoor. The implication must be that additional food supplies were available, presumably in the form of flocks and herds reared on the upland pastures. The arable farms cluster to the east of Dartmoor on the fertile 'brown soils' sheltered from extremes of climate by the mass of the moor itself.

It would appear that the large pastoral villages and the small arable farms are different responses to different environments, and it may well be that they represent two divergent subsistence economies, but the possibility remains that this is archaeological evidence of a transhumant society – the population leaving the scattered farmsteads of the east during the spring and summer, taking their herds and flocks to the wetter western pastures, to return again in time for harvest. Some form of transhumance is certainly implied by the small acreage of the eastern group of farms.

THE MIDLANDS, WALES AND THE NORTH

Much of what has been said of the settlement pattern and economy of southern Britain must apply to the rest of the country but at present the evidence is, to say the least, sparse. In Wales several inhabited cave sites of the period have been defined, e.g. Lesser Garth Cave, Radyr (Glam), and Culver Hole Cave, Llangenydd (Gower), but open settlements are rarer. The ring-work on Marros Mountain, Pendine (Carm), may have been occupied at this time, but the evidence is not conclusive and it may possibly belong to the later first millennium. The above-mentioned sites all produced pottery in the Late Bronze Age tradition but little is known of other aspects of the material culture and economy – except, of course, for the numerous bronze hoards.

The Midlands and north are no better known. Recent work at Mam Tor, Derbyshire, has however demonstrated the existence of a cluster of Bronze Age huts producing radiocarbon dates of 1130 ± 115 and 1180 ± 132 (1222, 1274 BC), sited on the top of a hill later enclosed by the bank and ditch of an Iron Age hillfort. At the neighbouring hillfort of Portfield, Lancs, the discovery of a Late Bronze Age hoard lends some support to the idea that many of the hilltops later fortified in the Iron Age may have originated as

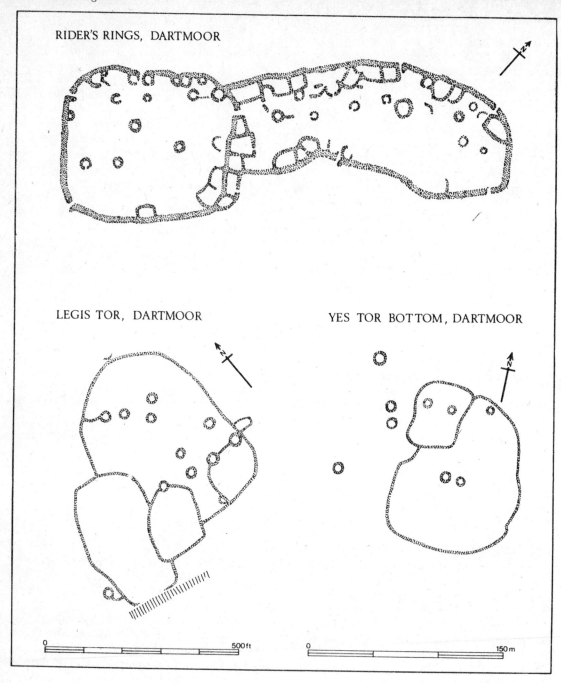

RIDER'S RINGS, DARTMOOR

LEGIS TOR, DARTMOOR

YES TOR BOTTOM, DARTMOOR

2:6   Villages on Dartmoor, late second to early first millennium (sources: *Rider's Rings*, Worth, 1935; *Legis Tor*, Worth, 1943; *Yes Tor Bottom*, Worth, 1943)

STANTON DOWN, DARTMOOR

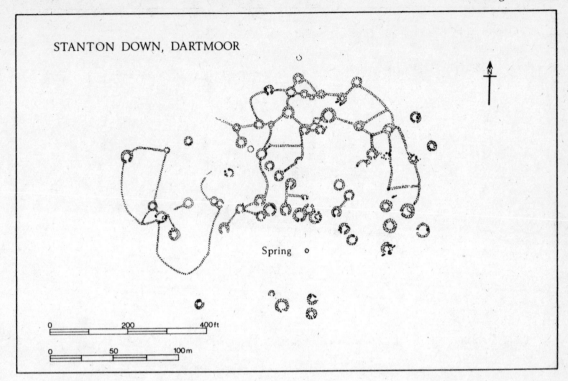

Spring

0   200   400 ft

0   50   100 m

2:7   A Dartmoor village of the late second to early first millennium (source: Baring-Gould 1902)

settlements even as early as the late second millennium. The same conclusions may be true of certain of the Scottish sites. At Traprain Law, for example, traces of an extensive Late Bronze Age settlement were discovered to underlie the subsequent Iron Age occupation. Other classes of settlement are less well known. Clusters of hut circles in the Yorkshire Dales, e.g. at Grassington, occasional cave deposits as at Covesea (Moray) and Heathery Burn, Co. Durham, the so-called crannogs of eastern Yorkshire and parts of Scotland, and the cellular stone houses of Jarlshof (Fig. 2:9), are all part of an extensive and varied settlement pattern about which few details are known. The general impression which these fragments provide is of well-established communities not unlike those of the south-east, which have adapted themselves closely to the more varied environments of the west and north. In the absence of positive evidence to the contrary, it would seem likely that the economy was largely dependent upon pastoralism, cereal-production playing a lesser but still significant

part. Views on this matter are, however, liable to modification in the light of current work on field systems in eastern Scotland.

POTTERY

The dating of pottery belonging to the period 1500–500 BC is fraught with difficulties, the detailed discussion of which is not directly relevant to this volume. Nevertheless, some generalisations must be made, if only to prepare the way for the more lengthy consideration of the later period in subsequent chapters. The south-east of Britain, south of the Severn-Wash axis, has produced a large amount of pottery of Middle to Late Bronze Age date which, until recently, was conventionally classed together under the general title of the Deverel–Rimbury culture (Preston and Hawkes, 1933), a name derived from two Dorset cemeteries excavated in the nineteenth century. Pottery of Deverel–Rimbury type has been recovered from two main contexts: cremation cemeteries and settlement sites of the types

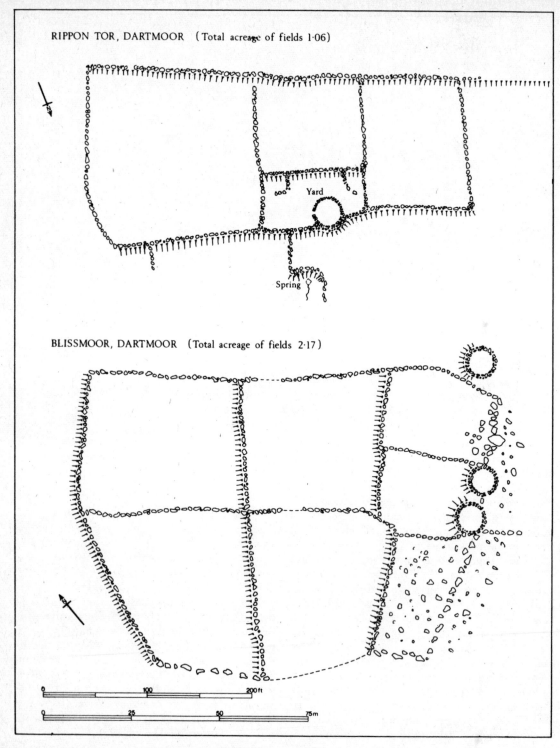

RIPPON TOR, DARTMOOR   (Total acreage of fields 1·06)

Yard

Spring

BLISSMOOR, DARTMOOR   (Total acreage of fields 2·17)

2:8   Dartmoor farmsteads of the late second to early first millennium (source: A. Fox, 1955)

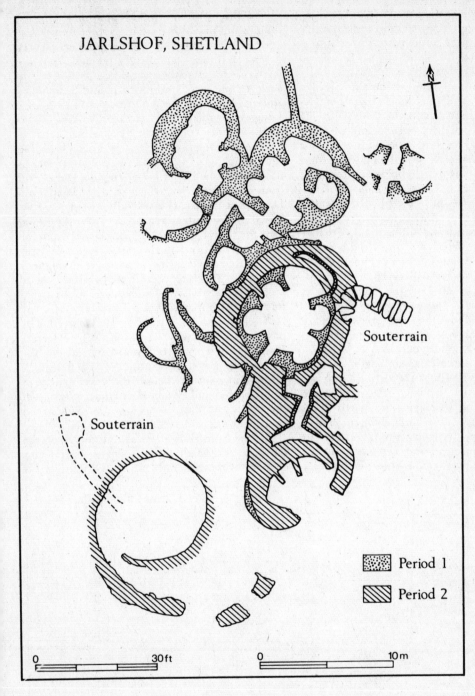

JARLSHOF, SHETLAND

Souterrain

Souterrain

Period 1

Period 2

0   30ft

0   10m

2:9   The Late Bronze Age homestead at Jarlshof, Shetland (source: Hamilton, 1956)

already described. At the cemeteries it is seldom found in any form of association with datable metalwork, but at the settlements bronze implements are occasionally found and can be used to provide broad date-brackets for the pottery.

An assessment of the associated bronzes (M. A. Smith, 1959) has shown that they ran broadly contemporary with the Montelius III phase of the north European Bronze Age, currently dated to 1200–1000 BC. This dating for an early stage of the Deverel–Rimbury culture gains further support from typological studies of the individual ceramic forms, which display a considerable degree of internal development from indigenous types independently dated to the middle of the second millennium. Further confirmation is offered by three radiocarbon dates. 1180 ± 180 (1274 BC) for the main phase of occupation at the Shearplace Hill settlement, 1243 ± 69 (1339 BC) for the homestead at Chalton, and 1000 ± 35 (1089 BC) for the Itford Hill settlement. Thus the date-bracket 1400–1000 may reasonably be proposed to contain the 'classic' Deverel–Rimbury culture.

Within the ceramic assemblages of this 'classic' phase it is possible to recognise a number of regional variations which partly reflect the basic folk tradition of region and partly local inventiveness (Fig. 2:10). These differences may be used to define regional groups. Thus in Devon and Cornwall lies the *Trevisker group*, in Dorset, south and west of the Stour, is the *South*

Dorset group (Calkin, 1964) and in south-east Hampshire and Wiltshire is the *Cranbourne Chase group* (Calkin, 1964). The contemporary pottery of Sussex differs significantly enough from the western groups to be considered as a separate *South Downs group*, and in Essex and Suffolk the *Ardleigh group* has been distinguished (Erith & Longworth, 1960). More detailed studies will no doubt characterise further regional variants.

The characteristic 'fine' wares which enable the regional groups to be defined do not seem to have lasted long after 1000. Indeed, the period from *c.* 1000 to 750, which can be called Late Deverel–Rimbury, is marked by an intense conservatism in pottery technology, during which time the barrel and bucket forms continued to be made but in a simplified range of types. Eventually, during the eighth century, new innovations appeared alongside traditional forms: large angular bowls were manufactured probably in imitation of imported bronze situlae, and a few vessels in peripheral Urnfield style occurred. The basic tradition was, however, still Deverel–Rimbury and may be considered to be the Ultimate phase of the continuum. These eighth-century innovations herald the development of an inventive and dynamic ceramic industry in the south and east of the country, which can properly be considered to be Iron Age.

In the Midlands, Wales and much of the north, pottery gradually ceases to be a significant element of the material culture and many areas

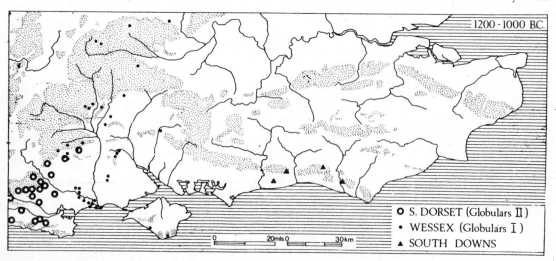

2:10   Distribution of Deverel–Rimbury pottery styles (sources: Calkin, 1964, and S. C. Hawkes, 1970; author)

become virtually aceramic. Several urnfields have, however, been recorded in central England, including a large cemetery at Bromfield, Salop, where a series of cremations has been dated to 1560 ± 180, 850 ± 71 and 762 ± 75, (1665, 934, 843 BC).

In the extreme north of Scotland, in the Hebrides, Orkneys and Shetlands, a well-established ceramic tradition, rooted ultimately in the third millennium but with French Urnfield influences, flourished throughout this period and well into the Iron Age.

THE BRONZE INDUSTRY

In the foregoing pages emphasis has been placed on the indigenous development of the British Late Bronze Age communities and the relative self-sufficiency of their subsistence economies. Superimposed upon this pattern of intense regionalism is a complicated and wide-flung trading system best exemplified by the distribution of bronze weapons and implements. Trading was on two levels: overseas trade, which brought in exotic types – often copied locally, and local trade, distributing the products of British smiths over more limited territories. This kind of specialist activity had a long ancestry in Britain; the Late Bronze Age was to see its ultimate development and the beginning of its decline.

The general assemblage of eleventh to tenth century date contains a wide range of implements, including flange-hilted, leaf-shaped swords based on imported Erbenheim and Hemigkofen weapons; leaf-shaped Ballintober swords; dirks; looped palstaves; experimental types of socketed axe; basal-looped spearheads; razors and ring-socketed sickles. Distribution of these types is broad but centres upon south-eastern England. In the south it is generally known as the Penard phase, after a Glamorganshire hoard; in Scotland it is represented in the Glentrool tradition. Trading connections were wide, linking England and Scotland to Wales, Ireland and the northern and western areas of France.

From the end of the tenth century until the middle of the eighth, Britain south of the Humber was served by bronze smiths casting a range of new implements in bronze with a high lead content, a technical innovation which was to last in the south for some centuries. These new types constitute what is known as the *Wilburton complex*: they include leaf-shaped swords with splayed V-shaped shoulders, long tongue-shaped chapes, simple socketed spearheads pegged into position on the shaft, late types of palstaves and socketed axes. Again trading connections were maintained between southern Britain and northwest France, but the new types do not appear to have penetrated far into northern England, Scotland, Wales and Ireland. In these regions, traditions and technology harking back to the preceding phases remained dominant. In northern Britain, for example, where the contemporary assemblage is known as the *Wallington complex*, some of the implements such as the side-looped spearhead and low-flanged palstave are close to types developed before the eleventh century. In Wales, too, early types continued in use to the eighth century, although late hoards in the Wilburton tradition are found in the upper Severn valley. A similarly retarded industry, called the *Poldar phase* (Coles, 1962a), has been defined for Scotland, where a number of Wilburton and Wallington types have turned up, but only in small quantities.

In the middle of the eighth century south and east Britain developed a series of new types in parallel with the western areas of France, with which trading contacts were maintained, but on a more intensive scale. The new assemblage, called the *carp's tongue sword complex* (Savory, 1948; Briard, 1965), includes the long sword with a narrowed point (after which the industry is named), characteristic bag-shaped chapes, knives of hog's back and triangular form, various types of socketed axe, socketed knives, pegged and socketed spearheads, various chisels and gouges, and several decorative attachments of which the so-called 'bugle-shaped' objects are the most characteristic (Fig. 4:2). In Britain the locally produced leaf-shaped sword of Ewart Park type occurs in considerable numbers throughout the whole of the country and serves as a linking feature between the carp's tongue sword complex of the south-east and the regional industries of the north and west, which can be defined largely upon typological variations in their socketed axes.

In addition to the cast bronze implements just described, vessels and shields of beaten bronze make their appearance in the British Isles from the mid-eighth century onwards, as a result of far-flung contacts with the Mediterranean and central Europe. The first of the vessels to arrive, the high-shouldered situlae known as Kurd buckets, find their way into Wales and Ireland, where some are modified by Irish smiths and later copied, giving rise to a distinctive Irish-British type which appears in small numbers in the north and west in the first half of the seventh century (Fig. 10:6). Broadly contemporary with this later development was the arrival of bronze cauldrons of Mediterranean type (class A cauldrons), which had developed ultimately from oriental prototypes firmly dated to 750–700 BC and are thought to have reached the British Isles by between 700 and 650 (Fig. 10:7).

The duality of the trading contacts between Britain and the continent implied by the importation of bronze vessels – a central European/Rhine route and a Mediterranean/Atlantic route – is also reflected in the origins of the beaten bronze shields, which give rise to local types widely distributed over most of the British Isles in the eighth century (Coles, 1962b). Other exotic types found their way in at this time, principally from central and northern Europe. Among these must be mentioned the first appearance of bronze fittings appropriate to horse harness, which surely implies the introduction of more sophisticated methods of harnessing and possibly the greatly increased practice of horse-riding. Such developments are largely in parallel with those discernible in Europe during the Hallstatt B phase of the Urnfield culture.

Many of the elements of eighth century metallurgy described above are represented in a remarkable founder's hoard discovered in 1959 at Isleham, Cambs, where some 6,500 fragments of bronze were found buried in a small pit cut into the chalk. A high percentage of the weapons belonged to the Wilburton complex but in addition a few objects of the carp's tongue sword complex were found, indicating that the hoard was deposited at the end of the Wilburton tradition. Additional support for a late eighth century date was provided by a few fragments of class A cauldrons and by a series of harness fittings which included cheek-pieces, annular strap-crossings and cruciform strap-crossings. Thus this single hoard exemplifies most aspects of the developed bronze technology and trading systems of the period, while at the same time the

presence of the bronze harness trappings introduces a new element, which we shall find recurring more frequently in hoards of the seventh and sixth centuries.

Behind the complexity and the detail of the early first millennium bronze industry, it is possible to discern several general trends, not the least of which is the development of numerous local schools of craftsmen specialising in the production of the more sophisticated objects such as the buckets, cauldrons and shields, all in beaten metal. The swords too, with their rapid and subtle evolution, were clearly made by specialists; many of these, to judge by the distribution pattern, were centred upon the lower Thames, where new foreign imports were evidently carefully studied and improved upon. Less skill would have been required for the production of the smaller cast implements and, as might be expected, intensive regionalisation is recognisable, representing the distribution of the products of single smiths or, at the most, small schools; craftsmen in the remoter parts sometimes worked in alloys and made types long outdated by advances in the more forward areas. In the south-east innovations kept appearing, partly because of native inventiveness and partly because of widespread trading contacts, particularly with northern and western France, which was maintained over several centuries. Thus by the end of the eighth century a wide range of weapons, tools, ornaments and other utensils was being manufactured and traded on an unprecedented scale; vigorous local production centres maintained high standards of inventiveness; and a common market existed between Britain and Atlantic Europe. Superimposed upon this was a well-defined pattern of smaller-scale trading with northern Europe across the North Sea. It was with this area that the first contacts with the Hallstatt C communities of the seventh century developed.

BURIALS

The best-known aspect of the culture of the thirteenth to eighth century is the burial rite. The dead were cremated and frequently, but by no means invariably, placed in urns, sometimes buried in urnfields of considerable size: more than 100 burials at Ardleigh, Essex; 104 at Moordown, Bournemouth and 100+ at Kimpton, Hants. In many cases it can be shown that urnfields grew up around earlier barrows, as at Steyning, Sussex, for example, where at least thirty-two urned and four un-urned cremations were inserted into an existing Middle Bronze Age barrow, and at Latch Farm, Hants, more than ninety cremations, mostly urned, were found in a similar relationship. Other examples are numerous. The Latch Farm excavation gives a clear indication of the range of burial ritual employed: frequently cremations were in up-ended urns placed in shallow pits; sometimes, however, the pots were set upright in the ground and in several cases subsidiary vessels, presumably containing offerings of food and drinks, were included. Some examples, usually those placed upright, were covered with stone slabs set flush with the surface of the ground and were therefore possibly intended to be visible. Two post-holes were also recognised, which might have belonged to wooden markers. The burials are usually clustered together without apparent order, but sometimes, as at Ardleigh and at Pokesdown, Hants, clusters and isolated burials were strung out in a linear arrangement as if to suggest the directional growth of the cemetery. At Barnes, Isle of Wight, between ten and fifteen urns were laid in a circle 12–15 ft (3–4 m) in diameter, implying a considerable degree of forward planning, unless it is assumed that all the cremations were interred at the same time.

Burial beneath barrows continued alongside the urnfield rite. In Wessex it is estimated that 12 per cent of the excavated barrows contained primary Deverel–Rimbury cremations but the barrows are generally only about half the size of the earlier barrows. A typical example was excavated at Plaitford, Hants, where two urns were found set in a shallow pit beneath a small cairn of clay, sand and pebbles, in which had been set a vertical marker post. Over the cairn had been heaped a circular mound 5 ft (1·5 m) high and 35 ft (10·7 m) in diameter. The use of a vertical marker post has also been noted at several urnfield sites.

In other parts of the country the urnfield rite was also practised. At Bromfield, Salop, an arc-shaped urnfield of urned and un-urned cremations has been totally excavated, producing three radiocarbon dates (p. 25). Another urnfield at Ryton-on-Dunsmoor, Warwickshire, yielded a single date of 751 ± 41 (832 BC). In Wales and Scotland urnfields are rare, but urned burials are often found as secondary interments in earlier barrows and cairns, and less frequently as primary burials beneath small cairns.

SUMMARY

The surviving archaeological evidence spanning the period *c.* 1400–700 BC provides a firm impression of massive continuity. We appear to be dealing with a conserving society which shows little sign of any form of innovation or inventiveness save in the specialised skill of bronze-casting – a skill which may reasonably be supposed to have been in the hands of a small group of itinerant specialists. Burial rite, settlement pattern and ceramic technology can have changed little for almost a millennium. But during the eighth century trading contacts expanded and intensified, bringing to Britain a flood of foreign products which were rapidly assimilated by British smiths, giving rise to a vigorous local industry, cheaper bronzes and a more widespread distribution. It was in this phase of innovation that the social, economic and technical changes which were to typify the Iron Age had their roots.

Regional Groupings: South and East

In this chapter and the next an attempt is made to offer a geographical and chronological framework which will allow the regional differences between the Iron Age communities of Britain to be described in a manner as objective as possible. There are several potential approaches which could have been adopted – pseudo-historical, chronological or cultural. All present difficulties. A pseudo-historical model couched in terms of invasion and folk movement would have imposed a pre-judged structure upon the evidence; a purely chronological system lacks sufficient absolute dates for calibration and would, in any event, take no account of spheres of contact or different rates of development; while a cultural model, in the style laid down by Childe, is extremely difficult to apply to the British material and is of very doubtful value in characterising a territory in which the communities are in close contact and share many systems in common. Accordingly, these conventional schemes have been rejected.

The framework given below relies very largely upon the characterisation of pottery styles and the definition of the areas in which the types constituting the style were commonly in use. The *style-zones* resulting from such a definition must represent an area of contact even if that contact implies little more than the marketing pattern from a single production centre. One advantage in using pottery as the basis for classification in this way is that it is relatively common over most of the south-east; moreover, as a plastic medium it is highly sensitive to change. A further advantage lies in the fact that regional sequences can be built up by means of stratigraphy and these can be linked to developments in neighbouring areas.

In this way an interrelated pattern of style-zones emerges, the individual components of which can be seen to develop at different rates in different areas.

The actual definition of a style-zone must necessarily be based on a detailed assessment of stylistic traits. While the intricacies cannot be enlarged upon here, the broad results are given below. Wherever possible, the style-zones have been named after two of the classic sites where the types are found. This kind of nomenclature has the advantage of being easy to remember while at the same time reflecting something of the geographical range of the zone. The use of two site-names also goes some way towards overcoming the objection that no single site can be typical. Finally, the individual style-zones are arranged in a chronological sequence to which some broad absolute dates are attached. These dates can be regarded only as an approximation but they are consistent with all the evidence at present available.[1]

EIGHTH AND SEVENTH CENTURY DEVELOPMENTS (Fig. 3:1)

The Ultimate Deverel–Rimbury culture (Fig. A:1)

Until the middle of the eighth century BC the pottery styles of south-eastern Britain continued in the tradition of the Deverel–Rimbury culture, but increased contact with the continent from about 750 onwards brought to the country a

---

[1] Because the quantity of illustrated material required to make this chapter intelligible would be somewhat cumbersome to include in the text, the pottery drawings have been brought together separately in appendix A.

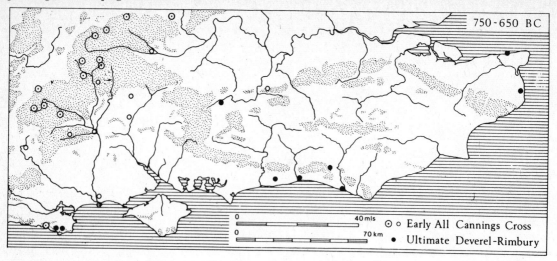

3:1   Distribution of eighth to seventh century pottery in southern Britain (source: author)

number of exotic artefacts, including bronze vessels which were widely copied in pottery to produce distinctive angular bowls totally alien to the earlier tradition.

The characteristic pottery types represented at Eldon's Seat (Encombe), on the Isle of Purbeck include bucket- and barrel-shaped urns, often with applied finger-tipped cordons, plain cordons or bosses, which derive from local Bronze Age forms. In addition, however, there were several examples of the angular bowl type, some of which are large enough to be considered to be copies of metal situlae. The same range of forms is known from several other Dorset sites. At Eldon's Seat, Chalbury and Kimmeridge the material is stratified beneath later assemblages which themselves date to an early stage in the Iron Age, probably the seventh to sixth centuries, a fact which tends to support an eighth to seventh century date for what has been called the Eldon's Seat I assemblage.

Along the Sussex downs a number of settlements belonging to this period are known, but in the absence of closed groups of stratified material it is necessary to distinguish them largely by typological considerations. Whetstones, were recovered from the two settlements on Plumpton Plain, Sussex, which are claimed to show signs of having been used for sharpening iron objects. If this evidence can be accepted, it would imply that they must date to not much earlier than 700.

The pottery from the sites was discussed in some detail by Hawkes (1935), who put forward the view that site A preceded site B, A dating from 1000 to 750 and B from 750 to 500. The principal differences in the two assemblages lay in the presence on site A of globular vessels with strap handles and incised decoration, related to the globular urns of the Deverel–Rimbury tradition, and their absence from site B. At site B, on the other hand, jars with high shoulders together with the characteristic carinated bowls appear, both of which look forward to later Iron Age forms. In spite of the recent trend to date sites of this kind considerably earlier, Hawkes's original arguments still seem to hold good, and if the dating were slightly adjusted to allow the change-over to centre upon 700 or 650 and not 750 the evidence of the iron-stained whetstones could be neatly accommodated.

The significance of the Plumpton Plain sites is considerable, for not only do their ceramic assemblages demonstrate chronological differences, they also emphasise a marked continuity. Thus the large bucket- or barrel-shaped urns with applied bosses or finger-printed cordons occur in quantity on both sites and remain a constituent of local assemblages which can be more firmly dated to the sixth and fifth centuries. The suggestion that the Plumpton Plain settlements should be updated brings with it further implications for other Sussex sites. The pottery from

Itford Hill, for example, is best paralleled by Plumpton Plain A, but that from New Barn Down is much closer to Plumpton Plain B. A detailed reassessment of the Sussex Bronze Age settlements, therefore, might well allow them to be arranged in a sequence stretching from before 1000 and continuing into the seventh or even the sixth century.

Large sceuomorphic carinated bowls, of the types considered here to belong to the eighth to seventh centuries, occur on a number of other coastal sites amid collections of pottery of various dates: at Kingston Buci, Highdown Hill and Castle Hill (Newhaven) in Sussex, and Mill Plain (Deal) and Minnis Bay in Kent. Related types are also known from the east coast at West Harling and Castle Hill, Scarborough. Coarse wares in Deverel–Rimbury tradition invariably occur alongside them, and from many of the sites items of bronze equipment of Late Bronze Age type are known.

The general impression which this evidence – albeit fragmentary and uneven – gives is that many of the communities occupying the south and east coastal regions of Britain began to produce pottery copies of the expensive bronze cauldrons and situlae which would have been traded widely along with other material of the carp's tongue sword complex. That the distributions of angular sceuomorphs and carp's tongue hoards are almost exactly coincident is therefore hardly surprising, nor is it difficult to understand why there is such a uniformity over so large an area. The same processes, perhaps even more intensified, were in force during the sixth century, but regionalisation in ceramic style gradually became apparent and the quality of the pottery considerably improved. These developments will be considered below.

The Early All Cannings Cross group (Fig. A:2)

In parallel with the coastal developments, a totally different ceramic style arose around the western fringes of the Wessex chalkland – a style which was to remain dominant in the area for several centuries. Since most of the sites continued in use throughout this period, it is very difficult to distinguish the earliest groups except upon typological grounds, but among the earliest types must be listed the large jars with evenly out-curved rims, and a rounded shoulder and body which in most cases is decorated with incised and stamped motifs, often in the form of stab-filled geometric shapes. The second distinctive type is the bipartite bowl with beaded rim and sharp shoulder angles, between which are bands of decoration, either stamped or incised. Sometimes these vessels are decorated with a coating of haematite burnished and fired to a shiny copper colour. Other types include large tripartite jars with sharp shoulders and flared necks, as well as a variety of coarse jars.

The classic site for the occurrence of these forms is All Cannings Cross in Wiltshire, where unfortunately the earliest assemblages were not distinguishable from the later material. Nevertheless, we may reasonably call the range of selected types the *Early All Cannings Cross group*. The discovery here of a tanged bifid razor and a fragment of Breton axe suggests an origin in the eighth or seventh century, but the bronzes could also have been residual material. Firmer dating evidence comes from the broadly contemporary site of Cow Down (Longbridge Deverill), Wilts, where a radiocarbon date of 630 ± 155 (708 BC) was obtained for wood charcoal collected from the post-holes of the main timbers of the earliest house.

While some of the ceramic forms can be explained away as indigenous copies of exotic metal types, the weak profiled jars with stabbed decoration stand out as something very new that cannot be easily paralleled except among Late Urnfield assemblages in eastern France and western Germany (Sandars, 1957, 225, Fig. 54; and Hatt, 1960, Fig. 68). Thus it is probable that an Urnfield element lies behind the origins of the Early All Cannings Cross group, but it is impossible at present to define the nature of the link more precisely. There is no firm evidence for a folk movement of any magnitude into the area, but limited immigration cannot be ruled out.

SIXTH CENTURY DEVELOPMENTS (Fig. 3:2)

The continuation of intensive trading contacts during the late seventh and sixth centuries introduced new types of metalwork into the country, among which were a series of fine carinated bowls (Fig. 3:3), like the elegant vessel with a sharp shoulder and furrowed neck found in a hoard at Welby in Leicestershire and dated to the early sixth century. These vessels

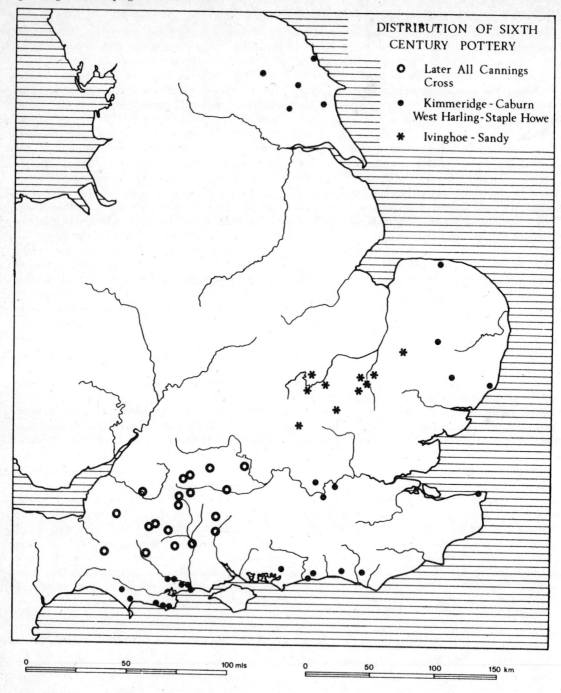

3:2   Distribution of sixth century pottery styles (source: author)

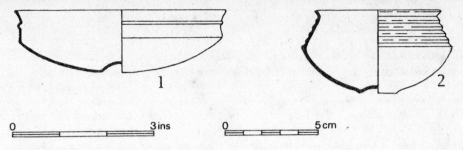

0 ——— 3 ins   0 ——— 5 cm

3:3   Bronze vessels serving as prototypes for angular pottery (source: 1   *Mindelheim*, Kossack, 1954: 2 *Welby, Leics Inv. Arch.* G.B. 24)

were immediately copied in pottery, giving rise to an extensive series of haematite-coated bowls centred on Wessex. Similarly, the tripartite jars with sharp shoulders and flaring necks may be seen to be copies of bronze containers, like the two from a seventh century hoard from Inverness recently rediscovered in a private collection. The presence in Britain of other metal vessels, such as the bipartite bowl with median neck cordon from the Mindelheim cemetery (Kossack, 1954), can also be postulated on the basis of their widely distributed ceramic copies. Thus it seems that the tendency to imitate bronze vessels, which began among the Ultimate Deverel–Rimbury communities of the south and east coastal regions, continued throughout the sixth century in parallel with a general improvement of ceramic technology and the gradual disappearance of traditional forms like the bucket- and barrel-shaped urns. Beneath the broad similarities of parallel development lie well-defined regional differences which must be described in detail.

The Later All Cannings Cross group

Many of the ceramic elements of the early group continued into the later period, but in general the tendency was for the large decorated jars to become less common and the smaller carinated bowls with furrowed shoulders to increase in number. Similarly, the technique of coating the vessels with haematite came into wider use. The general impression, then, is of a strong continuing local tradition, but one in which the relative proportions of the various types changed with time. There is as yet no good evidence for a stratigraphical distinction between the early and later phases of the group, but several sites would

appear, on typological grounds, to have been first occupied only during the later period.

The Kimmeridge–Caburn group (Fig. A:3)

Along the south coast of Britain a number of occupation sites can be recognised as producing a distinctive assemblage of material. The most characteristic vessels are the bipartite bowls, almost all of which have beaded rims and sharp shoulder angles, proclaiming their sceuomorphic origins. Median shoulder cordons occur widely, but furrowed and stamped decoration is restricted more to the western end of the distribution. Tripartite jars with flared rims, constricted necks and sharply angled shoulders, are also a feature of this group, as are coarser shouldered jars often with finger-tip or finger-nail impressions along the rim-tops and shoulders.

At Kimmeridge a well-stratified assemblage was recovered from an occupation site on the edge of a cliff, where Kimmeridge shale had been worked into armlets. Stratigraphically the group could be shown to succeed a layer containing pottery of Eldon's Seat I type (Ultimate Deverel–Rimbury) and at Eldon's Seat it could be argued that the Kimmeridge assemblage was probably current during the hiatus between phases I and II (Cunliffe, 1968b). In Dorset and Wiltshire there is a considerable degree of overlap between the All Cannings Cross and Kimmeridge traditions, but the Sussex sites show far less evidence of contact with the Wessex developments. Indeed, the traditions of the Ultimate Deverel–Rimbury style remain apparent throughout the sixth century. At sites like the Caburn and Stoke Clump the angular types occur alongside coarse vessels of devolved bucket and barrel type.

Traditional types likewise predominate among the assemblages from the farmstead at Weston Woods, Albury, Surrey, and from Minnis Bay, Kent, but at both of these sites occupation probably began in the late eighth or early seventh century and continued to the end of the sixth.

Dating depends largely upon typological considerations, but there is some additional independent evidence. Occupation at Weston Woods, Surrey, for example, produced a radiocarbon determination of 510 ± 110 (583 BC), an assessment totally in keeping with the typological dating of the pottery. Furthermore the semi-submerged settlement site of Minnis Bay, off the Kentish coast, has yielded a bronze hoard of the carp's tongue sword complex, but not in direct association with the occupation levels. Among the many items represented in the hoard is a fragment of a bronze cauldron which, taken together with a consideration of the other objects, would suggest a deposition date centring upon 600 BC, a date within the range to which some of the pottery would be assigned on typological grounds. It is not unreasonable, therefore, to suggest that the hoard was deposited during the main phase of occupation. While it must be admitted that the dating evidence for the individual sites is a little weak, taken together it consistently points to the bracket *c.* 650–500 for the developments categorised here as belonging to the Kimmeridge–Caburn group.

There is no reason to suppose that the ceramic innovation arose in response to an intrusion of people; the strong native undercurrent and the evidence of sceuomorphism together suggest an indigenous population absorbing new ideas. Burial rites also continued in native style: at the Caburn, immediately outside the palisaded settlement, a cremation was found placed in a large jar and buried in a pit covered by a low barrow. Similar cremations are recorded from East Anglia.

The West Harling–Staple Howe group (Fig. A:4)

The angular bipartite bowl form occurs on a number of sites in eastern England, invariably mixed up with quantities of pottery made in local traditions. At Staple Howe the native forms are usually jars with finger-impressed shoulders; at Scarborough, Yorks, which began a little earlier, finger-impressed neck cordons in Late Bronze Age tradition predominate; while at West Harling, Norfolk, both types occur in approximately equal quantities.

Dating evidence is provided at Staple Howe by a group of loosely associated bronze objects, including three Hallstatt C razors, a tanged chisel, part of a socketed axe and a small fragment of harness mount like those found at Llyn Fawr and Court-St-Etienne in seventh century contexts. A single radiocarbon date of 450 ± 150 (522 BC) from the site is in keeping with the character of the metalwork and pottery. The metal finds from Scarborough are not closely associated with the pottery but it seems reasonable to suppose them to be broadly contemporary. They include a tanged chisel like that from Staple Howe, a socketed axe, a flat-headed pin and two harness-rings – all paralleled in the Heathery Burn deposit, Co. Durham (p. 54) – which together suggest a date early in the sixth century or late in the seventh.

It now seems probable that the vessels found at the hillfort of Grimthorpe, which include jars with flared rims, shouldered jars and bowls, and simple hemispherical bowls, should be regarded as belonging to an early phase in the West Harling–Staple Howe tradition. The two radiocarbon dates for bones found in the ditch, 690 ± 130 and 970 ± 130 (769 and 1058 BC) were surprisingly early to the excavator, but when the similarities are pointed out between the Grimthorpe pottery and the vessels of the Ultimate Deverel–Rimbury tradition, a date in the seventh or eighth century would seem acceptable. Some further support is provided by a group of similar pottery from within and below a group of nine barrows on Ampleforth Moor, Yorks, which is also comparable to the sherds from the Heathery Burn Cave. Two radiocarbon dates were obtained: 582 ± 90 and 537 ± 90 (658, 612 BC), placing them fairly reliably in the seventh century.

At Ampleforth Moor the burial rite was cremation, the ashes being placed below small barrows, barely 5 ft (1·5 m) high and 24–32 ft (7·3–9·8 m) in diameter; each was surrounded by a ditch. The native tradition of cremation was also continued at Creeting St Mary, Suffolk, where a typical tripartite vessel decorated with plain cordons containing a cremation was found buried apparently without a covering barrow; while at Warborough Hill, Norfolk what appears to have been a cremation beneath a barrow was recorded.

While it is too early to be definite, it might eventually be necessary to divide the West Harling–Staple Howe group into an early and later phase: the early phase of Ultimate Deverel–Rimbury origin dating to the eighth to seventh century, including Ampleforth Moor, early Scarborough and Grimthorpe, the later phase of seventh to sixth century date being represented by the angular bipartite wares of the two type-sites.

It will be apparent that significant similarities existed between communities living in southern and eastern Britain in the sixth century. All areas showed a strong indigenous element overlaid by a parallel development in fine ceramics – a development which implies contacts with the continent – further emphasised by the presence of the Hallstatt C metal types at Staple Howe. Internal trade, perhaps by sea, is also suggested by the presence of large decorated jars of All Cannings Cross type at Minnis Bay, Kent, and Darmsden, Suffolk. While there can be little doubt, therefore, that the coastal regions were in close contact with each other – a contact which acted as a spur to innovation – inland areas like the Chilterns received little stimulus and appear to have developed along more isolated lines.

The Ivinghoe–Sandy group (Fig. A:5)

The recent excavation of the hillfort on Ivinghoe Beacon has brought to light a distinctive assemblage of pottery found in loose association both with the structure of the fort (p. 229) and with a group of bronze implements. Previously a number of isolated groups of broadly contemporary material were known from sites such as Sandy, Harrold, Kempston and Totternhoe – all in Bedfordshire – Hawthorn Hill, Herts, and several others, most of them unpublished; but apart from the material from Sandy, the finds were unassociated and mainly recovered under non-archaeological conditions.

The Ivinghoe pottery is generally coarsely made. The principal types include the shouldered bowl or jar with the rim-top out-curved and the shoulder sometimes ornamented with finger-impressions, jars with applied neck cordons impressed with finger-printing, round-shouldered jars with flared rims, open hemispherical bowls, and occasionally bipartite bowls and jars, one of which has incised decoration on the shoulder. The same range of types recur on the other sites mentioned but the bipartite bowl with rounded shoulder tends to be rather more common. There are obvious similarities between this group and the pottery from Scarborough, Minnis Bay, the Caburn, etc., the only significant difference lying in the general lack of the tightly moulded and cordoned vessels imitating bronze types. The impression which the pottery gives, therefore, is of a contemporary native tradition largely untouched by external influences.

Exactly the same conclusions can be reached from a study of the associated bronze work, which at Ivinghoe includes a tanged bifid razor, fragments of two swords probably of Ewart Park type, a ring, various mounts and studs, tweezers and several pins. To these may be added the winged axe found unassociated in 1929. All the bronze work falls within native Late Bronze Age tradition of the late eighth and seventh centuries, uninfluenced by obvious Hallstatt C techniques. On a conservative estimate, a date of about 650 BC might be suggested for the initial occupation of the site. Within this same general range of pottery can be placed the vessels recovered from the Totternhoe quarry, Beds, found together with a bronze vase-headed pin of Late Urnfield type. A similar pin was recovered from All Cannings Cross and an iron copy is known from Fifield Bavant, Wilts. The bronze examples cannot be dated too closely, since individual pins might have survived in use for some time, but a seventh to sixth century range would seem most likely.

Thus the evidence at present available suggests the existence of a regional group centred upon the Chilterns and the gravel terraces to the west, defined by pottery made in the traditional manner and by the continued use of Late Bronze Age metalwork. Exact dating is impossible, but the range 650–500 probably covers the main developments which the pottery style characterises.

The south-west peninsula

The seventh and sixth century cultures of the west of England are at present ill known. Early pottery similar to the southern and eastern assemblages has been found in small quantities at several sites, including Norton Fitzwarren and

Worlebury, Somerset, Dainton, Devon, and Bodrifty, Cornwall. The settlement at Kestor, Devon, may also belong to this general group but the assemblage is not sufficiently distinctive. No internal dating evidence is provided by these sites, but comparison with the pottery of the Kimmeridge–Caburn group suggests a broad contemporaneity. What the scarcity of sites implies – a sparse population, a general lack of contemporary pottery or the continuance of Bronze Age types – it is at present impossible to say.

THE FIFTH TO THE THIRD CENTURY (Fig. 3:4)

A most dramatic change in pottery styles came about towards the end of the fifth century, when well-made angular bowls and vessels appeared with pedestals copying the *vases carenées* and *vases piriformes* of the continental La Tène cultures. The influence of these ceramic innovations was felt most strongly in the Thames valley and eastern England, contributing to the regional assemblages called here the Long Wittenham–Allen's Pit group, the Chinnor–Wandlebury group and the Darmsden–Linton group. Further south in Sussex and west in Hampshire and Wiltshire, elements of the new types, though apparent, are more dimly reflected in the contemporary ceramic development. The mechanism by which these La Tène I types were introduced into Britain remains unclear. While

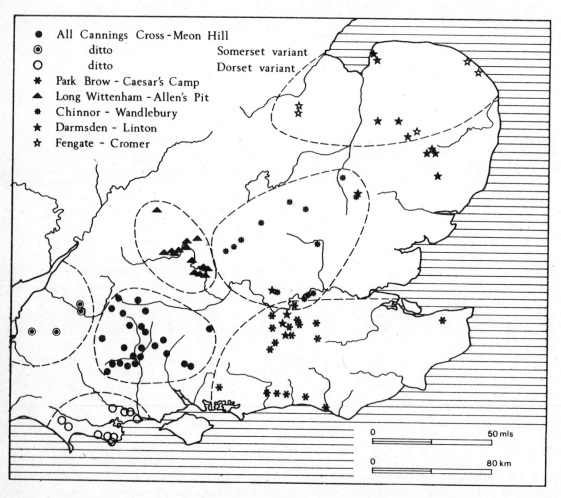

● All Cannings Cross - Meon Hill
◉ ditto   Somerset variant
○ ditto   Dorset variant
✱ Park Brow - Caesar's Camp
▲ Long Wittenham - Allen's Pit
✴ Chinnor - Wandlebury
★ Darmsden - Linton
☆ Fengate - Cromer

0   50 mls
0   80 km

3:4   Distribution of fifth to third century pottery styles (source: author)

it is possible that an actual folk movement took place, penetrating Britain by means of the Thames to introduce an alien population, it is no less likely that the new types emerged as the result of close trading relations between the two sides of the Channel. Since the nature of the evidence does not allow the problem to be resolved, it is preferable simply to characterise the regional groups as objectively as possible.

The All Cannings Cross–Meon Hill group (Fig. A:6)

The All Cannings Cross settlement continued in use for several hundred years following the initial occupation of the site in the seventh century. No stratigraphical distinction was made by the excavator between the early and late phases, but the later pottery can be distinguished on typological grounds and can be shown to be the same as that found at the Hampshire site of Meon Hill, where occupation did not begin until the late phase. At the more recently excavated settlement of Cow Down (Longbridge Deverill), Wilts, a stratigraphical distinction has been recognised between early All Cannings Cross pottery and later All Cannings Cross–Meon Hill group. The latter assemblage can therefore be regarded as distinct from and succeeding the earlier group.

There is a wide area of continuity between the two assemblages. In particular, the haematite coating of bowls continued on an extensive scale, but the bipartite form gave way to shouldered bowls with widely flaring rims. The commonest of these was still ornamented with furrowed shoulders, as in the earlier tradition, but other forms of shoulder decoration were now adopted, including groups or areas of diagonal lines and stroke-filled triangles, the decoration now being applied by shallow tooling with a blunt point before firing and not by incision or stamping. At a later stage a highly characteristic form of haematite-coated bowl was produced in central Wessex, with the angles of the body accentuated by cordons, between which various forms of geometric decoration were scratched on to the surface after firing and probably filled with white paste. Unlike the other bowl types, these scratched cordoned bowls were provided with a carefully moulded foot-ring to enable them to stand firmly. There can be little doubt that vessels of this type were made in a single production centre and distributed locally from there.

They do not replace the other types but occur beside them. In addition to the decorated bowls, several plain types with variously moulded profiles commonly occur but always with a haematite-coated surface.

The coarse ware types are restricted to plain shouldered jars, seldom with any form of decoration on the shoulder or rim, though not invariably so. Occasionally jars with horizontally or vertically perforated handles are found, and at a late stage plain bucket-shaped types come into more common use. A more exotic type, found twice at Swallowcliffe Down, Wilts, consisted of a high-shouldered jar with flaring rim and a narrow squat pedestal foot, made in a black fabric with a well-burnished surface. Since parallels with continental La Tène types are fairly close, it is possible that the Swallowcliffe vessels are local copies of imported types. The distribution of the principal types centres upon the Wessex chalkland extending from the Marlborough Downs in the north to the river Itchen in the east. The same assemblage also recurs as far south as Hengistbury Head. In south Dorset, south of the Stour, a more restricted range of types occurs, typified by the flared bowl and bipartite bowls with near-vertical concave sides (Fig. A:7). The assemblage is clearly within the broad tradition of the Wessex haematite-coated bowls but is outside the range of the centres producing the more characteristic decorated types.[1] A westerly extension of the generalised assemblage can also be recognised at the Somerset sites of Bathampton Down, Pagan's Hill, Banwell and South Cadbury (Fig. A:7). Like the south Dorset ceramics, there is some divergence from the typical central Wessex groups, but similarities in form and the use of haematite coating serve to link the two traditions closely.

Some indication of the date range covered by the assemblage is provided by a few stratified metal objects. From Maiden Castle comes a Viollier type Ia fibula dating to the second half of the fifth century, which may have arrived about 400 BC. The latest datable metal objects from All Cannings Cross are two local versions of the La Tène II fibulae of a type in use in the

[1] The largest groups of finds of this type occur at the hillforts of Chalbury and Maiden Castle (where it is called Maiden Castle A) and at Eldon's Seat, Encombe (where it has been referred to as the Eldon's Seat II assemblage).

fourth or even the third century, and the Meon Hill settlement has produced an iron La Tène II fibula of fourth century origin. This admittedly sparse evidence, taken in conjunction with typological considerations and sequence, suggests that the All Cannings Cross–Meon Hill group, together with its south Dorset and Somerset outliers, developed out of the late All Cannings Cross and Kimmeridge–Caburn groups, probably in the fifth century, and continued in use into the third or even the second century. Throughout this time there was, of course, internal development: the flared furrowed bowls were gradually replaced by the scratched cordoned bowls in the central areas and the coarse ware vessels lost their sharp-shouldered profiles, developing towards simpler barrel-shaped containers by the end of the period. There was also a noticeable preference for darker fired fabrics.

Other aspects of material culture, economy and settlement pattern are shared with the rest of south-eastern Britain, emphasising the cultural unity of the area. The only other distinctive Wessex artefacts are the local copies of the La Tène I fibulae with their bows decorated by a simple row of punched dots. Sixteen have now been found, all from the central Wessex area (Figs 14:7, 14:8). Clearly this was a local product made for a market of restricted size. Like the pottery, the fibulae serve to emphasise a sphere of contact, implying that the Wessex sites were linked by marketing ties.

The Park Brow–Caesar's Camp group (Fig. A:8)

The south-east of Britain, particularly the chalk areas of the North and South Downs, is scattered with settlement sites, most of them ill recorded but producing similar assemblages of pottery. The range of types is not wide but consistently includes bowls with well-defined shoulders and flaring rims, usually made in a dark well-burnished fabric. The coarse ware vessels consist of jars with rounded shoulders, upright or flaring necks and flattened rim-tops. Finger-impressions on the rims and shoulders sometimes occur, and occasionally jars and bowls are provided with squat pedestal bases.

The type-sites chosen to define the group were not extensively excavated but at the open settlement at Park Brow, Sussex, a bent silver ring of Viollier type Ic was discovered, which is hardly likely to have reached Britain before 270; while at Caesar's Camp (Wimbledon), Surrey, an assemblage of pottery was found associated with the rampart of a timber-laced hillfort of Hollingbury type (p. 229). Dating and internal development are difficult to assess in any detail, but on typological grounds it is probable that the finger-impressed coarse ware, which occurs in quantity at Caesar's Camp, is earlier than the plainer forms from Park Brow. The development would appear to be largely parallel with that of the All Cannings Cross–Meon Hill group in Wessex and probably covers the same time span, from the fifth to the third century.

The Long Wittenham–Allen's Pit group (Fig. A:9)

In the upper Thames valley and extending into the Cotswolds are a number of sites which have produced varied but distinctive assemblages of pottery including bowls with well-defined shoulders and flaring rims, fired usually to dark tones and well finished by smoothing or burnishing. The shoulders of these vessels were frequently decorated with shallow-tooled decoration in a variety of patterns resembling the contemporary Wessex examples; but, with the exception of occasional haematite-coated sherds which may be imported into the region, the decorated bowls are distinctive enough to be regarded as locally made. There are three major coarse ware types: weak-shouldered jars sometimes with finger-impressions on the shoulders, open bowls with heavy T-shaped rims, finger-impressed on the outside, and large shouldered jars with sharply flaring rims closely related to the tripartite jars of the early All Cannings Cross group. These are usually plain but occasionally the shoulders are tooled with simple geometric decoration.

Although good stratigraphical evidence is lacking from practically every site, it seems that the tripartite jars and some of the plainer, less flared bowls belonging to the beginning of the sequence overlap with the early All Cannings Cross and Kimmeridge–Caburn groups; then follows the development of the highly decorated bowls in parallel with the Wessex, All Cannings Cross–Meon Hill group. Towards the end of the period the bowl form becomes simpler in profile and less frequently decorated, while the coarser vessels take on a slacker and more barrel-shaped form. The picture is to some extent confused by regionalisation and by the differential distribution and by the differential distribution of the more elaborate types. Thus further from the Thames, in the eastern flanks of the Cotswolds, very few of the bowls are found and the coarse wares are of a very generalised form.

Internal dating evidence is lacking apart from a La Tène I fibula from Radley, Berks, but analogies with Wessex might suggest a beginning in the late sixth or fifth century and a development continuing as late as the third or second century.

The Chinnor–Wandlebury group (Fig. A:10)

The area occupied by this group approximates to that of the Chilterns, but extends in the north up to the Fen margins and in the south to the Thames valley and the Berkshire Downs. The pottery by which the group is characterised consists of bowls with flaring rims and shoulders frequently decorated with simple geometric patterns, often dot-filled triangles. At Blewburton Hill, Berks, and Chinnor, Oxon, rosette stamps were sometimes employed, the rosettes being arranged between pendent swags at Blewburton Hill; this mode of decoration is strictly limited in distribution. More common and more widely spread were the flared bowls, the lip splaying beyond the maximum diameter of the shoulder. These were invariably made in a black burnished fabric and were sometimes ornamented with a zigzag pattern scratched after firing. This type of bowl was often provided with a simple foot-ring base, a technique apparently learnt from the East Anglian group to be described below. The coarse ware jars were of normal shouldered type, sometimes with finger-impressions on the rim-tops and shoulders.

Both of the type-sites provide evidence of internal development. At Chinnor two phases of occupation were recognised. The first yielded a large number of bowls, mostly decorated with simple linear zigzag motifs or groups of lines, although some were ornamented with pendant stab-filled triangles frequently in association with stab-filled arcs, possibly imitating handles. The second phase, stratigraphically distinct from the first, included bowls in a brownish ware stamped with rosettes. In all probability, different production centres are indicated. At the hillfort of Wandlebury, Cambs, it was possible to relate a pottery sequence to two separate phases of the

fort construction. The earlier group contained the basic forms defined above but the later assemblage was more generalised, exhibiting few distinctive features but sufficiently similar to the first group to suggest a logical development from it. Clearly over such a large area, factors such as local development in isolation, as well as specialised production offering geographically limited distribution, tend to complicate the apparent unity of the region. A further possibility that cannot be ruled out is that some sites like Wandlebury may have continued to be inhabited as late as the first century, while the communities further south came under the influence of more advanced pottery traditions.

Dating with precision is impossible. Similarities to Wessex, the upper Thames and East Anglia suggest a broad contemporaneity which may have spanned the two centuries following 500, but no internal evidence is yet available.

The Darmsden–Linton group (Fig. A:11)

The east of England from the Wash as far south as the Thames supported a group of settlements linked by a common ceramic tradition typified by a large assemblage of pottery found at Darmsden in Suffolk. The most characteristic type of vessel is the bowl in a fine black burnished ware with a sharp narrow shoulder and a short upright or slightly flared rim. The shoulders are usually ornamented with deeply impressed horizontal grooves, while the bases may be rounded or provided with simple foot-rings. Similar bowls with more rounded shoulders also occur, together with larger bowls with widely flared rims. The jar forms are usually shouldered and frequently, but not invariably, decorated.

The little bowl form has certain similarities to La Tène I types on the continent, suggesting a fourth and third century date for their first appearance in this country. The similarity does not necessarily imply a folk movement into Britain at this time since trading contact would be quite sufficient to explain the likeness. Links with adjacent groups are demonstrated at several sites. At Sandown Park, Esher, Surrey, Darmsden–Linton pottery is found with types of Park Brow–Caesar's Camp forms and at Linton, Cambs, associations with Chinnor–Wandlebury wares are recorded. A general contemporaneity is therefore implied.

The Fengate–Cromer group (Fig. A:12)

In Norfolk and the Fen margins a few sites have been discovered yielding a group of well-made and highly decorated pottery typified by a large collection recovered from the habitation site at Fengate, Northants, and by a much smaller group discovered during a cliff fall at Cromer, Norfolk. At Fengate a typological sequence was proposed (Hawkes & Fell, 1945) starting with bowls with flaring rims and somewhat globular bodies, usually decorated with shallow tooling above and below the shoulder or girth. Associated with this early group were jars with sharp shoulders and finger-nail or finger-tip decoration on the rims and shoulders, and sometimes cordons at the junction of the neck and rim. But since the pottery of the middle group included bipartite bowls and the use of slashed cordons, presumably derived from earlier local traditions such as those evident at West Harling, it is possible that the typological arguments originally put forward should be reversed: the 'middle' group becoming the earliest, thus allowing for an indigenous development diverging from the forms of the local West Harling–Staple Howe group. Until closely stratified deposits are excavated, however, further discussion would be valueless.

Typologically the Fengate–Cromer group should be placed in the fifth century, before the development of the Darmsden–Linton group some time after about 400. Support for this view was provided by the discovery of a pin of sunflower-swan's neck type in one of the Fengate pits: these pins are normally regarded as being fifth century imports.

The Breedon–Ancaster group (Fig. A:13)

The ceramic and cultural development of the east Midlands between the Trent and the Welland is at present far from clear but it has long been possible to recognise a group of weak-shouldered jars, frequently scored on the outside with irregularly arranged lines. This general category has been referred to in the past as Trent valley A ware, following definition of the type at Breedon-on-the-Hill, Leics. At the time scored coarse ware jars were thought to be predominantly of the first century BC and later, but recent work has extended both the distribution and the time range.

The original Breedon excavations provided no close dating evidence for the pottery, but the most recent work (Wacher, 1964) has demonstrated a stratigraphical sequence suggesting occupation over a considerable period. Moreover, at Ancaster, Lincs, the excavation of a substantial open settlement, occupied by a community using scored jars, has yielded an iron involuted brooch and a bronze wire fibula with a four-coiled spring, high bow and recurved foot – characteristics which proclaim a La Tène I ancestry (May, 1966). While the brooches do not prove an early date, they are more likely to have been in use in the third or second century than much later. Typologically the pottery would not be out of place in a fourth or third century context.

The Arras group (Figs 15:2, 15:3)

The early La Tène contacts with most of southern Britain were on the basis of casual trading, but in eastern Yorkshire it is possible to distinguish a group of burials which have very close connections with France, implying some form of intrusive folk movement bringing with it burial traditions alien to those of the indigenous culture. These new burials are conventionally referred to as the Arras culture, after the Yorkshire barrow cemetery partially examined for the first time in 1815. The Arras cemetery provides evidence of most of the rites characteristic of the Yorkshire burials: there were several inhumations buried with the remains of carts; some were covered by barrows constructed within rectangular ditched enclosures; the barrow mounds were invariably small and the cemetery was large, containing between 100 and 200 graves. These elements are repeated on a number of sites, the more important of which include Dane's Graves, Driffield, Eastburn, Cowlam, Pexton Moor, Hunmanby, Huntow and Sawdon.

A distributional analysis of the rite of cart burial shows that two distinct methods were employed: either the carts were placed upright in the graves, sometimes with recesses cut for the wheels so that the body of the cart could rest on the ground surface; or the carts were dismantled, the wheels being placed flat. That burials of the first type were found on the limestone hills, while the second were restricted to the Wolds, suggests the possibility of some form of cultural distinction between the two areas – a suggestion further supported by the apparent absence of large cemeteries, as opposed to isolated barrows, on the limestone hills in reverse of the situation on the Wolds.

The surviving grave-goods can be divided into two groups: the cart- and harness-fittings, and personal ornaments and offerings. The first category covers a wide range of types including the iron cart-tyres, nave hoops and miscellaneous wheel-fittings, lynch pins to prevent the wheels from coming loose, bronze pole sheaths, three-link horse-bits and various terret-rings from the leather harnesses. Detailed comparisons with continental types (Stead, 1965, 28–45) show that while the British versions were closely related to them, they are nevertheless sufficiently distinctive to be considered the result of several generations of local development. Not one of the cart- or harness-fittings at present known can be regarded as a direct import from France.

Among the ornaments, on the other hand, there is an assemblage from Cowlam which is clearly of direct continental inspiration. It includes a fibula of Münsingen Ia type, a bracelet with 'tongue-in-glove' terminals, expanded at five points around the circumference, which can be paralleled in Alsace and Burgundy in early La Tène contexts, and a necklace composed of seventy blue and white beads. Again, parallels can be found for such necklaces in the phase Ia graves at Münsingen although they do occur later. The Cowlam burial is the earliest assemblage that can be defined within the Arras culture, probably dating to the early part of the fourth century: it might reasonably be thought to represent the burial of first-generation imported trinkets. The Cowlam bracelet and necklace are similar to finds from the Arras cemetery, where knobbed and ribbed bracelets of early La Tène type provide a further link with Burgundy and Switzerland. The remainder of the ornaments – the inlaid and involuted brooches, the incised bronze mirror, the ring-headed pins, finger-rings, pendants, toilet sets and toggles – all belong to a decidedly British tradition and must be later developments influenced more by internal British traditions than by continental ideas.

There can be little doubt that the Arras culture arose as the result of a folk movement into eastern Yorkshire early in the fourth century. Thereafter local development modified the culture, but as late as the first century BC its alien origins were still apparent. A careful consideration of the niceties of burial rite and the typology of the earliest group of artefacts has led Stead (1965) to propose a complex origin for the invaders, coming from the Burgundian area (where dismantled carts and the absence of weapons and pottery are similar to the British burials) via the Seine. In the Nanterre–Paris region part of the band remained to give rise to the Parisii while those destined for Britain moved on, to found another community in Yorkshire, known to Ptolemy as the Parisi: the coincidence is noteworthy. The cultural affinities of the Pexton Moor burial, with its rectangular enclosure ditches and wheel pits, may however indicate that some part of the immigrant force had connections with the La Tène group in the Champagne.

A close study of the Arras culture emphasises some of the problems involved in recognising immigrant communities by means of the archaeological record. Seldom is it possible to discover material of the first generation; what survives is more likely to belong to subsequent developments, which invariably diverge from the traditions of the homeland. Nevertheless, the Yorkshire evidence is impressive. It suggests small bands arriving, with little more than their personal equipment, and settling down among the natives in whose pottery traditions they shared. When time came for burial they maintained their own rituals, using a mortuary cart to bring the body to the grave and sometimes burying it with the dead. So strong were these religious practices that they remained dominant for several hundred years.

At present it is difficult to link the burial tradition of the Arras folk to other aspects of the material culture of the region, since so few occupation sites have been excavated. The pottery tradition, which must run broadly parallel to the burials, should post-date the Staple Howe assemblage (p. 34) but pre-date the simple coarse wares of the Dane's Graves–Staxton style (p. 47) which are predominantly second to first century BC in date. The class of large jars with upright or everted rims, like those from Kendall, Kilham and Atwick, might be considered to be of fifth to third century date on typological grounds, but sequential or absolute dating is at present lacking.

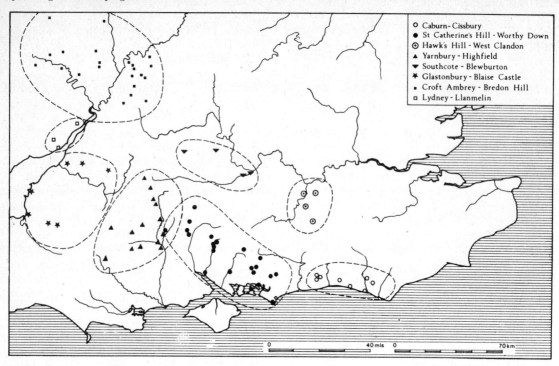

3:5   Distribution of second to first century saucepan pot pottery styles in southern Britain (the broken lines are added merely for emphasis) (source: author)

THIRD TO FIRST CENTURY DEVELOPMENTS

During the third and second centuries BC the pottery over a large area of southern Britain developed a remarkable degree of uniformity characterised by vertical-sided 'saucepan pots' and jars with rounded shoulders and beaded rims. Broadly speaking, this continuum covers Sussex, Hampshire, Wiltshire, Surrey, Berkshire, Somerset, Gloucestershire, the Welsh borderland and parts of south Wales. The only differences which can be recognised in the ceramic assemblages of these regions are minor variations of profile, regional decorative preferences and fabric variations. Recent petrological analyses have demonstrated with great clarity that differences of this kind are due almost entirely to the differential distribution of commercially produced wares and have little to do with significant cultural boundaries.

In Dorset and the south-west, and in the upper Thames valley, the Midlands and East Anglia, the contemporary ceramics do not form a part of the saucepan pot continuum. In these areas the bowl form tends to predominate, although it must be admitted that very little material is yet known from north of the Thames.

The southern British Saucepan Pot styles

To describe in any detail the range of pottery from each of the regional styles constituting the saucepan pot continuum is unnecessary here, since the illustrations of selected vessels (Figs. A:14–A:18) together with the distribution map (Fig. 3:5) summarise in a simple visual form the major points. Nevertheless, a few generalisations must be offered.

The Caburn–Cissbury style (Fig. A:14) has been so called after two partially excavated hillforts in Sussex. The main characteristic of the pottery is that it tends to be decorated with simple regular and asymmetrical curvilinear designs. The rims and bases of the 'saucepans' are frequently thickened, perhaps to imitate the strengthening of leather prototypes of which the vessels are copies.

The St Catherine's Hill–Worthy Down style (Fig. A:15), centred upon Hampshire, also shows signs of sceuomorphism in the frequent use of a decorative zone, incorporating oblique lines between rows of dots, presumably meant to imitate stitching. The group is also characterised by a greater predominance of jars, often similarly decorated, some of which are large while others have about the same capacity as the saucepan pots.

The Yarnbury–Highfield style (Fig. A:16) of Wiltshire differs from the Hampshire group in that narrow-necked jars frequently occur and the decorative motifs often incorporate simple tooled arcs springing from shallow depressions.

The Hawk's Hill–West Clandon style (Fig. A:16) is proposed to include the limited assemblages recovered from the relatively few sites in Surrey. Similarities to the Sussex types are apparent.

The Southecote–Blewburton Hill style (Fig. A:17) is distributed in the Berkshire Downs–Reading area. The basic pottery forms show considerable variation, reflecting influences both from the decorated hemispherical bowl types of the upper Thames and from Hampshire. The general preference in decoration is for rectilinear areas filled with shallow tooled lines or dots.

The Glastonbury–Blaise Castle Hill style (Fig. A:17) is a tentative descriptive title proposed for contemporary material found in Somerset. The Somerset area poses problems, largely because the third and second century developments are difficult to distinguish stratigraphically from the mass of highly decorated fabrics known collectively as *Glastonbury ware* which, on current estimates, are thought to post-date *c.* 150 BC (and will therefore be more appropriate to a later section). Nevertheless, behind the native Glastonbury tradition it is possible dimly to discern an earlier tradition, clearly linked to the saucepan pot styles and presumably contemporary with them. The decorated vessels from the hillfort of Little Solisbury, though at present unique, may lie towards the beginning of the sequence, and another early group from Blaise Castle Hill, Glos, was found in a pit with a La Tène I fibula, allowing the possibility of an early date. Other material from Camerton and

Worlebury, Somerset, and from Bury Wood Camp, Wilts, is limited in quantity and without useful associations. From the two villages of Glastonbury and Meare quantities of typologically early pottery are known, suggesting an occupation sequence beginning perhaps as soon as the third century, but it is not yet possible to isolate an early group stratigraphically.

The Croft Ambrey–Bredon Hill style (Fig. A:18) is represented in the Herefordshire–Cotswold region by occupation sites and hillforts producing pottery in the saucepan pot tradition which is decorated either with bands of stamped impressions below the rim or with a similarly placed zone of linear tooling. Until recently it was thought that the two styles represented different cultural groups of complementary dates, but the excavation at Croft Ambrey, together with a petrological examination of the fabrics (Peacock, 1968), has demonstrated that both types were contemporary and were the output of three production centres in the Malvern area, which developed to serve the needs of a region hitherto largely aceramic. The complexities of production and distribution which the study underlines are probably typical of those which existed over much of southern Britain at this time.

The Lydney–Llanmelin style (Fig. A:18) is centred upon the south Welsh coastal plain east of the Usk, where a group of sites producing a distinctive saucepan pot assemblage have been excavated. The range of decorative motifs is limited but includes chevron patterns and large oval-shaped stab marks which tend not to occur in other groups.

Dating evidence for these saucepan pot styles is not plentiful but stratigraphically they can be shown to post-date the assemblages of the fifth and fourth centuries, out of which they appear to have developed, and to pre-date Belgic and Belgic-influenced types of the first century. Individual associations include the La Tène I fibula from Blaise Castle Hill and a coin of Ptolemy V (204–180) from Winchester; neither provides close dating in its own right, but the coin at least implies that the pottery was in use in the second century or later.

Two radiocarbon dates are available from Longbridge Deverill (Cow Down), based on

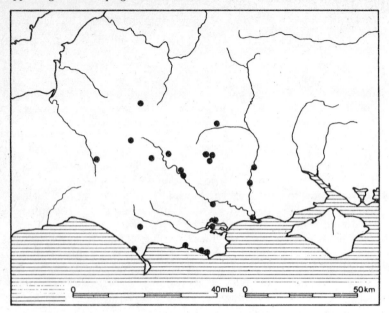

3:6   Distribution of Maiden Castle–Marnhull pottery (source: author)

wood charcoal from pit fillings: one pit is dated to 460 ± 140 (532 BC), the other to 490 ± 90 (563 BC). Both dates are at least 100 years older than would be expected and are difficult at this moment to explain.[1] Nevertheless, the occupation sequences at sites like the hillforts of Torberry, Sussex, and Croft Ambrey and at the Meare settlement show that the saucepan pot assemblage was in use over a considerable period of time, and a beginning earlier than that conventionally accepted might eventually prove to be correct.

Over the southern counties of Britain the end must have come with the introduction of the potter's wheel together with the changes consequent upon the folk movements of the period 150–50 BC. In Somerset and the south-west development continued largely unhindered, to give rise to the mature Glastonbury style, which may have lasted until the period of the Roman invasion – AD 43–47 – while in Gloucestershire, Herefordshire, Shropshire and south Wales the local style may have continued in use even later until those areas were gradually subdued by the Roman armies between 47 and c. 60.

[1] One possibility is that some of the charcoal was residual, deriving from the destruction of the earlier seventh century house. It is best, therefore, to regard the samples as potentially contaminated.

The Maiden Castle–Marnhull style (Figs 3:6, A:19)

From the lower reaches of the Wiltshire Avon west approximately to the valley of the river Brit and from the Channel coast to the river Ebble, a range of pottery is found typified by the large and well-stratified collection from the hillfort of Maiden Castle and from the open settlement at Marnhull. The forms and decoration readily distinguish the style from the adjacent saucepan pot groups. The commonest types are large ovoid jars with beaded rims and smaller bowls of similar shape. Some jars were provided with countersunk lugs, and occasionally open bowls with flat-topped rims occur. Decoration often takes the form of grooved scrolls, arcs or wavy lines. Sometimes single or grouped dimples are employed, either associated with other patterns or in isolation; less often shallow-tooled arcs occur. A consideration of the sequences and associations from the two type-sites leaves little doubt that the entire assemblage could easily have developed out of preceding traditions without necessarily postulating an invasion from the continent. Even the countersunk lugs, which were once thought to have derived from Brittany, are now best regarded as a local feature.

At what stage pottery of the Maiden Castle–Marnhull type began to develop its distinctive

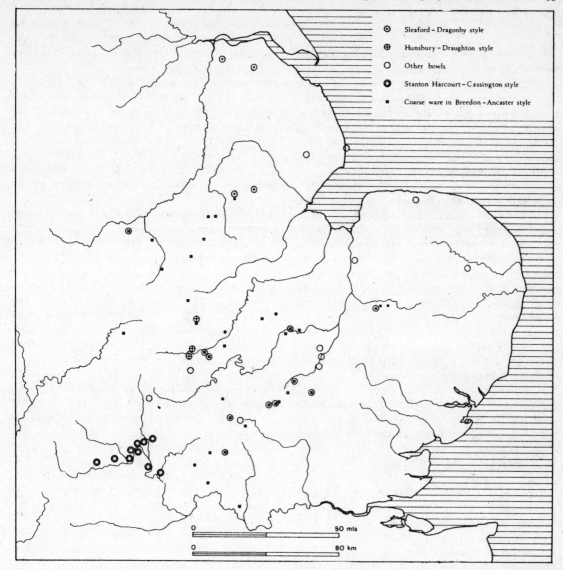

Key:
- ⊙ Sleaford – Dragonby style
- ⊕ Hunsbury – Draughton style
- ○ Other bowls
- ⊗ Stanton Harcourt – Cassington style
- ▪ Coarse ware in Breedon – Ancaster style

0   50 mls

0   80 km

3:7   Distribution of pottery styles in the East Midlands (source: author)

characteristics is difficult to say, but a beginning in the third or second century would allow a sufficient time span for the associated structural developments at Maiden Castle to take place. The end of the sequence was marked by the rapid evolution of better made and more sophisticated pottery of Durotrigian type which resulted from the introduction of the potter's wheel and resumed contacts with the continent towards the beginning of the first century BC.

The Midlands and eastern England (Fig. 3:7)
North of the Thames, in the east Midlands, the Chilterns and East Anglia, a number of stylistic groups of pottery appear in the third and second centuries, all sharing a common type of hemispherical bowl with a simple beaded lip, made in a dark well-burnished fabric. As a broad generalisation we might regard it as defining a bowl continuum complementary to the saucepan pot continuum further south. As might be

expected, several individual styles can be recognised.

The Stanton Harcourt–Cassington style (Fig. A:20)

In the upper Thames valley a change to dark well-burnished bowls became noticeable towards the end of the Long Wittenham–Allen's Pit style and eventually gave rise to an assemblage in which the black hemispherical bowl of the type found at Frilford, Berks, predominated. But Frilford bowls were usually highly decorated and there is some evidence to suggest that they belong to the century or so before the Roman invasion. It seems probable, therefore, that an intermediate stage exists, characterised by plain bowls together with the ultimate simplification of the coarse ware shouldered jar, and datable to the third and second centuries. Such a phase seems to be represented by the pottery from a number of Oxfordshire settlements, particularly the type-sites of Stanton Harcourt and Cassington.

To make a distinction in the development somewhere about 150–100 BC is, of course, arbitrary in so far as the internal development of the style is concerned, but it will be argued (pp. 84–6) that the appearance of elaborately decorated ceramics in an arc stretching from the south-west peninsula through the Oxford region to the Humber is a phenomenon of some significance, complementary to the dominance of plain pottery of Belgic type to the south-east.

The Hunsbury–Draughton style (Fig. A:21)

Extending north from the Oxford region along the Jurassic ridge into Northamptonshire it is possible to trace several groups of pottery containing bowl forms similar to those of the Stanton Harcourt–Cassington style. The vessels from the fourth phase of occupation at Rainsborough Camp, Northants, might reasonably be assigned to the Stanton Harcourt–Cassington style but further north at Hunsbury and Draughton, Northants, it is probable that the assemblages of the third and second centuries should be regarded as stylistically separate, since the subsequent development gives rise to highly distinctive decorated bowls (p. 85).

The large, but unstratified, collection from Hunsbury includes material dating from the third to second century BC until the first century AD. The fibulae – three La Tène I types and two of La Tène III – no doubt reflect the chronological range reasonably accurately. On typological grounds, the pottery too would seem to cover the same span. The coarse shouldered jars, the simple bead-rimmed bowls and probably the jars with perforated lug handles belong to the earlier period, while the elaborately decorated bowls develop later. The same sequence was recognised stratigraphically at Draughton. Thus the Northamptonshire development is parallel to that in the Oxford region but must take with it the same reservations about abitrarily dividing a sequence in order to separate a decorated phase.

The Sleaford–Dragonby style (Fig. A:22)

Between the Northamptonshire uplands and the Humber, several sites have recently come to light as producing a range of ceramics which typologically follow the Breedon–Ancaster group and are succeeded by wheel-turned Belgic forms which characterise the pottery of the Coritani. The predominant type is the bowl form with slightly everted rim, usually fired black and frequently burnished on the surface. Alongside the fine wares are found coarse shouldered jars made in a gritty ware. Some of the bowls are decorated with stamped circlets linked with arcs and swags impressed with a fine-toothed roulette wheel. At both of the type-sites these assemblages lie at the beginning of a sequence which develops uninterruptedly into the first century AD. The high technical quality and the uniformity of the fine wares suggest the probability of commercial production but it is too early to speculate on the number of production centres involved. That many of the decorative techniques continued to be practised after the introduction of Aylesford–Swarling types is an indication of the strength of the local traditions.

The Chilterns and East Anglia (Figs 3:7, A:23)

The ceramic material of the third and second centuries from the Ouse valley, the Chilterns and East Anglia is at present sparse and, with the exception of a few notable sites, poorly stratified. When groups are found, they are frequently mixed up with Belgic and later material; moreover, the vessels relevant to the period are rather generalised and ill-defined. There are, however, certain similarities which seem worth emphasising by classing most of the sites together under the same heading. Eventually it may be possible to define a series of separate styles.

The most distinctive pottery types, apart from a few imported saucepan pots, include wide-mouthed bowls with beaded lips, usually made in a dark highly burnished ware, and coarse ware jars frequently decorated with deeply scored lines. Decoration of the bowls is rare but includes the use of impressed dots and rouletted lines. The only unifying factor between the various sites is the existence of the heavily scored coarse jars, which recur frequently over the whole area from the Thames to Norfolk. Indeed, there is little difference between them and those from the Trent valley (Kenyon, 1950), suggesting some degree of parallel development. The predominant fine ware form, the globular bowl, is rarely decorated except at sites in the north, notably at Barley, Arminghall, Cambridge and Wareham. It may be that these sites will eventually be classed together as a group separate from the Chiltern area, which is distinguished from the north by a scattering of saucepan pots.

The style must have begun after the *floruit* of the Chinnor–Wandlebury Darmsden–Linton styles, but it is difficult to demonstrate the exact relationship between them. In all probability one developed imperceptibly into the other some time in the third century. During the first century the area gradually came under the influence of Belgic ceramic technology, which prevented the further advance of the purely native traditions.

The Dane's Graves–Staxton style (Fig. A:24)

In a detailed discussion of the metalwork of the La Tène cultures of Yorkshire, Stead (1965) has suggested a division into two phases. The first, characterised by the burial at Cowlam, is considered to have begun in the fifth century; the second phase, represented by the burials at Arras and Dane's Graves, is not earlier than the third to second century. The excavations of Dane's Graves and of the Driffield and Rigg's Farm burials have produced a collection of pottery belonging to a single stylistic group in which bucket-shaped vessels with thick bases and frequently with internally bevelled rims predominate. These types probably derive from vessels in the earlier Grimthorpe style, but some

influence from the saucepan pot style of the south, or indeed from contemporary and similar types in France, might possibly be represented. A settlement site producing pottery of this kind is known at Staxton, where a palisade trench was found together with pits and a quantity of occupation debris. How long the style continued in use is impossible to say, but it is unlikely to have outlived the end of the first century BC.

The south-west peninsula

There is very little that can be said of the material culture of the south-west peninsula, largely because of lack of suitable excavations. On sites like Bodrifty, Cornwall, where continuity of occupation may reasonably be expected, there are only a few sherds of generalised coarse wares which might be placed typologically before the appearance of the decorated Glastonbury wares. Some of the coarse pottery from Maen Castle, Cornwall could be regarded as of much the same date, belonging perhaps to the fourth or third century.

It is now generally agreed that the highly decorated wares began to be produced locally as early as the third century BC under the influence of styles prevalent at this time in Brittany. It is not impossible that skilled potters actually settled in the Lizard area of Cornwall and made vessels of local clay for the neighbouring communities, who had hitherto been virtually aceramic. The excavation at Castle Dore, Cornwall, has produced a range of pottery beginning with these early decorated wares and continuing into the first century BC but until more series of this kind have been produced, it will be difficult to arrive at a development sequence for the region. It is even more difficult to suggest absolute dates before cordoned wares begin to appear in the first century BC.

SUMMARY

Having described the ceramic development of the south and east in some detail, we may now briefly summarise the main trends. By the eighth century BC south-eastern Britain was occupied by stable sedentary communities whose roots lay far back in the second millennium. The pottery in use at the time, though showing certain regional differences, exhibited a remarkable degree of similarity over a wide area – a similarity due in part to several centuries of conservatism. The development of overseas trade, typified by the distribution of imported bronze implements and weapons belonging to the carp's tongue sword complex brought the coastal regions of the south-east into close relationship with each other. It was no doubt as part of these trading systems that metal vessels were introduced into the country, to be avidly copied by local potters. First of all, the large situlate buckets and cauldrons of the eighth and seventh centuries were imitated. These were followed in the seventh and sixth centuries by the importation of smaller carinated bowls, ceramic versions of which are found all round the coastal areas of southern Britain from Cornwall to Yorkshire, giving rise to the first distinctive styles of Iron Age pottery. Rapid and divergent ceramic development followed throughout the sixth and into the fifth century.

During the fifth century the influence of continental pottery types appeared in the region of the Thames and the adjacent areas to the north, suggesting at the very least some kind of direct contact between eastern Britain and the European mainland. South of the Thames this influence was slight. At about the same time, however, Yorkshire seems to have received a small number of immigrants from France bringing with them their distinctive style of burial rite involving the use of the mortuary cart. The incursion had little effect on pottery development in the area and its influence was restricted to Yorkshire.

From the fourth century until the end of the second, pottery styles developed locally. Although many different style-zones can be defined, two broad groupings emerge: one stretching from Sussex west across Wessex into the Cotswolds and the Welsh Marches, typified by straight-sided saucepan pots, and another in the Midlands spreading from the Thames valley to East Anglia and Lincolnshire, characterised by hemispherical bowls. The south-west began to develop its own distinctive styles, influenced to some extent by the forms currently in use in Armorica and Normandy. It was upon this pattern that the new cultural elements introduced in the period 150–50 BC impinged, dramatically altering the direction of local development by the technical innovation of the potter's wheel.

Regional Groupings: North and West

The communities of the highland areas of Britain differed in many ways from those of the south-east: settlement appears to have been generally sparser, a greater reliance was placed on pastoral activity, the material culture was poor, and pottery was very little used over most of the area except in the extreme north-west of Scotland. For these reasons, definition of regional groupings is more difficult, and in some places impossible, and even where there is some material basis for chronological or regional division, precise definitions comparable with those obtainable in the south-east can rarely be achieved.

For most of the north and west, bronze implement typology offers the only method at present available for assessing regional groupings in the seventh and sixth centuries BC. The groups so defined do little more than reflect spheres of contact but since these must imply some degree of cultural cohesion, or even uniformity, they may be thought to offer an initial albeit tenuous, basis for regional definition (Fig. 4:1). By the fifth century the organisation of specialist bronze industries had virtually disappeared. The development of hillfort architecture in many parts of the west and north provides some basis for regional grouping (Hogg, 1965, for Wales; Feachem, 1966, for east Scotland), but so few forts have been adequately excavated (in some areas even surveys are wanting) that stylistic groupings based on them are at best uneven and at worst misleading. Some of these problems will, however, be returned to later.

The rest of the material culture is, to say the least, sparse: pottery occurs but rarely and is seldom distinctive; other artefacts, such as spindle whorls and bone and iron implements, lack sufficient form or specialisation for typo-logical assessment. Thus we are at present without the means of defining regional groups or chronological phases for much of the north and west.

WALES

In the seventh and sixth centuries BC three distinctive bronze industries can be defined.

The Llantwit–Stogursey tradition

In south Wales, principally Monmouthshire and Glamorganshire and spreading into Somerset, Devon and Cornwall, a group of related domestic bronze implements has been defined and named after two of the important hoards (Burgess, 1969a, 19–21; also Fox & Hyde, 1939, 390; Savory, 1958, 37). Distinctive among the tools represented is the socketed axe with a heavily moulded lip, decorated with parallel ribbing on the two faces. The type is frequently found in association with a range of tools including socketed gouges and tanged chisels. Varieties of the axe also occur in the Llyn Fawr and Cardiff hoards together with horse harness-fittings indicating a seventh to sixth century date which is further supported by occasional associations with material of the carp's tongue sword complex. Scattered finds, a few hoards and occasional moulds for axes have turned up in south-west Britain, implying the use of the Severn estuary and western sea approaches for trading – no doubt in connection with the exploitation of Cornish tin – but the main distribution of hoards is centred upon south Wales.

No settlement sites of the period have yet been discovered, but the relatively fertile south Welsh

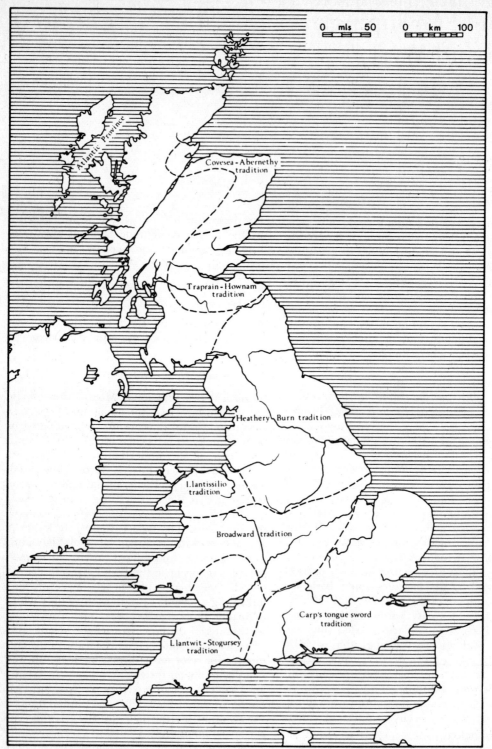

4:1   Distribution of the major bronze traditions in the seventh to fifth century (source: author)

plain in all probability supported a well-established agricultural economy which would have allowed a settled way of life comparable with that practised in the south and east. Whether or not pottery was in common use is a problem to which no answers can yet be given.

The Broadward tradition

The Broadward group, named after a Herefordshire hoard, can be defined in terms of an assemblage of weapons which includes swords of Ewart Park type, chapes and spearheads, among which a barbed variety is characteristic. The contrast between the predominantly domestic character of south-east Welsh hoards and the military nature of the Broadward hoards may possibly reflect a difference in social structure, but the total absence of occupation sites which can definitely be assigned to the period prevents any consideration of settlement pattern or economy. The area covered by the group extends from Pembrokeshire through central Wales into Cheshire and from here into the Welsh borderland, while some of the diagnostic weapons are found even further afield. The territory is well suited to a basically pastoral economy which would be consistent with a warlike society. The absence of pottery is another feature suggestive of pastoralism, since under such living conditions pottery would tend to break easily and would be better replaced by leather, wooden or metal containers. Indeed, there is clear evidence from the later forts in the Welsh borderland that the communities remained largely aceramic into the fourth or third centuries BC.

Northern Wales–the Llantissilio tradition

The northern corner of Wales appears to have been a technological backwater in the seventh and sixth centuries, receiving exotic types from Ireland and other parts of England and Wales rather than developing its own. A degree of conservatism is shown by the retention of the late type of palstave, which had been replaced by socketed axes elsewhere. Other aspects of the local culture are largely unknown but it is possible that the earliest phase of settlement at Castell Odo, Caerns, dates to as early as the sixth century. Here a palisaded enclosure, circular huts and pottery in the form of large jars with finger-impressed rims bear a general similarity to the cultural assemblage of southern Britain, but there is no need to assume (*pace* the excavator) that the site originated as the result of an alien intrusion from the south.

The famous Parc-y-Meirch hoard (Pl. 12 and pp. 133–4), containing horse harness-fittings of seventh century date, belongs geographically to this group. Its presence clearly demonstrates the extensive trading systems which, whether directly or indirectly via Ireland, allowed exotic north European objects to be transported to this relatively isolated territory.

In the period lasting from the fifth to the first century BC, the south Welsh coastal plain west of the Usk and the hills of Carmarthenshire and Pembrokeshire were densely settled. In Glamorganshire the settlement on Merthyr Mawr Warren, with its two La Tène I brooches, offers an insight into an occupation site of the third or second century where, in addition to the normal domestic rubbish, debris from bronze- and iron-working was recovered. Pottery, however, was far from plentiful and the few surviving vessels are hardly distinctive. A typologically earlier vessel recovered from Bacon Hole, Glam, hints at a well-established ceramic tradition. The pot, an elegant flared bowl with a carinated shoulder and decoration above, would not be out of place among the fifth to third century assemblages of southern Britain, but at present it stands alone in south Wales. The settlement sites of the southwest are better known, as the result of several large-scale excavations. At Coygan Camp, situated on a limestone promontory overlooking Carmarthen Bay, an open settlement producing Ultimate Late Bronze Age pottery was overlain by the construction of a small enclosure defended by two banks and ditches. To this phase probably belong two La Tène bracelets and a selection of plain bucket-shaped vessels, two of which were decorated with simple incisions forming pendant arcs. This type of decoration has similarities to the Lydney–Llanmelin style. Other Pembrokeshire excavations, at the cliff fort on St David's Head and at the hillfort of Moel Trigarn, produced little distinctive pottery, but a number of spindle whorls, decorated shale discs, hammer stones, glass beads and jet rings give some indication of the contemporary material culture.

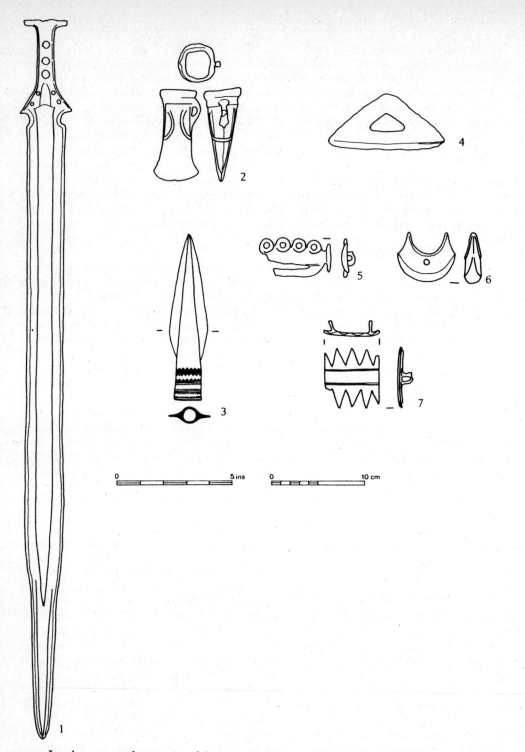

4:2 Implements and weapons of the carp's tongue sword complex. 1 Sword from the river Thames; 2 socketed axe from the Thames at Brentford, Middx; 3 socketed spear from Chingford, Essex; 4 knife from Eaton, Norwich; 5 'belt attachment' from the Thames at Sion Reach; 6 chape from Levington, Suffolk; 7 leather attachment from Watford, Herts (source: Burgess, 1969b)

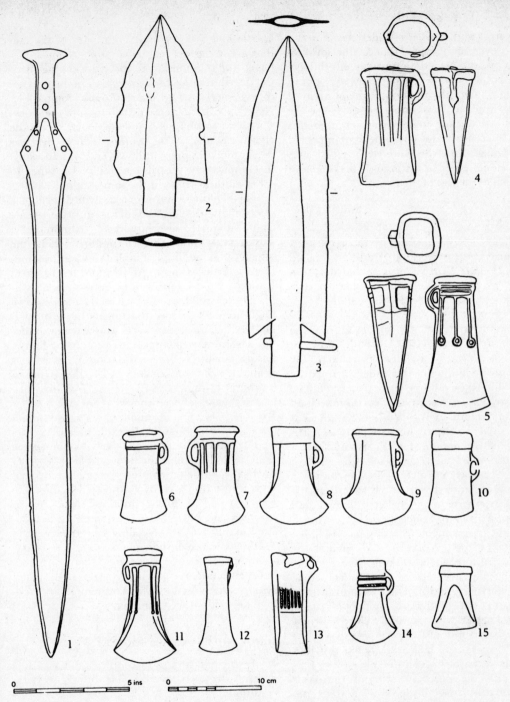

4:3 Implements and weapons of various bronze traditions in the seventh to fifth century.
1 Sword from Ewart Park, Northumberland; 2 spear from Broadward, Herefordshire;
3 spear from Plaistow Marshes, Essex; 4–15 socketed axes; 4 Llantwit Major, Glam;
5 ? from Leeds; 6 Dalduff, Ayr; 7 Shetland; 8 Tomintoul, Ban; 9 Culloden,
Inverness; 10 Mawcarse, Kinross; 11 Delvine, Perth; 12 Annan, Dumfries; 13 Carse
Loch, Kirkcudbright; 14 Birse, Aberdeen; 15 ? Angus (sources: 1–5 Burgess, 1969b;
6–15 Coles, 1962a)

In central and northern Wales the material culture is even more sparse than in the south of the principality. The communities seem to have been aceramic; moreover, since they were not in close contact with the materially richer areas of southern England, few imported artefacts are found. But that some contact was maintained is demonstrated by the duck-stamped pot imported to Pen Dinas from the Malvern region. This paucity alone serves to distinguish north Wales from much of the rest of the country.

NORTHERN ENGLAND

Throughout the seventh and sixth centuries a well-defined bronze-working tradition, called here the *Heathery Burn tradition*, served northern England, overlapping with the northern part of the West Harling–Staple Howe pottery style-zone.

The extensive collection of material from the Heathery Burn Cave, Co. Durham, may be regarded as typical of a range of artefacts; the maximum distribution of this range, defined by the Yorkshire type of three-ribbed socketed axe, was centred upon Yorkshire, Northumberland and County Durham with outliers in adjacent counties. The Heathery Burn deposit is particularly valuable, not only for its cart and harness fittings and bucket referred to below (p. 133), but also for the associated metal types, including a Covesea bracelet, a Ewart Park sword, spearheads of northern type, socketed knives and chisels and a group of Yorkshire socketed axes. A fragment of copper ingot, a casting jet and half a bronze mould for a Yorkshire axe suggest the probability of local metalworking. Non-metallic finds from the cave include jet armlets, stone spindle whorls, a range of bone tools and fittings, and five sherds of pottery belonging to coarse shouldered vessels with internally flattened rims.

There is a substantial overlap between the southern extension of the Yorkshire axe distribution, pushing down through Lincolnshire to East Anglia, and the northern part of the West Harling–Staple Howe group of occupation sites defined above on the basis of their distinctive pottery. At Staple Howe a Yorkshire axe, jet armlets and other items of the non-metallic material culture are shared with the Heathery Burn Cave, and again at Scarborough a Yorkshire axe was found on the settlement site. Such

associations are a salutary reminder of the fact that groupings defined on ceramic grounds may have little relationship to those depending upon the distribution of bronze types. The two classes of evidence are seldom mutually compatible. Nevertheless, the dense distribution of the Yorkshire axes emphasises a zone of contact from the eighth to the sixth century which deserves recognition. At present, however, it is impossible to compare the distribution of metal types to other cultural traits in the same region.

The Pennines show remarkably little evidence of occupation before the first century BC. Apart from the impressive hillforts at Almondbury, Yorks, and Mam Tor, Derbyshire, where the sequence alone implies a lengthy occupation, there is little to show. At Grafton, in the West Riding of Yorkshire, an open settlement was partly excavated, producing shouldered jars with finger-impressed rims and finger-tip decoration on the shoulder. Finer wares were few in number but several sherds appear to belong to slightly flaring bowls. No internal dating evidence was available, but on analogy with the styles of southern Britain, a date in the fifth to third century would be reasonable. Further west at Roomer Common a small barrow was found over a grave of broadly the same period.

The general impression given by the sparse material culture and the apparent lack of settlements is that the population was small compared with the south. Moreover, the evidence for the economy in the first century BC (pp. 203–6) suggests that pastoralism was widely practised. Presumably in the preceding centuries we are dealing with much the same pattern: small communities of herders moving their livestock between summer and winter pastures. In such a system material culture and settlement archaeology are seldom well represented.

SCOTLAND: SOUTH AND EAST

In the seventh and sixth centuries the area was covered by two overlapping bronze-working traditions.

The Traprain–Hownam tradition

The eastern coast of northern England and Scotland, from the Tyne north to the Esk in the county of Angus, exhibits some degree of cultural

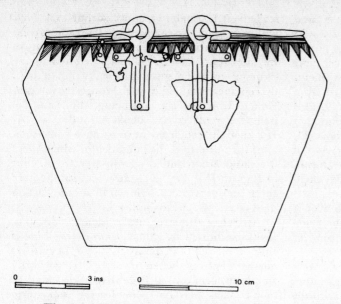

0   3 ins   0   10 cm

4:4   The Adabrock bronze bowl, Lewis (source: Coles, 1962a)

unity which can be defined principally through the distribution of locally manufactured bronze implements such as the Traprain Law type of socketed axe (Coles, 1962a) and British varieties of Hallstatt swords. To these should be added imported Hallstatt types, including a Hallstatt sword (Cowen's class b) from Cambuskenneth, Stirling, the Horsehope cart- and harness-fittings, the Adabrock bronze bowl (Fig. 4:4), razors from Traprain Law and Kinleith, Midlothian, and a group of sunflower swan's-neck pins (Fig. 10:13). Evidently close contact was maintained with mainland Europe throughout the period, allowing an unusually wide range of exotic material to reach this part of Britain.

Within this region a number of settlement sites have been discovered and a few excavated. Mostly they are palisaded enclosures containing one or more circular timber huts, similar in many ways to the early settlements of southern Britain. Two radiocarbon dates are now available: 510 ± 40 (585 BC) for charcoal from the palisade trench at Huckhoe, Northumberland, and 590 ± 40 (665 BC) for an occupation layer associated with the palisaded enclosure at Craigmarloch Wood, Renfrewshire. Together they leave little doubt that the metal objects, both imported and local, were contemporary with the early settlements, even though direct associations are not yet recorded. These early settlements and their

sparse and virtually aceramic material culture have been called the Hownam culture (MacKie, 1969, 21).

The Covesea–Abernethy group

Between the Firth of Forth and the Moray Firth, and overlapping with the northern distribution of the Traprain–Hownam sites, lies the Covesea–Abernethy group, which can be defined by both metal implements and distinctive techniques of hillfort construction. The metal types include the Covesea armlet with unevenly expanded terminals, a type thought to have been imported into Britain from northern Europe in the eighth to seventh century together with the pendant necklets of Braes of Gight and Wester Ord (Coles, 1962a, 39–44). Locally made products are also represented, including the short socketed axes with heavy multiple neck-mouldings, named after the Meldrum hoard, which are found in eastern Scotland mainly, but not invariably, north of the Forth.

From the Sculptor's Cave at Covesea, Moray, and Blamashanner, Angus, metalwork has been found in association with a widely distributed group of pottery belonging to the rather generalised flat-rimmed class. The north-east Scottish group is, however, sufficiently distinctive to be named Covesea ware, and is thought to have ultimately originated in northern Europe (Coles, 1962a, 44). If this derivation is correct, it would suggest some form of folk movement into north-east Scotland in or about the seventh century, introducing both pottery and the new metal objects. Such a view is further supported by a radiocarbon date of 590 ± 90 (665 BC) for beams and planks belonging to the initial occupation of the timber-laced hillfort at Finavon, Angus (Pl. 3a). The style of timber-lacing of this fort and of others from eastern Scotland is comparable in many details to structures found in Late Urnfield contexts in central and northern Europe. Thus the seventh century date proposed for Finavon is perfectly consistent with the view of an incursion from Europe during the seventh century or perhaps a little earlier (but see pp. 237–8).

While the bronze-working traditions were eventually replaced by iron-working, other aspects of the material culture together with the timber-lacing of forts continued in use over many centuries, giving rise to a broad continuum known as the Abernethy culture (MacKie, 1969, 16–21).

It will be evident from the foregoing paragraphs that the Traprain–Hownam tradition and the Covesea–Abernethy group have much in common. Hallstatt and Hallstatt-derived artefacts extend far into the Covesea–Abernethy region and the characteristic palisaded settlements are now being discovered north of the Firth of Forth. Similarly, Covesea-style flat-rimmed pottery has been found at an occupation site at Green Knowe in Peeblesshire, well within the distribution pattern of the Traprain–Hownam group, and indeed a variety of flat-rimmed pottery is also known from Traprain Law itself. The distribution pattern of the Meldrum and Traprain Law axes also overlaps, the Meldrum type extending across most of eastern Scotland from the border to the Moray Firth. In view of such a widespread similarity, it might be thought to be more reasonable eventually to treat the entire area as a single east Scottish group, abandoning the conventional terminology of a Tyne–Forth Hownam culture and a north-eastern Abernethy culture (MacKie, 1969, 20). At present, however, some semblance of the accepted system is retained here.

From the fifth to the first century the area stretching from Northumberland to the southern edge of the Highlands was covered with small settlements, usually groups of huts enclosed within palisades or earthworks. The radiocarbon dates now becoming available show that many of the sites must have been first inhabited in the sixth or even the seventh century but a high percentage remained in use throughout the pre-Roman Iron Age, the huts being rebuilt and the palisades replaced by banks and ditches. At Huckhoe the replacement must have come soon after the burning of the palisade, for which there is a radiocarbon date of 510 ± 40 (585 BC), but at Ingram Hill the bank, ditch and palisade are three centuries later, as shown by a radiocarbon date of 220 ± 90 (285 BC).

Apart from the structural evidence of development, calibrated by radiocarbon dates, there is little to be said of material culture or of cultural change. Pottery, when it occurs, is generally simple in form and of little diagnostic value. A few trinkets like La Tène fibulae and spiral finger- and toe-rings occur sporadically but generally the sites are poor and produce little. Since there is no evidence of any cultural change during the entire period from the seventh century BC until the Roman conquest, it is simpler to regard the later phases of the occupation as continuous with the earlier cultural groups, distinguishable only by absolute dating or by stratigraphical sequence.

SCOTLAND: NORTH AND WEST

Unlike the rest of northern Britain, the extreme north and west – including the coastal area north of the Firth of Clyde, Caithness and Sutherland and the Western Isles, Orkney and Shetland – were occupied by communities capable of producing distinctive pottery often of high quality. The ceramic traditions, rooted in third and second millennium types, developed throughout the first millennium, occasionally influenced by outside traits, well into the Roman era. Excavations at Dun Mor Vaul on Tiree and at Jarlshof and Clickhimin on Shetland provide firm stratigraphical sequences against which the ceramic and cultural development can be traced, while radiocarbon dates from Dun Mor' Vaul allow part of the sequence to be calibrated.

At Clickhimin continuous occupation from the seventh century BC until the sixth or seventh century AD enables the ceramic tradition to be seen in relation to the structural development of the site. In the pre-broch phase, which concerns us here, three periods have been isolated, of which the first two can be collated with the early occupation at Jarlshof.

Clickhimin I: seventh to sixth century The first period of occupation is represented at the type-site by the establishment of an oval stone-built house constructed in a technique dating back to the Neolithic period. Similar buildings were in use at Jarlshof at this time. Throughout the period the material culture was simple, consisting largely of heavy stone tools and a limited range of bone implements, but at Jarlshof a bronze smith established himself, his presence being indicated by fragments of clay moulds for swords, socketed axes and sunflower pins.

The range of pottery was restricted to barrel- and bucket-shaped jars, sometimes with flat-topped rims (Fig. A:35). At Jarlshof they were occasionally decorated with one or two plain cordons. These simple forms are closely related to the indigenous tradition of the Bronze Age.

Clickhimin II: sixth to fifth century The second phase was marked at Clickhimin by the establishment of a round house within the earlier enclosure and at Jarlshof by the construction of clusters of circular stone-built huts over the ruins of the earlier houses. The discovery of iron slag at Jarlshof shows that the new metal was not only in use but was being worked locally. There was now a marked change in the quality of the pottery, with the introduction of shouldered jars alongside the simple bucket and barrel shapes (Fig. A:35). Some differences, possibly chronological, exist between the vessels from the two sites: those from Clickhimin are finer and slacker in profile compared with the Jarlshof assemblage. Since many similarities exist between these Shetland types and contemporary pottery from the south and east of Britain, it has been suggested that a colonising movement from the south was the cause, introducing the round house tradition as well as knowledge of iron-working and improved ceramic technology. The evidence is inconclusive, however, since it may equally well be argued that the change was brought about by casual maritime trading rather than folk movement.

Clickhimin III: fifth to first century The third period

at Clickhimin, not represented at Jarlshof, was initiated by the construction of a stone ring-wall to defend the farmstead. The associated pottery was more varied in form than in the previous periods, the commonest types being ovoid jars with short everted or beaded rims (Fig. A:36). Four decorative techniques were employed: the internal fluting of the rims, the application of a plastic moulded strip in the neck angle, the deliberate curvilinear grooving of the inside of the base, and various forms of impressed or stabbed decoration – usually stab-filled pendent triangles, isolated impressed circlets and impressed arcs of circles. There is a strong regional character about the assemblage, but broad similarities with peripheral Urnfield wares in France hint at the possibility of some kind of maritime contact dating back to the fifth century.

Elsewhere in north-western Britain, well-stratified deposits of the seventh to first century are few, but beneath the broch at Dun Mor Vaul on Tiree an early midden deposit was recovered, sealing a living floor. The occupation rubbish included a quantity of pottery representing two main types: bucket and barrel urns, sometimes with simple geometric decoration stamped and scored beneath the rim, and smaller S-profiled vessels similarly decorated (Fig. A:34). Just above the midden a more angular vessel was found, its sharply everted rim and reddish slip-coated surface possibly echoing traditions current in southern Britain. Another settlement on Tiree, Balevullin, produced evidence of occupation during this period. The site of what appears to be a circular timber-built hut was associated with a range of pottery which bears certain similarities to pottery from eastern England dating to the sixth to fifth century. A few fragments of iron show that iron was used, even if not extracted locally.

The ceramic assemblages from the two sites on Tiree have a number of types in common with Clickhimin phases II and III which might be thought, on the internal evidence of sequence, to lie within the sixth to third centuries. The radiocarbon dates from Dun Mor Vaul are entirely consistent with this, ranging from 400 ± 110 (470 BC) for roots from the old ground surface and 445 ± 90 (515 BC) for charred grain to 280 ± 100 (345 BC) for animal bones belonging to a late phase in the midden occupation.

Protohistory to History, *c.*150 BC to AD 43

Until the middle of the second century BC the history of the British Isles cannot be written in terms of identifiable individuals and their actions. At best we have to be content to define groups of people through their artefacts, their structures and the effects they had on their environment. But the two centuries preceding the Roman invasion of AD 43 lie in the shadows of history – the literate world was encroaching. Broadly, the period can be divided into two: *c.* 150–55 BC and 55 BC – AD 43. In the first part, migrations and spheres of tribal influence can be distinguished, largely through the evidence of coin typology and distribution; by the second, following the invasions of Julius Caesar, we can write of the actual people, the kings and demi-kings of the British aristocracy and their relationship to each other and the Roman world, reflected in contemporary historical writings as well as in the numismatic evidence.

Before attempting to piece together the outline of late pre-Roman Iron Age history, something must be said of the nature of early coinage in Britain and of the assumptions based upon it. It is now generally accepted that Celtic coins remained close to their place of origin except in unusual circumstances – trade alone being insufficient to cause widespread dispersal. If this is so, the kind of distribution manifest in certain classes of Gallo-Belgic coins, in their homeland and in this country, must be explained in terms of the movement of people. Second, the strong traditionalism of design which prevailed allows tribal types to be clearly defined and their spheres of influence to be plotted. Using these criteria, it is possible to recognise a series of waves of incomings spreading from Belgic Gaul to Britain, while from well-defined territories in

Britain secondary ripples emanate. The current nomenclature, developed by D. F. Allen (1961a) talks of the intrusive coinage as Gallo-Belgic and the local developments as British.

We can safely follow Allen in assuming that closely defined distributions of Gallo-Belgic coins in Britain imply intrusive elements but the strength of the intrusions, whether aristocratic or peasant, requires other evidence to elucidate it further. More often than not, that evidence is not forthcoming. It is far less certain what peripheral developments in Britain mean, for while on the one hand they may reflect local movements of power, they are equally likely to result from a borrowing of the new idea by neighbouring communities. There is no simple answer; each case has to be considered on its merits. It is salutary to recall Allen's warning that in assessing the coin evidence one must remember that 'it is only part, and not always the most important part, of the historical record' (1961a, 98).

THE REFORMATION OF TRIBAL SOCIETY, 150–55 BC

Writing of Britain, Julius Caesar provides many invaluable fragments of information, not the least of which is that the maritime areas of Britain were raided and then settled by invaders from the Belgic areas of Gaul, who for the most part retained their tribal names. No dates are given but the settlement may reasonably be linked with the two earliest groups of Gallo-Belgic coins found here: Gallo-Belgic A (the so-called Bellovacian coinage), which originated in the area of the Somme and intruded into Kent and Essex, and Gallo-Belgic B (defaced Bellovacian dies) from the Somme–lower Seine

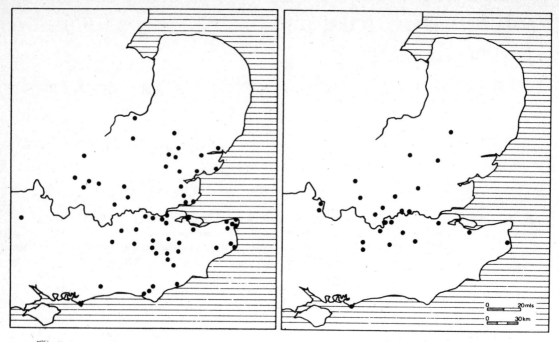

5:1   Distribution of Gallo-Belgic A and B coins (sources: D. F. Allen, 1961a and 1962)

region, which concentrates, in this country, on the Thames. Thus the distributions of the two groups (Fig. 5:1) are essentially complementary. Both types were current in Gaul between 150–100 BC and their British usage is likely to fall within this range.

If the people represented by the coin distribution are Caesar's raiders and settlers, it is reasonable to ask what, if anything, such an incursion brought with it besides the coins. A money economy, clearly, and no doubt some degree of reformed political organisation, but if the movement was essentially an influx of warrior aristocrats, it would be pointless to look for substantial changes in the indigenous folk culture. La Tène II-inspired luxury articles such as swords, anthropoid daggers, brooches and the pairs of bronze spoons might, however, be thought to represent the new order and it is conceivable that other changes, in social structure and warfare, which were taking place at about this time (pp. 305–8) could have resulted indirectly from the new incomings.

The next wave is reflected in the appearance of Gallo-Belgic C coin types (Fig. 5:2) originating in the region of the Somme and the Pas-de-Calais a little after 100 BC, which remained in

use for thirty to forty years. The British distribution is puzzling: less than a score of coins occur, spreading widely over the area south and east of a line from the Humber to the Test but concentrating on Kent, the main point of entry. They do, however, lie at the beginning of eleven separate British developments – British A-K, deriving directly from Gallo-Belgic C prototypes – as well as British L-N and YZ, which developed subsequently from British H and I. British A-D spread across the south from Surrey to Dorset; British E-G lie north of the Thames centring upon Essex; while British H-K are found further north in the east Midlands, Norfolk and the Wash to the Humber.

While it is clear that the Gallo-Belgic C issues imply continuing contacts with the continent, and the British derivations show the spread of the political and economic system of the Belgic communities to most of the south and east, it seems unnecessary to interpret the evidence in terms of a new invasion thrusting out into unconquered territory. The copying of Gallo-Belgic C coinage on such a vast scale, however, implies that a considerable prestige was attached to it at the time when areas peripheral to the main Belgic-dominated lands were coming under the

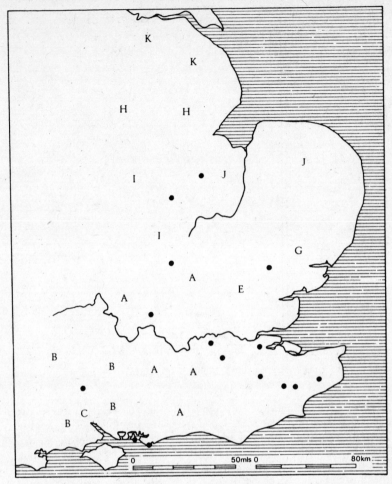

5:2   Distribution of Gallo-Belgic C coins (●) and their British derivatives (sources: D. F. Allen, 1961a and 1962)

influence of the new systems. A plausible context for these developments is provided by the reign of the high king Diviciacus (C. F. C. Hawkes, 1968). In 57 BC Caesar's envoys remembered him as overlord of Gaul and Britain. His reign fits neatly into the currency of Gallo-Belgic C coins (95–65) and the power that such a man must have wielded could have brought about the widespread belgicisation of south-east Britain. The actual mechanisms of such a process are beyond recovery: in some areas local chieftains may perhaps have adopted coinage to facilitate trade, whilst in others war-bands may have fought themselves to power, replacing the old aristocracy. At any event, the picture is one of change and turmoil.

Whilst the British coinages were developing, a new wave of Gallo-Belgic coins reached Britain. These were geometric quarter-staters known as Gallo-Belgic D; their period of currency lies in the thirty years or so before the invasions of Caesar. The influx was not particularly far-reaching for Britain but spread along the coast from Kent to Sussex (Fig. 5:3), giving rise to two new British types: British O in Sussex and British P in Kent. Certain elements of British O were adopted further west in Dorset, where they lie behind the development of the Durotrigian silver currency.

The relatively minor effects of Gallo-Belgic D were completely overshadowed by coins of the next wave – Gallo-Belgic E – which appear to

5:3   Distribution of Gallo-Belgic D and E coins (sources: D. F. Allen, 1961a and 1962)

have been introduced from the territory between the Nervii and Atrebates in the early sixties or late fifties, presumably in the turmoil resulting from the threat or actuality of the Roman advance through Gaul. In Britain the coins cluster in three groups: along the Sussex coast, from Kent to the upper Thames, and in Essex; but Gallo-Belgic E soon became the established coinage over most of the south-east. Such a dramatic influx must represent extensive new arrivals from northern Gaul: people like the chiefs of the Bellovaci who in 57 BC, so Caesar tells us, took refuge in Britain. But it was more than an aristocratic movement, for this was probably the period when the production of wheel-made La Tène III pottery really became established, contributing to the development of the archaeologically named Aylesford–Swarling culture which characterised the material assemblage of the Belgic south-east until the Roman conquest of AD 43. This, then, was the fluid situation when Caesar made his first sortie into the British Isles in 55 BC.

The growth of a warrior society in Britain in the centuries before *c.* 150 BC will be discussed

later (pp. 303–6); the material culture, the apparent social structure and the development of hillforts all point to the increasing commonness of warfare. The influx of bands of warlike people, particularly in the thirty years on either side of 100 BC, must have added to the ferment even if the incomings were at first numerically small. It is therefore reasonable to ask whether their effects can be found in the archaeological record.

In Wessex, on the fringe of the primary Belgic area, it would appear that major defensive measures were taken in the first century BC. At Danebury the east entrance (Pl. 5) was massively re-defended at about this time. Previously a simple timber gate had existed in the univallate defence. This was now replaced with a more massive construction set further back in the entrance gap, while in front two curved inner hornworks were built, creating a flint-walled approaching corridor 150 ft (46 m) long and 20 ft (6 m) wide along which any attacker would have had to run the gauntlet while defenders on the north inner hornwork could have rained down volleys of slingstones. The inner hornworks were further defended by two claw-like outer hornworks fronted by V-shaped ditches, which returned to join the main ditches of the fort. In the centre of these outer works was a dual-portal outer gate. The entire complex was brilliantly designed so that every part was clearly visible from the sling platform on the end of the north inner hornwork and all lay within the slingers' range of 200 ft (60 m). There can be little doubt that the concept was purely military. Some indication of the date is given by the discovery of a gold-plated Gallo-Belgic C coin from the top of the primary silt of the outer hornwork ditch. The coin was in a fresh condition and is hardly likely to have been dropped much after 70 BC. Judging by the degree of silting beneath it, a construction date of *c*. 100 BC would seem reasonable.

The eastern entrance of Maiden Castle was treated in an even more impressive way. After the initial phase of multivallation (phase III), the entire approach was remodelled (phase IV) with a complex of overlapping earthworks designed to create a circuitous approach protected by carefully sited platforms for slingers. The gates themselves (two separate gates) were set in long stone-walled corridors, close to one of which was a hoard of 22,000 slingstones. Dating is not direct but depends upon the total absence of coins. Since Durotrigian coins began to be minted in 70–60 BC, phase IV is like to pre-date this period and may well have begun about 100 BC.

There are a number of other, unexcavated, forts with similar complex outworks, e.g. Beacon Hill (Burghclere), Badbury, Hambledon Hill (Pl. 1), Yarnbury (Pl. 2a), etc., but their dating and sequence cannot easily be determined. Other forts in the area, where more limited excavation has taken place, frequently show late entrance modifications, invariably giving rise to a long corridor entrance. St Catherine's Hill, Winchester, can be interpreted in this way. So can the Caburn, Trundle, Torberry, Bredon and, further afield, the forts of the Welsh borderland and north Wales. Moreover, in these areas, even where excavation has not taken place, the present physical form of the earthworks frequently suggests the existence of similar long corridor approaches.

We have evidence, then, that over much of the south and west of Britain the defences of hill-forts were improved by the construction of either long corridor entrances or complex outworks or both. Wherever dating evidence is available, these refurbishings can be seen to belong to the period of the saucepan pot continuum, broadly second to first century, and there are indications from some sites that the construction date lies at about 100 BC or a little before. It must be stressed that the techniques involved in the rebuildings were not alien to the local traditions. Multivallation and simple forms of hornworks already existed in the south-west, and the earlier gate developments were moving towards the inturned or corridor form. Far more significant is the fact that it was always long-established sites that were brought into defensive order. While the nature of the evidence so far stated does not allow us to say that all the rebuildings were local responses to the same stimulus, it does point to intense defensive activity spread over a few decades at the most.

Evidence of defence prompts us to look for evidence of attack. It can indeed be found. At Worlebury and Bredon war cemeteries of mutilated bodies have been discovered close to the entrances; at Danebury the gate was destroyed by fire; while at Torberry the dry-stone walls flanking the entrances were thrown down deliberately, filling the hollowed roadway. These acts took place while saucepan pots were in use and must therefore reflect inter-tribal warfare or raiding, probably within the first half of the first century BC. It can hence be argued that certain parts of Britain offer evidence of stress in the period before Caesar's invasions. Distributions are informative. The new defensive activities spread along the South Downs, the Wessex chalklands, the upper Thames, the Cotswolds and into the south-west and the Welsh border areas – a distribution almost exactly complementary to the contemporary coinage intrusions of Gallo-Belgic A, B and C, which cover the North Downs and North Weald, the lower Thames, Essex and parts of Suffolk, spreading up to the Chilterns. Native defensive activity, in fact, forms an arc around the primary Belgic settlement area. It is not unreasonable, therefore, to suggest that in the period *c*. 150–80, when the new Belgic dynasties were establishing themselves in the south-east, the petty chiefs of the surrounding areas were busy protecting themselves and their territories against further westward expansion as well as against local aggression. The evidence for destruction and the establishment of the British coinages A-J strongly indicates the eventual emergence of Belgic-style rule in many of these areas.

THE CAMPAIGNS OF JULIUS CAESAR, 55 AND 54 BC

In 55 BC Britain was still very much of an unknown quantity to the Roman world, and even after interviewing traders Caesar could find out relatively little about it. To provide the necessary intelligence he sent a warship commanded by Volusenus on a reconnaissance mission with orders to find out as much as possible and return quickly. Meanwhile he set about preparing a fleet based upon the warships used the previous summer against the Veneti. Inevitably the Britons got wind of the preparations and sent envoys to offer hostages and thereby allegiance. Caesar's reaction was to extract promises of good behaviour and send them home, accompanied by Commius, a king of the Gaulish Atrebates who, Caesar tells us, was greatly respected in Britain. It is indeed conceivable that he was related to some of the immigrants of the previous ten years. His task was to warn the British leaders of the impending invasion and to persuade as many as possible to seek allegiance with Rome. The move was ill judged, however, and Commius was soon taken prisoner, only to be returned with suitable contrite regrets after Caesar had landed.

Eventually the expedition set sail for Britain in eighty transports carrying the two legions and another eighteen for the cavalry, accompanied by a large number of warships. The landing was opposed and difficult, not least because the Roman cavalry failed to arrive, but eventually a foothold was obtained and the army moved forward. Envoys were sent by the British chieftains and a temporary peace ensued, but was soon broken by the Britons when the Romans appeared to be in difficulty. Only after several indecisive engagements was Caesar able to extricate himself and sail back to the relative safety of Gaul with a large number of British hostages.

The campaign of 54 BC was more massively staged: over 800 ships were involved, transporting an army of five legions and 2,000 cavalry. The campaign was more extended than the previous year's and Caesar's account is more informative. In addition to details of the actual fighting, Caesar has much to say about the politico-military situation in Britain. Before the invasions a powerful local king, Cassivellaunus, whose territory lay to the north of the Thames, had been continually warring with neighbouring tribes. He had killed the king of the Trinovantes and had driven out his son Mandubracius, who fled to Caesar in Gaul. Yet as soon as the Roman threat appeared, personal animosities were forgotten and Cassivellaunus was elected the overall war leader of the resistance, commanding a vast confederate army. Even so, through sheer force of arms, Caesar managed to cut his way through Kent, crossed the Thames and took the battle into Cassivellaunus's kingdom. Gradually the British resistance crumbled and Cassivellaunus was reduced to guerrilla tactics and a scorched-earth policy. With the growing inevitability of Roman success, the unstable British alliance gradually broke up, the Trinovantes sending envoys to Caesar and promising to surrender if Mandubracius was returned and the tribe protected against Cassivellaunus. The immediate success of these negotiations brought over other tribes, including the Cenimagni, Segontiaci, Aucalites, Bibroci and Cassi (whose whereabouts and subsequent history are unknown); Caesar also obtained information leading to the location of Cassivellaunus's stronghold.

The last stages could now be fought out. As Caesar was attacking the oppidum, Cassivellaunus rushed orders to Kent ordering the four kings of the region, Cingetorix, Carvilius, Taximagulus and Segovax, to launch a surprise swoop on Caesar's naval base. The plan was sound but the attack failed and with it the British resistance. Cassivellaunus, using Commius as an intermediary, was forced to sue for peace, which Caesar granted (no doubt gladly) in return for hostages, the assurance of an annual tribute to Rome and on the understanding that Cassivellaunus should not molest Mandubracius or the Trinovantes. The arrangements having been settled, Caesar departed.

The episode is invaluable for the light it throws on the British scene. The country was split into innumerable tribal groups warring with each other and while in matters of national emergency a single war leader would be elected, old rivalries could lead to eventual betrayal. This is precisely the kind of picture one would expect after reviewing the coin evidence of the previous half-century; Caesar, however, provides us with names, motives and a story line. The proximity of Rome introduces a new factor into British protohistory: tribes in conflict could now ally themselves with Rome, as the Trinovantes had done, using the threat of Roman protection as a significant bargaining counter. Moreover, Roman life and luxury offered a new outlet for those who desired to enhance their own prestige. Thus political and economic ties with the continent increased and British history takes on a new clarity.

From first-hand accounts of Caesar's battles we learn much of Belgic fighting tactics. They possessed three forces: infantry, cavalry and charioteers, who seldom fought in close formation but usually attacked in open order interspersed with groups of reserves to cover the retreat or to relieve the fighters when they began to tire. Caesar found that fighting such a foe was difficult. Even greater problems were posed by the natives' use of chariots, of which Cassivellaunus had 4,000 under his control. Evidently this kind of warfare was new to Caesar. He describes how the Britons drove about wildly to create a din and to inspire fear whilst throwing their javelins at the enemy. They would then drive out through their own cavalry and jump down to engage the enemy on foot while the charioteers retired a short way, positioning themselves so as to be able to swoop in and rescue their masters if required. 'They combine', said Caesar, 'the mobility of cavalry with the staying power of infantry.' He goes on to describe how by daily training they became highly skilled – able to drive up steep inclines with horses at full gallop, checking and turning with ease. They could also run out along the chariot pole, stand on the yoke and get back into the vehicle with great speed. Altogether Caesar was impressed. But even so, the British defence could not stand up to Roman attack. Like the Celtic personality, it was daring, fierce and brave but lacked staying power. It was impetuous and instinctive rather than considered. When faced with the grinding solidarity of the Roman military machine, the British resistance melted into the forests to engage in guerrilla warfare. Even the two hillforts which Caesar mentions, possibly Bigbury in Kent and Wheathampstead in Hertfordshire (Fig. 5:4), were overrun by the army without much difficulty. British fighting techniques were geared far more closely to the rapid raids of inter-tribal fighting (as indeed were the defences of the hillforts) than to the relentless force of organised military imperialism.

The archaeological record of the first century BC and early first century AD is rich in the material trappings of war. Spearheads and swords abound; shields are less commonly represented because they would normally have been made of perishable wood, wickerwork and leather, but a number of examples of metal bosses and bindings occur[1] and towards the end of the period elaborate parade shields of highly decorated bronze are known, such as the famous examples from the Thames at Battersea and Wandsworth and from the river Witham (Pls 14, 19a, 19b). Other personal parade armour includes the magnificent helmet of bronze from Waterloo Bridge (Pl. 21). The chariots themselves, though largely of wood, are occasionally represented by metal fittings (Fig. 5:5) such as lynchpins, yoke mounts like the decorative bronze bulls from Bulbury, and the yoke terminals from Brentford (Middx), High Cross (Leicester) and Llyn Cerrig Bach. Several examples of nave bindings, also possibly from chariots, are known. Horse trappings too, including bridle-bits, strap buckles, rings and the unique pony cap from Torrs (Kirkcudbright), are generally widespread. To this list of warlike artefacts should be added two examples of the Celtic war trumpet – the carnyx (S. Piggott, 1959) – one from the Witham at Tattershall Bridge, the other from Deskford, Banff (Fig. 5:6). The carnyx is also clearly shown, held aloft by a horseman, on coins of Tasciovanus, Cunobelin, Eppillus and Dumnovellaunus (D. F. Allen, 1958, 44–5).

In spite of the warlike nature of society at this time, warrior burials are rare (p. 293). Four are known in Yorkshire from Bugthorpe, North Grimston, Grimthorpe and Eastburn; Norfolk has produced one at Shouldham, and more recently three have been found in the south at Whitcombe, Dorset, Owslebury, Hants, and St Lawrence, Isle of Wight. In all of these the normal procedure was for the body to be inhumed and accompanied by a sword, a shield, sometimes a spear and occasionally other fittings and offerings.

[1] Grimthorpe, Llyn Cerrig-Bach, St Lawrence, Tal-y-Llyn, Noel Hiraddng, Standfordbury, South Cadbury and Owslebury.

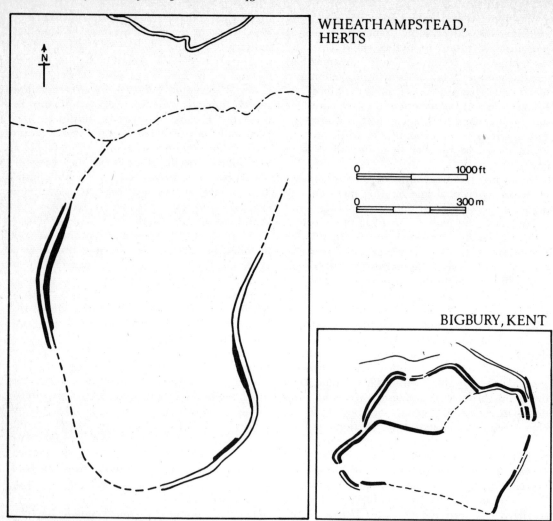

WHEATHAMPSTEAD,
HERTS

BIGBURY, KENT

5:4   First century BC fortifications (sources: *Wheathampstead*, Wheeler & Wheeler, 1936; *Bigbury*, Jessup & Cook, 1936)

Taking the evidence of the warrior burials together with the occurrence of warrior equipment, it can fairly be said that the archaeological record supports the texts in their implication that the later part of the British Iron Age was fraught with internal conflicts.

THE EMERGENCE OF TRIBAL KINGDOMS,
54 BC – AD 43

Commius, who was Caesar's mediator during the British campaigns, returned to Gaul in the late summer of 54 BC as a trusted and well-rewarded ally of Rome, but two years later he made a volte-face by supporting Vercingetorix, the leader of the Gallic rebellion, and was hunted down and almost murdered by the Roman authorities. Eventually, in about 50 BC, he fled to Britain to join his people already settled there. It was at this time that a new wave of Gallo-Belgic coins – Gallo-Belgic F – was introduced into southern Britain. Few of the original issues have been found, but the series soon gave rise to the extensive British Q coinage, with its characteristic triple-tailed horse on the reverse. British Q, in turn, developed into the first issues of Commius. The initial distribution of the British Q derivatives clusters upon the Sussex coastal plain and the middle Thames region, but further to the west, in Gloucestershire, the intrusive Gallo-Belgic type initiated a different development known as British R, which formed the starting point for the subsequent Dobunnic currency.

While there is no proof that the Commius of Caesar was the Commius of the coins, the

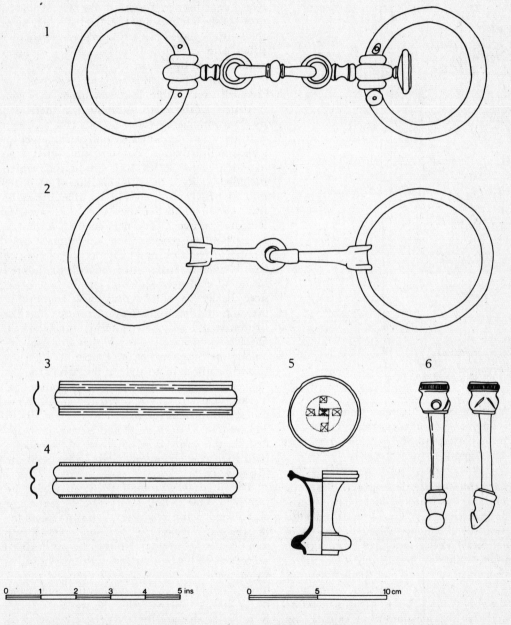

5:5   Chariot and harness fittings from Llyn Cerrig-Bach, Anglesey. 1, 2   bridle-bits; 3, 4 nave bindings; 5   yoke mount; 6   lynch pin (source: C.F. Fox, 1946)

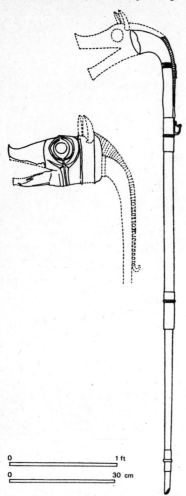

0 |————————————————| 1 ft
0 |————————————————| 30 cm

5:6   War trumpets. 1   the head from Deskford, Banff, restored as a carnyx-mouth; 2   the carnyx from Tattershall Bridge, Lincs, restored (source: S. Piggott, 1959)

chances are that we are dealing with the same man. In Britain the dynasty which he heads produced three later rulers: Tincommius, Eppillus and Verica, all of whom claimed to be sons of Commius. Since Verica was alive in AD 43, the relationship would only be possible if Commius, an active man in the middle of the first century BC, sired Verica in his old age and if Verica himself lived to his sixties. The problem is therefore not insuperable but an alternative explanation would be that the *Commi filius* legend used by both Eppillus and Verica should be interpreted

more loosely to imply grandson or even great-grandson. It is clear, however, that the Atrebatic dynasty founded by Commius emerged as the result of the last incursion of people into Britain from Gaul; Gaul was thereafter in Roman hands.

The developments of the next ninety years can be considered simply as a struggle between the two major power blocks – the Catuvellauni north of the Thames and the Atrebates largely to the south – played out at the expense of smaller tribes and carefully watched, and sometimes manipulated, by Rome.

The broad political events can be reconstructed with reasonable accuracy from the coin evidence. In the south Commius was succeeded by Tincommius in about 20 BC, and to begin with the coins remained virtually unchanged in style and distribution; but some time after 16 BC a totally new series was introduced which included one type based on an issue of Augustus minted between 15 and 12 BC. There can be little doubt that the dies were the work of Roman engravers. The change may imply an act of political reorientation, the hitherto anti-Roman Atrebates now allying themselves to Rome. Such a change fits well with the limited historical evidence available, for on three occasions before 27 BC Augustus was considering invasion and in 27 Dio Cassius records that the Britons would not come to terms. But by 13 BC Horace could state in an ode that Britons were among the suppliants of the Emperor. The continued pro-Roman attitude of the Atrebates was further reflected in the coinage of Eppillus and Verica, who not only adopted romanised types but styled themselves *Rex*. The fact that both Tincommius (before AD 7) and Verica (*c*. AD 42) fled to the protection of Rome is an added indication of the close political ties between the two powers.

The internal fortunes of the Atrebates can be traced in some detail. It is probable that there was always conflict between the contenders for the throne: the flight of Tincommius to Rome some time before AD 7 and the immediate succession by his brother Eppillus suggests inter-tribal feuding; indeed, Eppillus himself was to last for only a short period, minting coins from his capital at Calleva, before he was forced into Kent about AD 1 possibly by Verica. It may even be that Verica's exodus in AD 42 was the result of internal pressures rather than the aggressive policies of the Catuvellauni, as is usually supposed.

In their relation to neighbouring tribes they were no more successful. The closely related Dobunni appear not to have followed the Romanising lead offered by Tincommius; instead, they continued to mint coins in the old triple-tailed horse style and there is some evidence to suggest a political allegiance between them and the Catuvellauni beginning in the early first century AD. That the Catuvellauni also gained control over the entire northern half of the Atrebatic kingdom is shown by the large number of coins of Cunobelin (the Catuvellaunian leader) in the area, almost to the exclusion of Verican issues (Figs. 6:1, 7:1). The rule of Eppillus in Kent was also halted by Catuvellaunian expansion in about AD 20 – in fact by the time of the Roman invasion of AD 43 the Atrebates retained command of a much reduced territory stretching from mid-Sussex to the river Test.

The changing situation in Kent demonstrates clearly the delicate balance of power between the northern and southern dynasties. It was always a fragmented area and therefore susceptible. In Caesar's time there were four kings in power but the first to issue inscribed coins, Dumnovellaunus, seems to have controlled the entire area east of the Medway. Dumnovellaunus remained in command from about 15 BC until just before AD 7 when he was forced to flee to Rome, but during this time it appears that he gained command of the Trinovantes, ruling for a while from Camulodunum. In the decade before his final expulsion he was replaced in Kent by several local chiefs, including Vosenios and Sa[. . .]. It was during this confused period that Eppillus moved in only to be ousted, as we have seen, by the Catuvellaunian king Cunobelin some time about AD 20.

The political developments north of the Thames in the Catuvellaunian and Trinovantian territories are altogether more complex. In Caesar's time the two tribes were at war and this situation seems to have been resumed soon after the withdrawal, in spite of the treaty undertakings made by Cassivellaunus. Until 20 BC Catuvellaunian coins remained uninscribed, but at about this time King Tasciovanus, probably the son or grandson of Cassivellaunus, began issuing coins from the Catuvellaunian capital at Verulamium. A few years later he was minting coins in the Trinovatian capital of Camulodunum but only, apparently, for a short time. The implication seems to be that the Catuvellauni had established a shaky and short-lived control over the Trinovantes. Precise dating is impossible, but Frere has suggested (1967) that the aggressive move may have been encouraged by the Roman defeat on the Rhine in 17 BC, the subsequent rapid withdrawal being thought expedient when the emperor Augustus visited Gaul in the following year.

Tasciovanus continued to rule until the first decade of the first century AD, during which time the Catuvellauni had gained ascendancy over a vast territory stretching from east Kent, through the mid-Thames to the Ouse valley and beyond. For a while the Trinovantes in Essex remained unmolested, and after the period of Catuvellaunian rule, the Camulodunum mint issued coins of Addedomaros, followed in about 10 BC by those of the Kentish king Dumnovellaunus. As we have seen, Dumnovellaunus was forced to flee to Rome before AD 7. The cause of his departure is uncertain but the fact that soon afterwards the Catuvellaunian king Cunobelin, son of Tasciovanus, was issuing coins with the Camulodunum mint mark strongly suggests that the Trinovantes had finally been engulfed by the empire of their aggressive western neighbours. South of the Thames too, Catuvellaunian expansionist policies were felt: Kent succumbed to Cunobelin in the twenties of the first century AD while another son of Tasciovanus, Epaticus, was at about this time gaining control of the northern part of the old Atrebatic kingdom based on Calleva (Silchester). By the thirties the empire of Cunobelin had grown to immense proportions, covering the entire area of the initial Belgic settlement north of the Weald–Kennet line. It is no wonder that Suetonius refers to him as *Britannorum rex*.

The international politics of the period are a little obscure, but we do know that in AD 16 a group of Roman soldiers were returned to the emperor after being shipwrecked on the east coast – an act which suggests that some form of diplomatic relations existed. Moreover, the archaeological evidence leaves very little doubt that trading between Britain and the Roman world was brisk. In all probability, therefore, the Catuvellaunian confederacy as well as the Atrebatic kingdom was tied to Rome by treaty obligations. But with the death of Cunobelin in 40 or 41, and the succession of his two sons Togodumnus and Caratacus, the older order crumbled and restraint was thrown to the wind. In 43 the Romans attacked.

The broad outline of tribal history sketched above has been based almost entirely upon the evidence of the inscribed coinages of the south-east; it is, of necessity, simplified and incomplete but is supported here and there by scraps of documentary evidence and by the main stream of the archaeological background which shows the gradual romanisation of the material culture in the area. The importation of Roman luxury objects, in the form of pottery, metalwork and presumably food and wine, implies changing habits in the same way that the inscribing of coins, sometimes in Latin, and the blatant copying of Roman issues are strong indications of the desire to embrace the less tangible aspect of Roman culture.

So far we have been concerned only with those areas which came under the direct influence of Belgic immigration – areas settled by significant numbers of new people. Around this nucleus, from the Humber to the Exe, lies a crescent of belgicised tribes all minting coins and all, in varying degrees, influenced by the culture of the south-east: in Lincolnshire the Coritani, in Norfolk and parts of Suffolk the Iceni, in Gloucestershire and north Somerset the Dobunni, and in south Somerset, Dorset, west Hampshire and parts of Wiltshire the Durotriges. The material culture and economy of these individual regions will be discussed later but here something must be said of the history of each tribe as far as it can be deduced from its coinage. In a recent study of Icenian coins, D. F. Allen (1970, 14–15) has suggested that the Iceni were the leaders of a group of associated or federated tribes occupying Norfolk and parts of Suffolk and Cambridgeshire. Three distinct *pagi* can be recognised, at first all issuing different types of coins with respectively a boar (?), a face, and a pattern on the obverse, while their reverses depicted horses. The first of the Icenian rulers to inscribe his coins was Antedios, a contemporary of Cunobelin, who was probably ruling at the time of the Roman invasion and continued in power as the first of the Icenian client kings. That Antedios was issuing his silver coins at

three to the denarius implies a deliberate intention to conform to the Roman exchange rate. His reign ended *c.* AD 50 and thereafter appear a series of coins inscribed with the tribal name in the form ECEN and ECE. These must represent the issues of various centres minting under the overlordship of Prasutagus, whose death in AD 59–60 and the events consequent upon it sparked off the rebellion led by his wife Boudicca.

The coins of Antedios and Prasutagus developed from the earlier pattern-horse variety but alongside them the other *pagi* continued to mint their own issues for a while. The face-horse types continued into the fifties but the boar-horse variety ended early in the reign of Antedios with issues inscribed CANS-DVRO and ALE-SCA, possibly representing the names of the issuing magistrates or moneyers. The general impression which this study gives is of three basic factions gradually coming together, until by *c.* AD 50 total power had passed to Prasutagus.

North-west of the Iceni lay the Coritani (D. F. Allen, 1963). Their inscribed coinage, replacing British K, begins about AD 10 and continues until about 50 with a series of seven dual-inscribed issues: AUN-AST, ESUP-ASU, VEP-CORF, DUMNO-TIGIR-SENO, and then VOLISIOS paired first with DUMNOCOVEROS, then with DUMNOVEL-LAUNOS, and finally with CARTIVEL. It would seem, therefore, that the tribe was either a confederacy of two kingdoms ruling jointly or, more likely, a single unit ruled in the old Gaulish manner by two periodically-elected magistrates. The ease with which the Roman army subsequently passed through the area implies that by the time of the conquest the tribe was pursuing a pro-Roman policy.

The territory of the Dobunni, as we have seen, came under the influence of the Gallo-Belgic F staters introduced soon after the campaigns of Caesar, and soon developed a local series (British R) in parallel with the Atrebatic development (British Q), both of which bore the characteristic triple-tailed horse (D. F. Allen, 1961b). That this local development continued, even after Tincommius had proclaimed his pro-Roman leanings by adopting a new coinage in the Roman style, has been taken by some writers to suggest a split between the two tribes, the Dobunni thenceforth continuing their anti-Roman policies (Hawkes, 1961). About 10 AD an inscribed series of gold staters begins; except in one case, the inscription appears above the continuing motif of the triple-tailed horse. The rulers mentioned, in chronological order, are: ANTED, EISU, CATTI, COMUX, INAM, CORIO and BODVOC, some of the names appearing also on an extensive silver series. An anti-classical conservatism is apparent throughout. The coins of the last two rulers, Corio and Bodvoc, belonging to the period *c*. 40–50, provide an interesting contrast: Corio's issues, rooted firmly in tradition, are distributed largely in Somerset and north Wiltshire while Bodvoc's, based on Gloucestershire, are considerably more romanised, with an inscription in good Roman lettering replacing the herringbone motif on the reverse of the gold staters, and a redesigned head facing an inscription appearing for the first time on the regular silver issues. Evidently a split had occurred both in territorial rule and perhaps in ideology. One possible explanation can be seen in the light of Dio's remark that the 'Bodunni [presumably Dobunni] were subject to Catuvellaunian kings' (Book LX, Ch. 6). It could be argued that during a forward advance Cunobelin or his sons took over the northern territory and set up Bodvoc as a puppet ruler. An alternative and no less unlikely view is that in 43 the tribe was split in its reaction to the Roman advance, the northern half going over to Rome. Dio's reference to a 'Bodunnic' surrender whilst Aulus Plautius was marching through Kent would therefore apply to only a part of the original tribe. If this were so, the romanised issues of Bodvoc could be thought of as products of a client king under Roman licence. The problem is not susceptible of a simple explanation.

The last coin-issuing tribe to be considered, the Durotriges, formed a block across the south coast from the Exe to the Test and north into Wiltshire and southern Somerset. From the outset Durotrigian currency was silver, influenced no doubt by the silver currencies of Armorica – an area with which the tribe maintained close trading relations in the first half of the first century BC. The earliest coins derived elements from both British A and B and seem to have originated about 60 BC or a little earlier. Thereafter the coinage evolved along its own lines, totally uninfluenced by developments in the neighbouring Dobunnic and Atrebatic areas. With the exception of two coins bearing the name CRAB, all Durotrigian issues were uninscribed. The general impression given by the coins and strengthened by the archaeological evidence considered later (pp. 96–9) is that the tribe, or confederacy, maintained a rigid independence which was to persist into the early years of the Roman occupation.

The tribes which lay beyond this arc of belgicised territory were without coins and so far removed from the literate world as to be without recorded history until after the invasion of AD 43.

The coin evidence, aided by occasional literary references, shows that in the century between Caesar's comings and goings and the Claudian invasion of AD 43 distinct tribal entities had crystallised out, and it may be that the volume of internal warfare, if not of dynastic bickering had substantially decreased. In the Belgic-settled areas of the south-east there is little evidence of major hillfort refortification or occupation, and even in the peripheral areas, while many hillforts continued to be inhabited, none show signs of large-scale rebuilding. New types of defences were, however, erected to defend the urban nucleations based around the royal courts and mints. At Camulodunum massive linear dykes were thrown across the tongue of land between the river Colne and the Roman river, enclosing an area of 12 square miles (31·1 km²) while similar earthworks straddle the coastal plain around Selsey, near Chichester, in the territory of the Atrebates – their most extended form defines an area of 60 square miles (152·4 km²). Fragments of similar systems are found around the urban settlements of Verulamium and at Bagendon, Glos. Evidently the new defences involved new strategic concepts. Territories were now being defended – territories which included not only the main urban nucleus but also scattered satellites, individual farms, cultivation plots and pastures. It has sometimes been assumed that the earthworks were designed against threat of chariot warfare; in any event, they are massive enough to be considered as defensive rather than merely as territorial boundaries.

The death of Cunobelin and the accession of his more aggressive sons Togodunus and Caratacus in about AD 40, followed by the threat of Roman invasion first by Gaius (Caligula) in 41 and later by Claudius in 43, must have had a profound effect on British society. It is to this

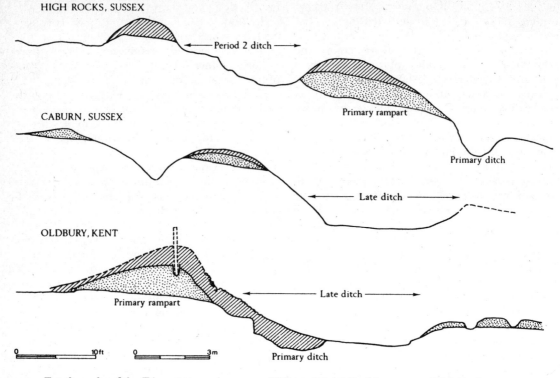

5:7 Earthworks of the Fécamp type (sources: *Oldbury*, Ward-Perkins, 1944; *High Rocks*, Money, 1968; *Caburn*, Wilson 1939)

period that a new wave of defensive activity belongs. In the south-east several hillforts show signs of refortification at this time (Fig. 5:7). At Oldbury in Kent the rampart was heightened and the ditch recut to a wide flat-bottomed form close in type to the Fécamp series of earthworks constructed in Gaul at about the time of Caesar's conquests. At Oldbury, however, a Claudian date is suggested by two sherds of Roman *mortaria* found in association with the modifications. The Caburn in Sussex has produced similar evidence, with a new ditch being dug in the characteristic flat-bottomed form outside the earlier lines. Here again a date close to 43 is indicated by sherds of a Claudian flagon found in the primary silt derived from the bank. Both sites show signs of destruction by fire. From this fragmentary evidence it is very tempting to suggest that both were late anti-Roman defences destroyed by the advancing armies in 43. The fort at High Rocks, Sussex, was also provided with a rampart and wide flat-bottomed ditch, this time *within* the earlier defences, there being

little space on the plateau outside to fit in the new circuit. Here, however, the dating evidence is less precise but points to a construction in the first century AD, quite possibly as late as the forties. Finally, at Danebury, Hants, the main fortifications were modified by the recutting of the ditch in flat-bottomed form and the heightening of the rampart some time after *c.* AD 30, a date based on the stratified pottery in upper fillings of the ditch immediately prior to recutting. Four, at least, of the existing forts in the south-east were therefore brought into defensive order in the period immediately preceding the invasion, and we may assume that more will eventually come to light as further excavations are undertaken.

Some writers (e.g. Cotton, 1961b, 66) have expressed doubts about the late dating of the Fécamp style in Britain, pointing out that such a view would require methods which evolved in Gaul a hundred years earlier to have lingered in the minds of the Britons for a disproportionately long time before being put into force. The fact that three of the four known examples are late does not, however, preclude the possibility that earlier examples will be found. Moreover, it has recently been shown (Boon, 1969) that the Fécamp method was used to defend an area of 85 acres (34·4 hectares) at Calleva probably in the year or two *after* the invasion of 43. That Fécamp defences were in use at the time of the invasion may now safely be accepted.

Further west indigenous techniques of defence were maintained. At Maiden Castle the earlier ramparts were refurbished, while at Hod Hill a hasty attempt at multivallation was being undertaken but was halted by the Roman advance of 43. A totally new bivallate earthwork appears to have been constructed at about this time at Boscombe Down West, Wilts, and there is some evidence of similar activity in many of the other hillforts of the south and west. The well-known reference to the Roman attack of the western forts (Suetonius, *Vesp.* 4), more than twenty of which Vespasian had to subdue in the campaign of 43–4, is supported by the evidence of slaughter at Maiden Castle and Spettisbury and by the ballista attack on Hod Hill. There can be little doubt that in the early forties feverish attempts were made to bring the old forts of the area into a defensive readiness, using techniques of fortification which owed nothing to Belgic ideas.

Basic fighting techniques seem to have changed very little between the invasions of Caesar and the Claudian conquest. Chariots were still in use at the Medway battle of 43, the battle against Boudicca in 60, and the routing of the Caledonians under Calgacus in 84. Indeed, Tacitus, while stating that the strength of the British armies lay in their infantry, admitted that 'some tribes also fought from chariots driven by noblemen and defended by their dependants' (*Agricola*, 12). The contemporary battle accounts still bear out the fierce but uncontrolled nature of the Briton at war but, as Tacitus remarks, 'they eventually failed because they are distracted between the jarring factions of rival chiefs. Indeed, nothing has helped us more in war with their strongest nations than their inability to co-operate. It is but seldom that two or three states unite to repel a common danger: fighting in detail they are conquered wholesale.' Evidently little had changed in a hundred years.

The Catuvellauni, Trinovantes, Cantiaci, Coritani and Iceni

Much of eastern England, from Kent to Lincoln-shire and from the coast inland to the Chilterns, came under the influence of cultural elements shared in common with the Belgic areas of the adjacent continent. Ceramic technology, burial rites, economy and socio-political structure showed only slight variation from one end of the region to the other. Nevertheless, below this apparent unity there lay five major tribal group-ings – the Catuvellauni, Trinovantes, Cantiaci, Coritani and Iceni – all recognisable through their distinctive coinages and all following definite political policies in relation to each other and to the eventual threat of Roman attack. Given only the material and structural evidence, it would have been very difficult to distinguish the Catuvellauni, Trinovantes, and Cantiaci: for this reason, they are described together as part of the archaeologically-defined Aylesford–Swarling culture. The Coritani and Iceni can be seen to differ in some material respects from the southern block and can thus reasonably be dis-cussed separately.

THE AYLESFORD–SWARLING CULTURE: THE CATUVELLAUNI, TRINOVANTES AND CANTIACI (Fig. 6:1)

The most readily recognisable of the British La Tène III cultural groupings has been named the Aylesford–Swarling culture after two Kentish cremation cemeteries excavated in 1890 and 1921 respectively. The relevant material was collated and received a detailed discussion in a paper by Hawkes and Dunning published in 1931; and more recently it has been reconsidered in the light of new finds, both British and con-tinental, by A. Birchall (1965). The culture is characterised by a distinctive range of pottery, usually wheel-made, together with the rite of cremation in flat graves. The associated metal-work is invariably La Tène III. The classic statement of the distribution of the group was provided by the distribution map of pedestal urns published by Hawkes and Dunning (1931, Fig. 7), which shows the vessels concentrating in Kent, Essex, Hertfordshire, Bedfordshire and the London area, with a few outliers further north and west. In the last forty years many more sites have been discovered but the pattern has not changed significantly. Thus in terms of the known tribes the Aylesford–Swarling culture is the folk culture of the Catuvellauni, the Trino-vantes and the Kentish kingdoms.

A reassessment of the evidence in the light of Allen's demonstration of second century Belgic incursions has failed to trace a significant body of material pre-dating Caesar's invasions. It is clear, therefore, that the developed culture (in the form defined here) cannot have been intro-duced by Caesar's invaders from Belgium along with the Gallo-Belgic A, B and C coinage. In Kent, however, Birchall has recognised an 'early' group of pottery, admittedly limited in quantity and extent, which could date to the pre-Caesarian period. The general impression which these detailed studies have given is that while at first the incomings were probably limited to an aristocratic element, by the middle of the century larger numbers of people were arriving, and their traditions and folk culture with them. After 45–50 immigration would have been halted by the progress of romanisation in Gaul, but internal local development would have con-tinued, with trade and other forms of social inter-course smoothing out differences and leading to

6:1   Distribution of coins of Cunobelin, demonstrating the maximum extent of Catuvellaunian influence (sources: D. F. Allen, 1961a and 1962)

the development of widespread cultural uniformity.

Pottery is the most characteristic artefact of the Aylesford–Swarling culture (Figs. A:25, A:26). It is usually of exceptionally high quality, most of it being wheel-made with an assurance and similarity of design which suggests commercial production on a large scale by specialists who, in the first instance, may well have been immigrants. Tall elegantly-shaped urns with pedestal bases, conical urns, corrugated vessels

and a wide range of elaborately cordoned and grooved bowls make up the bulk of the types, with butt beakers, tazze, platters and lids occurring less frequently. Also relatively common are the coarser narrow-mouthed jars with their outer surfaces wiped or scored to create crude patterns. This type probably originates in an earlier period but takes on a new formality with the introduction of the techniques of wheel-turning.

After 15–10 BC the locally produced vessels were supplemented by imported fine wares from

Gaul, Germany and the Mediterranean, including terra rubra and terra nigra platters, Gallo-Belgic butt-beakers, Arretine wares and eventually samian pottery, whilst from the middle of the first century BC wine was being imported in some quantity in large amphorae (p. 149). Some local copying of the imports occurred, particularly of the Gallo-Belgic beakers and platters, and it is probable that the production of the pale fabric butt-beakers of Gaulish type had begun at Camulodunum before the invasion of AD 43.

The culture is best known through its cemeteries and isolated burials, which form a significant part of the archaeological record. A few examples will suffice to demonstrate the range of burial rites. At Verulamium a typical cemetery has been excavated in its entirety close to the nucleus of the Prae Wood Belgic settlement (Fig. 6:2). Here no less than 463 individual cremations were discovered, usually placed inside an urn buried in a small pit, and often accompanied by one or more accessory vessels and by bronze brooches. Less frequently other grave-goods were buried, including mirrors, bracelets, keys, knives, shears, gaming pieces, spoons and toilet sets – in fact, a range of personal belongings appropriate to both males and females. Some of the burials, richer than others, were heaped up on the floor of larger grave pits, and several of

these were placed in the centres of rectangular ditched enclosures containing poorer satellite burials arranged in a circle around the principal grave. The cemetery also produced eighteen inhumations, of which sixteen were unaccompanied. Judging by the quantity of imported Gallo-Belgic wares, which are unlikely to have arrived in Britain much before 10 BC, the cemetery must have been in use throughout the half-century before the invasion of AD 43.

The large-scale excavation of the Verulamium cemetery allows the site to serve as a type example for La Tène III cremation cemeteries in general. To this category belong the two type-sites of Aylesford and Swarling, both of which are somewhat earlier than Verulamium. Neither site was excavated under modern conditions, and apart from the groups of grave-goods little is known of the general arrangement or plan of the cemeteries. At Swarling, however, two groups of cremations were found: an eastern group of nine and a west group of ten burials. Class distinctions were evident in the care with which some of the graves were dug, as well as from the number of accessory vessels provided and the occasional presence of fibulae. Grave 13 was outstanding in that the main burial was placed in an iron-bound wooden bucket together with two elaborate bronze fibulae, while standing around were six

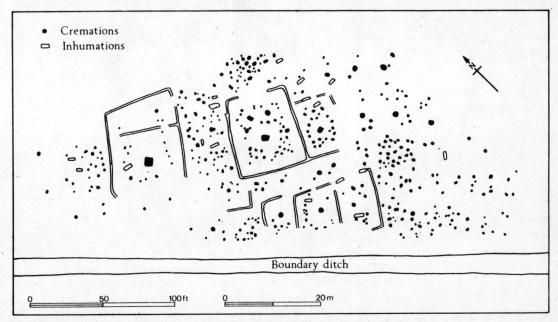

• Cremations
▭ Inhumations

Boundary ditch

0   50   100 ft   0   20 m

6:2   The cremation cemetery at Prae Wood, Verulamium, Herts (source: Stead, 1969)

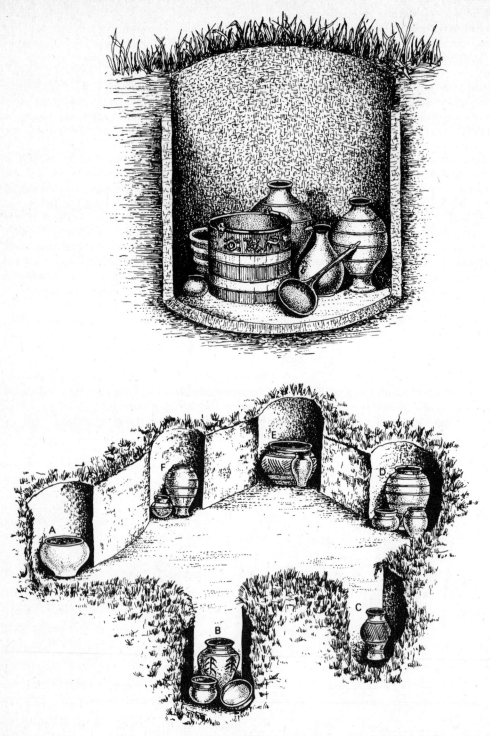

6:3   Burial groups of the cemetery at Aylesford, Kent (source: original illustrations, Evans, 1890)

pottery vessels, no doubt once containing offerings of food and drink. Such elaboration suggests the burial of a person of wealth and status.

Elaborate bucket burials were also a feature of the Aylesford cemetery, where three such groups can be reconstructed (Birchall, 1965, 243 ff.). Burial X contained a large wooden bucket bound with iron, together with six pots; burial Y was richer (Fig. 6:3), consisting of a circular chalk-lined pit within which lay a bronze-plated situla (Pl. 26a) containing the cremation and a fibula, a bronze oenochoe (jug) and patella, both of Italian manufacture, together with a number of pots (Fig. 6:3). The third burial, Z, produced a bronze-mounted wooden tankard with bronze handles surrounded, apparently, by five or six pots. Since the Italian bronze vessels and the brooch from grave Y are types well known on the continent in contexts dating to 50–30 BC, it may be assumed that the Aylesford burial dates to somewhere within the second half of the first century BC. The exact relationship of the three rich burials to the poorer cremations is unrecorded but the existence of circular settings of burials hints at the possibility of satellite arrangements comparable to those at Verulamium. Bucket burials, though few in number, occur widely in south-east Britain, at Old Warden, Harpenden, Great Chesterford (Pl. 26b), Lexden, Baldock and Welwyn Garden City as well as Aylesford and Swarling, all in the primary Belgic areas, with outliers at Hurstbourne Tarrant and Silkstead in Hampshire and Marlborough in Wiltshire (Stead, 1971). These three peripheral burials may represent a Belgic aristocracy penetrating outlying regions during phases of westward expansion.

North of the Thames a group of exceptionally rich cremation burials (Fig. 6:4) has recently been defined and named after the type-site of Welwyn, Herts (Stead, 1967). Six examples definitely belong to this group – Hertford Heath, Mount Bures, Snailwell, Stanfordbury, Welwyn and Welwyn Garden City – and a further eight sites in the same general area are possibly also of this kind. The Welwyn type burials may be characterised as cremations placed in large grave-pits with no covering mound (Fig. 6:5). The pits contain a wide range of grave-goods including at least one wine amphora (usually more, six being the maximum) and quantities of tableware, much of it imported. Some were provided with imported bronze vases, strainers and patellae, others with silver cups, while one produced imported glass dishes and containers. Clearly the dead person was being provided with sufficient food and wine to see him on his journey to the next world. Surprisingly, however, meat (or at least meat on the bone) was seldom found. Most burials contained a few other personal belongings such as buckles, bracelets, beads and gaming pieces, but weapons are conspicuously absent. Iron fire-dogs (e.g. Pl. 23), spits and in one case a tripod represent the dead man's hearth furniture in several of the graves. The imported material, particularly the Italian bronzes in the earlier graves and the Gallo-Belgic and samian vessels in the later, allow the burials to be arranged in a chronological sequence spanning the century between the invasions of Caesar and Claudius. Welwyn type cremations represent a tradition of aristocratic burial deeply rooted in the formative period of the Aylesford–Swarling culture north of the Thames.

Flat cremations are, however, not the only type of rich La Tène III burial in the south-east. At Lexden, Essex, close to Camulodunum, a large barrow, some 75 ft (22·9 m) in diameter, was excavated in 1927 and found to cover an enormous oval burial pit 27 ft (8·2 m) long (Fig. 6:6). In the pit had been placed a cremation together with a surprising range of grave-goods, including amphorae and other vessels, bronze chain-mail with silver studs, a bronze table, a pedestal for a statuette and a series of bronze figures including a cupid, a griffin, a bull and a boar. There were also fragmentary bronze-embossed plates, studs, hinges and other fittings, a series of decorative silver attachments, gold tissue and a silver medallion of the emperor Augustus cut out of a coin. One significant difference when compared with the Welwyn burials is that at Lexden there appears to have been a deliberate destruction of some of the offerings at the time of burial. Evidently the ritual basis of the Lexden burial differs in several respects from that of the Welwyn group.

Another barrow burial, but on a much smaller scale, was excavated in 1905 at Hurstbourne Tarrant, Hants. Here a mound 27 ft (8·2 m) across and 3·5 ft (1·1 m) high covered a burial group consisting of a cremation placed in a bronze-mounted wooden bucket, surrounded by

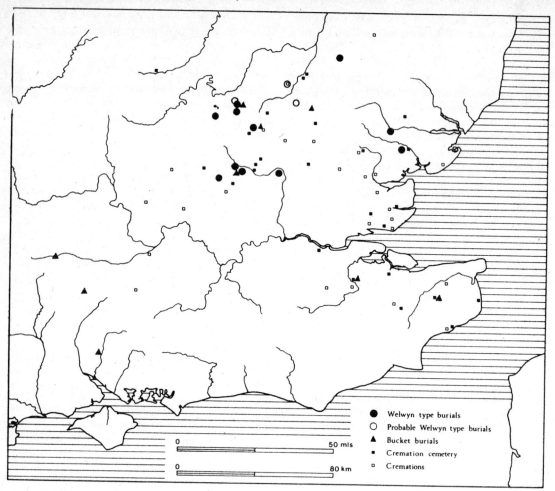

6:4 The cremation cemeteries of the Aylesford–Swarling culture (sources: various, including Peacock, 1971; Stead, 1967 and 1971)

twelve vessels, accompanied by a bronze brace-let, a thistle brooch and a vessel of brown glass. Both Lexden and Hurstbourne Tarrant belong to the fifty years or so before the Claudian invasion; Lexden, by virtue of the amphorae types, should be dated to the very end of the first century BC (Peacock, 1971).

From the foregoing summary it will be seen that the type of burial rite in the Belgic areas was varied but relatively consistent. It reflects a belief in the after-life and it mirrors very clearly the degree of social stratification which is known to have existed from the literary sources.

Within the Aylesford–Swarling culture there developed urban or proto-urban settlements at

Canterbury, Verulamium and Camulodunum, with several lesser known settlements like Rochester, where traces of a mint suggest a subsidiary centre of some importance. While it must be admitted that little is yet known of these Belgic oppida in Britain, the work at Verulamium has defined the main characteristics of this type of site (Fig. 6:7). The earliest nuclear settlement appears to lie on a gravel plateau above the river Lea at Wheathampstead, Herts, where massive earthworks flank at least three sides of an enclosure of some 90–100 acres (36–40 hectares) – the size of the average Romano-British town. Limited excavation within has demonstrated the presence of intensive occupation spanning the

WELWYN GARDEN CITY, HERTS

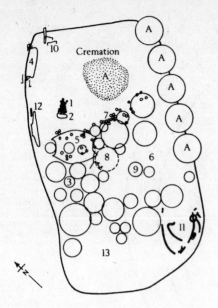

1 Gaming pieces
2 Beads and bracelet fragments
3 Silver cup
4 Bronze strainer
5 Bronze dish
6 Nail cleaner
7 Bronze studs
8 Wooden vessel
9 Wooden vessel
10 Wooden board with iron fittings
11 Wooden vessels with iron fittings
12 Triangular knife
13 Wooden object with iron fittings

A Amphorae

SNAILWELL, CAMBS

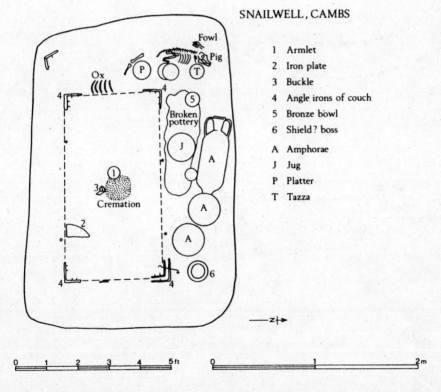

1 Armlet
2 Iron plate
3 Buckle
4 Angle irons of couch
5 Bronze bowl
6 Shield? boss

A Amphorae
J Jug
P Platter
T Tazza

6:5 La Tène III chieftain burials (sources: *Welwyn Garden City*, Stead, 1967; *Snailwell*, Lethbridge, 1953)

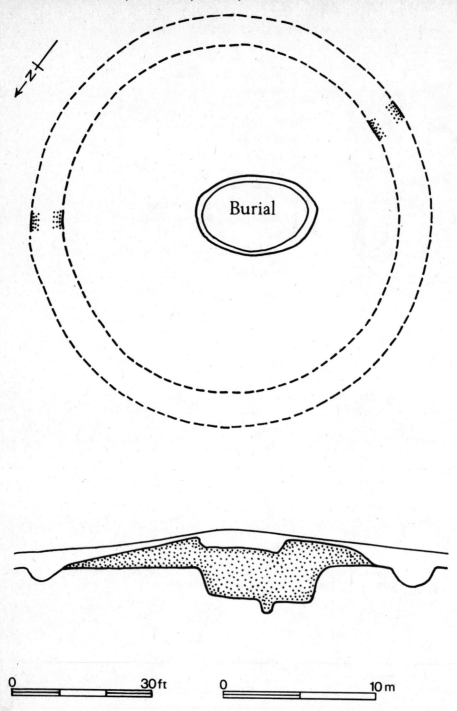

6:6   The Lexden tumulus, Essex (source: Laver, 1927)

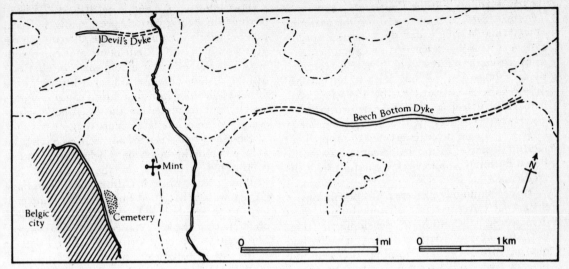

6:7 The Belgic occupation remains at Verulamium, Herts (source: Wheeler & Wheeler, 1936, with additions)

latter part of the first century BC but apparently ending before 15–10 BC (if the absence of Gallo-Belgic vessels, which began to be imported at about this time, is regarded as significant and reliable). It has been suggested, quite plausibly, that Wheathampstead was the oppidum where Cassivellaunus made his last stand against Caesar. Caesar tells us that British strongholds in general were densely wooded spots fortified with ramparts and ditches and that Cassivellaunus's stronghold was protected by forests and marshes and had been filled with a large number of men and cattle for their own protection. Wheathampstead would indeed fulfil these conditions, but the identification is unlikely ever to be proven.

The abandonment of Wheathampstead is matched by the growth of Verulamium, 5 miles (8 km) to the south-west and occupying a similar plateau position above the river Ver in the area of what is now Prae Wood. Plentiful imports were found showing that the site reached its maximum period of occupation in the first half of the first century AD. Instead of massive earthworks, the main inhabited area of the oppidum was enclosed by relatively slight ditches and palisades, altered on several occasions, within which lay the huts, drainage ditches and ovens of the settlement. Outside the boundary ditch flanking this nucleus was the cemetery referred to above. Other settlement areas must have existed nearby; one, found closer to the river

beneath the Roman town, produced the debris of a Belgic mint. Evidently the settlement was dispersed rather than concentrated at a single nucleated site. One further aspect of the local settlement pattern deserves consideration. From a point close to Wheathampstead as far as the river Ver opposite the Belgic settlement at Prae Wood runs a massive defensive bank and ditch known as Beech Bottom Dyke, the staggered line of which is continued by a lesser earthwork, Devil's Dyke, to the west of the river a little way north of the settlement. It seems probable that these banks and ditches form part of a series of dykes designed to defend and define the territory of the oppidum and its satellite settlements. As we shall see, systems of linear earthworks reach complex proportions at Camulodunum and in the Chichester region. The lack of such a development at Verulamium might be explained by the fact that the seat of Catuvellaunian government had moved to Camulodunum early in the first century AD, relieving Verulamium of its political importance. If so, the Beech Bottom Dyke/Devil's Dyke complex could be seen as an early stage in the development of territorial defences, arrested before the system could achieve its ultimate form.

Linear earthworks must be regarded as a new concept in defensive architecture arising late in the British Iron Age, partly as a response to new forms of warfare and partly, perhaps, from techniques introduced from the Belgic homeland. Tacitus (*Annals*, ii, 19), describing the assembly of a Germanic tribe called the Cherusci, specifically mentions their choice of a location hemmed in by a river and forests which were surrounded by deep bogs. On the one side without natural defences the neighbouring tribe, the Angrivarii, had constructed a 'broad earthwork as a boundary'. Here, surely, is a direct reference to large-scale linear defences erected to supplement natural obstacles in much the same way as the Beech Bottom complex makes careful use of the landscape.

If Verulamium represents the beginnings of linear defensive systems, Camulodunum must demonstrate the ultimate development (Fig. 6:8), for here a series of dykes, usually laid out in straight lines running between the Roman river and the river Colne, carve out a territory of some 12 square miles (31 km²). The system is so complex that more than one phase of construction must be involved. It is, in fact, possible to postulate an early nucleus in the Cheshunt Field area, where a Roman (and presumably pre-Roman) temple complex lies within a curved line of earthworks of early appearance. Only by extensive excavations, however, will the true complexity of the development finally be demonstrated. How many separate nuclear settlements lay within the territory is not known, but the Sheepen site, which has been examined by excavation (Hawkes & Hull, 1947), has yielded ample evidence of scattered huts of apparently circular and sub-rectangular form together with pits, ditches, the debris from a mint and masses of imported pottery. Here, evidently, lay a centre of some importance. The enormous quantity of imported wares found in one area has even suggested to the excavator the possibility of it being the actual residence of Cunobelin. Such an attribution, while possible, can never be proved.

The nucleated settlements of Kent are less well known, but beneath Canterbury Belgic occupation in the form of rectangular huts and drainage gullies has been found on both sides of the river Stour, whilst the discovery of coin-moulds at Rochester points to a second centre of some importance lying somewhere beneath the Roman town and overlooking the river Medway. Both of these settlements may well subsequently prove to be in the oppidum class. Several of the earlier hillforts of Kent were also re-defended during the Belgic period, presumably by local petty chieftains. Bigbury, near Canterbury, produced an impressive range of metalwork, including a series of tools, horse- and cart- (or chariot-) fittings, a slave chain, and hearth-fittings in the form of a fire-dog and a cauldron chain – objects which tend to underline the essentially aristocratic nature of the late occupation.

Re-use of hillforts does not seem to have been at all common in the primary Belgic areas. A few of the old structures on the Chilterns, like Wilbury, Ravensburgh Castle and Cholesbury Camp, were reoccupied but the settlement pattern, in so far as it is known, shows a marked preference for the less exposed valleys and woods. The politico-economic structure, which in much of the rest of Britain encouraged the continued use of the hillfort, seems here to have been largely superseded by people of different habits.

THE EAST MIDLANDS AND EAST ANGLIA: THE CORITANI AND ICENI

North and north-west of the primary Belgic areas, from the Chilterns across the valleys of the Ouse, the Nene and the Welland to the Trent, lies a large territory composed of varying soils, much of which was uncongenial for early settlement. The region can be defined as that dependent upon the river systems flowing into the Wash and Humber. The south-easterly limit is divided from the primary Belgic settlement area by the ridge of the Chilterns, the middle Thames valley lies at the southern extremity, while the western and northern limits approximate to the line of the Trent.

The settlement pattern and the material culture of much of the region are at present ill known, but by the second and first centuries BC farming communities had spread over considerable expanses of the river gravels. The ceramic development of the region was not dramatic: coarse hand-made jars, usually with high shoulders and upstanding rims, remained the dominant form, continuing in some areas to the first century AD. In the Oxford region the jars were generally without decoration, but over most of the rest of the area a percentage of them were roughly scored externally and the rims were often indented with finger-impressions (p. 46). Finer wares were characterised by the deve-

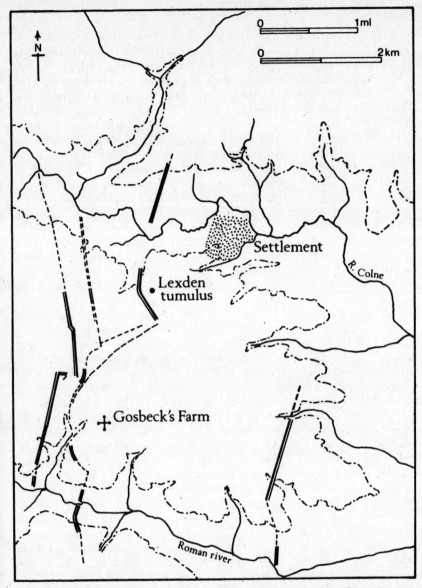

6:8   The major Belgic occupation remains of Camulodunum, Essex (source: Hawkes & Hull, 1974)

lopment of the wide-mouthed bowl, with a simple or proto-bead rim, usually fired to a dark grey colour with the surface burnished.

During the first century BC a number of regional variations became apparent, defined by the style in which the bowl form was decorated. In the Oxford region common motifs include pendent swags and arcs, drawn in a variety of ways often incorporating impressed circlets. In Northamptonshire the decoration tends to be freer and more lively, relying on the yin-yang or flowing scroll for its effect. These types cluster in the Hunsbury–Desborough–Draughton area but outliers have been found as far west as Cambridge. Closer to the Wash, around St Ives and extending into Lincolnshire as far north as Dragonby, rouletting is more commonly used but the quantity of material from this area is not great. In all probability, these regional variations in decoration reflect no more than the distribution of the products of specialist commercial manufacturing centres.

How long these ceramic traditions remained dominant is difficult to say. At Frilford, Oxon, it has been suggested that they continued well into the first century AD, while at Barley, Herts, occupation continued until the Roman conquest. Late occurrence of the indigenous tradition is not, however, universal for there is now indisputable evidence for the penetration of Belgic styles into the Lincolnshire–Leicestershire region, into the territory of a tribe which became known as the Coritani. Similarly, in the south, Catuvellaunian ceramics and coins spread across the Chilterns into Bedfordshire and into the Oxford region, implying an extension of Belgic domination emanating from the primary settlement areas, probably about the beginning of the first century AD. In parallel with this, the Iceni in Norfolk developed a Belgic-inspired coinage.

The Coritani (Fig. 6:9)

The territory of the Coritani as defined by the spread of their coinage lies between the rivers Trent and Nene – an area within which relatively few settlements have yet been found. Two nucleated occupation sites have, however, been extensively excavated. At Old Sleaford, a well-defined ceramic assemblage of Aylesford–Swarling type was recovered together with the debris of a mint, the latter implying a centre of some political and economic importance. Further north, at Dragonby, 7 miles (11·2 km) south of the Humber, another substantial settlement is currently being excavated. Here it has been possible to define several stages in the occupation sequence, beginning with a phase typified by decorated bowls and jars ornamented with arcs usually executed in rouletting and stamping. This phase was followed by the introduction of Aylesford–Swarling types during the second half of the first century BC. The merging of the two traditions gave rise to basically Belgic types, often decorated with rouletting in the native manner. The final stage came early in the first century AD with the importation of Gallo-Belgic butt-beakers, together with terra rubra and terra nigra platters.

Where the urban centres of the tribe lay is not yet clear. Old Sleaford with its mint was evidently of political and economic importance

and may indeed have been an oppidum; while beneath the Roman town of Leicester (Ratae) traces of pre-Roman occupation have come to light, suggesting the possibility of another substantial settlement, the limits and nature of which have still to be accurately defined.

Apart from Old Sleaford, Dragonby and possibly Leicester, the only other Coritanian site to be excavated on any scale is the enclosed settlement at Colsterworth, Lincs. The associated pottery shows that the site was occupied during the middle of the first century AD, beginning in the pre-Roman period. Since the number of huts occupied at any one time cannot be accurately assessed, the size of the social group is impossible to define, but in all probability the settlement was a small hamlet or large farm, rather more substantial than the earlier settlement site in the southern part of the Coritanian territory at Draughton, Northants, but well within the range of size of settlements in the south.

Allen was of the opinion (1963) that Coritanian coinage originated as the result of a separate colonising movement into Lincolnshire, either from the Kent/Essex region or direct from the continent, some time towards the middle of the first century BC: thereafter a distinctive series of local types developed. The pottery sequence at Dragonby tends to support the view of close contact with the south-east, but whether the Aylesford–Swarling types were introduced as the result of a folk movement or by the normal processes of trade remains to be defined. The existence of contact between the two areas is further emphasised by groups of imported Aylesford–Swarling brooches found at Dragonby and South Ferriby (S. C. Hawkes, 1964) and by the appearance in the north of butt-beakers of the kind made at Camulodunum. Contact in the reverse direction is represented by quantities of Coritanian coins found in the territory of the Catuvellauni.

The Iceni (Fig. 6:9)

The territory of the Iceni, as defined by the distribution of their coins, centred upon Norfolk stretching west towards the valley of the Nene. Practically nothing is yet known of the settlements of the period, although it appears probable that many of the earlier sites continued to be occupied. Defended enclosures are few and many

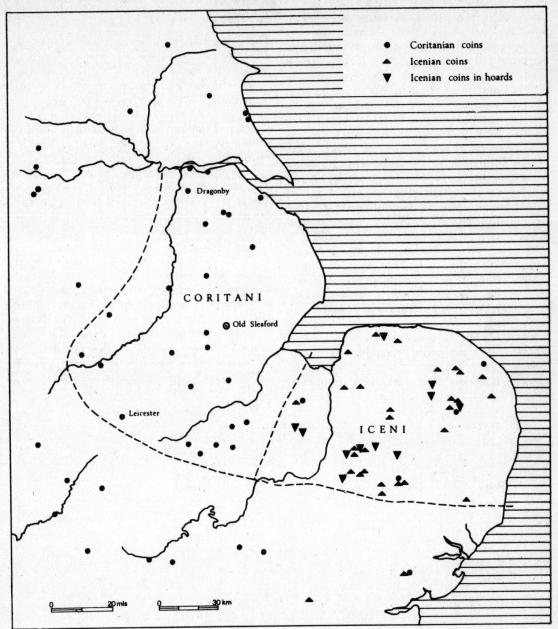

6:9   Distribution of coins of the Coritani and Iceni (sources: D. F. Allen 1963 and 1970)

originate before the first century BC, but at the multivallate fort of Wareham Camp pottery of the immediate pre-Roman period has been found in limited quantity. Other than this, and possibly the continued use of others of the camps, no major defended centre or oppidum is yet known in Icenian territory.

The material culture of the territory differs little from that of the Catuvellauni area. The ceramic sequence, as it is at present known, suggests strong influence from the Aylesford–Swarling culture, and in the first century AD

Gallo-Belgic imported wares were adopted in limited quantities. The most dramatic aspect of Icenian culture lies, however, in the wealth and display of the ruling classes. The famous hoards from Snettisham, Bawsey and North Creake together contain no less than fifty torcs and arm-rings of gold and electrum, while at Santon Downham, Ringstead and Westhall large collections of horse-trappings, including bits, terret-rings, harness mounts, lynch pins and other chariot fittings, have come to light. No other tribal area has yet produced such vivid evidence of opulent aristocratic display. This was the society which, less than twenty years after the Roman invasion, produced the energetic and almost successful war-leader Queen Boudicca.

It is not yet possible to assess the degree of belgicisation of the Icenian territory. The Belgic-derived coinage and the adoption of Belgic ceramics suggest close contact with Catuvel-launian and Coritanian culture, but whether this is the result of an incursion or simply trading contacts leading to acculturation is not clear. The fact that the Iceni probably took a pro-Roman line at the time of the invasion would suggest, however, that they were politically independent of the Catuvellauni.

THE UPPER THAMES VALLEY

The Oxford region forms a territory at present difficult to ascribe to any tribal group. Culturally the area lay in the north Thames ceramic zone, typified by coarse jars and open bowls frequently decorated with pendent swags and circlets (pp. 45–6). By the middle of the first century BC it appears, from the coin distributions, to have come under the sway of the Atrebates (British Q coins and a few scattered issues of Tincommius) but towards the end of the century coins of the Trinovantian and Catuvellaunian leaders Adde-domaros, Tasciovanus and later Cunobelin occur, to the virtual exclusion of Atrebatic issues, while over much of this area Catuvel-launian style pottery begins to spread.

By the early years of the first century AD the Catuvellaunian-dominated areas extended to the flanks of the Cotswolds, forming a boundary with the Dobunni somewhere in the region of Grims Ditch, a complex of earthworks built in the style of Catuvellaunian defensive dykes. The possibility remains that the earthworks define an actual frontier between the two tribes. The wider implications have been discussed in some detail by Hawkes (1961) and are referred to again below (pp. 121–2).

The Atrebates, Dobunni, Durotriges and Dumnonii

Around the area of primary Belgic (or more strictly Aylesford–Swarling) settlement lie a group of tribes which show some degree of belgicisation. Some eventually came under Catuvellaunian domination; others merely adopted certain of the cultural traits of their neighbours; while those furthest away were little influenced. Any attempt to describe the attributes of these tribal groups must begin with the assumption that their territory can be defined in terms of the coin distribution (that is, where coins exist) but it must be remembered that the political map was probably in a state of flux and that during the period with which we are concerned – some 150 years – there must have been many internal divisions and shifts of boundaries. Nevertheless many of the tribes exhibit a clear identity which they maintain over much of the period under discussion (see Fig. 7:11).

THE ATREBATES

The Atrebates began to take on a historical aspect when Commius arrived in Britain to join his people already here, after fleeing from Caesar. Numismatically the incursion seems to be represented by the few Gallo-Belgic F coins and the widespread British Q coinage which develops directly out of it. The main density of the distribution (Fig. 7:1) at this time covered Sussex, Hampshire, Surrey, north Wiltshire and much of the middle Thames, but by the time that the inscribed issues of Commius and his sons were minted, the area north of the Thames was no longer included. This could be interpreted as the loss of the trans-Thames territory at an early stage, but the point is difficult to prove. More certainty can be attached to the loss of the

Silchester region in about 25 BC, when the Catuvellaunian king Epaticus began to mint coins from Calleva. Thenceforth much of the northern part of the kingdom seems to have passed under Catuvellaunian domination.

The area of the original territory under Commius corresponds closely to the distribution of the saucepan pot wares belonging to the Sussex, Hampshire, Surrey and Wiltshire groups, hinting that some degree of cultural unity may well have existed in the pre-Caesarian period, stretching back into the second or even the third century BC. It was from this background that the new ceramic traditions of the Atrebates developed. Three new style-zones can be recognised, gradually emerging from indigenous traditions (Fig. 7:2). These may be defined as an Eastern group, extending along the Sussex coastal plain and downs approximately to the Arun; a Southern group, covering the rest of Sussex and Hampshire west to the Test; and a Northern group, centring on Salisbury Plain and spreading north to the edge of the Thames valley.

The Eastern group (Fig. A:29), is characterised by globular jars with a narrow mouth and outbent rim, some with flat bases and others with foot-rings. Another common type was the jar with a high shoulder, upright or slightly everted rim and a foot-ring base. Decoration was carried out variously with shallow tooling, rouletting, stamping, painting and the addition of applied cordons, to create horizontal zones of swags and arcs, or sometimes simpler rectilinear zones. It is possible to trace many of the forms and decorative elements back to the preceding saucepan pot tradition, but some influence from the Belgic areas of Kent may be thought to be apparent in the foot-ring types. That trans-Wealden contacts

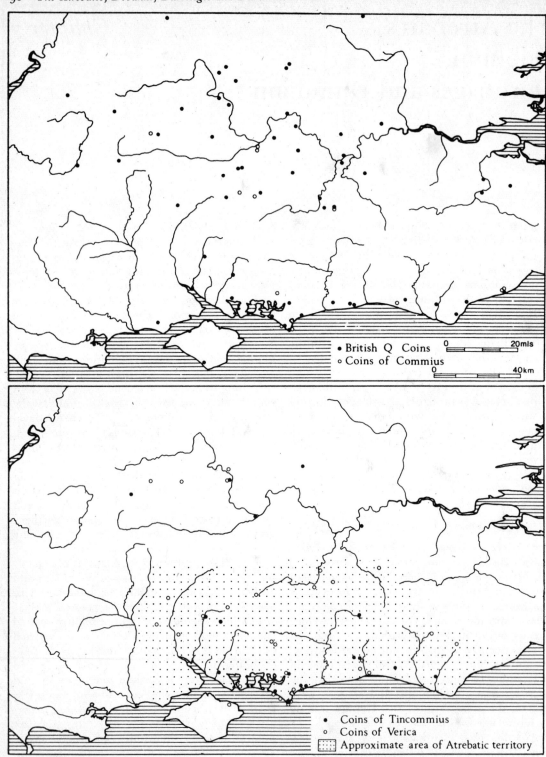

7:1   Distribution of coins of the Atrebates (sources: D. F. Allen, 1961a and 1962)

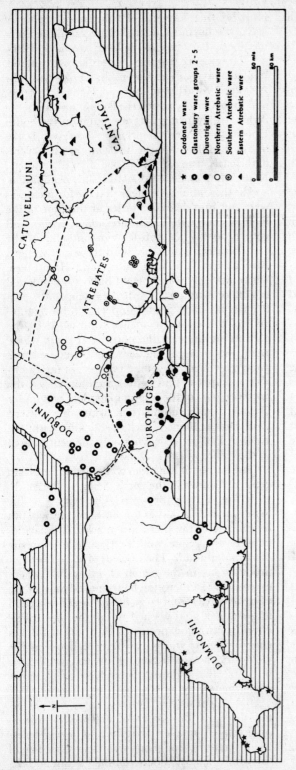

7:2 Pottery styles in southern Britain, first century BC to first century AD (source: author)

were maintained is clearly demonstrated by small numbers of these vessels found in the Aylesford–Swarling areas of Kent and Essex in contexts which show the broad contemporaneity of the two traditions. Various views have been put forward to explain the origins of this Eastern group but, in spite of the vague Armorican analogies, there seems to be no need to postulate an immigration to account for the development of the new style. Where stratigraphical evidence is available, continuity is the general rule both typologically and in terms of settlement area.

The South-western Atrebatic ceramic style (Fig. A:28), centred upon Hampshire and west Sussex, is typified by bead-rimmed jars with high shoulders and wide mouths, found together with high-shouldered bowls with simple upright rims, and necked jars often with a cordon at the junction of the neck and body. Less frequent (and occurring only in the first century AD) are local copies of Gallo-Belgic platters and butt-beakers. The North-western assemblage (Fig. A:28) is similar in many ways, but the bead-rimmed jars are frequently tightly grooved, and ovoid jars which hark back to the saucepan pot phase of the area occur together with rather larger quantities of Gallo-Belgic imports. There is nothing in either of the western assemblages to require an intrusive element (except, of course, the imported Gallo-Belgic wares, which were presumably the result of trade). All the basic forms and decorative styles were already in existence in the preceding saucepan pot phase, the only difference being that the Atrebatic wares were for the most part wheel-turned. The apparent differences, then, are best explained in terms of the introduction of the technological innovation of the potter's wheel rather than a significant folk movement.

The three broadly defined ceramic zones probably owe their identity partly to the indigenous folk tradition and partly to the distributional ranges of the production centres, but it is conceivable that the regionalisation in the later period also reflected a political fragmentation and realignment. On coin evidence it is possible to postulate the spread of Catuvellaunian control over much of the north-west zone, centred particularly upon the valley of the river Kennet. It is in this region that the two Catuvellaunian style burials were discovered, the bucket burial from Marlborough and the barrow cremation at

Hurstbourne Tarrant. Furthermore, coins of Tasciovanus and Cunobelin are far more common here than those of the later Atrebatic rulers.

The evidence from east Sussex is less dramatic, but we have already seen that links with the Aylesford–Swarling culture of Kent developed, and to this can be added the fact that a number of Aylesford–Swarling pots are found on the South Downs sites. More impressive, however, is the fate of the hillforts in the first century AD. Several of the east Sussex and Wealden sites, like those of Kent, show evidence of continuous occupation, and at the Caburn it is clear that the fortifications were put into defensive order at the time of the Roman conquest. The impression of unrest, and very probably an anti-Roman outlook, in the east contrasts noticeably with the south-western Atrebatic zone of west Sussex and Hampshire, where not only were the old hillforts abandoned but there is ample historical evidence of a pro-Roman alliance. Some support for the significance of this class of evidence is provided by the parallel situation in the north-west zone, where again many of the hillforts were occupied and some refortified. In summary, it is not unreasonable to suppose that by the time of Verica the northern part of the original kingdom was under Catuvellaunian domination while the eastern part had realigned itself politically with the Kentish kingdoms, leaving only the central area in the hands of the original dynasty.

The Atrebatic kingdom contained three urban centres: Calleva in the north, Selsey in the south, with Venta lying between. The nature of the Selsey centre is a matter for some speculation, but in general terms there are marked similarities between this region and the Catuvellaunian site of Camulodunum. The nucleus of the settlement probably lay in the region of Selsey Bill, where extensive coastal erosion has removed most of the evidence apart from large quantities of coins and fragments of gold washed up on the shore. The entire peninsula is protected by a series of dykes running across the gravel terrace between the valleys of the south-flowing streams, whilst the lines of the valleys themselves are further strengthened by north–south earthworks (Fig. 7:3). A recent survey (Bradley, 1971) has suggested three major phases of defence protecting progressively smaller territories, but nevertheless the intention throughout was clearly to defend the whole peninsula between the Lavant and the

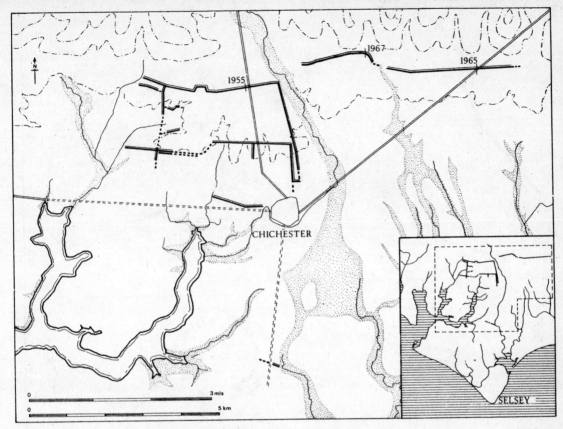

7:3 The entrenchments at Chichester, Sussex (source: Bradley, 1971)

streams flowing into Bosham harbour – that is, to protect the farmland belonging to the oppidum as well as the main nucleated settlement and its satellite farms. It was within the northern part of this territory that the Roman town of Chichester (*Noviomagus Regnensium*) was subsequently built, together with the large palatial building a mile (1·6 km) away at Fishbourne, which has tentatively been ascribed to the client king Cogidubnus (p. 120).

The nucleus of the northern centre, Calleva, was subsequently buried beneath the Roman town of Silchester (*Calleva Atrebatum*), but its existence is well attested by the discovery of large numbers of Celtic coins together with quantities of pre-Roman pottery, including imported amphorae, Gallo-Belgic wares and Arretine vessels (Boon, 1969). The site lies on a tongue of gravel projecting between the West End Brook and the Silchester Brook (Fig. 7:4). So far no earthworks can with certainty be assigned to the

pre-Roman phase, but an uncharacteristic bend in the outermost Roman circuit (the Salient) may belong to the earlier defences, while the massive lengths of dyke which command the approach to the promontory are best considered to be of pre-Roman date. Boon (1969) has tentatively divided the occupation of the site into three phases: I, the earliest occupation, *c.* 80 BC to the expulsion of Tincommius in about AD 5; II, the oppidum of Eppillus and possibly Verica, *c.* 5–25, during which time Eppillus minted coins with the mint-mark *Callev* and *Calle*; and III, the phase of Catuvellaunian domination, *c.* 25–43. In support of the last, Boon draws attention not only to the dense distribution of late Catuvellaunian coins in the area, but also to the discovery at Silchester of fragments of coin-moulds containing metal residues closer in composition to Catuvellaunian issues than to Atrebatic coinage.

The third oppidum at *Venta* (Winchester) lies largely beneath the Roman town (Fig. 7:5).

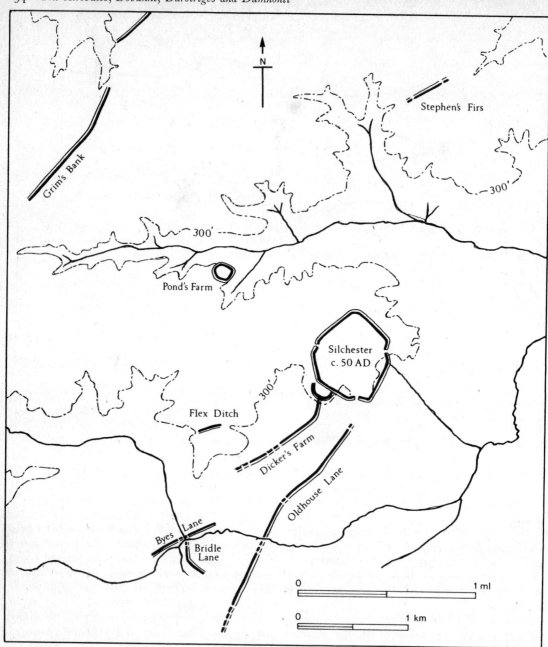

7:4   The siting of Calleva, Hants (source: Boon, 1969)

Intensive occupation of the valley-side began in the second to first century BC during the currency of saucepan pots. At this time a bank and ditch were constructed to enclose on the north, west and south sides an area in excess of 34 acres (13·8 hectares). The eastern limit is not known, but it is conceivable that the earthworks simply ran down the hill and terminated on the edge of the marshy river valley. Occupation within the enclosure was probably continuous but by the first half of the first century AD the nucleus had moved further towards the river, where frag-

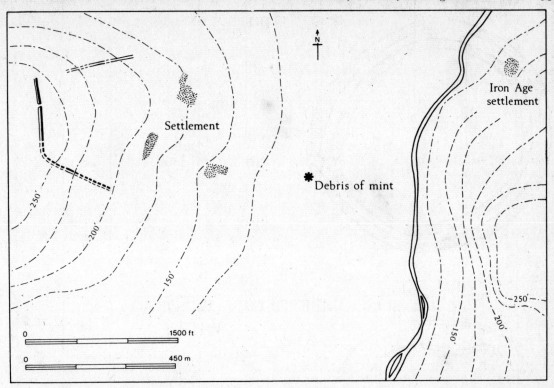

7:5   The siting of Venta, Hants (sources: Biddle 1966, 1967 and 1968, with additions)

ments of coin-moulds and quantities of Gallo-Belgic pottery suggest a settlement of some importance.

The three Atrebatic oppida so far considered may all have begun to be occupied in the pre-Caesarian period, but their siting and subsequent development show that they were not hillforts in the strict sense of the word. Some earlier hillforts did, however, continue to be maintained (Fig. 7:6). At Bury Hill, Hants, the original enclosure was remodelled in bivallate form, while at Boscombe Down West, Wilts, a bivallate enclosure of similar type was constructed towards the middle of the first century AD on a hitherto open settlement site. Chisbury, Wilts, may also belong to this class. Elsewhere in Wiltshire at Yarnbury, Ebsbury, Oldbury, etc. the earlier defensive circuits continued in use, but nothing is known of the refortification, if any, to which the sites were subjected. At Danebury, Hants, excavation has however shown that refortification dating to the middle of the first century AD was on a relatively insubstantial scale, consisting simply of recutting the ditch to create a wide flat-bottomed obstacle and heightening the rampart (Pl. 4). The refortification of the Caburn in east Sussex was carried out in much the same way. Whether or not all the refortifications were mounted in response to the Roman invasion threat it is impossible to say, but where dating evidence survives (e.g. the Caburn, Danebury and Boscombe Down West) the invasion period seems to be the most likely context.

Rather less is known of the settlement sites of this period, largely because excavations have seldom been on a large enough scale to uncover a reasonable sample of the ground plan, but at Worthy Down and Owslebury in Hampshire and at Casterley in Wiltshire substantial areas have been exposed, together with sufficient evidence to demonstrate a continuity of occupation from the time of saucepan pot tradition. These sites are complexes of ditched enclosures designed to create corral space as well as habitation areas (p. 161).

Burial rites within the Atrebatic area varied

BURY HILL, HANTS

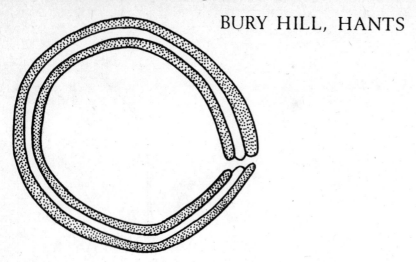

BOSCOMBE DOWN WEST, WILTS

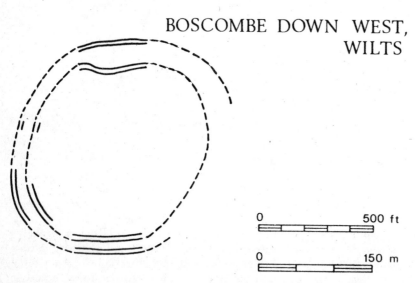

0 _____ 500 ft

0 _____ 150 m

7:6 Atrebatic enclosures (sources: *Bury Hill*, C. F. C. Hawkes, 1940b; *Boscombe Down West,* Richardson, 1951)

considerably. At Owslebury and St Lawrence, Isle of Wight, inhumation burials of warriors with their swords and shields were recorded in La Tène III contexts. In the northern part of the region, however, the Catuvellaunian style of cremation was practised, e.g. at Marlborough and Hurstbourne Tarrant, and over most of the rest of the area cremation was the general rule. To what extent this represents the gradual belgicisation of a hitherto inhuming society is difficult at the moment to say.

THE DUROTRIGES (Fig. 7:7)

The Durotriges were a close-knit confederacy of smaller units centred upon modern Dorset. To the east and north their boundaries with the Atrebates seem to have been marked by the Avon and its tributary the Wylye. Further west Ham Hill and South Cadbury lie within the Durotrigian sphere, but the Somerset levels and the valleys of the Parrett, Cory and Brue are best considered to belong to the territory of the

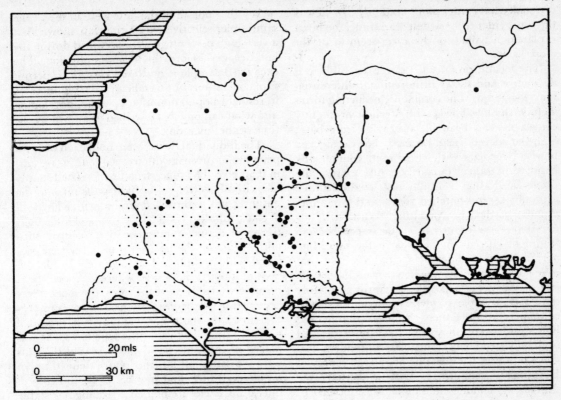

7:7 Distribution of coins of the Durotriges. Shaded area shows approximate extent of tribal group (sources: D. F. Allen, 1961a and 1962)

Dobunni. The extreme western limit is difficult to define with precision but it probably lay close to the Axe or even the Exe.

The territory thus defined exhibits a considerable degree of cultural unity with marked dissimilarities to the neighbouring Atrebatic culture. The cultural isolation of the area is reflected in its coinage. At an early stage, before Caesar's campaigns, the gold standard, introduced in the form of British A and B gold staters, was abandoned in favour of silver staters and quarter-staters, which remained the basic system until the later part of the first century AD. The adoption of a silver currency, admittedly based on Belgic types, was probably a response to well-developed trading connections with the Armorican peninsula, where silver was the basic exchange medium. The actual practice of trade is given some substance by the discovery of Durotrigian coins in the Le Catillon hoard (Jersey) and by the sporadic occurrence in the Durotrigian area of coins of the Armorican tribes the Coriosolites,

the Osismii, the Veneti, the Baiocasses and the Abrincatui (Fig. 10:18).

Whatever the true nature of the cross-Channel trading patterns, whether for metals, slaves or other perishables, it is evident that large quantities of pottery were being brought into the port on Hengistbury Head, Hants, from the adjacent French mainland. The two best-defined types are the finely turned, black burnished vessels known as Hengistbury class B ware (Fig. A:27), found on a dozen sites mostly in the Christchurch area, and graphite-coated fabrics found less frequently in the same region. Both types are well known in France as a result of Wheeler's pre-war campaign of excavations (Wheeler & Richardson, 1957), which demonstrated the existence of closely similar wares in contexts dating to the time of Caesar's conquest. As to the appearance of these forms in Britain, they may either be considered as 'the relics of a few shiploads of refugees at the time of the Caesarian conquest' or the 'commercial products of a somewhat earlier date' (ibid., 47). In view of the coin evidence for widespread trade, the latter explanation would, on balance, seem to be the more likely.

The locally produced ceramic assemblage is distinctive and shows little regional differentiation (Fig. A:30). The commonly occurring forms include shallow bowls with straight or slightly convex sides, a bead lip and a foot-ring base; high-shouldered bead-rimmed bowls; necked bowls; large jars with or without countersunk handles; handled tankards; and occasionally tazze. Decoration is usually restricted to simple wavy lines, cross-hatched zones, and sometimes the use of dots or rouletting. With very few exceptions, the forms can all be traced back to traditions current in the area in the preceding period, the main difference being, however, that much of the material was now wheel-finished. A few of the vessels, like the tankards, probably developed as copies of metal or wood-and-metal containers whilst others, such as the necked bowls and tazze, may well have been derived from imported Hengistbury class B products. The general impression given by an overall survey of Durotrigian ceramics is that a considerable degree of commercialisation was practised, possibly resulting from the absorption of specialist potters from northern France. Until a sufficient sample has been analysed, however, such an assumption must remain unproven.

Unlike the Atrebatic and the Aylesford–Swarling regions, where large newly built oppida surrounded by defensive dykes played an increasingly important part in centralising political power, in the Durotrigian territory trends towards urbanisation remained focused on the old hillforts. At Maiden Castle, the 45 acre (18·2 hectare) enclosure was tidied up, streets were metalled and defences maintained in good order, while the close-packed houses continued to be inhabited and rebuilt. An even more impressive demonstration of a Late Iron Age nucleated settlement is the fort on Hod Hill. Within its 52 acre (21 hectare) fortified area, the one wedge-shaped quadrant which has escaped modern ploughing is covered with traces of small circular huts, some of them with annexed enclosed yards and many of them associated with storage pits. Spacing tends to be haphazard but several well-defined street lines can be traced (Figs 13:15, 13:17). While it is evident even from the ground

survey that not all of the huts were in use at the same time, selective excavation has shown that a very high percentage were occupied during the last decades before the Roman invasion. The excavated sample is not large enough to permit firm conclusions but it indicates a rapid increase in resident population after *c.* 50 BC, developing into what can only be described as a town by the time of the invasion.

The individual houses were built each within a penannular drainage ditch *c.* 30–35 ft (9–10·5 m) in diameter. The superstructure consisted simply of a circular setting of upright posts set into the natural chalk and packed around with a low wall of chalk rubble, giving a living area of up to 20 ft (6 m) in diameter unimpeded by central supports. Many of the huts seem to have been provided with a cupboard immediately inside the door on the left-hand side, where weapons could be placed. In two of the huts this space was occupied by a bag of slingstones, and presumably the sling; in another it contained a group of harness-fittings; whilst in the fourth a spear was placed in the same position. Several of the huts were set within an attached yard, defined by an arc-shaped ditch and low bank. In the case of hut 56 the enclosure housed a rectangular stable suitable for two or three horses, with a space beside it adequate for parking a cart.

Hut 36 was unusual in that it lay in the corner of a sub-rectangular palisaded enclosure some 70 ft (21 m) across, the rest of the enclosed area containing timber structures of undefined form. Since it was this hut that appears to have been singled out for bombardment by Roman ballistae at the time of the invasion, the excavator may well be correct in his assumption that it was a chieftain's residence (Richmond, 1968). Its siting, in a prominent position close to the main street which ran towards the principal gate of the fort, is indicative of its importance.

Maiden Castle and Hod Hill are not unique among the Dorset forts. Hambledon Hill, for example, appears from a ground survey to have been equally as densely occupied as Hod, and the recent work at South Cadbury, Somerset, has demonstrated a similar urban aspect in the immediate pre-Roman period. The evidence is now sufficiently strong to leave little doubt that many, if not most, of the Durotrigian forts were in active use in 43 AD; it was, after all across this territory that Vespasian had to force his way, destroying one oppidum after another. Localised defence based on the forts does not necessarily mean that all the forts were permanently occupied on a large scale. It could be argued that the countryside population fled to the protection of the defences only when the threat of Roman attack occurred; indeed, it would be surprising if some such movement did not take place, swelling the population within. But even so, the archaeological evidence from Maiden Castle and Hod Hill suggests that permanent communities, well-rooted in the Iron Age past, were already inhabiting the forts.

The nature of Durotrigian settlement in the countryside is best demonstrated by three sites, all in Cranbourne Chase, Tollard Royal, Rotherley and Woodcuts (Fig. 11:6). Of these Tollard Royal provides the clearest picture, partly because it has been totally excavated and partly because it was not encumbered by a Roman phase of occupation. The economy of the farm lies well within the tradition of downland and mixed farming stretching back to the second millennium and must represent a typical homestead farm worked by a single family. The adjacent farms of Rotherley and Woodcuts are in much the same tradition, but would appear to represent somewhat larger establishments, perhaps holdings belonging to extended families (C. F. C. Hawkes, 1948). The early date of these excavations and the subsequent Roman occupation prevents a more detailed assessment of the Iron Age phase of settlement.

The aspects of Durotrigian culture so far considered owe practically nothing to influences derived from the Belgic culture of the south-east. This regionalism is further demonstrated by the continuance of the rite of inhumation, not only until the invasion but for some time afterwards. The famous war cemetery at Maiden Castle provides dramatic evidence for burial ritual in the hours following the Roman attack. The dead, thirty-eight of them, were all interred, somewhat hurriedly to judge by the positions of the bodies, but many of them were provided with a ritual meal contained in a pottery vessel placed beside the body in the grave. Rather less ceremony attended the mass burial at Spettisbury, where more than eighty bodies were thrown into a single pit, but this may conceivably have been a Roman tidying-up operation after a battle rather than an example of native burial practice.

The only two rich burials from the Durotrigian area were also inhumations. One, from Whitcombe near Dorchester, was the burial of a male warrior complete with sword, spear, La Tène II fibula, strap-rings, a spindle whorl and a hammer; the other, from West Bay near Bridport, was probably a female burial but all that remained were a few human bones, a pot and the handle of a mirror, exposed in a cliff-fall. Both lie within the traditions practised over much of southern Britain and appear to owe little to any particular regional culture or to intrusive elements.

While it is true to say that Durotrigian culture developed in its own characteristic way, little influenced by its eastern neighbours, trading contacts were nevertheless maintained. The production of armlets and vessels of Kimmeridge shale became a not inconsiderable cottage industry on the Isle of Purbeck (Calkin, 1949). Both finished products and raw shale were exported over some distance, to the Catuvellaunian area, for example – where it was turned into the elegant pedestal urns and tazze found in several of the rich burials. Salt-extraction too, which had already begun in the early part of the pre-Roman Iron Age, continued along much of the Dorset coast (Farrar, 1963), no doubt as a specialised commercial enterprise.

One of the most important trading centres on the fringe of Durotrigian territory grew up on Hengistbury Head (Fig. 7:8). Here, within the protection of the double dykes which cut off the neck of the promontory, there developed a complex entrepôt provided with a spacious anchorage and controlling the river routes into the heart of Wessex. Limited excavation has demonstrated the existence of a remarkably advanced metal industry represented by copper cake, a block of copper-silver alloy weighing more than 9 lb (4·1 kg), waste from copper casting and the remains of two cupellation hearths for the extraction of silver from argentiferous copper or argentiferous-cupriferous lead. An abundance of copper and silver coins is also strongly suggestive of a mint producing both struck and cast coinage, some of which continued in active circulation until the beginning of the second century AD. In many ways, therefore, Hengistbury Head could be considered to be the Durotrigian equivalent of the oppida of the south-east, but its marginal siting and heavy dependence upon overseas and

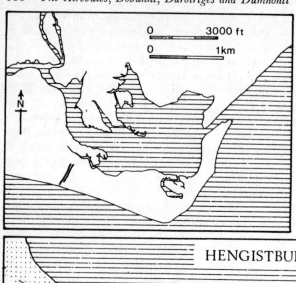

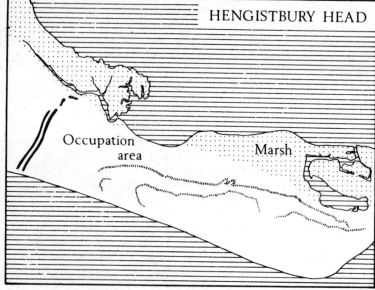

7:8   Hengistbury Head, Hants (source: Bushe-Fox, 1915)

coastal trade tend to contrast with the political centralisation implied by its Belgic and belgicised counterparts.

THE DOBUNNI (Fig. 7:9)

The distribution of Dobunnic coinage places the nucleus of the tribal territory in Gloucestershire, extending into north Somerset down to the Mendips, north and west Wiltshire, Oxfordshire west of the Cherwell and most of Worcestershire. The full extent of this area was defined by the earliest uninscribed gold coinage (British R) and continued to be the maximum extent of the Dobunnic nucleus until the Roman conquest (D. F. Allen, 1961b). In the last two decades before the invasion the territory appears to have been split between two ruling households. Comux, followed by Bodvoc, controlled the Gloucestershire – Oxfordshire – Worcestershire area, while Corio remained dominant in northern Somerset. It has been suggested (C. F. C. Hawkes, 1961) that the division had far-reaching political effects at the time of the invasion, but this matter will be returned to below (p. 122).

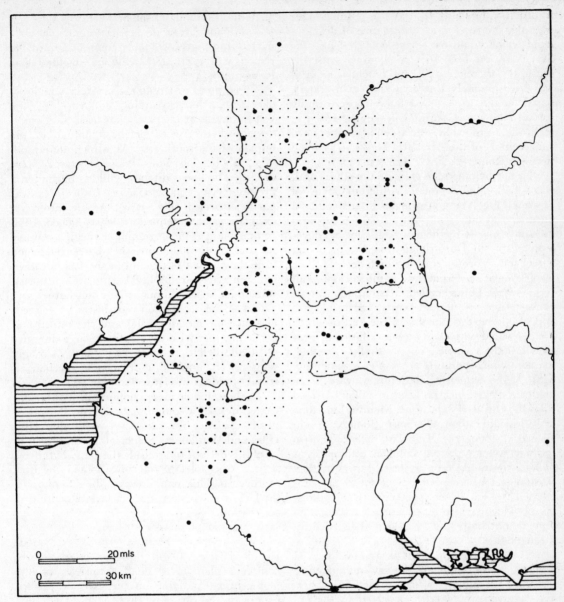

7:9   Distribution of coins of the Dobunni. Shaded area shows approximate extent of tribal group (sources: D. F. Allen, 1961a, 1961b and 1962)

A similar twofold division can be traced in the native pottery and its distribution in the first century BC (Fig. 7:2). North of the Bristol Avon the principal types included jars and saucepan pot shapes decorated with a zone of either linear tooling or stamping below the rim, types which recent petrological examination (Peacock, 1968)

has shown were manufactured in the Malvern area and exported widely, not only to the communities of the Cotswolds but also to the basically aceramic communities further west in the Welsh borderland (Fig. A:18). The form and style of decoration places these stamped and linear-tooled wares firmly within the saucepan pot tradition of the south. Indeed, it is possible to see over this entire area a convergence of development which could only have occurred had the Severn region been in close contact with the south. It is therefore surely no coincidence that it was over precisely this area that gold staters, based on the triple-tailed horse types, rapidly spread following Caesar's campaigns. The two territories seem to have remained in contact until Tincommius of the Atrebates began to develop ties with Rome (C. F. C. Hawkes, 1961).

The north Somerset region, on the other hand, was developing a totally different style of ceramics (Fig. A:33), growing ultimately out of a linear-tooled saucepan pot tradition (p. 43) and influenced partly by the new technological developments in the Durotrigian area, but involving a new and vigorous art style which derived some inspiration at least from the ceramics of Cornwall (Fig. A:32). This so-called Glastonbury ware is characterised by necked bowls, saucepan pots and simple bead-rimmed jars, the best of which are decorated with elaborate curvilinear or geometric designs carried out in shallow tooling, frequently incorporating areas of cross-hatching. Most of the Somerset Glastonbury wares were made from clays incorporating grit fillers derived from the Old Red Sandstone, Mendip limestone or Jurassic limestone, all of north Somerset origin (Peacock, 1969, 43). To what extent the two ceramic styles represent cultural differences is difficult to say. At the very least, however, they must reflect discrete spheres of social or commercial contact. Taken together with the numismatic evidence mentioned above, it could be argued that both areas retained their identity throughout.

It is impossible at present to say how long the indigenous traditions of pottery manufacture remained dominant. Wheel-turned Atrebatic and Catuvellaunian types occurred to the exclusion of earlier types at Bagendon, Glos, in the first century AD, while at several sites (including Meare, Camerton and Kingsdown Camp in Somerset, and Salmonsbury in Gloucestershire) these south-eastern varieties replace the local types within the few decades immediately before the invasion. The overall impression given by the present state of our knowledge is that acculturation was slow and patchy, particularly in Somerset, but that ceramics of south-eastern type were being introduced into the east Cotswolds soon

after the beginning of the first century AD. Even so, in many areas of the Dobunnic territory native traditions may have continued until the region was eventually subdued in the years following AD 43.

Those areas of Dobunnic territory which lay closest to the expanding influence of the Catuvellauni, particularly the east Cotswolds, developed earthwork defences similar to the oppida of the south-east. At Minchinhampton, Glos, about 600 acres (242·8 hectares) were defended by linear ditches, while at Bagendon a promontory of about 200 acres (81 hectares) was partly encircled (Fig. 7:10). At the latter site excavations have defined evidence of occupation commencing at the beginning of the first century AD and continuing until the sixties, by which time the civilian settlement at the Roman town of Cirencester, 3 miles (4·8 km) to the south-east, was under way. Although the exact nature and extent of the occupation remains to be defined, evidence for metalworking and the minting of coins, together with the relatively large quantity of Gallo-Belgic imported pottery, strongly suggests an important settlement, perhaps a tribal oppidum in Catuvellaunian style.

In the remoter areas, hillforts probably continued in use for some time – actively defended, if the evidence for massacres at Bredon Hill, Glos, and Worlebury, Somerset, is considered to be of this period; but outside the Cotswolds there is little trace of late refortification in the first century AD. This may, however, be due more to the lack of excavation than to lack of continued occupation.

A number of smaller settlements are known but very few have been extensively excavated. Langford Down, Oxon, however, offers a fairly complete plan of a small farmstead of the first century AD lying on the extreme eastern fringes of the territory (Fig. 11:8). Here two adjacent ditched enclosures both appear to have protected broadly contemporary circular huts, but the full extent of the enclosures could not be traced. Similarities lie with the complex ditched enclosures of the Atrebatic area. At Butcombe in Somerset, on the north flank of the Mendips, a farm of about this date has been excavated, yielding evidence of circular huts and associated pits of the late pre-Roman Iron Age. These belong to the first phase of a farming settlement which continued in occupation well into the Roman

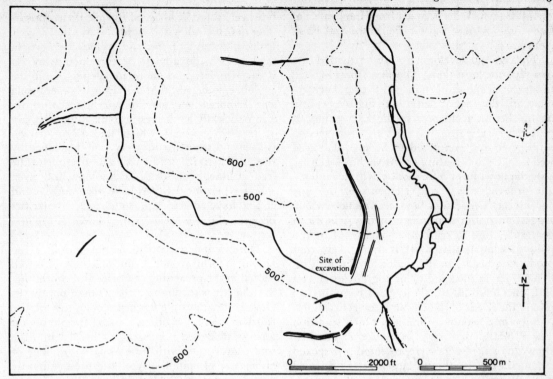

7:10   The siting of Bagendon, Glos (source: Clifford, 1961)

period.

The burial practices of the Dobunni are known from relatively few sites. At Barnwood, Glos, a cemetery containing a single inhumation together with a small cremation group suggests a mixture of traditions not necessarily contemporary. The survival of inhumation is further demonstrated by the Birdlip cemetery, Glos, where at least four inhumations were found in stone-lined graves covered by slabs of limestone and buried beneath cairns of stone 4–5 ft (1·2–1·5 m) high. The principal burial was of a female who was provided with an impressive array of grave-goods, including two bronze bowls, a silver brooch plated with gold, a bronze mirror, a necklace of amber, jet and stone, an animal-headed knife, a tubular bronze bracelet and four bronze rings.

With so little evidence to go on, it would be unwise to speculate too far but the survival of the inhumation rite, here as among the Durotriges, points to a strong indigenous element maintaining a pre-Belgic tradition in spite of the belgicisation of some of the principal centres like

Bagendon. Hawkes (1961) has shown that the coin evidence and an interpretation of the available archaeological material can together be used to build up an intricate pattern of political relationships between the Dobunni and their Atrebatic and Catuvellaunian neighbours, suggesting first a break with the Atrebates in *c.* 16 BC followed by allegiance with the Catuvellauni, which eventually led to the Catuvellaunian domination of the north at about the time of the invasion. A historical model of this kind may well provide a valid hypothesis to explain the political situation but it should not be allowed to obscure the basic non-Belgic tradition of an already stable society.

THE DUMNONII

The Dumnonii occupied the south-west peninsula probably as far east as the Parrett–Axe line. In this position of relative isolation, cultural contact with the eastern Belgic communities was almost non-existent and it is therefore hardly surprising that the area failed to develop a coinage of its own. Indeed, apart from the hoards at Carn Brae, Mount Batten, Penzance and Paul, coins are almost unknown.

The ceramic development can be divided into two separate traditions. The first, the so-called *Glastonbury ware*, was produced at several centres including the Lizard peninsula (Fig. A:32) and on the Permian outcrops of the Exe region. It probably originated in the third or second century BC and continued to be manufactured well into the first century BC. As we have seen (p. 47), the bowl form – frequently with an internally grooved rim – and elements of the fine curvilinear decoration are techniques which suggest an origin somewhere in the Armorican peninsula, but there is no evidence of actual pottery being imported. It is more likely that production began locally under foreign inspiration or even at the hands of immigrant specialists and, once established, the centres continued to supply the needs of the territory for generations.

Superimposed upon the Glastonbury tradition was a totally new style of pottery, generally known as *cordoned ware*, represented by necked jars, tazza-like bowls and large everted-rimmed jars, all ornamented with horizontal cordons, sometimes in combination with grooves (Fig. A:31). The pottery is well made and turned on a wheel. At Castle Dore cordoned ware could be shown to be generally later than Glastonbury ware, and there is ample evidence from Cornwall to show that cordoned ware traditions continued into the Roman period. The date of the introduction of the new style is difficult to define with precision but typologically it owes much to the ceramics of the Armorican peninsula. While it could be argued (C. F. C. Hawkes, 1966) that cordoned ware was brought in by refugees fleeing from Brittany in 56 BC as the result of Caesar's attack, it is equally possible that the new traditions were introduced gradually throughout the first half of the first century BC during the course of normal commercial contact. The two areas were closely related not only by trade but also politically, if we can accept Caesar's statement that the Armoricans summoned reinforcements from the adjacent coasts of Britain at the time of the Roman advance in 56. Other elements of the archaeological record also serve to emphasise a cultural unity between the two areas: promontory forts, or cliff castles, are common to both, as indeed are the fogous or souterrains. Again,

however, there is no need to link their appearance in Cornwall with a sudden influx of refugees. Indeed, several of the cliff castles were occupied before the advent of cordoned ware. It is far simpler, and more in keeping with the evidence, to suggest that the south-west peninsula and Armorica became closely related culturally and politically as the result of an intensification of trading contacts which had begun much earlier and were already very well developed by the third century BC. In such an atmosphere the free exchange of ideas, technology and even military personnel would have been normal and could have given rise to broad similarities between the two areas by the middle of the first century BC.

Dumnonian settlement of the period *c.* 100 BC–AD 50 forms part of a continuous pattern well rooted in the preceding centuries and continuing in some areas throughout the Roman period. In Devon the multiple-ditched enclosures of the third or second century remain the dominant form of defended homestead or hamlet into the first century AD, with little apparent change in either size of community or the predominantly pastoral economy. Thus Milber Down Camp, one of the few excavated sites in this category, remained in use well into the first century BC while later occupation into the Roman period continued outside the main enclosure. Similarly, at Castle Dore first century AD occupation is attested by cordoned ware. Further west, in Cornwall, rounds (i.e. small enclosed homesteads seldom exceeding 3 acres (1·2 hectares) in extent), which form a dominant element of the Roman settlement pattern, originate in the late pre-Roman period. At Crane Godrevy and Gwithian, cordoned ware has been found; and at the somewhat larger site of Carloggas, St Mawgan-in-Pydar, occupation began during the first century BC, while Glastonbury style wares were in use, and continued into the Roman period. It is estimated (Thomas, 1966, 88–90) that in Cornwall and south and west Devon between 750 and 1,000 rounds existed, with a density averaging one per square mile (2·6 per km²). Clearly they must represent the homesteads or small hamlets of an essentially non-nucleated population.

Another type of settlement which appears later, representing the same-sized social group, is the courtyard house – a central courtyard sur-

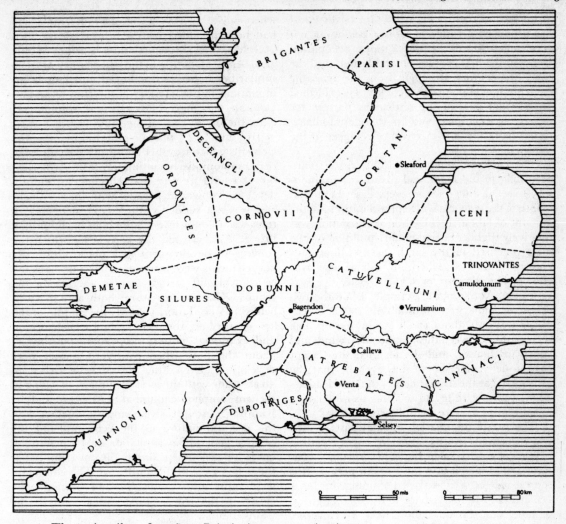

7:11 The main tribes of southern Britain (sources: various)

rounded by rooms, all enclosed within a massive stone wall. Sometimes courtyard houses were built within rounds (e.g. Goldherring) or were otherwise enclosed, but open villages like Chysauster are also known. The origin of the courtyard house is still a matter of uncertainty. While it is true that it could have evolved locally, parallels with Brittany may point to inspiration from abroad.

Further east, in Somerset, larger nucleated settlements are found at the sites of the so-called lake villages of Glastonbury and Meare. Estimates of size are difficult to determine but it has been argued (Tratman, 1970) that at Glastonbury twenty to thirty houses were in use at one

time. Settlements of this size are rare and it might be that they were the product of the unusual local environmental conditions.

The best defined category of hillforts in the south-west are the cliff castles, which densely ring the coasts of Cornwall and north Devon. Essentially, a cliff castle is a promontory projecting into the sea, the neck of which is defended by one or more series of banks and ditches. The obvious similarities between the cliff castles of south-west Britain and those of Brittany (Wheeler & Richardson, 1957) has frequently been used as an argument in favour of a Venetic invasion of Cornwall, but of the sites excavated, Maen Castle would appear to have originated at least as early as the second century BC. while Gurnard's Head has produced a range of fabrics beginning not very much later. At the Rumps occupation began in the first century BC and lasted until the early first century AD. Thus, from the available evidence it would appear that cliff castles formed an essential part of the settlement pattern for nearly three centuries and are therefore unlikely to be the result of the arrival of refugees in the mid-first century BC.

The enclosed areas of the cliff castles vary according to the shape and size of the promontory selected, but since in every case the actual length of the defences was kept to a minimum, the amount of labour involved on construction was relatively slight. Massive hillfort-building on the scale practised in the south-east is almost unknown, and even when an inland site was chosen, like Tregear or Chun Castle, size was restricted. At Chun, for example, while the two defensive walls were substantial, the area enclosed was only about 170 ft (52 m) across. The relationship between the homesteads (rounds and courtyard houses) and the fortified sites is not easy to determine, but it may well be that the forts served as the strongholds of the local leaders. They were not suited to serve as foci for larger social groups as were the hillforts in Wessex.

The rite of inhumation in small cists, which was practised in the area in the preceding periods (e.g. at Harlyn Bay and Trevone), continued unhindered into the Roman period. It is represented at several sites, including the large cemetery at Mount Batten and the smaller group of burials at Trelan Bahow near St Keverne, where one of the graves was of a rich female who had been provided with a bronze mirror, two bracelets, rings, brooches and a necklace of blue glass beads, all dating to the first century AD. The similarities between this burial and female inhumations in the territory of the Durotriges and Dobunni may suggest an element of unity underlying the burial rites of the south-west.

In summary, it may be said that many of the elements which together constitute the culture of the Dumnonii derive ultimately from Armorica, but it would appear that Dumnonian culture developed slowly in parallel with the continent and was not suddenly altered by incursions of refugees. The tin trade, stretching back into the Bronze Age, created the process by which the convergent development took place. Gradually new elements were introduced: first perhaps the concept of cliff castles, then prototypes for the group 1 Glastonbury ware, both arriving well before 100 BC. Later, towards the middle of the first century BC, the technique of wheel-turning and cordoned pottery appeared, possibly at about the time when courtyard houses were developing. Even after the Venetic defeat in 56 BC, trade with the west continued, bringing in the wine amphorae found at St Mawgan and the Rumps. These intrusive elements, together with the pastoral nature of the economy and the relative geographical isolation of the peninsula, led to a development totally dissimilar to that of the Belgic areas of the south-east. The Dumnonii were culturally, politically and economically closer to the tribes of Armorica than to the Catuvellauni.

The late Pre-Roman Iron Age in Wales and the North

Wales, the north of England and Scotland were far removed from the influences of the Belgic communities of the south-east and, unlike the tribes of the south-west (see Fig. 7:11), they remained out of contact with the active cross-Channel trade which modified and expanded the material culture of these areas. In fact, it is true to say that they remained largely isolated from continental influences until the second half of the first century AD, by which time Roman rule had penetrated all but the extreme north-west. For these reasons there is a considerable degree of cultural continuity and it is sometimes difficult to isolate material of the late pre-Roman Iron Age from that of the earlier period. Nevertheless the writings of the various Roman authors provide a valuable descriptive horizon from which to assess the social and economic changes of the preceding decades.

WALES

Any consideration of the cultural groupings and developments in Wales during the first centuries BC and AD is likely to be fraught with difficulty, largely because of the lack of large-scale excavation and the almost total absence of datable cultural material. Moreover, the inhospitable nature of much of the countryside has ensured that considerable areas remained uninhabited whilst elsewhere pastoralism was dominant. Together these factors mitigate against an adequate description of the material culture on a regional basis.

Knowledge of tribal groupings rests largely upon the writings of the geographer Ptolemy whose lists, taken together with descriptive accounts by Tacitus and other fragments of epigraphic evidence, show that Wales was divided into a minimum of five tribal areas roughly approximating to broad geographical divisions. In the extreme south-west, in Pembrokeshire and Carmarthenshire, were the Demetae. Next to them, from the Gower peninsula stretching along the coastal plain to the Wye and extending into the Black Mountains, were the Silures, whom Tacitus describes as ruddy-faced and curly-haired, reminding him of Iberians. In the north-west, centred on the Llyn peninsula, lay the Gangani, who were presumably related to a tribe of the same name living in north-west Ireland, while along the north coast lived the Deceangli. Lastly, between these four tribes were the Ordovices, occupying the mountainous area in the centre of the principality.

The Silures

The exact limits of Silurian territory cannot be precisely drawn but it is clear that the bulk of the tribe occupied the lowland coastal areas of Glamorganshire and Monmouthshire and the valleys of the Black Mountains with the river Wye forming the approximate boundary with the Dobunni. In all probability, the cluster of small defended settlements centred on the upper reaches of the Usk, in the heart of the Brecon Beacons, can also be regarded as belonging to a geographically isolated outpost of the Silures.

Material culture and settlement type have many similarities with those of adjacent territories. Some of the hillforts in the eastern part of the territory, such as Sudbrook and Llanmelin in Monmouthshire, are closely similar to Wessex sites; others are best paralleled by the multiple-ditched enclosures of the south-west peninsula;

while the cliff castles of the coastal group are identical to those of Cornwall. Environment, economy and commercial communications must have encouraged this parallelism. At Llanmelin a 5·5 acre (2·2 hectare) multivallate enclosure with a semi-inturned entrance was shown to have been in use during the local phase of the saucepan pot continuum, roughly second to first century BC, and there is some evidence of modifi-

cation after belgicised pottery had arrived on the site, probably during the first century AD. Occupation continued into the Roman period. A similar continuity into Roman times was demonstrated by the multivallate enclosure at Sudbrook, where the defences came late in the sequence, post-dating occupation containing first century BC saucepan pots. The levels contemporary with the defences contained a mixture of

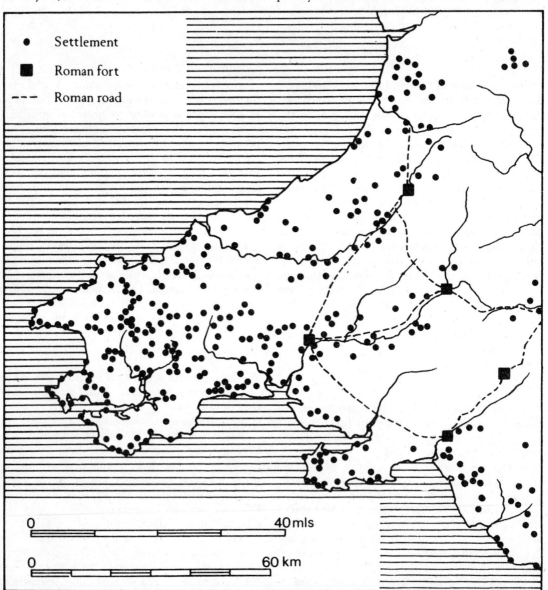

8:1   The distribution of settlement sites in south-west Wales (source: Ordnance Survey *Map of southern Britain in the Iron Age*)

first century AD pottery continuing until early Flavian times.

Both of the sites so far considered lie at the east side of the territory within easy reach of the effects of Dobunnic and Roman culture. Further west, however, along the Glamorganshire coast, the material culture is far less well represented. The three promontory forts to be excavated, the Knave, Bishopston Valley Fort and High Penard, have produced very little apart from a few imported sherds of group 3 Glastonbury ware, odd scraps of Roman pottery and a few indeterminate sherds. Nevertheless, there can be little doubt that the forts were inhabited during the last century of Silurian independence. The only settlement to be excavated on any scale is at Mynydd Bychan, a walled enclosure containing a group of circular huts. In the first period the buildings were of timber but later they were rebuilt in stone within walled courtyards. Occupation began in the latter part of the first century BC and continued probably as late as Flavian times, the later decades being characterised by the appearance of wheel-turned vessels manufactured in the Belgic manner but in an orange-buff fabric. Whether this represents local production or importation from Gloucester is not clear.

From the foundation of the Fosse frontier in AD 47, Silurian territory would have been in close contact with the Roman world, and the foundation of the fortress at Usk in c. 55–60, followed by several decades of campaigning before the final annexation in c. AD 74, would soon have brought the natives of the coastal plain into an intimate relationship with the Roman army. It may well have been under these conditions that the belgicised ceramics were introduced. The alternative, that widespread trade with the Dobunnii was practised before 47, while possible, is unproven.

The Demetae

The Demetae occupied the extreme south-west corner of Wales, probably extending along the valleys of the Tywi and Teifi into the foothills of the Cambrian mountains. Much of the more hospitable parts of this territory was densely scattered with small enclosed settlements, usually 1–3 acres (0·4–1·2 hectares) in extent, comparable in many ways to the rounds of Cornwall

(Fig. 8:1). Excavations at Walesland Rath, Pembs, have demonstrated the existence of a substantial community living in a cluster of circular huts from the first century BC into the first century AD. In the second century, after a period of abandonment, the site was reoccupied by a community existing in much the same way as before but now living in a simple rectangular stone building and using romanised pottery. Continuity of this kind may also be suspected at two other Pembrokeshire sites, Cwmbrwyn and Trelissey, where romanised buildings have been excavated inside apparently earlier earthworks, and at Coygan Camp, Carm, which remained in use into the sub-Roman period. This pattern of unhampered indigenous development spanning many centuries may well be even more deep-rooted. Indeed, the discovery of La Tène I bracelets at Coygan Camp tends to emphasise the antiquity of settled pastoralism in the area, but the extreme paucity of artefacts makes any assessment of material development and chronology a matter of difficulty for the pre-Roman phases.

Several observers have pointed out the relative lack of Roman military activity in the south-west of Wales, suggesting that the Demetae offered no resistance to the advance and therefore required no substantial holding force save a garrison based at Carmarthen. If this were so, it would explain the peaceful uninterrupted occupation of the peasant villages and hamlets – a process which, on present evidence, offers some contrasts to the settlement of the hostile Silurian territory.

The Ordovices, Gangani and Deceangli

The settlement pattern of north Wales appears to have been little affected by the events of the late pre-Roman Iron Age in the south-east of the country. The material culture remained as sparse as ever and many of the sites continued to be occupied well into the Roman period with little evidence of significant change. The Roman campaigns of AD 47–51 and indeed the Roman presence in Britain from AD 43 tend, however, to be reflected in the structural development of some of the defended sites. At Dinorben, Denbigh, it has been suggested that the final reconstruction of the ramparts on the south side of the fort (period V) could have resulted from

Roman threats in the neighbourhood, while at Castell Odo, Caerns, the slighting of the defences may have been carried out by the Romans in the last quarter of the first century AD.

Perhaps the most impressive feature of the settlement pattern of the area is the continued use of the hillforts like Tre'r Ceiri, Caerns, with their densely occupied interiors, and the development of large numbers of enclosed farmsteads usually working on average 15 acres (6·1 hectares) or so of associated terraced fields. While the exact origin of this system is still in some doubt (Hogg, 1966), it is clear that the social grouping and some aspects of the architecture must relate to pre-Roman tradition and it would indeed be surprising if many of the farms in use in the Roman period did not originate in the first century BC or even earlier. The problem is one of establishing calibrated sequences in a virtually aceramic region.

The Cornovii

According to Ptolemy, the territory of the Cornovii included both the cantonal capital at Viroconium and the legionary base at Deva (Chester), which in terms of modern counties would have meant that the tribe occupied Cheshire and Shropshire and probably parts of surrounding areas. To the south, their boundary with the Dobunni probably approximated with the river Teme, an east-flowing tributary of the Severn; in the east they would have met the Coritani in the Trent valley; and to the north the boundary with the Brigantes may have lain along the Mersey. The western limit of the tribal territory is far more difficult to define. The great number of defended enclosures in the hills and mountains of the Welsh borderland could equally well have been under Ordovician domination, but the structural pecularities of some of the larger forts (e.g. Old Oswestry, the Breiddin, Ffridd Faldwyn and Titterstone Clee) tend to link them more with the forts of the south and east, suggesting a zone of contact, although this does not necessarily imply that the borderland forts belonged to Cornovian territory. The absence of coins and the relative lack of cultural material makes the definition of the tribal boundary hereabouts uncertain.

In the century or so before the Roman conquest, the area seems to have continued to develop along earlier lines uninfluenced by social and economic development of the south-east. Many of the hillforts were kept in defensive order and a little pottery and fine metalwork was imported from outside the area but, like the other territories outside the aggressive range of the south-eastern chieftains and of their trading patterns, there was little change until the entire territory was annexed by the Roman army led by Ostorius Scapula, in and soon after AD 48.

NORTHERN ENGLAND

The Brigantes

The Brigantes occupied a vast territory in northern Britain stretching, according to Ptolemy, from sea to sea. Their northern boundary with the Selgovae, the Novantae and the Votadini probably lay a little to the south of the line later taken by the Hadrianic frontier, while their south-eastern flank fronted the Parisi, who occupied the Wolds and the Vale of Pickering north of the Humber, and the Coritani, who extended across the Trent valley possibly into the Peak District. The south-west boundary, with the Cornovii, is more difficult to define but probably crossed Lancashire in the vicinity of the river Weaver or Mersey.

Relatively little is known of the settlement pattern or economy of the tribe but the excavations at Stanwick, Yorks (Fig. 8:2), have suggested a predominantly pastoral way of life reflected not only in the dominance of cattle among the animal bones recorded but also by the absence of grain storage pits and the massive extent of the defences geared to protect expanses of well-watered pasture for livestock. Whether the pastoralism was nomadic or transhumant is impossible to decide on the present evidence. Cereals were produced, to judge by the fragment of a rotary quern discovered at Stanwick and by the early groups of fields in Wharfedale and the adjacent valleys, but even so, flocks and herds may well have been tended in upland pastures for much of the year. The use, well into the Roman era, of caves and isolated huts on the Yorkshire moors is an indication that a transhumant economy continued to be practised for many centuries.

A further indicator of a pastoral way of life is the retarded development of the ceramic tech-

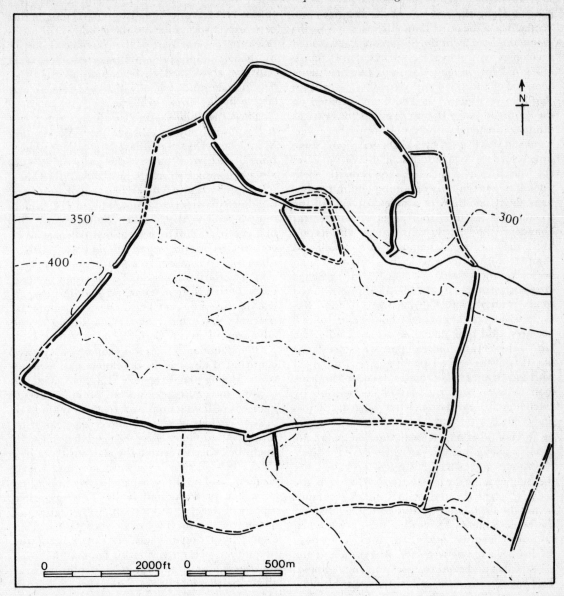

8:2   The fortifications at Stanwick, Yorks (source: Wheeler, 1954)

nology. Brigantian pottery consists almost entirely of coarsely made cooking and storage vessels, generally without decoration and of simple form, lacking distinctive characteristics. No doubt most of the containers were made of wood basketry and leather – materials more appropriate to the pressures of pastoral mobility. An example of an elegant wooden dish was found in a waterlogged deposit at Stanwick. That the population was not, however, entirely un-

appreciative of fine pottery is vividly demonstrated by the large percentage of imported wares found at Stanwick: of all the pottery recovered some 60 per cent consisted of samian ware, butt-beakers and other Roman imports from the south.

Of the various defended sites lying within Brigantian territory, only Stanwick has been adequately examined and published. Here, on a strategic junction of two major routes, one running along the east side of the Pennines into Scotland and the other branching west across the mountains by way of the Stainmore Pass, is sited a complex of massive earthworks more than 6 miles (9·6 km) in length overall. The first phase consisted of a fortified enclosure of some 17 acres (6·9 hectares) known as The Tofts, situated on the south side of a stream. The earthwork was dump-constructed without stone or timber revetment and was fronted by a V-shaped ditch. Some time before AD 60 an additional area of 130 acres (52·6 hectares) was enclosed, largely on the north side of the stream but containing within its confines about one-third of a mile (0·5 km) of the stream. At this time the earlier enclosure was abandoned and partly dismantled. The second phase defences were composed of a stone-faced rampart fronted by a wide flat-bottomed ditch not unlike those found sporadically in the Belgic area of the south-east. In the third phase, dated to about AD 72, a further massive extension was undertaken, adding some 600 acres (242·8 hectares) and now including about a mile (1·6 km) of the stream. The rampart was stone-faced like that of the second phase and was provided with an entrance in the south side, which appears soon to have been put out of commission by extending the ditch somewhat raggedly across the original causeway. Later additions to the south may be of post-Roman date and were not thought relevant to the early history of the site.

Wheeler has plausibly suggested (1954) that the Stanwick earthworks were developed as the rallying place of the anti-Roman resistance within the Brigantian territory. He suggests that the phase I enclosure was built *c.* 47–48, when Ostorius Scapula advanced into Flintshire, forcing a wedge between the Brigantes and the Welsh tribes and causing dissension among them. The dating of the phase I pottery would allow such an attribution. The second phase, dated to *c.* 50–60, may well have been consequent upon the irreparable split which occurred within the Brigantian kingdom, as a result of which the tribe was divided between a pro-Roman faction led by Queen Cartimandua and an anti-Roman party under the command of her husband Venutius. Wheeler suggests that Stanwick II was Venutius's base, from which the resistance to Rome was organised. When, in 71–2, the ninth legion under Petillius Cerialis began its final thrust north, Stanwick was once more enlarged (phase III) but after a hasty strengthening of the gate area it succumbed to the Roman army and Brigantia became part of the province. Thus, if this historical interpretation is correct, Stanwick must be considered to be a unique site, the development and style of which was determined largely by the threat of Rome.

The other hillforts in Brigantia are far less well known: only at Almondbury, Yorks, and Mam Tor in Derbyshire have large-scale excavations been carried out. At the former site – an already complex structure probably dating back to the third century or earlier – a phase of rebuilding was observed (Almondbury III) which must belong to the late first century BC or the first century AD. The refurbished defences were constructed in the *murus gallicus* style, with a timber-laced rampart retained between vertical stone faces. After a period of occupation producing imported Roman coins and Arretine ware, it was destroyed by fire. The destruction cannot be precisely dated but may well be linked to the advance of Petillius Cerialis.

The dominantly pastoral economy may have contributed towards the development of warlike traits among the Brigantes. Literary evidence relating to the first century AD provides several glimpses of the factions and rivalries within the upper echelons of society, and it may fairly be supposed that these reflect the deep divisions that might be expected within the clan structure of a tribe whose territory was so diverse and whose economy and wealth was based largely upon the possession of flocks and herds. The aggressive aspects of society are represented by a group of distinctive swords (Piggott's class IV) made, no doubt, by a single school of craftsmen for the Brigantian hierarchy, and by the scattered discoveries of horse-trappings including the remarkable hoard found at Stanwick in 1845 (MacGregor, 1962) which contained a sword, a wide range of chariot- and horse-trappings, and a number of fragments of personal equipment. While the exact nature of the Stanwick hoard must remain in doubt, it provides a vivid impression of the degree of wealth and display attained by the upper classes of Brigantian society by the end of their period of freedom.

The Parisi

On the east flank of the Brigantes lay the Parisi,

occupying the territory stretching from the Humber estuary to the north Yorkshire moors. The region was in close contact with northern France in the late fifth century, giving rise to the Arras culture (pp. 40–1 and Stead, 1965), which developed after a small-scale folk movement brought new people into the area – probably from the Seine valley. Stead has demonstrated a degree of continuity from the fifth or fourth century beginning until the Roman conquest, unhindered by any further continental contact – a fact which has led him to support the idea that the tribal name of Parisi given by Ptolemy in describing the situation in the first century AD must date back to the fifth to fourth century. He further points out that the closest parallels for the Yorkshire burials occur in the territory of the Gallic Parisii.

The cemeteries of the Arras culture at Dane's Graves and Eastburn continued in use throughout the first century BC and well into the first century AD. There was little change, except that metal associations were rare in the later periods and, where objects occurred at all, they related more directly to the developing styles of southern Britain. Pottery buried with the dead, however, became more common. One new element to appear in the area during the first century BC was the warrior burial – known from North Grimston, Bugthorpe and Grimthorpe, all sited along the western side of the Wolds. The presence of weapons and lack of indigenous features – such as the cart buried with the body, rectangular enclosures and barrows – suggest a different tradition and ritual. It is, however, quite unnecessary to define a separate culture (as Stead 1965, 84, where he calls it the North Grimston culture). It is simpler to regard the burials, which are similar to others found in various parts of Britain, as representing a general and widespread change. What exactly the new style of burial means is less clear; in all probability, it is little more than a change of fashion but the possibility that it signifies the presence of extra-tribal mercenary warriors should not be completely overlooked.

Little is known of the settlement sites or economy of the Parisi, but before the first century BC it seems probable that a dominantly pastoral economy was practised, resulting in a paucity of ceramics and a lack of well-defined occupation sites. It may be that the linear ditch systems of the Yorkshire Wolds, with their associated enclosures, are par of the pastoral tradition of this period. By the first century AD, however, a number of settlement sites appear, particularly in the Holderness region, suggesting a possible re-orientation of economy leading to a more settled way of life. Some of the settlements, like the ditched enclosures at Langton and Staxton, continued in use into the Roman period, and indeed the Langton settlement later developed into a small villa.

The quality of ceramic production improved throughout the first centuries BC and AD, probably under the influence of traditions emanating from the territory of the Coritani across the Humber. Such an improvement would be consistent with the gradual introduction of a more settled economy. The development can perhaps best be seen by comparing the coarse plain vessels from Dane's Graves with the later collection from an occupation site at Emmotland in Holderness (Brewster, 1963). The Emmotland vessels are not only better made and finished but are constructed in more positive forms, mostly jars with everted rims but occasionally bead-rimmed jars and small bowls reminiscent of the belgicised styles from the south. A scatter of Claudio-Neronian brooches from Parisian territory, together with the large quantity of imported Gallo-Belgic wares from North Ferriby, leaves little doubt that trading relations had been established with the south by the Claudian period, if not earlier. An awareness of the material advantages of romanisation may have been instrumental in encouraging the tribe to offer no resistance to the eventual penetration by the Roman army in 71–2.

SOUTHERN SCOTLAND: VOTADINI, NOVANTAE, SELGOVAE AND DAMNONII (Fig. 8:3)

Between the Tyne–Solway and the Clyde–Forth lines, which later approximated to the frontiers constructed under Hadrian and Antoninus Pius, four major tribal groups can be distinguished. The Votadini occupied the eastern coastal region and the lowlands between the Tyne and the Clyde, the Novantae covered the area of Galloway and Dumfriesshire, while the Selgovae lay between the two. North of the Novantae and stretching along the west coast to the Clyde was

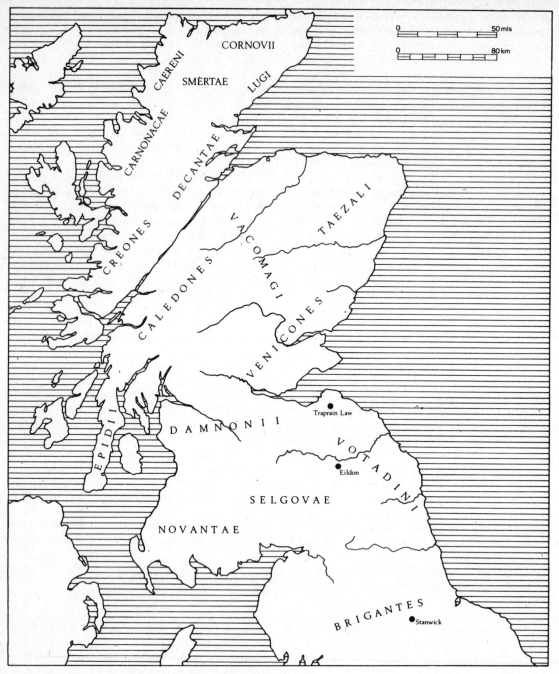

8:3   The main tribes of northern Britain (sources: various)

the territory of the Damnonii. How significant were the social and political differences between the groups at the time when they were distinguished by Roman writers in the first and second centuries AD it is impossible to say, except that the Votadini appear to have been more generously treated by the Romans than their neighbours the Selgovae, an observation which, if substantiated, might hint at a distinction between tribal policies. Nor is it possible to define how far back in time tribal distinctions can be traced, since there is no historical or numismatic evidence upon which to base conclusions. Any description of the area must, therefore, rely substantially on the form and distribution of settlement sites and upon the somewhat sparse material culture recovered by excavation.

While a very large number of settlement sites are known in the area, as a result of extensive field surveys carried out by the staff of the Royal Commission on Historical Monuments and by G. Jobey, it is extremely difficult to assign dates to them except for the earlier sites (pp. 206–8) for which radiocarbon determinations are now available. On typological grounds, however, two major classes of settlements and homesteads can be defined as belonging to the period stretching from the end of the pre-Roman Iron Age into the Roman era: 'scooped enclosures', consisting of walled enclosures containing huts and yards terraced into the natural slope of the hill, and settlements of stone-built huts. The latter are relatively common, particularly in the territory of the Votadini, but any apparent differential distribution may be due largely to different intensities in the archaeological field-work. The dating evidence obtained for some of these settlements suggests an initial occupation in the second century AD but this does not preclude an earlier beginning for others. The abandonment of many of the small hillforts and defended enclosures probably occurred throughout the first century AD, but no indisputable dating evidence survives and it may well be that some at least continued in use. By the end of their life, many of them had developed into multivallate structures, some with close-set defences, others with their ramparts more widely spaced in a manner similar to that of the multiple-ditched enclosures of south-west Britain.

Many of the larger oppida evidently continued to be occupied. The principal fort of the Votadini, the long-established Traprain Law in East Lothian, remained the tribal centre throughout the Roman occupation, but the Selgovian centre on Eildon Hill North, Roxburgh, seems to have been abandoned at the time of the Flavian advance. A general consideration of the forts of both the Selgovae and the Votadini tends to suggest a gradual amalgamation of nucleated communities at an increasingly restricted number of sites in a manner paralleled in southern Britain. This might well represent a growing political cohesion which eventually manifested itself in organised tribal attitudes to Rome. Herein might lie the reason why Agricola subdued the eastern areas of Scotland first before turning his attention to the more fragmented Novantae and Damnonii, where there are only four hillforts in excess of 6 acres (2·4 hectares) compared with thirteen in the territory of the Selgovae and Votadini.

A few brochs are known in Votadinian territory, with rather more spreading down the west coast into the lands of the Damnonii and Novantae. One can be shown to be secondary to the multivallate hillfort at Torwoodlee, Selkirk, while at Edin's Hall, Berwick, a broch follows a hillfort but is replaced by a stone-built settlement. Dates ranging from the first into the second century are indicated for the occupation of the southern brochs where there is sufficient material to be sure. Various suggestions have been made to explain the occurrence of brochs in the area, including the importation of broch-building mercenaries by the Votadini, following the first Roman withdrawal from Scotland, but the matter must remain beyond proof.

NORTHERN SCOTLAND (Fig. 8:3)

North of the Forth–Clyde line the names of some twelve tribes are recorded, but since they are not easy to differentiate historically or archaeologically it is simpler to describe the area and its settlements in general terms.

The Highland Massif, the homeland of the Caledonians, divides the area into two: the eastern coastal region occupied by the Venicones, the Vacomagi and the Taezali; and the north and west coasts and islands (the Atlantic province) settled by the Epidii, Creones, Carnoacae, Caereni, Cornovii, Smertae, Lugi and Decantae. In the north-eastern region the basic folk culture of the Abernethy complex continued largely unchanged. Defended settlement sites, duns, hillforts and occasional brochs occur but are relatively little-known in archaeological terms. It was through this area that the last campaigns of Agricola were fought, and it was somewhere here that the great army of the Caledonians under their leader Calgacus met its

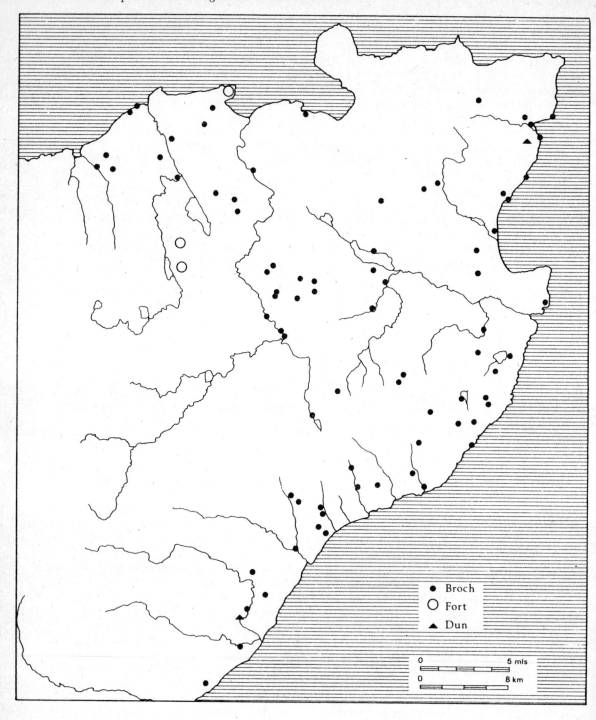

8:4   The distribution of brochs in Caithness (source: RCHM(S), *Caithness*)

defeat, leaving the countryside depleted for a generation or two. Events of this magnitude must have left their mark on the settlement pattern but it still remains to be defined.

The Atlantic province, largely untouched by Rome, continued to develop in relative isolation, giving rise to a range of highly distinctive structures and a material culture well adapted to the needs of the environment. Reassessing the evidence in 1934, Childe referred to the structures of the area as the *castle complex*, in order to emphasise the basic unity of the hundreds of small forts, duns and brochs which characterised the densely fortified landscape (Fig. 8:4). Broadly speaking, these 'castles' can be divided into duns and brochs, both of which can be further subdivided on the basis of their form siting and regional distribution (MacKie, 1965a, fig. 2). The details of these structures are considered in more detail below (pp. 219–22) and need not concern us now.

The material culture belonging to the settlements of the Atlantic province presents much the same variety as that of the contemporary sites in the South, with the one exception that iron was never plentiful. Bone was made into needles, awls, gouges, bobbins, long-handled combs, spindle whorls and dice; bronze was used for ring-headed pins and spiral finger-rings; while stone of various kinds continued in use for tool-making, for the production of armlets out of jet and for the manufacture of small vessels. Another similarity to southern Britain is that pottery was well made and relatively plentiful; moreover, it is susceptible to regional and chronological division. In the west several distinct styles have been defined; these include *Clettraval ware*, characterised by globular jars with everted rims, decorated by a finger-pinched girth cordon with concentric channelled semicircles in a zone above (Fig. A:74). Alongside the later stages of the development, *Vaul ware* appears in two basic forms: large barrel-shaped urns and smaller jars with an S-shaped profile and slightly everted rim; both types are often decorated with incised geometric patterns. Broadly contemporary with the Vaul wares are the barrel-shaped *Balevullin* vessels with finger-printed girth cordons, sometimes ornamented with simple incised patterns.

In the northern area of Orkney, Shetland, Caithness and Sutherland incised and cordoned wares are almost entirely lacking. Instead, the commonest types are tall jars with small beaded or everted rims, sometimes with well-burnished surfaces, which developed out of the pre-broch wares at Clickhimin and can therefore be referred to as the *Clickhimin IV* style. The type is widespread in the north and occasionally penetrates into the west. The main feature is the shouldered jar with internally-fluted everted rim (Figs A:35, A:36). Sometimes cordons are applied at the junction of rim and body and a few examples have bases internally impressed with patterns of finger-marks.

Very few well-stratified sites have yet been adequately examined in the Atlantic province but the range of material now available from Clickhimin, Jarlshof, Dun Mor Vaul, etc. is at last allowing the copious material culture to be arranged in a sequence related to structural development. A first assessment of this has recently been offered by MacKie (1965a, fig. 6) but until more excavation has been undertaken, details of sequential development and regionalism will remain obscure.

Childe believed that the broch culture arose as the result of intrusive elements emanating from south-west Britain (1935a, 237–9 and 1946, 94). This view was expanded by Sir Lindsey Scott (1948), who attempted to show that the pottery, as well as the architecture and the rest of the material culture, could be derived directly from the south-west and that in his view the entire culture was introduced by 'colonists'. More recently, MacKie (1965a) has argued convincingly for the indigenous development of the broch and the wheel-house together with much of the ceramic tradition, but still retains the belief (1969) in an immigration from the south some time in the first century BC. As D. V. Clarke (1970) has shown, however, the supposed evidence for immigration is far from satisfactory and can all be explained in terms of trade and other forms of peaceful contact not requiring folk movement. While the problem is by no means solved, the case for indigenous development under the influence of widespread trading contact seems to be gaining ground.

By the time of the Roman invasion, the Northern and Western Isles were very strongly defended by more than 500 local chieftains living in their broch towers. The fact that in AD 43 a treaty was concluded between the Roman fleet and the Orcadian chieftains is perhaps indicative of their significance in the eyes of the Roman commanders. The treaty probably continued to be honoured, for when Agricola destroyed the mainland resistance in the battle of Mons Graupius in AD 84, he was able to claim that the conquest of Britain had been completed, though not before the islands had been visited by the Roman fleet.

In the ensuing peace the fortifications were gradually dismantled and were replaced by wheel-houses representing a resurgence of the native traditions of domestic architecture. Local economy flourished at first and trading relations were maintained with the Roman world, during which time luxury goods like glass and pottery together with a few coins trickled in, but with the collapse of Roman law in the south a decline set in and the material culture became much simpler until it was once more reduced to a level not unlike that of the Late Bronze Age.

The Establishment
of Roman Control

The military history of Britain in the first century AD has received considerable attention from archaeologists and historians and need not be enlarged upon here, but it is necessary, for the sake of our theme, to examine the reaction of the native tribes of Britain to the threat and actuality of Roman rule.

In the early years of the forties the attitudes of the southern tribes towards Rome were divided. The huge confederacy dominated by the Catuvellaunian royal house – which spread from Kent to Gloucestershire and covered the Home Counties, Essex, Hertfordshire and parts of Bedfordshire, Cambridgeshire and Suffolk – maintained a firm anti-Roman policy; so, too, did the communities of the Salisbury Plain region (?once Atrebates) and the individualistic Durotriges of Dorset. Pinned between this axis and the southern coast there remained a small enclave of Atrebates, ruled by Verica, who appear to have maintained their Romanophile leanings until the moment of the conquest. Beyond the anti-Roman arc were tribes of uncertain allegiance: the Iceni, the Coritani, parts of the Dobunni and the Dumnonii, some of whom, fearing the aggressive tendencies of the Catuvellauni, may well have been inclined to throw in their lot with Rome. In short, the country was divided.

Tension was further heightened by the accession of the two Catuvellaunian leaders Togodumnus and Caratacus in or very soon after AD 40, following the death of their father Cunobelin. The instability which must have been created by a change of leadership after so many years of unified rule may well have led to internal divisions within the tribe, in addition to a feeling of unease in the surrounding areas. In about 42 Verica, the old king of the Atrebates,

fled to Rome to ask for the help of the emperor Claudius. No doubt Verica would have provided the emperor and his advisers with an up-to-date assessment of the political situation in Britain. Moreover, his flight could have been interpreted by the Roman propaganda machine as the expulsion of a trusty friend and ally in whose interests military intervention in Britain was required.

The invasion began towards the end of April AD 43 with the massing of the Roman army in Kent. After several unsuccessful skirmishes in east Kent, Caratacus and Togodumnus withdrew their army behind the river Medway and there pitted the whole weight of the British resistance against the Romans. For two days the river line was held but Roman superiority of arms eventually triumphed. The battle was decisive. British opposition melted away; Togodumnus subsequently died in battle while Caratacus moved to the west to continue the fight, eventually ending up as a resistance leader in south Wales among the Silures. The dramatic collapse of centralised opposition in the south-east was rapidly followed up by the Roman advance across the Thames and the drive on the Catuvellaunian capital at Camulodunum, led by the emperor himself. By the end of July Catuvellaunian dominance had been totally smashed and all that remained was to mop up pockets of resistance and establish military control.

The relative ease of the initial stages of the advance depended to a large extent upon a stable left flank, a stability which was provided by the buffering effect of the Atrebatic enclave in Sussex and east Hampshire. Had it not been for the presence of this friendly tribe, the hostile elements of the south-west would have created a potential threat to the extended Roman supply lines across Kent. It was, then, very much in the Roman interest to ensure the political stability of the area. The flight of Verica to Rome implies unrest but whether as the result of Catuvellaunian expansion or of internal differences is unknown. The Roman attitude was clear enough, for almost immediately there appears in the area a client king, Tiberius Claudius Cogidubnus, who was later to style himself 'king and legate to the emperor in Britain'. While it is possible that he was left by Verica to hold on to the reins of government in his absence and was therefore already in power when the Romans landed, it could be argued either that he was a Roman nominee selected at the time of the invasion from among the ruling household or, more likely, that he was a member of the Atrebatic aristocracy living in exile who was brought in by the army. An explanation in these terms would account for the rapid and dramatic Romanisation of the kingdom in the thirty years following the invasion. Whatever the precise explanation, there is a good case for suggesting the landing of a military detachment in the Chichester region in parallel with the main advance through Kent to stabilise the area and keep an eye on dissident elements. Such a force could have brought the king with it and established his right to rule by its very presence. A strongly pro-Roman client king could have been used as a diplomatic tool to persuade neighbouring rulers, uncertain of their allegiance, to support the Roman cause. Indeed it may have been through the good offices of Cogidubnus that a king of the Dobunni, probably Boduocus (Bodvoc), capitulated while the Roman army was still fighting its way across Kent.

Cogidubnus was a success as a client king, for Tacitus records his faithful support of Rome into the seventies or eighties. Two inscriptions from Chichester serve to emphasise the extent of romanisation. One records the erection of a statue, probably equestrian, to Nero in AD 58, while the second, a dedicatory slab from a temple to Neptune and Minerva erected to the honour of the Divine House of the Emperor, probably in the early eighties, gives Cogidubnus the title *legatus augusti*, which he may have been granted as a supporter of Vespasian following the upheavals of AD 69 (Cunliffe, 1971a). It can also be plausibly argued that the great palatial building at Fishbourne, Sussex, may have been the residence of the king in his later years. In total, the evidence for rapid and thorough romanisation is impressive but that Cogidubnus may at first have had difficulty with his subjects is hinted at by the growing evidence of military remains at Chichester, the possibility being that the king may have required a supporting garrison to establish and maintain his control at least in the early years of his reign. Nevertheless, from the Roman point of view the arrangement was a resounding success, as Tacitus puts it (*Agricola*, 14), 'an example of the long-established Roman custom of employing even kings to make others slaves'.

The Durotriges offered a more intractable problem. They remained culturally isolated from the tribes of the south-east and in place of unified government it may well be that the tribe was split into smaller units owing allegiance to local chieftains. At any event it fell to Vespasian, leading the *Legio II augusta*, to hack his way, one hillfort at a time, across Durotrigian territory late in 43 or early in 44. After taking the Isle of Wight, fighting thirty battles and destroying more than twenty hillforts, he could claim to have conquered two powerful tribes. Archaeological traces of the campaign are vivid (Fig. 9:1). At the time, forts like Hod Hill and Maiden Castle were being actively strengthened in archaic defensive styles, and it is probable that many of the other Dorset sites were being brought into defensive order to meet the threat. Actual attack can be demonstrated at several forts. At Hod Hill the chieftain's hut was softened up by ballista fire from a tower sited close to the defences, as is shown by the concentration and distribution of iron ballista bolts around the hut. How the inhabitants responded is unknown, but shortly afterwards the fort was cleared and a Roman garrison housed in one corner. Maiden Castle succumbed to a violent attack in which a number of its defenders were cut down in close fighting or killed by ballista fire, their bodies later to be buried hurriedly but in native style in a cemetery at the east entrance. At Spettisbury, on the other hand, a number of bodies together with fragments of their equipment were bundled unceremoniously in a large pit, possibly at the hands of the Roman army tidying up after an attack. As more of the Dorset hillforts are excavated similar evidence will no doubt come to

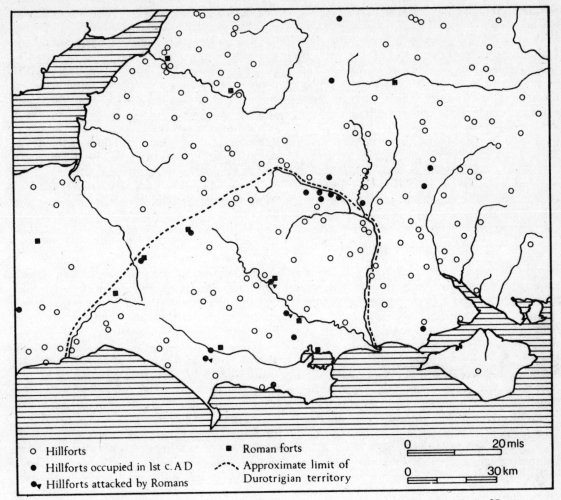

9:1   Native and Roman forts among the Durotriges (source: Ordnance Survey Map of Iron Age Britain, with additions)

light although not necessarily all were assaulted at this time. Tiresome though this method of warfare must have been to the Romans, it posed little real difficulty, for the hillforts of the south-west were designed to withstand local raids rather than Roman aggressive siege. Nevertheless, the strength of the resistance demanded the garrisoning of a number of separate contingents at strategic points throughout the territory, simply to remind the Durotriges of the military presence.

The reference in Suetonius's account of the conquest of *two* tribes in the south-west raises problems to which there are at present no clear answers. It is generally assumed that the second

tribe were the Dumnonii but the early military dispositions hardly support this. On balance, it would seem more reasonable to suppose that the area referred to was Salisbury Plain north of the Nadder and west of the Test, which had originally been under Atrebatic domination but may, by the time of the conquest, have split with the pro-Roman rulers and become allied with one of the anti-Roman tribes – either the Dobunni or the Durotriges. Alternatively, it might be argued that the area was under some form of Catuvellaunian control. At any event, many of the hillforts of the region appear to have been maintained in defensive order, although firm archaeological evidence of attack is at present wanting. At Danebury, as we have seen, the defences were remodelled in the Fécamp style adopted in the Belgic areas of the south-east at Oldbury, High Rocks and the Caburn, while on Boscombe Down West a totally new multivallate enclosure was constructed towards the middle of the first century. That the region was regarded as administratively, and presumably culturally, separate from the surrounding tribes is shown in its classification by the Roman authorities as part of the administrative region of the Belgae.

The political situation among the Dobunni at the time of the invasion can be seen reflected in their coinage. The tribal territory seems to have been split into two: one area, centred upon Gloucestershire, was ruled by Boduocus (Bodvoc) whose coins, modelled on Roman types, suggest a potential pro-Roman attitude, while to the south, in north Somerset, the more traditional coinage of Corio was dominant. The division between the two types of coinage could be interpreted as representing pro-Roman and anti-Roman factions, in which case it would have been Boduocus whose submission was received, possibly through Cogidubnus, while the Roman army was fighting its way through Kent. It has been suggested that by AD 43 this Gloucestershire faction was coming under the domination of the Catuvellauni and was therefore all the more ready to throw in its lot with Rome. Corio in north Somerset may well have fended off Catuvellaunian aggression and may therefore have been less inclined to side with the invaders. The fact that his territory was subsequently absorbed into the artificial *civitas Belgarum* is an indication of his opposition to, and suppression by, Rome. Both territories were, however, soon garrisoned as part of the military frontier zone based on the line of the Fosse Way running parallel to the Severn–Trent axis.

The northern neighbours of the Catuvellauni, the Iceni of East Anglia, submitted to Rome immediately after the initial stage of the invasion, their leader, or leaders, being among the eleven kings who offered their support to Claudius. On the basis of the coin evidence recently reassessed by Allen (1970), one of these kings is likely to have been Antedios, whose coins were circulating in part of Icenian territory in the thirties and forties alongside an uninscribed series of face-horse silver coins, presumably representing the issues of another royal household. Antedios was

probably still alive in AD 47 at the time of a local uprising inspired by the Roman desire to disarm the tribe, but he may have died or been replaced soon afterwards. He was succeeded by Prasutagus, whose coins were inscribed with the tribal name ECENI and ECE implying some kind of general overlordship of the tribe, but the survival of separate factions is demonstrated by a series of late coins inscribed SUBIDASTO–ESICO. The client kingdom came to a dramatic end with the death of Prasutagus in AD 60 and the revolt, led by his wife Boudicca, consequent upon it (p. 125).

The political attitudes of the two remaining tribes in the Midlands, the Coritani and the Cornovii, are not recorded but the apparent ease with which the Roman frontier was constructed across the land belonging to the former and close to the territory of the latter would suggest some kind of treaty relationship. Quite possibly the Coritani, along with the Iceni and Dobunni, were suffering from the expansionist policies of the Catuvellauni and regarded the Romans as the lesser of the two evils.

Thus by AD 47 the most civilised part of Britain – that area south and east of the Fosse frontier – had been thoroughly subdued by the army and, apart from the client kingdoms of the Iceni and the Regni (as the southern Atrebates were called), the region was now under direct military control (Fig. 9:2). To the west and north were less congenial regions, difficult to conquer and of uncertain productive capacity. These evidently lay beyond Roman territorial desires, but those tribes immediately adjacent to the frontier had to be brought into some form of relationship with the new government. The Dumnonii in the south-west peninsula were probably quite friendly: they had, after all, been trading freely with foreigners for years. Moreover, the frontier successfully isolated the peninsula and rendered the tribe of little potential danger. In the Midlands were the Dobunni, part of whose territory lay inside the military zone and who were therefore forced to behave, and the Cornovii, with whom a treaty had probably been negotiated. Finally, across the north of Britain 'from sea to sea' was the vast confederacy of the Brigantes, whose loyalty to Rome was at most times evident but precarious. Thus the Dobunni and Cornovii were employed as buffer states against Wales, while the Brigantes served to absorb pressures from the northern tribes.

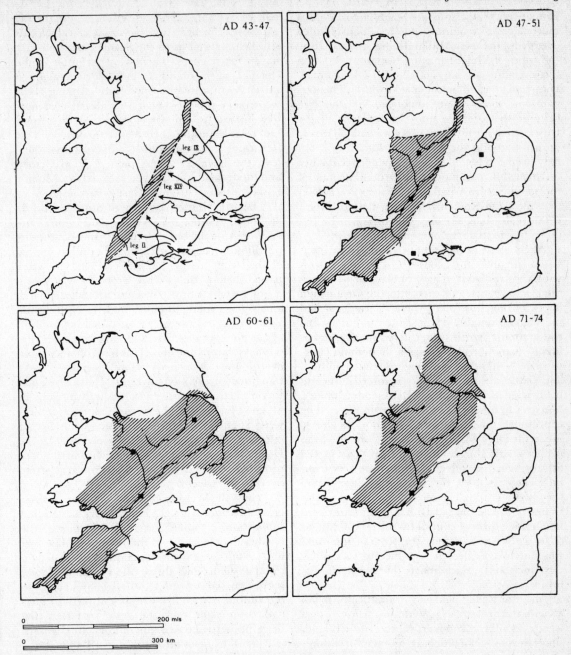

9:2 The Roman conquest of southern **Britain**; **the** military zone is shaded; black squares indicate legionary bases (sources: various)

Native resistance had been virtually wiped out in the south-east but, with the powerful Catuvellaunian leader Caratacus, the focus of the anti-Roman movement passed to south Wales to the territory of the Silures whence, in the winter of 47–8, Caratacus launched a fierce attack against a tribe allied to Rome – presumably the Dobunni in the Severn valley. This event, and the growing strength of the British resistance which it represented, forced the new

Roman governor Ostorius Scapula to adopt a more aggressive military policy which entailed occupying the west Midlands and thus isolating the tribes of Wales from the Brigantes. To gain the necessary mastery of the Bristol Channel, Dumnonia had to be occupied as well. The preparations did not go unnoticed by the free Britons: the advance into the territory of the Deceangli in north Wales was greeted by a minor uprising among the Brigantes, some of whom may have considered their independence further threatened by this move, while the disarming of the south-eastern tribes, a necessary precaution to protect the Roman rear, was met with by a revolt in Icenian territory which had to be put down by an auxiliary detachment.

After these preparations had been consolidated and the consequent unrest dealt with, the army moved against Caratacus, first in Silurian territory and then into the Ordovician lands of north Wales where Caratacus had moved, presumably to be closer to his escape route to the north. After a while Caratacus finally abandoned his guerrilla tactics and chose to make a stand at a strongly fortified hilltop. The battle was lost and he was forced to flee to the Brigantes, whose queen Cartimandua handed him over to the Roman authorities in AD 51. The capture of the war-leader did not, however, mean the end of Welsh resistance, which was to last for nearly thirty years more. In 51 or 52 the Silures defeated a legion, inflicting very considerable casualties, but during the later fifties they were gradually worn down by the continuous campaigning of Didius Gallus and kept under some form of control by the establishment of forts. But at this time the Roman intention was not to conquer: it was merely to destroy resistance and thus remove the threat to the frontier.

Imperial policy changed dramatically in AD 58 with the arrival of Q. Veranius, whose orders were evidently to conquer the rest of Britain. A single season's campaigning among the Silures was sufficient to smash their resistance once and for all, and when the next season's campaign began in 59 (under the command of Suetonius Paulinus) the army was able to concentrate on the north, presumably weakening the resistance of the Ordovices before marching against the Druid stronghold on Anglesey, described by Tacitus as a 'source of strength to the rebels'

(*Agricola*, xiv) – a reference, no doubt, to the widespread respect, and power which the Druids still held as well as to the island's function as a haven for refugees. Tacitus's description of the storming of the island is vivid: 'The enemy lined the shore in a dense armed mass. Among them were black-robed women with dishevelled hair like Furies, brandishing torches. Nearby stood the Druids raising their hands to heaven and screaming dreadful curses.' Overcoming their fear, the Roman soldiers pushed on to victory and destroyed 'the groves devoted to Mona's barbarous superstitions' (*Annals*, xiv, 30).

The annexing of Anglesey meant the end to organised resistance in Wales, but before consolidation could be undertaken, the Boudiccan rebellion broke out, requiring the full attention of the army in the south-east. Fourteen years passed before the Welsh problem was faced again, by which time old wounds had healed and a new generation of fighters had emerged. From 74 to 77 Julius Frontinus campaigned to and fro across the principality, suffering some serious setbacks, but by the end of his term of office most of the area had been subdued and it only remained for the next governor, Julius Agricola, to complete the work by a single campaign in AD 78. Thereafter the Ordovices and Silures were kept in the firm grip of a complex of permanent forts and roads. Other tribes like the Demetae of the south-west, who are never recorded to have opposed Rome, were left to develop in peaceful isolation.

Whilst the Welsh tribes on the western border of the province were gradually being beaten into submission, trouble broke out among the northern confederacy of the Brigantes. The first hint of unrest (*discordiae*) occurred in 47–8 as a result of the Roman thrust into Flintshire. It was serious enough to compel the Roman general to return, but 'after a few who began the hostilities had been slain and the rest pardoned, the Brigantes settled down quietly' (Tacitus, *Annals*, xii, 32). The use of the word 'discord' to describe the uprising tends to suggest internal troubles, which were probably put down by the ruling house without the need for Roman help. It was probably a minor incident but it heralded the split between the pro-Roman and anti-Roman factions which was eventually to destroy the confederacy.

Caratacus must have been relying on the

strength of the anti-Roman feeling when in 51 he fled into Brigantia 'seeking the protection of Queen Cartimandua', but he had misjudged the situation and was immediately turned over to the Roman authorities. Such an act is best seen as an attempt by the queen to demonstrate a loyalty to Rome and to underline her own position of power in the eyes of the army of occupation. She had, after all, just witnessed the overwhelming successes of the Roman forces in Wales; some token of loyalty may have been deemed necessary to prevent Roman intervention in her kingdom.

Within the next seven years, however, the unified rule of the confederacy began to split up. A quarrel broke out between Cartimandua and her husband Venutius, both of whom had previously been loyal to Rome. Civil war followed, Venutius immediately assuming an anti-Roman position and, by doing so, taking upon himself the mantle of resistance leader of the free Britons. Cartimandua 'by cunning stratagems, captured the brothers and kinsfolk of Venutius' (Tacitus, *Annals*, xii, 40), which understandably annoyed him and led him to invade her part of the kingdom. The position became so serious that it was eventually necessary for a Roman legion to be sent some time about 57–8, with the purpose of keeping the two sides apart.

Matters finally came to a head during the confusion in the year 69. 'Inspired by the differences between the Roman forces, and by the many rumours of civil war that reached them, the Britons plucked up courage under the leadership of Venutius who, in addition to his natural spirit and hatred of the Roman name, was fired by personal resentment towards Queen Cartimandua' (Tacitus, *Hist.*, iii, 45). One of the reasons for Venutius's evident distaste for his wife was that she had married his armour-bearer Vellocatus. 'So Venutius, calling in aid from outside, and at the same time assisted by a revolt among the Brigantes themselves, put Cartimandua into an extremely dangerous position.' Cartimandua was forced to ask the Roman administration for military assistance but even the intervention of a substantial contingent of cavalry and infantry could do little more than snatch the queen from danger. Thus by *c.* 70 'the throne was left to Venutius, the war to us'.

The narrative of Tacitus leaves very little doubt that the north was now in a state of wide-spread open rebellion led by the Brigantes, backed up by tribes extending far north into the interior. For the Roman province to the south the situation was serious. Immediately Vespasian had gained the throne and the civil disturbances were at an end, the new governor of Britain, Petillius Cerialis, began a three-year campaign in the north from 71–4. 'After a series of battles, some not uncostly, Petillius had operated, if not actually triumphed, over the major part of the [Brigantian] territory' (Tacitus, *Agricola*, xvii). During this time Brigantian resistance must have been smashed and Venutius defeated, for in spite of a lull of five years or so while Wales was being subdued, there was little further trouble in the area when Agricola began his thrust to the far north. By the early eighties the whole of Brigantia was enmeshed in a close-knit network of forts and roads, which divided the old confederacy into a multiplicity of easily patrolled fragments.

In the three decades during which the Roman armies were forced to subdue the warlike peoples of Wales and the Pennines, the romanisation of the south-east was being completed, but in spite of a deliberate and well-used programme employing client kings, making substantial monetary loans to noble families, founding *coloniae* and undertaking elaborate programmes of urban building, progress was by no means smooth. The first hints that all was not well occurred in AD 47, when some of the Icenian tribesmen, objecting to being disarmed, organised a resistance movement and constructed fortifications. The revolt was easily put down but it must have shown the authorities that a certain instability existed in the client kingdom of the Iceni.

Trouble came to a head in 59–60 with the death of Prasutagus. He was rich and in his will he had adopted the normal procedure of making the emperor joint heir with his two daughters, but it is evident from what followed that the Roman administration intended to absorb the client kingdom into the province, quite probably because it was regarded as a point of instability. The Icenian nobles, led by Boudicca, resisted with the result that a military detachment was sent in; 'the first outrage was the flogging of his wife Boudicca and the rape of his daughters; then the Icenian nobles were deprived of their ancestral estates . . . these outrages, and the fear of worse now that they had been reduced to the status of a province, moved the Iceni to arms' (Tacitus, *Annals*, xiv, 32). The time was ripe for rebellion, for a new generation of fighters had grown up, the Roman army was heavily occupied in Anglesey and there was a growing dissatisfaction with Roman fiscal measures.

The Iceni were not alone: their neighbours to the south, the Trinovantes, joined in together with 'other tribes who were unsubdued by slavery' (ibid., 32), implying help from beyond the Fosse frontier, perhaps from the Brigantes. The Trinovantes had a particular reason for dissatisfaction, for it was at the site of their tribal capital, Camulodunum, that the Romans had established a *colonia* which entailed the appropriation of thousands of acres of the surrounding farmland for the veterans now settled there. To make the situation even worse, the government had built a temple to the Emperor Claudius in the *colonia* – no doubt in an attempt to refocus the religious feeling of the natives on the empire and away from Druidic nationalism. The policy misfired.

The revolt which followed was violent: London, Camulodunum and Verulamium were destroyed, the ninth legion was driven back and the Procurator fled to Gaul. 'The Britons had no thought of taking prisoners or selling them as slaves, nor for any of the usual commerce of war, but only of slaughter, the gibbet, fire and the cross. They knew they would have to pay the penalty: meantime they hurried on to extract vengeance in advance' (ibid., 33). It is evident that, in the initial stages, the rebellion succeeded more by its fury than by its planning. Gradually, as the impetus was dissipated, the power of the rebels waned and eventually Boudicca was forced to accept a set battle at a site chosen by the Roman commander, Suetonius Paulinus, probably because winter was approaching and food supplies were running short. British fighting tactics had changed little since the invasions of Caesar: cavalry and infantry were mixed up, chariots were still used, and women and children came along as spectators to watch the fight. It was a classic contest with British enthusiasm pitted against Roman order. Inevitably British resistance broke: 'The Romans did not spare the women, and the bodies of the baggage-animals, pierced with spears, were added to the piles of corpses. It was a glorious victory equal to those of the good old days: some estimate as many as

80,000 British dead . . . Boudicca ended her life with poison' (ibid., 37).

The situation did not ease with the British defeat. 'The territory of all tribes that had been hostile or neutral was laid waste with fire and sword. But famine was the worst of the hardships, for they had omitted to sow crops. . . .' The events of 60–61 must have reduced eastern England to a virtual desert, and not until Suetonius was replaced could the process of reconstruction begin. Indeed, it was to take ten years before the province was stable enough for renewed military activity in the north.

As we have seen, much of Brigantia was explored by Cerialis in 71–4 and some part of the area must have been thoroughly garrisoned, sufficient at least to prevent further trouble from recalcitrant tribesmen. With the arrival of the new governor, Julius Agricola, in the summer of AD 78, a new forward policy was initiated. After tidying up the occupation of north Wales, Agricola could concentrate on the conquest of the north (Fig. 9:3). He spent the campaigning season of 79 consolidating the somewhat tentative occupation of Brigantia, probably as far north as the Tyne–Solway line. By a series of minor plundering raids followed up by bribes, he was able to take control of the entire region, including some tribes which had previously been outside the Roman sphere of interest. The ease with which Brigantia was thus absorbed is a clear reflection of the success of the Cerialian campaigns and presumably of the spread of the enervating luxuries of romanisation from the south. The spirit of resistance and the unity of the area had been smashed.

To the north of the Brigantes lay three tribes: the Novantae of the south-west Lowlands, the Selgovae in the centre and the Votadini occupying the east coast. Since it was probably from these tribes that Venutius had received help ten years earlier, they were clearly regarded as a potential threat to the security of the Roman province and had to be brought under Roman control. Accordingly, in 80 Agricola marched north, forcing his way to the river Tay. After wintering in Scotland, he spent the next year building forts and roads with the evident intention of consolidating the Clyde–Forth line as a frontier. 'This neck was now secured by garrisons, and the whole sweep of country to the south was safe in our hands. The enemy had been pushed

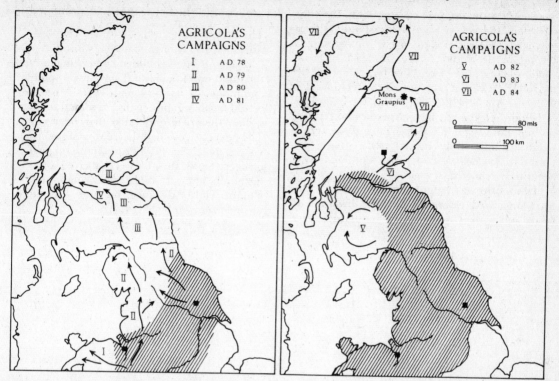

9:3 The Roman conquest of northern Britain; the military zone is shaded; black squares indicate legionary bases (sources: various)

into what was virtually another island' (Tacitus, *Agricola*, xxiii). Much of the military activity in the Lowlands was concentrated in Selgovian territory, where presumably the main resistance lay. The tribal oppidum on Eildon Hill appears to have been slighted at this time, and the principal Roman fort of the whole northern system was built close by at Newstead. The Votadini, on the other hand, were less harshly treated: fewer forts were established in their territory and their tribal capital on Traprain Law was allowed to remain in occupation. The Novantae of south-western Scotland, together with other more remote tribes, were the subject of a separate campaign in 82, at the end of which Agricola stood on the shore and looked across to Ireland, estimating that it could be conquered and held with a single legion and a few auxiliaries.

So far the army had met with little organised opposition, but when in the next spring they moved north again along the eastern coastal plain beyond the Tay, Caledonian resistance began to gel. Even with the support of sea-borne supplies and reinforcements, Roman communications were seriously stretched, but gradually forts were established at the mouths of the glens to bottle up the tribesmen in the mountains, and the Roman hold strengthened. Once they had overcome their initial surprise at the speed of the Roman advance, the Caledonians began to organise a more aggressive resistance, culminating in the attack on a Roman fort which only narrowly escaped destruction. 'With unbroken spirit,' says Tacitus, 'they persisted in arming their whole fighting force, putting their wives and children in places of safety and ratifying their league by conference and sacrifice' (*Agricola*, 27).

Thus by the beginning of the summer of AD 84 the scene was set for the final confrontation between the two armies at Mons Graupius. 'The Britons, undaunted by the loss of the previous battle, welcomed the choice between revenge and enslavement ... Already more than 30,000 of them made a gallant show, and still they came flocking to the colours' (Tacitus, *Agricola*, xxix).

To the Caledonians, pushed literally to the edge of Britain, this was clearly the last stand. As their war-leader Calgacus is reported to have said in his pre-battle oration: 'We, the last men on earth, the last of the free, have been shielded till today by the very remoteness of the seclusion for which we are famed . . . but today the boundary of Britain is exposed; beyond us lies no nation, nothing but waves and rocks.' Even if the actual words are those of Tacitus (*Agricola*, xxxii), it is tempting to believe that the sentiments are accurately reported.

The battle was fought, the Britons lost: the final organised resistance of free Britain had fallen and with it 10,000 British casualties. The last words must be left with Tacitus (ibid., 38):

The Britons wandered all over the country-side, men and women together, wailing, carrying off their wounded and calling out to the survivors. They would leave their homes and in fury set fire to them . . . sometimes they would try to organise plans . . . sometimes the sight of their dear ones broke their hearts . . . The next day revealed the quality of the victory more clearly. A grim silence reigned on every hand; the hills were deserted, only here and there was smoke seen rising from chimneys in the distance and our scouts found no one to encounter them.

Continental Trade and Contact

The title of this chapter to some extent prejudges the mechanisms by which a wide range of artefacts, manufactured on the continent, arrived in Britain. Clearly there was organised trade, with well-defined processes and, no doubt, recognised exchange rates; this much is evident from the surviving documentary references. But there were many other means by which exotic material could be imported, ranging from folk movement to gift exchange and bride-price. Archaeological methods can seldom distinguish precisely between these systems. In the discussion to follow, the scope of the evidence is laid out in chronological order and, where it is thought to be appropriate, some of the wider implications of the material are discussed.

Britain had always been receptive of two separate routes of contact: one from central and northern Europe across the North Sea, the other from the Mediterranean and Iberia by way of the Atlantic to south-west Britain and the Irish Sea. These dual approaches were maintained throughout the Iron Age and indeed recur in the fifth and sixth centuries AD. Superimposed upon the broad pattern of major routes were separate processes which influenced the intensity or volume of contact. These are more difficult to isolate: they might involve political policies which deliberately encouraged or hindered relationships, or social factors such as the development of a conserving, inward-looking society lacking the motivation to engage in commerce. Economic pressures would also have contributed to the complex situation. Occasionally these separate factors can be isolated with some degree of certainty but frequently they remain confused and ill-defined.

EUROPEAN CONTACTS: SEVENTH AND SIXTH CENTURIES (Fig. 10:1)

The beginning of what can reasonably be called the Iron Age in Europe is linked to the development of the Hallstatt Culture, characterised by the appearance of a horse-riding aristocracy using a long slashing sword and frequently burying their dead in timber-built tombs beneath barrows. Some of the burials are very rich, containing trappings belonging to the chieftain's horses as well as a cart upon which the body may have been transported to the grave, along with weapons and selected items of personal equipment. Rich burials of this type cluster in Czechoslovakia and southern Germany but are known sporadically across most of central Europe, modified types spreading into central and southern Belgium. What their sudden appearance means is not immediately clear. Some writers have proposed an invasion of an eastern aristocracy, ultimately from the Steppes, spreading west and gaining overlordship of the Late Urnfield communities. In support of such a view, close parallels are drawn between the harness-fittings and burial rites in the two areas; moreover, the rapid spread of the burials over Europe would be consistent with the concept of a mobile warrior aristocracy. Against this view, however, it can be argued that the characteristic long sword of the Hallstatt warriors owes nothing to eastern Cimmerian influence (Cowen, 1967) and is best seen as the invention of the Late Urnfield bronze smiths in response to cavalry warfare. Similarly, there is nothing new about rich burial rites involving the use of vehicles. Earlier examples are known in central and northern Europe but only incompletely, since

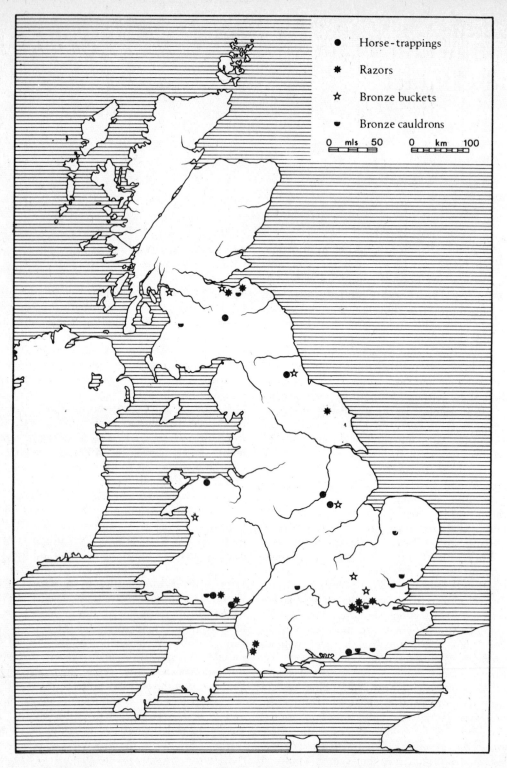

10:1　Distribution of selected types of Hallstatt metalwork, Ireland omitted (sources: various, including Hawkes & Smith, 1957, with additions)

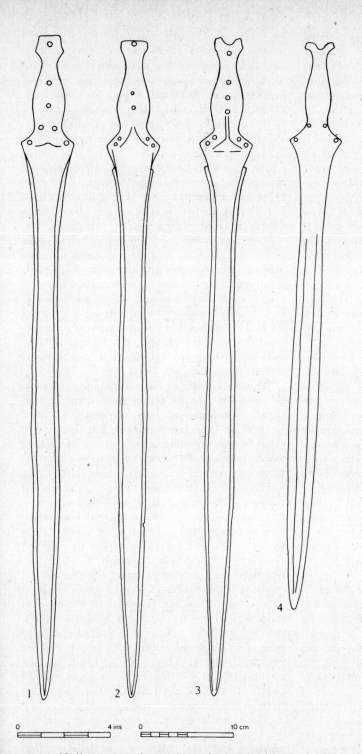

10:2 Hallstatt swords. 1 Brentford, Middx (type A); 2 Henley, Oxon (type B); 3 Newcastle upon Tyne (type C); 4 Cambridge (type D) (source: Cowen, 1967)

the cremation ritual has destroyed much of the evidence. Extending these arguments, another model can be constructed which supposes that the Hallstatt aristocracy is simply an indigenous upper class adopting the rite of inhumation and making an increased use of the horse as a cavalry animal. The arguments for and against these two views cannot be paraded in full here, but it should be remembered that they are potentially the black and white extremes of a highly complex social situation, which must have differed between one area and another.

In Europe the chronology of the period is now tolerably well known. In the central area of southern Bavaria, Hallstatt C began about 720 BC and reached its full development by about 700 (Kossack, 1954, and Dehn & Frey, 1962). The period lasted for about a hundred years and by *c.* 600 it was superseded by the Hallstatt D phase. To what extent there was a time-lag in the spreading of artefacts into western Europe and Britain, it is impossible to say. Mariën (1958), writing of the Belgium burials at Court-St-Etienne, considers the first intrusive Hallstatt C types to have arrived about 675, but it should be emphasised that the artefacts concerned are closely similar to those found at the beginning of the period in Bavaria, and there is no reason why they should not have reached Belgium nearer 700 – the two areas are, after all, only 300 miles (480 km) apart. Similarly, there *need* be no recognisable time-lag between technological developments in central Europe and their appearance in the British Isles. Unless other evidence is forthcoming, it is simpler to assume that Hallstatt C artefacts reached Britain during the time of their currency in Europe, that is, between 700 and 600 BC.

The most characteristic weapon of the Hallstatt period is the long slashing sword of bronze, of which two varieties have been identified: the Mindelheim type, found exclusively in central and northern Europe, and the Gundlingen type, a far more common weapon spread over the whole of Europe. In a recent detailed study (1967), Cowen has distinguished four broad classes of Gundlingen sword on the basis of their hilt form (Fig. 10:2). Of his classes a and b, both continental productions, twelve are known from Britain – eight of them from the Thames area; but with the possible exception of the sword from Ebberston, Yorks, none are from closed archaeo-

logical contexts. Once established in Britain, the new weapon-type was closely copied by the local swordsmiths, giving rise to Cowen's types c and d, of which twenty-seven recognisable examples are known in Britain and two from the continent. In parallel with this development, various composite and hybrid forms were manufactured locally as native inventiveness took over, culminating in the evolution of the *Thames type* of sword, which represents the eventual dominance of the native traditions over the foreign. The type proved to be popular not only in southern Britain but also in north-western Europe, where some fifteen exported examples have been recognised.

The long sword was kept in a sheath of wood or leather terminating in a metal chape, the sides of which were splayed out into wings so formed, it is suggested, to enable a mounted warrior to keep the end of the sheath steady with his left foot whilst drawing the sword with his right hand. The chapes, like the swords, are characteristic of continental burials and occur sporadically in Britain; there are eight known from England and ten from Ireland (Fig. 10:3).

The occurrence of the swords and chapes in Britain (Fig. 10:4) requires an explanation. Clearly a number of weapons must have been brought in from the continent, but conversely, once British manufacturing centres had developed, home-produced varieties were exported. Without special pleading, simple trading mechanisms could explain the entire pattern. In support of this, it must be stressed that whereas a very high percentage of continental finds come from graves, no burial find is known in Britain – with the possible exception of the ill-recorded discovery at Ebberston in Yorkshire, where two swords and a chape were found together with a quantity of human bones. Even if this is accepted as a typical Hallstatt C burial in continental style, it need not necessarily represent a foreign warrior aristocrat. Hallstatt swords must have been worn by British nobles. The evidence of the swords, therefore, is best explained in terms of a continuation of the existing trading systems between Britain and northern Europe, which had been in operation for centuries.

The seventh century saw the importation of a wide range of harness- and cart-fittings from northern and central Europe and their eventual deposition here in hoards, together with locally produced tools and weapons and sometimes

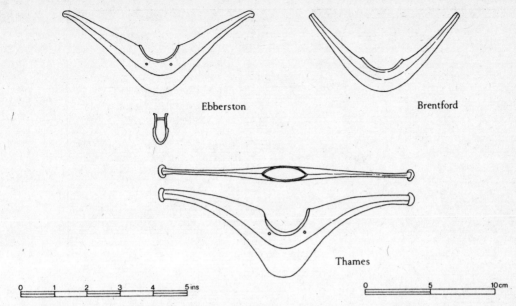

Ebberston

Brentford

Thames

10:3 Hallstatt chapes (sources: *Ebberston*, Burgess, 1969b; *Brentford*, Wheeler, 1929; *Thames*, R. A. Smith, 1925)

imports from western Europe (Fig. 10:5). Hoards of this kind are therefore of considerable significance in establishing synchronisms between local industry and datable foreign products. While it must be admitted that close dating is extremely difficult, the hoards can be divided into a loose sequence stretching throughout the eighth to the seventh century. At the beginning of the sequence must be placed the famous collection of material found beneath a layer of stalagmite on the floor of the cave at Heathery Burn, Co. Durham. In addition to socketed spears, socketed axes, knives, gouges, awls, a bifid razor, and a range of bone and stone artefacts, there were recovered a group of bronze cart- and harness-fittings (Fig. 10:5). The cart-fittings consisted of eight bronze bands, presumably for binding the ends of the axles of a wheeled vehicle. Similar objects are recorded in Late Urnfield contexts in central Europe dating to the eighth century or a little later. The harnesses are now represented by a bronze strap-distributor (i.e. a disc with perforated vertical sides to allow leather straps to cross at right angles), a ribbed disc with attachment loops, two large disc-shaped mountings and a group of bronze rings of various diameters. In addition, two cheek-pieces of bone were found. Dating evidence is provided by a bronze bucket (Fig. 10:6) of a type in use in the first half of the

seventh century – a date which corresponds well with the Ultimate Urnfield character of the material.

The strap-distributor and the looped disc can be closely paralleled at two other hoards from Welby, Leics (Fig. 10:5), and Parc-y-Meirch, Denbigh (Pl. 12), which together with the Horsehope hoard from Peeblesshire (Fig. 10:5) constitute a closely similar group of horse-equipment hoards broadly datable to the middle of the seventh century. At Welby five strap-distributors were found, together with a perforated looped disc and double-looped harness fitting identical to those from the other two hoards. Other central European types at Welby include two T-shaped handle attachments for a cauldron and a small carinated bronze bowl with furrowed decoration on the shoulder (Fig. 3:3), of a type which is frequently reproduced in pottery in southern England. The local bronze industry was represented by socketed axes, a spear and a sword.

The Parc-y-Meirch hoard is altogether more substantial, containing some ninety individual pieces among which is a group of harness-trappings including double-looped fittings and strap-distributors as well as jingle-jangles composed of kidney-shaped plaques of bronze joined loosely together with bronze rings (Pl. 12). This type of bridle decoration is represented in

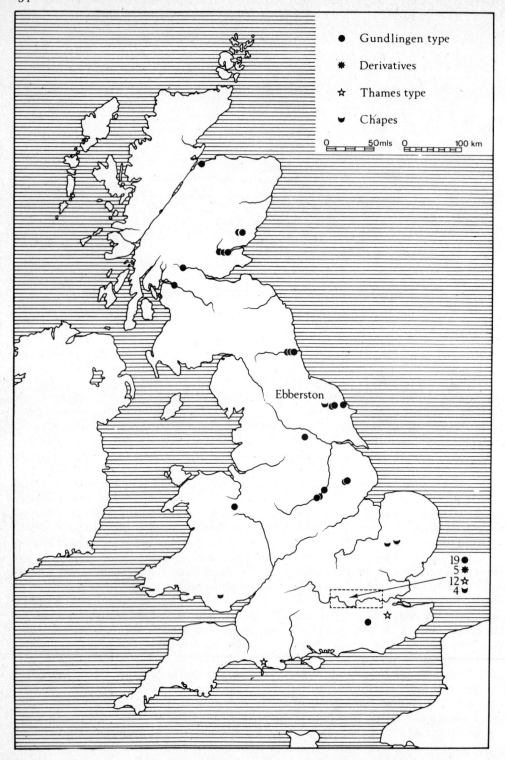

10:4   Distribution of Hallstatt swords and chapes, Ireland omitted (source: Cowen, 1967)

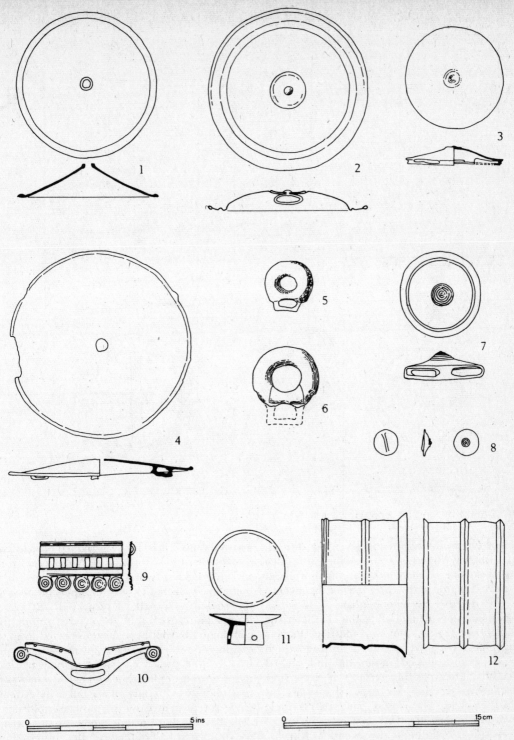

10:5   Selection of Hallstatt horse-trappings and cart-fittings. 1   Newark-on-Trent, Notts;
2, 9, 10   Llyn Fawr, Glam; 3, 4, 8, 12   Heathery Burn, Co. Durham; 5, 7   Welby, Leics;
6, 11   Horsehope, Peebles (sources: 1, 3, 4, 8, 12 *Inv. Arch.* G.B.; 2, 9, 10   Grimes, 1951;
5, 7   Powell, 1950; 6, 11   S. Piggott, 1955)

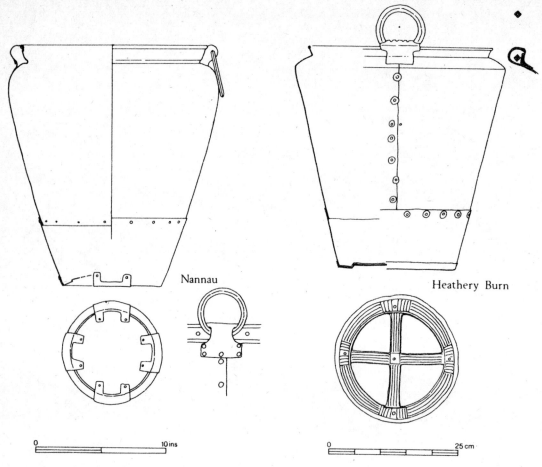

Nannau

Heathery Burn

10:6   Bronze buckets (source: Hawkes & Smith, 1957)

Scandinavia in the eighth and seventh centuries, and a slightly different form of the same idea appears in one of the south Belgian burials at Court-St-Etienne in the early part of the seventh century. In the Horsehope hoard a range of harness-rings occur, including the characteristic double-looped ring, but in addition Piggott (1955) has recognised several cart-fittings which include a dish-shaped mounting and ribbed discs, the latter possibly serving as decorative attachments for the axle caps of a small (or model) vehicle. The closest parallels for these pieces are among the Hallstatt cart burials of Czechoslovakia, dating to the seventh century.

Of the later seventh century hoards, by far the most significant is the collection of material recovered from the bottom of an ancient lake at Llyn Fawr in Glamorganshire. Local products are well represented by five socketed bronze axes, four of them of a distinctive Welsh type, three socketed sickles, two of bronze and one of iron, and three socketed chisels. It is possible that the socketed iron spearhead recovered was also of local manufacture, but the type is simple and could equally well have been imported from the continent, where identical forms were in use. Clearly, the presence of a local type of sickle made in iron implies that iron extraction was by now under way, if only on a small scale. Atlantic trade is represented by two bronze cauldrons of class B1 (Pl. 11) – a type which first came into use in the first half of the seventh century. North European Hallstatt C types (Figs. 10:5 and 10:8) include an iron sword with hilt plates of bone, two bronze cheek-pieces, three bronze discs or phalerae from harness decorations, an openwork

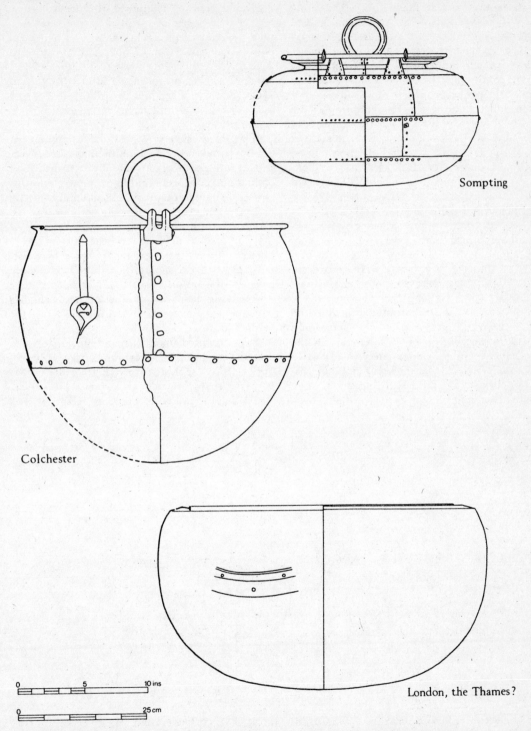

Sompting

Colchester

London, the Thames?

0   5   10 ins

0   25 cm

10:7   Bronze cauldrons (sources: *Sompting*, E. C. Curwen, 1948; *Colchester and London*, Hawkes & Smith, 1957)

harness mount, a belt hook and a crescentic razor. All the types can be very closely paralleled in early Hallstatt C burials in southern Germany and Belgium, particularly at Court-St-Etienne. So close are the parallels that direct importation from the continent is the only reasonable explanation for the presence of these objects in western Britain. Precise dating for the deposition of the hoard is, of course, difficult since there is no way of assessing how long the individual items had been hoarded, but the fact that all appear to be broadly contemporary and identical to continental types hints at a date not far removed from the middle of the seventh century. By this time, then, iron production was established.

A second hoard to show an association between Late Bronze Age types and iron comes from Sompting, Sussex, where the remains of a class B2 cauldron (Fig. 10:7) were recovered, together with seventeen axes and a Hallstatt phalera of hollow conical form. To one of the axes adhered a mass of corroded iron. On the basis of the cauldron, a date of 650–600 would seem to be most likely, but a later date in the sixth century cannot be completely ruled out.

Several other but less closely datable discoveries of harness- and cart-fittings have come to light. Phalerae of Hallstatt type have been recovered from the Thames at Brentford, Middx, with masses of bronze work of Late Bronze Age type. A phalera of similar date with a central perforation came from a hoard at Newark-on-Trent, Notts (Fig. 10:5), together with socketed axes and spears, and a hoard at Cardiff, Glam, produced an axle cap and two Hallstatt C razors as well as various implements in the local Bronze Age tradition.

This brief survey of the more significant hoards leaves very little doubt that throughout the seventh century, harness- and cart-fittings of continental type were finding their way into this country in some quantity and not infrequently ending up in scrap hoards along with local types. The mechanisms by which this material arrived are impossible now to recover. Conceivably horses and their tack were being traded together, perhaps with carts, but we cannot completely rule out the possibility that a few people were now making their way into the country, bringing with them the outward and visible signs of their aristocracy.

Superimposed upon this trade in aristocratic military equipment, was the importation of minor objects such as razors (Fig. 10:8) (C. M. Piggott, 1946), swan's neck pins (Fig. 10:9) (Dunning, 1934) and brooches (Fig. 10:10)

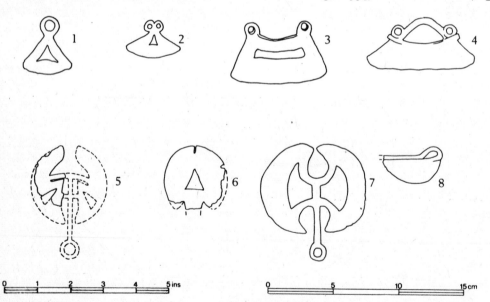

10:8   Selection of Hallstatt razors. 1, 6   Cardiff, Glam; 2   Llyn Fawr, Glam; 3   river Thames at Richmond, Surrey; 4, 5, 8   Staple Howe, Yorks; 7   Midlothian (sources: 1, 6 Nash-Williams, 1933a; 2   Grimes, 1951; 3, 7   C. M. Piggott, 1946; 4, 5, 8   Brewster, 1963)

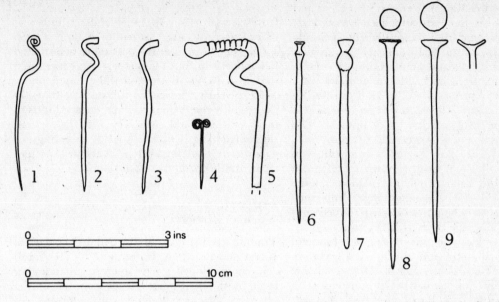

10:9 Bronze pins. 1 Hammersmith, London; 2 Brighton, Sussex; 3 Portslade, Sussex; 4 Dorchester; 5, 7 All Cannings Cross, Wilts; 6 Totternhoe, Beds; 8, 9 Heathery Burn, Co. Durham (sources: 8, 9 *Inv. Arch.* G.B.; rest author)

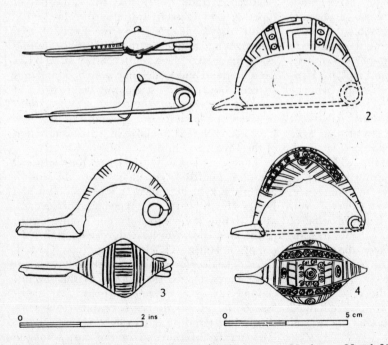

10:10 Hallstatt fibulae. 1 Hod Hill, Dorset; 2 York; 3 North Wraxall, Wilts; 4 Box, Wilts (sources: 1, 4 R. A. Smith, 1925; 2 *Antiq. Journ.* XII (1932), 454; 3 Cunnington & Goddard, 1934)

(Harden, 1950). Razors from the Llyn Fawr and Cardiff hoards have already been mentioned; others have come from the settlement at Staple Howe, Yorks, unstratified from early occupation sites on Ham Hill and South Cadbury and as isolated finds from half a dozen or more sites. Razors are frequently found in Hallstatt burials on the continent, where they must represent a standard piece of a warrior's equipment. The British finds do not, however, come from burials.

Swan's neck pins occur sporadically in Britain. In all, about ten are known, mainly from the south but, apart from the examples at the settlement site of All Cannings Cross, Wilts, they are not generally found in closely stratified contexts, and since the type is likely to have continued in use for some time, it is not a very useful chronological indicator. Even less certainty attaches to the large number of Hallstatt fibulae from Britain. Not one has been recovered in an Iron Age context, but the number is so great that some at least must have found their way into Britain in the seventh or sixth century, on the dresses of visiting womenfolk or as traded trinkets.

In north-eastern Scotland a more substantial group of intrusive metal types has been found, constituting what is called the Covesea phase of the local metal industry (Coles, 1962a). Dominant among the types which define the phase are simple penannular armlets with their terminals expanded outwards, a type found in Late Urnfield contexts in north-western Europe, whence it is suggested they were imported to Scotland. In two important hoards, Wester Ord, Ross, and Braes of Gight, Aberdeen, Covesea armlets were found associated with penannular necklets with free-swinging loops and pendants. These too have close north European parallels dated to *c*. 700 BC. In a third hoard of some significance, from Blamashanner, Angus, three Covesea armlets were found with a Late Urnfield type of bronze bowl and an iron ring, demonstrating beyond doubt the overlap between the Covesea phase and the use of iron. Other associations showed that Covesea types were used in parallel to an already vigorous indigenous bronze industry, the various phases of which are named after the hoards at Adabrock, Ballimore and Tarves (Coles, 1962a).

While a north European origin can be demonstrated for the Covesea types, the nature of the contact is far less clear. It has been suggested

that the distinctive flat-rimmed pottery found at Covesea itself, Blamashanner and a number of other sites is of Late Urnfield derivation (Coles, 1962a, 44), hinting at the possibility of a limited folk movement, but the pottery is so generalised that firm assumptions cannot be based on it. More recently, however, radiocarbon dates in the seventh century for the timber-laced forts of north-east Scotland (MacKie, 1969) have considerably strengthened the idea of an immigrant community bringing their architecture, pottery styles and bronze types with them.

ATLANTIC TRADE: SEVENTH TO SIXTH CENTURIES

Trading contacts along the Atlantic coasts of Iberia and France to Britain had by the eighth century developed a new intensity, manifesting itself in the south-east of the country in the hoards of the carp's tongue sword complex. It is now clear that this trade was maintained throughout the seventh and well into the sixth century, running therefore in parallel with the Hallstatt C incomings. It was along these old-established trade routes that the cauldrons of types A and B were introduced (Hawkes & Smith, 1957), class A (two from England, two from Scotland and seven from Ireland) beginning in the first half of the seventh century, class B (six from England and Wales, one from Scotland and sixteen from Ireland) originating before 650 and arriving for a century or so after. Associations between the cauldrons and Hallstatt C types have been referred to above in the consideration of the Llyn Fawr and Sompting hoards.

That some at least of the carp's tongue sword complex hoards occur later than the eighth century is clearly shown by the fact that the Bexley Heath hoard – the type hoard of the complex – is now known to contain a Thames sword of the kind shown to have developed in Britain out of the Hallstatt C Gundlingen type (Cowen, 1967). The development is unlikely to have taken place much before the middle of the seventh century at the earliest, and the hoard may therefore be as late as the sixth century. The continental material similarly offers support for this later dating of the end of the carp's tongue complex. A Hallstatt C razor in the Île Guenoc hoard, Finistère (Briard 1957, Fig. 28), and a radiocarbon date of 559 ± 130 (634 BC) for

Saint-Guganen Loudéac, Côte du Nord, are suggestive evidence for the continuation of trade into the seventh to sixth century.

On both sides of the Channel there appeared at this time large numbers of small non-functional axes with rectangular sockets and unprepared cutting edges, known as Breton or Armorican axes. Altogether in Armorica alone, it is estimated that 188 hoards contained this type exclusively, producing some 20,000 individual specimens (Giot, 1960, 158), and the type is found widely in south-east Britain. The opinion now is that they formed some kind of currency and continued to be used as such into the fifth century or even later. At Saint-Martin-des-Champs, Finistère, Breton axes were found in association with an iron ingot, demonstrating a late survival. The axes, then, are the last manifestation of the Atlantic bronze trade, out of which grew the sophisticated trading contacts first mentioned by classical writers in the fourth century, to which Caesar refers in some detail a few centuries later.

EUROPEAN CONTACTS: SIXTH TO FIFTH CENTURY

In central Europe the change to the Hallstatt D

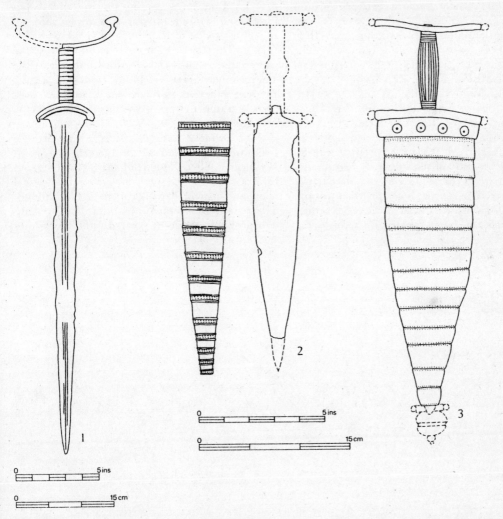

10:11 Hallstatt D weapons. 1 river Thames; 2 Battersea, London; 3 Mortlake, Surrey (sources: 1 R. A. Smith, 1925; 2, 3 Jope, 1961a)

stage of culture took place a little before 600 BC. By this time the central areas of development, typified by the rich chieftains' burials, had shifted west into the middle Rhine and Moselle region and into Burgundy – areas which now benefited from the new trade routes along the Rhône that had opened up following the foundation of the trading port of Massilia (Marseilles). Trading systems were by this time well established between central Europe and the Mediterranean world, and luxury goods belonging to wine-drinking and feasting rituals were being imported from the Greek and north Italian workshops, eventually finding their way into the tombs of the aristocracy. Trading contacts between Britain and the continent appear to have been less intensive in the sixth and early fifth century than they had been in the preceding hundred years, but nevertheless a number of imported metal objects of Hallstatt D type are known.

The Thames was evidently an important point of entry, to judge by the number of new types found in the London area. From the Thames came a short iron sword with an antennae-shaped hilt (Fig. 10:11) (R. A. Smith, 1925) characteristic of sixth century continental types, and from the same general provenance was recovered a simple hemispherical bronze cauldron of Hallstatt D type (Hawkes & Smith, 1957) which can be paralleled on many west/

central European sites, more commonly in the second half of the century (Fig. 10:7).

The long-established school of swordsmiths in the Thames region, who by now were manufacturing their own varieties of the Hallstatt C imports, soon absorbed the idea of the Hallstatt D short dagger – a type in use in the early sixth century in Württemberg – and began to manufacture their own elegant versions with an improved method of suspension using twin loops at the back of the sheath to strengthen the attachment to the belt (Fig. 10:11 and Pls 14, 16 and 17). The industry continued to flourish until about 300 BC, influenced in its later stages by new La Tène ideas coming in after about 450 (Jope, 1961b). A comparable example, showing the same process of adoption and rapid modification of Hallstatt D ideas, is exhibited by the representative of a class of fibulae found in the Thames near Hammersmith (Hodson, 1971). Evidently there must have been schools of craftsmen working in the area, always receptive of new continental ideas.

More widely flung contacts with northern Italy are emphasised by the bucket, dug up at Weybridge, Surrey, made of strips of corrugated bronze rivetted together along a single vertical seam and provided with two movable handles. The type is well known in western Europe and was probably made in north Italian workshops

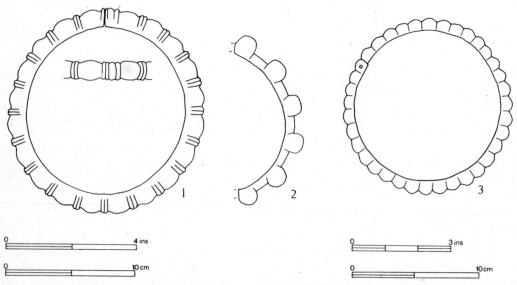

0   4 ins

0   10 cm

0   3 ins

0   10 cm

10:12 Hallstatt bracelets and neck-rings. 1 Scarborough, Yorks; 2 Cold Kitchen Hill, Wilts; 3 Clynnog, Caerns (sources: 1 R. A. Smith, 1934; 2 *DMC*; 3 Grimes, 1951)

some time in the sixth century whence, directly or indirectly, it reached Britain.

Other west European or Mediterranean objects found in Britain include about eighty examples of continental fibulae dating to the period of the eighth to fourth centuries (Harden, 1950). It is of course, impossible to be sure when they were imported. Some of them may have arrived during the Roman period or even later in the collections of travellers, but many must have been imported into Britain during the time when they were current on the continent. Other personal ornaments of Hallstatt type, including neck- and arm-rings of bronze with 'nut' moulded decoration, occur less frequently. One was found close to an early occupation site at Scarborough, Yorks, and another unassociated example is recorded from Clynnog, Caerns (Fig. 10:12). The general type does not seem to have been widely copied by local craftsmen.

Another class of imported material is pottery. Several finds of Mediterranean vessels have been made in Britain, but again the date of their importation is, without exception, unknown since no examples have yet been found on stratified occupation sites. Several vessels have been dredged from rivers, including a Greek Black Figure kylix from the Thames near Reading, which is reliably dated on stylistic grounds to the late sixth century (Boon, 1954, 178). From the same river, at Barnes, an Italic handled cup of the seventh century was dug out of the river bank, and from Barking Creek came a Greek hydriskos of the sixth century (Harden, 1950, 321–2). A squat lekythos of fourth century date was also recovered from Billingsgate. Finally, mention should be made of a group of three Greek vessels, one of them an Attic drinking cup of the late fourth century, which were found together in an artificial cave at Teignmouth, Devon, during the last century. It must be stressed that none of these finds need represent Iron Age importation, but there is nothing inherently difficult in supposing that some Mediterranean vessels found their way into southern Britain during the course of normal trading expeditions.

Scotland appears to have maintained direct contact with northern Europe at this time as shown by the distribution of distinctive sunflower-swan's neck pins (Fig. 10:13): eight from Scotland, one from Ireland and one from Fengate, Northants. Coles (1959) has shown that the genesis of the type – the fusing of the Hallstatt swan's neck pins and the Irish–Scandinavian sunflower pins – probably took place in north

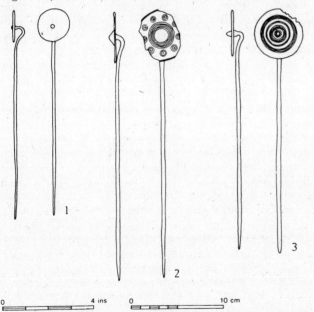

10:13 Sunflower-swan's neck pins. 1 Tarves, Aberdeen; 2 Loch Broom, Ross; 3 Campbeltown, Argyll (source: Coles, 1959)

Germany in the sixth and fifth centuries. From there the idea penetrated to Scotland. Two associated finds, the hoards from Grosvenor Crescent, Edinburgh, and Tarves, Aberdeen, show that the pins were in use at the same time as bronze swords of Ewart Park type, still manufactured in the Late Bronze Age tradition.

It can be seen from the above paragraphs that imported material of Hallstatt D date is sparse in Britain, but sufficient survives to imply continuous contact with the continent throughout the sixth and early fifth centuries. Nothing in the surviving archaeological record need, however, be explained in terms other than of casual trade.

CONTACTS BETWEEN BRITAIN AND THE
CONTINENT: FIFTH TO SECOND CENTURY

From the fifth to the second century, contacts between Britain and adjacent parts of the continent were maintained. Metalwork in the new La Tène style, which developed in Europe towards the beginning of the fifth century, found its way into the country largely as the result of trade. Many of the incoming types were copied by local craftsmen, giving rise to specifically British varieties. In Yorkshire, however, a more extensive cultural assemblage appears to have been introduced, including not only metal types but alien burial customs best paralleled among the La Tène cultures of France. This group – referred to as the Arras culture – has been considered in some detail above (pp. 40–1).

The sixth century production of a distinctive series of daggers and dagger sheaths in the Thames region (p. 142 above) was evidently carried out by local craftsmen influenced at first by Hallstatt D prototypes but soon evolving their own improved techniques and style. Production continued throughout the fifth and fourth centuries absorbing, after about 450, La Tène improvements, which were being developed in parallel on the continent. The earliest of these La Tène-inspired sheaths, one discovered at Chelsea, is so close to northern French types of the mid-fifth century while evidently itself of British manufacture that the British craftsman must have responded directly to new continental ideas. Close contact appears at only this time; thereafter the British and French traditions diverged, hinting at the beginning of some degree of cultural isolation. The eighteen daggers of La Tène I type found in Britain, mainly in the Thames area, can be arranged in a typological sequence lasting until the late fourth century. Among the latest to be made was the scabbard from Wisbech (Pl. 18), decorated in a freehand curvilinear style with S-shaped scrolls arranged in lyre and palmette patterns about a central ridge. This must be regarded as a provincial version of an art style current in Europe during the fourth century, from which early beginnings British Celtic art eventually developed.

About 300 BC a marked change in weapon fashions took place. Daggers ceased to be made and the long sword came once more into its own. None of the surviving swords can be regarded as definite imports except possibly the finely decorated version from the river Trent at Sutton, Lincs, which is closely similar to examples belonging to the Swiss sword style. Even the scabbard from Standlake, Oxon, (Pl. 15), which has close connections to continental technological tradition, is best regarded as a British production standing at the head of a long development series lasting throughout the rest of the pre-Roman period. What is perhaps most impressive about the British swords is their complete isolation from continental development. This fact, together with general lack of imported varieties, might well suggest that for the most part Britain now lacked the close contacts with the continent which it had previously maintained during the seventh and sixth centuries.

Personal ornaments are found scattered over much of southern Britain but in no great numbers. The earliest of the La Tène types to appear are the characteristic fibulae (Pl. 22a) with a high arching bow, a large four-coiled spring and a catchplate of similar size made by bending the foot back parallel to touch the bow (Fig. 10:14). The bow is often decorated with simple curvilinear or stamped decoration, and the foot is usually expanded into a disc shape decorated with stamped or incised decoration, or very occasionally inlaid with coral. Altogether, some fourteen examples of this type are recorded in Britain. Typologically they belong to a late phase in period 1a of the Münsingen[1] sequence,

[1] The cemetery at Münsingen, near Berne, has produced a series of graves which can be arranged in a sequence based largely upon their position relative to the horizontal stratigraphy of the cemetery. Detailed analysis and cross-dating have enabled reliable dates to be attached to specific artefacts (Hodson, 1968).

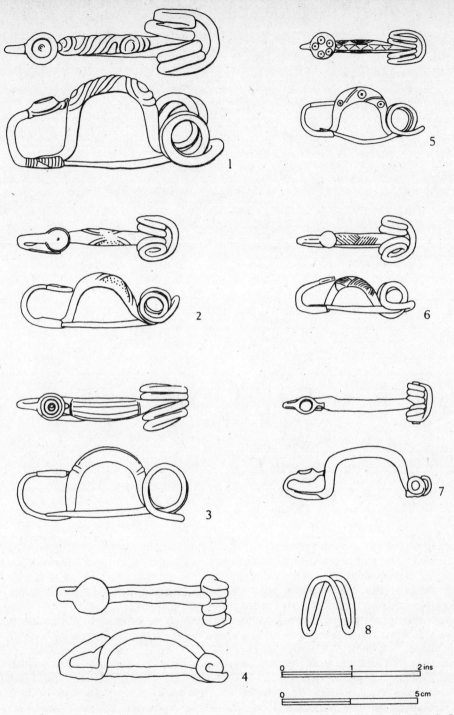

10:14　La Tène fibulae and a bent silver ring. 1　Box, Wilts; 2, 6　Blaise Castle Hill, Glos;
3, 7　Merthyr Mawr Warren, Glam; 4　Merthyr Mawr Warren, Glam; 4　Findon Park,
Sussex; 5　Water Eaton, Oxon; 8　Park Brow, Sussex (sources: 1, 5　R. A. Smith, 1925;
2, 6　Rhatz & Brown, 1959; 3, 7　Grimes, 1951; 4　Fox & Wolseley. 1928; 8　R. A. Smith,
1927)

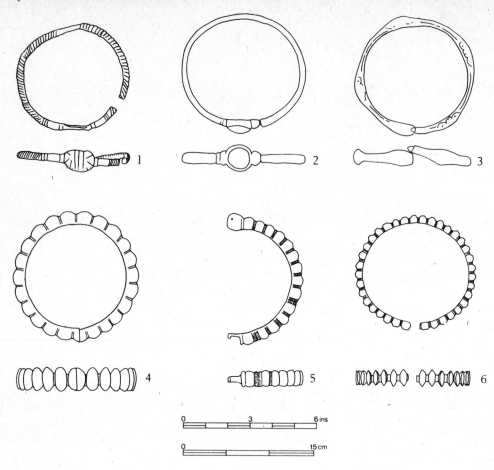

10:15   La Tène bracelets. 1   Coygan Camp, Carm; 2, 4   Arras, Yorks; 3, 6   Cowlam, Yorks; 5   South Ferriby, Lincs (sources: 1   Wainwright, 1967a; 2–6   Stead, 1965)

currently dated to 400–350, and are therefore unlikely to have arrived in Britain much before the mid-fourth century. Relatively few brooches of Münsingen 1b phase (350–280) are recorded, but one famous example, an iron version of a 1b disc-footed type, was recovered from a pit together with pottery at the Sussex settlement of Findon Park. Two others are known from the Thames at London and from Wallingford, Berks. Thereafter imported La Tène types are very rare, and apart from a bent silver ring characteristic of the Münsingen 1c phase (280–200) from Park Brow, Sussex (Fig. 10:14), imports of the third and second centuries are virtually unknown; indeed, the emphasis in Britain is upon local development from 1a types largely uninfluenced by continental trends until the incursion of La

Tène III types about 100 BC and after. The evidence from the brooches tends, therefore, to support the sword development in suggesting a phase of regionalisation in the third and second centuries.

Bracelets of La Tène types are not common in Britain outside the territory of the Yorkshire Arras culture, where two basic types are found: the relatively plain version with a 'tongue-in-glove' fastening and the more elaborate knobbed and ribbed type with a thick and often heavy body formed into adjacent bosses or ribs (Fig. 10:15). The plain types occur once at Cowlam and four times at Arras, both Yorkshire graves. The only other examples to be found are the pair of bracelets with circular bezels from Coygan Camp, Carm, but here the fastening is simple and not specially tongued. The knobbed and ribbed types are rather more widely spread.[1] It is difficult to be certain how many of these bracelets are direct imports and how many are locally made, but most of the specimens can be paralleled among La Tène I and early La Tène II contexts in eastern France and Switzerland, whence it is likely they were derived.

Trading contact between the west of Britain and the Atlantic coasts of Gaul and Iberia is well attested both in the classical literature and in the archaeological record. The Roman poet Avienus, in his poem *Ora Maritima*, uses scraps of information taken from a very early account of the Atlantic seaways known as the Massaliote Periplus, which describes the journeyings of the Tartessians and the Carthaginians from southern Iberia to Brittany, Ireland and Britain (Albion) for purposes of trade. After Tartessos was conquered by the Carthaginians, in the early fifth century, the Greek city states which had previously been supplied with tin from Iberia began to look further afield for their vital supplies. One Greek merchant, Pitheas sailed to Brittany along the Atlantic route between 330 and 325 recording his experiences, which now survive only in the writings of later Roman authors such as Strabo. Nevertheless, sufficient appears in these secondary sources to show that the tin-producing areas of the south-west were in constant contact with the Iberian and Mediterranean world from the fifth century onwards, no doubt following upon trading traditions already established in ancient times.

Archaeologically, contacts along the Atlantic sea route are attested by three fibulae of Iberian type, two from an inhumation cemetery at Harlyn Bay, Cornwall (Fig. 10:16), and one from Mount Batten overlooking Plymouth Sound, Devon. Characteristically the brooches are provided with a knob-ended crosspiece for the pin to pivot on, a high bow and an upturned foot ornamented with a large disc head. In Spain the type is equivalent to La Tène I, suggesting arrival in Britain some time in the fourth century or a little later. A more dramatic example of Iberian

[1] Five knobbed and two ribbed types are known from eastern Yorkshire. Others are recorded from South Ferriby, Lincs, Mount Batten, Devon, Cold Kitchen Hill, Wilts, Hengistbury Head, Hants – all unstratified – and from the ditch of the hillfort of Llanmelin, Mon.

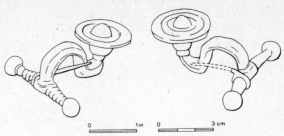

10:16 Fibulae of Iberian type from Harlyn Bay, Cornwall (source: H. O'N. Hencken, 1932)

contact is a small bronze statuette found on the shore at Aust close to the site of the Severn Bridge (Pl. 22b). The figure, a female, is provided with a crescentic headdress and has eyes enlivened by inset glass beads. Spanish parallels suggest a fourth or third century date but the Aust figurine is without association or context. Nevertheless, it is tempting to see it as an imported object brought in during the early La Tène period.

Thus the documentary and archaeological evidence together emphasise the continuance of well-established patterns of trade along the Atlantic sea routes from the fifth to the second century. It may have been by these means that some, at least, of the large number of early Greek coins arrived in Britain. The distribution pattern now extends across much of southern and eastern Britain, but rarely have the coins come from undoubted Iron Age contexts (Laing, 1968). While it remains a possibility that some of them may have come in during the Roman period or as later collectors' items, many must have arrived during the pre-Roman period in the wake of Atlantic trade. Only one, a coin of Ptolemy V (204–181 BC) from Winchester, has so far been found stratified in an Iron Age level (Cunliffe, 1964, 75).

It was possibly by the Atlantic route that the remarkable hanging bowl found in a stone cist at Cerrig-y-Drudion, Denbigh, was brought into the country (Fig. 10:17). The vessel is hemispherical in shape, with a horizontal flange to which were attached four chains for suspension. It was clearly meant to be viewed from below, since the under surfaces of the flange and the bowl are decorated with an elaborate scheme of incised palmettes and acanthus half-palmettes

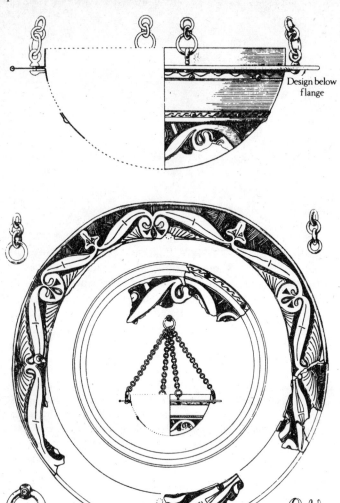

10:17 / The Cerrig-y-Drudion hanging bowl from Denbigh (source: reproduced from Smith, 1926)

thrown into prominence by a cross-hatched 'basketry' background. The style of decoration has much in common with the Celtic art styles of western France, whence it may have been derived some time in the fourth century. This piece, at present the oldest example of Celtic art in Britain, must lie at the beginning of a series of exotic imports which provided much of the inspiration for the British craftsmen whose schools were soon to develop to serve the aristocratic market.

TRADE IN THE FIRST CENTURY BC AND EARLY FIRST CENTURY AD

Trading contacts between Britain and the adjacent continent seem to have intensified after about 100 BC. In the south, one of the principal points of entry was the port of Hengistbury Head in Hampshire, with a subsidiary centre probably at Mount Batten near Plymouth, Devon. Strabo and Caesar expressly refer to cross-Channel trade controlled by the Armorican tribe called the

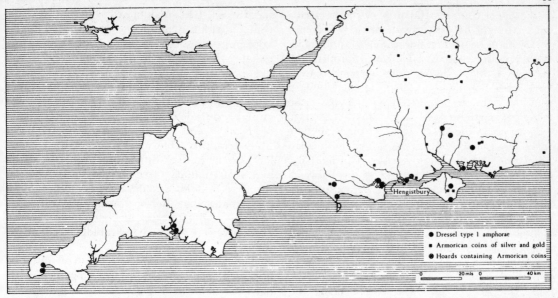

10:18　Map of pre-Roman imports of amphorae and Armorican coins into southern Britain via the Atlantic seaways (sources: D. F. Allen 1961a and 1962; Peacock, 1971)

Veneti, with whom some of the British communities maintained close diplomatic relations. The coin evidence, however, tends to emphasise the importance of other Armorican tribes, if the distribution of their coins in Britain can be interpreted in this way (Fig. 10:18). Venetic issues are rare, but gold coins of the Namnetes, the southern neighbours of the Veneti, turn up at Hengistbury and further inland near Swindon, while base silver issues of the Coriosolites are frequently found along the south coast together with issues of the Baiocasses, Redones, Unelli and Osismii (Allen, 1961a, 119). This pattern implies lively cross-Channel contacts throughout the first half of the first century BC.

These contacts are further emphasised by the appearance at and around Hengistbury Head of typical Armorican and Norman pottery, in particular the characteristic graphite-coated vessels and the elegant wheel-made cordoned vessels referred to in this country as Hengistbury class B ware. In Britain the distribution of these exotic fabrics clusters closely around Hengistbury Head. Trade through the port is also demonstrated by the appearance here of the rare type of wine amphora of Dressel's type 1A, which was used as a container for importing Italian wine. Apart from a number found at Hengistbury Head and isolated examples from Green Island (Poole harbour), Dorset, and from Ventnor, Isle of Wight, the type is otherwise unknown in Britain, and indeed is not recorded in Brittany. The implication would seem to be that shiploads of Italian wine were being brought direct to southern Britain along the Atlantic sea routes, bypassing the Venetic middlemen. One load at least foundered off Belle-Île, Morbihan, where the wreck complete with cargo still lies (Peacock, 1971).

The Roman conquest of Gaul in the middle of the first century BC, and in particular the savage reprisals which Caesar wrought against the Veneti and other maritime tribes, seem to have brought the cross-Channel trade to an end. At Hengistbury Head and neighbouring Dorset sites, a few examples of the later Dressel 1B amphorae are found, but these were probably coming into use in the decade or two before Caesar's campaigns and need not imply that trade continued after the mid fifties. All the evidence at present available suggests that after Caesar's raids, the south and south-west were without direct commercial outlets to the neighbouring Roman world.

In the last hundred years before the Claudian conquest, the Belgic areas of south-eastern Britain seem to have developed a lively trade with Roman Gaul. Throughout the second half of the first century BC, Italian wine was imported in large quantities (as the widespread occurrence of Dressel type 1B amphorae shows), and along with the wine came the tableware appropriate to its consumption. Bronze jugs (oenochoe) and bronze patellae, found in the burials at Aylesford and Welwyn, were imported from the Ornavasso region of northern Italy some time between 50 and 10 BC, while silver cups of Augustan date were brought in only to be buried with dead chieftains at Welwyn and Welwyn Garden City. Bronze bowls and wine-strainers, probably of Gaulish or Italian manufacture, were also introduced. In return, an impressive range of British produce was exported to the Roman market, notably the 'corn, cattle, gold, silver, hides, slaves and clever hunting-dogs' listed by Strabo.

From about 10 BC until the conquest of AD 43 the volume of trade seems to have increased. Fine Gallo-Belgic tablewares were being imported in quantity, together with smaller consignments of Arretine vessels made in northern Italy: later samian ware from southern Gaul, reached Britain. A limited number of glass vessels also made an appearance at this time. Wine too continued to be imported in bulk, as well as increasing quantities of fish sauce and olive oil from the Spanish province of Baetica, the two delicacies arriving in characteristic amphorae (Peacock, 1971). In addition to food, wine and tableware, other luxury goods appeared, like the set of glass gaming pieces from the burial at Welwyn Garden City and the small medallion of the Emperor Augustus found in the tumulus burial at Lexden – the latter surely a diplomatic gift of some kind. In fact, in the few generations before the conquest, the wealthy members of south-eastern British society must have been able to enjoy much the same range of Roman consumer luxuries as their distant relations now living across the Channel in Roman Gaul.

SUMMARY OF CONTINENTAL CONTACTS
FROM THE SEVENTH CENTURY BC TO THE
FIRST CENTURY AD

Standing back from the great mass of evidence briefly surveyed in the foregoing pages, it is possible to make a number of broad generalisations. From the middle of the eighth century until the middle of the fourth it would seem that the British Isles maintained vigorous trading contacts with the continent, demonstrated by the appearance in these islands of a large number of metal types ranging from personal ornaments like pins and bracelets to swords and horse-harness fittings. Much of this exotic material is of central and north European origin, but the old-established trade routes along the Atlantic coasts of France and Iberia (and ultimately the Mediterranean) continued to be used, particularly by the traders distributing bronze weapons and tools manufactured in the local Atlantic Bronze Age styles. Imported types did not, however, materially alter the traditional range of weapon- and tool-types although many of the new ideas were adopted and rapidly modified by the British craftsmen.

The appearance in the seventh century of imported Hallstatt C swords together with harness- and cart-fittings might be thought to imply an incursion of a mobile, horse-riding aristocracy from continental Europe. No positive trace of a large-scale folk movement into Britain survives, and the virtual absence of the characteristic Hallstatt burial rite in Britain argues that no such movement took place except perhaps in north-eastern Scotland, where techniques of hill-fort building and a dense scatter of foreign metal types might be thought to indicate an actual movement of people. The general picture to emerge is therefore of a broadly parallel development between Britain and the continent, the two areas being in a close trading relationship with each other, encouraging a free flow of ideas while indigenous traditions remained dominant.

Free interchange with the continent was maintained throughout the fifth and fourth centuries, allowing the importation of luxury objects such as daggers and swords, by means of which elements of the contemporary continental art styles first appeared in Britain. Along with the more expensive types came a scattering of trinkets including fibulae, bracelets and occasionally rings. Throughout this period the Atlantic trade routes to and from south-western Britain were maintained, the principal export being Cornish tin for the Mediterranean world. Occasional references to the tin trade in classical literature suggest that the system was well established and flourishing. No doubt equally complex trading patterns linked the south-east of the country to adjacent parts of the continent.

Some time just before 400 BC a group of pastoralists appear to have migrated from France to eastern Yorkshire, establishing a community which maintained its identity until, and even after, the Roman invasion. Apart from this one instance, there is no evidence to support the idea of a widespread invasion.

The material culture and settlement pattern of the third and second centuries suggest that continental contact decreased during this period, allowing the British communities to assume an intensely regional aspect reflecting little of the European developments. Contact was re-opened by settlers arriving from the Belgic areas of northern Gaul towards the end of the second century. From this time until the Caesarian campaigns in the fifties, south-western Britain shows signs of intensive trade with the Armorican peninsular and beyond. But after Caesar's conquest of Gaul this trade ceased, to be replaced by even more intensive contacts between the Roman world and the pro-Roman tribes of eastern Britain, which were maintained until the conquest of AD 43.

The Settlement Pattern and Economy of the South and East

When Aulus Plautius founded the Fosse frontier in the years AD 44–7, he was simply emphasising a geographical truth: Britain could be divided into two parts about a line drawn along the Jurassic ridge from Lincoln to Lyme Bay. To the south and east lay a densely settled region depending to a large extent on the production of grain; to the north and west settlement was sparse and there was greater reliance on pastoral activity. To the Roman military mind the south-east was clearly the part to become a province, for grain was an immensely valuable commodity and arable farmers, because of their dependence upon the seasons, were sedentary and thus easier to control. Admittedly, Plautius was seeing Iron Age Britain at its most developed stage after a hundred and fifty years or more of close contact with the continent, but this basic economic division held good for the earlier period and played a considerable part in influencing the density and the distribution of settlements.

Settlements are so closely bound up with the nature of food-production and the food-producing capacity of the soil that it is impossible to divorce the two aspects completely. In the early part of this chapter, the emphasis will be upon the settlements themselves from a structural chronological and social point of view; their significance in terms of the economy will be considered towards the end of the chapter. Similarly, it is necessary here to make a somewhat arbitrary distinction between settlements and hillforts, whereas in fact there is a degree of overlap between them. Hillforts, however, whatever their origins, are distinguished by the strength of their defences and by the size of the social unit responsible for them. These matters will be considered again later.

THE SETTLEMENTS (Fig. 11:1)

The ridge of Jurassic limestone which runs diagonally across Britain from the Humber to the vicinity of Exeter provides a convenient western limit for the densely settled region of the south-east. Geographically the land is varied, but the lighter soils of the limestone area, the chalk uplands and the river gravels were particularly conducive to Iron Age agricultural techniques, and were accordingly more often selected for settlement in preference to the less hospitable sands and the more densely wooded clay areas. It is on the chalklands of Wessex and the Sussex Downs that most of the excavated sites lie.

The characteristics of the settlements belonging to the thirteenth to sixth centuries have already been referred to in some detail above (pp. 11–17). Normally the inhabited area was enclosed by a bank in which timbers of a palisade or a thickset hedge were based (although traces do not always survive), and each enclosure was provided with a gate of simple construction. Within the enclosed area, which averaged 1–2 acres (0.4–0.8 hectares) was a simple circular hut, or sometimes more than one, arranged so as to leave sufficient space around for the more domestic activities of the farm to be carried out. Sometimes, as at New Barn Down, Sussex, the total settlement consisted of only two enclosures, but at Plumpton Plain A, Sussex, there were found to be at least three broadly contemporary huts arranged along a trackway, while at Itford Hill, Sussex, seven or eight conjoined enclosures were found with at least three more isolated huts scattered further away. Evidently, while some settlements were individual farmsteads, others may have taken on the aspect of hamlets or even small villages.

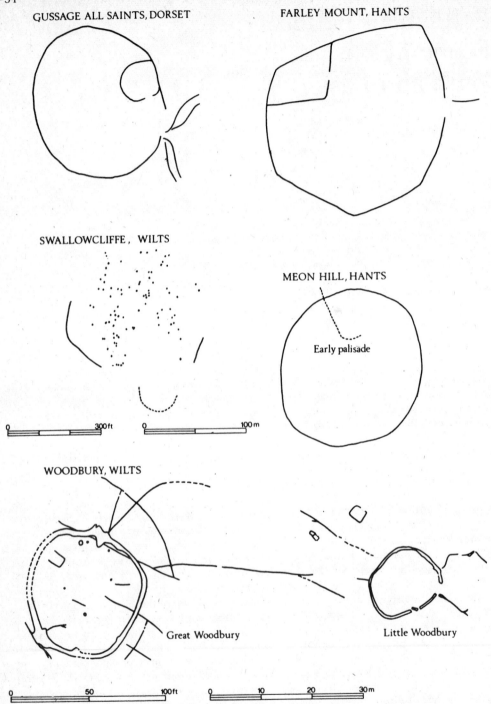

GUSSAGE ALL SAINTS, DORSET

FARLEY MOUNT, HANTS

SWALLOWCLIFFE, WILTS

MEON HILL, HANTS

Early palisade

WOODBURY, WILTS

Great Woodbury

Little Woodbury

11:1   Plans of Wessex settlements (sources: *Gussage All Saints and Farley Mount*, Bowen & Fowler, 1966; *Swallowcliffe*, Clay, 1925; *Meon Hill*, Liddell, 1933; *Woodbury*, Bersu, 1940)

The settlement at Shearplace Hill, Dorset, which belongs to the late second millennium, was enclosed by a substantial and well-cut ditch backed by a bank with no signs of a palisade but possibly capped by a thorn hedge. Ditches are also present at Boscombe Down East, Wilts, and various sites on the Marlborough Downs; but at the Sussex sites, most of which are early first millennium in date, ditches (if they occur at all) are insignificant features, the emphasis being placed more upon the palisade embedded in a bank. This may, of course, be a regional peculiarity rather than a chronological development, but the universal emphasis on palisades from the seventh century until the fourth or third century suggests that the period *c.* 1000–800 saw a change of fashion, the fenced enclosures gaining favour over enclosing ditches. The available evidence, such as it is, may therefore point to the gradual indigenous development of the palisade idea.

PALISADED ENCLOSURES

Palisaded enclosures containing settlements of various sizes are a common feature in eastern Scotland (pp. 206–9), but a widespread, if sporadic, occurrence over the rest of Britain is sufficient to show that enclosures of this kind were a normal element in the mid-first millennium settlement pattern. The most extensively excavated of the southern British palisaded settlements is Little Woodbury, Wilts, where two phases in the continuous occupation of the site can tentatively be recognised (Fig. 11:2). In the first phase the farm was enclosed by a palisade traced only on the east side, where a four-post gate – the principal entry to the compound – was uncovered. Within lay a single large circular hut 45 ft (13·7 m) in diameter, with its entrance porch aligned exactly upon the gate.

The extent of the palisaded enclosure is unknown, but the ditched enclosure which replaced it defended about 4 acres (1·6 hectares), which may well approximate to the area of the original. Within the enclosure many domestic activities have left their mark. Behind the house lay a large irregular working hollow where grain-parching and cooking were probably carried out. Seed corn was stored in rectangular four-post granaries, usually placed around the periphery of the enclosure, while hay, and possibly seed corn in the ear, was hung up on two-post racks to dry. At a later stage, in the third or second century, grain storage in large underground silos became

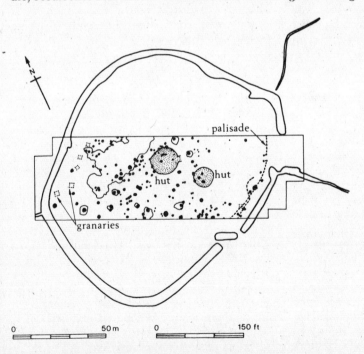

widespread; these pits, later used for rubbish disposal, were found in large numbers. A high proportion of those from Little Woodbury relate to the later phase of the site's occupation. In addition, one must suppose that other aspects of the day-to-day routine were carried out within the enclosure – processes such as the grinding of corn, spinning, weaving, leather-working, basketry, etc., and on occasions animals in need of special attention may have been temporarily tethered inside.

The date of the early phase occupation cannot be given with precision, but the earliest assemblage of pottery belonged to the All Cannings Cross - Meon Hill style, the maximum use of which centres on the fourth and third centuries. A few scraps of Kimmeridge–Caburn wares might suggest a beginning within the fifth century or a little earlier, but these fragments may be nothing more than the survival of archaic types.

The second Wiltshire site to have begun life as a palisaded enclosure is Swallowcliffe, where the initial occupation is approximately contemporary with that of Little Woodbury. The excavation, however, was carried out before the development of modern techniques and apart from pits little else of structural significance was found. In Hampshire the excavations at Meon Hill near Stockbridge (Fig. 11:1) provided further evidence of a palisaded settlement, again related to the All Cannings–Meon Hill style of pottery. As at Little Woodbury, the old palisaded enclosure was replaced by a bank and a ditch of hillfort proportions. A further example of just such a replacement occurred at the Caburn, Sussex, in the phase pre-dating the hillfort. Here little of the early plan can now be recovered, but a length of palisade trench outside the entrance to the later fort and two huts just inside, together with several pits, represent the initial phase producing pottery of the Kimmeridge–Caburn style of sixth or fifth century date.

Excavations at other hillforts have occasionally suggested the pre-existence of palisaded settlements. Blewburton Hill, Berks, Winklebury, Hants, and Wilbury, Herts, have all produced some evidence of early palisades but work has never been on a sufficient scale to show whether or not the later defences exactly followed the lines of the earlier enclosures. If so, it would have to be supposed that fenced enclosures exceeding 15

acres (6·1 hectares) in extent were being built in the middle of the first millennium.

Two other sites deserve mention: at Hollingbury and Park Brow, both in Sussex, trenches belonging to palisaded enclosures of rectangular plan have been partly excavated. Three sides of the Park Brow enclosure – some 100–120 ft (30–37 m) – were examined, while at Hollingbury only one side 150 ft (46 m) long with a central entrance came to light. Since the plans are therefore incomplete and the enclosed areas have not been extensively excavated, speculation as to function is difficult, but these may have been specialised structures, perhaps even religious enclosures, and not settlement sites at all.

Sufficient has been said to show that in the period from the sixth to the third century settlements in southern Britain were frequently surrounded by fences bedded in palisade trenches. Since the emphasis of the earlier first millennium enclosures was also upon a vertical timber barrier rather than ditches or banks, it is not unreasonable to suppose that the later palisades were an indigenous development. Details of the settlements themselves are few, but most of those recorded enclosed individual farms and most of the farms of the period may well have been palisaded. Evidently, some rather more substantial areas, which later became hillforts, were also enclosed in this way.

EARTHWORK-ENCLOSED SETTLEMENTS

At Little Woodbury, Meon Hill and the Caburn, palisades were replaced by ditched enclosures during the time when saucepan pots were in use, that is, the third to first centuries on current reckoning. The class of earthwork-enclosed settlements which they typify can usually be shown to belong to this later period.

Little Woodbury in its later phase can be taken as a type-site for the class (Pl. 7a). Excavation has shown that the palisade was replaced by a ditch some 11 ft wide by 7 ft deep (3·4 m by 2·1 m), which must once have been backed by a rampart of chalk dug from it. The ditch enclosed a roughly circular area some 4 acres (1·6 hectares) in extent, provided with a single wide entrance, apparently without a gate, from which two linear ditches radiated out like antennae. Closely similar enclosures are known at a large number of sites (Fig. 11:1). In all cases where excavation has been undertaken, the enclosures have proved to belong to the time when saucepan pots were in use, and all show signs of intensive occupation comparable to Little Woodbury, though in few other cases have the interiors been excavated on a sufficient scale to enable houses to be discovered. Areas range from about 1·5 acres (0·6 hectares) at Mancombe Down, Wilts, to about 6 acres (2·4 hectares) at Farley Mount, Hants (Pl. 8) a range which may well reflect the status of the individual owner and the size of his holding. This type of settlement is widespread not only on the chalkland of Wessex but over much of southern Britain.

A somewhat smaller ditched enclosure found at Draughton, Northants (Fig. 11:3), was rather more closely packed with houses than the Wood- bury type. Total excavation has demonstrated the existence of three huts ranging from 34 to 19 ft (10·4 to 5·8 m) in diameter, fitted tightly in- to a circular enclosure only 100 ft (30 m) across, leaving very little room for the range of activities which went on in the southern farms. Another settlement of the same type but belonging to the first century AD was examined at Colsterworth, Lincs (Fig. 11:4). It consisted of a ditched en- closure measuring 240 by 210 ft (73 by 64 m) across, containing two clusters of circular huts of varying dates, the largest being some 44 ft (13·4 m) in diameter. Storage pits, working

hollows and timber granaries were absent, sug- gesting that these settlements reflect a different economic substructure from the farms of the chalklands and gravels.

Few of the enclosed settlements of the river gravels have been adequately excavated, but in the Welland valley at Tallington (site 37) a rectangular ditched enclosure 215 ft by 160 ft (65·5 m by 48·8 m) lying alongside a trackway has been almost totally excavated, revealing most of the aspects of the Little Woodbury economy with the exception of the house (quarried away) and grain storage pits, which would have been impossible to construct in the wet gravelly soil: grain must therefore have been stored in above-ground containers. Rectangu- larity is not a common feature among the settle- ments of the period but it recurs sporadically, for example on Down Barn West (Winterbourne Gunner), Wilts, where there is an enclosure very similar to the Tallington site in size and in the placing of the gate at one corner. Down Barn West has not been excavated on any scale but at least one pit was found inside and the possibility of others cannot be ruled out. Whether or not the site was permanently occupied, however, is a problem which only large-scale excavation can answer.

Why the change-over from palisades to banks and ditches took place some time in the third or

DRAUGHTON, NORTHANTS   WEST HARLING, NORFOLK

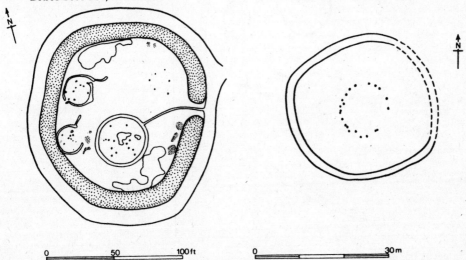

11:3 Plans of settlement sites at Draughton and West Harling (sources: *Draughton*, Grimes, 1961; *West Harling*, Clark & Fell, 1953)

second century is impossible to say. Maintenance time cannot have varied very much, and the defensive qualities of a bank and ditch of these proportions are only marginally better than those of a stout and well-maintained palisade. Since no major cultural break can be defined, and indeed continuity of settlement site is impressive, it must be concluded that the changes were the result of fashion and internal development in parallel with the changes in hillfort architecture, which will be considered later.

'Banjo' enclosures (Fig. 11:5)

A second type of earthwork-enclosed site, usually about 0·5–1 acre (0·2–0·4 hectares) in extent, occurs in Wessex and sporadically elsewhere

(Perry, 1966 and 1970). Characteristically these sites are provided with a single entrance, to which runs a roadway defined on either side by V-shaped ditches 3 or 4 ft (c. 1 m) deep. Frequently the roadway joins a linear ditch at right angles at a distance of between 150 ft and 300 ft (45 m and 90 m) from the enclosure. At Blagdon Copse, Hants, a limited excavation undertaken at the junction of the road ditches and the linear ditch showed that both had been planned in relation to each other and were therefore broadly contemporary.

The planning and construction of the 'banjo' enclosures and the so-called 'spectacle' sites, which are essentially two conjoined banjo enclosures, strongly imply that they were designed principally to aid the collection, selection and

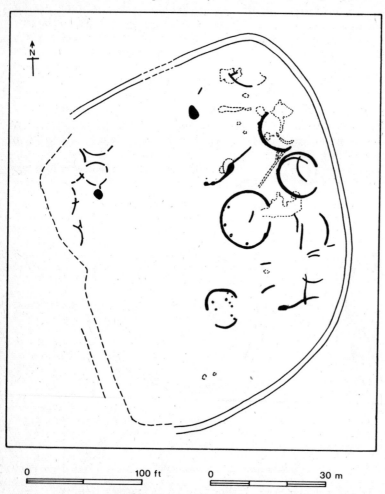

11:4   Plan of Colsterworth, Lincs (source: Grimes, 1961)

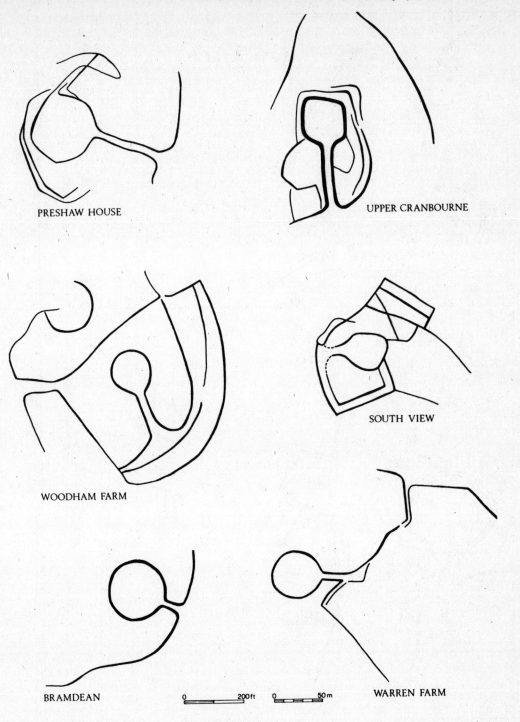

PRESHAW HOUSE

UPPER CRANBOURNE

WOODHAM FARM

SOUTH VIEW

BRAMDEAN

WARREN FARM

0   200ft   0   50m

11:5   'Banjo' enclosures in Hampshire, drawn from air photographs (source: Perry 1966, 1970)

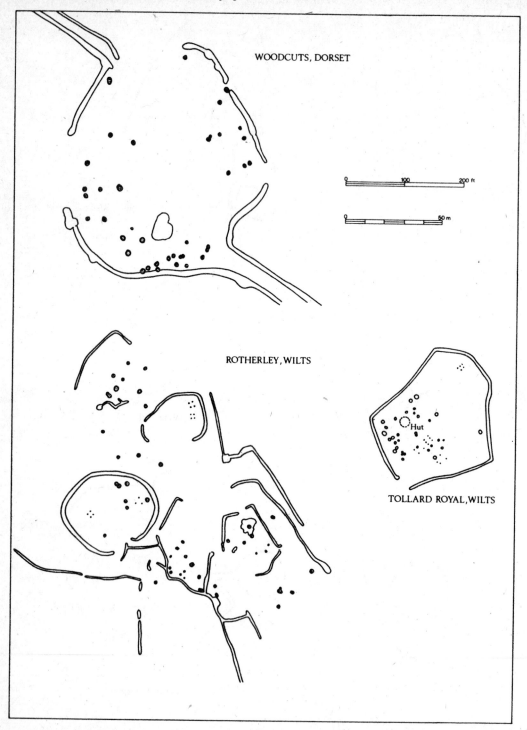

11:6   Settlements on Cranbourne Chase (sources: *Rotherley Down and Woodcuts*, Pitt-Rivers, 1887; *Tollard Royal*, Wainwright, 1968)

temporary corralling of cattle. But in the single example in which the interior has been sampled by excavation – Bramdean, Hants – evidence of occupation has been discovered, raising the question of whether they may have served as habitation sites. The evidence is not yet sufficient to be conclusive and until the interior of one of the banjos has been totally stripped, the question must remain open.

At both Blagdon Copse and Bramdean the primary phase of construction is associated with saucepan pots of the second or first century BC, implying that some at least of the banjos are late in date. It is possible that they developed out of the ideas inherent in the 'antennae' ditches associated with the entrances of some of the Little Woodbury type of enclosures.

DITCHED ENCLOSURES OF THE FIRST CENTURY BC AND FIRST CENTURY AD

The tradition of surrounding farmsteads with a simple enclosing ditch was maintained in some areas, notably Dorset, into the first century AD. The classic example of such a settlement is Tollard Royal on Cranbourne Chase, Wilts (Pl. 7b), where total excavation has exposed the complete ground plan of the farm (Fig. 11:6), consisting of a kite-shaped ditched enclosure of about an acre (0·4 hectares) in extent, provided with a single entrance. Inside were found a single hut, thirty-five storage pits of varying capacity and three or four granaries. One of the most impressive features of the plan is the large open area within the enclosure, where presumably flocks and herds could have been temporarily corralled. The basic plan, clearly a direct continuation of the traditional Little Woodbury type, is further reflected in the neighbouring settlements of Rotherley and Woodcuts, which continued in use little changed well into the Roman period.

A rather more extensive type of settlement, found sporadically in the south, is represented by the Wessex examples of Worthy Down, Hants, Owslebury, Hants, and Casterley Camp, Wilts (Fig. 11:7). All three sites are characterised by a complex series of ditches which define enclosures of varying sizes and shapes, some used for habitation, some (e.g. at Owslebury) for burial, others presumably for livestock. The plan of Casterley Camp is particularly informative for here it is possible to recognise the careful placing of entrances so as to allow maximum inter-use of enclosures. Such an arrangement would have been of value at those times during the year when flocks and herds needed to be brought together and sorted for culling, castrating or redistribution. The development of these complex ditched enclosures as an adjunct to settlements suggests the increased importance of stock-rearing – a matter which will be returned to again later (pp. 174–9).

Settlements of a similar kind can be traced by aerial photography on the gravel river terraces of the Midlands but few have been extensively examined except for Langford Downs, Oxon (Fig. 11:8). Further excavation in these areas will probably show that complex ditched enclosures are a common type of settlement in the late pre-Roman period.

HOUSES (Fig. 11:9)

Houses of the late second and early first millennia are now well known, principally from the excavation of the Sussex settlements. Characteristically they are simple circular structures averaging 20 ft (6 m) or so in diameter, constructed of a series of upright timbers placed somewhat irregularly in a circular or oval setting; central supports were seldom employed and indeed were not necessary for structures of such small span. Where huts have been terraced slightly into a sloping hillside, it is evident that the upright timbers did not form the outer wall of the hut but were simply supports for the sloping rafters, the lower ends of which probably rested on the outer edge of the terrace, which in some cases was up to 5 ft (1·5 m) away from the ring of vertical timbers. Thus two areas were created: a central area with a high roof-line where the principal activities of the house were carried out, and a surrounding area between the posts and the wall of the hut which could have served as storage or sleeping space. Approximate calculations for the small hut N from Itford Hill, Sussex, show that 150 ft² (14 m²) were available for 'living' and 200 ft² (19 m²) for sleeping and storage. Few of the early huts show any great refinement in structure but substantial door-posts and short porches are known.

CASTERLEY CAMP, WILTS

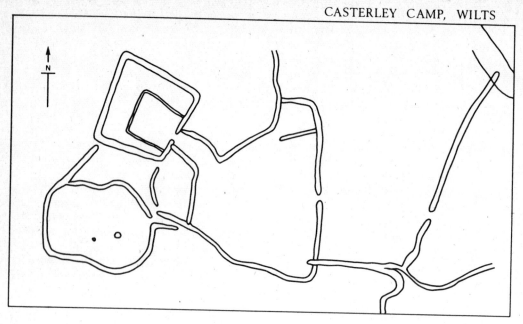

WORTHY DOWN,   HANTS

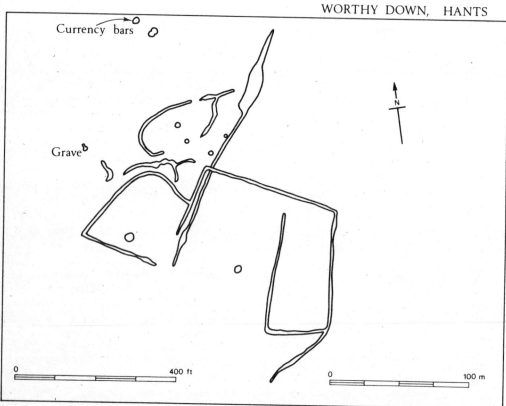

11:7.   Ditched enclosures of the first century BC to the first century AD (sources: *Casterley Camp*, Cunnington & Cunnington, 1913; *Worthy Down*, Dunning, Hooley & Tildesley, 1929)

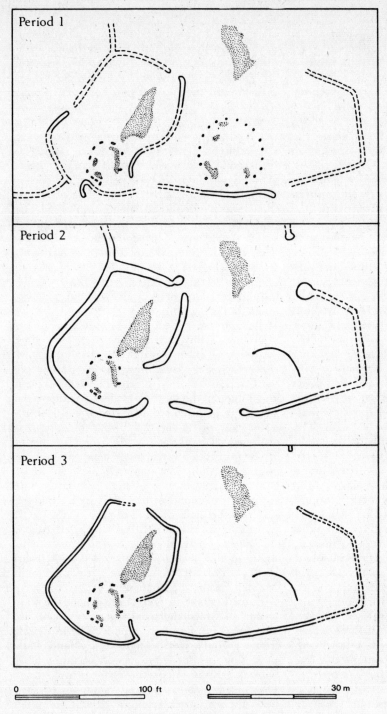

Period 1

Period 2

Period 3

0 ⟼ 100 ft   0 ⟼ 30 m

11:8   The development of the settlement at Langford Downs, Oxon (source: A. Williams, 1947)

This basic house type continued in use throughout the Iron Age. The sequence at Eldon's Seat (Encombe), Dorset, spanning the period from the seventh to the fifth century, shows a gradual increase in diameter from 18–20 ft (6 m) up to 29 ft (9 m) for the latest house. There was also a trend towards a more regular spacing of timbers and one hut was provided with an entrance porch. The latest house was very regularly constructed, and the spacing of the vertical posts in relation to the edge of its platform implies that they served not only as rafter supports but also as the wall timbers. Simple houses of this kind continued into the second or first century BC, for example at Little Woodbury, house 2, which can be shown to belong to the saucepan pot period.

In parallel to the tradition of simple ring-post houses, more complex structures developed. House 1 at Little Woodbury, Wilts, offers one of the clearest examples (Fig. 11:9). Here two concentric circles of posts were erected, the inner circle being more massive and taking most of the weight of the roof timbers, the outer circle taking the slighter posts. The house is further complicated by the central setting of four timbers which served to support the centre of the roof and probably, at the same time, stood above the roof-level to create a louvre for smoke to escape. The Little Woodbury plan is essentially only a modification of the early houses mentioned above, in which the total enclosed area was divided into a central region and peripheral space. Little Woodbury shows the additional modification of a substantial porch or entrance passage 15 ft (4·6 m) long. Provided with an inner and outer door, it would have created a trap to prevent cold air from sweeping in.[1] The overall diameter of the house, 46 ft (14 m), compares with two other large houses of the same general type, one from Cow Down (Longbridge Deverill), Wilts, and the other from Pimperne Down, Dorset, both 50 ft (15 m) in diameter. All three houses belong to the period from the sixth to the fourth century; at present no house of comparable size or complexity has been found in the latter part of the Iron age.

A structure of rather different type was found at West Harling, Norfolk. In plan it consisted of a circular ditch broken by two wide causeways, with an internal bank with corresponding openings. Within lay a mass of post-holes which probably belonged to a house-like structure. One interpretation suggests that the roofed area was annular about a central open yard (R. R. Clarke, 1960, 95), but it would be simpler to reconstruct it as a conventional circular house standing within a ditched enclosure, the ends of the rafters resting on the bank. The possibility that it was a religious building is unlikely in view of the presence of hearths and drainage gullies, which would argue for domestic use. Another West Harling house was of a more conventional structure (Fig. 11:3): a circular setting of posts about 38 ft (11·5 m) in diameter. This too was built in the centre of a circular ditched enclosure about 110 ft (33·5 m) across.

Penannular or completely circular ditches surrounding huts are known on several sites, including Overton Down, Wilts, Sandown Park (Esher), Surrey, Heathrow, Middx, Camerton, Somerset, and Barley, Herts. The type, though uncommon in the south, is evidently widespread. The gully or ditch would serve to collect rainwater running off the roof, either to conserve it or prevent it from flooding the house in times of heavy rain. Such an arrangement would have been a necessity on impermeable soils as at Draughton, Northants, where a circular enclosing gully was found to be linked by a drainage gutter to the main ditch of the enclosure.

In the western part of the region, particularly in Dorset where stone was readily available, many of the houses were provided with dwarf walls of dry-stone work. In the case of one hut at Maiden Castle, the stone outer wall would have been used to bed the ends of the rafters, the main weight of which must have been taken on the concentric setting of large posts. The hut circle from Chalbury, Dorset, on the other hand, while possessing an outer dry-stone wall, was apparently without central timbers, but while it could easily have been spanned by rafters supported only upon the wall itself, verticals without post holes may once have existed. Thus there is little structural difference between the huts built wholly of timber and those in which some dry-stone work has been incorporated.

---

[1] It has been suggested (Tratman, 1970) that the ground plan of the main house at Little Woodbury was produced in more than one phase, the internal setting of four posts and the entrance passage representing rectangular structures differing in date from the circular building. On balance, the original interpretation of the excavator, given above, seems preferable.

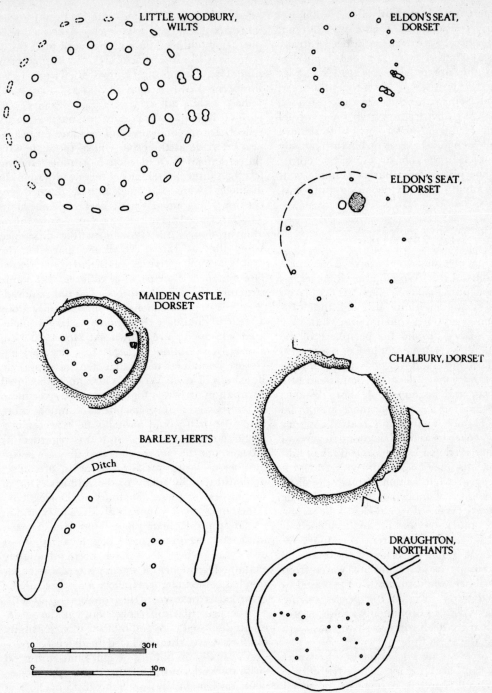

11:9 Plans of southern British houses (sources: *Little Woodbury*, Bersu, 1940; *Maiden Castle*, Wheeler, 1943; *Eldon's Seat*, Cunliffe, 1968b; *Chalbury*, Whitley, 1943; *Barley*, Cra'ster, 1961; *Draughton*, Grimes, 1961)

The internal arrangements of the individual houses vary considerably. Frequently, but not invariably, there were hearths either centrally placed, as at Maiden Castle, or more usually to one side, as they are in the houses at Eldon's Seat and West Overton Down; less frequently bread ovens occur. Some of the huts were also provided with drainage gullies leading from the centre of the hut out of the entrance, possibly to remove rainwater which may have seeped in through any central gap left in the roof structure. Sometimes small storage pits or even buried ceramic containers are found, in which food and liquids may have been stored.

SETTLEMENT SIZE AND SITING

Many of the sites described above were single farming units. Little Woodbury, whatever its social implications, had only one centrally placed hut in use at any one time (although the possibility remains that other contemporary huts may have been placed around the periphery of the enclosure). With its fine early house, 4 acre (1·6 hectare) farmyard and massive grain storing capacity, it must have been the homestead of a wealthy man and his family. A short distance from the excavated site lay a far more substantial ditched enclosure, known as Great Woodbury (Fig. 11:1), covering an area of about 10 acres (4 hectares) and enclosed by a massive ditch of hillfort proportions some 20 ft (6 m) wide and 12 ft (3·6 m) deep. A single section through the ditch revealed pottery of saucepan pot type in the primary silting. While it would clearly be wrong to base too much on this limited evidence, it could well be argued that Great Woodbury replaced Little Woodbury. Certainly, the relatively small percentage of saucepan pot wares from Little Woodbury would suggest that it ceased to be occupied fairly early in the period during which these types were commonly in use; moreover, it is hardly likely that the two sites were occupied at the same time.

By virtue of its non-defensive siting, Great Woodbury can hardly be regarded as a hillfort, but it may well represent a stage in the social development of the owning family, moving from the old site to the new when wealth had increased sufficiently to allow a new building programme to be undertaken. If these speculations are correct, there is no need to suppose that the actual size of the homestead community had increased; a larger area enclosed and a more massive ditch need be nothing more than status symbols. Massive enclosures for apparently single homesteads are known elsewhere, as at Pimperne Down, where the large house is retained within an 11·5 acre (4·7 hectare) enclosure. Thus size of enclosure does not necessarily reflect size of community. The same point can also be made at the other end of the scale with the settlement at Draughton, Northants. Here no less than three houses, one of them 33 ft (10 m) in diameter, were crammed into a ditched enclosure about an acre (0·4 hectares) in extent. The farm need have been no less significant or affluent than Little Woodbury, the difference being that at Little Woodbury space for the arable farming activities was included whereas at Draughton, by virtue of a different economic structure, extensive yard space was not required.

While the settlements of single-family units appear to dominate the landscape, larger nucleated settlements are known. At Hog Cliff Hill, Dorset, a rambling 26 acre (10·5 hectare) enclosure contained more than ten huts, and on Boscombe Down West, Wilts, an unenclosed occupation area was found to extend over more than 16 acres (6·5 hectares) – much more extensive than would normally be expected of a single farm. Both sites must be regarded as villages, but the fact remains that they are few in number. A larger social grouping is, of course, demonstrated by many of the hillforts. One of the earliest of these, Chalbury in Dorset, contained more than seventy individual huts, and in its latest pre-Roman phase Hod Hill, Dorset, must have been even more populous. In almost every case where forts have been adequately examined, evidence of intense internal occupation has come to light. Hillforts may therefore be regarded as the towns of the Iron Age (pp. 254–9).

The principal difference between the settlements discussed here and hillforts is one of siting. Hillforts were always placed in defensive positions, usually on hilltops or spur-ends with good visibility and control of the main approaches, while settlement sites were chosen to be close to the arable land. Even the massive ditch of Great Woodbury cannot disguise the fact that the site has little tactical significance. The close relationship between settlement and arable land is demonstrated on a number of sites, but the Farley

Mount enclosure in Hampshire is perhaps one of the more dramatic, showing acres of rectangular 'Celtic' fields spreading out regularly from the boundaries of the settlement. It is tempting here to think of both fields and settlement being laid out at the same time to colonise a piece of virgin downland.

It is difficult to generalise about the overall pattern of rural settlement, largely because adequate area surveys are practically unknown. On the South Downs, however, in the area of Chalton, Hants, a detailed field study has shown a remarkable density of occupation sites, many of them sited by choice on the shoulders of east-facing slopes, linked to each other and to their fields by a network of trackways. In an area of 2 square miles (5 km²) eleven settlements are known, some barely a quarter-mile (0·4 km) from their neighbours. Such a density is not universal even on the chalk, for in a comparable survey of the Marlborough Downs based on the parishes of West Overton and Fyfield, only three settlements were found in a block of 5 square miles (12·9 km²), the average distance between them being about a mile (1·6 km). Detailed figures for areas of river gravels are not yet available but in the upper Thames region, where extensive gravel digging, coupled with a series of archaeological excavations, has brought to light a number of sites, substantial settlements occur as close as 1–2 miles (1·6–3·2 km) from each other.

None of these figures can be regarded as totally reliable since discovery is a chance factor, however much the chances are increased by intensive field-work. Even when the settlement pattern is thoroughly known, there can be no assurance that all the sites were in use at the same time, nor is it possible to compare the sizes of individual settlements; even so, it is now tolerably clear that on favoured land like the chalk downs and the river gravels substantial farms were closely spaced. The pattern of settlement may not have been unlike that of west Wales today.

SUBSISTENCE ECONOMY

Over most of the inhabited parts of south-east Britain, grain-production formed the basis of the economy. Throughout the second millennium barley was the principal crop, in particular the naked variety (*Hordeum tetrasticum*), but late in

the second and early in the first millennium two changes became apparent: first, naked barley was replaced by the hulled variety (*Hordeum hexasticum*) so that by the mid-first millennium the percentage of the naked type had been reduced to less than a third, and second, wheat began to increase in popularity, rising to about 45 per cent of the total production during the Iron Age. It was not, however, the traditional emmer (*Triticum dicoccum*) that came back into common use but a newly introduced variety of wheat called spelt (*Triticum spelta*). Both spelt and hulled barley are species which can be sown in the autumn and will ripen a little in advance of spring-sown varieties. The advantages are obvious: some sowing can be carried out in the otherwise dull autumn season after main harvest, thus spreading the work load, while the harvest season will be extended, yielding a fresh supply of corn at just the time when the winter's stores would have been running low. The change of emphasis to spelt and hulled barley can therefore be seen as a refinement of some significance in the simple traditional arable techniques hitherto practised.

Other cereals were grown on a much smaller scale. Rye, another first millennium introduction, occurred sporadically in Wessex and oats of both the wild and cultivated varieties are recorded from various sites, but only in very small proportions. It was during the later part of the Iron Age that the Celtic bean (*Vicia faba*) appeared in the Somerset villages; exactly when it was introduced cannot yet be ascertained, but it is at present unknown in contexts pre-dating the second century and may therefore have been quite a late introduction. Finally, club wheat (*Triticum compactum*) and chess (*Bromus* sp.) occur consistently but in relatively small quantities.

Corn was probably cut with reaping hooks (Fig. 11:10) just below the ear when it was still not completely ripe, and carried back to the farmstead for drying on racks, which are represented archaeologically by pairs of post-holes to support vertical framing timbers. After being allowed to dry out naturally, the ears were parched (heated artificially), probably to loosen the grain from the husk to facilitate threshing. It is generally assumed that temporary ovens built of cob were constructed for the corn-drying process, but an alternative explanation is that drying may have been carried out on a larger scale on skins spread over pre-heated flint nodules. The indirect heat which the flints would have imparted would have been quite sufficient to dry the ears to the necessary degree, with the added advantage of keeping the grain away from the direct source of heat, thus cutting down risk of combustion. That accidents did happen, however, is shown by quantities of charred grain from various sites, including deposits from pits at Itford Hill, Sussex, Fifield Bavant, Wilts, Totternhoe, Beds, and Little Solisbury, Somerset. This type of process would explain the vast quantities of fire-crackled flints ('pot-boilers') which are found on most of the settlement sites, usually lying in thick layers mixed up with charcoal in the so-called 'irregular working hollows'. Indeed the working hollows may well be the sites where parching was carried out.

As soon as the ears were dried, they would in all probability have been threshed before storage,

but it is not inconceivable that some of the corn may have been stored in the ear. Such a deposit is claimed to have been found in the hillfort of Little Solisbury, but details are obscure. Two forms of storage were employed (Fig. 11:11): the bulk of the grain, probably about two-thirds or more of the crop, which would have formed the food supply for the community during the winter and the early spring, was placed in underground storage silos constructed in pits of beehive, barrel or cylindrical shape and usually averaging 6 ft (1·8 m) deep. Pits dug into the solid chalk were not necessarily lined. Although some form of wicker lining tends to cut down wastage through mould growth by keeping the grain away from the damp sides of the pit, the degree of caking together of the outer crust of grain would not have differed greatly between lined and unlined pits so long as an airtight seal of clay or marl was placed over the pit mouth. The effort involved in providing each of the grain storage pits with a

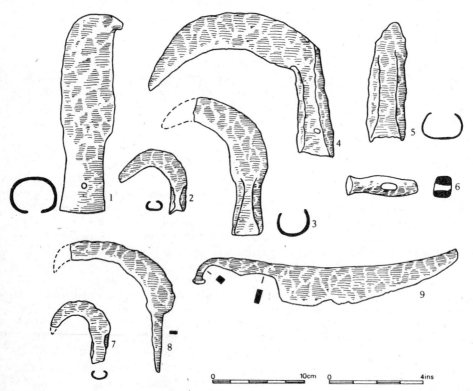

11:10   Iron tools. 1   bill-hook from the Caburn, Sussex; 2, 3, 4, 7, 8   reaping hooks from Barbury Castle, Wilts; 5   ploughshare from the Caburn, Sussex; 6   hammer from the Caburn, Sussex; 9   knife from Barbury Castle, Wilts (sources: *Barbury Castle*, MacGregor & Simpson, 1963; the *Caburn*, Curwen & Curwen, 1927)

Storage pits

Granaries

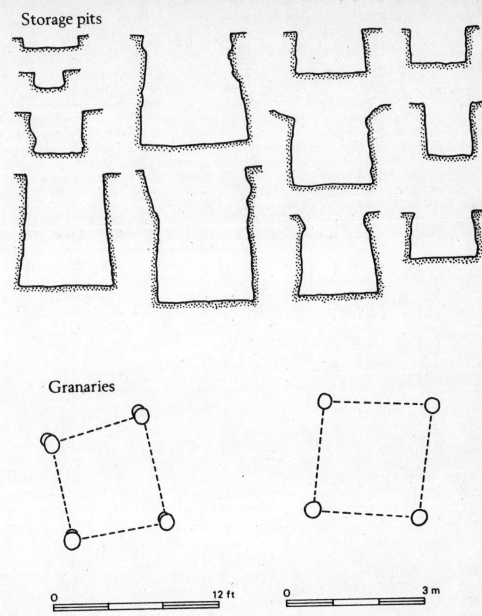

| 0 | | | 12 ft |
| 0 | | | 3 m |

11:11   Selection of storage pits and granaries from Little Woodbury, Wilts (source: Bersu, 1940)

wicker lining may well have been considered unnecessary – at least in the chalk areas, where the sides were firm and tolerably dry. Wicker linings have, however, been recorded at Dane's Camp, Worcs, Poxwell, Dorset, and Worlebury, Somerset, but there is nothing to show that these pits were used for storing grain rather than other commodities. Some pits were lined with dry-stone work, but these are restricted to areas where stone commonly occurs. On the Isle of Portland about seventy stone-lined pits of beehive shape were discovered, narrowed at the top so that they could be easily closed by a single slab. One of them contained a mass of carbonised grain.

Various types of flooring have also been recorded, ranging from stone and wood to clay and sand.

A variety of pit forms are known, no doubt reflecting an equally wide range of function in addition to grain storage. Some, lined with clay, may have served for water storage, being linked by gullies to the eaves-drips of roofs; some were perhaps vats for such processes as tanning; while others may have been used as larders where dried or smoked meat may have been stored.

The grain selected as seed corn for the following year – possibly as much as a third of the annual harvest – would have been subjected to a different treatment. After being dried naturally on racks and then threshed, the seed would have been placed in granaries raised above ground on four or, less often, six massive

posts (Fig. 11:11). All that survive archaeologically are the settings of holes, usually averaging 8–10 ft (2·4–3·0 m) apart, but one must suppose that the vertical framework took a raised floor and walls suitable for retaining the seed either stored loose or in the ear. A raised floor would have been the obvious way of keeping the grain away from the damp soil, while at the same time making it difficult for rodents to attack the supply. Granaries occur widely over most of south-east Britain. Frequently, as at Little Woodbury, they were built on the periphery of the settlement, often against the boundary to keep them as far removed as possible from the domestic activities of the settlement and the potential threat of fire. Not all of the four- or six-post buildings were necessarily granaries; regular

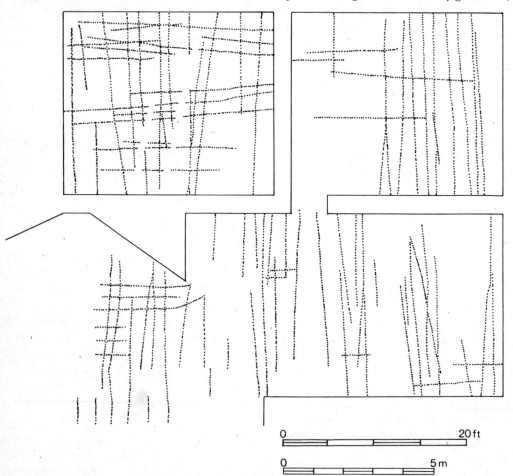

0 ———— 20 ft

0 ———— 5 m

11:12   Plan of plough ruts discovered beneath a lynchet on Overton Down, Wilts (source: P. J. Fowler, 1967)

arrangements of rectangular structures found inside some hillforts have more the appearance of houses (p. 256), while it has been suggested that some of the isolated examples may possibly have been platforms for the exposure of the dead (Ellison & Drewett, 1971). In settlements like Little Woodbury, however, explanations in terms of granaries or store buildings seem more reasonable.

Throughout the winter the underground silos would have been opened as required to feed the occupants but the granaries of seed corn remained sealed until spring sowing began about March. At this stage the roaming flocks and herds would have been driven off the fields to feed on the upland pastures, while the fields were manured with household refuse brought out from the farm and spread about the land.

If the fields had been heavily grazed or trampled by animals, ploughing may have been unnecessary. In most cases, however, ploughing was undertaken using the simple iron-shod crook or bow ard (without a mould-board to turn the sod), the effect of which would have been simply to scratch a furrow in the soil. The excavation of Celtic field surfaces is now bringing to light evidence of actual ploughing in the form of the bottoms of the individual furrows scored into the bedrock. At Overton Down, Wilts (Fig. 11:12), the remnants of furrows belonging to at least five ploughings have been examined. Although the pattern is necessarily incomplete, because the ard would not always bite deep enough to scratch the chalk, sufficient survives to show that the individual furrows were about a foot apart, and that in all probability the field was ploughed in two directions at right angles, to break up the soil sufficiently for sowing. Very approximate estimates for the work involved in each ploughing can be arrived at by considering an average-sized Celtic field about 70 yards (64 m) square, ploughed by an ard drawn by two oxen travelling at about 2 miles an hour. It would take between six and eight hours to complete the area: in other words, a field could be ploughed in a day. The Overton Down field is not necessarily of Iron Age date (it could belong to the Roman period) but there is little doubt that the practices recognised there are exactly comparable to the pre-Roman situation. Indeed, evidence is now accumulating from various parts of the country to show that this basic system of arable produc-

tion dates back to the second and third millennia BC, and probably remained little changed until the end of the Roman period.

In addition to using the ard for cultivation, hand-digging with a wooden spade was undertaken. At the second millennium site at Gwithian, Cornwall, individual spade-marks were found in the headland of the ploughed fields and at the sixth century site at Weston Wood (Albury), Surrey (Fig. 11:13), two small plots were recognised, measuring 23 by 28 ft (7·0 by 8·5 m), each composed of parallel furrows dug into the sand apparently with a spade. The close relationship between the cultivated areas and the houses of the settlement would suggest that they were garden plots comparable to those attached to the Cornish villages of the first century BC.

Iron Age fields, where they can be defined, are usually squarish in shape and bounded by lynchet banks created largely by the process of ploughing, which encouraged particles of soil to move down the slope to form a positive lynchet, at the lower edge of ploughing, leaving a negative lynchet at the upper edge. That the lynchets formed at all implies the continuous ploughing of defined areas over a period of many years. Little is yet known about the mechanism of primary land division, but fences, hedges, marking stones or posts, and gullies or setting-out banks were all used to define the original limits of the fields. After the first ploughing or two the land was probably cleared of large stones and flints, which would have been thrown to the edges of the fields thus adding to the permanence of the boundaries. As ploughing continued, lynchets increased in size until gradually the stage was reached when the uncultivated slopes of the banks themselves would have been extensive enough to be used as strips of pasture between arable plots. As a general rule, therefore, it may be said that as arable farming developed within a given area of hill slopes, the actual arable acreage must have decreased with the growth of lynchet slopes. If the thick soil of the lynchets was allowed to support the scrub and woodland which would tend to grow naturally, the areas of potential pannage and forage for pigs and cattle would have gradually increased.

The colonisation of wasteland was systematic in many areas. The fields around the Farley Mount settlement have a distinctly well-planned regularity about them, and around the hillfort

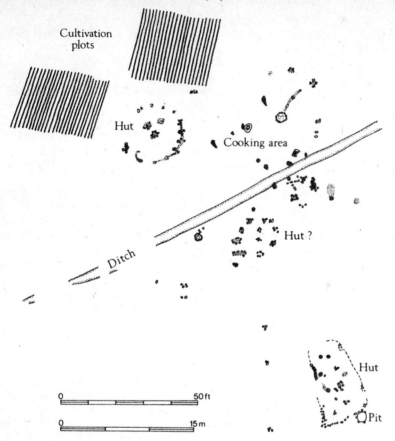

Cultivation
plots

Hut

Cooking area

Hut ?

Ditch

0   50 ft

0   15 m

Hut

Pit

11:13   Plan of the settlement and cultivation plots at Weston Wood, Surrey (source: J. M. Harding, 1964)

of Sidbury, Wilts, hundreds of acres of ordered field systems are known, pre-dating linear earthworks linked to the fort. It is difficult to resist the assumption that at times during the first millennium massive and concentrated programmes of land clearance and distribution were undertaken.

Arable farming on the scale outlined above could not have been maintained without considerable flocks and herds to provide manure for the fields. Cattle and sheep were reared in large numbers while pigs played a subsidiary role. The cattle were the small Celtic short-horns (*Bos longifrons*), about the size of modern Dexter cows; the sheep were a small straggly variety, not unlike the modern Soay type.[1] In addition to the three basic farmyard animals, dogs were kept, probably as pets and work-animals, and small

horses or, more correctly, ponies about 12 hands (120 cm) high, rather like an Exmoor pony, were reared mainly for traction.

Statistics based on the quantities of animal bones found on occupation sites give some idea of the relative importance of the different species, but it must always be remembered that the bones can do no more than represent animals butchered at the homestead. If, for example, sheep were kept solely for wool, their bones would tend to be scarce in such deposits. In broad terms, however, there appears to have been a gradual increase in the numbers of sheep relative to cattle during the first millennium. At the Cranbourne Chase sites of South Lodge Camp, Martin Down Camp and the Angle Ditch, the percentage of cattle in the total faunal assemblage varies between 48 and 67 per cent, the lower figure being abnormally depressed by exceptionally large numbers of deer and dogs,

---

[1] Goats were also kept but it is difficult to distinguish them from sheep on the basis of their skeletal remains.

while in the first century BC village at Glastonbury sheep outnumber oxen by almost seventeen to one. It is of course possible that the assemblages are affected to some extent by the different functions of the sites or by environment, but the general trend towards sheep-rearing is clear enough. The same story is told by the collection of bones from Eldon's Seat (Encombe), Dorset, where between the seventh and fifth centuries the proportion of sheep increased from 40·7 to 61·7 per cent and cattle correspondingly declined from 50·6 to 28·3 per cent.

The relative increase in the numbers of sheep throughout the first millennium is probably linked to the spread of downland arable. To maintain the enormous acreages of fields farmed during the Iron Age, flocks and herds would have been essential in providing manure for the land. Sheep would have been the obvious choice, for not only could they survive for long periods on the Downs without water, but they were also relatively easy to maintain over the autumn and winter. From September until December they could be turned loose on the stubble without the need for special feeding and from December until March or April, when the pastures began to grow again, straw fodder carted to the fields would have been sufficient to keep them alive. For the remainder of the year, from April to August, there would have been ample pasture for the flocks to grow fat on in the fields left fallow and, if this failed, on the open downland. The symbiosis between sheep and fertile arable land cannot be over-stressed: it is no exaggeration to say that without large flocks, grain-production on its Iron Age level would have been impossible to maintain.

Sheep also had other uses: at various times they could provide wool and milk, and eventually meat, bone, sinew and skin. Relatively few were slaughtered in the first year – only 9·2 per cent at Encombe and about the same percentage from Hawk's Hill, Surrey – and over 40 per cent of the flock lived to more than two years of age at both sites. These figures were not universal, however, for at Barley, Herts, 39 per cent were killed in each of the first two years. One possible explanation is that at Barley the slaughter of yearlings reflects a reliance on sheep as a meat source, the carcasses being salted down for winter, while in the south sheep were kept more for their wool and manure, mutton being of secondary im-

portance. Clearly, there were regional variations in farming practice which need to be worked out in detail when further data become available. In spite of the numerical advantage of sheep, mutton was not consumed in very large quantities compared with beef. The average weight of a sheep was only about 125 lb (56·7 kg), while that of a cow might be as much as 900 lb (408·2 kg). Thus at Hawk's Hill the 57 per cent of sheep produced only 23 per cent of the meat supply while the 17 per cent of cattle yielded 53 per cent. The figures are of course approximate, but they emphasise the fact that for the most part the Iron Age farmers of the south were beef-eaters.

Cattle were far more difficult to maintain than sheep. They needed constant watering and from December until March they would have required protection from the weather in corrals and enclosures and provision of regular feeds of straw, hay or leaf fodder. It would seem unlikely that the beasts were brought into the actual farmstead enclosures unless special provision was made to keep them well clear of the domestic fittings and houses, as seems to have been the case at Farley Mount, where the corner of the 6 acre (2·4 hectare) enclosure was divided off by another length of ditch, presumably to protect the house. At Little Woodbury, Wilts, no internal divisions are known, but the antennae ditches in front of the main entrance could well have enclosed a stockyard. The advantages in having the stock close by during the winter months are obvious: not only could they be protected from raiders and wild animals, but the constant foddering and watering which would have been necessary could more easily have been carried out from the home farm. Foodstuffs for the cattle would have proved no problem; hay would have been important, so too would leaf fodder cut in the spring and stored throughout the summer. Nor must the significance of straw be overlooked. If, as we have assumed, the harvest was undertaken before the cereals had ripened, the straw would have retained a far greater nutritional value. Indeed, this may be one of the reasons for the early harvesting which necessitated drying and roasting before threshing. Straw and hay may have been stacked on the two-post racks which occur so frequently, while leaf fodder would probably have been stored in underground silos.

In addition to their value as meat- and milk-producers, cattle were used for many kinds of tractions, in particular ploughing. For these reasons, the tendency was to keep the herd to maturity. Of the 39 individual animals recognised at Hawk's Hill, only 3 were killed in the range 0–6 months and 16 were older than 3 years when they died or were slaughtered. At Eldon's Seat the figures were comparable: of the 28 represented, 17 had reached maturity. Apart from the plough teams and the bulls kept for breeding, the main herd was probably composed of cows kept in milk during the spring and summer months, when they would have been allowed out to browse in the forest fringes, the pastures and the steep faces of the lynchets. Their very presence implies the provision of water in reasonable quantities, possibly collected and conserved in dew-ponds. No certain traces of Iron Age dew-ponds have been recognised, but their existence on the Downs can hardly be doubted. At the settlement on Park Brow, Sussex, a structure suggestive of an ancient dew-pond was found in close relationship to the trackway which joined the various sites. If it is indeed Iron Age in date, its siting would have suited it admirably to the pastoral needs of the community.

Pigs of a domesticated variety played a significant part in the economy. Normally numbers were low: 3·5 and 4·0 per cent in the two periods at Eldon's Seat, 1, 0 and 9 per cent on the Cranbourne Chase sites, but rising to 22 per cent at Hawk's Hill and 33 per cent at Highfield, near Salisbury, Wilts. The range is interesting, since it must indicate a considerable variation of practice in the reliance placed on the animal. Settlements close to tracts of woodland on nearby clay soils, in river valleys, or on steep hangers, would have been able to maintain large herds of swine without much trouble, but where pannage was sparse, on the more open Downs, pig-rearing would have been difficult and consequently numbers were much lower.

Hunting appears to have been of little significance. Red deer, roe deer and fallow deer are all recorded on settlement sites, but since shed antlers were collected for tool-making, percentages are unreliable. Various birds are known, including duck, swan, raven, blackcock and red grouse (?), and occasionally small mammals like water voles and hedgehogs turn up in reliable archaeological contexts; fish, apart from a chub from Little Woodbury, are virtually unknown. On the coasts, however, shellfish were collected in great quantity.

Dogs were general purpose animals used for hunting, herding and probably as pets. They occur widely but little reliable work has yet been carried out on the various breeds represented. At Highfield about twenty dogs were found (22 per cent of the total animal bones), of which five were of foxhound type, one like a retriever and one rather smaller than a fox terrier. Evidently selective breeding was by this time well under way. The large number of dogs from Highfield is puzzling. The site does not appear to have religious connections, which could have accounted for ritual killings, but some of the bones showed knife-cuts possibly resulting from the collection of sinews, which may be thought to indicate some form of industrial activity.

The importance of animal husbandry to the economy was considerable. It is therefore not surprising that specialised structures were designed and built to cope with the problems of looking after the flocks and herds. In the late second millennium various enclosures, commonly referred to as pastoral enclosures, were erected in Wessex (pp. 14–16). The same types of structure continued in use into the middle of the first millennium. The small rectangular earthwork on Harrow Hill, Sussex, with opposed gated entrances and palisade set into a shallow bank, serves as a convenient type-site. Finds were sparse but some pottery of sixth century type was found together with an unusual quantity of ox skulls. The excavators estimated that if the density of bones found in their limited excavation was typical of the enclosure as a whole, there must have been at least a thousand oxen present. That the bones were almost entirely skulls hints at a ritual significance, but an alternative suggestion, not necessarily exclusive of the first, is that beasts were collected here for slaughter, the carcasses being carried off and the useless heads left.

A closely similar earthwork of the same date was found on Portsdown Hill, near Portsmouth, Hants (Fig. 11:14). Here, however, the enclosure could be shown to succeed, but not necessarily replace, a linear boundary comprising of a gully flanked on either side by timber fences. Land boundaries of this kind were probably a relatively common feature of the first millennium

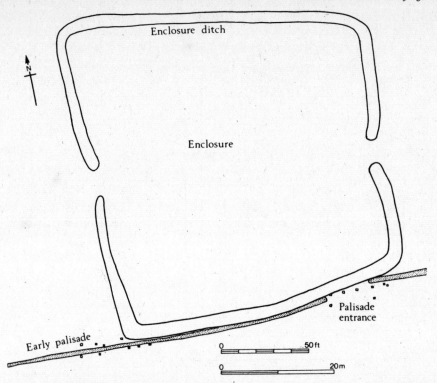

11:14   The pastoral enclosure on Portsdown Hill, Hants (source: Bradley, 1969a)

landscape (another was found at Winterbourne Dauntsey, Wilts), but the slight nature of their earthworks tends to militate against their easy recognition. Since the construction of the Portsdown enclosure blocked an entrance in the palisade, its siting may have been deliberate. It is tempting to see the fence as a kind of boundary to prevent cattle from straying from one area of pasture to another; an enclosure built hard against a fence would have offered distinct advantages at times when cattle were being herded towards the corral. Another, unexcavated, example of this kind of arrangement lies on the crest of Bow Hill, Sussex (Fig. 11:15), where a rectangular enclosure can be seen to be linked to a length of linear earthwork.

A recent survey of rectangular earthworks in Berkshire (Cotton, 1962) has shown them to have a range of dates from Late Bronze Age to Roman, and a similar variety of function is implied. Nevertheless, the examples discussed above are sufficiently similar in form, siting and date to suggest a common function: they are not precisely rectangular, they belong to the early part of the Iron Age and they are sited on tracts of pasture, sometimes connected to linear boundaries. Similar but unexcavated examples are known at Ladle Hill, Hants (Fig. 11:15) and at Chalton, Hants. In the latter example two separate areas of pastureland each have a rectangular enclosure at one end, close to trackways leading through the adjacent fields. The evidence, such as it is, suggests that these are specialised stock enclosures sited so that they could be used for the collection of cattle or sheep at those times when it became necessary to divide the herd for calving, castration or selective culling.

At a later stage, possibly as late as the second century BC, the banjo enclosure described above (p. 158) had developed, no doubt as an improvement on the old arrangement. The characteristic of the banjo, the long ditched causeway leading from a linear boundary to the enclosure, if suitably divided by temporary fences and hurdles, would have been of considerable value in the sorting and selecting of stock. The very numbers of these enclosures scattered over Wessex tend to

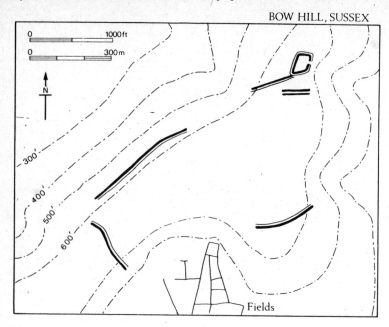

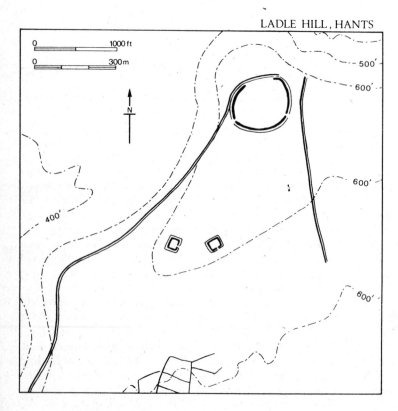

11:15   Rectangular enclosures and associated pastureland (sources: *Bow Hill*, author; *Ladle Hill*, S. Piggott, 1931)

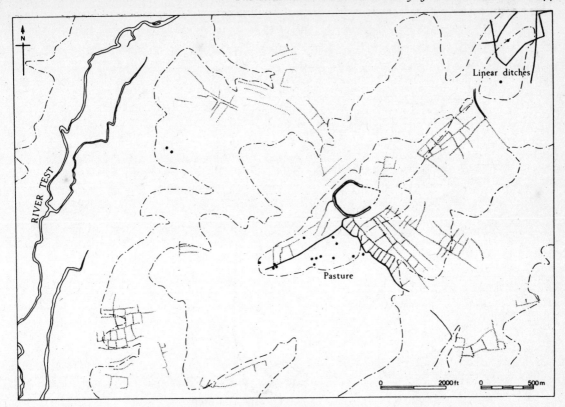

11:16   The landscape around Woolbury, Hants; contours at 200 ft and 400 ft O.D. (source: author)

suggest a reorientation of economy towards more pastoral pursuits.

The hillforts, with their enclosed nucleated settlements of considerable size, would have needed provision for corralling stock. The Trundle, Sussex, shows one way in which this was done. The fort itself lies in the centre of a tract of open land clearly divided from the arable fields by earthwork boundaries crossing the spurs; thus cattle could be kept throughout the winter within sight of the ramparts, facilitating their feeding and protection. A somewhat different arrangement was provided at Danebury, Hants (Fig. 13:13). In the first stage an annex of about 3 acres (1·2 hectares) was added to the side of the fort, but this was eventually replaced when the entire circuit was surrounded by a relatively minor ditch linked to a ditched droveway which can be traced for some distance from the entrance, passing through an extensive field system, the fields running up the enclosing ditch. In the new arrangement, dated to the second or

first century BC, the total area enclosed was increased to 27 acres (11 hectares). A variation of this arrangement can be seen at the adjacent fort of Woolbury on Stockbridge Down (Fig. 11:16), where two linear ditches run up to the fort, defining an area of pasture in front of the main gate and dividing it from the neighbouring arable fields. Although the arrangement of these three sites differs in detail, the overall result is the same: the creation of an extensive tract of enclosed pasture close to the fort and divided from the nearby arable. Within the pasture the entire herd of cattle belonging to the community could have been corralled in safety throughout the winter.

The use of linear ditches to divide up the land is a well-known feature of the Wessex landscape. Many of the boundaries must date back to at least the beginning of the first millennium. At Quarley Hill, Hants (Fig. 11:17), excavation has demonstrated the superimposition of a hillfort, dating to the fifth to fourth century, above part

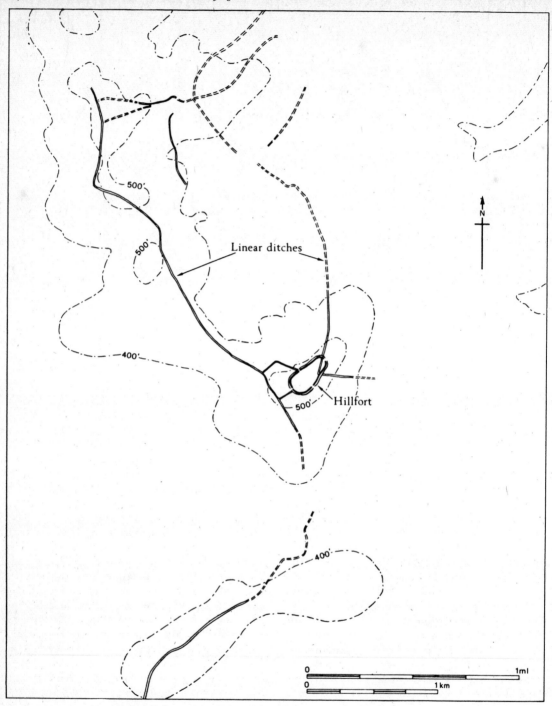

Linear ditches

Hillfort

11:17   Quarley Hill, Hants and its 'ranch boundaries' (source: Hawkes, 1939c)

of a system of ditches which appear to converge upon the hilltop, while other parts of the same system are contemporary with the fort. Similarly, at Ladle Hill, Hants, a 'ranch boundary' seems to precede the construction phase of the unfinished camp. Elsewhere boundaries can be shown to belong to the late second to first century, e.g. at Sidbury Hill, Wilts, where some at least of the great series of converging ditches date to a phase contemporary with the latest stage of hillfort development. The boundaries of this group are of particular interest since they appear to cut indiscriminately across areas of field systems, implying that part of the arable land at least had gone out of use by this time. The function of the ranch boundaries is obscure but they were clearly intended to divide up the land into well-defined tracts, sometimes laid out from a focus, as at Sidbury Hill, sometimes apparently concerned to take in a stretch of river valley like the system on either side of the river Bourne above Salisbury in Wiltshire. One implication is that a rigorous system of land division was imposed upon the landscape; another is that the territories thus defined were at certain times during the year turned over for stock-grazing.

The linear ranch boundaries of central Wessex are a response to the need to divide large areas of undulating upland. Elsewhere, along the ridges of the North and South Downs and the Chilterns, short lengths of bank and ditch, sometimes multiple, were employed. These cross-ridge dykes and spur dykes, as they are called, defined rigid territories of land which must have had political or tenurial significance but they would also have served as convenient pastoral boundaries between one farm and the next, and sometimes they can be shown to divide arable from pasture. These earthworks and their relationship to the landscape dserve more detailed investigation than they have at present received.

Sufficient has been said to show that the pattern of mixed farming as practised in the south and east of Britain was a complex process involving a close inter-relationship between the arable and pastoral aspects of the system. One was wholly dependent upon the other, but throughout the first millennium there were changes which can dimly be recognised through the archaeological record. Grain-production became more diversified with the introduction of spelt, bread wheat, oats and rye towards the beginning of the period, and at the same time there was a greater reliance on hulled barley. The new types would now allow autumn sowing as well as spring, with all the attendant advantages. Storage methods also changed: in the first half of the millennium pits were relatively seldom used, but after the fourth or third century massive underground silos were commonly constructed where subsoil was suitable, taking up to 40 bushels (14·5 hectolitres) of grain. The change may, however, be more a response to political conditions than to economic factors. As arable fields colonised the waste, so larger flocks of sheep became more necessary to maintain the fertility of the land. Cattle continued to play an important part in the economy and it is possible that towards the end of the period they began to take on an even greater significance. The digging of ranch boundaries indiscriminately across fields, the provision of enclosed pasture around some of the hillforts, and the apparent increase in stock enclosures of banjo type, all point to the growing importance of cattle. If this is in fact the case, and it must be admitted that the evidence is by no means conclusive, the change may be linked to changes in the nature of society which were becoming apparent in the third to second centuries (p. 305).

The discussion of the subsistence economy of the south-east has necessarily been based on evidence derived largely from downland excavations. It is therefore biased towards one environment. Where, however, faunal material is available from elsewhere, e.g. the Isle of Purbeck, the same general pattern appears to hold good. Settlement plans and structures from the gravel sites as far afield as the Welland valley also bear out the impression that mixed farming of Little Woodbury type was widespread over the whole of the south-east. Future research, particularly in the field of faunal studies, will do much to highlight the regional variations which must inevitably have existed.

The Settlement Pattern and Economy of the North and West

The economy and the settlement pattern of the communities living beyond the Jurassic ridge varied considerably from area to area, depending partly upon geography and climate, and partly upon the previous cultural history of the region. Some areas were populous, others barren. In contrast to the south and east, therefore, we must consider each region in turn.

THE SOUTH-WEST PENINSULA

The south-west peninsula has a distinctive character unlike any other area of Britain. Bounded on three sides by the sea and separated from Wessex by the marshlands of Somerset, its communities developed along peculiar lines influenced more by the structure and food-producing potential of the land than by external stimulus. The peninsula is dominated by six areas of moorland: the sandstone uplands of Exmoor in the north-east and the granite masses of Dartmoor, Bodmin, Hensbarrow, Carnmenellis and Penwith – all providing a light, if not particularly fertile, soil more suitable for pasture than for arable farming. Between these upland masses lie the Culm measures of middle Devonian and the Permian rocks yielding an intractable clay soil generally unsuitable for prehistoric settlement.

In chapter 2 the principal types of settlement centring upon the Dartmoor massif and dating to the late second and early first millennia were discussed. Briefly, they included large enclosed villages, sometimes with attached stockpens, sited around the south and west limits of the moor; open villages with huts linked by stone walls found in much the same area; and small farmsteads of one or two huts associated with a few embanked fields. This last type is concentrated on the more protected and correspondingly drier eastern edges of the moor. The dating of these Late Bronze Age settlements is notoriously difficult, for while there can be little doubt that many of them began to be occupied in what is conventionally the Bronze Age, the upper limit of dating is difficult to define. In some cases they may have continued in use as late as the latter half of the first millennium. Two Dartmoor settlements have, however, produced artefacts suggesting an Iron Age date – Kestor, near Chagford, and Foale's Arrishes (Figs 12:1, 12:2). Both settlements comprise a group of huts scattered among small rectangular fields with a single larger hut protected by an enclosing wall. Strictly, this type of site is little more than an agglomeration of small farmsteads but their close spacing and the provision of a single more impressive house might suggest that we are dealing with hamlets or even villages, in which some form of class structure prevailed. A tighter nucleation can be recognised at other undated sites such as Broadall Lake in the upper Yealm valley, Devon, where ten circular huts were grouped along the side of two fields.

The excavation at Kestor (A. Fox, 1955) has provided a valuable insight into the form of a settlement which might tentatively be dated to the fifth or fourth century BC (Fig. 12:1). One of the isolated huts, lying at the junction of three field walls, was totally excavated. It was a simple structure, some 27 ft (8·2 m) across internally, enclosed by an outer wall to take the lower ends of the rafters, which were further supported by a circular setting of posts and a central post to hold up the crown of the roof. Internal fittings were restricted to a hearth and an area of cobbling

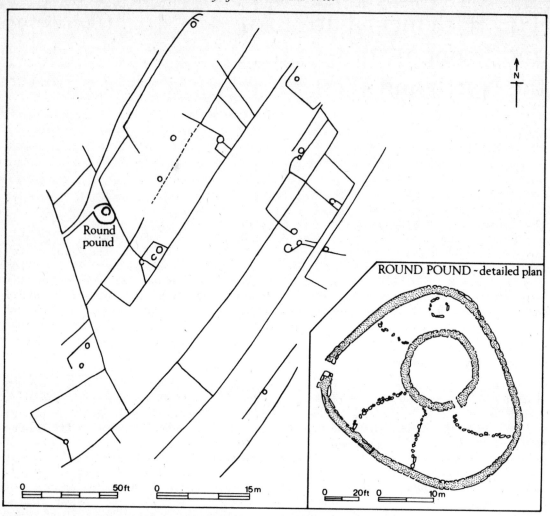

12:1   The settlement at Kestor, Devon (source: A. Fox, 1955)

close to the entrance. The larger hut, built towards the centre of the enclosure known as the Round Pound, was 37 ft (11·3 m) across internally and of a more complex structure, but here too internal posts acted as roof supports – the difference being that a central opening seems to have been provided, with a drip-pit beneath to collect and drain away rainwater. The reason for the opening was that the hut was used for iron smelting and fumes therefore had to be removed. Inside were found a small bowl furnace filled with iron slag and nearby a forging pit, presumably for reheating the bloom prior to the hammering necessary to remove impurities. The hut was enclosed within an oval stone-walled

pound 100–110 ft (30–33 m) across, provided with a single narrow doorway opening on to a terraced drove road which ran between the surrounding fields. A second, much smaller hut lay close to the pound wall but was completely undated and may indeed belong to the medieval period. While it would be wrong to argue from the evidence of one site alone, the fact that the largest hut belonged to the iron smith might be an indication of the high status in which the community held such a man.

The close relationship between the pound, the trackway, the other huts and the fields leaves little doubt that all functioned together. Indeed, it was possible for the excavator to show that the ancient plough-soil stopped 6 ft (1·8 m) clear of one of the huts and that a slight negative lynchet had been formed, demonstrating clearly that the field had been ploughed after the hut had been constructed. Near by, the plough-soil was found to overlie a layer of peat, which was shown by pollen analysis to belong to the sub-Atlantic period – a time when the climatic conditions were becoming much wetter. The Kestor settlement and its fields therefore belonged to a community which colonised an area of virgin moorland after the middle of the first millennium, at a time when climatic deterioration had already set in. In all probability, it was one of the last inroads to be made on the moor before wetter weather drove the long-established population from the uplands.

The presence of fields and the discovery of a saddle quern are sufficient to show that arable farming was practised, but the field systems tend to be far more limited in extent than those of the south-east, implying – but by no means proving – that corn-production was of subsidiary significance. Of the pastoral aspects of the economy little can be said: animal bones are destroyed by the acid moorland soils and relevant artefacts, apart from a spindle whorl from Kestor, are exceedingly rare. Flocks and herds must, however, have been a dominant feature of the early first millennium economy, to judge by the large pounds of Late Bronze Age date, and in all probability pastoral activities continued to be of first-rate importance throughout the latter part of the period – as, indeed, the multiple-enclosure forts to be described below imply.

Scattered huts among small rectangular fields is a pattern of settlement reflected over most of the south-west peninsula from Dartmoor to Land's End, but while many such sites are known, few have been excavated outside Dartmoor itself. One site, Bodrifty on Mulfra Hill near Penzance, Cornwall (Fig. 12:4), has how-

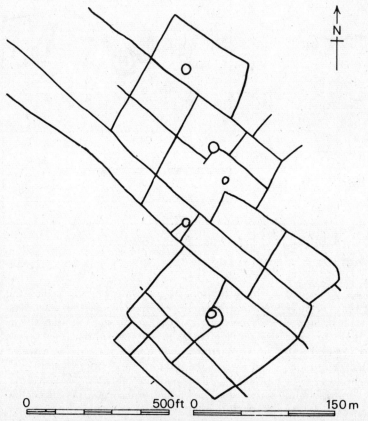

N

0   500ft   0   150 m

12:2   The settlement at Foale's Arrishes, Devon (source: Radford, 1952)

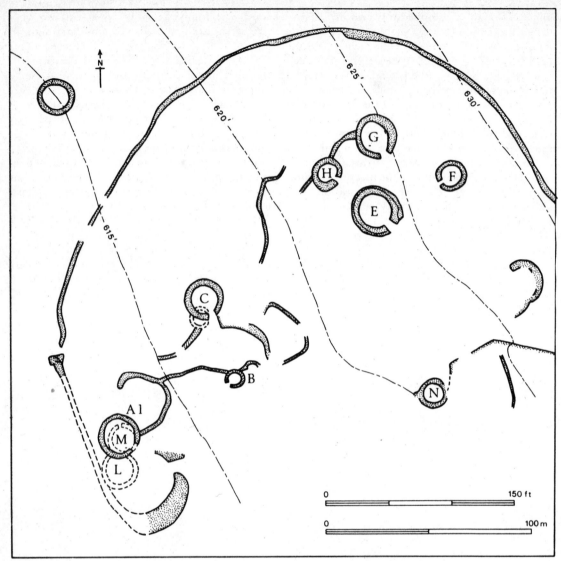

12:3   The settlement at Bodrifty, Cornwall. Letters refer to the identifications in the excavator's report (source: Dudley, 1957)

ever provided some details in response to limited excavation. Here more than twenty simple circular huts were spread over a tract of land ¼ mile (0·4 km) across but at least nine clustered together and were later enclosed by a pound wall built probably in the second or first century BC at about the time when some of the huts show signs of rebuilding. In the original pre-pound settlement, beginning perhaps as early as the sixth or fifth century, the individual huts were joined by lengths of walling rather like the technique employed on some of the Dartmoor villages such as Stanton Down. The huts themselves (Fig. 12:4) are closely similar in structure to the Dartmoor examples, with wide stone walls, central hearths and sometimes internal settings of posts to help support the rafters in the case of the larger buildings. The excavation produced few finds, but spindle whorls and saddle querns give some hint of the agricultural and pastoral activities of the community. The significance of Bodrifty lies in the relatively large quantities of pottery recovered, ranging from types which would not be out of place in sixth to fifth century contexts in Wessex to jars of the second to first centuries decorated in a local version of the Glastonbury style. The ceramic evidence allows the possibility that occupation continued well into the first century AD.

Thus the Dartmoor and Cornish settlements are very close in details of planning, structure and economy, but on Dartmoor there is no evidence to suggest that occupation continued after the third or second centuries, since no trace

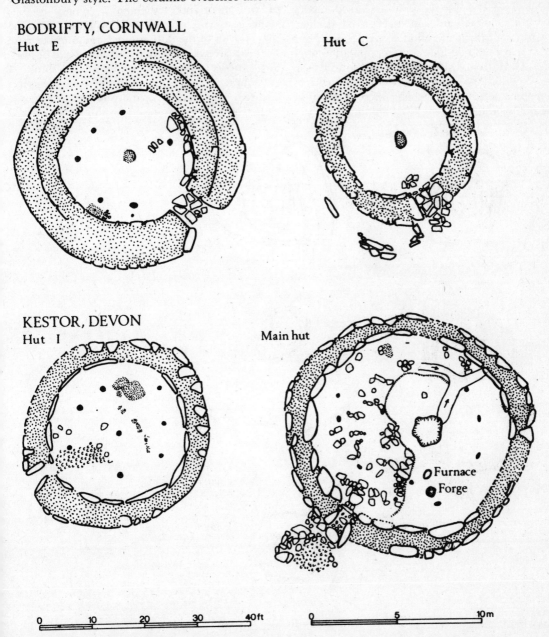

12:4 House plans in south-west Britain (sources: *Bodrifty*, Dudley, 1957; *Kestor*, A. Fox, 1955)

of Glastonbury style pottery has ever been found nor do any of the sites show signs of Roman use. The contrast with Cornwall is striking but can be explained if it is assumed that the onset of sub-Atlantic conditions forced the inhabitants of the high moors to abandon their traditional farm-lands, while those living around the fringes of the less elevated and more hospitable Cornish moors were able to continue and even expand their territories. If this contention is correct, it would mean that a considerable shift of population took place away from Dartmoor and Bodmin Moor over a period of a century or two. It is necessary, therefore, to consider where these dislocated pastoralists might have settled. Significantly, the

lowland areas of Devon and eastern Cornwall are densely scattered with settlements commonly referred to as multiple-enclosure forts (Figs 12:5, 12:6), evidently designed for pastoral com-munities and (where evidence is available) not built until the second or first century BC. It is tempting to see these structures as the successors of the moorland settlements, colonising the richer low-lying soils of the Devon and Cornish hills, but until the dating of a large number has been discovered it would be unwise to be too dogmatic as to their origins and relationships.

Characteristically, the multiple-enclosure set-tlements are often sited, more for pastoral con-venience than for strength, on hill-slopes or the

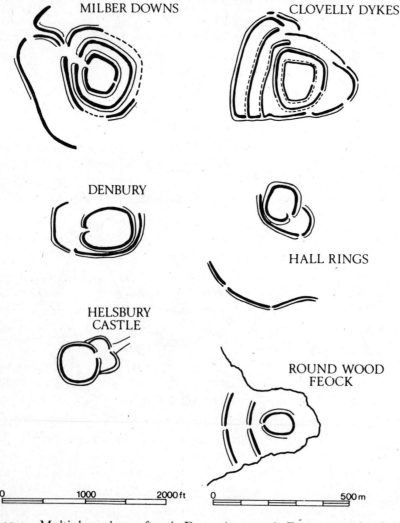

12:5   Multiple-enclosure forts in Devon (source: A. Fox, 1953 and 1961b)

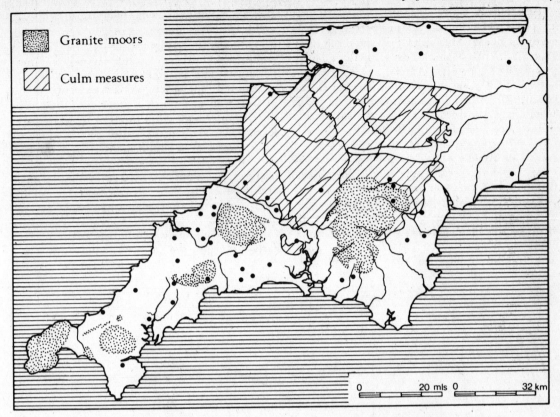

Granite moors

Culm measures

0   20 mls   0   32 km

12:6   Distribution of multiple-enclosure forts in south-west Britain (source: A. Fox, 1961b)

ends of ridges overlooking springs or river valleys (Pl. 3b). Normally the inner enclosure, between 0·5 and 4 acres (0·2 and 1·6 hectares) in extent, is defended by a fairly massive bank and ditch laid out in a circular or sub-rectangular plan with a single entrance in one side. The additional enclosures were created in several ways (Fig. 12:5). At Milber Down Camp, Devon, two outer banks and ditches were arranged concentrically with the inner earthwork, both enclosing a considerable additional acreage. An even more impressive example of this type is Clovelly Dykes, where two enclosures are concentric with the main camp and two additional areas are attached to one side of the outermost, thus providing four separate enclosed areas in addition to the central element. All were interlinked with entrances, the main entrance being so sited as to give easy access to nearby springs. A variation on this type can be seen at Castle Dore, Cornwall, Denbury, south Devon, and at several other sites where the outer enclosure is pendent upon the inner, the

two ramparts being close-spaced for part of their length but diverging widely towards the entrance to form an outer enclosure. A third type occurs in which the main camp is provided with a separate annex attached to the side with the entrance. Strictly, the little fort at Blackbury Castle, Devon, belongs to this class, but here the passage between the two entrances was flanked by banks and ditches, giving rise to the so-called barbican approach. More distant cross-banks were also extensively used, usually to cut off the neck of the promontory or spur upon which the main enclosure was situated. This type of arrangement frequently enclosed a substantial acreage, which almost invariably included springs or streams.

The intention behind the siting and planning of these settlements is clear enough: the inner enclosures, some of which were comparable in size to enclosures of Little Woodbury type though others were smaller, presumably formed the inhabited area where the owner and family lived while the outer enclosures were designed to protect the homestead pastures and their watering-places. They are, in fact, nothing more than the defended homesteads of a predominantly pastoral community. Animal bones seldom survive in the acid soils of the area, but in the absence of Celtic field systems flocks and herds would have provided much of the food for the inhabitants. The material culture is not particularly well represented in the archaeological record but spindle whorls occur consistently and signs of moderate wealth appear at Milber Down Camp in the form of an iron dagger handle, and at Castle Dore, where armlets of bronze, shale and glass and five glass beads have been found. Hints such as these, together with the amount of effort which construction of the earthworks must have required, suggests that the multiple-

enclosure settlements were probably the homesteads of a wealthy class of society who, judging from the associated pottery, lived in the area from about the third or second century BC until perhaps as late as the Roman conquest.

Another type of habitation site occurs widely in Cornwall and north-west Devon, usually in hilly country 200–400 ft (60–120 m) above sea-level. These settlements, called rounds in Cornwall, consist of a simple banked and ditched enclosure, seldom exceeding 2 acres (0·8 hectares) in extent and sited invariably on good arable land (Fig. 12:7). Inside there are usually a few huts built close against the bank. Several have been excavated: the round at Trevisker, Cornwall, containing two huts of the second or early first century BC, superseded an earlier unenclosed settlement dating back to the second

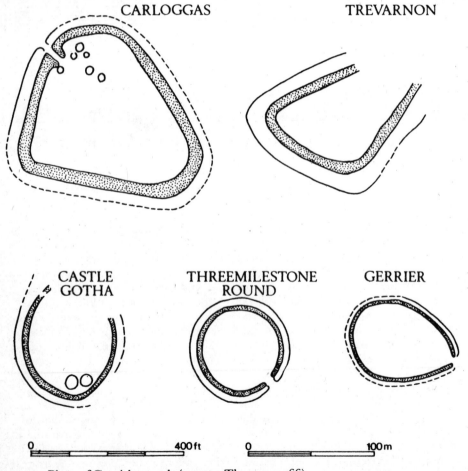

12:7   Plans of Cornish rounds (source: Thomas, 1966)

millennium, while at Castle Gotha, Cornwall, the 1·5 acre (0·6 hectare) enclosure and its two huts, built late in the second century BC, continued in occupation for about 500 years. Detailed field-work in west Cornwall (Thomas, 1966) has shown that rounds were densely distributed, varying from one per 0·84 square mile (2·1 km²) to one per 1·75 square miles (4·5 km²), but since only a few have been excavated, it is impossible to say that all were in use at the same time; many of them may not have been built until the Roman period. Nevertheless, as a settlement type rounds were probably widespread before the first century BC.

A different type of settlement, the so-called courtyard house, is found on the high ground in west Cornwall. This is essentially a central paved courtyard surrounded by rooms and byres, the whole complex being enclosed with a massive stone wall, usually with a single entrance leading into the yard. Houses of this kind are normally provided with adjacent fields or cultivation plots.

When courtyard houses occur in clusters, as they do at Chysauster (Fig. 12:8), the appearance is not at all unlike a deserted medieval village. Whether single or in groups, courtyard houses are usually unenclosed but several sites are known where houses are contained within a round (Fig. 12:9). At Porthmeor at least three houses and their gardens were enclosed in this way at a date subsequent to their erection, while at Goldherring the round contained a single house with its cultivation plots outside. Where evidence of date is available, it is generally found that courtyard houses began in the first century BC and continued in use throughout the Roman era. The origin of courtyard houses is still a matter of uncertainty, but inspiration from the Armorican peninsula is likely to have contributed to their development.

Another type of settlement to be considered is the so-called lake village of which the best known examples are Meare and Glastonbury, situated in the Somerset levels. Both sites were excavated

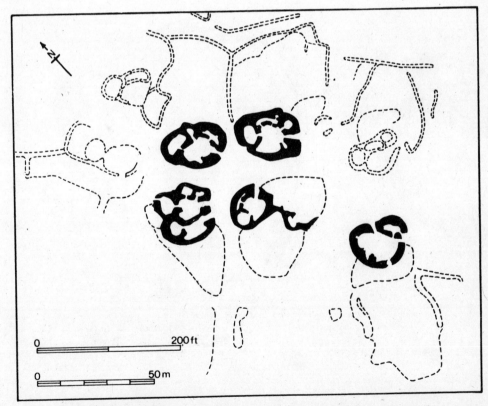

12:8   The village of Chysauster, Cornwall (source: H. O'N. Hencken, 1933)

some years ago, Glastonbury between 1892 and 1907 and Meare West 1910–33, before the intricacies of detailed stratigraphical studies were fully appreciated, but a series of recent studies by Godwin (1941 and 1955) on the problems of environment, Avery (1968), reporting on a re-examination of Meare East, and Tratman (1970), reassessing Glastonbury, have gone some way in improving our understanding of the nature and chronology of the settlements.

The recent work at Meare East has demonstrated a considerable length of occupation, beginning in the third century BC with a cluster of circular wooden huts built on the desiccated surface of a raised bog adjacent to the Meare and Westhay Island, a few hundred feet from the open water. In the second century the area was abandoned, presumably in favour of a nearby settlement on drier land, the old site being used as a refuse tip. Later, for some undefined reason, hundreds of tons of clay were dumped over the middens while occupation continued nearby into the first century AD, by which time the area was being subjected to fresh-water flooding. One problem to emerge from the new excavations is the exact location and form of the main settlement and the relationship of the east village to the near-by west village, where some forty huts of a settlement at least twice that size were excavated. It has not yet been established whether the date range and development of the west village is at all comparable with the eastern site.

The Glastonbury village has been almost totally excavated but its development is no less obscure. In its final form it extended over a roughly triangular area measuring some 400 by 300 ft (122 by 91 m) enclosed by a sinuous palisade. In all, the sites of some ninety huts have been defined, but it is unlikely that all were occupied at the same time. The village appears to have been founded on a shelf of peat flanked along the east side by the original course of the river Brue, towards which an embanked causeway reached out. The situation is broadly comparable to Meare East but the peat surface

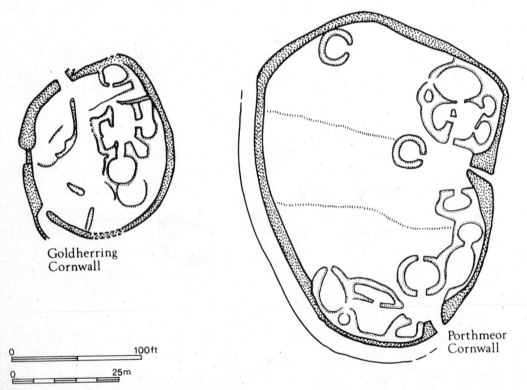

Goldherring
Cornwall

Porthmeor
Cornwall

0 — 100 ft

0 — 25 m

12:9   Courtyard houses built into rounds (sources: *Goldherring*, Guthrie, 1969; *Porthmeor*, Hirst, 1936)

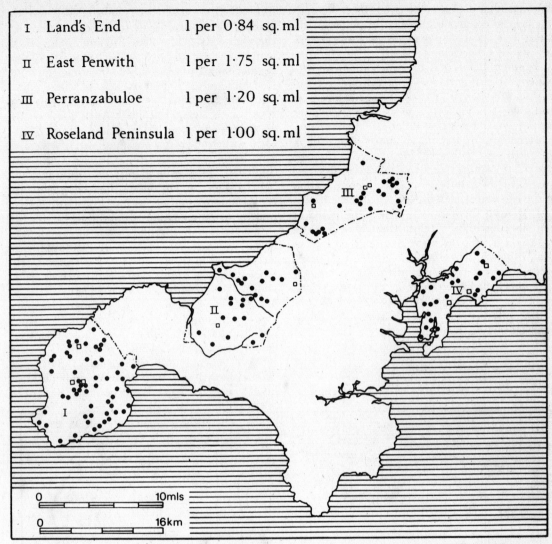

I Land's End 1 per 0·84 sq. ml

II East Penwith 1 per 1·75 sq. ml

III Perranzabuloe 1 per 1·20 sq. ml

IV Roseland Peninsula 1 per 1·00 sq. ml

0   10mls

0   16km

12:10 Settlement density in Cornwall: ● homesteads □ hillforts (source: Thomas, 1966)

beneath the earliest levels of the village was considerably wetter. Tratman (1970) has suggested that the original settlement comprised a group of rectangular timber-framed buildings some 10 ft (3 m) square, quoting as evidence various rectangular settings of posts as well as sections of morticed timber evidently belonging to rectilinear panels. His view has much to commend it, particularly in the light of recent discoveries in the Welsh borderland hillforts and at Danebury, Hants. In its later stages the village consisted of circular clay-floored huts with central hearths which were replaced at frequent intervals. The hut walls were usually constructed of close-set vertical timbers with wattlework in between; doorways were often provided with thresholds and paved approaches.

It is difficult to assess the size of the villages but Tratman's tentative analysis of Glastonbury suggests twenty to thirty houses in use at any one time. The material culture points to a range of specialist activities being carried out; indeed, it may be thought that these settlements possess the attributes of proto-urban communities.

The large hillforts of Wessex type are rare west of the Exe. The south-east is a hillfort-

dominated landscape surrounded by farms relying heavily on arable production, while in the
south-west isolated settlements of pastoral type
(the multiple-enclosure forts) and mixed farming
types (the rounds) replace open settlements and
villages which showed the same range of specialisation (Fig. 12:10). Clearly the social structure
and political organisation of the two areas must
have been different, a difference further emphasised later by the total absence of coinage in
the south-west. It is tempting to suggest that the
pastoral-dominated economy of the south-west
prevented the growth of political centralisation
to the extent to which it developed in the south-
east. Instead, there arose a society composed of
individual lordships of approximately equivalent
status, covering most of the area. In the extreme
west, however, where arable farming was practised to a greater extent, individual farmsteads
were as closely spaced as in the south-east. Here
the larger cliff castles possibly served as the
centres upon which the farming community
were dependent (Fig. 12:11).

SOUTH AND WEST WALES

The southern coastal area of Wales stretching

from the Usk valley to Pembrokeshire was in
many ways similar in its settlement pattern to
the south-west peninsula of England, a similarity
which can be explained, in part at least, by the
geomorphological likeness of the two areas. The
Carboniferous and Triassic rocks of Glamorganshire and Monmouthshire and the Ordovician
rocks of the western counties give rise to soils
comparable to those of Devon and eastern Cornwall, while the craggy coastline west of Swansea
Bay could easily be mistaken for Cornwall.
Similarly, the predominantly north-south flowing rivers tend to cut the territory lying between
the mountains and the sea into strips and blocks,
making communication by land difficult.

Unenclosed hut groups, generally undated,
occur in Carmarthenshire and Pembrokeshire
but they are ill known compared with the Dartmoor sites. One group, partly excavated in 1899,
lay on the top of Moel Trigarn in the Precelly
Mountains. Recent aerial photography has
shown that some of the huts pre-date the multiple
walls of the later hillfort and must therefore
belong to an open settlement of some size.

Multiple-enclosure settlements of the types
defined in the south-west occur in some number
in all four of the south Welsh counties. Site loca-

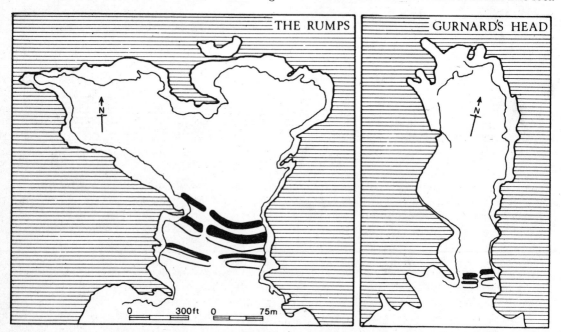

12:11   Cornish cliff castles (sources: *the Rumps*, Brooks, 1964; *Gurnard's Head*, A. S. R. Gordon, 1941)

tion again indicates a preference for valley-sides dominating springs or streams, suggesting that here, as in the south-west, the enclosures were constructed by predominantly pastoral communities more concerned with watering their flocks and herds than with purely military considerations.

The west country round also has its counterparts in the raths of south-west Wales. It is estimated that of the 580 hillforts in Wales about 230 enclose less than an acre, and of these three-quarters lie in the south-west. While it is true that many were occupied in the Roman period, and some may even have been constructed then, a high percentage probably date back to the Iron

Age. Total excavation of Walesland Rath near Haverfordwest, Pembs, provides a unique insight into the structure and development of this type of establishment (Fig. 12:12). Here an oval-shaped area, 210 by 160 ft (64 by 49 m) internally, was enclosed by a bank and ditch pierced by two entrances. The south-west gate was massively constructed with three pairs of timbers which must have once supported a tower, while the western entrance was flanked by dry-stone walling, with its gate set back within the line of the ramparts. Internally the enclosure was packed with timber structures, including at least six circular timber huts, several of which show signs of rebuilding on a number of occasions. A

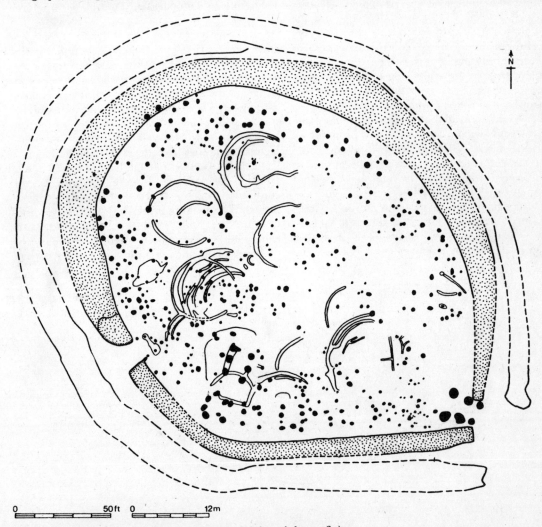

0   50ft   0   12m

12:12   Walesland Rath, Pembs (source: Wainwright, 1969)

more unusual type of building was constructed from three pairs of large timbers; this resembles the structures found in the Wessex and Welsh borderland hillforts. The provision of an eave-drip trench around it shows that it was roofed and may possibly have been a house but does not necessarily preclude the possibility of its serving as a granary in this context. More remarkable was the maze of post-holes arranged in alignments around the periphery of the enclosure close to the rampart. Though difficult to interpret in detail, they must belong to substantial timber ranges not unlike those found in the Shetland fort of Clickhimin. It may be that such a layout will prove to be more common in the south-west than hitherto supposed. Dating evidence at Walesland Rath was sparse but the first phase can be assigned to the first century BC or a little earlier, while the second phase, defined by the rebuilding of the rampart on a more massive scale and the blocking of the west gate, began in the early part of the first century AD. Occupation continued into the third century.

A second excavated site belonging to the same category is Coygan Camp, sited on a promontory of Carboniferous limestone overlooking Carmarthen Bay (Fig. 12:13). An initial occupation, tentatively assigned to the eighth to second century, was followed by the construction of the enclosure bank and ditch. Two entrances were provided: a north-west gate, the approach to which was further protected by a length of additional rampart built across the neck of the

promontory, and a south-west entrance leading down to the marshy pasture at the base of the hill. Contemporary internal structures were not found, nor was the material culture particularly rich, apart from producing a pair of bronze La Tène bracelets, but a large quantity of animal bones were well preserved in the alkaline soil. The collection from the enclosure phase shows that numerically cattle predominated, amounting to 64 per cent of the total, with sheep/goats a mere 16 per cent, closely followed by pigs at 15 per cent. Allowing for the fact that a single cow produced about seven times the meat yield of a sheep, it will be evident that the basic diet was beef, the intake of mutton and pork being negligible by comparison. The relative importance of meat to grain cannot be assessed, but quern-stones were very rare and storage facilities unrecorded. In all probability, the inhabitants were pastoralists, using the fertile pastures of the neighbouring Devonian soils and the marshland fringes at the foot of the hill for rearing and maintaining large herds of cattle. The proximity of the sea provided an additional food-source: fish bones were not preserved but shellfish were collected in quantity from the estuary of the Taf and from the rocky pools at the base of the Pendine Cliffs. Like Walesland Rath, Coygan Camp continued to be occupied well into the Roman period. The neighbouring sites of Trelissey and Cwmbrwyn, both earthwork enclosures, also contained substantial Roman style masonry buildings. It is not unreasonable to suggest that

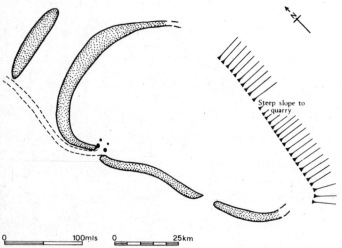

Steep slope to quarry

0   100mls   0   25km

12:13   Coygan Camp, Carm (source: Wainwright, 1967a)

here too we are dealing with Iron Age settlements which remained in use for some centuries after the Roman conquest.

Few of the rath-like enclosures in Glamorganshire or Monmouthshire have been adequately excavated, with the notable exception of Mynydd Bychan, Glam, overlooking the Ewenny valley, where a small enclosure was found to contain a group of timber-framed circular huts, probably dating to the first century BC. Rebuilding in stone took place in the middle of the first century AD (Fig. 12:14).

Many of the promontories of south-west Wales were defended by banks and ditches, turning them into the equivalent of the Cornish cliff castles (Fig. 12:15). Several have been partially examined by excavation. On St David's Head, Pembs, a complex rampart protected a small group of six conjoined stone-walled huts 15–20 ft (4·5–6·0 m) in diameter, excavated in 1900. The material culture was sparse but whetstones, spindle whorls, hammer stones and fragments of iron were found together with a few glass beads and decorated shale pendants. No precise evidence of the date range of the settlement has come to light. At the Knave, a promontory fort near Rhossili in Glamorganshire, two widely spread ramparts protected a clifftop, the inner area of which was barely 150 ft (46 m) across. Pottery akin to the wares in the Glastonbury style suggests a date in the first century BC but occupation could well have begun much earlier. The quarter-acre (0·1 hectare) promontory fort at Bishopston valley, Glam, produced pottery of similar date together with samian ware, suggesting a continuation of occupation into the Roman period, and finally, at High Penard, Glam, a 2 acre (0·8 hectare) promontory fort with widely spaced ramparts was examined, but yielded only Roman objects.

The exact status of these smaller promontory forts is in some doubt but the Knave and High Penard could strictly be classed as multiple-enclosure settlements modified to suit a promontory position, while the areas enclosed by many of them correspond to the raths on inland sites. It is doubtful, therefore, whether the promontory forts should be regarded as economically or socially distinct from the other types of enclosure. It is simpler to suppose that most of them are merely variants of the multiple-enclosure and rath types.

In summary, it may be said that the settlement pattern and economy of south and west Wales had much in common with Devon and Cornwall, the reason being chiefly that the climate and geomorphology of both areas encouraged the development of basically pastoral economies, which in turn directly influenced the nature of the social structure. The emphasis appears to be on individually defended homesteads, sometimes large enough to house not only the owner and family but also a considerable entourage. The absence of large hillforts strongly suggests a lack of centralised government. Cattle-rearing played an important part in the economy, the animals no doubt serving as a manifestation of wealth which could be treated as currency. In the more mountainous regions sheep may have been more significant but positive evidence is at present lacking. The position of cereal-growing is similarly uncertain: querns have been found but no extensive traces of Celtic field patterns have been recognised in the area. At present, all that can be said is that limited corn-growing is likely but unproven.

NORTH WALES

The study of the settlement pattern of north Wales is made difficult by the almost total absence of dating evidence from the many excavated sites, but the high quality of the field-work carried out, particularly in Caernarvonshire, makes it possible to describe in some detail the basic settlement forms belonging to the pre-Roman Iron Age.

Discussion must begin with the small multivallate enclosure of Castell Odo near Aberdaron, Caerns (Fig. 12:14), where as a result of extensive excavation a development sequence can be recognised, beginning with an open settlement composed of several circular timber houses associated with a small quantity of pottery similar in some forms to southern British assemblages dating to the fifth or fourth century. At some stage while the huts were in use, work began on the construction of a timber palisade, but it appears never to have been completed – a fact which might be linked to the destruction of one of the houses by fire. In the third phase the settlement was enclosed by a bank of earth surrounding an area approximately 250 ft (76 m) across, in which were built several circular huts of stone.

MYNYDD BYCHAN, GLAM

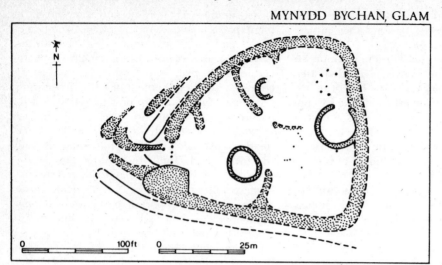

CASTELL ODO, CAERNS

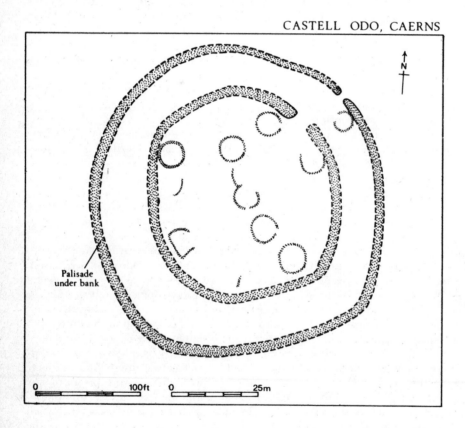

12:14   Welsh settlement sites (sources: *Mynydd Bychan*, Savory, 1954 and 1956; *Castell Odo*, Alcock, 1961)

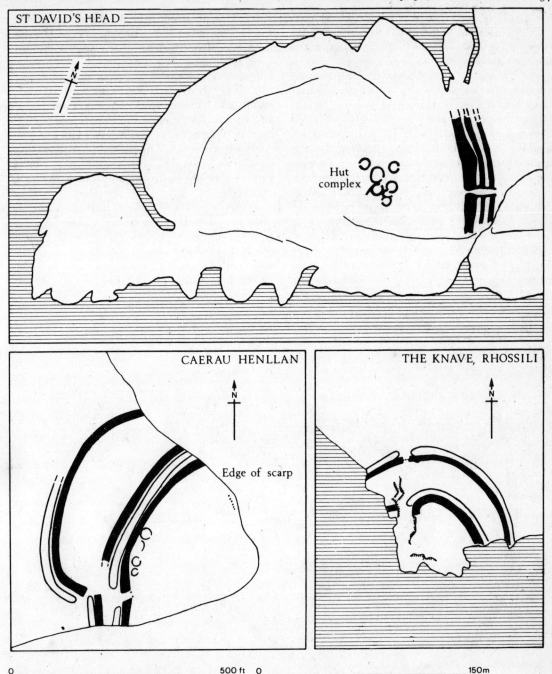

12:15   Welsh promontory forts (sources: *St David's Head, Pembs,* Baring-Gould, Burnard & Enys, 1899; *Caerau Hellan, Card,* ordnance survey; *The Knave, Glam,* Williams, 1939b)

Later still the bank was revetted back and front with dry-stone walling and a new, similarly constructed bank was erected inside it, leaving a space of about 40 ft (12 m) between the two. Finally, possibly as the result of the Roman invasion, the defences were slighted and circular stone houses were built over them.

In terms of size and social structure, Castell Odo compares closely with the raths of south-west Wales. In all probability, it developed as the homestead of the local chieftain's family, providing perhaps some protected accommodation for dependants within the enclosure. The intervallum space created later could well have served as a safe corral for stock, functioning in much the same way as the multiple-enclosure forts of the south-west. Elsewhere in north Wales this type of small defended settlement is by no means common, but several are found in the Aberdaron peninsula and along the coastal strip. Further inland at Dinas Emrys, Caerns, traces of a fenced settlement, possibly of similar type, have been recognised. It has been suggested that the palisade idea and the use of timber were alien traditions introduced by Hallstatt warriors. Admittedly timber-work of this kind is not known in earlier contexts in the region, but this may be due more to absence of evidence than evidence of absence. The palisade tradition could equally well have developed in Britain (p. 156); it is not necessary to invoke Hallstatt invaders to explain it.

A second class of enclosed homesteads, generally known as concentric circle sites, has been recognised in Caernarvonshire. A typical example, Llwyn-du-Bach, consists of a circular stone-built hut 29 ft (9 m) across, with two concentric enclosing walls 85 and 200 ft (26 and

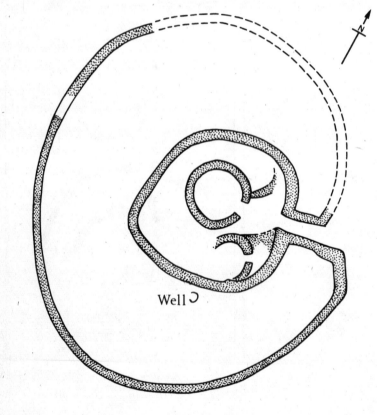

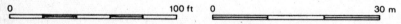

12:16　Settlement at Llwyn-du-Bach, Caerns (source: Bersu & Griffiths, 1949)

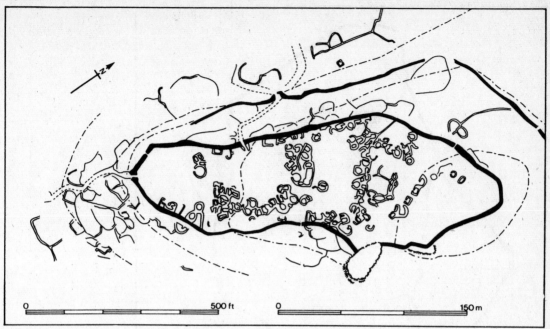

12:17   Plan of Tre'r Ceiri, Caerns (source: Hogg, 1962)

60 m) in diameter (Fig. 12:16). Suitable corral space was provided between the outer and inner walls while the inner enclosure contained the domestic features. No indication of dating was found but it has been suggested (Hogg, 1966) that concentric circle sites belong to the pre-Roman Iron Age and may have formed the prototype from which some at least of the native Roman Iron Age enclosures developed.

One of the most dramatic aspects of the north Welsh settlement pattern, is the development of large hilltop settlements defended by stone walls. The evidence from the Caernarvonshire forts of Garn Boduan. Tre'r Ceiri and Conway Mountain (Figs 12:17, 12:18) shows that many of them were occupied by sizable communities of between 100 and 400 people living in circular stone-walled huts, there being some twenty to eighty huts in each settlement. Normally the huts were totally enclosed by dry-stone ramparts but occasionally, as at Carn Fadrun, Caerns, a considerable part of the settlement lay on the surrounding slopes. Further east at Dinorben, Denbigh, a settlement of comparable size was recognised, but in this case the huts were of timber and some at least pre-dated the construction of the hillfort.

There is yet little evidence bearing on the economy of the region. At Dinorben sheep were numerically more common than cattle but exact percentages are not recorded. The implication is that at first the sheep-runs of the mountains were more widely used than the pastures of the Clwyd valley. By the Roman era the emphasis had been reversed. Sheep may have been of importance in the pre-Roman period in other parts of the region, for the mountainous landscape would have been more conducive to the rearing of sheep than cattle. Herein may lie one of the reasons why the multiple-enclosure forts of the south-west are rare in the north, for sheep would not have required the same corralling facilities as cattle. It may also be relevant that spindle whorls, reflecting the importance of wool, are more commonly found on the occupation sites of the north. The significance of grain-production to the economy is difficult to assess, but saddle querns were surprisingly common at Dinorben, Castell Odo and Conway Mountain, although at other sites they are absent. That the region possessed a fine grain-growing potential was shown by extensive development of arable farming under Roman domination. It may well be that large-scale cultivation began a few centuries earlier.

The occurrence of large hillforts in some parts

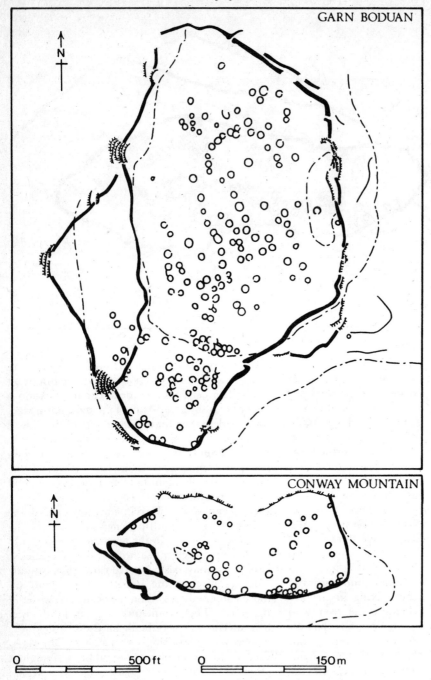

12:18   Plans of two Caernarvonshire hillforts (sources: *Garn Boduan*, Hogg, 1962; *Conway Mountain*, Griffiths & Hogg, 1957)

of the region suggests a centralisation uncommon in the predominantly pastoral areas of the south-west. It is possible, however, that they represent the kind of complex social organisation which was potentially possible in a community practising mixed farming based on grain-growing and sheep-rearing – an economy closely similar to that of south-eastern Britain. If so, the occurrence of hillforts is not surprising. Hogg (1966) put forward the suggestion that the hillforts were permanently occupied on the grounds that the houses within were substantially built and no houses have been found in the surrounding lowlands. Nevertheless, the possibility remains that they were used only as the summer refuge of people following a transhumant way of life, their winter farms being sited on the rather more hospitable lowlands (Alcock, 1965). The virtual absence of lowland farms may be more apparent than real, for many of the Roman period homesteads might well have begun in use before the conquest; the fact that no distinctive pre-Roman artefacts have been found may only reflect the widespread dearth of the surviving elements of the pre-Roman material culture. That transhumance was practised to some degree seems likely, but there are difficulties in accepting the hillforts as positive evidence for it. Migration to upland summer pastures would tend to disperse rather than nucleate population, although it could of course be argued that raiding was more prevalent in the summer months, making communal defence necessary. At present, it must be admitted that the problems are rather too many to allow firm conclusions to be reached: more statistical evidence is required of the composition and age-range of the flocks and herds from various sites. Sadly, this kind of data has seldom been published in the past.

THE WELSH BORDERLAND

The wide strip of countryside west of the Dee–Severn axis, extending into the foothills of the Welsh mountains, has produced abundant evidence of pre-Roman Iron Age occupation, but almost entirely from the excavation of large hillforts; no small homesteads have yet been examined, although in the upper reaches of the Severn and the foothills of the Berwyn Mountains enclosures of less than 3 acres (1·2 hectares) abound, as they do between the Wye and the

Usk in the south.

Several of the excavated forts show signs of rebuilding and extensive occupation over a considerable period of time, and in the southern part of the area at least, many of the basic elements of the south-eastern economy are found. The most thoroughly excavated of the forts, Croft Ambrey in Herefordshire has produced ample evidence of extensive grain-production: quantities of charred grain were found in various levels, saddle querns were common, and a number of four-post granaries were uncovered together with storage pits in the later periods. The animal bones show that sheep were the most numerous but cattle and pigs occurred in quantity. There is also evidence that horse meat was eaten and fresh-water mussels were collected. That a very high percentage of the animals were mature when killed suggests that flocks and herds were kept more for their milk and wool than for their meat. The production of woollen clothing is further emphasised by the discovery of spindle whorls and loom-weights. A similar picture can be reconstructed for the hillforts of Sutton Walls, Heref, where cattle predominated – 41 per cent compared with 38 per cent sheep and 16 per cent pigs. A weaving comb and several loom-weights are added evidence of wool-production.

The significance of stock-rearing to the economy is shown by the provision of annexes at several of the forts. Croft Ambrey offers an example of a simple annex attached to one side, enclosing about 7 acres (2·8 hectares) – an area equivalent to that of the main camp. A more complex pattern occurs at Old Oswestry, Salop (Fig. 12:19), where in a late period subdivided enclosures were added to either side of the main entrance; these were later contained within a bank and ditch which enclosed the entire fort. Functional explanations are difficult, but the later circumvallation would have provided a considerable protected acreage of pasture in the lee of the fort similar to the situation at Danebury, Hants. The divided enclosures are harder to understand in their present form but had suitable provision been made for entrance, they might have served as stockpens.

The similarity between the basic economy of the southern borderland and south-eastern Britain is striking but there is no need to explain it in terms of invasions into the area from the south. A simple parallel development guided by

CASTLE HILL, ALMONDBURY, YORKS

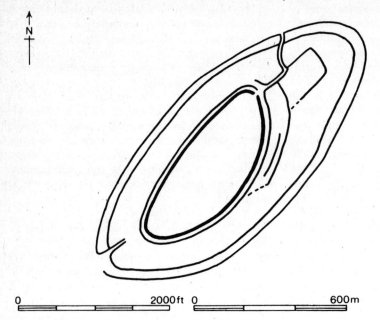

OLD OSWESTRY, SALOP

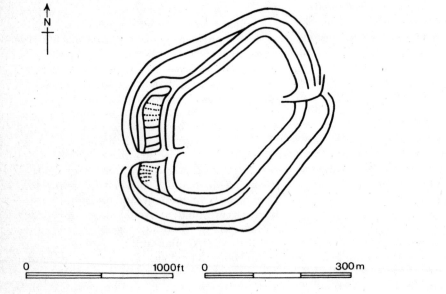

12:19   Hillforts with outer cattle corrals (source: Varley 1950b)

the similar food-producing potential of the two environments is likely to be the main reason.

North of the Wye and Teme valleys, however, the economic basis may prove to have been differently orientated: the land is mountainous and is dissected by narrow river valleys, suited more to stock-rearing than cultivation. It may be significant that it is in precisely this area that the small enclosed settlements, comparable to those of south-west Wales, abound. The more isolated forts of this area, like Titterstone Clee and the Wrekin in Shropshire, have not produced the range of domestic material common in the southern part of the region, but this may in part be due to the limited nature of the excavations. Nevertheless, their uncongenial siting, and the total absence of surface indications of huts where they might legitimately have been expected to survive on the stony hilltops, strongly suggests that some of the forts at least were temporary refuges for livestock and herders. It is not impossible, therefore, that a degree of transhumance was practised in some areas, the population living most of the time in the smaller enclosed settlements. Of the unexcavated hillforts of this northern area several, including Earl's Hill, Salop, and the Breiddin, Montgomery, are multiple enclosures providing adequate protected pasture for flocks and herds of considerable size.

Tentatively, therefore, we may suggest a divergence in the economies of the borderland: emphasis in the southern area was on mixed farming, combining cereal-growing with sheep-rearing and the maintenance of substantial herds of cattle and swine, while in the northern area pastoral activities took predominance over cultivation. It may be of some significance that pottery, widely used in the later period in the southern area, was virtually unknown in the north. Among the mobile northern pastoralists, leather and wooden containers would have been used in preference to breakable pottery, whereas to the more sedentary cultivators of the south, mass-produced pottery appears to have been a sought-after commodity.

THE MIDLANDS

The triangle of country west of the Avon–Soar–Trent, east of the Severn–Dee and south of the Pennines is composed of vast tracts of Keuper marl, Triassic sandstones and coal-measure shales, highly unconducive to pre-Roman Iron Age settlement. Apart from the river gravels and the more fertile sandstone and limestone hills, the area appears to have been largely unsettled. The only site excavated in any detail is the hillfort of Breedon-on-the-Hill, Leics, sited on a hill of Magnesian limestone overlooking the valleys of the Soar and Trent. No internal buildings were recognised, but occupation appears to have been extensive. Pits, possibly for storage, and a number of quern-stones suggest that grain-production was widely practised. The quantity of animal bones recovered was not large but cattle were numerically more common than sheep (50 per cent compared with 36 per cent), underlining the importance of the pastures along the Soar valley. The use of sheep as wool-producers is, however, reflected in the discovery of a weaving comb.

If the evidence derived from Breedon-on-the-Hill is typical of the area as a whole, it would seem that where settlement occurred in the Midlands the economy was generally similar to that of the south-east, but clearly far more evidence is required before definite conclusions can be reached.

THE PENNINES AND THE NORTH OF ENGLAND

The North of England can be considered as two separate areas: an eastern region, consisting of the chalk Wolds and the limestone Moors divided from each other by the Vale of Pickering, and a western region of which the Pennines themselves form the greater part. Between the two lie the valleys of the Swale and the Ouse, which follow the wide band of Triassic sandstone and marls. In neither region has much evidence of economy or settlement pattern come to light but, as the result of limited excavations, certain generalisations are possible.

The best known of the Yorkshire Wold settlements, is the site of Staple Howe, situated on a chalk hillock overlooking the Vale of Pickering (Fig. 12:20). Here a farmstead dating to the sixth and fifth centuries has been substantially excavated, revealing an oval palisaded enclosure, subsequently remodelled, containing several huts and a massively constructed five-post rectangular granary. The excavator has suggested that in the

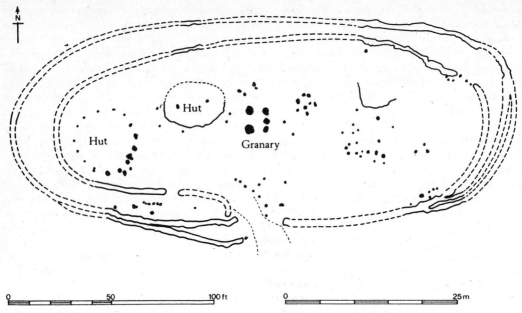

12:20   Settlement site on Staple Howe, Yorks (source: Brewster, 1963)

first phase the only hut in use was an oval structure which was subsequently replaced by two circular huts. While the circular huts are of generalised type similar to those found over most of southern Britain, the oval hut is more unusual: its roof appears to have been constructed around a horizontal ridge-post supported on two verticals, while the lower ends of the rafters would have rested on the ground or upon dwarf walls constructed of turf or chalk. In addition to large quantities of pottery and a range of imported bronze objects referred to above (p. 34), the surviving material remains included masses of animal bones, principally of cattle, sheep and swine, together with an amount of carbonised grain, all of which proved to be club wheat (*Triticum compactum*).

The same general pattern of economy is reflected in the evidence from the hillfort of Grimthorpe, which occupies a somewhat similar position on the west edge of the Yorkshire Wolds overlooking a low-lying area of densely-wooded Keuper marl. Within the defences of the fort were found eight four-post granaries, emphasising the importance of cereal-growing. The animal bones showed a preponderance of cattle – 55 per cent compared with 25 per cent sheep; pigs (7·8 per cent) were only a little more plentiful than horses (7·3 per cent). If these figures are

corrected for actual meat yield, beef consumption would be seen to amount to about 82·4 per cent of the total meat intake. A more detailed examination of the cattle bones shows that more than 70 per cent of the herd was maintained over two winters before eventual slaughter. Sheep, on the other hand, were killed off at a constant rate. The implications are clear enough: the economy was sufficiently stable for extensive over-wintering, a fact which in itself adds support to the view that corn-growing, producing straw fodder, played a significant part in balancing the complex processes of food-production. Clearly, then, mixed farming was practised – indeed, there is very little difference between the socio-economic basis of Staple Howe and Grimthorpe and that of a typical Wessex farm, except for the absence of querns and storage pits. Since, however, storage pits were rare or unknown among the southern sites in the sixth and fifth centuries, their absence from the contemporary Yorkshire sites is hardly surprising. The lack of querns is a little puzzling, but this may be nothing more than an accident of survival.

While the settlement pattern and economy of the Yorkshire chalk hills closely resembled that of the southern downlands in the seventh to fifth centuries, the same does not appear to be true of the later period. In Yorkshire there is nothing to compare with the expanding farming economy and settlement pattern of the south. It could be, of course, that the sites have not yet been found, but an alternative and more attractive hypothesis is that the incursion of the La Tène immigrants in the late fifth century halted local development, or at least changed its direction. Until settlements of the period have been defined and excavated, the nature of the later Iron Age farming pattern of the area must remain unknown, but the paucity of permanent settlements and the occurrence of linear earthworks associated with rectangular enclosures, which may be of this date, hint at the possibility of a more pastoral and nomadic existence. The matter, however, is at present beyond proof.

West of the Vale of York lie the Pennines, offering three basic environments to potential settlers: the upland limestone areas of Derbyshire and the Yorkshire Dales, the acid ill-drained moors of the coal-measures and millstone grit, and the wide valleys floored with glacial drift which dissect the range. Little is known of the area in the pre-Roman Iron Age, but several large hillforts are recorded. At Castle Hill (Almondbury), Yorks (Fig. 12:19), overlooking the valley of the Holme, substantial annexes were added close to the main entrance of the fort, and later an outer series of banks and ditches were constructed to enclose the annexes and the original fort together with a considerable acreage of protected pasture. Such an arrangement, which has parallels in the Welsh borderland and Wessex, strongly suggests the increasing importance of livestock, which needed protection.

Further north the overriding importance of stock-rearing is emphasised by the remarkable development of the fort at Stanwick, Yorks, in the first century AD in parallel with Roman political and military manoeuvres further south. The relatively small earthworks of the first phase, an enclosure 17 acres (6·9 hectares) in size lying alongside a stream, were extended to cover 130 acres (52·6 hectares), including a stretch of the stream bank, some time about 50 or 60 AD. Later, about 70 AD, a subsequent enlargement added a further 600 acres (242·8 hectares) to the protected pasture, together with about a mile of river valley. Wheeler (1954) argues convincingly that the works were carried out by the anti-Roman faction of the Brigantes led by Venutius, to provide safety for the tribe and its herds as the Roman advance pressed nearer.

The cultural assemblage from Stanwick, recovered largely from the excavation of a circular hut and a series of drainage gullies within the first phase defensive circuit, emphasises to the pastoral nature of the economy. The total absence of storage pits and granaries and the discovery of only one small fragment of quern suggest that cultivation was of relatively little significance. Of the animal bones recovered, 40 per cent were cattle, 23 per cent sheep/goat and 16 per cent pig. The siting of the fortifications, enclosing meadows and pannage, was clearly designed for the benefit of the cattle and pigs, the animals which yielded the greater percentage of the meat; sheep were of subsidiary importance.

While it must be admitted that Stanwick may be somewhat atypical, because of the political pressures under which it was largely constructed, there can be little doubt that by the first century AD the basic economy of the Pennine area was pastoral and semi-nomadic. Nevertheless, the limestone hills and valleys between the rivers Wharfe and Greta, where intensive field-work has been carried out, were densely settled (Raistrick, 1939) and there is no reason to suppose that other limestone areas were any less thickly inhabited (Fig. 12:21). Three types of settlement have been defined, the most common being the isolated hut, or sometimes a pair, set in a small embanked enclosure with a field or two nearby (Fig. 12:22). This type is found mainly on the limestone plateau. The second type of settlement is the larger nucleation of huts which might reasonably be referred to as a village. One of the best-known examples, at Grassington in Wharfedale, consists of about 2 acres (0·8 hectares) of huts and enclosures associated with about 80 acres (32·4 hectares) of rectangular fields. The third type of site is the inhabited cave, quite often with a group of small fields laid out close by. The nature of the economy seen through the material culture is clear enough: grain was grown but in relatively small quantities, the principal food-sources being meat and milk from the flocks and herds. The relative percentages of cattle and sheep are uncertain, but the equipment of spinning and weaving occurs in quantity and the limestone pastures would have been far better suited to sheep than to cows.

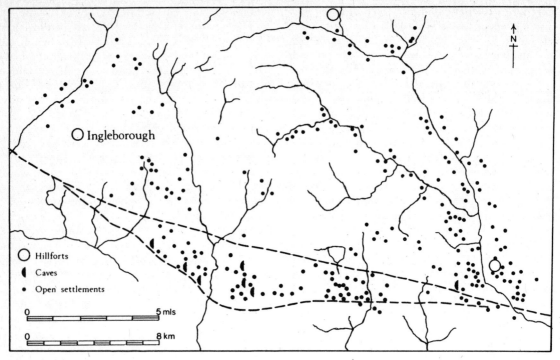

O Ingleborough

O Hillforts

❮ Caves

• Open settlements

0   5 mls

0   8 km

12:21   The distribution of settlements in the Wharfedale area of Yorkshire (source: Raistrick, 1939)

Although most of the sites in the area are difficult to date and many were occupied throughout the Roman period, it is inconceivable that none of them should have begun earlier. Indeed, in all probability the Roman settlement pattern closely reflected that of the preceding period. It cannot, however, be demonstrated that there were no substantial changes in the economic system consequent upon the conquest. All that can be safely said at present is that the land supported a considerable population who, by the Roman period at least, were cultivating fields as well as maintaining flocks and herds. Until the large-scale excavation of some of the settlements has been undertaken, further conclusions are impossible.

The general absence of hillforts in the northern Pennines, with the exception of Ingleborough, Yorks, is notable. Presumably the pastoral nature of the economy prevented the development of politically cohesive tribes requiring defended foci. The dissected nature of the landscape would also encourage the isolation of smaller groups.

THE TYNE–FORTH REGION

The settlement pattern of the eastern part of northern Britain, centred upon the Tyne–Forth region but extending to the north and south of it, is well known as the result of intensive field-work (Jobey, 1962a, 1965, 1966a, 1966b and 1971; RCHM(S) *Peeblesshire* and *Roxburghshire*), backed up by limited but carefully planned excavation. Most of the known sites now lie in the foothills of the main mountain ranges, on marginal land which has escaped recent ploughing, but aerial photography is now showing that occupation extended on to the richer boulder clays of the lowlands, where all surface indications have long since disappeared.

The commonest form of settlement, numerous examples of which are now recorded, is the palisaded enclosure (Fig. 12:23): a circular, oval or sub-rectangular area surrounded by a continuous palisade trench in which close-spaced vertical timbers were wedged. A variety of plans are known (Figs 12:24, 12:25). At one of the largest of the sites, White Hill, Peebles, two con-

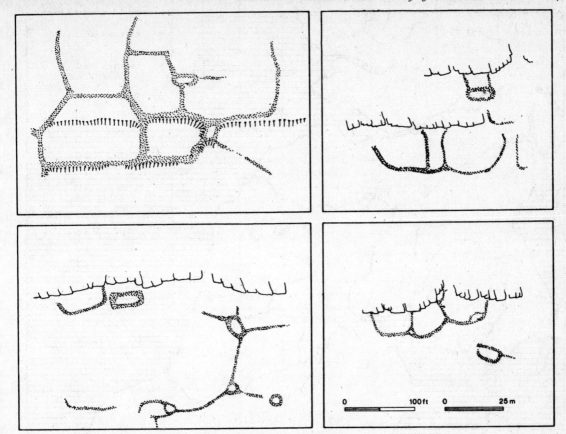

12:22   Settlement sites in the Pennines (source: W.B., 1938)

centric palisades were erected 20–50 ft (6·1–15·2 m) apart, the inner enclosing an area of 1·75 acres (0·7 hectares). Hayhope Knowe, Roxburgh (Fig. 12:25), follows much the same arrangement, the only difference being that here the inner palisade was double, while at Castle Hill (Horsburgh), Peebles, both inner and outer palisades were double. The examples mentioned so far were all provided with simple opposed entrances, but others are known with only one entrance. At the thoroughly excavated site of West Brandon, Co. Durham (Fig. 12:26), the simple double palisade ended in four large gate-posts in the centre of one side, and at Harehope, Peebles (Fig. 12:25), a single central gate was provided in each of the two periods represented; in the second, however, it was flanked with substantial timber-built towers. Harehope is atypical in another way since the palisades, instead of being set in a rock-cut trench, were bedded in a shallow bank of soil and rubble. While it may be true that this was a modification developed with time, the method of construction is not unlike that practised in Late Bronze Age contexts in southern Britain.

Stylistically the palisaded settlements have parallels among early sites further south which belong to the seventh to fourth centuries. A radiocarbon date for charcoal from one of the palisade trenches at Huckhoe, Northumberland, provided a reading of 510 ± 40 (585 BC) while the palisade at Burnswark has been dated to 500 ± 100 (574 BC). Clearly, then, the northern palisades are of the same broad date as those in the south. A further point of similarity is that some of them were later rebuilt as earthwork-enclosed sites. A good example of such a refurbishing can be seen at West Brandon, where a ditch was dug outside the palisades, the rampart without revetment being piled up behind, sealing

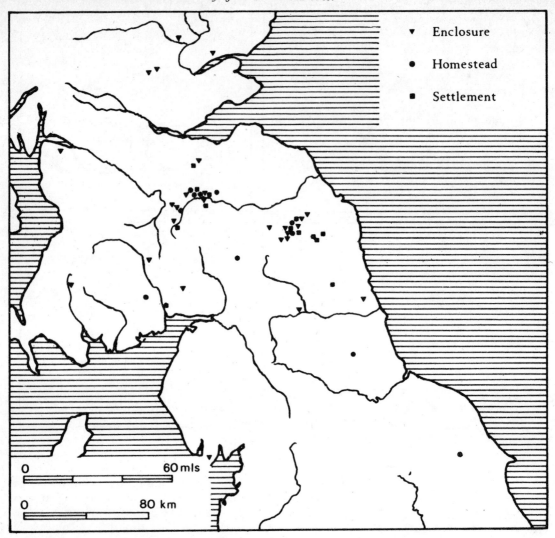

12:23   Distribution of palisaded homesteads and settlements in northern Britain (source: Ritchie, 1970)

the original palisade trenches. At Huckhoe both the inner and outer lines of palisade, 50 ft (15 m) apart, were replaced by stone-faced ramparts, while at Castle Hill (Horsburgh) the two palisades were again echoed in later earthworks but enclosed a more restricted area.

In all these examples and the many others that are known, there is little positive evidence for dating the change in enclosure style. At Huckhoe the earthworks must have been built immediately after the destruction of the palisade by fire in the sixth century, but radiocarbon dates of 245 ± 90 (311 BC) for Brough Law and 220 ± 90 (285 BC) for Ingram Hill, both in Northumberland, show that not all the earthworks were as early.

A point worthy of emphasis is that many of the sites, both palisaded or earthwork-enclosed, were provided with multiple lines of defence, commonly 50 ft (15 m) or so apart. While there can be no certainty on the matter, it is very tempting to see such an arrangement as the deliberate provision of protected corralling space for livestock, on analogy with the multiple-enclosure forts of the south-west. Pastoral activities must have played a significant part in the economy but the general absence of faunal material renders any assessment of the composition of flocks and herds impossible. Cultivation was by no means neglected, as the four saddle querns from West Brandon and the rotary quern from Harehope show. Huckhoe has also provided evidence of what could be interpreted as a four-post granary, but the storage pits and corn-drying hollows of the south are entirely lacking and no field systems of definitely pre-Roman date have yet been defined. Thus, although the superficial resemblances to the settlements of southern Britain are impressive, the economy seems to have been more pastorally orientated.

The size of the settlements varies considerably from homesteads of one house like West Brandon to hamlets or even villages like the sixteen houses of Hayhope Knowe. Houses are invariably circular, ranging from about 20 to 50 ft (6 to 15 m) in diameter (Fig. 12:27). The simplest are merely circular settings of posts like Harehope house 1 and the house which pre-dates the palisades at West Brandon. A slightly more complex arrangement occurs at Glenachan Rig where a central post was provided to support the roof and the lower ends of the rafters were bedded in a shallow trench, thus providing some storage space behind the verticals. The earliest house in the palisaded enclosure at West Brandon is even more elaborate, with a roof taken on three con-

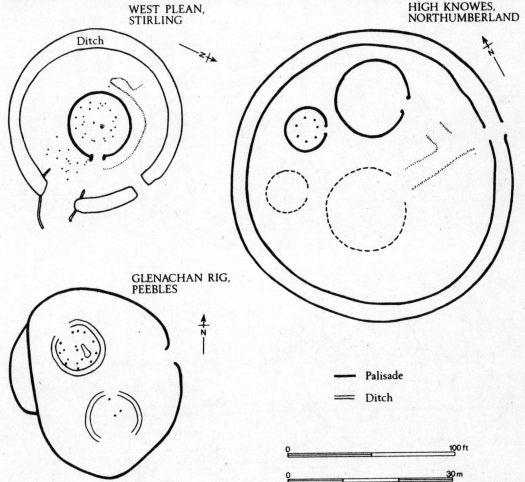

WEST PLEAN,
STIRLING

HIGH KNOWES,
NORTHUMBERLAND

GLENACHAN RIG,
PEEBLES

—— Palisade

== Ditch

0 — 100 ft

0 — 30 m

12:24 Comparative plans of palisaded enclosures (sources: *West Plean*, Steer, 1958; *High Knowes*, Jobey & Tait, 1966; *Glenachan Rig*, Feachem, 1961)

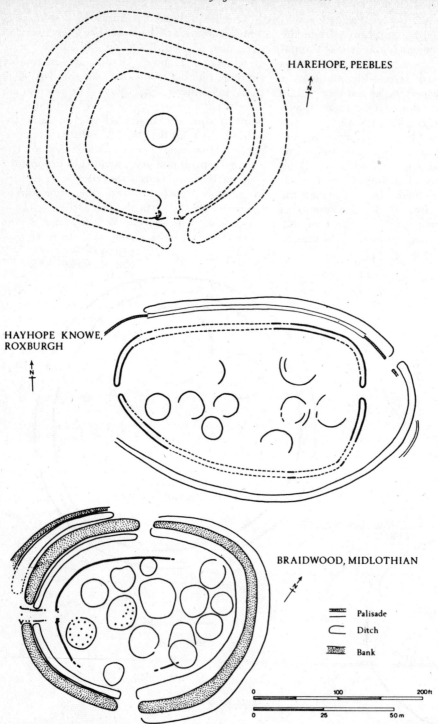

HAREHOPE, PEEBLES

HAYHOPE KNOWE, ROXBURGH

BRAIDWOOD, MIDLOTHIAN

	Palisade
	Ditch
	Bank

0　　　　100　　　　200ft

0　　25　　50 m

12:25　Comparative plans of palisaded settlements (sources: *Harehope*, Feachem, 1962; *Hayhope Knowe*, C. M. Piggott, 1951; *Braidwood*, S. Piggott, 1960)

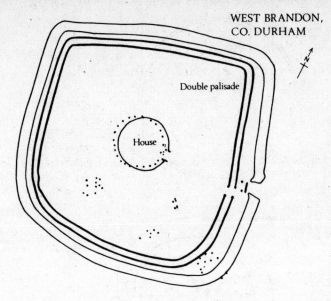

WEST BRANDON,
CO. DURHAM

Double palisade

House

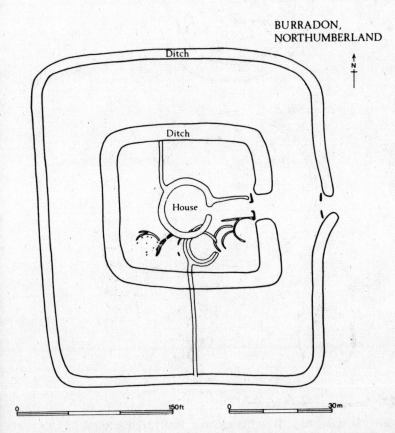

BURRADON,
NORTHUMBERLAND

Ditch

Ditch

House

0   150ft   0   30m

12:26   Comparative plans of rectangular enclosures (sources: *West Brandon*, Jobey, 1962b; *Burradon*, Jobey, 1970)

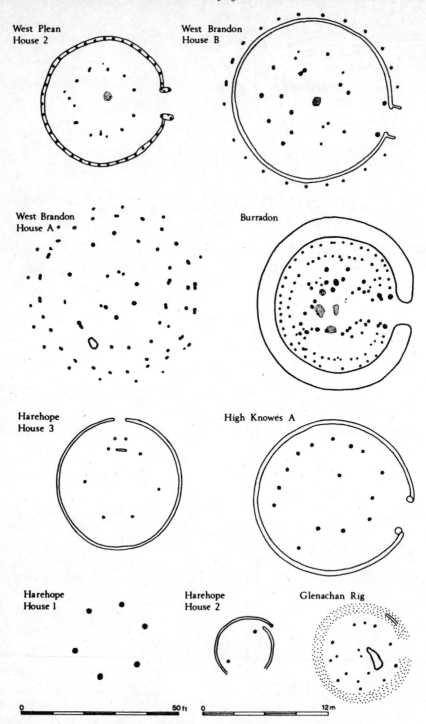

12:27   Types of north British house plans (sources: *West Plean*, Steer, 1958; *West Brandon*, Jobey, 1962b; *Burradon*, Jobey, 1970; *Harehope*, Feachem, 1962; *High Knowes*, Jobey & Tait, 1966; *Glenachan Rig*, Feachem, 1961)

centric circles of posts, the outermost being 50 ft (15 m) in diameter. Beyond this is a further set of stake-holes, perhaps to tie down the roof-timbers, while the entrance passage seems to have been provided with double doors. In size and sophistication, the house rivals Little Woodbury, Wilts, and Pimperne Down, Dorset.

The earliest house at West Brandon was replaced by a structure of similar size, the outer wall of which was bedded in a continuous trench. Inside, a multiple setting of individual posts would have supported the main weight of the roof, while again an outer setting of stakes was provided, presumably as anchors for the rafters. A closely similar house was found at West Plean in period 2 – similar even to the extent of having the same type of short porch. The period 3 house at Harehope belonged to this general category but in this case it would appear that the outer wall was made of split timbers erected as a continuous wall rather than wattle infilling between individual posts.

A later development, well-represented among settlements discovered in Northumberland, is the appearance of stone-walled huts set in enclosures sometimes overlying the defences of hillforts (Fig. 12:28). Such settlements are normally so sited as to make use of sheltered slopes, comfort being more important than defensive potential. Some regional differences are evident. In the Cheviot foothills the usual type of enclosure is circular, containing a number of huts fronting on to a sunken yard which is sometimes paved. Further south in Northumberland rectilinear plans prevail, the enclosures containing four or five round huts opening on to a pair of cobbled yards divided by a central pathway leading to the rear of the enclosure. The huts show no significant variation in size or complexity, suggesting little social differentiation, but in some areas larger settlements arise as the result of gradual growth and addition to a basic nucleus. Nucleation of this kind is not, however, common and the normal settlement unit remained throughout more appropriate to the family and the extended family than to more complex social groupings.

Dating evidence, where it exists, shows that many of the sites were occupied during the second century AD – a fact which, together with the rectangularity of the plans, has suggested direct Roman inspiration — but the recent discovery of a rectangular enclosed homestead at Burradon, Northumberland (Fig. 12:26), dating to the middle of the first millennium BC shows that little can be based on plan alone. In all probability, enclosures with stone-walled huts developed out of the strong local tradition and may even have come into use before Roman interference in the area. There is often an element of continuity in choice of site between the small defended hillforts and the settlements: on some occasions the settlements actually overlie lengths of the disused defences. In such a case it is possible that a direct continuity of occupation took place. Elsewhere, the proximity of settlements to hillforts could be interpreted as a community moving to a more hospitable site nearby when need for defence was removed.

Another type of settlement, less well known, is the so-called 'scooped enclosure': a group of hut platforms terraced into the hillside and enclosed by a bank or wall (Fig. 12:28). Dating is at present uncertain but typologically a Late Iron Age or early Roman context would seem to be most likely.

The replacement of palisades with earthworks has given many of the early homesteads and settlements the appearance of hillforts, but not only do most of them not exceed 3 acres (1·2 hectares) in overall extent, the siting of many is clearly not defensive. For this reason, there is frequently considerable uncertainty in the use of the term 'hillfort' in Scotland: many of the 1,500 or so recorded (at least three-quarters of them in the Tyne–Forth region) are no more than rampart-enclosed homesteads and settlements. To avoid confusion, the phrase 'minor oppidum' has been used (Feachem, 1966) to describe fortifications of a more massive size, 6–40 + acres (2·4–16·2 + hectares) in extent, sited with an eye to the defensive possibilities of the land. These are far less numerous – some fourteen within the region under discussion. Many of them enclosed massive settlements: more than 500 houses within the 40 acres (16·2 hectares) of Eildon Hill North, Roxburgh, it is estimated, and at least 130 within the 13 acres (5·3 hectares) of Yevering Bell, Northumberland.

These Scottish sites with their ten to twelve huts per acre were three times more densely settled than those of north-west Wales. Excavation of Traprain Law, East Lothian, which at one time reached 40 acres (16·2 hectares), has shown that here at least occupation began in the

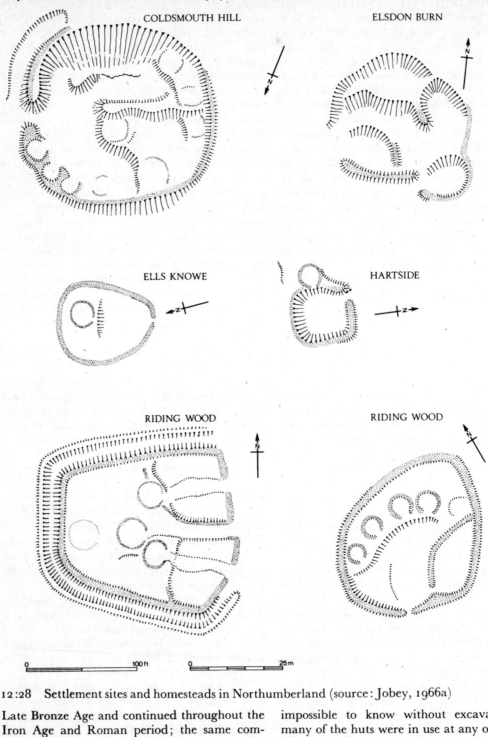

12:28   Settlement sites and homesteads in Northumberland (source: Jobey, 1966a)

Late Bronze Age and continued throughout the Iron Age and Roman period; the same complexity of occupation may well be true of the other large oppida of the region. It is therefore impossible to know without excavation how many of the huts were in use at any one time or what the density of occupation was in the Iron Age compared with the Roman period. It is not

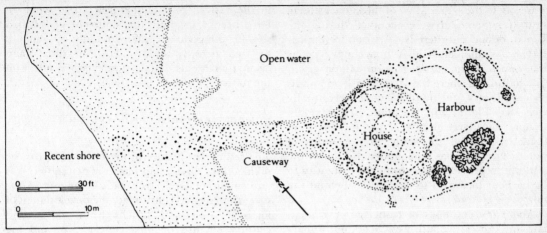

Open water

Harbour

House

Recent shore

Causeway

0   30 ft

0   10 m

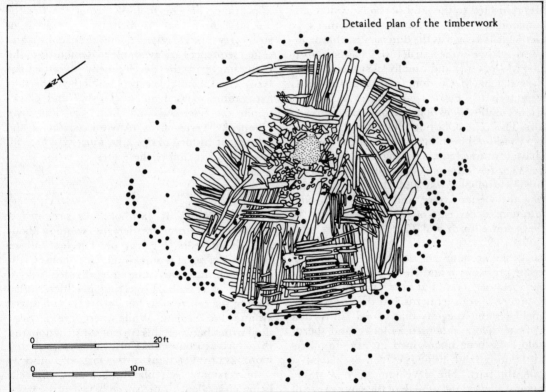

Detailed plan of the timberwork

0   20 ft

0   10 m

12:29   Milton Loch, crannog I (source: C. M. Piggott, 1955)

unreasonable, however, to suppose that by the later part of the Iron Age these oppida had developed into large nucleated settlements which in some way commanded the allegiance of the inhabitants of the surrounding countryside.

In south-west Scotland, in the territory of the Novantae and Damnonii, a more specialised type of settlement known as the crannog developed. Crannogs were usually built at the edge of lochs and consisted of artificial islands composed of layers of brushwood and rubble revetted around the edges by vertical piles and surfaced with oak logs. Upon these platforms a single hut usually stood, the whole structure being joined by a causeway to the shore. Most of the known sites in south-west Scotland were occupied during the Roman period but there is no reason to suppose that all were built after the Roman conquest. The best known of the crannogs is on Milton Loch, Kirkcudbright, where the artificial island and its associated jetty and small harbour were totally excavated (Fig. 12:29). The platform was largely occupied by a large circular hut 42 ft (12·8 m) in diameter, divided internally into a series of rooms. The hut was surrounded by a narrow platform to provide access from the causeway to the harbour facing on to deep water behind the hut.

About ten crannogs of Iron Age or Roman date are known in south-west Scotland, apparently restricted to the land of the Novantae and Damnonii. In much the same area another type of settlement known as the dun occurs, characterised as a stone-walled structure enclosing up to 4,000 ft² (370 m²) and usually of sub-circular or sub-oval plan (M. Gordon, 1969). Duns normally possess rebated entrance passages, as well as various combinations of mural galleries, cells and stairs. This type of fortified homestead probably has a considerable antiquity but some are known to have continued in use during the Roman Iron Age. Very few duns occur in the territory of the Votadini and Selgovae but they are common along the western coast and islands, and concentrations occur east of the Highlands in the valleys of the Forth and Tay.

The basic economy of southern Scotland in the late pre-Roman and Roman Iron Age is not clearly understood but the not infrequent occurrence of rotary querns and the appearance of field systems suggests that cereal cultivation was extensively practised. Flocks and herds would have been maintained in large numbers and hunting and fishing evidently played a significant part. The development of a stable economy allowed the growth of the same range of settlement type – homesteads, hamlets and oppida – as appeared in the south. Even constructional details of the palisades and houses can be closely paralleled in Wessex. Where differences occur, they result from the different physical provisions required for pastoral-based rather than cereal-based subsistence. Little evidence of change can be recognised before the Roman conquest in the late first century AD but thereafter,

in the eastern part of the area, there seems to have been a gradual abandonment of fortified sites for the greater comfort of more congenially situated farms. In the west, however, the Roman occupation seems to have had even less effect on the native culture.

NORTH-WEST SCOTLAND AND THE ISLANDS

The settlement history of the north-west can be divided into three main phases: open settlements and small enclosed farmsteads belonging to the seventh to second century BC, the development of fortified duns and brochs from the second century BC into the first century AD, and the appearance of wheelhouses during the first or second century AD. While many hundreds of structures survive, relatively few archaeologically tested sequences are available to demonstrate the early stages in the development of settlement type, with the notable exception of the important excavations carried out at Jarlshof and Clickhimin on Shetland and Dun Lagaidh near Ullapool, Wester Ross. Any discussion of the settlement history of the area must rely heavily on a consideration of these sites.

Pre-broch settlements

The excavations at Jarlshof have provided a sequence of pre-broch settlement spanning about a thousand years (Fig. 12:30). The first village consisted of several stone-built oval houses (Pl. 9a). Each hut was internally divided into a number of cells by projecting partition walls, leaving the centre clear for a general living space around the hearth. While there are obvious similarities between this type of construction and the courtyard houses of Cornwall, it is probably more accurate to think of the Jarlshof houses as stone versions of circular timber huts, the cells being equivalent to the space between the main roof supports and the outer walls in the more sophisticated types of timber structures.

Rebuilding was carried out on several occasions, and at an early stage a souterrain (or underground storage cellar) was constructed beneath the courtyard of one of the houses. Later the house was totally rebuilt as a circular structure averaging 24 ft (7·3 m) across, with cubicles set into the wall and a large souterrain

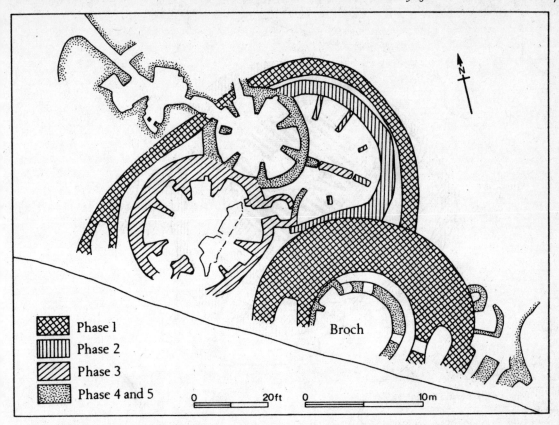

Phase 1

Phase 2

Phase 3

Phase 4 and 5

Broch

0 _____ 20ft

0 _____ 10m

12:30   Plan of the settlement at Jarlshof, Shetland, from the construction of the broch (source: Hamilton, 1956)

opening out of one side. At about the time that the first souterrain was built, angular pottery with flat rims came into fashion and iron began to be used. Whether or not these innovations represent a single significant cultural change, or are simply the result of gradual development under some external influence, remains uncertain.

A similar sequence has been recognised beneath the broch of Clickhimin 22 miles (35.2 km) north of Jarlshof (Fig. 12:31). The earliest settlement (period I) consisted of an oval cubicled house built entirely of stone, belonging to the Late Bronze Age. This was replaced by a large roundhouse (period II) associated with carinated pottery like that from Jarlshof. Eventually (period III) the house was encircled with a defensive fort wall, inside which lay a blockhouse, to protect the entrance. At this time the accommodation was greatly increased by the construction of timber ranges around the inside

of the fort wall, probably standing to a height of two storeys with stalls below and living space above. The blockhouse is a remarkable structure (Fig. 12:32). Originally it would have been three storeys high with an attached timber-built range behind. At ground floor level a central passage was provided in the masonry leading to the dwelling space behind, while at first floor level a door gave access between the rooms of the timber range and mural cells constructed within the thickness of the blockhouse masonry; the second floor was probably a wall-walk to provide a vantage point. Blockhouses of this kind are known at two other Shetland sites (Fig. 12:33), at Ness of Burgi, Sumburgh, and on an islet in the Loch of Hunter, Whalsey. At both sites the structures appear to have been integral with the main defensive wall, a situation which may have been intended at Clickhimin but never achieved. In the final pre-broch phase at Clickhimin (period IV), after repair of the outer fort wall

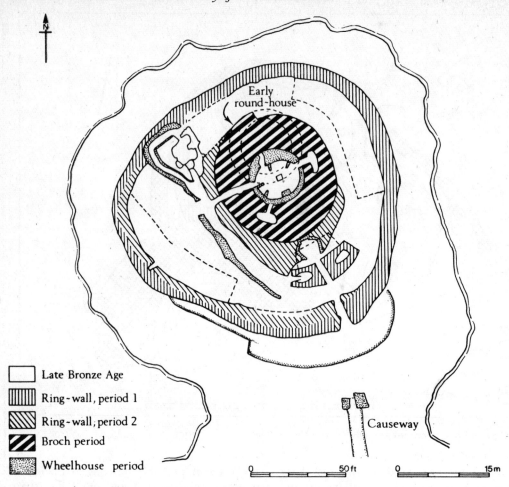

N

Early
round-house

☐ Late Bronze Age

▥ Ring-wall, period 1

▧ Ring-wall, period 2

▨ Broch period

░ Wheelhouse period

Causeway

0   50 ft   0   15 m

12:31   Plan of the settlement at Clickhimin, Shetland (source: Hamilton, 1968)

and the demolition of the timber ranges, work began on the construction of an inner ring-wall around the island, butting up to the original Iron Age circular hut, which remained in use. The work was, however, unfinished by the time that the broch was constructed.

The Clickhimin sequence is of immense value in that it presents a complete and unbroken development spanning the pre-broch period from the seventh to the first century. It has been suggested (Hamilton, 1968) that the blockhouse architecture should be considered to be immediately ancestral to the development of the brochs, implying that brochs originated somewhere in the Northern Islands – perhaps on Orkney, where the building stone is eminently suitable. The problem, however, is a difficult one

and will be considered again below (p. 222).

Elsewhere in north and west Scotland, evidence of pre-broch occupation is scarce, but roundhouses provided with souterrains and associated with the angular pottery of Jarlshof type are also known on the mainland at Kilphedir, Sutherland, for which radiocarbon dates of 150 ± 80 (215 BC) and 420 ± 40 (491 BC) are now available. Similar houses and pottery are recorded on the Calf of Eday, Orkney. The settlements of the west coast and Western Isles are less well known, but at Dun Mor Vaul on Tiree (Argyll) a pre-broch midden of the fifth to third century has been examined, and at Dun Lagaidh near Ullapool a vitrified fort with radiocarbon dates of 490 ± 90 and 460 ± 100 (565 and 532 BC) has been shown to pre-date a broch.

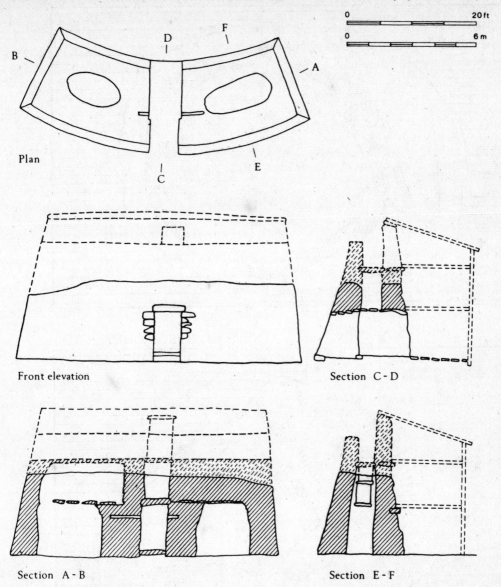

0   20 ft

0   6 m

Plan

Front elevation

Section C - D

Section A - B

Section E - F

12:32   The blockhouse at Clickhimin, Shetland (source: Hamilton, 1968)

Neither site has, however, produced much evidence of material culture or economy.

Broch and duns (Pl. 10b)

The principal feature of the Late Iron Age landscape in north and west Scotland is the density of small fortified sites which Childe (1935a) referred to as the 'castle complex'. These fortified sites can be divided into two main types: duns and brochs.

Duns are essentially small dry-stone walled enclosures seldom exceeding 4,000 ft² (370 m²) in internal area. The walls, originally about 10 ft (3 m) high, were normally solid but some were provided with mural galleries or simple mural cells. Brochs, on the other hand, were generally taller, rising to 30 ft (9·1 m) or more in height, and are characterised by the cellular nature of their wall structure, which consisted of two concentric skins about 3 ft (0·9 m) apart, held to-

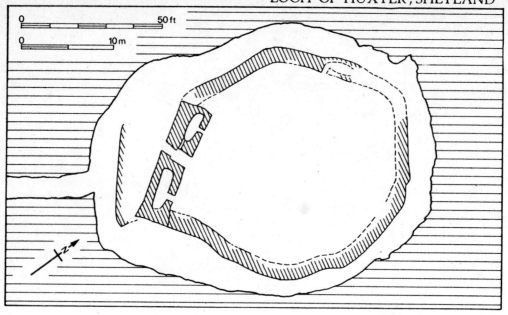

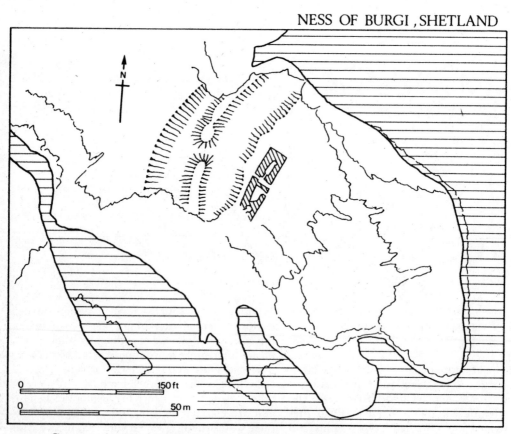

12:33   Comparative blockhouses (source: Hamilton, 1968)

BROCH OF MOUSA, SHETLAND

BROCH OF DUN TRODDAN, INVERNESS

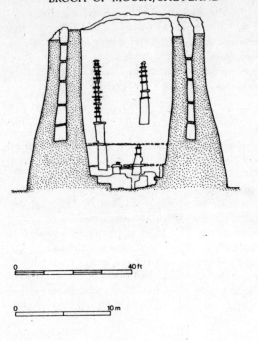

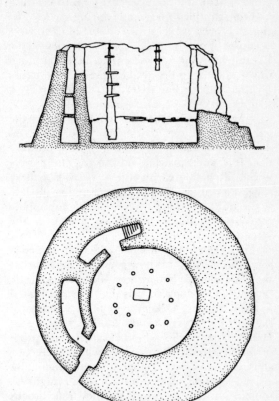

12:34 Brochs (source: Curle, 1927)

gether by rows of stone lintels inserted every 5 or 6 ft (1·5 or 1·8 m) in vertical intervals and bonded into both walls (Fig. 12:34). The result of this structure was the creation of superimposed mural galleries interlinked by stone staircases. The outer walls are always built solid, with no openings save the single entrance, but in some examples the inner wall-face is broken by vertical openings divided by horizontal lintels placed at intervals. The main entrance is always a long narrow passage passing through both walls, frequently with a cell or guard-chamber opening off one side of the passage.

The inner wall-face is usually provided with at least one ledge or sacrament 5 ft (1·5 m) or so above the floor level, apparently to support a gallery, the inner edge of which is taken on a setting of posts (MacKie, 1965a, 104–5). The alternative view, that the sacrament took the gable-ends of a high pitched conical roof supported by the vertical posts, should not be completely rejected, particularly when it is remembered that some brochs contain internal features like hearths which would benefit from roofing.

Regional varieties of brochs have been defined (MacKie, 1965a, 105–10), but the details cannot be examined here except to say that those of Caithness, Sutherland and Orkney tend to be more sophisticated in structure. Another difference is one of siting: while those in the Western Isles are usually built in isolation, the northern group more often stand in fortified enclosures of masonry or earth-and-rubble construction. One variety, which may prove to have a significance when considering the origin of brochs, is the broch-like structure sited on the edge of a promontory or precipice so that one side of the building can be omitted or represented by a low parapet. This has been called a semi-broch.

From stratified finds made during the excavation of brochs, it is clear that many of them were occupied throughout the early centuries of the Roman Iron Age and some may have continued in use later. Two brochs have produced samples yielding radiocarbon dates: at Dun Ardtreck, a semi-broch on Skye, an assessment of 55 ± 105 (115 BC) was obtained for charcoal from the rubble foundations. From Dun Mor Vaul on Tiree, dates of AD 60 ± 90 (AD 5) for a primary floor level and AD 160 ± 90 (AD 105) for rubble which accumulated in the first wall gallery suggest a construction and use spanning the late first century AD. Thus it is reasonable to suppose that broch-building may have begun in the second or first century BC.

The origin of the brochs has been a matter of some dispute but it is now generally agreed that they developed somewhere in the Atlantic province. One suggestion is that they originated in the Caithness–Orkney region, in the area of their greatest concentration (Childe, 1935a, 204; Hamilton, 1962, 82); another is that they arose in the west, possibly on Skye, where there is a considerable variety of stone structures including a concentration of semi-brochs which might be thought to be ancestral to the true brochs (MacKie, 1965a, 124–6). In support of this latter view, it has been argued that the broch was more appropriate to the defence of the small pockets of farmland typical of the western Highlands and Islands and is strictly alien to the more open countryside of Caithness and Sutherland. The matter is unlikely to be resolved until a more substantial series of radiocarbon dates becomes available.

Several excavations should be mentioned because of the light they throw on the relative position of brochs in the structural development of the individual sites. In each case there is clear proof of a degree of continuity. At Dun Mor Vaul the broch was shown to have been built on a site already occupied for several hundred years, but at Dun Lagaidh, Ross and Cromarty, the later structure was built over part of a vitrified fort for which a sixth century radiocarbon date is available, suggesting a period of abandonment between periods of occupation. Clickhimin, Shetland, provides the most complete sequence of fortification at present available; the broch was

built late in the history of the site but the presence of the earlier blockhouse, which embodies several of the constructional techniques of the broch-builders, evidently represents a stage of construction towards the beginning of the complex sequence which must lie behind the eventual emergence of the fully-fledged broch.

Wheelhouses (Pl. 10a)

The wheelhouse represents a totally different type of structure, which occupies the same area as the brochs and is broadly contemporary with them. A wheelhouse is a circular stone-built hut, the interior of which is divided by radial stone piers projecting from the wall but leaving the interior clear. The piers presumably supported the roof of wood and turf in much the same way as internal settings of vertical posts would have done in the timber-built houses of the south. In some examples, known as aisled wheelhouses, the piers are free-standing but are joined to the outer wall by lintels.

Some wheelhouses, like Tigh Talamhanta (Allasdale) and Clettraval in the Hebrides (Figs 12:35, 12:36), were built as free-standing houses surrounded by a farmyard enclosure containing working areas as well as subsidiary structures like byres or barns. At Jarlshof, Shetland, on the other hand, the first aisled wheelhouse was built into the yard attached to the broch with a byre close by (Pl. 9b). This building is of particular interest because in its original stage the roof was supported on vertical timbers which were only later replaced by free-standing stone piers. Later still the original aisled wheelhouse was dismantled and replaced by a conjoined pair of wheelhouses, superbly built with radial piers corbelled out at the top to roof the individual bays. Jarlshof, then, appears to demonstrate the entire sequence of wheelhouse development. Elsewhere on Shetland, as for example at Clickhimin, most of the wheelhouses were found to be inserted into brochs.

While there is some evidence to suggest that elements of wheelhouse architecture were developing on Shetland before the brochs, possibly in the third and second centuries BC, the major occurrence of the type dates to after the brochs had begun to go out of use as defended structures. The range of stratified Roman imports suggests a second to third century AD date.

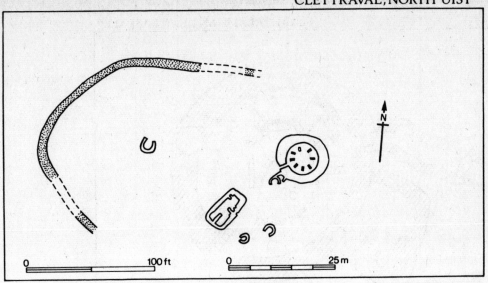

CLETTRAVAL, NORTH UIST

0   100 ft

0   25 m

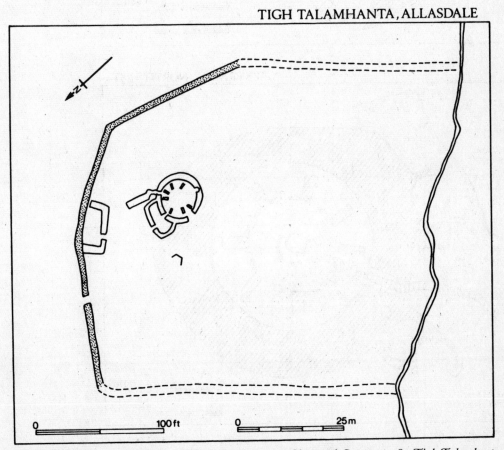

TIGH TALAMHANTA, ALLASDALE

0   100 ft

0   25 m

12:35   Farmsteads in north-west Britain (sources: *Clettraval*, Scott, 1948; *Tigh Talamhanta*, Young, 1955)

TIGH TALAMHANTA , ALLASDALE

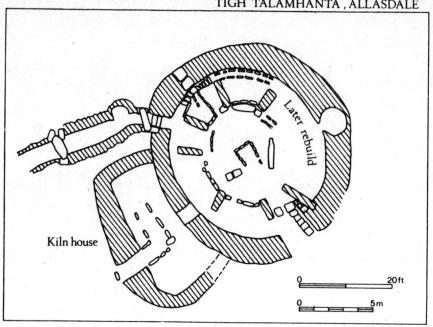

CLETTRAVAL, NORTH UIST

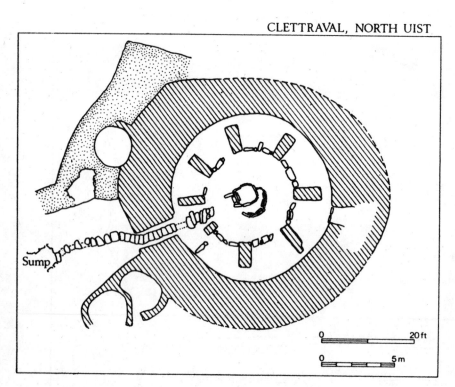

12:36   Wheelhouses (sources: *Clettraval*, Scott, 1948; *Tigh Talamhanta*, Young, 1955)

The economy of the north and west was largely self-sufficient: sheep and cattle were kept, cereals were grown, while the sea provided seals, whales, fish, limpets and sea birds. Throughout the period, tools tended to be made in local materials like bone, slate and quartz, while utensils were manufactured in pottery, steatite and presumably leather. Apart from a restricted range of bronze and iron tools and ornaments, metal was never common.

It seems, therefore, that for much of the early part of the Iron Age, communities lived peacefully in open settlements but gradually defences multiplied, giving rise to a densely fortified landscape in which almost every homestead was defended. Such a process may well have developed in parallel with the increased emphasis on defence apparent in most other parts of the country. There is no need to introduce the idea of an alien breed of 'castle-builders' to explain a process which in all probability was the result of widespread pressures created by internal social development. Over much of the western area the land was broken into isolated fertile pockets by natural barriers such as mountains and deep inlets. Inevitably, in such conditions, communities tended to remain isolated and settlements failed to nucleate.

Some time in the second or first century BC a specialised type of fortified house – the broch – emerged, perfectly adapted to the requirements of society and its environment. It is hardly surprising that it spread (possibly at the instigation of expert builders) over the whole of the Atlantic province, even into areas like Caithness and Sutherland, where the more gentle undulating land might be thought to be less suitable for such a specialised form of fortification. Brochs continued to dominate the landscape into at least the second century AD, but in the more peaceful conditions which then arose they ceased to be built and were superseded (and sometimes physically replaced) by wheelhouses, which represented the resurgence of the indigenous house type, deeply rooted in the native building traditions of the area.

Throughout the period under discussion the communities of the Atlantic province remained dependent on the sea as a means of communication as well as for food-gathering and protection. While the sea linked the far-flung parts of the province together, it seems to have isolated it from the rest of the country.

SUMMARY

From the above survey it will be apparent that the communities living in the north and west of Britain were far more diverse in their life style than those of the south-east, but the coarseness of the archaeological evidence allows only the more obvious differences to be dimly seen. There does, however, appear to be a correspondence between basic economy, settlement pattern and social structure. In those areas which were predominantly pastoral, like Devon and south and west Wales, strongly defended homesteads emerged packed into a densely populated landscape, suggesting a fragmented society based on small kin groups having little overall centralised control. In other areas, like the Tyne–Forth region and the Welsh borderland, a more mixed economy involving corn-production created communities rooted for centuries to their homesteads. Stability led to the formation of larger political groupings and the emergence of coercive power, which is reflected in the construction of large tribal hillforts. Elsewhere there are hints of well-established transhumant economies which would require seasonal gatherings and an element of nucleation, discernible perhaps in the settlement patterns of north Wales and the Pennines.

Against this regional variation there was change. In Devon climatic deterioration appears to have caused the depopulation of the moors, forcing the people to exploit the lusher pastures of lower-lying areas, breaking down the transhumant way of life and allowing the development of a more stable pastoralism reflected in the numerous defended homesteads. In eastern Yorkshire, an area where there are signs of a mixed economy of south-eastern type in the sixth to fifth century, the arrival of new communities from France seem to have imposed a more pastoral way of life, which remained dominant until the first century BC.

The true picture must have been one of infinite variety, ever-changing at different rates in different regions. At present we can only begin to comprehend its complexity, but each new discovery will allow a finer texture to emerge.

The Development of Hillforts

England, Scotland and Wales together can boast about 3,000 structures classed loosely under the heading of hillforts and other defended enclosures. Many more than half are small sites of 3 acres (1·2 hectares) or less which need be little more than defended homesteads: these include the rounds of the south-west peninsula, the raths of south Wales and the numerous homesteads and small settlements of eastern Scotland. As a broad generalisation, it may be said that the bulk of the hillforts proper are concentrated in the south-east, in those areas in which cereal-production played a significant part in the economy – in such a way as to hint that the emergence of hillforts may be an indirect result of a stable populaton. Their very existence implies surplus labour working under coercion, but whether that coercion was the good of the state or the power of a ruling class are matters reserved for more extensive discussion later (ch. 16).

In spite of the impressive nature of the monuments, relatively few have been extensively excavated, and where excavation has taken place, it is normally only the structure of the rampart that has been examined. Many sites were dug before the subtleties of internal timber-work were understood, and frequently trenches were too narrow and too few to provide decisive evidence bearing on the presence or absence of internal structure. Even so, a number of sites have yielded some meaningful results and this evidence can be synthesised into a general pattern of development relevant to most areas of the country.

THE STRUCTURE OF HILLFORT DEFENCES

A. Earth and timber structures in England and Wales

Palisades One of the earliest kinds of defensive barrier employed on sites of hillfort size was the palisade of close-set timbers embedded in a continuous foundation trench without ditches or the banking up of spoil behind. This is clearly the same technique as that used on the smaller settlements (discussed above, pp. 155, 206–9), which developed out of a tradition of fencing going back to the beginning of the first millennium or earlier. Wherever excavation has been adequate, palisades, if they occur, can be shown to precede earthwork defences. At the Breiddin, Montgomery, the palisade lies at the beginning of a complex development and the evidence of associated finds suggests that a seventh or even eighth century date might not be out of place. The palisade at Blewburton Hill, Berks, antedates by some time the construction of a timber-laced rampart, and the same interpretation is possible for the foremost palisade at Bindon Hill, Dorset. At Winklebury, Hants, Skelmore Heads, Lancs, Wilbury, Herts, and Eddisbury, Cheshire, short lengths of early palisades have been found, again in early contexts pre-dating the subsequent developments on these sites.

Although in the examples noted above the later defences generally follow the earlier palisades at the points excavated, there is no positive proof that the lines were coincident throughout. The rather more extensive excavations at Hembury, Devon, have however demonstrated that here the defences of the later fort follow what appears to be an earlier palisade more or less exactly on at least two sides of the circuit (Fig. 13:1). Admittedly, the interpretation of the

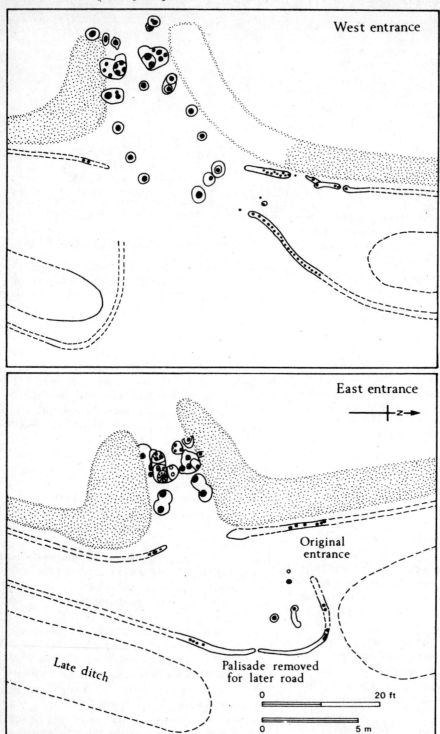

West entrance

East entrance

Original
entrance

Late ditch

Palisade removed
for later road

0   20 ft

0   5 m

13:1   The palisaded enclosure at Hembury, Devon (source: Liddell, 1935b)

sequence is not straightforward but the outer palisade would appear to be the earliest feature, since at the position occupied by the later east entrance it was refilled at the point where the new roadway crossed it. The implication here, then, is that the construction of the earthwork defences followed hard upon the abandonment of the palisade. Both the later entrances were placed close to the sites of the palisade entrances, but the digging of the later ditches has obscured some of the details. Even so, the palisades can be seen to curve back inwards and at the east entrance there is some evidence to suggest a timber structure within the incurve not at all unlike the towers of the second period gate at Harehope in Peeblesshire.

Large palisaded enclosures can therefore be seen generally to precede hillforts, sometimes by a considerable period of time. No absolute dates can yet be given but it is known from the smaller palisaded homesteads of the north that the method of defence was being practised in the seventh century (pp. 206–9) and the finds from the Breiddin might point to an origin here going back even a century earlier.

The Ivinghoe Beacon style of timber strengthening (Fig. 13:2) In parallel with the palisaded enclosures a second type of defence developed known at present from Ffridd Faldwyn, Montgomery, Ivinghoe Beacon, Bucks, Grimthorpe, Yorks and Dinorben, Denbigh. At Grimthorpe rubble and soil from a relatively shallow U-shaped ditch was retained between two rows of timber about 8 ft (2·4 m) apart, the timbers in each row being placed at about the same spacing, thus forming a rough grid which would have allowed cross-bracing to keep the structure rigid. Between the verticals of both the back and front rows one must imagine a close boarding of planks or halved timbers to prevent the rubble fill from spilling out. Although dating evidence is by no means decisive, it is now becoming clear that simple box ramparts probably predate the conventional beginning of the Iron Age. The box ramparts at both Ffridd Faldwyn and Dinorben lie at the beginning of long development sequences: at Dinorben a radiocarbon date of 945 ± 95 (1032 BC) was obtained for a pre-rampart layer, while charcoal derived from the first box rampart was dated to 895 ± 95 and 765 ± 85 (980 and 846 BC) Grimthorpe also provided

two early dates for bone samples recovered from the partially silted ditch: 690 ± 130 and 970 ± 130 (769 and 1058 BC). No dates are available from Ivinghoe Beacon but the metalwork from the fort lies within the eighth to seventh centuries. Taking this evidence together, there is a degree of consistency about the overall pattern, suggesting initial occupation in the ninth to seventh centuries. Thus the earliest hillforts in Britain must have developed in parallel with those of the European Urnfield cultures. Strictly, the box rampart could be thought of as a double palisade, of the type well represented in northern Britain (pp. 206–9), filled with earth and rubble. The nature of this relationship both structurally and chronologically remains to be further examined.

The Hollingbury Camp style of timber strengthening (Fig. 13:2) A simple development following the rubble-filled timber wall of Ivinghoe Beacon type was the addition of a sloping rampart behind the inner face of the inner row of timbers. This would have provided two additional advantages: ease of access at all points and an added strength and rigidity. While at Hollingbury Camp, Sussex, the bank was slight – barely 8 ft (2·7 m) wide – backing a timber wall of the same width, in the first phase of Danebury, Hants, the 7 ft (2·1 m) wide timbering was backed by a far more substantial structure almost 30 ft (9·1 m) wide. At Maiden Castle, Dorset, the timber structure of period I was 12 ft (3·6 m) wide, with a bank of equivalent width behind, standing to a maximum height of 4·5 ft (1·4 m). Clearly, there were considerable variations in proportion.[1]

Wandlebury, Cambs, is a particularly important example demonstrating a sequence of development (Fig. 13:3). In the first period a box-type rampart was constructed with timber faces 13 ft (4·0 m) apart, the front timbers being placed at 2·5 ft (0·76 m) intervals, and those of the bank face even closer. Whether or not a lacking ramp was built will never be known,

---

[1] At Buckland Rings, Hants, limited excavation suggested two rows of timbers as much as 19 ft (5·8 m) apart, set within an earthwork of 30 ft (9·1 m) width overall. While it is not impossible that the walls were laced together with cross-members, the considerable width might argue against this.

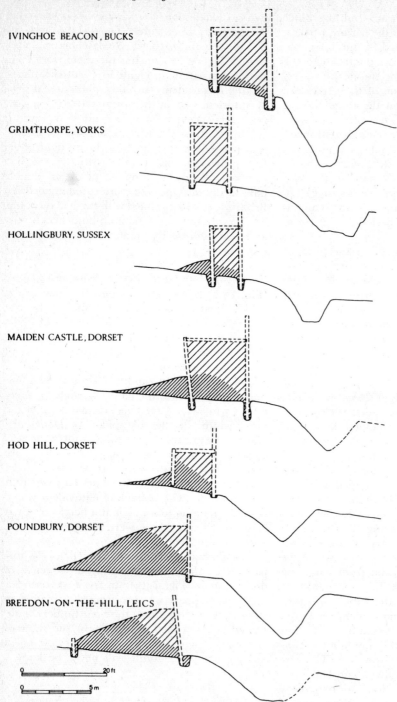

IVINGHOE BEACON, BUCKS

GRIMTHORPE, YORKS

HOLLINGBURY, SUSSEX

MAIDEN CASTLE, DORSET

HOD HILL, DORSET

POUNDBURY, DORSET

BREEDON-ON-THE-HILL, LEICS

13:2   Comparative sections of box ramparts and their derivatives (sources: *Ivinghoe Beacon*, Cotton & Frere, 1968; *Grimthorpe*, Stead, 1968; *Hollingbury Camp*, E. C. Curwen, 1932; *Maiden Castle*, Wheeler, 1943; *Hod Hill*, Richmond, 1968; *Poundbury*, Richardson, 1940; *Breedon-on-the-Hill*, Wacher, 1964)

THE STRUCTURAL DEVELOPMENT
OF WANDLEBURY, CAMBRIDGESHIRE

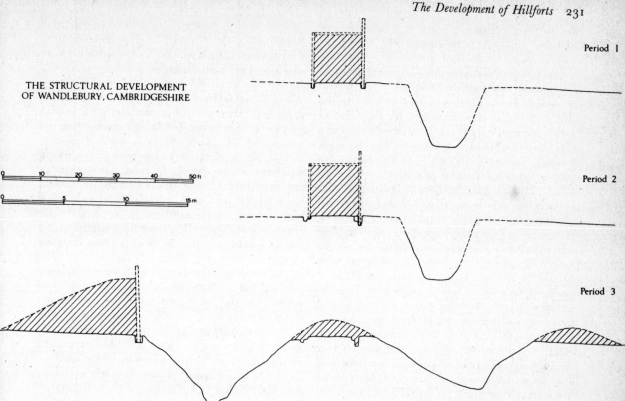

Period 1

Period 2

Period 3

13:3 The development of the defences at Wandlebury, Cambs (source: Hartley, 1957)

since a later ditch would have dug it away. In the second phase the rampart was rebuilt 14 ft (4·3 m) wide, with the timbers in both rows set at 9 ft (2·7 m) centres, again possibly with a backing rampart. In the third major phase a totally new rampart was thrown up *behind* the original work, fronted by a ditch. This third period work was constructed in a style to be described below as the Poundbury style (p. 232). Thus, what was presumably a Hollingbury type of rampart had an extended use at Wandlebury. Its replacement is, however, a reminder that timber had a relatively short life and major rebuilding would have had to be carried out perhaps as often as every decade or two if the defences were to be kept in good order.

The dating of this type of construction technique is tolerably well known. At Hollingbury Camp pottery of the sixth to fifth centuries has been found within the fort, but not in direct relationship to the rampart, while at most of the other sites the associated material lies consistently within the fifth to third century range.

The Hod Hill type of timber strengthening (Fig. 13:2) The first phase of the defences of Hod Hill, Dorset, possessed an internal structure at present unique. A rampart some 32 ft (9·7 m) wide was fronted by a continuous palisade trench in which were placed vertical timbers, no doubt backed by horizontal timber cladding. Within the body of the mound was found a second row of individual timbers, the bases of which did not penetrate the natural subsoil; to these the front fence would presumably have been anchored. The defences differ from the more normal Hollingbury Camp type in that the inner timbers were supported only by the spoil of the rampart itself. In an excavation less skilfully observed, they may well have passed unnoticed.

It is tempting to see the constructors of Hod Hill adapting time-honoured building methods in the realisation that the inner timbers were needed only to anchor the fronting fence, postholes specially cut into the bedrock being no longer required. Dating is difficult on the published evidence, but some time after the local fifth to third century pottery had gone out of common use would seem most likely.

The Poundbury type of timber strengthening (Fig. 13:2) The logical development following the breakthrough at Hod Hill was to further modify the nature of the inner timbering. At Poundbury, Dorset, controlled excavations demonstrated a 30 ft (9·1 m) wide rampart fronted by a palisade of closely spaced timbers 3 ft (1 m) apart. No trace of internal timbering, either vertical or horizontal, was seen. It may, of course, be that the trenches were so sited as to miss inner verticals, but this is unlikely. A more reasonable explanation is that the front face was attached only to horizontal beams embedded within the body of the rampart: these would have been extremely difficult to trace and would have appeared only under ideal conditions. It is inconceivable that the fence could have withstood the thrust without some such back-pinning.

The third phase of Wandlebury, Cambs, which demonstrably replaces the rampart of Hollingbury type, was of a similar construction. The same technique appears to have been adopted at Yarnbury, Wilts, Titterstone Clee, Salop, Cissbury, Sussex, and probably in the second phase of Hembury, Devon, replacing the palisaded enclosure. Breedon-on-the-Hill, Leics, presents a slight variant: in the first phase here, the fronting fence was of closely placed timbers, with the tail of the rampart 25 ft (7·6 m) away revetted by individually bedded posts. While the possibility of cross-bracing from front to rear must be borne in mind, timbers in excess of 25 ft (7·6 m) would seem to be an unnecessary extravagance. In all probability the excavator was correct in supposing that the rear posts did nothing more than prevent the back slope from eroding, in which case shorter horizontal binding timbers could have been used to anchor the front face. Caesar's Camp (Wimbledon), Surrey, poses a somewhat similar problem. Two narrow sections observed under rescue conditions brought to light evidence of front and rear timbers 27 ft (8·2 m) apart. As at Breedon-on-the-Hill, it is possible that the back row was a separate supporting fence distinct from the front, but the question must remain open.

The dating of the Poundbury technique is difficult to ascertain with precision: at Wandlebury it is later than the Hollingbury style and associated with pottery which could centre upon the fourth to third centuries. The evidence from the other sites, such as it is, does not conflict with this broad generalisation.

The glacis style In the constructional variations described, the overriding consideration was to provide a vertical wall of timber confronting the outside world, protected by a ditch dug some feet in front of it. Yet, however the backing structure was modified, the basic flaws in design remained: the timber would soon rot and would have to be replaced (a difficult task in such circumstances); it could easily be fired by an enemy; and the gradually crumbling lip of the ditch would eventually loosen the fronting timbers.

All these problems were overcome by a new method which appears to have been widely adopted in the south and east some time in the third century or soon after. Ditches were dug deeper and the rampart face was sheered back at an angle following the ditch side, thus creating a continuous slope from the bottom of the ditch to the crest of the rampart at an angle of 30–45 degrees. At Hod Hill, Dorset, the overall distance from top to bottom was 58 ft (17·4 m) and at Danebury, Hants (Pl. 4), 53 ft (16·1 m), while at Maiden Castle, Dorset, it reached 83 ft (25·2 m). Covered with a loose scree and capped by a breastwork of timber or flint, the approach would have been daunting to the attacker. The only maintenance problem was to keep the ditch clear of silt. This would have been undertaken periodically, the scree being thrown out on the downhill side creating a spoil bank sometimes referred to as a counterscarp. In one section at Danebury, it was possible to trace evidence of eleven different periods of addition to the counterscarp bank, each representing a periodic clearing-out operation.

Glacis style defences can be shown to replace timber structures at a number of sites from the Dorset forts to Poundbury, Maiden Castle and Hod Hill to as far north as Breedon-on-the-Hill in Leicestershire, and it will be shown below that some early stone-built forts were also remodelled in this way. Dating evidence, where it survives, shows that glacis defences were in use in the south during the time when saucepan style pots were being manufactured, centring therefore on the second and first centuries; but at Croft Ambrey,

Heref, in the Welsh borderland dump-constructed ramparts were in use from the beginning of the occupation sequence, which probably started in the fifth or even the sixth century. There is evidence from the south that here too dump ramparts without revetting were established by the sixth century. Such a rampart was found at Balksbury, Hants in a seventh to sixth century context, at Quarley Hill, Hants, dating to the fifth to fourth centuries and at St Catherine's Hill, Hants, a little later. On present evidence, therefore, it is simpler to assume that the technique of defending a site with a bank of spoil and a ditch was long established, dating back into the second millennium, and that after a brief period when timber- and stone-faced ramparts predominated, the older technique came back once more into common use and persisted in some areas until the Roman conquest.

At Maiden Castle six subsequent extensions and modifications all adopted the basic glacis style, and at Hod Hill there were three phases. Evidently the glacis was regarded as the ultimate in defensive tactics until the wide flat-bottomed ditches of Fécamp style were introduced in the first century AD (pp. 71–3).

Multivallation Superficial surface examination of the British hillforts shows that many of them were provided with more than one rampart and ditch; such forts are listed on the Ordnance Survey *Map of Southern Britain in the Iron Age* as multivallate. The term is confusing, however, for it covers several different situations. The multiple-enclosure forts of the south-west, while strictly multivallate, were so because extra lines of banks and ditches were required to enclose space for livestock. Danebury, Hants, is termed multivallate for much the same reason. Other forts like Wandlebury, Cambs, Bredon Hill, Glos, the Caburn, Sussex, and Croft Ambrey, Heref, give the appearance of multivallation because of their growth or shrinkage and not necessarily from a general policy of extending the line of fire. Thus, surface assessment alone can seldom be decisive. Nevertheless, deliberate multivallation for the purpose of defence can be demonstrated on sites like Maiden Castle, Dorset, beginning in phase III and reaching its ultimate development in phase IV. At Hod Hill, Dorset, it is possible to trace the development of multivallation, starting in stage IIa (the first glacis

remodelling) with the construction of a palisade in front of the ditch. Subsequently a second ditch was begun but not finished, the spoil being thrown up over the line of the palisade, which was now isolated between the two ditches. Whether or not the palisade belongs to stage IIa, the fact remains that multivallation came late in the development of the fort and, as the excavator has suggested, may have been initiated and subsequently abandoned at the time of the Roman advance in AD 43.

A somewhat similar situation occurred at Buckland Rings, Hants where, in spite of large-scale levelling, it was possible to trace a fence outside the line of the inner ditch and in front of an outer ditch. No evidence of a rampart behind or sealing the fence-posts survived. At what stage the outer features were constructed it is impossible to say, but in all probability they were added to the original construction, and it is possible that the Buckland Rings sequence is a direct parallel to Hod Hill.

Generally it may be assumed that multivallation was a late development in most areas, sometimes – as at Hod Hill – not appearing until the first century AD but certainly at least a century earlier at Maiden Castle. At Rainsborough Camp, Northants, it has been argued that the second rampart and ditch date to as early as the fifth century, but the evidence can be variously interpreted and is best regarded as unproven.

In all probability, development varied in different areas of the country and in different geographical situations. Two or three banks and ditches thrown across a neck of land to protect a promontory do not necessarily have to be related to the same time or philosophy of warfare as the multiple girding of Maiden Castle. Thus, while most true multivallation was late, one may expect considerable variation between one part of the country and another. One final point is clear: there is now no need to suggest that intrusive ideas were the cause – local inventiveness is quite sufficient.

B. Stone and stone-and-timber defences in England and Wales (Figs 13:4, 13:5)

Although palisaded structures were constructed in areas where good building stone occurs naturally, later developments in these regions

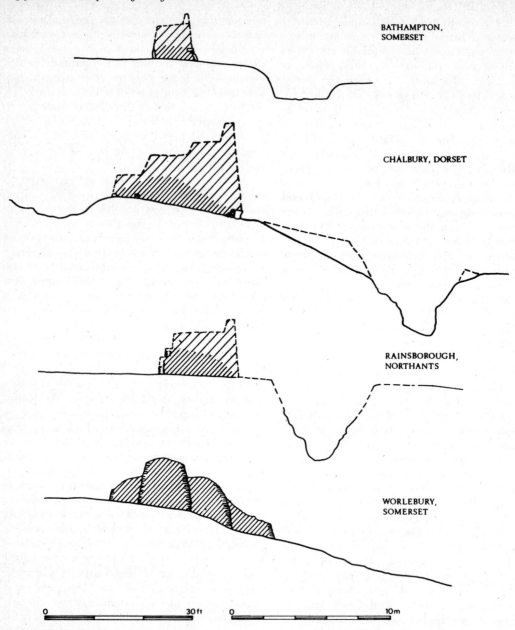

BATHAMPTON, SOMERSET

CHALBURY, DORSET

RAINSBOROUGH, NORTHANTS

WORLEBURY, SOMERSET

0   30 ft   0   10 m

13:4   Stone-faced ramparts (sources: *Bathampton*, Wainwright, 1967b; *Chalbury*, Whitley, 1943; *Rainsborough*, Avery, Sutton & Banks, 1967; *Worlebury*, Dymond, 1902)

usually adopted the technique of dry-stone walling, with or without internal timber binding. Unfortunately, horizontal timbers are far less easy to trace archaeologically than verticals, and it is therefore a distinct possibility that a higher proportion of the stone-faced ramparts were timber-laced than is at present apparent. Nevertheless, for the purpose of this discussion a distinction will be made between those where no timbering was observed and those known to have been timber-laced.

One of the earliest of the simple forts possessing

TIMBER LACED RAMPARTS

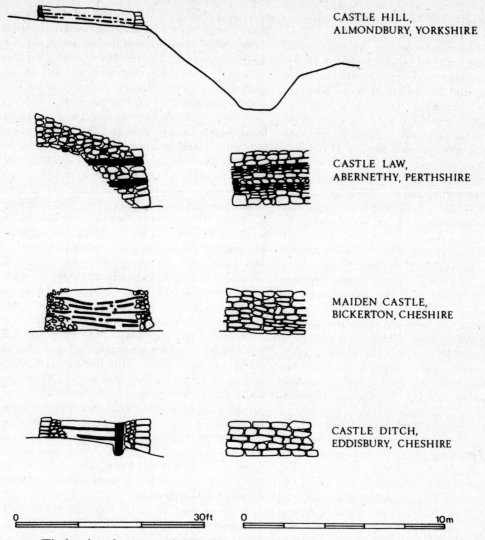

CASTLE HILL,
ALMONDBURY, YORKSHIRE

CASTLE LAW,
ABERNETHY, PERTHSHIRE

MAIDEN CASTLE,
BICKERTON, CHESHIRE

CASTLE DITCH,
EDDISBURY, CHESHIRE

| 0 | | | 30ft | 0 | | | 10m |

13:5   Timber-laced ramparts (source: Varley, 1950b)

a rubble rampart encased at the front and back with dry-stone walling is Chalbury, Dorset (Fig. 13:4), where the total thickness of the rampart was 20 ft (6·1 m). Since associated pottery leaves little doubt that the defences belong to the fifth to fourth centuries, Chalbury is presumably the stone-built equivalent of the timber box rampart of Maiden Castle I, only 3 miles (4·8 km) away. A similarly early date has been proposed for the first fort at Rainsborough Camp, Northants (Fig. 13:4), where the stone-faced rampart, 17 ft (5·2 m) wide at the base, was reduced in width by two steps at the back.[1] The thickness of the ramparts between the wall-faces varies from fort to fort but is usually between 16 and 24 ft (4·9 and 7·3 m). The enclosure at Bathampton Down, Somerset, was however protected by a wall only 9·5 ft (2·9 m) wide, divided by a 12 ft (3·6 m) berm from a wide flat-bottomed ditch. At Worlebury, Somerset (Fig. 13:4), on the other

[1] The excavator's suggestion that a similar stepping was adopted at the front carries less conviction.

hand, the overall thickness of the main stone wall was 38 ft (11·5 m); but this was apparently created by several additions or rebuildings at the back and front of a wall of normal width.

At several sites in the south, stone-structured ramparts were replaced by glacis style defences. This is particularly well demonstrated at Llanmelin, Mon, and at Rainsborough Camp; in both cases, excavation has shown that the major remodelling in glacis style came late in the occupation of the site. One apparent exception to the rule is the much-quoted Bredon Hill, Glos; here the usual interpretation is that the inner rampart, built in a dump-constructed or glacis style, was followed by the outer rampart, stone-faced and fronted by a berm and U-shaped ditch. There are difficulties with this interpretation, not the least being that the two entrances through the outer rampart were almost blocked by the inner defences. If, however, the supposed constructional sequence is reversed, this problem would be overcome and the development of the rampart styles – first stone-faced then glacis – would be in accordance with the general pattern elsewhere, Bredon Hill being no longer the exception. The fact that the outer rampart and ditch were slighted opposite the entrance in the inner rampart might be thought to provide further support for the reinterpretation.

Outside the south and east of Britain, the stone facing of the rampart seems to have survived to the time of the Roman invasion. In north-west Wales, Tre'r Ceiri, Garn Boduan, Carn Fadrun and Conway Mountain in Caernarvonshire all maintained their stone wall defences until the last, but the glacis style was adopted at some of the Welsh borderland sites like the Wrekin, Salop, and Croft Ambrey, Heref, and even penetrated as far north as Dinorben, Denbigh.

A combination of timbering and stone facing has been recorded on several southern British sites close to stone outcrops. In the outworks of the phase II east entrance at Maiden Castle, Dorset, dry-stone facing was employed instead of split timber or planks as a revetting material between vertical timbers erected in the general tradition of the timber box rampart of the first period; while at South Cadbury, Somerset, exactly the same technique was employed in the second Iron Age defence, the only difference

being that here an inner row of verticals was used to prevent the tail of the rampart from spreading. It should be emphasised that in both cases stone walling was being used only as a filling material in place of timber and not as an integral part of the rigid structure. This is essentially a local development, parallel to the Hollingbury–Hod Hill–Poundbury types, in areas where stone was readily available.

Further west and north, in an arc spreading from the Cotswolds through the Welsh borderland and Cheshire into Yorkshire, a series of partially excavated forts provides clear evidence of the use of timber- and stone-structured ramparts. Some of the forts like Castle Ditch (Eddisbury), Cheshire (Fig. 13:5), and Ffridd Faldwyn, Montgomery, began as simple palisaded enclosures which were replaced by box-constructed timber ramparts employing vertical and horizontal timbering. Between the front verticals infilling was usually by dry-stone walling in the manner of South Cadbury and Maiden Castle. The same technique was used in the first and second phases of the rampart at Castle Hill (Almondbury), Yorkshire (Fig. 13:5). In all three cases the forts were later rebuilt using a rubble rampart laced with horizontal timbers and fronted, both inside and out, by dry-stone walling unbroken by timber verticals. Dinorben provides a comparable sequence but with the timber-laced stone rampart (period II) following a timber box-constructed type. Two radiocarbon dates for charcoal from the destruction of the laced rampart, 535 ± 85 and 420 ± 70 (609 and 491 BC), would suggest a sixth century date for its construction and use.

Some of the forts in the west and north, such as Leckhampton Hill and Crickley Hill in Gloucestershire, Maiden Castle (Bickerton) in Cheshire (Fig. 13:5), and Corley Camp in Warwickshire, began with horizontally timber-laced ramparts fronted by continuous dry-stone facings and many underwent subsequent modification.

From the above description, it will be seen that the use of stone and timber followed a series of complex patterns which are only now being gradually sorted out. Tentatively, however, we may define a phase in which stone was used as an infilling material in box-constructed ramparts of Ivinghoe Beacon and Hollingbury Camp type, spanning the period from the seventh to the fourth century. In the west and north of England, the technique of lacing the ramparts with horizontal timbers and facing them back and front with stone walls soon emerged locally, probably as a development from the earlier style. The dating evidence, such as it is, shows that the technique was being practised in the sixth and fifth centuries. Eventually the use of horizontal timbers was abandoned and ramparts were built with stone facings only, in a simple style which probably originated earlier and continued in use in some parts throughout the Iron Age. Finally, in southern England and occasionally elsewhere, stone-constructed ramparts were eventually replaced by the glacis style. At present this generalised scheme fits all the available evidence but regional and chronological differences may be expected to complicate the issue.

C. The stone and timber forts of Scotland

The Scottish hillfort development is in some respects different from that of the rest of Britain. Like the south, some forts began as palisaded enclosures, but after these had gone out of use, vertical timbering is virtually unknown again. In the north the characteristic rampart structure is the rubble-and-earth core faced inside and out with dry-stone walling, the whole bonded by rows of horizontal timbers which project through the outer, and sometimes the inner, wall-face. At Abernethy, Perth (Fig. 13:5), two rows of rectangular beam-holes 10–12 in (24–30 cm) square appeared through the outer wall-facing of the innermost rampart: the lower row was 2–3 ft (60–90 cm) above the ground, the second row 2 ft (60 cm) above the first. The outer rampart proved to be of the same construction, but in neither the inner nor the outer rampart did the timbers penetrate the inner wall-facing. It is impossible to say how extensive the use of longitudinal timbering was, since only at Abernethy are the timbers recorded. Ditches do not seem to have been an integral part of this kind of defensive scheme.

Half a dozen or so forts have produced direct evidence of timber-lacing but more than sixty of the Scottish sites belong to what is called the vitrified class, all examples showing signs of widespread burning of the timber-lacing causing the core material of the rampart to become discoloured and to fuse. The exact nature of the timber structure of most of these forts has not been recorded, but at Finavon (Pl. 3a) and Monifieth in Angus, and Castle Law (Forgondenny), Perth – all forts timber-laced in the Abernethy style – vitrified material was found in the rampart cores. In all probability, therefore, we are dealing with a single class of horizontally timber-laced ramparts, some of which were fired. Whether the firing was deliberately carried out by the builders to consolidate the rampart, or by attackers, is a matter of some debate (summarised in Cotton, 1955, 94–101), but the potentially destructive nature of a fire, the unevenness of the firing within individual sites, and the relatively slight firing of many of them would suggest accident or attack rather than design.[1]

There has been much discussion as to the date and origin of the Scottish forts (Cotton, 1955) but most of it is now rendered obsolete by the production of a group of radiocarbon dates (MacKie, 1969). For charred beams or planks from behind the wall at Finavon an estimate of 590 ± 90 (665 BC) was obtained, with supporting dates of 410 ± 80 (480 BC) and 320 ± 90 (390 BC) for subsequent levels. At the vitrified fort of Dun Lagaidh, Wester Ross, a carbonised branch under the fort wall gave an estimate of 490 ± 90 (565 BC) but at Craigmarloch Wood in Renfrewshire a date of 35 ± 40 (95 BC) was obtained apparently for a timber-laced rampart which replaced a palisaded enclosure. The sample does not, however, seem to have been securely linked to the construction period and charcoal from beneath the wall provided a date of 590 ± 40 (665 BC). Together the evidence is impressive: there can now be little doubt that many of the forts must originate in the seventh or even the eighth century, while the discovery of La Tène artefacts from some of the excavated examples shows that occupation continued for several centuries.

The Abernethy style forts originate, therefore, at the time when contacts between Scotland and the Hallstatt cultures of Europe were at their height. Similarities have been noted (S. Piggott, 1966, 7) between the Scottish style of timber-

---

[1] These vitrified forts should be compared with the burnt timber-laced ramparts of the west, e.g. Dinorben, Denbigh, Crickley Hill and Leckhampton Hill, Glos, and Bower Walls Camp, Somerset, where the limestone rubble cores have been turned to lime by the intensive heat.

lacing and the method employed on the Swiss site of Wittnauer Horn in both its Hallstatt B3 (Late Urnfield) and its Hallstatt C/D phases, and at Montlingerberg, another Late Urnfield fort in Switzerland. It is indeed tempting to suggest that the concept of using only horizontal timbers together with dry-stone walling was introduced into northern Britain from continental Europe at the time of these maximum cultural contacts, but positive evidence is lacking.

Not all the Scottish forts were provided with timber-laced ramparts. Several of the fortified enclosures examined in the Cheviots, including Howham Rings, Hayhope Knowe and Bonchester Hill in Roxburghshire, were enclosed by simple stone-faced ramparts without internal timbering. At Kaimes Hillfort, Midlothian, the recent series of excavations has demonstrated the replacement of a timber-laced rampart with a simple stone-faced structure; twigs from its core were radiocarbon dated to *c.* 298 ± 90 (365 BC), thus suggesting a fourth century date for the change in style at this site.

SUMMARY OF HILLFORT DEFENCES
(Diagram A)

Controlled excavation, together with a substantial series of radiocarbon dates, is beginning to provide a sequence for the development of defensive structures which is consistent over the whole country. The tradition of building defensive palisades appeared in most parts of Britain by the ninth century and continued to be employed probably into the seventh. In the south of Britain the use of palisades runs parallel with the construction of box-framed earth and timber ramparts of Ivinghoe type, which developed a backing rampart (Hollingbury style) after the sixth century. At present these types, incorporating vertical timbers, are unknown in the north. The seventh century saw the appearance in Scotland of the timber-laced rampart with external stone faces, a style of construction which was also adopted in western Britain as far south as the Bristol Avon. Which area, if any, can claim priority in the use of timber-lacing is uncertain. On one hand, it could be argued that the technique was introduced into Scotland from abroad, spreading to the south later, but an equally plausible explanation is that it was a British invention originating somewhere in the

Cotswold–Welsh border area out of the box rampart idea. At present this latter hypothesis seems the more reasonable but the matter will only be solved when more radiocarbon dates are available.

By the fourth century timber-lacing had ceased to be practised, and over most of the stone-producing areas of northern and western Britain, ramparts were constructed simply of stone-faced rubble. In the south, however, the vertical revetment of ramparts with close-spaced timbers persisted (Hod Hill and Poundbury types) probably throughout the third and even into the second century. During the first century old-established methods of building ramparts from dumped earth with a sloping face became widespread over much of the south and parts of the south-west. Eventually, by the first century AD, a new type of flat-bottomed ditch (Fécamp type) was introduced into the south-east, possibly from northern Gaul.

ENTRANCES

Hillforts were provided with one or, less usually, two entrances which were necessarily the weak links of the defensive circuit. It is hardly surprising, therefore, that much care and attention were lavished on these points, the entrances frequently being remodelled and rebuilt on more occasions than the main lines of the defences. A substantial number of entrances have been excavated on a reasonable scale. These, together with an examination of the earthworks of unexcavated examples, allow some general inferences to be drawn, and collated sequences can now be built up for the chalk downs of the south and the Welsh borderland.

In the south two sites, Torberry in Sussex and Danebury in Hampshire, offer continuous sequences spanning the period from the fifth or fourth to the first century BC. These can be used in conjunction with the results from other excavations to produce a consistent picture of entrance development relevant for most of the south-east of the country.

One of the earliest known gates, that belonging to the hillfort of Ivinghoe Beacon, Bucks, is a relatively simple structure consisting of a short timber-lined passageway 11 ft (3·4 m) long and of equivalent width, set back slightly at the end of a courtyard formed by turning the ends of the

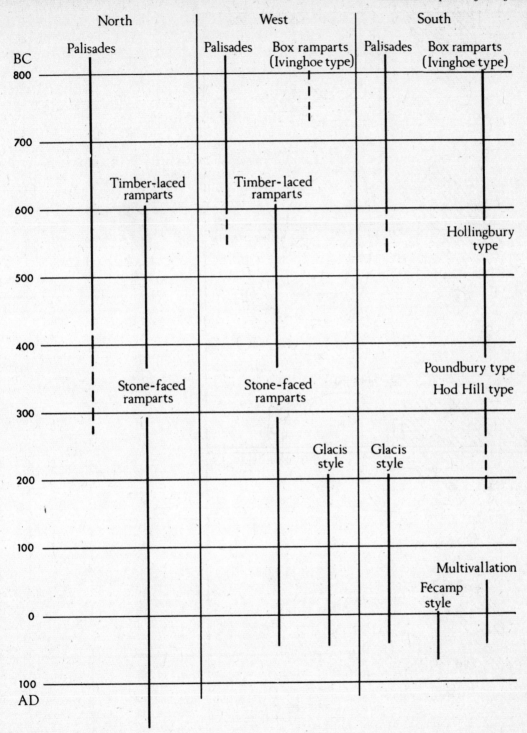

Diagram A Summarised development of hillfort defences

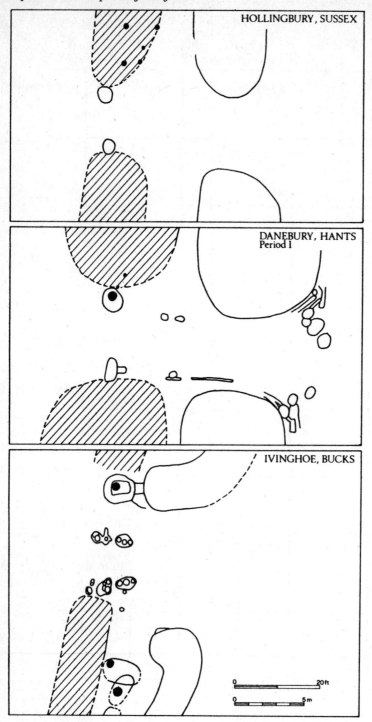

13:6   Single-portal entrances (sources: *Hollingbury Camp*, E. C. Curwen, 1932; *Danebury*, author; *Ivinghoe Beacon*, Cotton & Frere, 1968)

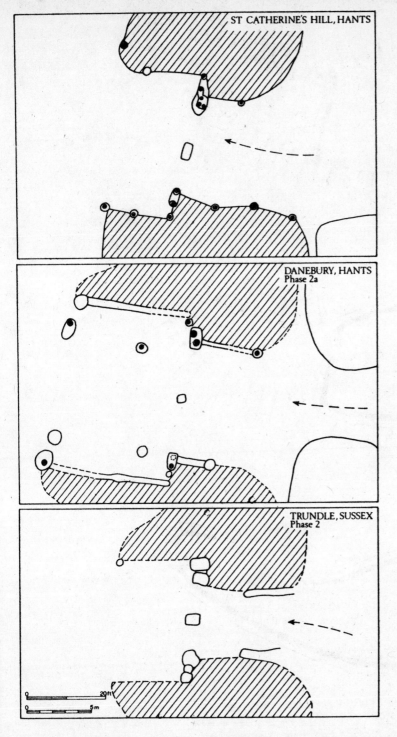

13:7 Dual-portal entrances (sources: *St Catherine's Hill*, Hawkes, Myres & Stevens, 1930; *Danebury*, author; *the Trundle*, E. C. Curwen, 1931 (author's reinterpretation))

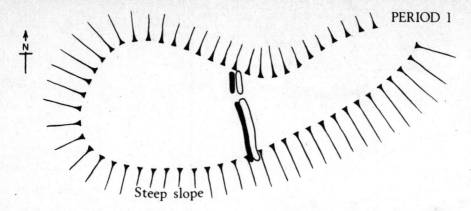

PERIOD 1

N

Steep slope

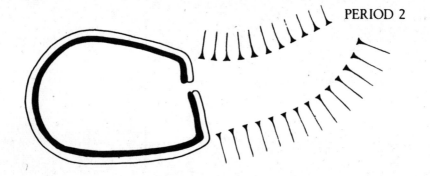

PERIOD 2

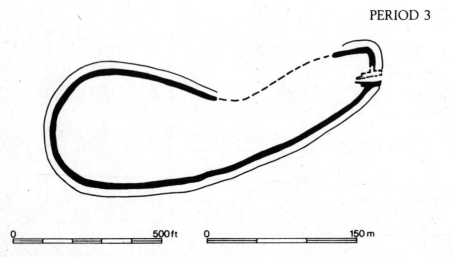

PERIOD 3

0   500ft   0   150m

13:8   The development of the hillfort of Torberry, Sussex (source: author)

ditch inwards (Fig. 13:6). The exact arrangement is not altogether clear but in all probability the rampart abutted on the timbers flanking the passage, although the possibility of additional side passages cannot be ruled out. An even simpler timber structure was provided at the east gate of Hollingbury Camp, Sussex (Fig. 13:6). Two vertical timbers 12 ft (3·7 m) apart were set at the inner side of a gap in the box-constructed rampart; on them the gates would have been hung. This arrangement is exactly comparable to the first gate of Danebury, which probably dates to the fifth or fourth century (Fig. 13:6).

The second phase at Danebury represents the development of a more complex gate (Fig. 13:7), embodying the idea of the dual-portal carriageway, which was maintained in use throughout several phases of rebuilding. Gates of almost exactly similar plan were in use in the first phases of St Catherine's Hill, Hants, and at the Trundle, Sussex. A simpler form of the same basic concept, but with only a single passageway, was found in the first period at Torberry[1] in the rampart which cut off the neck of the promontory defining the original defended area (Fig. 13:8). The entrance, which lay on the north side of the ridge below the crest, consisted of a simple gap in the rampart, the ends being revetted with a continuous palisade of posts, with the large post-holes for the gate set a little in front, about 5 ft (1·5 m) apart. The ditch-ends were askew to each other so that the approach would have to be oblique. From the gateposts shallow palisade trenches ran forward to the ditch-ends. This same type of arrangement can be traced, with modifications, at Quarley Hill, Hants, and at Yarnbury, Wilts. The main feature of both the dual- and single-portal entrances is that the gates themselves were set halfway along the entrance passage on line with the crest of the ramparts. Dating is fairly consistent: on the basis of sequence and associated pottery they should all fall within the fourth century, possibly lasting into the third.

In the second period at Torberry the earthwork was carried around the summit of the hill,

enclosing about 5 acres (2·2 hectares) (Fig. 13:8). The first entrance continued to be used at this time but in the third period the cross-defence and entrance were abandoned and partly dismantled while the fort was extended eastwards, continuing the contour works of the second period along the sides of the ridge and enclosing a further 3 acres (1·2 hectares). The entrance through the new circuit lay on the axis of the ridge. In its original form the ditch-ends were placed askew to each other to form an oblique approach, but other details were obscured except for a row of posts which would have revetted one of the rampart-ends, creating a passageway 50–60 ft (15–18 m) long. The exact siting of the gate at this stage has been lost. The intention of the new entrance is, however, clear enough: the creation of a defended corridor extending into the fort between the rampart ends.

The same appears to be true of other entrances. At Danebury, the third period entrance was provided with a simple dual gate set back at the end of a revetted corridor 43 ft (13 m) long, while at the Trundle the gate of the second phase lay at the end of a corridor 50 ft (15 m) long. Much the same arrangement seems to have been constructed at the inner entrance at Yarnbury and at Blewburton Hill, Berks. Little dating evidence is available but in terms of the individual sequences a third to second century date is probable.

In the final stage at Torberry (phase four) the entrance was remodelled on a massive scale (Fig. 13:9): the ditch-ends were walled across and filled in and the corridor was flanked on either side by substantial dry-stone walls 10–12 ft (3·0–3·6 m) wide extending into the camp for 90 ft (27 m). At the inner end of the gradually narrowing passage lay the gate, represented by two post-pits. Both phases three and four were associated with saucepan pots, showing that the creation of the corridor entrances lay within the second and first centuries BC. Much the same development was found at Danebury (Pl. 5), where in the fifth period a long corridor approach to the gate was created by turning the ends of the rampart outwards to form a passage 150 ft (45 m) long, and building around them, as protection, a pair of claw-like hornworks containing an outer gate (Fig. 13:11). From a platform created on the crest of the out-turned rampart it would have been possible for the defenders to

[1] Torberry was excavated between 1956 and 1958; the final report has not yet been published but plans of the overall development and of the main gate are given here (Figs. 13:8, 13:9).

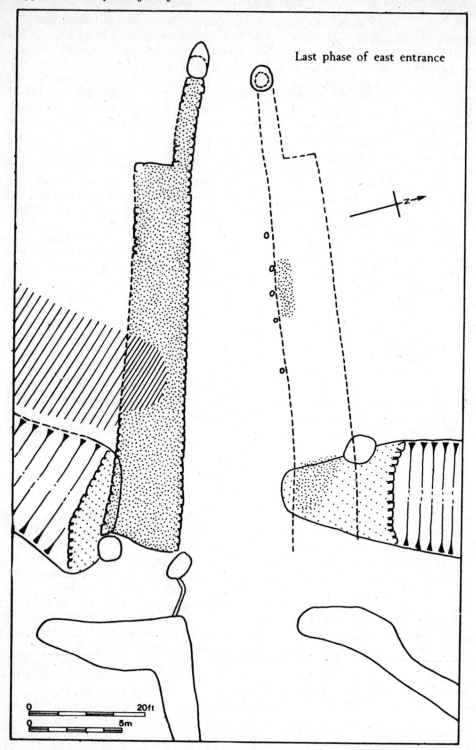

Last phase of east entrance

13:9   The last phase of the main entrance of Torberry, Sussex (source: author)

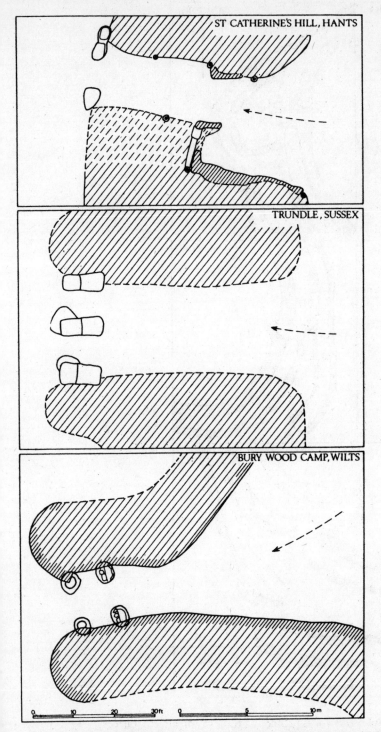

13:10   Inturned entrances (sources: *St Catherine's Hill*, Hawkes, Myres & Stevens, 1930 (author's reinterpretation); *the Trundle*, E. C. Curwen, 1931; *Bury Wood Camp*, King, 1967)

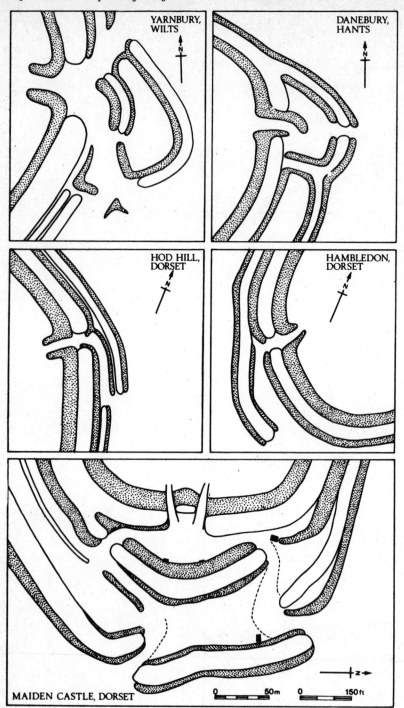

13:11   Comparative plans of complex outworks protecting hillfort entrances (sources: *Yarnbury*, M. E. Cunnington, 1933; *Hod Hill and Hambledon Hill*, Richmond, 1968; *Maiden Castle,* Wheeler, 1943; *Danebury*, author)

control both gates and the entire compass of the entrance earthworks, as well as the approach to the fort.

Corridor entrances were common throughout the hillfort areas of southern Britain (Fig. 13:10). At the neighbouring sites of the Trundle and St Catherine's Hill, long inturned corridors were now created out of the earlier gate structures, while at Bury Wood Camp, Wilts, the north-east entrance seems to have been first built in this style. Normally the corridor was constructed by turning the ends of the rampart into the camp as at Torberry, but in some cases, for example Buckland Rings, Hants, the Caburn, Sussex, and Llanmelin, Mon, partial or full multivallation contributed to the length of the defended approach, while at other sites like Danebury the corridor effect was created by out-turning the earthworks and protecting them with outer horn-works. A prime example of such an arrangement is the east entrance of Maiden Castle, Dorset (Pl. 2b), in phases II and III. Here (Fig. 13:11) any would-be attacker would have been confronted by a long tortuous corridor approach of more than 240 ft (73 m), winding in and out between earthworks which shielded strategically placed artillery platforms designed, no doubt, to be manned by defenders with slings.

A somewhat simpler method, with the same overall advantages, entailed the construction of a single flanking earthwork attached to one side of the entrance and running parallel to it (Fig. 13:11). This type can be most clearly seen at the Steepleton Gate of Hod Hill, Dorset, where a hornwork, unfinished presumably because of Roman attack, was added in front of an already inturned gate, creating a corridor of 300 ft (90 m) overall length. The same technique was employed at the neighbouring Hambledon Hill (Pl. 1) and, in a modified form, at Rawlsbury and Badbury Castle, all in Dorset; the outworks of Yarnbury, Wilts, (Pl. 2a), in their latest form would have created a similar general effect.

Wherever dating evidence is available, simple inturned corridor entrances of the Torberry type seem to date to the end of the second or beginning of the first century BC and even the more complex earthworks of Danebury belong to the same period, but the addition of flanking outworks is generally a later development, quite possibly not appearing in the south-west until the first century AD. Flanking works designed to deflect frontal attack are a far more sophisticated reaction to defence than the building of long corridors. It remains to be seen whether it was threat of Roman attack in AD 43 or earlier inter-tribal fighting which sparked off the development.

Turning now to the sequence in the Welsh borderland hillforts, the work at Croft Ambrey, Midsummer Hill and Credenhill Camp in Herefordshire and Ffridd Faldwyn, Montgomery, when collated allows the main development trends to be isolated (Stanford, 1971b). The earliest gate is a simple single-portal type found at Ffridd Faldwyn in association with a box rampart and tentatively dated to the eighth and seventh centuries. This was replaced by a series of twin-portal gates spanning the sixth to fourth centuries. Croft Ambrey, where occupation began towards the end of the sixth century, was also provided with a succession of twin-portal gates of broadly similar type.

During the fourth or early third century, timber guard-rooms came into common use, appearing at Midsummer Hill and probably Credenhill Camp, but soon to be replaced by stone-built guard-chambers of a kind which were also added to the Croft Ambrey gate. Guard-chambers are well represented among the hill-forts built in the stone areas of north Wales and the Welsh Marches, and extend south into Northamptonshire (Fig. 13:12). Strictly, two different types can be recognised: chambers added immediately behind the ramparts – as at Rainsborough, Northants, Castle Ditch (Eddisbury), Cheshire, Leckhampton Hill, Glos, and Dinorben, Denbigh – and those built at the ends of long corridor entrances like Titterstone Clee and the Wrekin, Salop, and Pen-y-Corddyn Mawr, Denbigh. No positive evidence is yet available to suggest whether or not there is a chronological difference between the two types. If we accept the fourth to third century dating suggested by Stanford for the appearance of guard-chambers at Croft Ambrey, Midsummer Hill and Credenhill Camp, and if the long corridor type of entrance plan was adopted in this area in parallel with its late second century appearance in the south, then there must be a difference in date between the two types. The problem is one which may eventually be solved by further excavation and radiocarbon dating.

One characteristic of the corridor entrances of the south, which recurs in the Welsh border

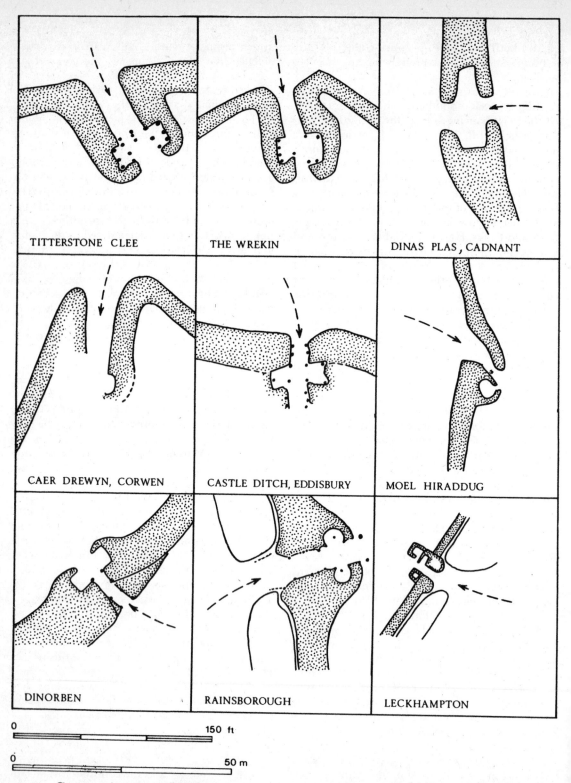

TITTERSTONE CLEE

THE WREKIN

DINAS PLAS, CADNANT

CAER DREWYN, CORWEN

CASTLE DITCH, EDDISBURY

MOEL HIRADDUG

DINORBEN

RAINSBOROUGH

LECKHAMPTON

0   150 ft

0   50 m

13:12   Comparative plans of hillfort entrance guard-chambers (source: Gardner & Savory, 1964, with amendments and additions)

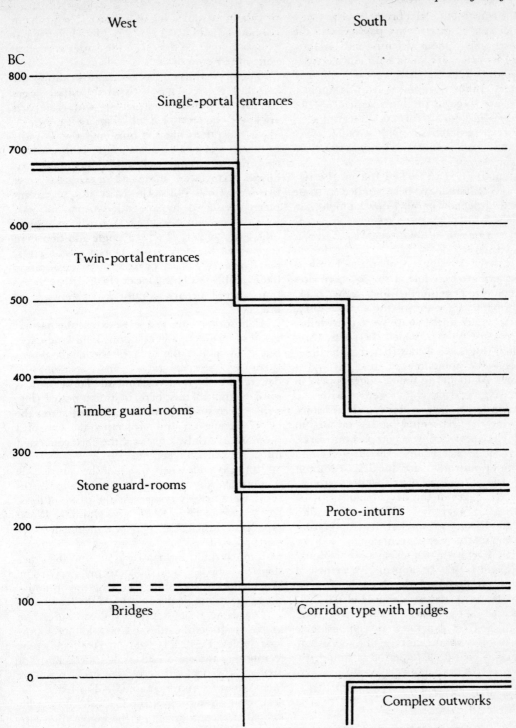

West

South

BC
800

Single-portal entrances

700

600

Twin-portal entrances

500

400

Timber guard-rooms

300

Stone guard-rooms

Proto-inturns

200

Bridges   Corridor type with bridges

100

0

Complex outworks

Diagram B   Simplified summary of the main trends in hillfort entrance development

sites, is the construction of a bridge over the gate linking one side of the entrance passage with the other, providing obvious defensive advantages. In the south bridges are found with long corridor entrances dating to the late second and early first century. In the west similar features appear, also at a late stage in the local sequence – for example at Midsummer Hill and Croft Ambrey – associated at the latter site with a radiocarbon date of 50 ± 100 (110 BC). The consistency in dating is impressive.

In summary, it may be said that in the two areas where hillforts have been studied in some detail, a well-defined parallel development can be recognised, although there are some apparent differences in dating in the early stages. Divergence in structural detail begins in the fourth century with the development of guard-chambers in the western group, while at the southern sites the gates tend to be set further and further back. Just before the beginning of the first century, many of the gates in the south were remodelled as long corridor types in which the gates, combined with bridges, were constructed at the inner ends of corridors sometimes as much as 150 ft (45 m) long. At about this time bridges appear in the western group, possibly together with the limited adoption of the corridor type of entrance plan. During the first century AD several forts in the south were provided with complex outworks, perhaps as a defence against threat of Roman attack, but outworks are not a common characteristic of the forts of the western group.

The main stages in the development can be summed up in Diagram B. When more radiocarbon dates become available, particularly from forts in the south, greater refinements will be possible, and with further excavation regional variations will no doubt appear. Nevertheless, the general similarity of development over a large area tends to suggest a degree of parallelism, reflected also in basic hillfort structure, which can best be explained by supposing a community of common culture and persistent contact over a considerable period of time.

REGIONAL DIFFERENCES IN THE
PLANNING AND SITING OF HILLFORTS

In the same way that the vernacular architecture of medieval Britain differs from region to region, so too it is possible to recognise peculiarities in

the planning and siting of hillforts. The problem cannot be discussed in any detail here but attention must be drawn to the larger and more generalised groupings.

The normal hillfort of southern Britain – the so-called contour type – is in its initial stages usually a univallate structure with ramparts enclosing the crest of a hill (Figs 13:13, 13:14). With exceptions like Cissbury and the Trundle in Sussex and St Catherine's Hill, Hants, where the original circuits were not subsequently enlarged, many were increased in size. At some, like Yarnbury, Wilts, the early fort was completely replaced by an entirely new rampart roughly concentric with the first (Pl. 2a), while others were enlarged with a single addition as in the case of Maiden Castle, Dorset (Fig. 13:15), and Torberry, Sussex, or more than one addition like Hambledon Hill, Dorset (Pl. 1). Multivallation, where it occurs, can usually be shown to be late.

Contour forts are to a large extent the natural result of fortifying a gentle downland landscape, but even within the area of the chalk downs there are steeper ridges and promontories demanding different treatment. Torberry is a good example of this: here, in its first period (Fig. 13:8), a cross-defence was constructed across the ridge, cutting off and protecting the end of a promontory; only later was the fort converted into a conventional contour work.

In the Weald, where much of the countryside is more sharply dissected by streams, promontories were usually chosen for the siting of forts. In the case of High Rocks and Hammer Wood (Iping) in Sussex (Fig. 13:16), multiple defences were constructed across the neck of the ridge with much slighter earthworks around the other slopes where the land falls steeply away. The Wealden forts were simply making the optimum use of the defensive possibilities of the landscape.

The same general principles can surely be applied to the cliff castles of Cornwall and southwest Wales (Figs 12:11, 12:15). Headlands projecting into the sea needed only short lengths of artificial defences cut across the neck to render them virtually impregnable. Admittedly, the structural similarities of the Cornish cliff castles as well as certain aspects of the material culture (pp. 104–6) show strong links with the Armorican peninsula – an area of similar geomorphological structure. But the absence of cliff castles in Corn-

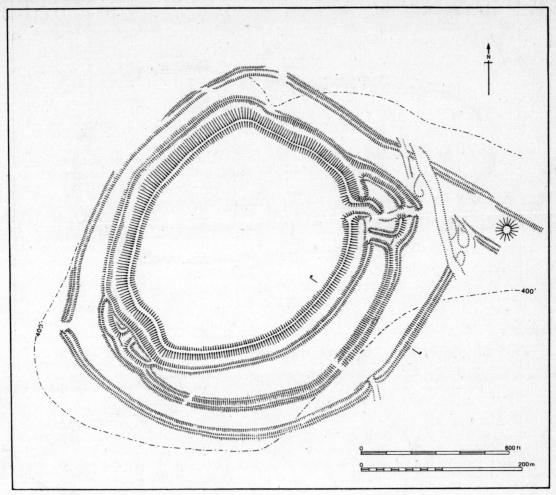

13:13   Danebury, Hants (source: author)

wall would have been more culturally significant than their presence, for the structure of the countryside demands this type of fortification.

While geomorphology is a significant factor in the siting and form of hillforts, geological considerations, particularly the availability of good building stone, can sometimes have a direct effect on actual structure and perhaps on form. In the Cotswolds it is possible to trace a group of relatively small univallate forts of almost circular plan – including Lyneham, Ilbury, Idbury Camp and Chastleton in Oxfordshire and Windrush Camp, Glos – which contrast with the vast enclosures of more than 50 acres (22·3 hectares), usually sited on ridges, like Norbury Camp (Northleach) and Nottingham Hill, Glos (Rivet,

1961, 33). Exactly what factors were involved in the evolution of these two classes is not clear but economic and social considerations may well have been important, while the circular form of the smaller category may have been encouraged by the availability of building stone.

Economic factors were of considerable significance in influencing fort type. It has already been emphasised (pp. 186–8) that the multiple enclosure forts of the south-west peninsula and south-west Wales were a response to the predominantly pastoral economy of these regions, but it would be more accurate to regard them as fortified homesteads. The adding of annexes to the larger forts, however (a response to the same economic pressures), gives several of the forts in

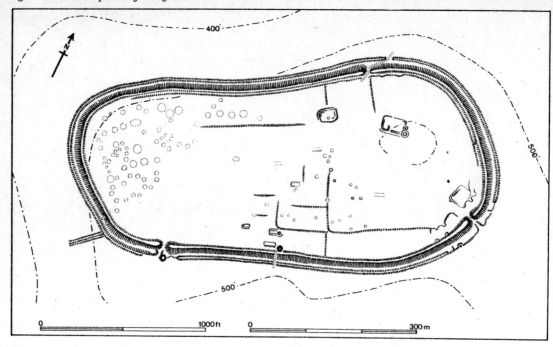

13:14   Cissbury, Sussex (source: Curwen & Williamson, 1931)

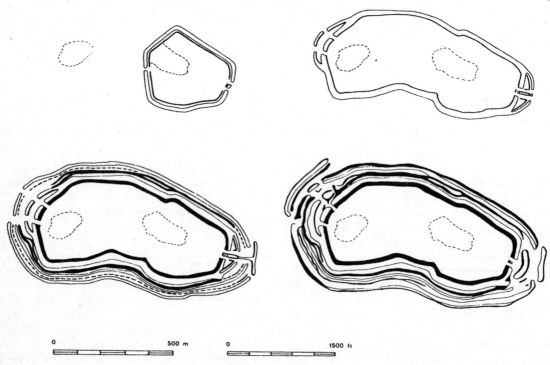

13:15   The development of Maiden Castle, Dorset (source: Wheeler, 1943)

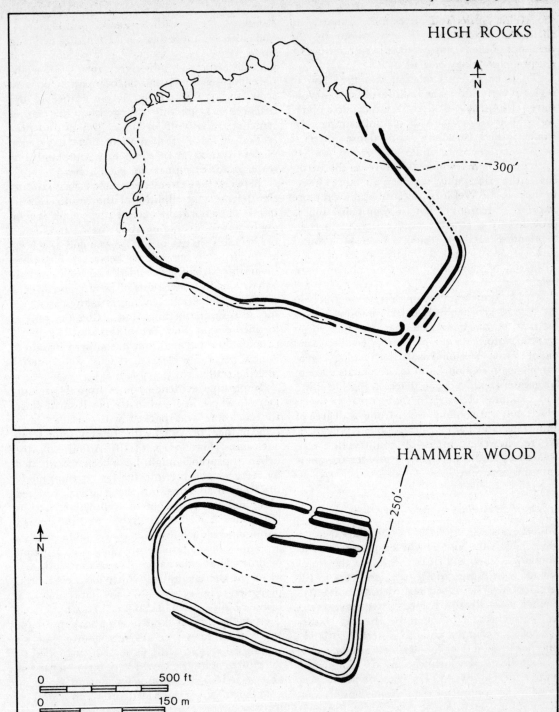

13:16 Wealden promontory forts (sources: *High Rocks*, Money, 1968; *Hammer Wood*, Boyden, 1957)

the Welsh borderland an overall similarity to them but a similarity brought about by the demands of the farming economy rather than by culture, chronology or geology.

To some extent, isolation can give rise to regional variations. The hillforts of Caernarvonshire (Hogg, 1962) demonstrate this particularly well. Their large size, hilltop siting, simple drystone walled structure and dense internal occupation serve to unite the group and to distinguish them from the structures in the northeast of the principality, which relate more closely to those in the Welsh borderland. An even more impressive demonstration of regionalisation is provided by a recent consideration of forts in Scotland (Feachem, 1966) where by ground survey alone several distinctive types of plan, clustering significantly together, have been recognised.

This brief survey may have erred too much on the side of geographical determination, but in the past too much emphasis has been placed on cultural/historical explanations when discussing hillfort form. Regional isolation, geology, geomorphology, economy and social structure are of far greater significance in determining the siting and planning of forts. In those areas between which cultural contacts were strong, a degree of uniformity and parallel development prevailed. Where, however, areas of countryside were isolated by natural features, a greater regionalisation is apparent.

THE FUNCTION OF HILLFORTS

Hillforts vary considerably in size – a variation which must, in its extremes at least, be related to function. At one end of the scale are the small defended enclosures from 1 to 4 acres (0·4 to 1·6 hectares), which are best regarded as individual fortified homesteads. These, as we have seen, are concentrated particularly in the south-west of the country and in eastern Scotland, but homesteads or hamlets of similar size without the massive fortifications are widespread in the south-east as well. Fortification in this case is essentially a result of the socio-economic condition of the region. At the other end of the scale are the massive straggling structures covering 60 acres (24·3 hectares) or more like Bathampton Down, Somerset, with 80 acres (32·4 hectares), Ogbury, Wilts, with 62 acres (25·1 hectares),

Walbury, Berks, with 87 acres (35·2 hectares), and others – altogether about ten sites centring upon Wessex but extending into Sussex and Gloucestershire (Wainwright, 1967b). The apparent absence of internal occupation on any scale and the relatively simple nature of the defences and gates might suggest that this class of structures was built for the collection and protection of cattle; that most of them were conveniently sited to be close to pastureland and water is added support for such a view.

Between the extremes are those forts sited with the defensive possibilities of the countryside in mind. They normally exceed 4 or 5 acres (1·6 or 2·2 hectares), averaging about 10–15 acres (4·4–6·1 hectares) in extent but occasionally reaching as much as 50 acres (22·3 hectares). They are invariably strongly defended and, where excavated, usually show signs of occupation over a considerable period, leading in many cases to a sporadic strengthening and extension of the fortified circuit. Few forts of this kind have been extensively excavated, but in southern Britain it is now becoming clear that dense and ordered internal settlement prevailed.

Impressive evidence comes from Hod Hill, Dorset, where in its ultimate pre-Roman stage the enclosure was packed with circular huts, some of them provided with annexes, some set in enclosures (Figs 13:17, 13:18). Admittedly, the urban appearance might have been accentuated by refugees pouring into the fort at the time of the Roman advance, but the relatively ordered planning, the provision of well-defined streets (Crawford & Keiller, 1928, 36), and the limited dating and sequence evidence available suggests a planned development spreading over a period of time. The remarkable plan of the south-east sector of the enclosure, which has never been ploughed (Fig. 13:17), gives the impression of a heavily built-up urban complex as it would have been at the time of the Roman attack in AD 43. More than forty-five circular houses can be recognised which, if the same density applied to the entire enclosure, would have meant a total of about 270 houses. Allowing for some to represent abandoned or replaced structures and a unit of three persons to a house, the potential population can hardly have been less than 500 and may have approached 1,000.

Although it could be argued that Hod Hill was a special case, the urbanised appearance

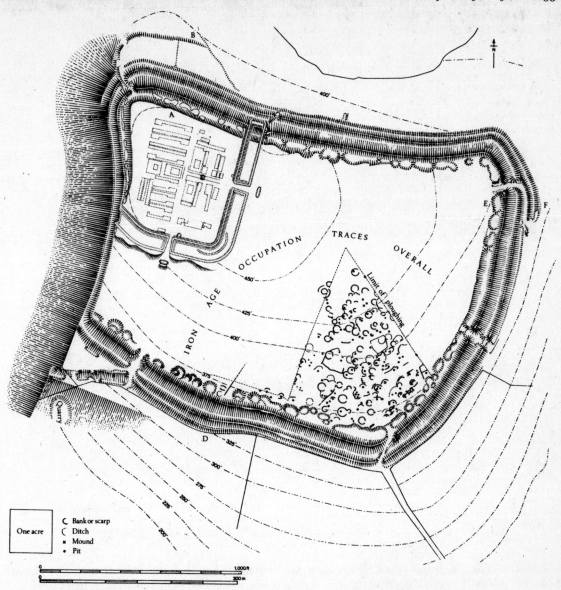

13:17   Hod Hill, Dorset (source: reproduced from RCHM, *Dorset*, vol. iii)

being created by the political unrest of the first century AD, there can be no doubt that the intensive occupation of the Dorset and Somerset hillforts dates back to at least the fourth century BC. At Chalbury, Dorset (Fig. 13:19), a simple fort apparently occupied for only a short time contained between seventy and a hundred hut-circles. Similarly, excavations at Maiden Castle, Dorset (Fig. 13:20), and South Cadbury, Somerset, have yielded indisputable evidence of close-spaced internal occupation spanning the period from the fourth century BC to the Roman conquest. It is therefore fair to suppose that a proportion at least of the forts of the south were continuously, or at least frequently, inhabited on a large scale. It is sometimes difficult to distinguish between truly continuous occupation and sporadic occupation in times of stress, but since there is no evidence for periods of abandonment it is simpler to assume that occupation con-

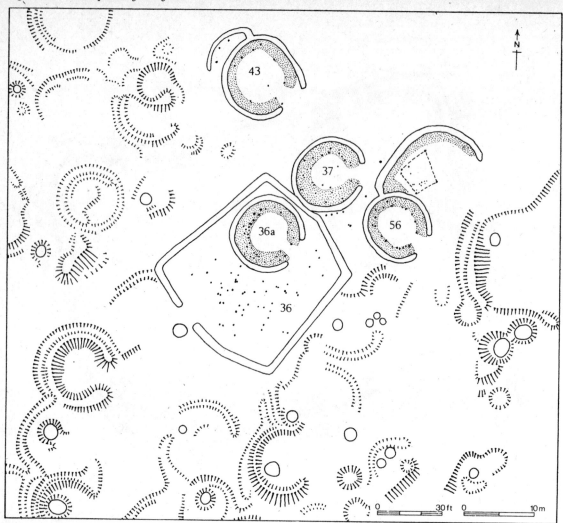

13:18   Details of the excavated huts in Hod Hill, Dorset (source: Richmond, 1968)

tinued without a break from foundation to abandonment.

Dramatic evidence of planned internal occupation has recently been discovered in four hillforts: Croft Ambrey, Credenhill Camp, and Midsummer Hill, in the Welsh borderland, and Danebury in Hampshire. In each site extensive internal excavation has revealed an area of regularly laid out rectangular timber buildings arranged in rows along streets. At Danebury five rows of building have been exposed, positioned end to end in lines parallel to the rampart (Pl. 6). The buildings were all four- or six-post structures measuring on average 10 by 12 ft (3·0 by 3·5 m)

and spaced at intervals of 7–12 ft (2–4 m) from each other. The buildings seem to have faced on to streets and backed on to areas reserved for the construction of storage pits. The three western hillforts have produced much the same arrangement except that the buildings were invariably of four-post construction. At Credenhill Camp three rows were uncovered, the average spacing between buildings being 11·5 ft (3·5 m) with pathways 15 ft (4·5 m) wide. Two types of building were represented: rectangular structures some 12 by 8 ft (3·7 by 2·4 m) and square buildings some 9 ft across (2·7 m). In all four sites two features stand out: the regularity of the planning

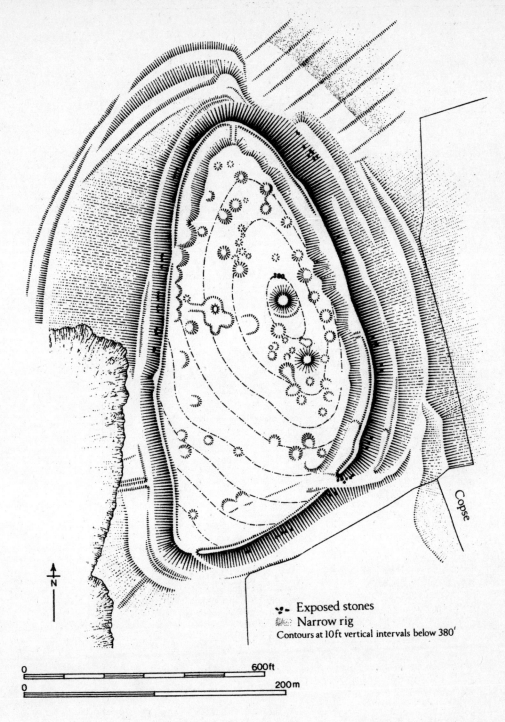

Exposed stones
Narrow rig
Contours at 10ft vertical intervals below 380'

0   600ft

0   200m

13:19   Chalbury, Dorset (source: reproduced from RCHM, *Dorset*, vol. iii)

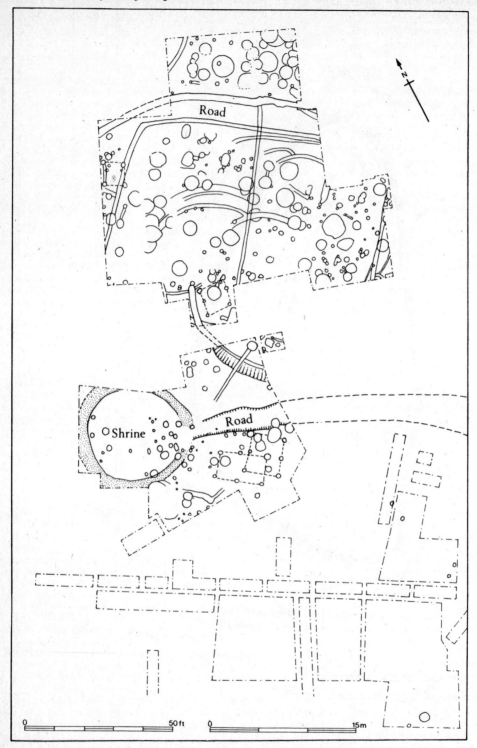

13:20   The settlement plan within Maiden Castle, Dorset (source: Wheeler, 1943)

and the fact that the buildings were constantly rebuilt in the same positions sometimes as many as six times. There can thus be no doubt of overall planning control and of continuous occupation.

These surprising discoveries raise three basic problems: why is the internal planning of Hod Hill with its round huts so different? should we expect the entire enclosed areas to be filled with rectangular buildings? and what is the function of these structures? The problem of Hod Hill cannot be solved without further excavation. One explanation might well be that the south-western forts were culturally different and maintained a tradition of round house building throughout the Iron Age, but a more likely alternative is that the circular houses at Hod Hill are all late, perhaps belonging to the first century AD, and that below them rectangular buildings remain to be found. The fact that early six-post rectangular buildings are recorded at South Cadbury, pre-dating circular houses, and at Maiden Castle, might be thought to strengthen this argument.

As to the density of rectangular buildings within the hillforts, it should be remembered that the areas so far excavated are all close to ramparts and it may well be that these regular streets of small rectangular structures are usually arranged peripherally within the forts, the central areas being planned or used in a different manner. If this is accepted as a possibility, any assessment of population based on the samples so far available must be regarded as totally unreliable. Nor can it be assumed that the rectangular buildings were all used as houses. Some may well have been storage buildings of the granary type. Work now currently in progress can, however, be expected eventually to throw light on these problems.

From the above discussion, it will be seen that elements of organised planning are a feature of hillfort interior layout. Little is yet known of planning on a larger scale but a few examples of specialised buildings and street patterns have been recorded. Streets are known at Hod Hill, one of them leading from the Steepleton Gate to the hut (36a) in a rectangular enclosure (Fig. 13:18), which is usually interpreted as being the chieftain's hut at the time of the Roman conquest. Elsewhere in the fort, a certain logic prevails in the general siting of the individual buildings. At Maiden Castle the main street entering the east gate ran through the fort directly to a circular stone-walled hut 30 ft (9 m) in diameter (Fig. 13:20). The fact that the hut was replaced in the Roman period by another circular structure that lay immediately adjacent to the Romano-Celtic temple hints at the possibility that the pre-Roman building possessed some religious connotations: its imposing approach certainly singles it out as a structure of some significance. This arrangement is also reflected at South Cadbury, where a processional way leads to what is undoubtedly a shrine or temple (p. 295). These two sites provide a reminder that sanctuaries are to be expected as an integral part of hillfort occupation; others of pre-Roman date are known at Heathrow, Middx, and at Pilsdon Pen, Dorset, while the presence of later Romano-Celtic temples within forts might imply a continuity of religious practice from the pre-invasion period.

Apart from temples, evidence of specialisation within hillforts is not yet impressive. At some forts like Balksbury, Hants, and Grimthorpe, Yorks, the four-post granaries tend to be placed just inside the ramparts, but this may well be more an accident of discovery since excavation has tended to concentrate on these areas. Only at South Cadbury has evidence of specialist activity, in the form of a metalworkers' quarter, been recognised, but there can be little doubt that specialisation must have occurred in other forts; it is only the lack of substantial area excavation that has prevented its discovery.

In other parts of Britain, hillforts show signs of an equally dense internal settlement. North Wales has several such sites, including Dinorben, Denbigh, and Garn Boduan, Carn Fadrun, Conway Mountain and Tre'r Ceiri in Caernarvonshire, each with numbers of huts ranging from nineteen to over a hundred (Figs 12:17, 12:18). A. H. A. Hogg's assessment of their significance has led him to propose a population density averaging about fifteen persons per acre (Hogg, 1962, 22–3), which in terms of actual numbers gives a maximum of about 400 people living in Garn Boduan at any one time. L. Alcock (1965, 194), reconsidering the same evidence, offers the suggestion that the population approximated more closely to 700, a density averaging twenty-five per acre. Clearly, figures of this kind are open to many sources of error, but the order of magnitude is interesting since it approximates to the rough figures suggested above for Hod Hill. Hogg and Alcock differ again over the problem of permanent residence, Alcock preferring to suppose transhumance between forts and the lowland settlements. Certainly, the extreme climate of the region might weigh on the side of transhumance, but comparisons with the Wessex forts show little difference. The matter is highly complex and cannot easily be solved without far more extensive excavation.

Most of the large Scottish oppida show similar signs of intensive occupation rising to more than 300 houses within the 40 acres (16·2 hectares) of Eildon Hill North, Roxburgh, the capital of the Selgovae. Allowing for undiscovered huts in the area beneath a plantation, R. W. Feachem (1966, 79) estimates the population to be between 2,000 and 3,000. Further south, at Yevering Bell, Northumberland, a 13 acre (5·3 hectare) enclosure contains about 130 huts which, if all were occupied at the same time, might point to a community of at least 500 souls. The same functional problems arise in Scotland as in Wales: were the forts permanently occupied or not? The answer is not yet forthcoming.

Sufficient has been said to show that many of the hillforts of southern and western Britain took on the character of small towns, each having a substantial and permanent population, organised internal planning, 'monumental' architecture and provision for specialists. It is difficult to resist the conclusion that many of them were truly urban in both appearance and function. In the highland areas of Wales and Scotland, the same pattern of dense occupation seems to hold good but the possibility of a transhumant aspect, at least in the life of some sections of the community, cannot be ruled out.

The mechanisms by which these nucleated settlements came into being will be considered in more detail later (ch. 16). Here it is sufficient to say that by the third to second centuries a stable pattern was beginning to emerge in the south and east of the country. While certain centres were reaching prominence, others were being abandoned; thus social and economic territories were beginning to crystallise out.

Any consideration of territorial boundaries must be to a large extent subjective but two areas, the South Downs and the Chilterns, lend themselves to easy consideration. The chalk downs east of the river Test are divided up into blocks by south-flowing rivers, the swampy valleys of

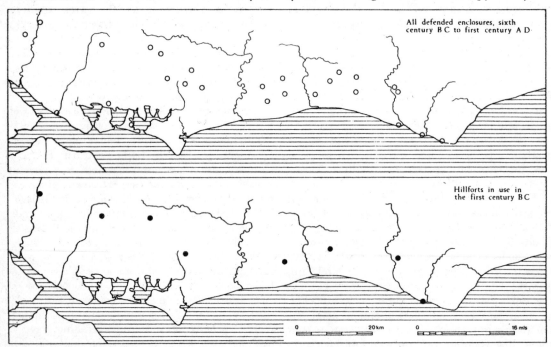

13:21   Hillforts on the South Downs (source: author)

which must have been major obstacles in the pre-Roman period. On each of the blocks of downland was one major hillfort occupied in the latter part of the Iron Age (Fig. 13:21). Other forts are known but they can usually be shown to have gone out of use before the third or second century BC – unlike the major forts, which continued to be occupied and modified into the first century or later. Gradually, then, in each of the natural territories one centre gained supremacy over the rest and outlived them, to become the natural focus of the region.

The same pattern appears to hold good for the eastern Chilterns (Fig. 13:22) but the situation is complicated by the fact that the chalk ridge is seldom dissected by rivers except in the case of the Cam and the Lea. Nevertheless, the scarp slope rivers created partial natural barriers, which were projected across the ridge by artificial boundaries composed of lines of banks and ditches; Dray's Ditches, Beds, the only boundary of this kind to be examined, has proved to be a complex structure composed of multiple ditches and timber stockades originating probably as early as the late second millennium. Within all but one of the six territories thus defined lies a single major hillfort (Dyer, 1961). Subsidiary forts are known in three of the regions, but the absence of adequate excavations prevents any firm conclusion as to their date or development. The general impression given by this pattern, however, is that the eastern Chilterns were subjected to the same social and economic pressures as the South Downs, leading eventually to the domination of each territory by a single fort.

The chalk plain of Wessex can be regarded in much the same way. Fig. 13:23 shows the area with each of the major forts known or suspected to have been occupied in the first century BC to the early first century AD. Each clearly commands a territory, the limits of which are frequently partly defined by rivers. The sizes of the territories vary between 30 and 50 square miles (77·7 and 129·5 km²) but average a little over 40 square miles (103·3 km²), thus demonstrating a remarkable consistency.

The three different regions briefly outlined here may be regarded as being among the clearest examples of a situation which can be paralleled over most of the country. But it would be wrong to think of hillforts and their territory as a rigid system imposed upon the countryside.

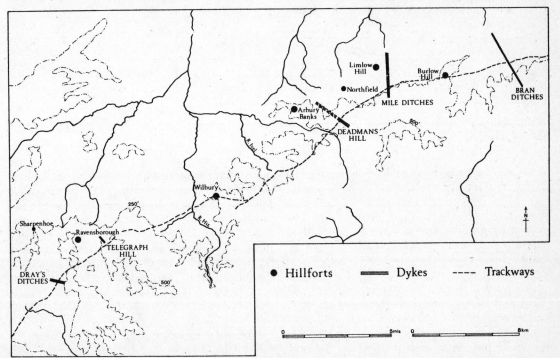

13:22　Territorial boundaries in the eastern Chilterns (source: Dyer, 1961)

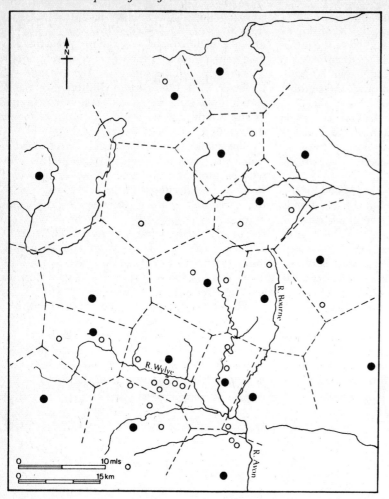

13:23 Hillforts in central Wessex (Wiltshire), with theoretical territories constructed on the basis of Thiessen polygons (source: author)

Wherever the evidence is sufficiently detailed, it points to a gradual evolution which frequently leads to a single centre gaining dominance, sometimes at the expense of other fortifications. The nucleation of power, and presumably population, within a natural or artificially defined territory must reflect a growing sophistication in political structure (p. 305).

A strongly defended hillfort implies two things: coercive power in the hands of society's leaders and the need to protect the community from attack. It could be argued that forts were essentially objects of display with no military significance, but while some element of display may well have been involved, there can be little

doubt that the siting and construction of the forts was carried out with a firm eye on the defensive potentialities of the situation. In some cases military pressures led eventually to multivallation which, it has been suggested, was a response to the introduction of sling warfare. Slings were certainly commonly used in southern Britain in the latter part of the pre-Roman period, but the occurrence of clay slingstones at Kimmeridge, Dorset, and Swallowcliffe Down, Wilts, shows that slings were in use for two or three centuries before, for hunting or aggressive purposes. It is simpler to suggest that fighting became more common, with the result that slings were more widely used for attack and defence, forcing the gradual adoption of more complex patterns of defensive architecture.

A study of hillforts, therefore, allows social change to be recognised: territories were being more closely defined and warfare was increasing. Together with other classes of evidence, it is possible to use these generalisations to outline, admittedly rather hazily, the revolution which society was undergoing in the second half of the first millennium BC (pp. 303–6).

Craft, Industry and Art *Chapter 14*

The manufacture and distribution of consumer goods in Iron Age Britain was a complex process involving trade and production on several different levels. Beneath the all-embracing pattern imposed by overseas trade, which remained a significant factor throughout, there lay two systems of no lesser importance: specialist localised production, with its own limited spheres of distribution, and home production geared to the needs of the immediate kin group. The latter satisfied the bulk of the population's needs.

HOME INDUSTRIES: WOOL, LEATHER, CARPENTRY AND BASKETRY (Fig. 14:1)

One of the most widely practised of the home crafts was the manufacture of woollen fabrics, which seems to have been carried out in most parts of the British Isles, presumably on a part-time basis within each household. Exactly how the fleece was removed from the sheep is a matter of some debate, in view of the absence of shears in all but the very latest Iron Age deposits, but an iron knife would have proved adequate and it is possible that the objects known as weaving combs may have been used for plucking out the wool. After cleaning, the wool would have been combed, probably with bone and antler combs, and then spun into yarn on a simple hand-spindle weighted with a whorl of stone or baked clay. It was probably at this stage that dyeing was undertaken, using vegetable dyes of which no trace has survived.

The nature of the loom used in Britain is still a matter of uncertainty but in all probability it was of the upright warp-weighted type. No archaeological trace of the structure survives in this country, with the exception of the loom-weights of clay and stone used for keeping bunches of warp threads taut and of even tension. Some simple machinery would have been used for shedding, i.e. parting the warp threads to allow the weft to be woven through – a process probably carried out with a shuttle of wood which may have been provided with a tip made from a pointed metapodial or tibia bone. The tamping down of the weft could most efficiently have been carried out with a wooden sword, although comb beaters (i.e. weaving combs) or pin beaters, in the form of hafted bone points, may sometimes have been used.

For the manufacture of braids, tablet weaving may have been practised. This is a method which requires the use of bone or wood plates perforated with two or more holes close to the edge to control the positioning and spacing of the warp. The technique was widely used in Scandinavia during the pre-Roman Iron Age and also during the Roman period in Britain, but the only indisputable evidence of earlier use in this country is a group of triangular weaving tablets found in Iron Age contexts at Wookey Hole, Somerset. Even so, the process was probably generally practised.

The more durable artefacts connected with spinning and weaving are found over much of the country throughout the pre-Roman Iron Age, and many of them can be traced back into the second millennium. A weaving comb (or a plucking comb) is known in a Middle to Late Bronze Age context at Shearplace Hill, Dorset, and functionally similar objects made of antler are found in Neolithic contexts. Similarly, loom-weights of cylindrical form made from baked clay are a recurring component of Middle to Late Bronze Age assemblages, and the type continues

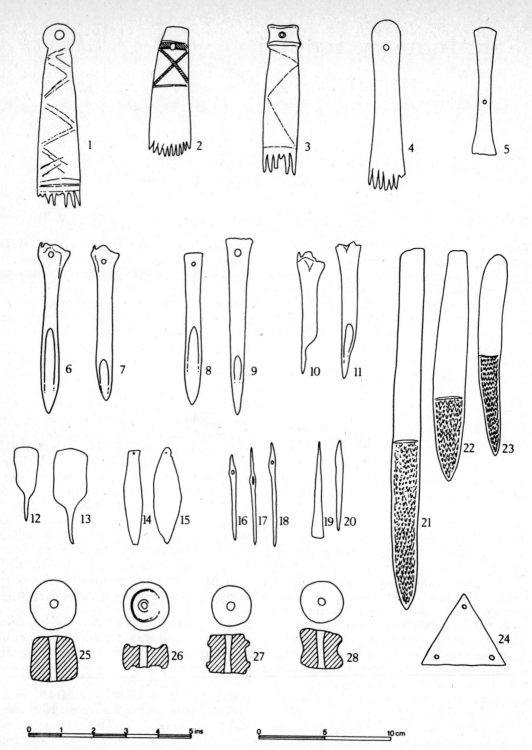

14:1 Bone and ceramic equipment connected with spinning, weaving and the preparation of skins. 1–23, 25–8 All Cannings Cross, Wilts; 24 Wookey Hole, Somerset (sources: *All Cannings Cross*, M. E. Cunnington, 1923; *Wookey Hole*, Balch, 1914)

into the Iron Age, eventually to be replaced by the more characteristic triangular variety. Even the bone threading points are sporadically found in pre-Iron Age contexts. There can therefore be little doubt that the manufacture of woollen cloth was an old-established craft in Britain and, to judge by the dense distribution of artefacts concerned with spinning and weaving, most households were geared to supplying their own requirements.

The weaving of organic materials other than wool would have been equally widely practised, although little evidence survives today. Basketry is implied by the impressions of basketwork on a pot from Dun Croc a Comhdlach, on North Uist, and some kind of matting made from rushes was found in a pit at Worlebury, Somerset. These few survivals do scant justice to the fact that basket-making and matting must have been common occupations during the prehistoric period, particularly in those areas in which pottery was scarce. Another occupation, the production of fishing-nets, would presumably have been carried out on a large scale, but apart from a few netting needles and lead and stone net-weights no trace survives.

Leather-working was of no less importance to the community than the production of woollen fabrics. The manufacture of a serviceable leather garment or container would have involved three separate stages: first the removal and cleaning of the skin, then tanning, and finally the making up of the finished article. These processes can be expected to leave little archaeological trace but general purpose iron knives would have been quite sufficient for skinning and cutting, whilst the stretching out of the pelt would probably have involved the use of wooden or bone points. Fatty substances rising gradually to the surface were scraped off, possibly with the use of the rib-knives (ribs thinned down to give a good scraping edge) so commonly found on occupation sites, whilst the removal of the hair was probably undertaken using a comb or scraper. The actual process of tanning could have been carried out in vats or in specially lined pits, using preparations containing oak bark and oak galls, as the principal sources of tannin. The elder Pliny mentions the importance of the trade in oak galls for this purpose in the first century BC, and indeed a small quantity of galls were found in a pit of the second century BC at Chalton, Hants,

suggesting their deliberate collection. At present this is the only evidence for what can hardly be doubted to have been a process commonly practised throughout the period. Finally, the manufacture of the finished articles would have required only iron knives and bone needles, both of which are commonly found in domestic contexts.

While clothing and harness would have been the principal leather goods to be manufactured, containers must have been made for use alongside, or instead of, ceramics. To a pastoral community frequently on the move, leather vessels were far more practical than pottery. Indeed, it is possible to see in the decoration of some of the second century pottery in Hampshire what might well be a sceuomorphic representation of stitching, the diagonal lines representing the thread, the shallow dots being the needle-holes (Fig. A:15). Moreover, the form of the saucepan pots would be more appropriate to leather work or bark-work than to a ceramic medium. The use of leather containers is likely to have been more widespread than we can ever demonstrate.

Other home crafts employing organic materials would have included carpentry and hurdle-making – about which very little is known at this period, although in the Somerset marsh villages of the second and first century both crafts were well developed. That the structural carpentry of the earlier period was advanced is implied by the complex nature of some of the earliest houses like West Brandon, Co. Durham, Little Woodbury, Wilts, and Pimperne Down, Dorset, where a detailed knowledge of the properties of timber would have been essential to produce stability and permanence. Hurdle-work must have been equally well advanced since hurdles were presumably used to serve as walling for some of the houses. Some storage pits, too, may have been wicker-lined but only at Dane's Camp, Poxwell, and Worlebury has such a lining been recognised.

METALWORKING: IRON, COPPER, TIN, LEAD, SILVER AND GOLD

The home crafts referred to so far could have all been practised using material locally available, the collection of which would have been a simple matter. Iron-smithing, on the other hand, involved more complex mechanisms, for while

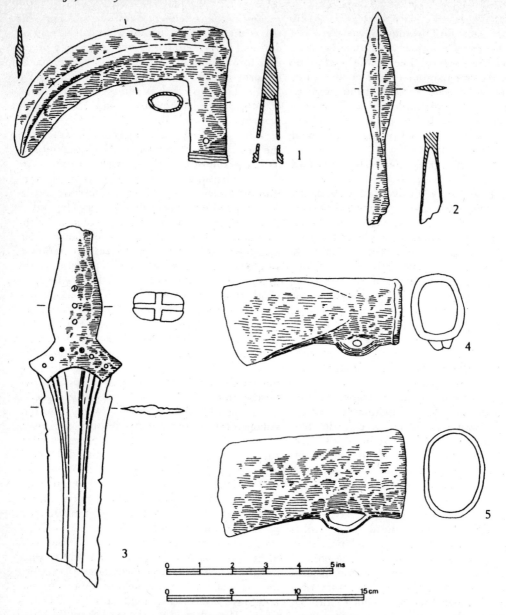

14:2 Early types of iron weapons and implements. 1–3 sickle, spear and sword from Llyn Fawr, Glam; 4 axe from Walthamstow, Essex; 5 axe from Cold Kitchen Hill, Wilts (sources: *Llyn Fawr*, Grimes, 1951; *Walthamstow*, Smith, 1925; *Cold Kitchen Hill*, author)

most areas of Britain lay within relatively easy reach of iron deposits, some element of specialist extraction must have been involved.

The discovery at Llyn Fawr, Glam, of an iron sickle made in close imitation of a native bronze prototype establishes beyond reasonable doubt that iron products were being manufactured in Britain probably as early as the middle of the seventh century (Fig. 14:2). This is not the only evidence: at Sheepen Hill (Colchester), Essex, a cauldron of the early seventh century was found, together with a small iron stud (Hawkes &

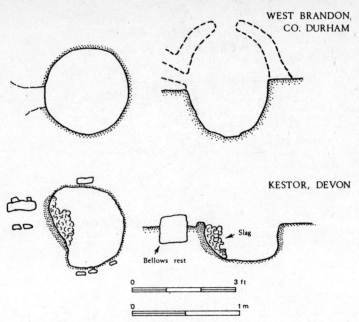

WEST BRANDON,
CO. DURHAM

KESTOR, DEVON

Slag

Bellows rest

0   3 ft

0   1 m

14:3   Iron-smelting furnaces (sources: *Kestor*, A. Fox, 1955; *West Brandon*, Jobey, 1962b)

Smith 1957, 161), and the Sompting hoard from Sussex, of the later seventh century, also contained a mass of corroded iron of undistinguishable form. Iron, then, was a component of some seventh century hoards and the Llyn Fawr sickle shows that competent blacksmiths were at work. The change-over from one metal to another must have been gradual, and it is only to be expected that to begin with old bronze types were copied in the new metal. The single-looped socketed axe made in iron appears on a number of sites as disparate as Scotland, the Berwyn Mountains, Cold Kitchen Hill, Wilts and Walthamstow, Essex (Fig. 14:2), but in no case has such an implement been found in a stratified context. It, might, however, be relevant that the Cold Kitchen Hill axe came from a site producing quantities of pottery of sixth or even seventh century date.

How extensively iron was used in the seventh, sixth or even fifth century is impossible to say. The survival of Late Bronze Age types on several Iron Age sites suggests that its introduction was gradual and that old traditions lingered for centuries. Indeed, it was not until the fourth to third centuries that the metal began to come into use on any scale. Smelting and forging seem generally to have been carried out at the home-

stead. Two examples serve to emphasise the point (Fig. 14:3). At Kestor, Devon, in the large hut already described (pp. 181–2), a small bowl furnace some 12–18 in (30–45 cm) in diameter was found dug to a depth of 9 in (23 cm) below the floor. On one side lay a flat stone, possibly functioning as a bellows-rest. Within the furnace were found charcoal and cinders with a high iron content. Nearby was a larger pit discoloured by intense heat, which may have been used to reheat the bloom for forging. The second example comes from the early palisaded homestead of West Brandon, Co. Durham, where two simple bowl furnaces were discovered, each about 12 in (30 cm) in diameter and 8 in (21 cm) deep. One of them was provided with a groove, in which the *tuyère* would have been placed, and contained the broken-up remains of a clay dome, showing that it had been at least partially enclosed.

While only about half a dozen furnaces have been found (Tylecote, 1962, 194), other evidence of iron-smelting – such as slag, cinder or iron ore – is more widespread and leaves little doubt that iron extraction and forging was a normal home craft and not solely a skill in the hands of specialists. The processes involved in extraction were simple enough: the crushed ore, mixed with

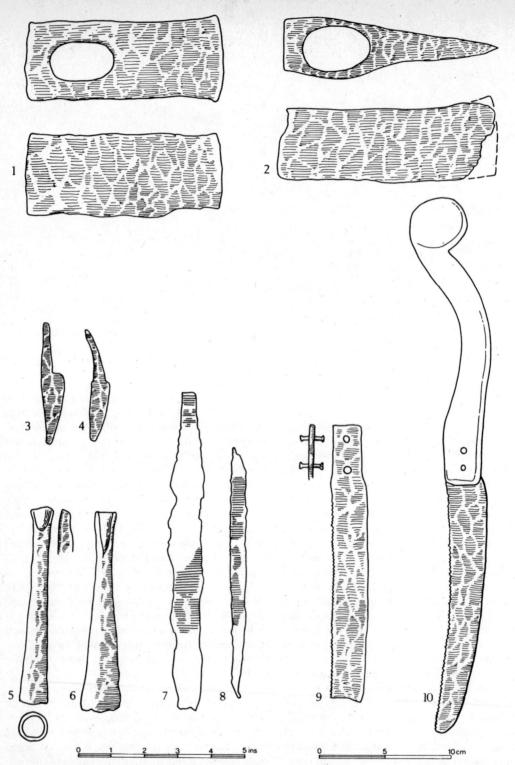

14:4 Selection of iron tools. 1 hammer from Bulbury, Dorset; 2 axe-hammer from Bulbury, Dorset; 3, 4 knives from All Cannings Cross, Wilts; 5, 6 gouges from All Cannings Cross, Wilts; 7, 8 files from Glastonbury, Somerset; 9 saw from Barley, Herts; 10 saw from Glastonbury, Somerset (sources: *Bulbury*, author; *Glastonbury*, Bulleid & Grey, 1917; *All Cannings Cross*, M. E. Cunnington, 1923; *Barley*, Cra'ster, 1961)

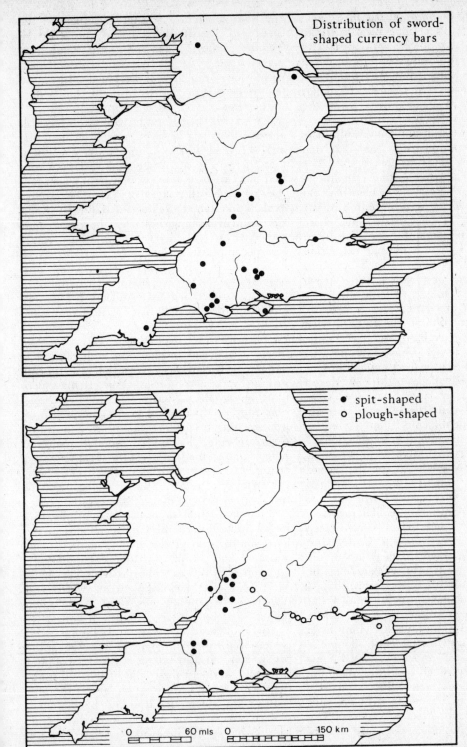

Distribution of sword-shaped currency bars

- ● spit-shaped
- ○ plough-shaped

0   60 mls   0   150 km

14:5   Distribution of iron currency bars (source: D. F. Allen, 1968a)

charcoal, would have been placed in a bowl furnace which may then have been partially covered with clay. Gradually, with the aid of bellows, the temperature would have been raised to above 800°C, at which point the reduction of the oxide would have taken place, the metal itself remaining as a spongy mass while the molten slag drained to the bottom of the furnace. On cooling, the reduced iron bloom would have been removed and continually heated and beaten until the remaining slag was forced out. The bloom was then ready for forging into implements or weapons. There seems to have been no deliberate attempt to strengthen the iron by the addition of carbon or phosphorus, but where stronger phosphorus-containing or carburised iron was produced by the normal extraction process, it may well have been selected for manufacture into weapons or tools requiring strong cutting edges (Fig. 14:4).

The extraction processes were sufficiently simple for the production of iron to be carried out on a part-time home basis, and over a large part of the country it would have been possible for most communities to extract enough ore for themselves from nearby deposits. Moreover, iron was not consumed in large quantities, since broken implements could be re-forged into replacements with little difficulty. Thus a complex system of trade and specialisation would not have been necessary except in those areas far away from ore deposits. Nevertheless, by the second and first centuries BC ingots of iron appear, and frequently turn up in hoards. There are two types, broadly speaking: rhomboidal ingots of continental type, of which only two have been found in Britain on Portland Bill, Dorset, and currency bars, widespread in the south of the country (Fig. 14:5). Currency bars can be divided into four different types. Sword-shaped bars, with a short pinched-up hilt and a flat blade usually between 31 and 35 in (78 and 89 cm) long, are found in an area stretching from Hampshire and Dorset in the south along the Jurassic Way to the Humber (Pl. 13a). Spit-shaped bars, usually much narrower than the sword-shaped versions and with a shorter pinched end, are concentrated in the Cotswolds and Somerset, with an outlier in Anglesey. The third variety, plough-shaped bars, are usually 1·5–2·5 in (4–6 cm) wide and about a quarter-inch (1 cm) thick, roughly pointed at one end

and with short raised wings or flanges at the blunt end. Distributionally they cluster in the Thames valley, spreading into Kent and the Midlands. The last type are bayleaf-shaped, with a long semi-circular sectioned hilt; only a few are known, principally from the Cambridgeshire region.

Much has been written on the subject of currency bars (e.g. more recently Tylecote, 1962, 206–11; Allen, 1968a), leading to the conclusion that there were many regional variations and that, since many of them were carefully hoarded, they are likely to have been of value. The simplest explanation is therefore that the bars represented a medium of exchange or barter, the iron content providing an actual as well as an agreed value. Further implications might be that they were manufactured by specialist iron-smelters and were traded to the neighbouring communities within restricted regions, the bars being then either hoarded as a form of wealth or manufactured into implements. The very existence of the bars, whatever their regional variations may mean, is sufficient to show that iron extraction had in part become a specialist skill in south-east Britain by the second century BC. It may, perhaps, be significant that practically all occupation sites producing indisputable evidence of iron-smelting in this area are third century or earlier in date. Tentatively, therefore, we may suggest that in the south-east the third to second centuries saw a growth of specialist extractors, the farms and villages now receiving ingots of metal rather than digging out their own ore.

The production of artefacts from the raw metal probably remained in the hands of the local smiths, who produced the common tools, weapons and fittings for the community, a selection of which are illustrated in Fig. 14:4. More specialist products such as swords and daggers were generally the work of craftsmen organised in distinct schools (pp. 279–80).

Itinerant trading was a well-established pattern in the preceding Late Bronze Age for the production and distribution of bronze tools and weapons. No doubt these long-established traditions were maintained until as late as the fifth century, by which time iron was beginning to replace bronze as the common everyday metal. Bronze, however, continued to be used for the manufacture of vessels and for trinkets such as brooches, rings, bracelets, harness-trappings and other decorative fittings, but on a much more limited scale than before. No longer do we find founders' hoards scattered over the country, but instead small-scale production, probably in the hands of specialists resident in the larger centres. Archaeological evidence for their presence in pre-first century BC contexts is rare but crucibles are recorded from various sites (Fig. 14:6)

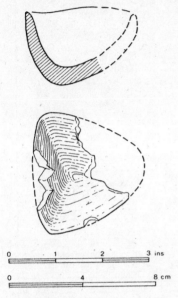

14:6   Bronze-working crucible from Breedon-on-the-Hill, Leics (source: Kenyon, 1950)

including Glastonbury and Meare in Somerset, probably within the first century, and a bronze workers' area has been defined at South Cadbury, Somerset. It is only with the development of the urban and semi-urban centres like Hengistbury Head, Hants, and Camulodunum, Essex, that large-scale metallurgical activities can be recognised.

The products of individual craftsmen can occasionally be traced distributed over a restricted territory. In Wessex, for example, there appears to have been a workshop producing a distinctive local version of the La Tène I fibula, with incised lines and impressed dots on the bow (Fig. 14:7). Some fifteen have been found, all within a 30 mile (48 km) radius of Salisbury in Wiltshire (Fig. 14:8). Although the actual production centre of the type is unknown, it is tempting to think in terms of a single bronze-worker settled somewhere in the area, supplying local needs in the fourth or third century. Small-scale manufacturing of this kind is likely to have been the normal pattern for much of the country wherever communities were sufficiently large to have supported a non food-producing specialist.

Until the fifth century or a little later, bronze scrap hoards were common in most parts of the country, particularly the south-east, but thereafter they disappeared. The extraction of copper would however have been maintained in Cornwall, north Wales and the Welsh borderland, Scotland and Ireland, and tin continued to be extracted from the Cornish deposits – in both cases by traditional techniques now more than 1,000 years old. Details of the extraction sites and processes are at present unknown but ingots of the refined metals must have been widely traded, particularly to the populous south-east.

Tin was exported to the continent. The elder Pliny (*Nat. Hist.*, iv, 30, 104) tells us that the fourth century historian Timaeus reported that 'the island of Ictis, where tin is to be got, is six days' sailing from Britain further inwards'. Similarly, Diodorus Siculus, referring to the voyaging of the explorer Pytheas in the late fourth century, states:

> In Britain the inhabitants of the promontory called Belerion are particularly friendly to strangers and have become civilised through contacts with merchants from foreign parts . . . They prepare the tin, working the ground in which it is produced very carefully . . . they beat the metal into masses shaped like an ox hide and carry it to a certain island lying off Britain called Ictis (v, 22).

Although there is still some doubt as to the exact identification of Ictis, the impression of a well-

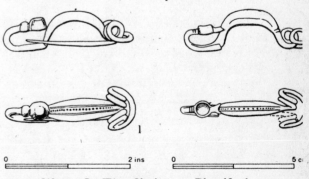

14:7   Wessex La Tène fibulae. 1   Blandford, Dorset; 2   Avebury, Wilts (source: Smith, 1925)

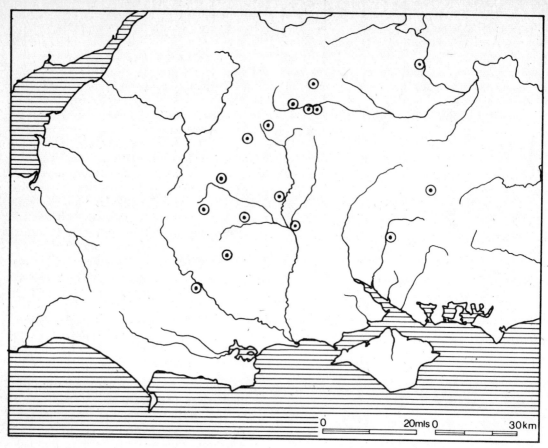

14:8   Distribution of Wessex fibulae (source: M. J. Fowler, 1954)

developed tin trade between Cornwall and the civilised world is evident – tin was being produced for the export market as well as home consumption. To what extent copper continued to be exported in the first millennium cannot now be ascertained.

Lead was not of great significance in the pre-Roman period. Admittedly, in the Late Bronze Age it was added to the bronze used for implements distributed in the south-east and lead objects are found sporadically on occupation sites of the Iron Age, but it was never extensively used. Only in the first century BC contexts at Glastonbury are any number of lead objects found, and here the metal was usually restricted to double perforated net-sinkers and spindle whorls. Lead is unlikely to have been extracted for its own properties, but as an additive to bronze to improve its casting properties it would have been of some value. Later, when silver was

being extracted from argentiferous galena by the process of cupellation, lead would have been a by-product which could have been put to use locally. The finds from Glastonbury imply the working, albeit limited, of the Mendip lead deposits, but of the exploitation of ore deposits elsewhere – in Shropshire, Flintshire, Derbyshire and Yorkshire – little is known before the Roman period.

Silver was extracted in limited quantities, but intensive production did not develop until the first century BC, when the demand for coinage increased in the south-east and the metal was used alloyed with gold to make torcs. Gold too is rare before the first century. Objects of Irish gold made in the Late Bronze Age tradition were still finding their way into Britain in the seventh and sixth centuries, but it was the social and economic development of the first century BC that encouraged more widespread exploitation.

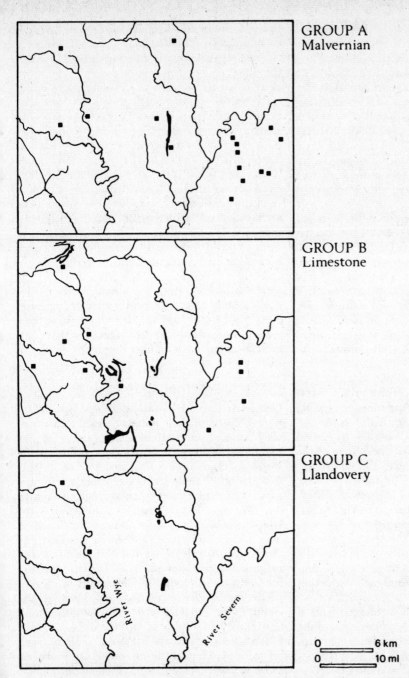

GROUP A
Malvernian

GROUP B
Limestone

GROUP C
Llandovery

14:9 Distribution of west Midlands pottery groups. The outcrop of the parent rock is shown in black (source: Peacock, 1968)

POTTERY PRODUCTION

In south-east Britain the production of pottery was on a considerable scale. As the discussion in chapters 3 and 7 will have shown, well-defined regional styles can be recognised from an early date – a fact which might be thought to imply some degree of commercial production, at least of the finer wares. Types like the scratched cordoned bowls of Wessex, made in very fine blackware with an evenly applied haematite-coated surface, fired red and scratched after firing in simple geometric patterns, are so similar to each other and so restricted in their distribution that it is inconceivable that they were not manufactured in a single centre. The same may be said with less certainty of much of the early fine ware in the south, but until a detailed programme of petrological examination has been undertaken on this early material, it would be unwise to speculate further.

The later pottery of two regions – the stamped and linear tooled ware of the Welsh borderland and Gloucestershire, and the highly decorated Glastonbury ware of the south-west – has been examined in detail with these problems in mind (Peacock, 1968 and 1969). Both groups date largely to the first century BC but manufacture began in the preceding century or even a little earlier. On the basis of the filling material added to the clay, the linear tooled and stamped ware of the west can be divided into four groups: group A contains igneous and metamorphic rock derived from the Malvern Hills; group B1 is gritted with a Palaeozoic limestone; group B2 with a Mesozoic limestone, probably from the Jurassic outcrop; and group C contains a crushed sandstone from the Llandovery beds west of the Malverns. The types belonging to all four groups, while generally similar, can be shown to have distinctive features and some degree of differential distribution can be observed (Fig. 14:9). The implication seems to be that within one culturally related area, specialist potters were at work in at least four centres supplying the ceramic needs of the communities living within 50–80 miles (80–128 km) from the production centres.

Much the same pattern has emerged from a petrological study of the Glastonbury ware of the south-west (Fig. 14:10). Six different groups have been recognised, each with distinctive typological characteristics and a restricted distribution pattern. Only in the case of group 1, which contains gabbro inclusions and must therefore have been made in Cornwall, is there any evidence of widespread trade, some of the vessels of this category reaching Devon, Somerset and Hampshire. If this kind of analysis is extended, the stylistic considerations which serve to dis-

tinguish the regional groups of the saucepan pot continuum (p. 42) may prove to result from the work of separate manufacturing centres in much the same way.

It is, then, becoming increasingly clear that the manufacture of fine pottery was a specialist craft by the first century BC and the probability remains that specialisation in some regions dates back to the fourth century or even earlier. Nothing is yet known of the production centres themselves, but it is unlikely that elaborate kilns existed since simple bonfire firings would have been quite sufficient to produce the wares: little archaeological evidence of manufacture can therefore be expected to survive. Some degree of commercial production does not, of course, exclude home production, and indeed it is probable that a reasonably high percentage of the local coarse wares were home-made in the earlier periods, but by the second and first centuries even the plainer and simpler vessels take on a mass-produced appearance, suggesting that commercial enterprise was now dominant.

SHALE, JET AND LIGNITE

Certain areas of the country developed specialisations because of their mineral wealth. In Cornwall some communities were geared to the extraction of tin at an early date and later the Wealden population specialised in iron extraction. In other areas stone was exploited for the manufacture of trinkets such as rings and bracelets. The best-known centre of this kind is the Isle of Purbeck in Dorset, where the black or dark-brown oily shale, known as Kimmeridge shale, was quarried from the cliffs and taken to neighbouring occupation sites for manufacture into armlets. Judging by the number of sites producing evidence of shale-working in the vicinity, the industry was well-established and must have had a sizeable output. Excavations at Eldon's Seat (Encombe), Dorset, have allowed the various stages in the manufacturing process to be worked out (Pl. 13b). First, it seems that large slabs of shale were brought to the site, possibly threaded on poles for ease of carrying. Then, with the aid of simply struck knives of flint, flat discs some 5 in (13 cm) across were carved out. The next stage involved either boring a central hole or cutting out a core, creating a ring which could gradually be whittled down

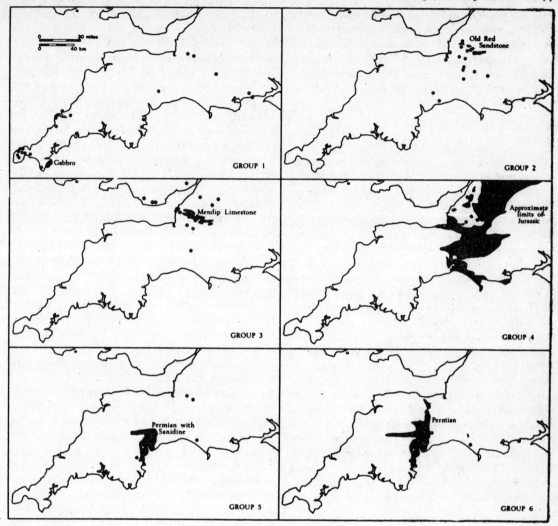

14:10   Distribution of Glastonbury ware (source: Peacock, 1969)

and finally ground to form finished bracelets, armlets, anklets or, occasionally, pendants.

The Kimmeridge shale industry flourished throughout the Iron Age and Roman period, but from the sixth to the second century, techniques of manufacture changed little. It was only after the introduction of lathe-turning in the first century that the nature of production began to take on a more commercial aspect. The distribution of Kimmeridge shale artefacts spread over much of central southern Britain but does not seem to have been particularly extensive outside a 40 mile (72 km) radius from Purbeck.

In northern Britain the place of shale was

taken by jet, a black shiny rock found in the upper lias exposed on the Yorkshire coast between Ravenscar and Port Mulgrave. The crude jet seems to have been taken to occupation sites and worked, in much the same way as shale, into bracelets, finger-rings and pendants, a number of which were found at Staple Howe in fifth century contexts. The discovery of jet or lignite bracelets at the Heathery Burn Cave in County Durham shows that production was under way as early as the seventh century. Jet trinkets are also found in later contexts among the Arras culture burials of eastern Yorkshire and it is well known that production continued into the Roman period. Jet was also popular in Scotland as far north as the Orkneys. It is, however, possible that more than one source of material was exploited and that the more northerly finds were derived from deposits in Scotland. Until a programme of chemical analysis is undertaken, the problem will remain unresolved.

SALT

One of the more important of the consumer products of Britain was salt, the principal source of which was seawater. Salt would have been required not only as an essential part of the diet but also as a preservative for meat stored during the winter. Evidence for salt extraction is now well known around much of the south-east coast of Britain, particularly the low-lying areas of Lincolnshire, Norfolk, Essex, Hampshire and Dorset (Riehm, 1961; Nenquin, 1961; Farrar, 1963), and as a result of the abundant but somewhat fragmentary evidence now available, the main stages in the extraction processes are reasonably clear, though not everywhere represented (Fig. 14:11).

Seawater was first encouraged to flow into large evaporation pans, probably at the beginning of the summer, and allowed to stand to evaporate, suitably covered from the rain, until autumn. The crust of crude salt and the underlying salt-impregnated clay were then broken up and roasted in an open fire to facilitate the next stage, which involved dissolving the salt from the resulting granular mass using a strong brine

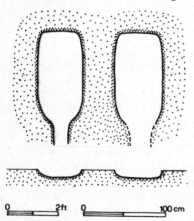

14:11   Salt-boiling hearths at Ingoldmells, Lincs (source: Baker, 1960)

solution and then decanting off the salt-rich liquor which was evaporated in large boiling pans, supported on clay bars. At Ingoldmells on the Lincolnshire coast, the pans were about 2 ft (60 cm) long and appear to have been subdivided by internal partitions so as to pre-form the resulting salt cake into uniform-sized cubes. (Riehm, 1961, 187). More often, however, the damp crystalline salt seems to have been scooped out and packed into porous clay moulds, which were probably warmed to 60–70°C to complete the drying operation. At Halle in Austria, where a number of complete moulds have been found, it is evident that standard sizes were aimed at so that the resultant salt-cakes would have been of equal value. It follows that the simplest way to market the salt would have been in the moulds. Insufficient data are available from the British sites to show whether or not the same standardisation applied here but in all probability it did.

The division between the initial extraction of the salt and its packaging and drying is emphasised by two sites in the Isle of Purbeck, Dorset – Hobarrow Bay and Kimmeridge (Calkin, 1949, 56–7) – both of which occur on the tops of cliffs overlooking shelving beaches. Since it would have been impracticable to carry seawater to them for evaporation, it is more reasonable to suppose that pans and evaporation tanks lay on the beach, the damp salt being carted to the cliff-top site for drying and packing in clay moulds ready for distribution. Hobarrow Bay produced a range of briquettage including parts of rectangular trays and cylindrical tray supports, associated with masses of burnt shale, while at Kimmeridge in a similar context hemispherical bowls were recovered, together with cylindrical vessels cut in halves partially or totally before firing (Fig. 14:12). The former belong to a well-known type of drying mould found on many of the saltworks, but the half-cylinders are more puzzling. Some, which were completely cut through before firing, could conceivably have been bound together during the drying process, to be then sliced in two, together with their salt-cake, to produce two half-measures; while those cylinders which were only incompletely separated could easily have been cracked apart after the contents had dried. Admittedly, both explanations seem to be over-complicated but it is difficult to suggest a simpler process. Whatever the final outcome of the problem, the fact

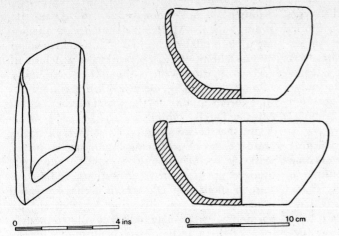

0 —— 4 ins   0 —— 10 cm

14:12   Salt-containers from the Isle of Purbeck, Dorset (source: Calkin, 1949)

remains that the cliff-top sites were concerned predominantly with drying the salt and not with its primary extraction, which must have been carried out on the beaches.

Both Hobarrow Bay and Kimmeridge belong to the early part of the Iron Age, dating to as early as the fifth century. At Paulsgrove, in Portsmouth harbour, Hants, a production centre of the fourth or third century has been found. Sites of the second to first centuries are more common, occurring at Wyke Regis (Dorset), Hayling Island and at many locations around the fringes of Langstone (Hants) and Chichester harbours. The Lincolnshire industry seems to have begun in the early part of the period – perhaps the fourth or third century to judge by the few sherds of associated pottery (Baker, 1960, figs 1 and 2) – and to have continued into the Roman period, while the even more extensive centres on the Essex coast span the first century BC to first century AD, possibly beginning earlier. A similar date range can be assigned to the group in Poole harbour, Hants. The extent and duration of most of the production centres speaks of an intensive industry becoming more important as time proceeded. There can be little doubt that in the later centuries at least salt extraction was carried out by specialists working full time and supplying the needs of a considerable inland market.

SPECIALIST SCHOOLS OF METALWORKERS

The crafts and industries discussed so far were designed to serve the immediate needs of the community, providing clothing, tools, utensils, salt and a few trinkets such as brooches and bracelets made of metal and stone. Luxury products were scarce before the second century BC, perhaps implying that the development of a class society requiring expensive forms of display had not proceeded far – a matter which will be discussed below (pp. 305–6). Without surplus wealth and the desire for display there could be little patronage, and without patronage schools of artist-craftsmen are unlikely to have flourished. That some specialists were at work, however, is evident. The production of cauldrons and buckets in the west, probably Ireland (Hawkes & Smith, 1957), in the seventh and sixth centuries is a reflection of the feasting aspects of a heroic society, and the elaborate harness-fittings and cart-trappings (pp. 132–6) show that some members of society were sufficiently wealthy to indulge in such luxuries, all of which were the products of craftsmen working in the old Bronze Age traditions.

The most impressive evidence of a continuous tradition of inventive craftsmanship is provided by the swords and daggers in the river Thames region, so densely distributed that there can be little doubt of their local origin. Production began in the late second or early first millennium with the manufacture of local bronze types copied from continental imports. Later in the seventh century the Hallstatt C Gundlingen sword developed in continental Europe and was immediately taken up locally, leading to the production of a series of distinctively British types (Cowen, 1967). In the sixth and fifth centuries new continental trends, particularly the appearance of iron daggers of Hallstatt D1 date, were quickly absorbed and there arose a British dagger series which spanned the period until the end of the third century (Jope, 1961a). Thereafter swords, influenced by continental La Tène II types, became common again.

The evidence of the Thames daggers argues convincingly for a highly skilled workshop geared to the aristocratic market of the fifth and fourth centuries, turning out exquisitely made iron daggers in elaborate bronze sheaths (Pls 14, 16 and 17). This British development runs parallel to continental sword and dagger production which, from the fourth century, provided a medium for the practice of the decorative techniques belonging to the general repertoire of the La Tène artist. In Britain no well-established schools existed at this time but a few of the dagger sheaths bear simple decoration. Those from the Thames at Windsor and at Wandsworth have openwork chapes while the entire scabbard from the Thames at Hammersmith is formed in an openwork technique (Pl. 16b). These pieces show a high degree of skill but are hardly comparable to the decorative art style appearing at this time on the European mainland. The scabbard from Minster Ditch near Oxford comes nearer to continental styles, with a somewhat halting attempt at a flowing pattern (Pl. 14), but by far the most impressive of the early British pieces is the scabbard of a dagger found in the Wisbech area, Cambs (Pl. 18). It is decorated in the rocker-tracer technique, with a simple attempt at depicting linked palmettes and fat, fleshy scrolls, comparable to work of the continental Waldalgesheim style and datable to about 300 BC. Together, the Minster Ditch and Wisbech scabbards lie at the beginning of the insular British art style, influenced no doubt by imported La Tène pieces like the Cerrig-y-Drudion hanging bowl from Denbighshire and by trinkets like the arm-ring from the Newnham Croft burial in Cambridgeshire (Jope, 1961b).

A slightly later piece, belonging to the beginning of the third century, is the more assured and elegantly worked sword scabbard from Standlake, Oxon (Pl. 15 and Case, 1949). Although probably of British manufacture, several structural details – such as the iron chape binding – are comparable to continental examples of the Middle La Tène period, suggesting a close relationship with European developments. The tip-plate too, worked in a pelta with end scrolls, dimly reflects the split palmette motif of mature Waldalgesheim work but is infinitely superior in quality to the first falterings of the Minster Ditch example.

By the second century BC schools of native craftsmen were producing highly accomplished works of art. Of these the famous parade shield dredged up from the river Witham in Lincolnshire in about 1826 (Pl. 19b) is perhaps the most remarkable for the bringing together in one harmonious work of a number of isolated themes, some of them archaic, which ultimately derive from southern Gaul and Italy (Jope, 1971). There can be little doubt of its local British production, for several peculiarities of the decoration can be found on earlier works in the area and continue to reappear on later products.

The same river has yielded another superb example of decorative art of much the same period in the form of a bronze mounting from the mouth of a scabbard. Like the shield, the Witham scabbard involves the same combination of gentle three-dimensional moulding and delicate incised curvilinear designs carefully planned with a great love of the asymmetric. These themes recur again on two shield bosses recovered from the Thames at Wandsworth (Pls 19a and 20) which, though of the same date range or a little later, are evidently the work of different craftsmen. Of the two mountings the circular boss (Pl. 20) is the most dramatic, its surface decorated with a pair of great birds, wings outstretched and tail feathers trailing behind, each so arranged and selectively illustrated as to be a mirror image of the other. With its careful use of repoussé and incised ornament, this must be considered among the masterpieces of British Celtic art.

To this same tradition of second century aristocratic art must be added the so called Torrs chamfrein from Kirkcudbrightshire which now, as the result of detailed study, can be seen to be a pony cap to which two horns have subsequently been attached (Atkinson & Piggott, 1955). The cap itself is decorated in repoussé with bilaterally similar patterns based on the open-looped pelta motif, each ending in a superbly executed bird's head with evident similarities to the Wandsworth

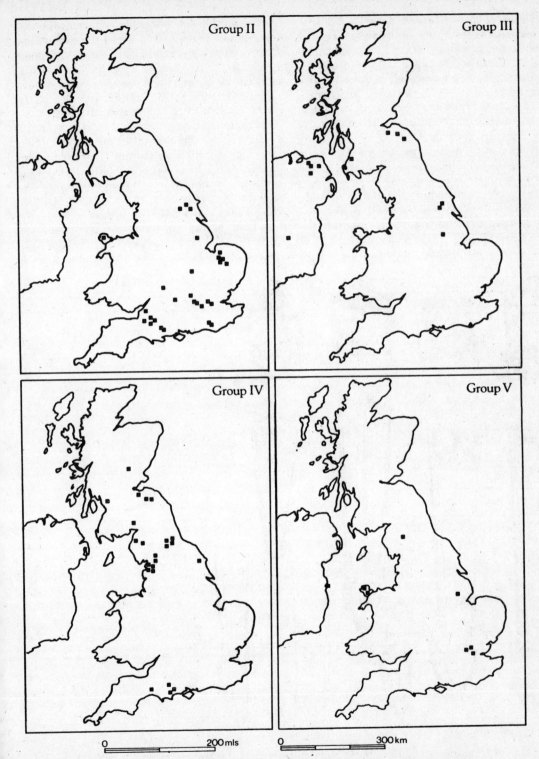

14:13   Distribution of British versions of La Tène swords (source: S. Piggott, 1950)

shield boss. The two bronze horns found with the pony cap may well originally have served as terminals for drinking horns. Both end in recurved birds' heads moulded in relief, originally with inset eyes of glass or coral, not at all unlike the repoussé birds' heads depicted on the cap. The sides of the horns were decorated with finely incised asymmetric curvilinear designs, many details of which – particularly the use of tightly coiled spirals to fill in the leaves – can be paralleled on the other objects decorated in the Witham–Wandsworth tradition.

The pieces belonging to the Witham–Wandsworth–Torrs group described here are the major items of an artistic tradition, centred in the east of England, which was providing articles of display for the aristocratic market in the second

century BC. The fineness of the craftsmanship and delicacy of the material leaves little doubt that these objects were created for parade purposes under the patronage of very wealthy clients. That all of them ended up in rivers or bogs suggest that after their earthly uses they were eventually dedicated to the gods.

The production of parade gear continued throughout the first centuries BC and AD. Two famous pieces, the helmet from Waterloo Bridge and the shield from Battersea, both dredged up from the Thames, serve as a demonstration. The Waterloo Bridge helmet (Pl. 21), found in 1868, consists of a cap made from sheets of repoussé-decorated bronze to which are attached two horns also of sheet bronze, each terminated by a separated cast button. The decoration, of slack

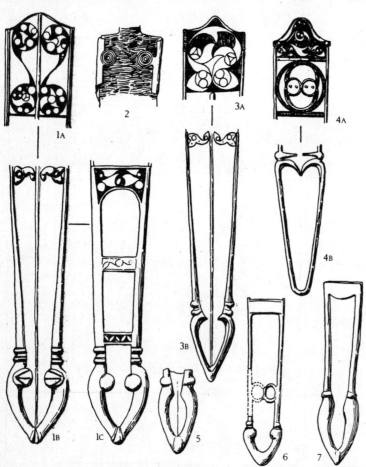

14:14 Group II swords. 1, 2 Hunsbury, Northants; 3 Meare, Somerset; 4 Amerden, Bucks; 5 Woodeaton, Oxon; 6, 7 Spettisbury Rings, Dorset (source: reproduced from S. Piggott, 1950)

asymmetric tendril motifs partially filled in with areas of hatching carried out with a rocked tracer tool, was constructed around six discs scored to take roundels of red enamel or cupric glass. Stylistic similarities between the helmet decoration and a group of gold torcs found in eastern England (below) would suggest a date in the first century BC but the use of glass roundels is a technique recurring again on the Battersea shield, which should belong to the decades immediately before the Roman conquest. For this reason the helmet might be thought to date to the later years of the first century BC.

The Battersea shield came to light in 1857. While it shows a certain overall similarity to the Witham shield, the waisted form of the body and the rigid symmetrical design suggest strong Roman influence. Similarly, the technique of pressing semi-molten red glass into the openwork roundels, which are then attached by means of pitch and rivets, is more appropriate to the immediate pre-Roman period. The Battersea shield, then, can be seen to be one of the last of the great parade art-works to be made before the conquest; it stands at the end of a tradition lasting at least three centuries which must have provided a livelihood for generations of master-craftsmen, as well as inspiration for many lesser men.

The works which have been mentioned so far were essentially the masterpieces of the east British workshops but it would be wrong to give the impression that all art was the preserve of the very wealthy. Throughout the first centuries BC and AD there developed a large number of centres producing specialised artefacts, sometimes enlivened with decorative motifs, which would have been within the price range of a much larger percentage of the population. Swords provide a good illustration of the point. From the end of the third century swords came back into fashion once more, replacing daggers as the general purpose weapon. Stylistic and structural consideration of the later Iron Age sword types has allowed a number of groups to be recognised, each occupying a fairly distinct geographical region (S. Piggott, 1950). Some types had a much wider distribution than others and many styles, once developed, remained in use up to the time of the Roman conquest, but there can be little doubt that several well-defined regional schools were at work serving the needs of their local communities (Figs 14:13, 14:14, 14:15).

Much the same pattern is suggested by the study of other luxury goods. Brooches, mirrors, tankards, bowls and a wide range of harness-trappings must all have been produced by specialist craftsmen skilled in the art of bronze-work and enamelling, and capable of practising, and sometimes developing, the elements of the insular British art style. Where and how these men worked is at present uncertain but the discovery of bronze-worker's tools at South Cadbury, Somerset, points to the existence of a workshop inside the hillfort. In all probability, each of the large nucleated centres was capable of supporting one or more full-time specialists but this need not imply that all craftsmen were attached to sedentary communities. The occasional discovery of hoards of scrap metal like that from Ringstead in Norfolk is a reminder that the itinerant tinker-craftsman may well have continued to play a part in late pre-Roman Iron Age society.

Among certain classes of metalwork it is at last becoming possible to distinguish the products of specific workshops, if not of individual craftsmen. A dramatic illustration of this is provided by the torcs of gold and electrum found mainly in eastern England in three famous hoards at Snettisham, Norfolk, Ipswich, Suffolk (Pls 24 and 25), and Ulceby, Lincs, and as isolated finds at Bawsey, Sedgeford (Pl. 25) and North Creake, also in Norfolk. Others have come from further afield, from Clevedon, Somerset, Needwood and Glascote (Tamworth), Staffs and Netherurd, Peebles (Fig. 14:16). The actual form of the torcs varies: they may be tubular, of twisted rods, plaited rods or braided strands, while the terminals are either of plain loops or decorated with cast curvilinear ornament.

A range of structural and stylistic peculiarities serves to inter-relate the group so closely that it is difficult not to consider them to be the work of one school. On those with decorated terminals, for example, there are three distinctive elements: curved ridges, filling in the style of 'matting' and small spherical bosses sometimes decorated with finely executed punch-marks, while notched ridges occur less frequently. These stylistic tricks are found on all except the examples from Bawsey and Ulceby. But the Bawsey torc, with its simple two-strand twisted body and plain loop terminals, is of a kind found in the Ipswich

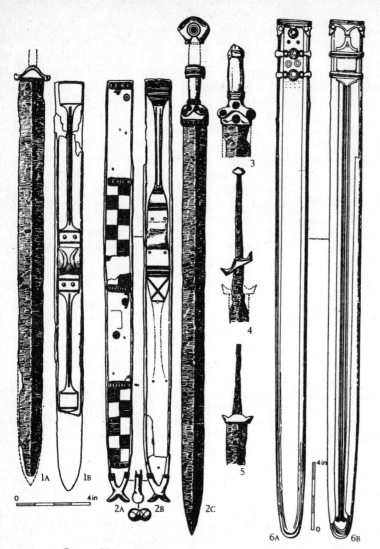

14:15   Group IV and group V swords. 1   Sadberge; 2   Embleton; 3   Thorpe, Yorks;
4, 5   Newstead (1–5 all group IV); 6   river Thames at Battersea (group V) (source: reproduced from S. Piggott, 1950)

hoard while of the two torcs from Ulceby one, with double-loop terminals, is paralleled at Snettisham, the other of plaited rods is similar to one found in the Ipswich hoard. Admittedly, the structural similarities are less decisive than the decorative links but the overall impression to be gained from these comparisons is of a single production centre in the first century BC specialising in the manufacture of goldwork for the immensely rich aristocratic market of East Anglia. The fact that the Waterloo Bridge helmet shares

many decorative techniques in common with the torcs might hint at some diversification of output.

A rather less exotic class of neck-rings, somewhat later in date than the Snettisham–Ipswich types, can be defined in the south-west (Megaw, 1971): these have been called the Wraxall class, after the best example of the group. Their main characteristic is that the neck-rings were cast in two separate halves which were then hinged together at one end and provided with a simple clasp at the other. The cast decoration was

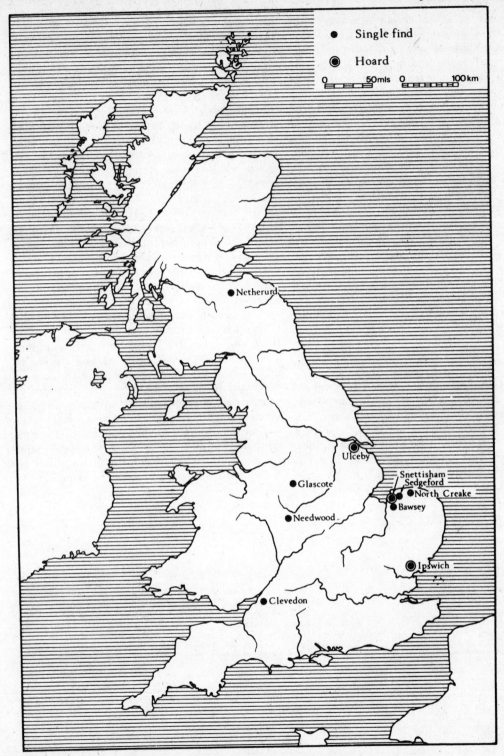

14:16 Distribution of gold and electrum torcs (source: author)

further enhanced with incisions to bring out the main theme of elongated S-curves set against dot-filled backgrounds. In all, some seven examples are known, all single finds and all coming from south-west Britain: one from Somerset, one from Cardiganshire, one from Cornwall and four from Dorset. Together they must represent the output of a somewhat second-rate workshop producing for a local market probably in the first century AD.

These two examples, the East Anglian gold torcs and the south-western bronze neck-rings, show that the regional distributions of some of the craft schools or workshops are capable of definition by stylistic analysis where sufficient distinctive material is available. By the first century AD, however, the workshops had proliferated to such an extent that copying between one craftsman and another became common and it is doubtful if the work of many more of the individual schools will ever be isolated with any degree of certainty.

COINAGE

The production of coinage, which became increasingly common after the beginning of the first century BC, must have involved the work of specialists. Whether or not metal was extracted by them is a matter for debate but the cupellation hearths and block of copper-silver alloy found at Hengistbury Head, Hants (p. 99), might have resulted from the activities of moneyers. Their principal task would have been the measuring of the correct amounts of raw metal and the production of blanks by melting down the mixture in the clay coin-moulds, examples of which have appeared on a number of sites. The blanks would then have been struck individually between dies. The basic production method required relatively little skill but the engraving of the dies must have demanded rather more ability. Indeed, on some occasions there is evidence of Roman or Gaulish die-cutters at work designing coins for Tincommius and Verica. Not all coins were struck; some were cast in clay moulds the details of which do not survive, but a study of the Potin coins of Kent (D. F. Allen, 1971) has suggested the use of relatively simple multiple moulds allowing a strip of coins to be cast in one process. For the more conventional types of cast coins, however, rather more complex techniques must have been adopted.

The production of coins was the last of the craft skills to be introduced into Britain before the Roman conquest. It embodied old techniques such as the extraction, alloying and casting of metal, but in addition it required much that was new: careful measurement, the development of engraving – often of high artistic merit – and an awareness of literacy. The sophistication of techniques fossilised in the production of a coin symbolised the complexity of the social and economic system for which the artist-craftsman of the first century AD was now working.

Death and the Gods

The evidence available for studying the religious beliefs and burial rituals of the Iron Age communities varies considerably both in volume and quality, and in its geographical spread over the country. There are three basic categories which can be called upon: direct archaeological data in the form of structures, cemeteries and ritual deposits; literary references concerned largely with the Druids; and less tangible assumptions which can be drawn from the limited place-name evidence and from a back projection of the religious scene of the post-conquest period. Together this material offers the impression of a highly complex religious pattern pervading the everyday life of the people and ever present in one form or another.

BURIAL CUSTOMS

It has frequently been said that little trace survives of the burials of the Iron Age period in Britain, and by comparison with the large cemeteries of the continental communities this might at first sight appear to be so, but when the material evidence is amassed, there emerges a very well-defined series of ritual practices which can be seen to change with time and to differ according to regional folk traditions and external influence.

The principal method of disposing of the dead in the first part of the first millennium BC was cremation, the ashes being buried, either urned or un-urned, in cemeteries which sometimes originated at the sites of older barrows. Occasionally ashes were buried under individual barrows, usually much smaller than those of the second millennium (pp. 26–7). These practices continued throughout the seventh, sixth and probably fifth centuries. Many urnfields show signs of continued use and, in all probability, most of the old-established burial grounds were maintained well into the fifth century. Since, however, a high percentage of the later cremations were buried without grave-goods or pottery containers, there is nothing with which they can be dated unless by a series of radiocarbon assessments.

The disposal of the dead in urns placed under small individual barrows is well attested in the seventh to fifth centuries. Sometimes cemeteries of barrows are found, like the small group of round barrows on Ampleforth Moor, Yorkshire (Fig. 15:1), which have produced pottery characteristics of the seventh century together with two confirmatory radiocarbon dates. The barrows were simple, ranging from 24 to 32 ft (7·3 to 9·7 m) in diameter and less than 5 ft (1·5 m) high; each was surrounded by a shallow ditch. Burial was probably by means of cremations placed in small pits or scattered on the original ground-surface. Other apparently isolated barrow burials are known scattered over southern Britain. Beneath slight mounds at the Caburn, Sussex, Buntley and Creeting St Mary, Suffolk, and Warborough Hill, Norfolk, ashes have been found in pottery urns of the Kimmeridge–Caburn type, which would suggest a date in the sixth century. Burials of this kind are direct descendants from preceding Bronze Age traditions.

Inhumations of this early period are much rarer. One possible example has been found under a barrow at Beaulieu Heath in the New Forest, Hants. The barrow, barely 15 ft (4·6 m) in diameter and surrounded by an irregularly cut ditch, was built of turf surviving to a maximum height of 2 ft (0·6 m). On the original

SKIPWORTH COMMON, YORKS

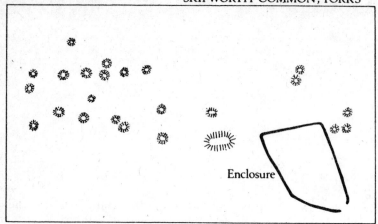

Enclosure

AMPLEFORTH MOOR, YORKS

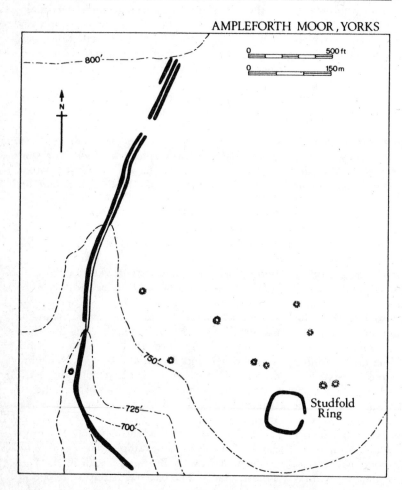

Studfold
Ring

15:1 Yorkshire cemeteries (sources: *Skipworth Common*, Stead, 1965; *Ampleforth Moor*, Wainwright & Longworth, 1969)

ground-surface beneath the mound lay the remains of several wooden planks, a bronze ring, smaller fragments of bronze, two small pieces of iron and a sherd of a coarse shouldered jar of early Iron Age type. While no interpretation can be offered with assurance, it is *possible* that the remains represent a cart burial of Hallstatt type, the bones of the inhumation having been totally destroyed by the acidity of the soil.

A second, though ill recorded, inhumation burial was discovered at Ebberston in Yorkshire in 1861 and briefly reported to a meeting of the British Archaeological Association held in that year. The account describes a bronze sword (of Hallstatt C type) and its chape, found 'together with another sword and a quantity of human bones'. Both swords were broken into four pieces. It is impossible to be sure now of the nature of the find, but the apparent ritual breaking of the swords is a feature which can be paralleled among continental burials and might be thought to support the idea that the Ebberston deposit was a genuine inhumation in Hallstatt C style. If so, it is the only example yet known in Britain.

A surprising difference exists between Britain and the continent in the seventh and sixth centuries. On the continent most of the Hallstatt swords known come from burials, whereas in Britain all except for Ebberston come from rivers. One possible explanation of this phenomenon is that in Britain the dead were cremated and disposed of, with their equipment, in rivers. This would account both for the riverine distribution of swords and chapes and the relative lack of burial grounds. Such a hypothesis is impossible to prove but the ritual is well attested among more recent primitive societies and need occasion no surprise.

By the fifth century it seems that cremation was being replaced by inhumation in some areas. In Yorkshire a new pattern of burial ritual was introduced from France, presumably by a group of settlers, resulting in what has been called the Arras culture (pp. 40–1), which is represented now almost entirely by its burials (Fig. 15:2). Three separate ritual practices are represented: the grouping together of small barrows in large cemeteries; the occasional rite of cart burial; and the practice of surrounding individual barrows with a rectangular ditched enclosure. Several barrow cemeteries are known (Fig. 15:1), ranging from small clusters to larger groups such as Eastburn (75), Scarborough Park (170) and Dane's Graves (up to 500). The individual barrows were usually small, up to 30 ft (9 m) in diameter, and normally covered crouched inhumations, although very occasionally extended inhumations and even cremations have been found. In most cases the barrows were surrounded by circular ditches but in seven cemeteries rectangular ditches were recorded.[1]

Generally the burials were without grave-goods but richer graves occur sporadically, and more rarely mortuary carts were buried with the dead.[2] A brief description of four of these cart burials will serve to illustrate their main features. The cart burial at Dane's Graves (Fig. 15:3) lay beneath a barrow some 27 ft (8·2 m) in diameter, in a rectangular grave-pit about 2·5 ft (0·76 m) deep and measuring 8·5 by 7·5 ft (2·6 by 2·3 m). The deposits consisted of two crouched inhumations laid on the bottom of the pit together with the remains of a dismantled cart and several items of harness-fittings. The 'king's barrow' at Arras was a little larger, covering a circular grave-pit 11–12 ft (*c.* 3–3.5 m) in diameter, in which had been placed a single extended inhumation with the bodies of two horses, one laid on either side. The wheels from the cart had been removed and propped against each of the horses while the harness-trappings, including two harness-loops, five terret-rings and two horse-bits, were placed together with the two lynch pins in the western half of the grave. Close to the head of the burial had been placed two pigs' heads, presumably as an offering to the spirit of the deceased.

Another example of a cart burial, the only one to be excavated under modern conditions, was found at Garston Slack, near Driffield, in 1971. Here the inhumed body had been placed on the bottom of the grave-pit and covered with the funerary cart. The two twelve-spoked wheels had been removed and laid on either side of the body. The grave-goods included the harness-trappings, consisting of a bit and terret-rings, a whip, a

---

[1] Arras, Cawthorn Camps, Hutton Buschel Moor, Pexton Moor, Seamer Moor, Skipworth Common and Thorganby (Stead, 1965).

[2] The best-attested cart burials occur at Arras (three), Dane's Graves, Beverley, Hunmanby, Middleton-on-the-Wold, Huggate, Cawthorn Camps, Pexton Moor and Garston Slack. Possible examples are recorded at Seamer Moor and Hornsea (Stead, 1965).

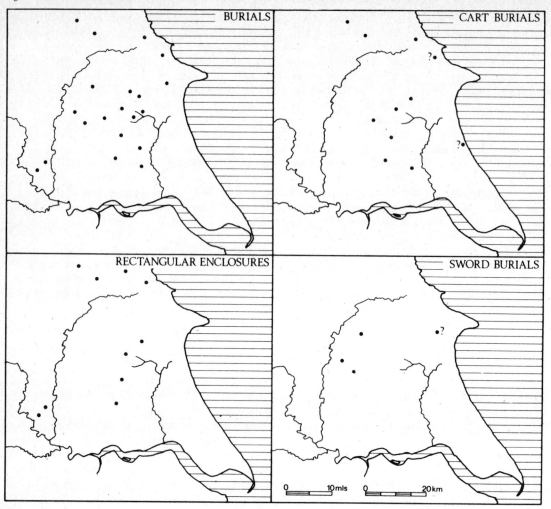

15:2   The Arras burials in Yorkshire (source: Stead, 1965, modified with additions)

bronze buckle and a pig's head included as an offering.

Most of the carts had been dismantled at the time of burial, but at Pexton Moor the cart was buried intact, with its wheels set into two oval pits dug into the bedrock (Fig. 15:3). The barrow in this example was surrounded with a rectangular ditched enclosure.

The principal elements of the Yorkshire cart burials can therefore be seen to be inhumation – either extended or contracted, the burial of the mortuary cart itself, the deposition of some or all of the harness-fittings, the occasional ritual sacrifice and burial of the horses, and the provision of some personal ornaments and food offerings. These features can all be paralleled among contemporary continental burials but the rarity of pottery and weapons in the Yorkshire group serves to distinguish the area.

Apart from the Arras group in Yorkshire, evidence for cart burial elsewhere in Britain is rare, though not absent. At Mildenhall, Suffolk, an extended inhumation was found, possibly under a barrow, accompanied by a long iron sword, an axe and a gold torc and flanked by the skeletons of two horses. No fittings of a cart appear to have been found, but the discovery was made some years ago and is ill recorded; the likelihood that significant details passed unnoticed is extremely high. An even more

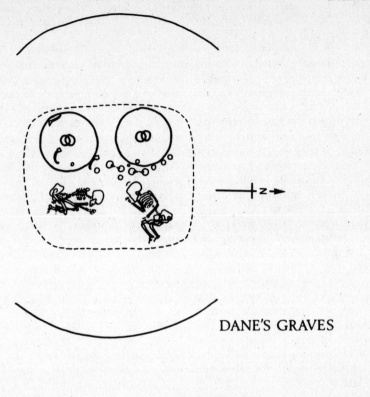

DANE'S GRAVES

PEXTON MOOR

ARRAS

0   20 ft

0   5 m

0   50 ft

0   15 m

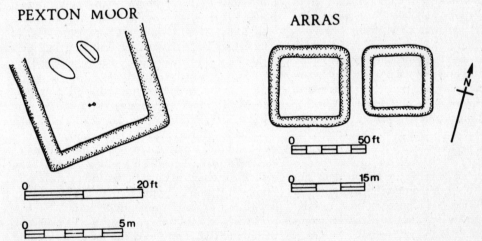

15:3   Burials from Arras, Dane's Graves and Pexton Moor in Yorkshire (source: Stead, 1965)

interesting burial was found at Newnham Croft, Cambs, where a contracted inhumation was recovered accompanied by three brooches, one of which was penannular, a bracelet, part of what may be the head-harness for a pony, and four simple bronze rings. Dating cannot be precise but on stylistic grounds the decorated bracelet is thought to belong to the second century. Again, there is no positive evidence for a cart. A third example comes from Fordington, just outside Dorchester in Dorset, where the bones of a man and a horse were found in 1840 together with a bronze bit of Iron Age type. The fact that only three possible cart burials have been found outside Yorkshire is a fair indication that the rite was not widely adopted in Britain.

In western and northern Britain, inhumation burial was often in stone cists, which were sometimes arranged in large cemeteries. In the south-west four substantial cemeteries have been found at Mount Batten, Devon, and Harlyn Bay, Trelan Bahow and Trevone in Cornwall but, apart from a single cist excavated at Trevone in 1955, details of general cemetery layout and of the individual graves are again insufficiently recorded. Nevertheless, certain details emerge: the bodies were usually, though not invariably, buried in contracted positions in their stone-lined graves, and it would appear that the cists were sometimes arranged in rows. Grave-goods were frequently included but were usually restricted to personal equipment such as pins, bracelets and fibulae, though occasionally more expensive items such as mirrors, necklaces and bronze vessels were included. The surviving material from these sites in Devon and Cornwall would suggest a date range spanning the fourth to first centuries or even later.

Cist burials are recorded sporadically from other parts of Britain. In Wales, for example, the famous bronze hanging bowl from Cerrig-y-Drudion, Denbigh, was found in a cist which may have been constructed originally for burial, while in Scotland many of the burials which can, on the basis of their grave-goods, be assigned to the Iron Age have been found in cists, either isolated or arranged in cemeteries as at Cairnconan, Angus. Inhumations of this kind continued in use into the second and third centuries AD.

Over much of south-east Britain, careful burial was by no means common before the first century BC. Indeed, evidence is now rapidly accumulating to suggest that bodies were commonly disposed of with little ceremony. On a number of settlement sites, both open farms and hillforts, complete articulated bodies have often been found tucked away in old disused storage pits which were being used for the disposal of rubbish. Occasionally it could be argued that these pit burials were deposits of ritual significance, as for example at Maiden Castle and Hod Hill in Dorset, where they seem to have been sited beneath extensions to rampart defences or

entrance earthworks, but more normally the intention seems to have been merely to dispose of the bodies with the minimum of effort.[1]

A number of settlement sites have produced evidence of even more casual treatment of dead bodies. Isolated human bones are frequently found in rubbish deposits and in some cases articulated parts of human carcases have been found in pits along with other occupation debris At Wandlebury, Cambs, for example, a child's body less the legs was apparently wrapped in a cloth or sack and thrown into a pit, while at Danebury odd limbs and pieces of human trunk occur sporadically. In one case at Danebury, Hants, a deliberate deposit was created in a specially dug elongated pit in which had been placed three legs, part of a trunk and a lower jaw. Unlike the other pits, this one had been left open for some time, the fragments of body remaining exposed to view. It is difficult to resist the conclusion that the deposit had some kind of ritual overtones.

Another factor of some significance is the apparent interest shown in the human head (a matter which will be returned to below. On several occupation sites skull fragments are noticeably more common than other human bones. Thirty-two fragments of human skulls were found at All Cannings Cross, Wilts, four of which had been deliberately cut out, one perforated for suspension, the others polished by use. Similarly, at Lidbury, Wilts, a piece of cranium had been carefully shaped and perforated. It must be assumed that skulls were selected for some kind of special treatment, which eventually resulted in token pieces being retained by individuals, perhaps as good-luck charms.

One explanation which would account for the ease with which human bones found their way into occupation deposits is that the dead may have been exposed rather than buried. Such a practice was common among certain primitive tribes and frequently took the form of exposing the bodies on raised platforms set aside in special enclosures close to the settlement. Under these conditions, the removal of skulls for ritual purposes would have been facilitated and the

[1] Examples include Worlebury, Somerset, Wandlebury, Cambs, Danebury and Worthy Down, Hants, Maiden Castle, and Cow Down (Longbridge Deverill), Boscombe Down West, Yarnbury, and Battlesbury, all in Wiltshire.

appearance of human bones in rubbish deposits is easier to understand. A further attraction of this theory is that it would help to explain the relative lack of cemeteries in south-east Britain throughout much of the period from the fifth to first century.

While it is true that few cemeteries are known outside the Arras culture of Yorkshire and the cist graves of the south-west, isolated examples of individual burials have been found from time to time. Towards the end of the period from the second century BC until the first century AD, a class of richer burials can be defined. Of these the warrior burials form a distinctive group, characterised by the rite of male inhumations accompanied by weapons in shallow graves without barrows. The grave found at North Grimston, Yorks, in 1902 was one of the richest: besides the body it contained an iron sword, a short sword with anthropomorphic hilt, bronze and iron rings, fragments of a jet ring, part of a bronze tube and a skeleton of a pig. The warrior at Owslebury, Hants, was similarly provided with his long iron sword in a wooden sheath together with rings and a scabbard hook for attaching it. By his side was a spear, broken so as to fit into the grave, while the body appears to have been covered with a wooden or leather shield of which the central bronze boss now survives. These two examples demonstrate most of the characteristics of the group as a whole, the others being summarised in the table on p. 294. There is no need to assume that warrior burials have any particular cultural or geographical significance: it is simpler to regard them as representatives of a social class that existed during the second century BC over the whole of south-east Britain. In Yorkshire these warriors might be regarded as the successors of those buried with their carts in the preceding fourth to third centuries.

Parallel with the warrior burials there appear a number of rich female burials, usually characterised by the presence of mirrors, beads, bronze bowls and other trinkets appropriate to female attire.[1] One of the best recorded of the group was discovered at Birdlip in Gloucestershire in 1879. Three cist graves were found, the centre one containing a rich female, with a male on either side. Her body was extended and over her face a large bronze bowl had been placed; a smaller bowl lay nearby. The other grave-goods included a gilded silver fibula, four bronze (?) dress-rings, a bronze armlet, a superb knife with a bronze animal-head terminal, a necklace of amber, jet and marble, and an engraved bronze mirror. The rich female burials at Trelan Bahow, Cornwall, and Mount Batten, Devon, were also interred in cists, placed in larger cemeteries. A variation occurs at Colchester, Essex, where the body had been cremated and the ashes buried in a pedestal urn alongside a range of accessory pottery vessels. The metalwork, including an engraved mirror, a bronze bowl and a bronze pin, serves to link the grave to the general category of rich female burials but, like the warrior burials, there is no need to attach any cultural significance to the type; they merely represent the standard practices involved in burying moderately wealthy women. The tradition of including mirrors with the departed can be traced back to the fourth to third centuries at Arras in Yorkshire, where two graves contained mirrors. The graves at Mount Batten are probably of first century BC date, while the Birdlip and Colchester groups date to the first century AD.

There is a third type of inhumation which might be considered sufficiently distinctive to be regarded as involving a separate ritual practice. At Burnmouth in Berwickshire and Deal in Kent extended inhumations have been found, each provided with a pair of bronze spoons. In each pair one spoon was marked with a cross, the other had a small hole punched to one side. Spoons of this kind have been found in various parts of Britain.[1] Some occur in contexts which might suggest ritual deposits. At Crosby Ravensworth in Westmorland a pair were discovered by a spring in a bog; at Penbryn in Cardiganshire another pair had been buried under a pile of stones; the river Thames produced a single spoon and some of those from Ireland were probably

---

[1] These occur at Arras, Yorks, Birdlip, Glos, Bridport, Dorset, Trelan Bahow, Cornwall, Mount Batten, Devon, and Colchester, Essex. The mirrors from Bulbury, Dorset, Billericay, Essex, and Desborough, Northants, may also have come from burials.

[1] The sites producing pairs of spoons are Burnmouth and Deal; Llanfair, Denbigh; Penbryn, Cardigan; Crosby Ravensworth, Westmorland; Weston, Somerset; and two sites in Ireland. Single spoons come from Ireland, the river Thames, and Upper Thames Street, London. A female grave with a pair of spoons is known in France at Pogny, Marne.

	Sword	Metal chape or bindings	Attachment rings or hooks	Spear	Metal shield fittings	Food offering	Other grave-goods
North Grimston Yorks	× ×		×			×	Jet ring, bronze tube
Bugthorpe, Yorks	×	×					2 bronze discs and 2 bronze studs
Grimthorpe, Yorks	×	×		×	×		Bronze disc and 16 bone 'shroud' pins
Thorpe, Yorks	×	×					
Clotherholm, Yorks	× ×						
Shouldham, Norfolk	×						
St Lawrence, I.O.W.	×	×			×		
Owslebury, Hants	×		×	×	×		
Whitcombe, Dorset	×	×	×	×			Brooch, chalk pommel

Grave-goods found with warrior burials

from bogs. It is difficult to resist the conclusion that these spoons were in some way connected with ritual procedures. If so, it may be that those with whom they were buried were involved in the practice of religion. This is, of course, pure speculation but it is not too much to expect that the graves of the religious leaders of the community may have been distinguished in some way, as were those of the aristocratic class.

Over much of the British Isles inhumation remained the basic rite up to the time of the Roman conquest. In the territory of the Durotriges, for example, a group of victims of the Roman advance were hastily buried in a cemetery at Maiden Castle. Even though the military situation was tense, trouble was taken to inhume the bodies in specially dug graves and to provide them with ritual meals buried alongside in pottery containers. Inhumation rites were very deeply rooted in Durotrigian territory, and even after the Roman conquest, when cremation became the norm, the bulk of the population continued to be buried in the old inhumation manner.

In the belgicised areas of the south-east, cremation became common from the beginning of the first century BC. The normal practice was to bury the ashes of the deceased in an urn in a well-defined cemetery area. A wealth differential is clearly reflected in the nature of the ancillary equipment buried with the ashes. The simpler graves were without grave-goods but a reasonable percentage were provided with small articles such as brooches and other personal trinkets. The richer individuals were buried either in or with bronze-plated buckets[1] and occasionally, as in the case of the rich graves at Aylesford and Swarling in Kent, other bronze vessels were included (p. 79). In Essex and Hertfordshire, a group of extremely rich burials have been defined, characterised by a deep grave-pit containing considerable volumes of wine stored in amphorae together with the vessels and other equipment appropriate to its consumption. The ritual belief behind such aristocratic burials was evidently to provide the dead man in the afterlife with the means of feasting and amusement to which he had been accustomed on earth. Burials of this kind were being undertaken in eastern England from the middle of the first century BC until the Roman conquest (p. 79).

In summary, it may be said that the burial patterns recognisable in the British Isles were complex. Basically, however, cremation rites in the old Bronze Age style continued into the fifth century. Thereafter inhumation became widespread, with specialised techniques such as cart burial occurring in some areas, while social stratification eventually became apparent in most parts of the country. From the beginning of the first century BC the rite of cremation became established in the south-east of the country, the burials demonstrating a considerable variation in wealth, closely reflecting the nature of the class society of the times.

Behind this broad development there lies the hint that the ritual of exposure rather than burial was being practised in southern Britain between the fifth and first centuries. How such a ritual would fit into the general development of British society is difficult at present to see, but it remains a distinct possibility that a continuity existed from the mortuary-house tradition of the Neolithic period throughout the second millennium, when bodies may have been stored prior to cremation, into the Iron Age. The problem is one of considerable interest but it requires more

---

[1] Bucket burials include: Aylesford and Swarling, Kent, Chesterford, Essex, Hurstbourne Tarrant and Silkstead, Hants, Marlborough, Wilts, Old Warden, Beds, Harpenden, Welwyn Garden City and Baldock, Herts (Stead, 1971).

evidence to elucidate it than is at present available.

RELIGIOUS AND RITUAL LOCATIONS

The ritual centres of the Iron Age can be divided into two major types: shrines incorporating some kind of man-made structure, and natural locations such as springs, streams or clumps of trees.

The clearest example of the few shrines at present known was found inside a ditched enclosure at Heathrow, Middx, along with a number of domestic buildings (Fig. 15:4). The temple consisted of a central *cella*, defined by trenches in which timber uprights had been set, surrounded by an 'ambulatory' constructed of individual close-set posts, the whole building being little more than 30 ft (10 m) square. The similarity between this structure and the later Romano-Celtic temples is so striking that there can be little doubt of the Roman form being modelled upon pre-conquest styles. Another rectangular shrine, similar in many respects to the Heathrow temple, has been uncovered towards the centre of the hillfort of South Cadbury, Somerset (Fig. 15:4). The surviving part of the South Cadbury shrine is a small *cella* with an attached porch, comparable in size to Heathrow but apparently without the surrounding ambulatory. Its ritual connotations were further emphasised by the discovery of a number of animal burials in shallow pits lining the approach.

The discovery of two examples of shrines within fortified enclosures raises the possibility that many of the hillforts may have contained religious centres, though the religious association of the buildings may not always be evident. In Maiden Castle, Dorset, the building which is evidently the shrine is a simple circular stone-walled structure lying at the end of one of the streets leading into the fort from the east gate (Fig. 15:4). The only hint of ritual activity is an infant burial just outside the door, but the fact that the building was reconstructed in the Roman period alongside a rectangular Romano-Celtic temple is a strong indication of the religious continuity of the particular location. It raises the possibility that many of the Roman temples sited in hillforts may have been constructed on the sites of pre-Roman shrines.

Continuity of this kind is not restricted to hill-

HEATHROW, MIDDX

SOUTH CADBURY, SOMERSET

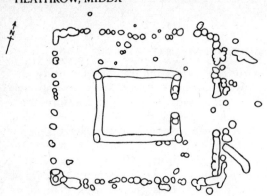

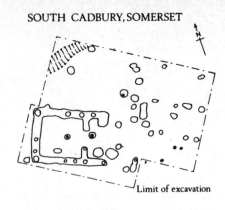

Limit of excavation

FRILFORD, BERKS

MAIDEN CASTLE, DORSET

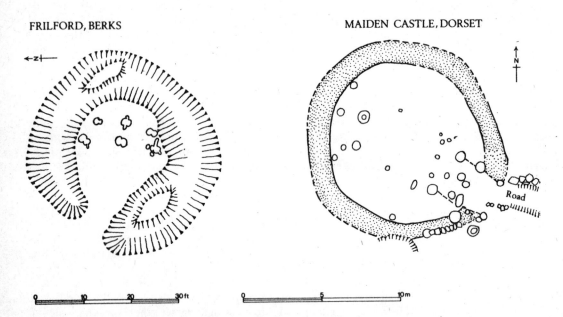

Road

15:4 Temples and shrines (sources: *Maiden Castle*, Wheeler, 1943; *South Cadbury*, Alcock, 1970; *Heathrow*, Grimes, 1961; *Frilford*, Bradford & Goodchild, 1939)

forts. A sequence of structures almost identical to the Maiden Castle arrangement has been exposed at Frilford, Berks, where a rectangular and a circular Roman temple were found to succeed an earlier religious centre, the circular Roman building lying above a penannular ditched enclosure of Iron Age date which contained a setting of six post-sockets (Fig. 15:4). Evidently Frilford served as a ritual centre for some decades before the Roman invasion. Much the same sequence must be true for the religious site at Worth in Kent, but apart from votive model shields from the Iron Age levels beneath the Roman temple (Fig. 15:5), little survives of the pre-Roman ritual aspects of the site. In all probability, the continuity of temple locations between the Iron Age and Roman periods will prove to be widespread when the early levels beneath Roman structures are more fully explored.

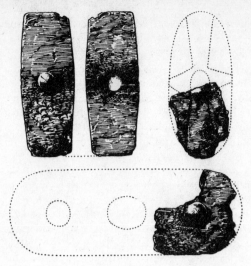

15:5 Votive model shields from Worth, Kent
(Scale ⅓) (source: reproduced from Klein, 1928)

Sacred locations unmarked by shrines must have abounded in Britain, as in the rest of the Celtic world. Springs, bogs and rivers would have been the obvious foci for ritual practices, as well as other striking natural features such as large rocks, very old trees or groves of trees. In all of these places the gods were thought to live and there they had to be served or placated.

Direct archaeological evidence for such locations is seldom forthcoming but many of the items of metalwork recovered from bogs and rivers may well have been offerings deliberately dedicated to the spirits of the place. The enormous numbers of exotic objects from the Thames and the smaller, but no less impressive, collections from other rivers like the Witham and the Tyne probably originated in this way. Bog deposits are also relatively common in some parts of Britain; among these must be included the large collection of metalwork thrown into the Lake at Llyn Cerrig-Bach on Anglesey, and the hoard of material, including two cauldrons, from Llyn Fawr in Glamorganshire. The pair of bronze ritual spoons from Crosby Ravensworth, Westmorland, and the pony cap and horns from Torrs in Kirkcudbrightshire, were also bog deposits. Besides the Llyn Fawr find, several other cauldrons from Britain, including a recently discovered example from Feltwell in Norfolk, and others from Ireland had been thrown into bogs. Tankards too were sometimes found in rivers and bogs, like the famous

Trawsfynydd tankard from Merionethshire and the vessel from Shapwick Heath, Somerset. The list of metalwork from these locations is impressive not only for its length but for the very high quality of the material. One must suppose that a surprisingly high percentage of society's wealth was dedicated to the gods in this manner.

While the discovery of fine metalwork tends to pinpoint sacred places besides bogs or rivers, the sacred groves mentioned by the classical writers are more difficult to locate. Some help is, however, provided by the distribution of the Gallo-Britannic word *nemeton*, which means a sanctuary in a woodland clearing. The word occurs in several Romano-British place-names in different parts of Britain, such as *Vernemeton* near Lincoln, *Medionemeton* in southern Scotland, and *Nemetostatio* near North Tawton in Devon. The Roman name for the thermal spring at Buxton, *Aquae Arnemetiae*, also includes the element, suggesting that the spring was in use as a religious centre long before the invasion. That so many *nemeton* elements are incorporated in Roman place-names in Britain is an indication of the large numbers of sacred woodland clearings of pre-conquest date, the memory of which lingered on.

DRUIDS AND THE GODS

The practitioners of religious ritual in Britain, as in Gaul, were the Druids. Caesar believed that Druidic religion originated in Britain, whence it was introduced to the continent: 'Even today', he says, 'anyone who wants to make a study of it goes to Britain to do so' (*Gallic Wars*, vi, 14).

The Druids served Celtic society in various ways: they were responsible for administering and guiding the religious life of the people, supervising ceremonies and sacrifices and divining the future from such omens as the death struggles of a sacrificial victim. They also maintained the theory and practice of the law and were the teachers of the old oral traditions of the people, holding schools where the novices learnt verses off by heart. Caesar reports (ibid., 15):

They seem to have established this custom for two reasons: because they do not want their knowledge to become widespread and because they do not want their pupils to rely on the written word instead of their memories; for once this happens, they tend to reduce the effort they put into their learning.

The literary evidence relating to the Druids can frequently be used to enhance and explain the archaeological material. Belief in the after-life, which is demonstrated by the provision of grave-goods with the dead, is referred to several times. Caesar says that the one idea that the Druids wanted to emphasise above all others was that souls do not die but pass from one body to another as each body dies. Pomponius Mela, writing in the first century AD, elaborates on this belief: because of their very strongly held views on the after-life, he says, (*Place of the World*, iii, 19):

> they burn and bury with their dead the things they had owned while they were alive. In the past they even used to put off the completion of business and the payment of debts until they had arrived in the next world. Some even went so far as to throw themselves willingly on to their friends' funeral pyres in order to share the new life with them.

A firm conviction about immortality was of particular encouragement to those required to act bravely in battle, as several classical writers were quick to point out.

Pomponius Mela writes of Druids teaching in caves or inaccessible woods, while Tacitus mentions 'groves devoted to Mona's [Anglesey's] barbarous superstitions', implying that at these places human sacrifice was carried out. An altogether more gentle ritual is, however, described in some detail by Pliny the elder. The passage is worth quoting at length because of the insight it gives into ritual beliefs and practices which would otherwise be unrepresented in the archaeological record.

> They choose groves of oak for the sake of the tree alone and they never perform any sacred rite unless they have a branch of it. They think that everything that grows on it has been sent from heaven by the god himself. Mistletoe, however, is very rarely found on the oak and, when it is, it is gathered with a great deal of ceremony, if possible on the sixth day of the moon . . . They choose this day because, although the moon has not yet reached half-size, it already has considerable

influence. They call the mistletoe by the name that means all-healing.

He goes on to describe the cutting of the mistletoe with a golden sickle by a white-robed Druid, followed by the ritual sacrifice of two white bulls, and concludes: 'They believe that if the mistletoe is taken in a drink, it makes barren animals fertile, and is a remedy against all poison' (*Nat. Hist.*, xvi, 249). Later Pliny mentions other herbs which, if collected under certain conditions, possessed curative properties: selago (or sabine) warded off evil and could cure eye diseases, while a marsh plant, samolus, was regarded as a charm against cattle disease. Mistletoe, selago and samolus are just three which Pliny happens to mention but hundreds of other herbs must have been endowed with magical properties about which the Druids would have known and taught.

Many of the classical accounts refer to the Druids carrying out human sacrifice. Ritual killing for the purpose of augury is mentioned by Diodorus Siculus and Strabo, while the mass sacrifices of men and beasts, burnt to death in cages made of branches, are described in some detail by Caesar and Strabo. Strabo also records ritual deaths by archery and crucifixion, and Tacitus, describing the destruction of the Druid centre on Anglesey in AD 59, justifies the Roman attack by saying of the Druids that 'it was their religion to drench their altars in blood of prisoners and consult their gods by means of human entrails' – words calculated to conjure up a sense of horrified distaste among his sophisticated Roman audience. One wonders whether the partly dismembered child from Wandlebury or the human limbs and torso from the 'ritual pit' at Danebury were in any way connected with Druidic practices. The only other archaeological evidence for ritual is the decapitation of bodies, like those found at Bredon Hill, Glos, and the setting up of heads on gates as witnessed by the skull found near the entrance to the Stanwick fort in Yorkshire. Decapitation is, however, more likely to have been a normal part of the battle scene than the preserve of the priestly cult.

The Druids mediated between men and their gods, of whom there were many. Caesar gives the clearest picture of the Celtic pantheon by equating the native deities with their nearest Roman counterpart (*Gallic Wars*, vi, 17–18): 'Their main god', he says, 'is Mercury; they have many images of him. They consider him the inventor of all arts, the god of travellers and of journeys and the greatest god when it comes to obtaining money and goods.' He then goes on to describe the lesser gods: Apollo who wards off disease, Minerva presiding over work and art, Jupiter the ruler of the heavens, and Mars the god of war. 'When they have decided to go to battle, they generally promise the captured goods to Mars. When they are victorious, they sacrifice the captured animals and make a pile of everything else.' Perhaps some of the ritual deposits from rivers and bogs were votive dedications made to the god in thanks for victory.

The iconography of Britain before the conquest, reflected largely in the Roman formalisation of the situation, shows that an immense number of local or tribal gods existed, each known by regional names and each endowed with specific qualities. Caesar's broad summing up, linking the Celtic deities to their nearest Roman counterpart, was little more than rationalisation of an exceptionally complex and bewildering pattern. After the Roman conquest the gods were frequently depicted in various guises, sometimes as a disembodied head, which must have represented a generalised portrait of divinity, and sometimes with specific characteristics. One of the more common types is the horned god which, depending upon his attributes, might variously represent the war-god Cernunnos (as Mars), Mercury, who Caesar says was the most commonly illustrated, or sometimes the hunting god Silvanus. Among the female deities the old triad of mother goddesses frequently occurs, particularly in the north and west, representing a deep-seated traditional belief in the power of three, a belief further emphasised by the occasional discovery of triple-faced heads.

Besides sculptural representation, the old gods are often named on dedicatory altars and other inscriptions. The names might include tribal deities like Brigantia or more widely respected gods like Camulos, the powerful war-god, whose shrine probably lay in the defended area at Camulodunum – perhaps at the site of Gosbecks Farm, an important cult centre in the Roman period. Other gods were more specific to certain localities, like Sulis who, later paired with Minerva, presided over the sacred spring at Bath; whereas others possessed more prescribed skills: Taranis the thunder-god or Nodens the cloud-maker. Some deities were rather more generalised in their stated powers: Nemetona and Mars Rigonemeta were respectively the goddess and god of the sacred grove, while Leucetius was simply 'the shining one'.

The list of gods is very long: each tribe must have had its own pantheon of favourite deities and every one of the many thousands of sacred locations would have been the special preserve of a local god whose name and presence would have been part of the natural awareness of the local community. It would have been difficult to travel far in Iron Age Britain before coming into contact with some sign of the gods, for religion and superstition pervaded all aspects of pre-Roman life.

Society and
Social Change

In the preceding chapters we have been concerned to examine change within the strict limits imposed by material remains and structural evidence, but there can be little doubt that the changes discernible in this way, and through the numismatic evidence, reflect – albeit dimly – aspects of social change within an increasingly complex socio-economic system. From the middle of the first century BC literary evidence allows a rather closer examination of these changes, adding a new dimension to patterns built up from the purely archaeological remains. But from the moment of the Claudian invasion, native institutions and developments are deflected and in some places destroyed by the forced growth of the Roman capitalist system. By examining post-conquest society and comparing it with the changing situation of the preceding century seen through the eyes of Caesar and Tacitus, it is possible to discern trends and directions of change, the backwards projection of which can be used as a framework of reference for hypotheses constructed around the material remains of the earlier pre-literate period.

THE BACKGROUND, 3500–750 BC

Before the development of Iron Age society can be examined, it is necessary to say something of the more distant past. For almost three thousand years, before the introduction of the technique of iron-working, communities had lived by a broadly similar mixed farming economy which allowed a living standard sufficiently above subsistence level for the production of a surplus. Throughout the third millennium and into the second, the surplus was absorbed by the construction of monumental buildings such as henge monuments, collective tombs and causewayed camps – the range of which implies the emergence of an *élite*. Causewayed camps, which are best seen as places of communal gathering – the foci of tribal groupings, show that some of the surplus was ploughed back into the institutionalisation of society, but the immense amount of labour involved in the construction of henges and associated religious structures is a dramatic indication of the dominating power of the theocracy. Similarly, the collective tombs, whether megalithic or earth-built, must represent considerable coercive power in the hands of either a religious *élite* or a secular ruling class. It must also be remembered that the monuments themselves represent far more than consolidated physical labour, for the conceptual thought behind some of the more sophisticated structures implies a knowledge of mathematics and astronomy which could only be maintained, developed and communicated by specialists.

Superimposed upon these complex systems of specialisation were lesser systems involving craftsmen in the extraction of raw materials and the manufacture and trading of artefacts, of which the polished stone axes offer the most readily demonstrable example.

With the introduction of metal-working and the assimilation of new ethnic groups towards the beginning of the second millennium, trading, both internally and with the continent, increased in volume and larger numbers of artisan-craftsmen emerged, offering an increasingly widening range of tools, weapons and luxury goods. The changes which this brought about in society soon became apparent: surplus could now be used to acquire objects of metal, while material wealth reflected in such possessions became a mark of individual status. The emergence of the rich Wessex culture burials soon after 1700 BC can best be interpreted in these terms. In parallel with the rise of individual wealth there appears to be a decline in the power of the theocrats to command society's surplus: collective tombs cease to be used and built and the great religious monuments show little sign of maintenance after the middle of the second millennium.

The funerary record of the next thousand years, with its emphasis on simple urned cremations, the gradual polarisation to cemeteries and away from individual burials, and the omission of luxury objects buried with the dead, gives little hint of social development or change except to suggest a levelling-out in society and perhaps a decrease in concern for the after-life. Settlement pattern archaeology has little more to offer but, where evidence is available, incipient nucleation is sometimes indicated. The over-riding impression given is of a society in a state of dynamic conservatism, but this does not mean fragmentation. Foci, in the tradition of the Neolithic causewayed camps, probably continued to be maintained. There are indications of such a centre at Danebury, Hants (Fig. 16:1), and many of the hilltops defined by partially enclosing earthworks may have been used as meeting places well back into the second millennium. Some of them continued to serve as tribal centres after the construction of hillforts within them, and the presence of Romano–Celtic temples in many is an indication of con-

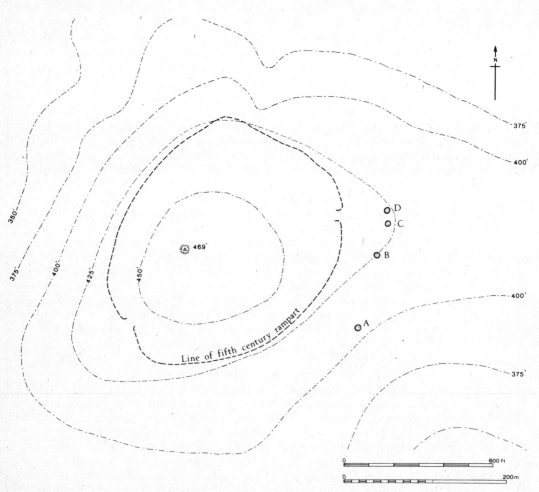

16:1 Ritual pits at Danebury, Hants (source: author)

tinued use, with the religious overtones becoming dominant.

EARLY IRON AGE SOCIETY, 750–100 BC

Until the eighth century the bronze industry, though flourishing locally and developing contacts with the adjacent parts of the continent, was essentially insular and geared to the demands of British communities, but from the middle of that century overseas trade expanded both geographically and in volume. New types were introduced from further afield and inspired British schools to adopt elements of the new ideas into their own repertoires. Society now began to emerge from an extended period of conservatism into one of innovation.

In parallel with these technological changes, the nature of the basic food-producing economy, after remaining much the same for several thousand years, began to develop with the introduction of varieties of cereals which could be sown in the winter. The advantages were considerable, for not only was it now possible to spread the sowing but the harvest period was also extended. Spreading the work-load and providing a more assured food supply released new productive forces; settled farming communities increased in number, colonising virgin land, and there is evidence of a gradually increasing population.

From the eighth century onwards, trade with the continent continued but, measured in sheer bulk of surviving artefacts, it appears to have decreased in volume after the sixth or fifth century. It is probable that the intensity of internal trading also decreased with the decline in the demand for bronze and the corresponding increase in the everyday use of iron – a material which could be extracted and worked locally in most parts of the country. Thus, by the middle of the first millennium a greater stability was emerging in the south and east of the country, characterised by a regionalisation suggesting the evolution of more closely defined groupings, which may well have recognised their own identity in relation to their neighbours. The appearance of regional pottery styles, probably representing spheres of distribution from commercial centres, may reflect the early stages in the emergence of formalised tribal territories.

Within the regional groupings of the mid-first millennium it is difficult to isolate the lesser social configurations with any degree of certainty, but the smallest socio-economic unit was undoubtedly the single family occupying a small farm set amid its fields or pastures. In some instances settlement plans suggest groups of extended family size and even clan groups living in loosely nucleated hamlets. In the south and parts of the east, fields were physically adjacent to the farms, implying that arable land was probably held in private ownership. Less certainty attaches to pasture but the appearance of the so-called ranch boundaries at about this time is suggestive of organised land division between clan groups. Some degree of communal organisation is also implied by the fact that many of the boundaries are laid out from foci. Moreover, there can be little doubt that each group of clans had its own *locus* or meeting place – frequently a hilltop or plateau defined by earthworks – where at certain times of the year communal meetings could be held associated with the redistribution of livestock, the organisation and reallocation of pasture, the worship of the gods and the taking of political decisions (Fig. 16:2). A social pattern of this kind is not very different from that implied by the Neolithic causewayed camps, or by the *loca* of the Scottish tribes, recorded in the Ravenna Cosmography, a seventh century document reflecting the situation of the third or fourth century AD.

While it is true that at this stage there is very little positive evidence of a hierarchical structure (and it would be possible to present society in terms of a kind of primitive communism), there are indications that some settlements may have been richer than others. Sites like South Cadbury, Somerset, Harting Beacon and Highdown in Sussex, which were later to be defended, have all produced an array of bronze and gold objects unusual among the material from normal settlement sites of the early first millennium. The status of such settlements is difficult to define in the absence of plans of the contemporary structures, but it is tempting to see in them the emergence of a hierarchy based on a wealth differential.

From the fifth century onwards, society began to exhibit an increasing tendency towards aggression brought about, partially at least, by pressure on land resulting from an increase in population. Weapons become more common;

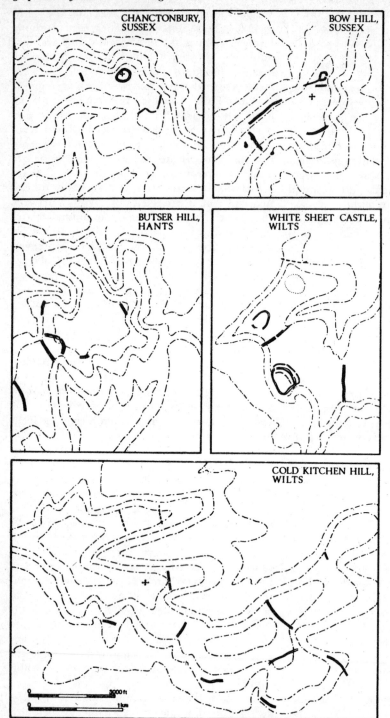

16:2   Potential locations for the origin of hillforts. All plans are oriented with north at the top; contours at 100-ft intervals (source: author)

the burying of grain in underground silos may reflect the need for safer storage; and most of the settlements replaced their enclosure fences with earthworks, frequently of defensive proportions.

More impressive still is the rapid growth in the number of strongly defended hillforts, which frequently seem to be constructed at already existing foci: some on the sites of causewayed camps, some within earthwork-defined plateaus, some at religious centres, some at the points of convergence of ranch boundaries and some on the sites of rich settlements. While it is at present difficult to be definite as to which type of focus was the most commonly chosen, on the present showing it would appear to be the settlement sites. If, as we have suggested, these represent the homes of an aristocracy, their conversion into forts (as distinct from enclosed homesteads) is a strong indication of the emergence of a warrior leadership with coercive power over, and presumably responsibility for, a group of clans. To begin with, there were many such forts in the south, but gradually certain sites increased their influence at the expense of others, until by late in the second century the landscape was dominated by a smaller number of very strongly defended centres, each commanding an average 30–40 square miles (77–103 km²) of land. The late first millennium, then, saw the focusing of power upon relatively few centres.

What all this implies in terms of society is more difficult to say, particularly in the absence of large-scale hillfort excavation, but it would appear that the interiors of many forts took on the appearance of towns. Put one way, it could be supposed that as centres for regional government they accumulated around themselves a substantial population – a centripetal movement encouraging traders and specialists to centralise, giving rise to a balanced urban community. An alternative view, however, might be that the forts were the centres of feudal manors peopled by the servants and retainers of the lord, the emphasis being on the dependence of the people upon one man. It may well be that elements of both views will eventually turn out to be relevant, always supposing that the archaeological evidence is sufficiently clear.

In the surrounding countryside there seems to have been relatively little significant change. Most of the old-established farms continued in use and many new ones were founded; a range in

status is also apparent, with some centres growing to considerable proportions and parading substantial defences. The picture is consistent with an increasing population and with the development of a stratified society.

The emergence of a warrior aristocracy provided a climate in which skilled craftsmen could work under the patronage of rich men able to pay for their products. It is hardly surprising that decorative art, when it appears in the second and first centuries BC, is applied almost invariably to warrior gear: to swords, daggers, shields, helmets, war-trumpets, pony armour and trappings, and to chariot-fittings. Only occasionally are domestic or feminine articles, like bowls, mirrors and brooches, highly decorated. But the development of an aristocratic art seems to have inspired the parallel growth of a more humble folk art, less ostentatious but no less satisfying, as the ornamentation on pottery and wooden vessels will bear witness.

It may fairly be said, therefore, that throughout the second half of the first millennium, much of the surplus produced by society was absorbed into the development of a rigid class structure which consumed labour, to construct and maintain defences, and wealth, to supply the increasingly extravagant demands of the ruling class. It is indeed probable that by the first century BC the aristocracy of the south-east had become totally divorced from a productive role in society and would estimate their wealth in terms of prestige and cattle, like the rulers of contemporary Gaulish and Germanic tribes. It is tempting to see the provision of corral space around many of the hillforts and the reallocation of land, suggested by the linear boundaries laid out from some of the forts, as the direct result of such a social specialisation. In simple economic terms, this could mean a dichotomy between the peasant agriculturalist and the warrior pastoralist. Such a simple terminology is, however, likely to obscure the true complexity of the situation.

The discussion so far has been concerned principally with the development of the south-eastern area of the country, where the evidence of settlement pattern and sequence is rather more fully preserved, but much of what has been said is probably relevant to other regions where a similar range of small settlements and hillforts occur in environments conducive to the production of surplus food. This would include the

Welsh borderland, north Wales and the eastern areas of lowland Scotland. Elsewhere, different settlement patterns, reflecting different subsistence economies, probably indicate divergent social developments.

In the south-west peninsula and south-west Wales the multiplicity of small, strongly defended homesteads belonging to communities mainly concerned with herding, together with the relative lack of large occupied hillforts, would suggest a less centralised form of government, each of the major homesteads representing an independent authority. The same kind of pattern occurs in the north and west coastal areas of Scotland and the Islands, where by the end of the first millennium large numbers of brochs are found, each presumably serving as the castle of a single or extended family. Since the earlier developments in these areas are unknown in detail, it is impossible to place the patterns of the final stages in perspective except to contrast the strongly defended nature of the later sites with the more open earlier settlements. Such a contrast is consistent with the pressures consequent upon an overall increase in population.

Over much of the Midlands, together with the Pennines, settlement appears to be thin. While paucity of evidence must be partly the result of a general lack of intensive field-work rather than an actual absence of sites, it is noticeable that there are relatively few hillforts compared with the south and east. Evidently socio-economic development in the two regions must have been different. It may well have been about the Midland and northern communities that Caesar was thinking when he offered the sweeping generalisation: 'Most of the tribes in the interior do not grow corn but live on milk and meat and wear skins.' However much this is regarded as an overstatement, it can hardly be doubted that herding played an important part in the economy. A scattered population and a pastoral economy, for which there are hints in the archaeological record, would have created relatively little need for centralisation except in times of national disaster, when war-leaders like Cartimandua and Venutius would have been elected. Thus it is probable that the political structure of the region was loose-knit, and there may indeed have been very little change in society between the early first millennium and the conquest by Rome.

The bellicose nature of the upper echelons of Iron Age society would have absorbed much of the surplus produced by the workers, but a percentage of the national product must have gone towards the maintenance of the priesthood. Little is known of the position of religion before the first century BC but Caesar was in no doubt that the well-established rituals of the Druids were deeply rooted in British tradition. The Druids needed no monumental structures, since apparently sacred groves and other ritual locations were sufficient for their celebrations, but the existence of such a complex and extensive community of non-productive religious specialists would have required an output well above subsistence level from the food-producers. It is tempting to see the Druids of the early to mid-first millennium (or their predecessors) officiating at the communal gatherings held at the various *loca* mentioned above and later, as the semi-urban hillforts became established, perhaps taking up residence and using the shrines which began to be built among the houses. Yet however true this may be, the fact remains that much of the religious activity of the Druids must have been based on purely rural locations such as springs, rivers and other notable natural features.

By the first century BC the Druids were playing a vital part in society, not only in the religious and cultural lives of the people, but politically, in being the only nationalising influence available to transcend the fragmented nature of British Celtic society. They were held in high regard by the population and were exempt from military service though, when forced to fight, as they were when Roman troops under Suetonius Paulinus invaded Anglesey in 59 AD, they were ready to do so. The Druids, then, formed an extra-tribal *élite* responsible for maintaining the oral traditions of the people and for organising the religious life and calendar.

LATE IRON AGE WARFARE AND SOCIETY, *c.* 100 BC–AD 43

From the beginning of the first century BC the nature of southern British society becomes clearer. We are at last made aware of people and their deeds – seen largely through the eyes of a few Roman observers, whose concern was to describe a contemporary situation rather than to analyse social changes. Even so, these accounts are of immense value, not least because they provide a fixed point against which the developments of the previous centuries can be assessed. Not only did the hundred years between the invasions of Caesar and Claudius see the culmination of many of the processes which had begun long before, but during this time the sophisticated Celtic society of the south-east, now in a state of almost perpetual war, began to fragment and decline.

The Celts at war is a subject well documented not only by contemporary Roman writers but also by Roman craftsmen, using stone and bronze to depict individuals and scenes of which they or their informants had had first-hand experience. To this the archaeological record is now adding much that was previously unsaid. All the evidence considered, we must accept Strabo's view that the Celts were war-mad. In perhaps the most vivid of all the writing on Celtic warfare, Polybius (*Histories*, II, 28-9) describes how the mass of the armies drew up, the opposing chariots driving up and down the enemy ranks, the warriors shouting hysterically to scare their opponents, while behind them the sides of the wagons drawn upon their flanks were beaten violently to increase the overall uproar from the bellowing horns and screaming fighters. Then the second stage began: the warriors would be driven into the field and there would alight to deliver personal challenges to their opposite numbers, bolstered up by much boasting. It was only in the last phase, after the individual contests were at an end, that general battle would commence.

Fighting methods changed and with continued contact with the Roman world the old heroic tradition died out; chariots too gradually became obsolete, although Poseidonius (in Diodorus, v, 29) still records their use in Gaul in about 100 BC and chariots are depicted on Celtic coins as late as 100-90 BC. By the time Caesar's campaigns began in 58, however, they were unknown, their place being taken by cavalry, while in Britain charioteering remained an important means of fighting well into the first century AD.

There is much less direct evidence available concerning the structure of Late Iron Age society, but most of the ancient writers who discuss Britain were agreed that the southeastern communities were very much like the Gauls. 'In both countries you will find the same ritual, the same religious beliefs,' wrote Tacitus, 'and there is the same hardihood in challenging danger, the same subsequent cowardice in shirking it' (*Agricola*, II). Describing their physical appearance, Caesar remarks that 'all the Britons dye their bodies with woad, which produces a blue colour' and that 'they wear their hair long, and shave the whole of their bodies except the head and the upper lip' (*Gallic Wars*, V, 14, 3). Tacitus gives rather more details of ethnic type, distinguishing between the large-limbed red-haired Caledonians, who he thought were of Germanic origin, and the swarthy curly-haired Silures, having much in common with the inhabitants of the Iberian peninsula.

Caesar is quite specific about the marital customs of the primary Belgic area. 'Wives,' he said, 'are shared between groups of ten and twelve men, especially between brothers and between fathers and sons, but the offspring of these unions are counted as the children of the man with whom a particular woman cohabited first' (ibid., 14, 4). It is evident from his discussions of Gaul that Celtic womenfolk had few rights: they could be tortured if their husbands died in suspicious circumstances, and husbands at all times held the right of life or death over their wives and children. But while this may be generally true of the tribes with whom Caesar came into contact, it is possible that beyond these areas different social conventions held sway. In Britain outside the primary Belgic areas, for example, we hear of two famous queens, Boudicca of the Iceni and Cartimandua of the Brigantes, both of whom served as political and military leaders. Perhaps, in these peripheral regions, the remains of an older matriarchal society survived.

Enough has been said above to show that society in south-east Britain (and very probably the whole country) was rigidly stratified into an aristocratic upper class and the mass of the people. In Gaul Caesar recognised three classes: the peasants, who he says were virtually slaves, the knights, and the Druids, who served as the religious leaders and teachers of society. A similar structure is probable for Britain. The knights could depend on the allegiance of a group of followers who would serve and fight for their leaders. There must have been many forms of relationship between master and followers but one, described by Pausanias, is of particular interest: he writes of the *trimarcisia*, which consists of three horsemen – the leader and his two squires, whose function it was to protect him and provide him with a fresh horse when necessary. In such a scheme the importance of the dependants to their lord was self-evident. When, in about AD 69, the Brigantian queen Cartimandua lured away her husband's 'armour-bearer', it may be that she was doing much more damage than simply humiliating him. The break-up of his *trimarcisia* (if this is what it was) could have had far-reaching effects on his efficiency as a military leader.

Caesar probably overstated his case by suggesting that the bulk of the peasants were little better than slaves. Indeed, the settlement pattern evidence from Britain leaves little doubt that a wide social spectrum existed. Even so, the number of large fortified enclosures in various parts of the country implies that the aristocracy possessed massive powers of coercion over the peasant classes in general. Slaves certainly existed. Strabo lists them as one of the principal British exports, while gang-chains for linking the necks of captives have been found at Llyn Cerrig-Bach, Anglesey, and at several sites in the Belgic settled areas of the south-east, including Bigbury, Kent, Verulamium, Herts, Camulodunum, Essex, and Barton, Cambs. Slaves were a valuable commodity in the Roman world and it is hardly surprising that British chieftains should capitalise upon the fact. Since slaves, in the true sense of the word, were of little significance in Celtic society, it can plausibly be argued that slave-raiding, inspired by the profit motive, developed as trade with the Roman world increased following Caesar's conquest of Gaul.

The picture of the society of the first century BC built up from the documentary sources tends to be static, but when seen against what had gone before and in the light of the new pressures to which society was being subjected, certain trends can be isolated. The already warlike aspect of southern society was greatly intensified first by the folk movements, which increased both the population and the tension in the years around 100 BC, and later by the Roman raids led by Caesar in 55 and 54 BC. These two periods of crisis led to two different responses: the first seems to have encouraged fragmentation, giving rise to a number of warring factions, each concerned to carve out and maintain its own territory; while the second required national leadership, which it temporarily obtained in the person of Cassivellaunus. But even a war-leader of the stature of Cassivellaunus could not hold together the disparate parts of the British resistance movement for long, particularly in the face of Roman diplomacy.

The Caesarian interlude introduced a number of new factors to the British scene: it brought home the reality of large-scale invasion; it provided a new and powerful weapon in the form of potential treaty relationships with Rome; it opened up vast new markets, not least for the consumption of slaves; and it provided the model of Roman capitalism, which must have proved attractive to the British aristocracy. All of these factors would have added to the turmoil. Unrest and war, resulting in the acquisition of profitable slaves, would have become even more commercially desirable.

The numismatic evidence gives some idea of this quality of dynastic rule throughout the last decades before the invasion. In the south-east tribal units were well defined and were ruled by kings, generally appointed on a hereditary basis, but there seems to have been a considerable mobility among the aristocracy, brought about partly by inter-tribal quarrels and partly by the imperialistic attitude of tribes like the Catuvellauni. In the regions peripheral to the primary Belgic territories, it is possible that a different form of government prevailed. The Coritanian coinage hints at rule by dual magistrates – a system known in Gaul. Similarly, the rapid succession of names recorded on the coins of the Dobunni and Iceni could be interpreted as rulers elected for a period of office, a structure for which there are again Gaulish precedents. In other parts of the country more primitive forms of government may have been in force. The proliferation of hillforts in the south-west and the way in which Vespasian had to fight his way, one fort at a time, through the area suggests the possibility of a fragmented leadership.

Aside from all this, most parts of southern and eastern Britain gradually developed the appearance of urbanised civilisation, with the growth of large oppida serving as trading centres, mints and seats of government. The adoption of elements of Roman culture was rapid. Vast quantities of wine were imported, together with the utensils and receptacles appropriate to its consumption; Roman engravers were employed to restyle the coinage of some dynasties, and complex treaty relationships were entered into. The south-east was fast becoming Romanised.

The ease with which the area was overrun by the army of Aulus Plautius between AD 43 and 47 is in some part a measure of this incipient Romanisation – after all, 'eleven kings' were prepared to throw in their lot with Rome immediately. The economy and social structure of the area had developed so far that effective resistance was no longer possible or, in the minds of many, desirable. The abortive attempt by the Catuvellaunian army, led by Togodumnus and Caratacus failed. Togodumnus was killed while Caratacus was forced to beat a retreat to the west, where the pleasures of the Roman life style were largely unknown. There, among the mountain tribes of Wales, he stirred up such trouble that Ostorius Scapula was forced to take action by occupying a considerable area of the Midlands before routing out the troublemaker, who was finally captured as the result of native treachery.

Other war-leaders followed: Boudicca in 60 leading the rebellion in eastern England, Venutius about ten years later leading the Brigantes against the advance of Cerialis, and ultimately Calgacus opposing the final thrust of Agricola into Scotland. On each occasion the British tribes showed an ability to unite under one leader, but resistance was seldom sustained for long and inevitably collapsed without lasting effect. The furious impetus of the Boudiccan rebellion and the total lack of forward planning is perfectly in keeping with what is known of the Celtic character.

As the areas of conflict moved away from the south-east, Roman civilisation rapidly took root. In a vivid and cynical piece of prose Tacitus explains, with obvious relish, the processes of social change:

> To induce a people, hitherto scattered and uncivilised, and therefore prone to fight, to grow pleasurably inured to peace and ease, Agricola gave private encouragement and

official assistance to the building of the temples, public squares and private mansions. He praised the keen and scolded the slack, and competition for honour proved as effective as compulsion. Furthermore, he trained the sons of the chiefs in the liberal arts and expressed a preference for British natural ability over the trained skill of the Gauls. The result was that in place of distaste for the Latin language came a passion to command it. In the same way, our national dress came into favour and the toga was everywhere to be seen. And so the Britons were gradually led on to the amenities that make vice agreeable – arcades, baths and sumptuous banquets. They spoke of such novelties as 'civilisation' when really they were only a feature of their enslavement. (*Agricola*, 21)

Much of this would have been true of the lowland areas of the province. The Roman money economy, and the ease of trading which the *pax Romana* made so possible, would have allowed the easy accumulation of wealth. In the Roman hierarchical system social and administrative status was totally dependent on money qualifications. Moreover, land could now be bought. These new factors brought about a total revolution in society: the old clan system, with its dynastic leadership based on prestige and birth, gave way to capitalism. But in the highland areas much of the order would have prevailed. The survival of the Gaelic and Welsh law and literature with its echo of the Celtic past is sufficient to demonstrate the fact, but in many ways an even more dramatic reminder is found in the seventh century document, the Ravenna Cosmography, which lists for Scotland a number of *loca* – the meeting places for the northern tribes in the third century AD. These tribal foci are part of a social tradition which we have been able to trace back to the beginning of the first millennium, and which must have been distantly rooted among the Neolithic communities of the third millennium. They symbolise above all the strong undercurrent of tradition which characterises so much of British prehistory.

Problems, Methods and Models

Chapter *17*

Until recent years it has been usual to explain the British archaeological record in terms of invasion from the continent. This kind of model has frequently been used to give structure to the British Iron Age (pp. 2–7). It was, after all, merely an extension backwards of the historic situation: the Roman invasion of AD 43 was a well-attested fact, as were Caesar's invasions of 55 and 54 BC. Before that, we are told by Caesar of an influx of Belgae, peoples from Gaul, settling in the coastal areas of Britain. It was not an illogical step, therefore, to suppose that a series of such incursions extended back deep into British prehistory, each marked by a recognisable change in the archaeological record. Moreover, such a view could also be supported where necessary by references to the great upheavals and folk movements affecting the contemporary European mainland and reported by classical writers.

In the nineteen-twenties and thirties 'invasion' became almost synonymous with changes in pottery styles. Thus it was thought that the southeast received the major part of the continental expansion largely because, one suspects, little pottery was then known from the rest of Britain. Invasion hypotheses became so inherent in archaeological thinking that it was unusual at this time for an excavation report to be written without considerable reliance on a pseudo-historical model. The model not only supported the data, it encased it.

Whenever the material has been studied objectively, as in the case of Hodson's examination of the 'Marnian invasion' (Hodson, 1962), conventional invasion models have seldom stood up with the probable exception of the incursion into Yorkshire initiating the Arras culture. The problem, nevertheless, is more complex: it may reasonably be asked whether the archaeological record *need* reflect invasion, even if invasion occurred; Caesar's Belgic immigration is notoriously difficult to define in conventional terms. Without the explicit statement of incursion, one might be tempted to explain the changes in the archaeological record in terms of increased trading relations had Caesar not specifically said, 'People came to raid and stayed to till.' Since there is no reason to suppose him wrong, the archaeological and numismatic evidence can be adapted to the theory of multiple incomings. Even the well-established Arras 'invasion' is not as strongly founded as one might think, largely because the equipment of the first-generation settlers has seldom been found and the intrusive culture must be seen only through its subsequent diluted developments.

Thus we are forced to ask whether it is permissible to use an invasion hypothesis at all where there is no direct supporting historical evidence. Strictly, I think the answer is 'yes', but only in exceptional cases where all other models seem inferior; even then, invasion should be presented as only one of a series of possible explanations. We must not allow prehistory to become dominated by pseudo-history again. This is not to say that we should not attempt to recognise 'events' (I use the word 'event' to refer to a series of linked happenings occurring closely together in time). It used to be thought that the appearance of hillforts in southern Britain constituted an event – a response to the stimulus of invasion. This has since been largely disproved. Might it not be, however, that the late second century abandonment, sometimes associated with the destruction, of many of the southern hillforts, occurred at approximately the same time as a result of a related series of political happenings? If so, this would be an event, requiring a political model as an explanation. The settlement pattern evidence, notably that obtained from the detailed excavations of hillforts, is particularly susceptible to analysis and explanation of this kind, and probably presents a far more fruitful field for studying political change than the propounding of generalised invasion theories which can seldom be substantiated.

It has long been recognised that the Iron Age communities of Britain formed regional groups, which used to be thought to result from the settlement of different bands of invaders. Now it is seen that regionalisation is caused by a variety of factors, not the least of which is simply the ease or otherwise of geographical communication between one area and another. A simple scheme for defining the principal groups has been given in chapters 3 and 4 and need not be repeated here. What does need emphasising, however, is that it owes little to conventional methods of defining 'culture' as laid down by Childe. In 1939, Christopher Hawkes called for 'cultural' definition within the Iron Age, while in 1964 Hodson went some way towards defining basic folk cultures for southern Britain, to be followed by MacKie for the north in 1969. However, apart from underlining the basic unity of Iron Age culture over the country as a whole, there seems to be little value in pursuing the concept further. The communities of Britain were in such close contact and shared so many systems in common that their similarity far outweighs the significance of their differences. The only value in defining minor regional variations, as has been done above, is to provide a broad framework for descriptive purposes. To suppose that significant cultural differences existed between communities using different types of pottery would be to misunderstand the evidence entirely.

So far, then, it has been suggested that the two basic models hitherto commonly used in British archaeology, namely invasion hypothesis and the concept of culture, are of little value in ordering the available evidence beyond the definition of localised 'events' and of regional style groupings. This does not, however, exhaust the methods of presenting and analysing the data.

One valuable approach seems to be the examination of the evidence for settlement pattern and subsistence economy (cf. chapters 11–13). A surprising quantity of material survives covering the whole country and showing regional variations which can be linked to environment as well as change with time. The sophisticated techniques of the 'new geography', such as central place theory and the various other kinds of locational analyses, will no doubt prove to be of some value when applied to these data. Nevertheless, it will first be necessary to improve the nature of the basic evidence by intensive field-work and limited excavation. It is no use constructing elaborate models based on sites that cannot be shown to be in contemporary use. Nor is it of much value to propound general laws about the settlement pattern of a region while the bulk of the sites remain to be discovered. This is not, however, a cry of despair, simply a warning that data collected according to the rules of the thirties are not likely to be of much immediate value when using the tools of the seventies. But for all that, in some areas such as the north-west where the survival of the settlement pattern is high, considerable advances may soon be made in our understanding of settlement dynamics. Eventually we may hope to have a series of models for different regions at different times which will provide us with a far better idea of the delicate relationships between man and his environment.[1]

Major advances can be expected concerning the mechanisms of trade and exchange, when geographical models are applied. Already the work on pottery fabrics is making it possible to trace the differences between local marketing and long-distance trade, while superimposed on this are the mechanisms of overseas trade, which may eventually be quantifiable. The fact that a reasonable documentary background exists will provide a useful control for the potential theoretical models.[2]

Finally, the problems of social structure and social change remain to be tackled. The great wealth of the documentary evidence makes the

[1] For the first attempts at this kind of analysis, see Newcomb, 1968 and 1970, for the south-west peninsula, and Hogg, 1971, for problems of hillforts. Hogg's analysis, however, assumes that all forts were in use at the same time. This is demonstrably not so for the south-east of England.

[2] Models for trade and exchange are briefly discussed in Collis, 1971a and 1971b, and Hogg, 1971.

task both attractive and hazardous. In the brief outline attempted in chapter 16, a few generalisations have been offered, many of which may eventually have to be modified or abandoned. Yet the exercise is worthwhile, if only to show that behind the popular myth of the 'Celtic nation' there was great variety and sometimes rapid social change. When we know more of demographic matters, we will be in a better position to discuss the causes of change which as yet we can still only dimly observe.

This book attempts to survey our present knowledge in a style as free as possible from imposed models. This seems to be the simplest and clearest approach at the moment: it loosens the joints and allows the data to find their own shape – indeed, it may be that simple descriptive treatments will remain the standard way of presenting complex material of this kind. What it must not obscure or hamper is the immense amount of work which remains to be done in discovering the relationships between aspects of the data not yet connected. The painstaking process of producing theoretical models, collecting new data, testing the models, and modifying them, must continue and will inevitably add much to our general understanding.

In so far as it is possible to look towards the next few decades to guess at the direction which Iron Age studies will take, it seems tolerably certain that far more emphasis will be given to studying entire landscapes and understanding the relationships of their intrinsic elements. This means two things: thorough field-work, together with schemes of large-scale and sometimes total excavation. Linked to this must come a more intensive study of animal bones in an attempt to understand the basis of animal husbandry – a subject yet barely touched by competent scholars. When these studies are in progress, problems of demography and the dynamics of change will at last come within the orbit of what it is possible to study. There are, of course, many related topics which must be examined in parallel with this type of broad programme. The production and distribution of pottery is still a great potential source of new information, and we know almost nothing of the physical type of Iron Age man himself even though skeletal material is not as rare as it was once thought to be.

The questions which we are asking of our material today are far more complex than those posed in the past: they concern change and equilibrium. The methods of study are necessarily more arduous and lengthy, but if the subject is to progress rather than accrete, we must not be afraid to undertake projects requiring broader vision and rigorous discipline.

Pottery *Appendix A*

In many chapters, particularly 3 and 7, it has been necessary to refer extensively to assemblages of pottery. Pottery is vitally important for the establishment of sequences, the definition of regional groupings and for throwing some light on the complexities of commercial production and trade. It has therefore been decided to illustrate a representative selection of the major groups. Where vessels have been drawn from the original material by the author, the source is given as 'author'; when they are drawn from published sources, the publication is cited. Reference to the site list (Appendix C) will, in the case of unpublished material, give the present location of the collections. All drawings are at ¼ the original size.

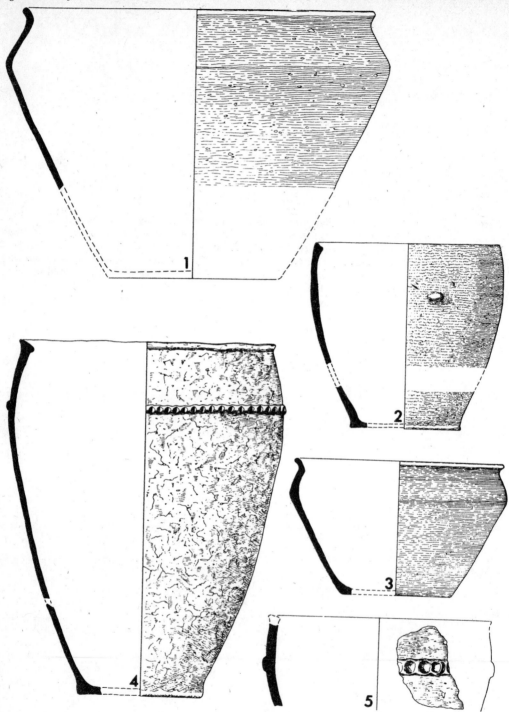

A:1   The Ultimate Deverel–Rimbury tradition: eighth to seventh centuries. 1–5   Eldon's
Seat (Encombe), Dorset (source: Cunliffe, 1968b)

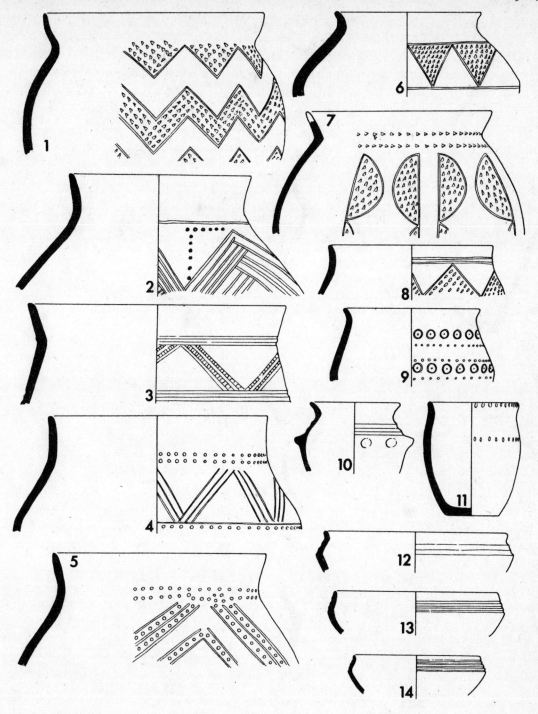

A:2   The Early All Cannings Cross group: eighth to seventh centuries. 1–11   All Cannings
Cross, Wilts; 12–14   Cold Kitchen Hill, Wilts (source: author)

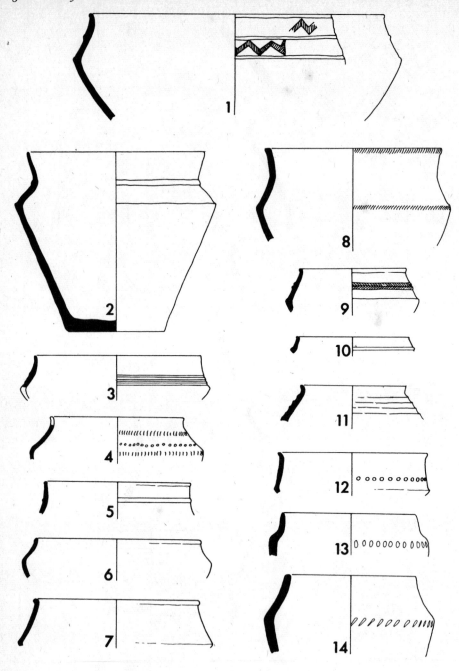

A:3   The Kimmeridge–Caburn group: sixth century. 1–2   the Caburn, Sussex; 3–7   Kimmeridge, Dorset; 8–9   the Caburn, Sussex; 10   Hollingbury Camp, Sussex; 11   Kingston Buci, Sussex; 12–14   Kimmeridge, Dorset (source: author)

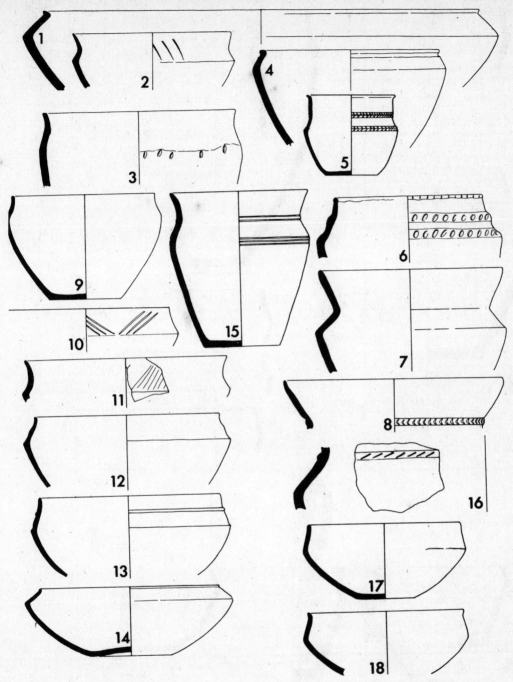

A:4   The West Harling–Staple Howe group: sixth century. 1–4   Staple Howe, Yorks;
5   Buntley, Suffolk; 6–14   West Harling, Norfolk; 15   Creeting St Mary, Suffolk;
16–18   Minnis Bay, Kent (sources: 1–4   Brewster, 1963; 5–18   author)

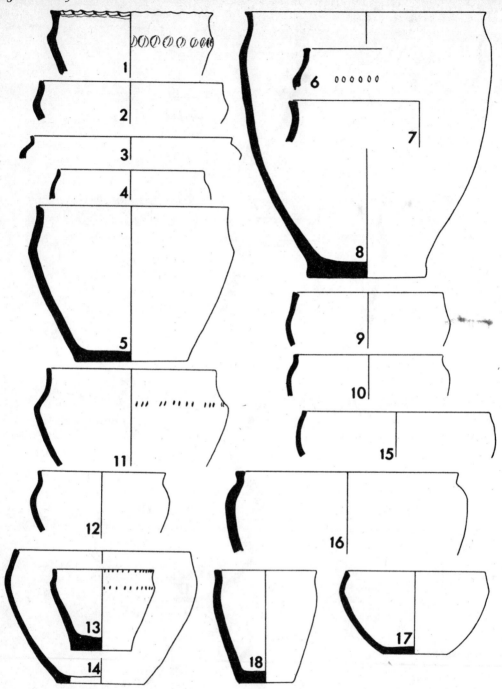

A:5   The Ivinghoe–Sandy group: sixth century. 1–4   Sandy, Beds; 5   Chippenham, Cambs;
6–8   Sandy, Beds; 9–10   Green End Road, Cambs; 11   Grantchester, Cambs; 12
Kempston, Foster's Pit, Beds; 15   Totternhoe, Beds; 16–18   Harrold, Beds (source: author)

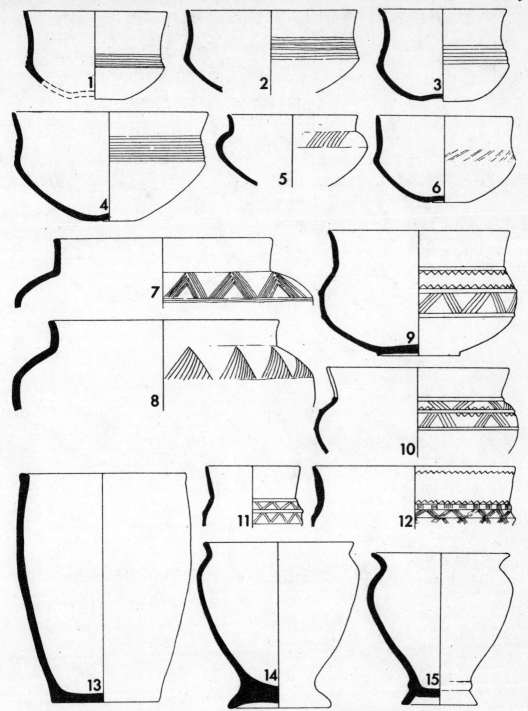

A:6   The All Cannings Cross–Meon Hill group: fifth to third centuries. 1   Winchester, Hants; 2   Boscombe Down West, Wilts; 3–4   All Cannings Cross, Wilts; 5   Boscombe Down West, Wilts; 6   All Cannings Cross, Wilts; 7–8   Boscombe Down West, Wilts; 9   All Cannings Cross, Wilts; 10   Meon Hill, Hants; 11   Yarnbury, Wilts; 12   Quarley Hill, Hants; 13   Boscombe Down West, Wilts; 14–15   Swallowcliffe, Wilts (source: author)

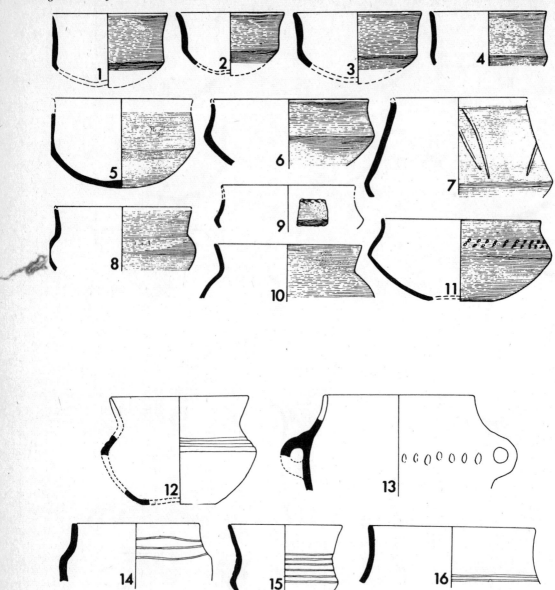

A:7 Dorset and Somerset variants of the All Cannings Cross–Meon Hill group: fifth to third century. 1–11 Eldon's Seat, Dorset; 12–13 Pagan's Hill, Somerset; 14–16 Bathampton Down, Somerset (sources: 1–11 Cunliffe, 1968b; 12–16 author)

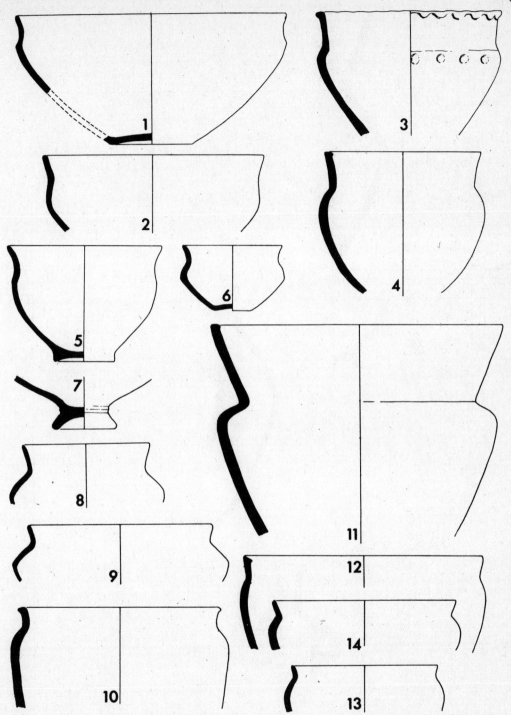

A:8   The Park Brow–Caesar's Camp group: fifth to third centuries. 1   St Catherine's Hill,
Guildford, Surrey; 2–3   Caesar's Camp (Wimbledon), Surrey; 4   St Martha's Hill, Surrey;
5   Chertsey, Surrey; 6   St George's Hill (Weybridge), Surrey; 7–13   Park Brow, Sussex;
14   Muntham Court, Sussex (source: author)

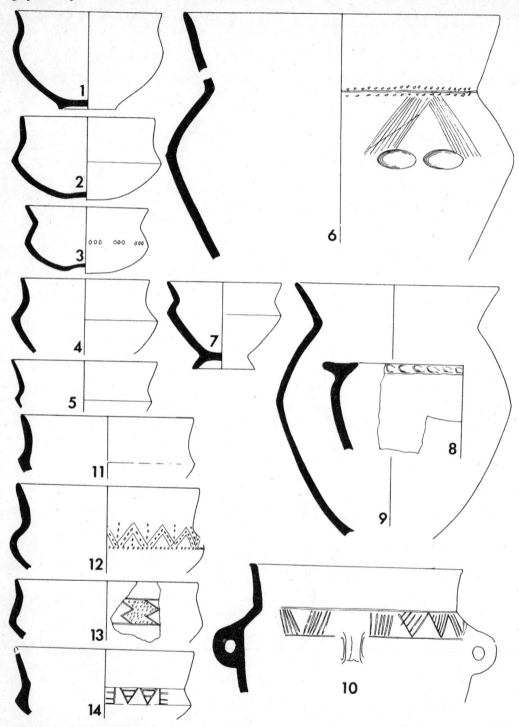

A:9   The Long Wittenham–Allen's Pit group: fifth to third centuries. 1   Chinnor, Oxon;
2–5   Long Wittenham, Berks; 6   Allen's Pit, Oxon; 7   Chinnor, Oxon; 8   Mount Farm,
Oxon; 9   Long Wittenham, Berks; 10   Allen's Pit, Oxon; 11   Mount Farm, Oxon; 12
Dennis Pit, Old Marden, Oxon; 13   Bampton, Oxon; 14   Witham, Berks (source: author)

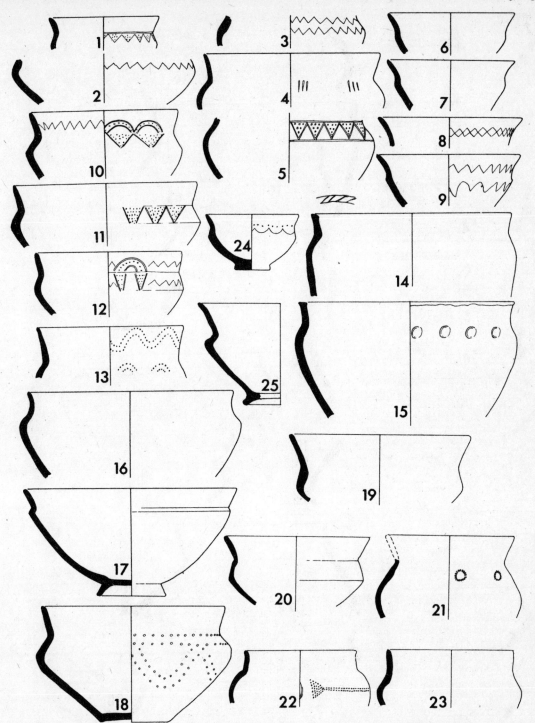

A:10   The Chinnor–Wandlebury group: fifth to third centuries. 1–2   Bledlow, Bucks; 3–5 Ellesborough, Bucks; 6–9   Great Wymondley, Herts; 10–13   Chinnor, Oxon; 14   Great Wymondley, Herts; 15   Chinnor, Oxon; 16–17   Wandlebury, Cambs; 18   Linton, Cambs; 19–23   Blewburton, Berks; 24   Chinnor, Oxon; 25   Mortlake, Middlesex (source: author)

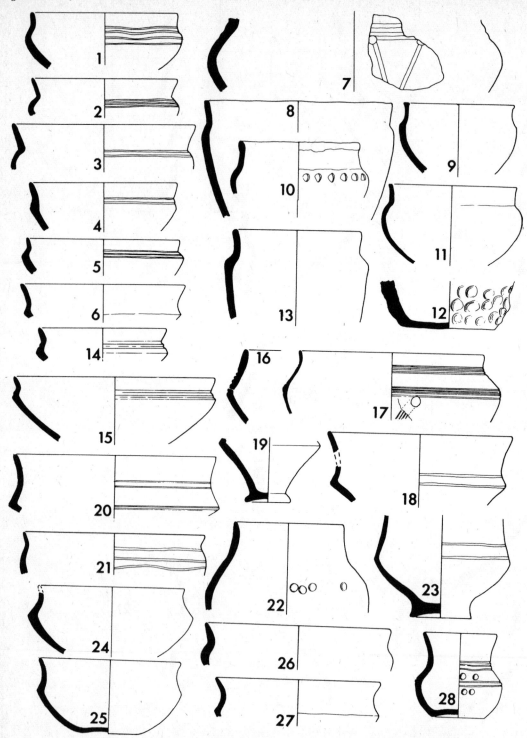

A:11   The Darmsden–Linton group: fifth to third centuries. 1–9   Darmsden, Suffolk;
10   Hawk's Hill, Surrey; 11–15   Linton, Cambs; 16–18   Hinderclay, Suffolk; 19   Linton,
Cambs; 20   Leigh Hill, Cobham, Surrey; 21–22   Linton, Cambs; 23–24   Feltwell, Norfolk;
25   Leigh Hill, Cobham, Surrey; 26–27   Hawk's Hill, Surrey; 28   Esher, Surrey (source: author)

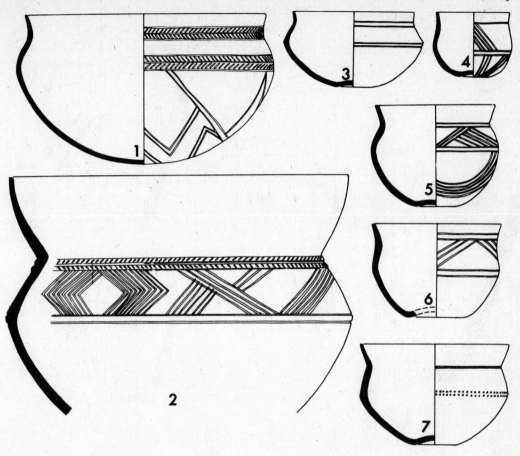

A:12 The Fengate–Cromer group: fifth to third centuries. 1 Cromer, Norfolk; 2–7 Fengate, Northants (source: author)

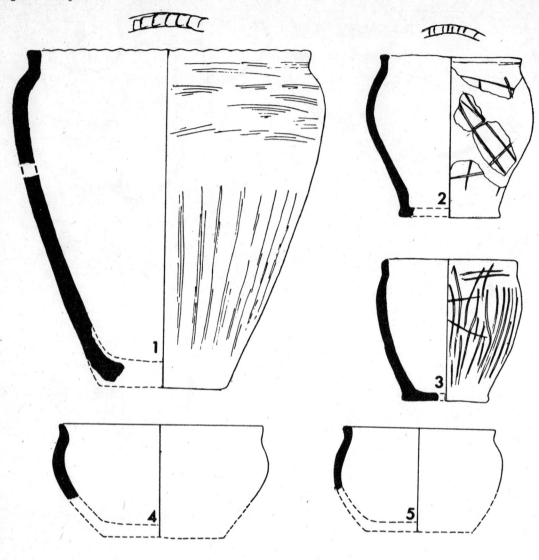

A:13   The Breedon–Ancaster group: ?fifth to second/first century. 1–5   Breedon-on-the-Hill, Leics (source: Kenyon, 1950)

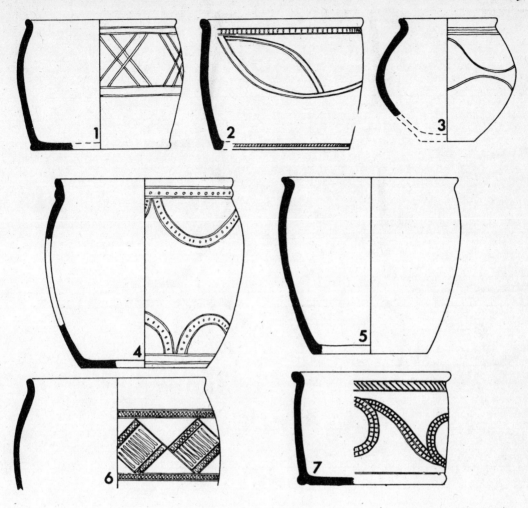

A:14 The Caburn–Cissbury style: third to first centuries. 1 Cissbury, Sussex; 2 Elm Grove, Brighton, Sussex; 3 Cissbury, Sussex; 4–5 Park Brow, Sussex; 6 Newhaven, Sussex; 7 the Caburn, Sussex (source: author)

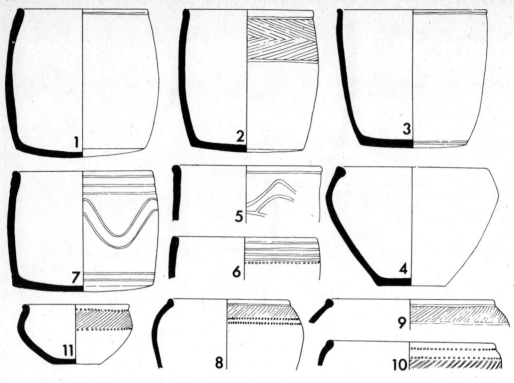

A:15   The St Catherine's Hill–Worthy Down style: third to first century 1   Twyford Down, Hants; 2–4   St Catherine's Hill, Hants; 5–6   Twyford Down, Hants; 7   Trundle, Sussex; 8–11   Worthy Down, Hants (source: author)

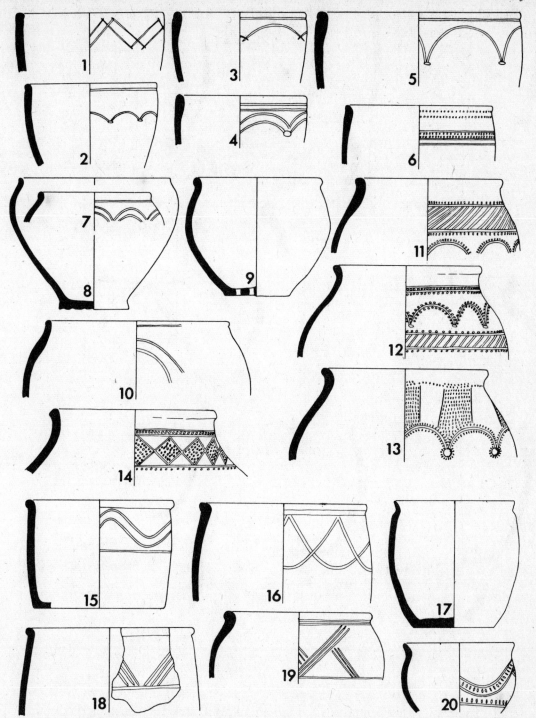

A:16 The Yarnbury–Highfield style (nos 1–13) and the Hawk's Hill–West Clandon style (nos 15–20): both third to first centuries. 1 Yarnbury, Wilts; 2 Highfield, Wilts; 3–4 Yarnbury, Wilts; 5 Fifield Bavant, Wilts; 6 Yarnbury, Wilts; 7 Highfield, Wilts; 8–10 Fifield Bavant, Wilts; 11 Yarnbury, Wilts; 12 Highfield, Wilts; 13–14 Yarnbury, Wilts; 15 Hawk's Hill, Surrey; 16–17 West Clandon, Surrey; 18 Hawk's Hill, Surrey; 19 West Clandon, Surrey; 20 Hawk's Hill, Surrey (source: author)

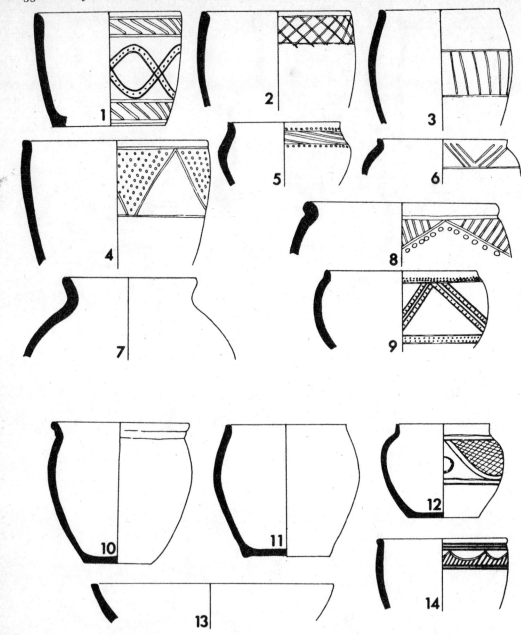

A:17 The Southcote–Blewburton Hill style (nos 1–9) and the Glastonbury–Blaise Castle style (nos 10–14): both third to first centuries. 1–3 Blewburton Hill, Berks; 4 Knighton Hill, Berks; 5–6 Theale, Berks; 7–8 Southcote, Berks; 9 Blewburton Hill, Berks; 10–11 Worlebury, Somerset; 12 Read's Cavern, Somerset; 13 Blaise Castle, Glos; 14 Read's Cavern, Somerset (source: author)

A:21 Decorated bowls of the Frilford and Hunsbury type: first century BC to first century AD.
1 Hatford, Berks; 2 Cassington, Oxon; 3 Boxford Common, Berks; 4 Frilford, Berks;
5 Iffley, Oxon; 6 Wokingham, Berks; 7 Cassington, Oxon; 8 Frilford, Berks; 9–10
Hunsbury, Northants; 11 Draughton, Northants; 12 Hunsbury, Northants (source: author)

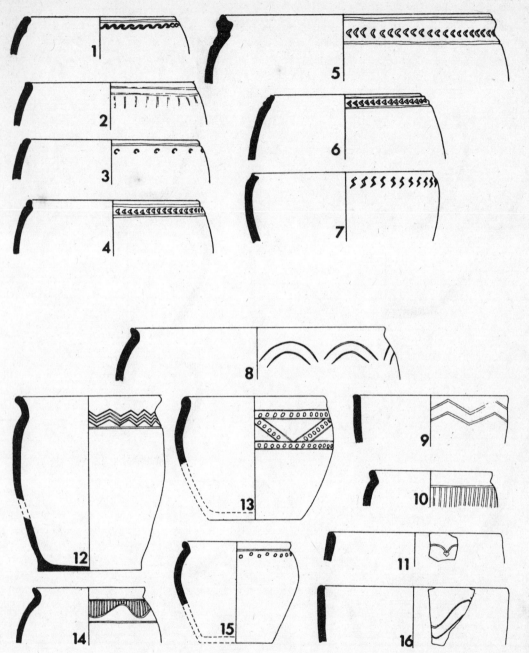

A:18 The Croft Ambrey–Bredon Hill style (nos 1–7): fifth/fourth to first centuries: the Lydney–
Llanmelin style (nos 8–16): third to first centuries. 1–6 Sutton Walls, Hereford; 7 Cleeve Hill,
Glos; 8 Lydney, Glos; 9 Llanmelin, Mon; 10 Lydney, Glos; 11–12 Llanmelin, Mon;
13–15 Lydney, Glos; 16 Llanmelin, Mon (source: author)

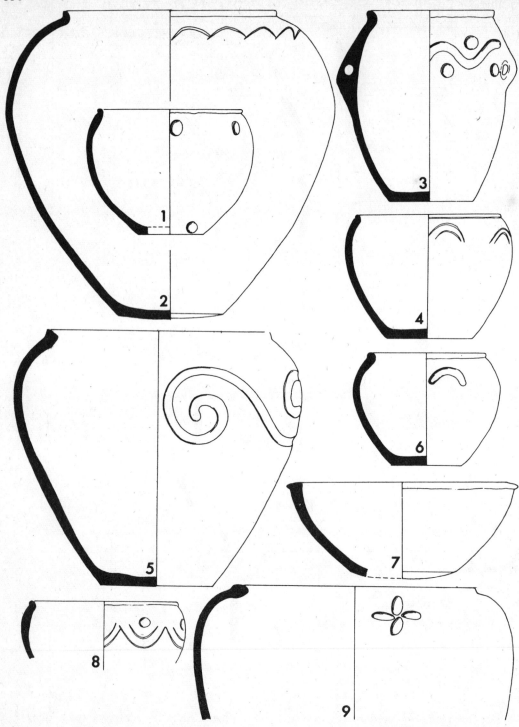

A:19   The Maiden Castle–Marnhull style: third to first centuries. 1–9   Maiden Castle, Dorset (source: author)

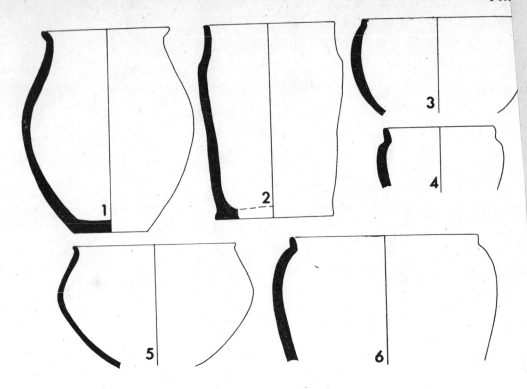

A:20   The Stanton Harcourt–Cassington style: third to first centuries. 1   Frilford, Berks; 2   Chastleton, Oxon; 3–4   Cassington, Oxon; 5   Yarnton, Oxon; 6   Mount Farm, Oxon (source: author)

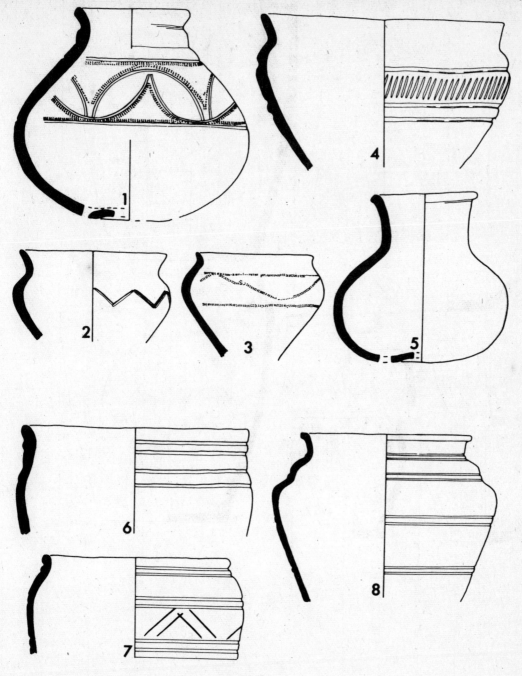

A:22 The Sleaford–Dragonby style: first century BC. All from Dragonby, Lincs: 1–5 early, ?pre *c.* 50 BC; 6–8 later, *c.* 50–10 BC (source: May, 1970)

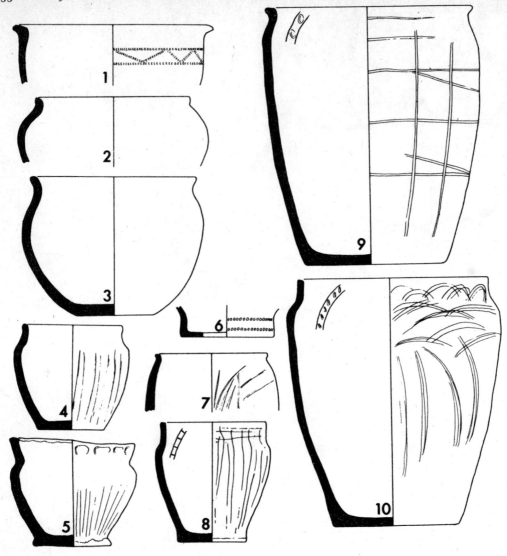

A:23 Bowls and coarse ware from eastern England: third to first centuries. 1 Abington Pigotts, Cambs; 2 St Ives, Hunts; 3 South Wilson, Bucks; 4 Slough, Bucks; 5 Abington Pigotts, Cambs; 6 St Ives, Hunts; 7 Houghton, Hunts; 8–10 Barley, Herts (source: author)

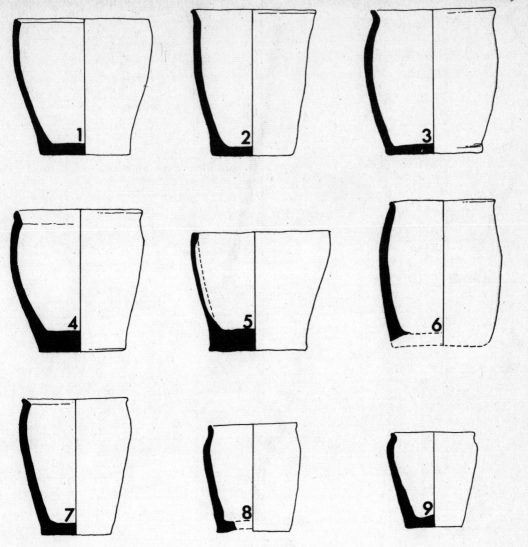

A:24 The Dane's Graves–Staxton style: third to first centuries. 1–6 Dane's Graves, Yorks; 7–9 Driffield, Yorks (source: Brewster, 1963)

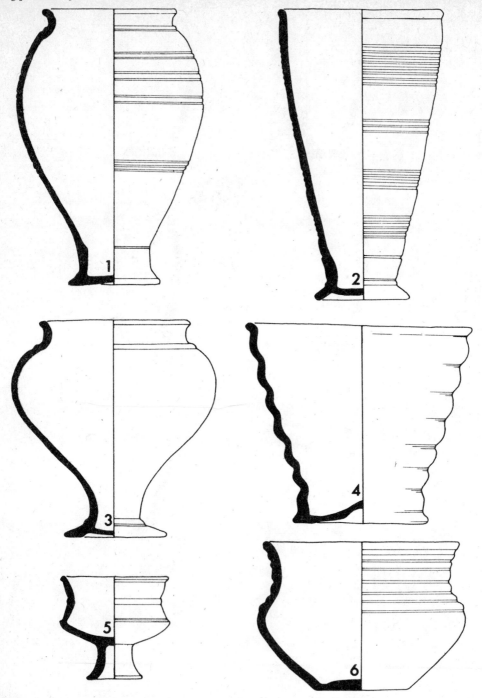

A:25   The Aylesford–Swarling style: *c.* 50 BC–AD 43. 1–7   Swarling, Kent (source: Birchall, 1965)

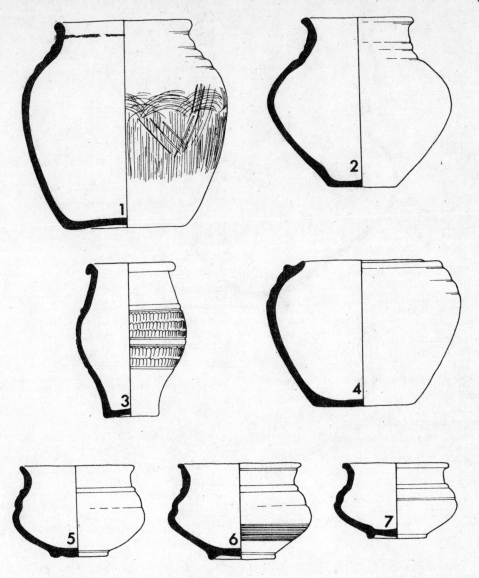

A:26   The Aylesford–Swarling style: *c.* 50 BC–AD 43. 1–4   Swarling, Kent; 5   Welwyn, Herts; 6   Aylesford, Kent (source: Birchall, 1965)

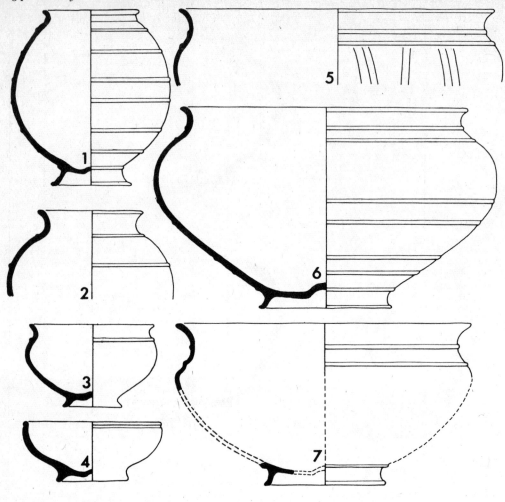

A:27 Imported Hengistbury class B ware: first century BC. 1–7 Hengistbury Head, Hants
(source: Bushe-Fox, 1915)

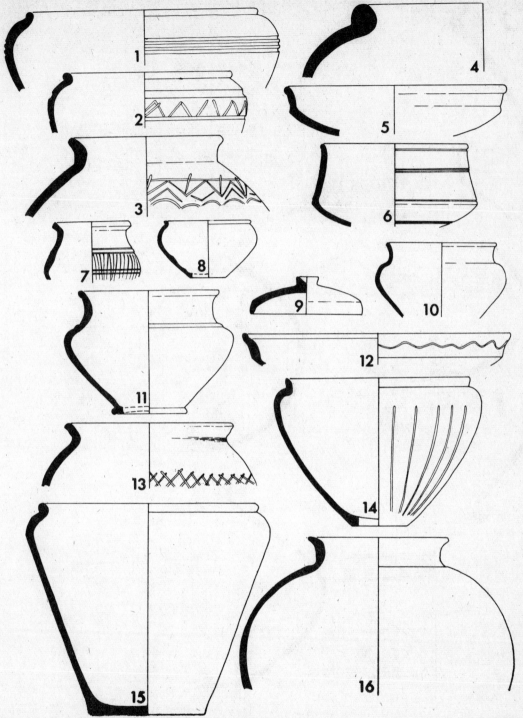

A:28 Northern and Southern Atrebatic types: *c.* 50 BC–AD 43. 1 Oare, Wilts; 2 Boscombe Down West, Wilts; 3–10 Oare, Wilts; 11–12 Worthy Down, Hants; 13 Winchester, Hants; 14–16 Horndean, Hants (source: author)

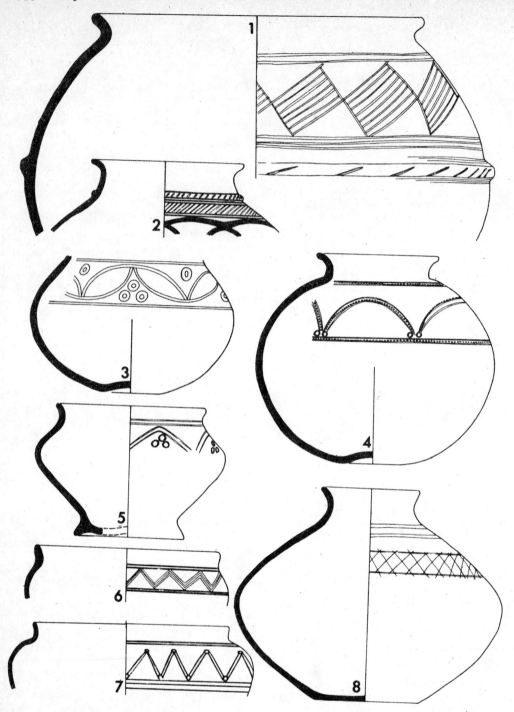

A:29   Eastern Atrebatic types: *c.* 50 BC–AD 43. 1   Broadwater, Sussex; 2   Horsted Keynes, Sussex; 3   Langenhoe, Sussex; 4   Saltdean, Sussex; 5   Little Horstead Lane, Sussex; 6   Glyne, Sussex; 7   Charleston Brow, Sussex; 8   Asham, Sussex (source: author)

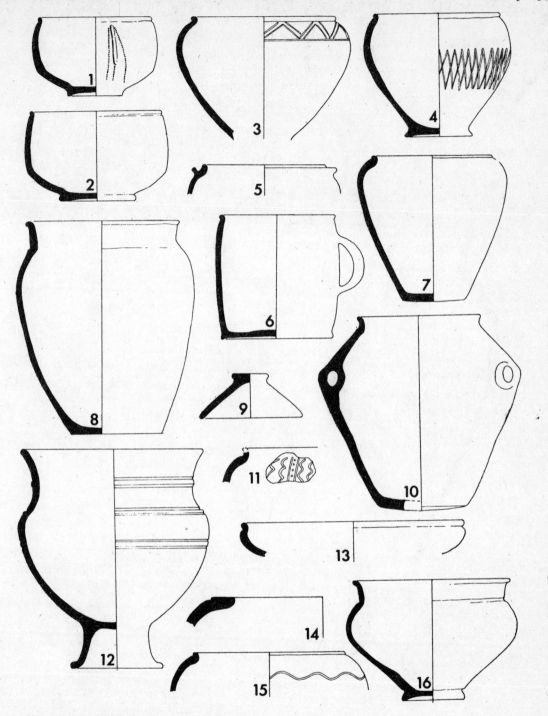

A:30 Durotrigian types: *c.* 50 BC–AD 43. 1–10 Maiden Castle, Dorset; 11 Fitzworth, Dorset; 12–16 Maiden Castle, Dorset (source: author)

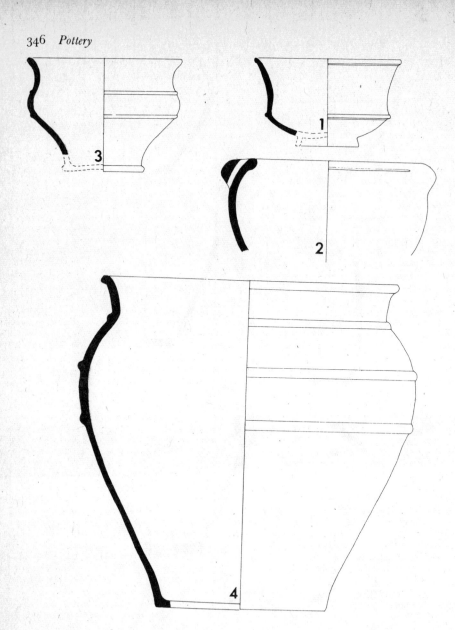

A:31 Cordoned ware types: *c.* 50 BC–AD 43. 1–4 Carloggas Camp, St Mawgan-in-Pydar, Cornwall (source: Threipland, 1957)

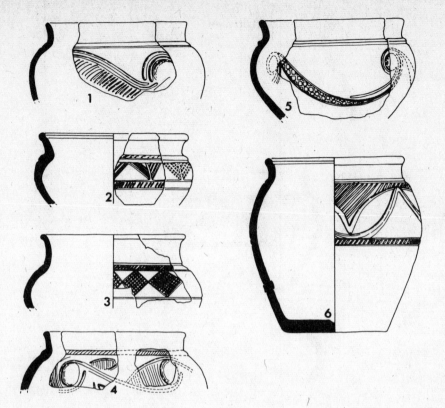

A:32   Glastonbury ware types (group 1): ?second century BC. 1   Castle Dore, Cornwall;
2–3   Carloggas Camp, St Mawgan-in-Pydar, Cornwall; 4–5   Castle Dore, Cornwall;
6   Carloggas Camp, St Mawgan-in-Pydar, Cornwall (sources: *Castle Dore*, Radford,
1951; *Carloggas Camp*, Threipland, 1957)

A:33 Glastonbury ware types (group 2): first century BC to first century AD. 1–2 Glastonbury, Somerset; 3 Wookey Hole, Somerset; 4 Meare, Somerset; 5–8 Glastonbury, Somerset (sources: *Glastonbury*, Bulleid & Gray, 1917; *Meare*, Bulleid & Gray, 1948; *Wookey Hole*, Peacock, 1969)

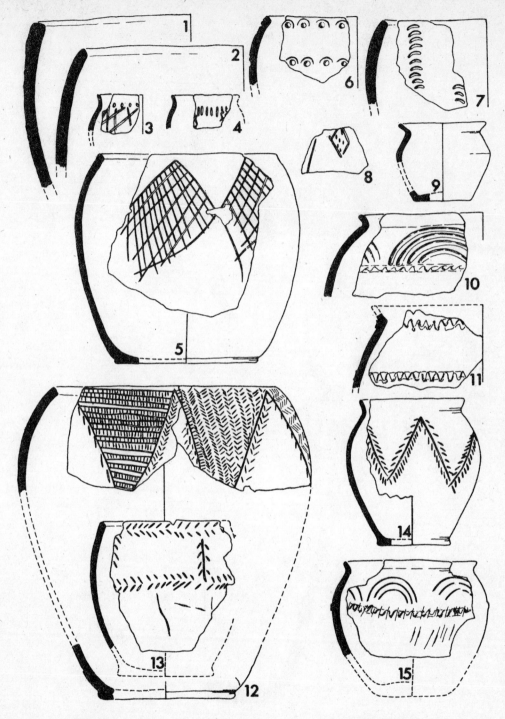

A:34 Pre-broch pottery: sixth to first century. Dun Mor Vaul, Tiree (source: MacKie, 1965b)

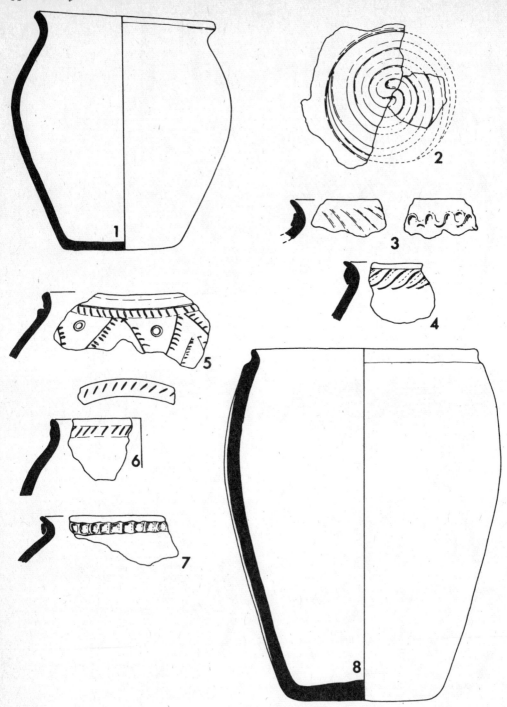

A:35   Pottery from Shetland. 1   Clickhimin (Late Bronze Age); 2–3   Jarlshof (Late Bronze Age); 4–6   Clickhimin (first Iron Age farm); 7–10   Jarlshof (village II = first Iron Age farm); 11–12   Clickhimin (fort period) (sources: Hamilton, 1956 and 1968)

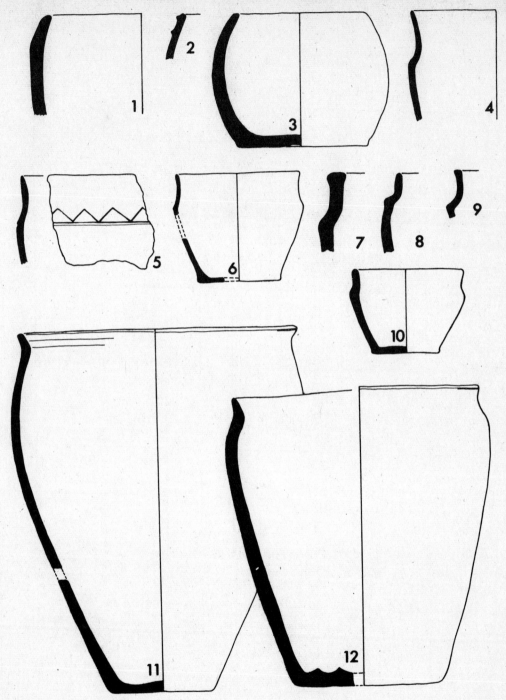

A:36 Pottery from Orkney and Shetland. 1–4 Clickhimin (fort period); 5–6 Orkney (broch pottery); 7 Clickhimin (broch pottery); 8 Jarlshof (wheelhouse pottery) (sources: Hamilton, 1956 and 1968)

Selected Radiocarbon Dates[1]   *Appendix B*

Over the past ten years radiocarbon dates for the first millennium BC have gradually become more plentiful. In general terms, it may be said that those now available form a remarkably consistent group which enhances and in no way conflicts with other categories of archaeological evidence. Dates have been quoted liberally in the text in radiocarbon years BC, calculated on the 5568 half-life, with an assessment calculated on the preferred half-life of 5730 in brackets afterwards. For convenience, the dates are listed separately here together with their laboratory numbers. No attempt has been made to correct to absolute years based on the bristlecone pine recalibration, since for dates within the Iron Age range the margin of error is too great to allow for significant positive reassessment.

	5568 half-life	*5730 half-life*
I SOUTHERN BRITAIN		
Chalton, Hants		
Charcoal from a Middle Bronze Age hut site	1243 ± 69 (BM-583)	1339 BC
Itford, Hill, Sussex		
Charred grain	1000 ± 35 (GrU-6167)	1089 BC
Longbridge Deverill (Cow Down) Wilts		
a. Wood charcoal from post-hole of house 1 in enclosure 2	630 ± 155 (NPL-105)	708 BC
b. Wood charcoal from post-hole of house 2 in enclosure 2	500 ± 90 (NPL-106)	574 BC
c. Wood charcoal from loom post-hole of house 2 in enclosure 2	420 ± 95 (NPL-107)	491 BC
d. Wood charcoal from pit 7	460 ± 140 (NPL-108)	532 BC
e. Wood charcoal from pit 37	490 ± 90 (NPL-109)	563 BC
Shearplace Hill, Dorset		
Miscellaneous charcoal and animal bone from Middle Bronze Age hut	1180 ± 180 (NPL-19)	1274 BC
Weston Wood (Albury) Surrey		
Carbonised cereal from a pit	510 ± 110 (Q-760)	583 BC
II THE MIDLANDS AND WALES		
Bromfield, Salop		
Bronze Age cremation cemetery: charcoal from three separate cremations	1560 ± 180 (BIRM-64)	1665 BC
	850 ± 71 (BIRM-63)	934 BC
	762 ± 75 (BIRM-62)	843 BC

	5568 half-life	*5730 half-life*
Midsummer Hill Camp, Heref		
a. Charcoal from quarry ditch associated with first gate	420 ± 190 (BIRM-142)	491 BC
b. Carbonised grain associated with destruction of eighth gate	50 ± 100 (BIRM-143)	125 BC
Dinorben, Denbigh		
a. Charcoal from occupation layer below period 1 rampart	945 ± 95 (V-123)	1032 BC
b. Charcoal from collapsed beam north-east of period 1 rampart	895 ± 95 (V-122)	980 BC
c. Charcoal, ?derived from period 1 rampart	765 ± 85 (V-125)	846 BC
d. Charcoal, ?from destruction of period 2 rampart	535 ± 85 (V-124)	609 BC
e. Charcoal from timber-lacing of period 2 rampart	420 ± 70 (V-176)	491 BC
Ryton-on-Dunsmoor, Warwicks		
Charcoal from a cremation	751 ± 41 (BIRM-26)	832 BC

III   NORTH-EAST BRITAIN

	5568 half-life	*5730 half-life*
Ampleforth Moor, Yorks		
a. Charcoal from ground-surface beneath barrow 3	582 ± 90 (BM-369)	658 BC
b. Charcoal from ground-surface beneath barrow 7	537 ± 90 (BM-368)	612 BC
Burnswark, Northumberland		
a. Charcoal from palisade	500 ± 100 (GaK-22036)	574 BC
b. Charcoal from gateway timber of ?hillfort	525 ± 90 (I-5314)	599 BC
Brough Law, Northumberland		
Charcoal from beneath rampart	245 ± 90 (I-5315)	311 BC
Craigmarloch Wood, Renfrew		
a. Charcoal from palisaded enclosure	590 ± 40 (GaK-995)	665 BC
b. Core of vitrified wall	35 ± 40 (GaK-996)	95 BC
Finavon, Angus		
a. Charcoal from low in fallen rubble	410 ± 80 (GaK-1222)	480 BC
b. Occupation layer of fort	320 ± 90 (GaK-1223)	390 BC
c. Beams and planks along inner wall-face	590 ± 70 (GaK-1224)	665 BC
Grimthorpe, Yorks		
a. Bones from ditch	690 ± 130 (NPL-136)	769 BC
b. Bones from ditch	970 ± 130 (NPL-137)	1058 BC
Huckhoe, Northumberland		
Charcoal from palisade trench	510 ± 40 (GaK-1388)	585 BC
Ingram Hill, Northumberland		
Charcoal from settlement site with palisade: beneath bank	220 ± 90 (I-5316)	285 BC
Kaimes Hillfort, Midlothian		
a. Twigs from core of rampart 2	(Not published) (GaK-1971)	365 BC
b. Wood from wall of hut circle 3	(Not published) (GaK-1970)	1191 BC
MacNaughton's Fort, Kirkcudbright		
Charcoal in palisade trench enclosing wooden roundhouse	280 ± 100 (GaK-808)	345 BC

	5568 half-life	*5730 half-life*
Mam Tor, Derby		
a. Interior occupation	1130 ± 115 (BIRM-192)	1222 BC
b. Interior occupation	1180 ± 132 (BIRM-202)	1274 BC
Staple Howe, Yorks		
Charred grain	450 ± 150 (BM-63)	572 BC

IV NORTH-WEST BRITAIN

Dun Ardtreck, Skye		
Charcoal from rubble foundations of semi-broch	55 ± 105 (GX-1120)	115 BC
Dun Lagaidh, Wester Ross		
a. Carbonised branch under vitrified fort wall	490 ± 90 (GX-1121)	565 BC
b. Burnt grain associated with burning of timber fort	460 ± 100 (GaK-2492)	532 BC
Dun Mor Vaul, Tiree, Argyll		
a. Roots from old ground-surface below broch	400 ± 110 (GaK-1092)	470 BC
b. Charred grain from pre-broch level	445 ± 90 (GaK-1098)	515 BC
c. Bones from midden under outer wall	280 ± 100 (GaK-1225)	345 BC
d. Primary floor in broch wall gallery	AD 60 ± 90 (GaK-1097)	AD 5
e. Rubble in wall gallery	AD 160 ± 90 (GaK-1099)	AD 105
Kilphedir, Sutherland		
a. Charcoal from hut 3	420 ± 40 (GU-299)	491 BC
b. Charcoal from hut 5	150 ± 80 (L-1061)	215 BC
c. Charcoal from hut 5	114 ± 55 (GU-11)	176 BC

[1] For a brief explanation of the use of radiocarbon dates and a list of dates relevant to British archaeology, see *Archaeological Site Index to Radiocarbon Dates for Great Britain and Ireland* (British Council for Archaeology, 1971).

List of Principal Sites

The major sites mentioned in the text above are listed here in alphabetical order, together with their more significant bibliographical references or, if unpublished, the source of the information or location of the finds. No attempt has been made to list all of the references for each site, nor have sites of only passing significance been included.

Abington Pigotts, Cambs   *C. F. Fox, 1924*

Abernethy, *see* Castle Law, Perth

Adabrock, Lewis   *Coles, 1962a, 48–50*

Allasdale, Isle of Barra   *Young, 1955*

All Cannings Cross, Wilts   *M. E. Cunnington, 1923*

Allen's Pit (Dorchester), Oxon   *Bradford, 1942a*

Almondbury, *see* Castle Hill, Yorks

Alnham, *see* High Knowes, Northumberland

Ampleforth Moor, Yorks   *Wainwright & Longworth, 1969*

Ancaster, Lincs   *May, 1965–9*

Angle Ditch, *see* Handly Down, Dorset

Ardleigh, Essex   *Erith & Longworth, 1960*

Arminghall, Norfolk   *Clark, 1936*

Arras, Yorks   *Stead, 1965; Greenwell, 1906*

Asham, Sussex   *E. Curwen, 1930*

Atwick, Yorks   *Greenwell & Gatty, 1910; Brewster, 1963, 143*

Aust, Glos   *Ellis, 1900; R. A. Smith, 1925, 148*

Aylesford, Kent   *Evans, 1890; Birchall, 1963, 1965; Stead, 1971*

Bacon Hole, Glam   *A. Williams, 1939a*

Badbury, Dorset   *Crawford & Keiller, 1928*

Bagendon, Glos   *Clifford, 1961*

Baldock, Herts   *Stead, 1971*

Balevu'lin, Tiree, Argyll   *MacKie, 1965c*

Balksbury, Hants   *J. Hawkes, 1940; Wainwright, 1970*

Bampton, Oxon   *Savory, 1939*

Banwell, Som   *Unpublished: Taunton Museum*

Barbury Castle, Wilts   *MacGregor & Simpson, 1963*

Barley, Herts   *Cra'ster, 1961*

Barn Down West, Wilts   *Fowler, Musty & Taylor, 1965*

Barnes, Isle of Wight, Hants   *Preston & Hawkes, 1933*

Barnwood, Glos   *Clifford, 1934*

Bathampton Down, Som   *Wainwright, 1967b*

Battersea, London   *C. F. Fox, 1958, Pls. 14, 16*

Battlesbury, Wilts   *Chadwick & Thompson, 1956*

Bawsey, Norfolk   *Maryon, 1944*

Beacon Hill (Burghclere), Hants   *Williams-Freeman, 1915*

Beaulieu Heath, Hants   *C. M. Piggott, 1953*

Bexley Heath, Kent   *Inv. Arch. G.B. 8th Set (1960), 53*

Bigbury, Kent   *Jessup & Cook, 1936*

Billericay, Essex   *C. F. Fox, 1958, 96*

Bindon, Dorset   *Wheeler, 1953*

Birdlip, Glos   *Bellows, 1881; Green, 1949*

Bishopston Valley, Glam   *A. Williams, 1940*

Blackbury Castle, Devon   *Young & Richardson, 1955*

Blagdon Copse, Hants   *Stead, 1970*

Blaise Castle Hill, Glos   *Rhatz & Brown, 1959*

Blamashanner, Angus   *Coles, 1962a, 98–9*

Bledlow, Bucks   *Head & C. M. Piggott, 1944*

Blewburton Hill, Berks   *A. E. P. Collins, 1947 and 1953; Collins, A. E. P. & F. J.. 1959; Bradford, 1942c*

Blissmoor, Dartmoor, Devon   *A. Fox, 1955*

Bodrifty, Cornwall   *Dudley, 1957*

Bonchester Hill, Roxburgh   *Curle, 1910; C. M. Piggott, 1952*

Boscombe Down East, Wilts   *Stone, 1936*

Boscombe Down West, Wilts   *Richardson, 1951*

Bower Walls Camp, Som   *Cotton, 1955, 85–6*

Boxford Common, Berks   *Peake, Coghlan & Hawkes, 1932 and 1933*

Braes of Gight, Aberdeen   *Coles, 1962a, 94–5*

Braidwood Fort, Midlothian   *Stevenson, 1949; S. Piggott, 1960*

Bramdean, Hants   *Unpublished excavation: B. Perry*

Bredon Hill, Glos   *T. C. Hencken, 1938*

Breedon-on-the-Hill, Leics   *Kenyon, 1950; Wacher, 1964*

Breiddin, Montgomery   *O'Neil, 1937; Musson, 1970*

Brentford, Middx   *C. F. Fox, 1958, Pl. 3*

Brentford, Old England, Middx   *Wheeler, 1929*

Bridport (West Bay), Dorset   *Farrar, 1954*

Broadall Lake, Devon   *A. Fox, 1955*

Broadwater, Sussex   *E. C. Curwen, 1954*

Bromfield, Salop   *Information from excavator: S. Stanfield*

Buckland Rings, Hants   *C. F. C. Hawkes, 1936a*

Bugthorpe, Yorks   *Greenwell, 1877; Stead, 1965, 104*

Bulbury, Dorset   *E. Cunnington, 1884*

Buntley, Suffolk   *Unpublished: pottery in Ipswich Museum*

Burnmouth, Berwick   *Craw, 1924*

Burradon, Northumberland   *Jobey, 1970*

Bury Hill, Hants   *C. F. C. Hawkes, 1940b*

Bury Hill, Glos   *Davies & Phillips, 1929*

Bury Wood Camp, Wilts   *King, 1961, 1962 and 1967*

Butcombe, Som   *P. J. Fowler, 1970*

Caburn, the, Sussex   *Curwen & Curwen, 1927; Wilson, 1938 and 1939; C. F. C. Hawkes, 1939a*

Caesar's Camp (Wimbledon), Surrey   *Lowther, 1947*

Cairnconan, Angus   *Jervise, 1863*

Calf of Eday, Orkney   *Calder, 1939*

Calleva (Silchester), Hants   *Boon, 1969*

Cambridge, Cambs   *Cra'ster, 1969*

Camerton, Som   *Wedlake, 1958*

Camulodunum (Colchester), Essex   *Hawkes & Hull, 1947*

Canterbury, Kent   *Frere, 1954*

Cardiff, Glam   *Nash-Williams, 1933a*

Carloggas (St Mawgan-in-Pydar), Cornwall   *Threipland, 1957*

Carn Fadrun, Caerns   *RCHM, Caernarvonshire, III, no. 1650*

Cassington, Oxon   *Leeds, 1935; Harden, 1942*

Castell Odo, Caerns   *Alcock, 1961*

Casterley Camp, Wilts   *Cunnington, M. E. & B. H., 1913*

Castle Ditch (Eddisbury), Cheshire   *Varley, 1950a*

Castle Dore, Cornwall   *Radford, 1951*

Castle Gotha, Cornwall   *Saunders, 1961*

Castle Hill (Almondbury), Yorks   *Varley, 1939*

Castle Hill (Horsburgh), Peebles   *Feachem, 1966*

Castle Hill (Newhaven), Sussex   *C. F. C. Hawkes, 1939b*

Castle Hill (Scarborough), Yorks   *R. A. Smith, 1928 and 1934*

Castle Law, Midlothian   *Childe 1933; Piggott, S. & C. M. 1954*

Castle Law, Perths (*see also* Forgondenny)   *Christison & Anderson, 1899*

Cerrig-y-Drudion, Denbigh   *C. F. Fox, 1958; R. A. Smith, 1926*

Chalbury, Dorset   *Whitley, 1943*

Chalton, Hants   *Cunliffe, 1970*

Charleston Brow, Sussex   *Parsons & Curwen, 1933*

Chastleton, Oxon   *Leeds, 1931b*

Cherbury, Bucks   *Bradford, 1940*

Chertsey, Surrey   *Unpublished: Guildford Museum*

Chippenham, Cambs   *Leaf, 1936*

Chinnor, Oxon   *Richardson & Young, 1951*

Chisbury, Wilts   *M. E. Cunnington, 1932a*

Chisenbury Trendle, Wilts   *M. E. Cunnington, 1932b*

Cholesbury Camp, Bucks   *Kimball, 1933*

Chun, Cornwall   *Leeds, 1927*

Chysauster, Cornwall   *H. O'N. Hencken, 1933*

Cissbury, Sussex   *Curwen & Williamson, 1931*

Cleeve Hill, Glos   *Gray & Brewer, 1904*

Clettraval, North Uist   *Scott, 1948*

Clickhimin, Shetland   *Hamilton, 1966 and 1968*

Clotherholm, Yorks   *Manby, 1963*

Clovelly Dykes, Cornwall   *A. Fox, 1953*

Clynnog, Caerns   *Grimes, 1951*

Cock Hill, Sussex   *Ratcliffe-Densham, H. B. A. & M. M., 1961*

Colchester, Essex   *Fox & Hull, 1948*

Cold Kitchen Hill, Wilts   *Cunnington & Goddard, 1934*

Colsterworth, Lincs   *Grimes, 1961*

Conway Mountain, Caerns   *Griffiths & Hogg, 1957*

Corley Camp, Warwicks   *Chatwin, 1930*

Covesea (Sculptor's Cave), Moray   *Benton, 1931*

Cowlam, Yorks   *Stead, 1965, 105; Greenwell, 1877*

Coygan Camp, Carm   *Wainwright, 1967a*

Crane Godrevy (Gwithian), Cornwall   *A. C. Thomas, 1964*

Crayford, Kent   *Ward-Perkins, 1938*

Credenhill Camp, Heref   *Stanford, 1971a*

Creeting St Mary, Suffolk   *R. R. Clarke, 1939*

Crickley Hill, Glos   *Unpublished excavation*

Croft Ambrey, Heref   *Stanford, 1967*

Cromer, Norfolk   *R. R. Clarke, 1960, Pl. 20*

Crosby Ravensworth, Westmorland   *Way, 1869*

Culver Hole Cave, *see* Llangenydd, Gower

Cwmbrwyn, Carm   *Ward, 1907*

Dainton, Devon   *Willis & Rogers, 1951*

Danebury, Hants   *Unpublished excavation: author*

Dane's Camp, Worcs   *Unpublished excavation*

Dane's Graves, Yorks   *Stead, 1965, 105: Greenwell, 1906; Mortimer, 1911*

Darmsden, Suffolk   *Cunliffe, 1968a*

Deal, Kent   *Woodruff, 1904*

Denbury, Devon   *A. Fox, 1961b*

Dennis Pit (Old Marden), Oxon   *Unpublished: Ashmolean Museum*

Desborough, Northants   *C. F. Fox, 1958*

Deskford, Banff   *S. Piggott, 1959*

Dinas Emrys, Caerns   *Savory, 1961*

Dinorben, Denbigh   *Gardner & Savory, 1964; Savory, 1971*

Down Barn West (Winterbourne Gunner), Wilts   *Fowler et al., 1965*

Dragonby, Lincs   *May, 1970*

Jarlshof, Shetland   *Hamilton, 1956*

Kaimes Hill, Midlothian   *Childe, 1941; Simpson, 1969*

Kempston, Beds   *Unpublished: Bedford Museum*

Kendall, Yorks   *Brewster, 1963*

Kestor (Chagford), Devon   *A. Fox, 1955*

Kilham, Yorks   *Brewster, 1963*

Kilphedir, Sutherland   *DES, 1963, 50; 1964, 51*

Kimmeridge, Dorset   *Davies, 1936; Calkin, 1949; Cunliffe, 1968b*

Kingsdown Camp, Som   *Gray, 1930*

Kingston Buci, Sussex   *Curwen, E. & E. C., & Hawkes 1931*

Knap Hill, Wilts   *Cunnington & Goddard 1934*

Knave, the, Glam   *A. Williams, 1939b*

Knighton Hill, Berks   *S. Piggott, 1927*

Ladle Hill, Hants   *S. Piggott, 1931*

Langenhoe, Essex   *Ward-Perkins, 1938*

Langford Downs, Oxon   *A. Williams, 1947*

Langton, Yorks   *Corder & Kirk, 1932*

Latch Farm, Hants   *C. M. Piggott, 1938a*

Leckhampton, Glos   *Burrow, Paine & Knowles, 1925; and recent unpublished excavation*

Legis Tor, Devon   *Baring-Gould, 1896; Worth, 1943*

Leigh Hill (Cobham), Surrey   *R. A. Smith, 1908, 1909b*

Lesser Garth Cave (Radyr), Glam   *Grimes, 1951*

Lexden, Essex   *Laver, 1927*

Lidbury, Wilts   *Cunnington, M. E. & B. H., 1917*

Linton, Cambs   *Fell, 1953*

Little Horstead Lane, Sussex   *Wilson, 1954*

Little Solisbury, Som   *Dowden, 1957 and 1962; Falconer & Adams, 1935*

Little Woodbury, Wilts   *Bersu, 1940; Brailsford, 1948 and 1949*

Llanfair, Denbigh   *E.L.B. 1862*

Llangenydd (Culver Hole Cave), Gower   *Grimes, 1951, 110*

Llanmelin, Mon   *Nash-Williams, 1933b*

Llwyn-du-Bach, Caerns   *Bersu & Griffiths, 1949*

Llyn, Cerrig-Bach, Anglesey   *C. F. Fox, 1946*

Llyn Fawr, Glam   *Fox & Hyde, 1939; Crawford & Wheeler, 1921*

Loch of Hunter (Whalsey), Shetland   *Hamilton, 1968*

Longbridge Deverill (Cow Down), Wilts   *S. C. Hawkes, 1961*

Long Wittenham, Berks   *Savory, 1937*

Lydney, Glos   *Wheeler, R. E. M. & T. V., 1932*

Maen Castle, Cornwall   *Cotton, 1959*

Maiden Castle (Bickerton), Cheshire   *Varley, 1935 and 1936*

Maiden Castle, Dorset   *Wheeler, 1943*

Mam Tor, Derby   *Jones & Thompson, 1965; Coombs, 1967 and 1971*

Mancombe Down, Wilts   *Fowler, Musty & Taylor, 1965*

Marlborough, Wilts   *C. F. Fox, 1958, 69; Stead, 1971, 279*

Marnhull, Dorset   *A. Williams, 1951a*

Marros Mountain (Pendine), Carm   *Grimes, 1951*

Martin Down Camp, Dorset   *Pitt-Rivers, 1898*

Meare, Som   *Bulleid & Gray, 1948 and 1953; Avery, 1968*

Meon Hill, Hants   *Liddell, 1933 and 1935a*

Merthyr Mawr Warren, Glam   *Grimes, 1951, 126–8*

Midsummer Hill Camp, Heref·   *Stanford, 1966–71*

Milber Down Camp, Devon   *Fox, Radford, Rogers & Shorter, 1952*

Mildenhall, Suffolk   *R. R. Clarke, 1939, 43*

Mill Plain (Deal), Kent   *Material largely unpublished: British Museum*

Milton Loch, Kirkcudbright   *C. M. Piggott, 1955*

Minchinhampton, Glos   *Clifford, 1961, 157*

Minnis Bay, Kent   *Worsfold, 1943*

Minster Ditch, Oxford   *Jope, 1961a*

Moel Hirradug, Flint   *Hemp, 1928*

Moel Trigarn, Pembs   *Baring-Gould, Burnard & Anderson, 1900*

Monifieth (the Laws of), Angus   *Neish & Stuart, 1860*

Mortlake, Middx   *Unpublished: London Museum*

Mount Batten, Devon   *Bates, 1871*

Mount Bures, Essex   *C. R. Smith, 1852*

Mount Farm, Oxon   *Myres, 1937*

Muntham Court, Sussex   *Unpublished excavation*

Mynydd Bychan, Glam   *Savory, 1954 and 1956*

Needwood, Staffs   *Leeds, 1933a*

Ness of Burgi (Samburgh), Shetland   *Hamilton, 1968*

Newark-on-Trent, Notts   *Inv. Arch. G.B. 36 (1958)*

New Barn Down, Sussex   *E. C. Curwen, 1934b*

Newhaven, Sussex, *see* Castle Hill, Newhaven

Newnham Croft, Cambs   *C. F. Fox, 1923, 81*

North Creake, Norfolk   *R. R. Clarke, 1951a*

North Grimston, Yorks   *Mortimer, 1905; Stead, 1965, 111*

North Ferriby, Yorks   *Corder & Pryce, 1938*

Norton Fitzwarren, Som   *Langmaid, 1971*

Oare, Wilts   *M. E. Cunnington, 1909*

Ogbourne Down, Wilts   *C. M. Piggott, 1942*

Ogbury, Wilts   *Crawford & Keiller, 1928*

Oldbury, Kent   *Ward-Perkins, 1944*

Oldbury, Wilts   *H. Cunnington, 1871*

Old Oswestry, Salop   *Varley, 1950b*

Old Sleaford, Lincs   *Unpublished excavation*

Old Warden, Beds   *Dryden, 1845*

Oliver's Camp, Wilts   *M. E. Cunnington, 1908*

Overton Down, Wilts   *P. J. Fowler, 1967*

Owslebury, Hants   *Collis, 1968*

Pagan's Hill, Som   *ApSimon, Rahtz & Harris, 1958*

Parc-y-Meirch, Denbigh   *Sheppard, 1941*

Park Brow, Sussex   *R. A. Smith, 1927; Hawley, 1927*

Parkle Lane, Samersham, Cambs   *Unpublished: Cambridge Museum*

Paulsgrove, Portsmouth, Hants *Unpublished excavation*

Penbryn, Cardigan *E.L.B., 1862*

Pen Dinas (Aberystwyth), Cardigan *Forde, Griffiths & Hogg 1963*

Penigent Gill, Yorks *W.B., 1938*

Pen-y-Corddyn, Denbigh *Gardner, 1910*

Pexton Moor, Yorks *Stead, 1965, 95*

Pilsdon Pen, Dorset *Gelling, 1970 and 1971*

Pimperne Down, Dorset *Harding & Blake, 1963*

Plaitford, Hants *Preston & Hawkes, 1933*

Plumpton Plain, Sussex *Holleyman & Curwen, 1935*

Pokesdown, Hants *Clay, 1927a*

Portfield, Lancs *Longworth, 1968*

Porthmeor, Cornwall *Hirst, 1936*

Portland, Dorset *RCHM, Dorset, II, Part 3, 605–6*

Portsdown Hill, Hants *Bradley, 1969a*

Poston, Heref *Anthony, 1958*

Poundbury, Dorset *Richardson, 1940*

Poxwell, Dorset *Wacher, 1968*

Prae Wood Cemetery (Verulamium), Herts *Stead, 1969*

Preshute Down, Wilts *C. M. Piggott, 1942*

Quarley Hill, Hants *C. F. C. Hawkes, 1939c*

Radley, Berks *Leeds, 1931a and 1935*

Rahoy (Morvern), Argyll *Childe & Thorneycroft, 1938*

Rainsborough Camp, Northants *Avery, Sutton & Banks, 1968*

Rams Hill (Uffington), Berks *Piggott, S. C. & C. M. 1940*

Ravensburgh Castle, Herts *Dyer, 1970*

Read's Cavern, Som *Palmer, 1922 and 1923; Langford, 1924 and 1925*

Rider's Rings, Devon *Worth, 1935*

Rigg's Farm, Yorks *Brewster, 1963, Fig. 81*

Ringstead, Norfolk *R. R. Clarke, 1951b*

Rippon Tor, Dartmoor, Devon *A. Fox, 1955*

Roomer Common, Yorks *Waterman, Kent & Stickland, 1954*

Rotherley Down, Wilts *Pitt-Rivers, 1888*

Rumps, the, (St Minver) Cornwall *Brooks, 1964, 1966 and 1968*

St Catherine's Hill, Hants *Hawkes, Myres & Stevens, 1930*

St David's Head, Pembs *Baring-Gould, Burnard & Enys 1899*

St George's Hill (Weybridge), Surrey *Lowther, 1949*

St Ives, Hunts *Unpublished: St Ives Museum*

St Lawrence, Isle of Wight, Hants *Stead, 1968, Fig. 19*

St Martha's Hill, Surrey *Lowther, 1935*

St Mawgan, *see* Carloggas Cornwall

Salmonsbury, Glos *Dunning, 1931*

Saltdean, Sussex *E. C. Curwen, 1954*

Sandown Park (Esher), Surrey *Burchell & Frere, 1947*

Sandy, Beds *Unpublished: Bedford Museum*

Santon Downham, Suffolk *R. A. Smith, 1909a*

Sawdon, Yorks *Stead, 1965*

Scarborough, *see* Castle Hill, Yorks

Scarborough Park, Yorks *Mortimer, 1895*

Sedgford, Norfolk *Brailsford, 1971*

Selsey, Sussex *White, 1934; E. C. Curwen, 1954, 257–8*

Shapwick Heath, Som *Gray, 1940*

Shearplace Hill, Dorset *Rhatz & ApSimon, 1962*

Sheepen Hill (Colchester), Essex *Hawkes & Smith, 1957, 161*

Sheepslights, Dorset *Calkin, 1949*

Shenbarrow, Glos *Fell, 1962*

Shouldham, Norfolk *Clarke & Hawkes, 1955*

Sidbury, Wilts *Applebaum, 1955*

Silkstead, Hants *Note, JRS, xxviii (1938), 196*

Skelmore Heads, Lancs *Powell, 1963*

Sleaford, Lincs *see* Old Sleaford

Snailwell, Cambs *Lethbridge, 1953*

Snettisham, Norfolk *R. R. Clarke, 1955*

Sompting, Sussex *E. C. Curwen, 1948*

South Cadbury, Som *Alcock, 1968, 1969 and 1970*

Southecote, Berks *Piggott & Seaby, 1937*

South Ferriby, Lincs *S. C. Hawkes, 1964*

South Lodge Camp, Dorset *Pitt-Rivers, 1898*

South Wilson, Bucks *Unpublished: Aylesbury Museum*

Spettisbury, Dorset *Gresham, 1939*

Standlake, Oxon *Akerman & Stone, 1857; Bradford, 1942b; Riley, 1947*

Stanfordbury, Beds *Dryden, 1845*

Stanton Down, Devon *Baring-Gould, 1902*

Stanton Harcourt, Oxon *Grimes, 1944; A. Williams, 1951b*

Stanwick, Yorks *Wheeler, 1954*

Staple Howe, Yorks *Brewster, 1963*

Staxton, Yorks *Brewster, 1963, Fig. 91*

Steyning, Sussex *Burstow, 1958*

Stoke Clump, Sussex *Cunliffe, 1966*

Sudbrook, Mon *Nash-Williams, 1939*

Sutton, Lincs *C. F. Fox, 1958*

Sutton Walls, Heref *Kenyon, 1954*

Swallowcliffe Down, Wilts *Clay, 1925 and 1927b*

Swarling, Kent *Bushe-Fox, 1925*

Tallington, Lincs *W. G. Simpson, 1966*

Tal-y-Llyn, Merioneth *Savory, 1964; Spratling, 1966*

Tattershall Bridge, Lincs *S. Piggott, 1959*

Teignmouth, Devon *A. Fox, 1956*

Theale, Berks *C. M. Piggott, 1938b*

Thorney Down, Wilts *Stone, 1941*

Thorpe, Yorks *Stead, 1965, 68*

Thundersbarrow, Sussex *E. C. Curwen, 1933*

Tigh Talamhanta, *see* Allasdale

Titterstone Clee, Salop *O'Neil, 1934*

Tollard Royal, Wilts *Wainwright, 1968*

Torberry, Sussex *Unpublished excavation*

Torrs, Kirkcudbright   *Atkinson & Piggott, 1955*
Torwoodlee, Selkirk   *S. Piggott, 1951*
Totternhoe, Beds   *C. F. C. Hawkes, 1940c*
Traprain Law, East Lothian   *Feachem, 1958*
Trawsfynydd, Merioneth   *J. R. Allen, 1896*
Trelan Bahow, Cornwall   *H. O'N. Hencken, 1932, 120*
Trelissey, Pembs   *Thomas & Walker, 1959*
Tre'r Ceiri, Caerns   *Hogg, 1962*
Trevone, Cornwall   *Dudley & Jope, 1965*
Trundle, Sussex   *E. C. Curwen, 1929 and 1931*
Twyford Down, Hants   *Stuart & Birbeck, 1936;*
   C. F. C. Hawkes, 1936b
Ulceby, Lincs   *Leeds, 1933a*
Ventnor (Gills Cliff), Isle of Wight   *Benson, 1953*
Verulamium, Herts (*see also* Prae Wood)   *Wheeler,*
   R. E. M. & T. V., 1936
Walesland Rath, Pembs   *Wainwright, 1969*
Wandlebury, Cambs   *Hartley, 1957*
Warborough Hill, Norfolk   *Clarke & Apling, 1935*
Wareham, Norfolk   *Gray, 1933*
Welby, Leics   *Powell, 1950*
Welwyn, Herts   *R. A. Smith, 1912; Brailsford, 1958b*
Welwyn Garden City, Herts   *Stead, 1967*
West Bay, *see* Bridport, Dorset
West Brandon, Co. Durham   *Jobey, 1962b*
West Clandon, Surrey   *Frere, 1946*
Wester Ord, Wester Ross   *Coles, 1962a, 129–30*
Westhall, Suffolk   *R. R. Clarke, 1939*
West Harling, Norfolk   *Clark & Fell, 1953; R. R.*
   Clarke, 1960

Weston, Som   *Craw, 1924, 147–9*
Weston Wood (Albury), Surrey   *Harding, 1964*
West Plean, Stirling   *Steer, 1958*
Wheathampstead, Herts   *Wheeler, R. E. M. &*
   T. V., 1936
Whitcombe, Dorset   *Unpublished: Dorset County*
   Museum
White Hill, Peebles   *Feachem, 1966*
Wilbury, Herts   *Applebaum, 1951*
Winchester, Hants   *Cunliffe, 1964; Biddle, 1966,*
   1967 and 1968
Winklebury, Hants   *C. M. Piggott, 1940*
Winterbourne Dauntsey, Wilts   *Stone, 1935*
Wisbech, Cambs   *Jope, 1961a*
Witham, Lincs   *Jope, 1971*
Wokingham, Berks   *Unpublished: Ashmolean Museum*
Woodcuts, Dorset   *Pitt-Rivers, 1887*
Wookey Hole, Som   *Balch, 1914 and 1928*
Woolbury, Hants   *Crawford & Keiller, 1928*
Worlebury, Som   *Dymond, 1902*
Worth, Kent   *Klein, 1928; C. F. C. Hawkes, 1940a*
Worthy Down, Hants   *Dunning, Hooley & Tildesley,*
   1929
Wrekin, Salop   *Kenyon, 1943*
Wyke Regis, Dorset   *Bailey, 1963*
Wytham, Berks   *Bradford, 1942a*
Yarnbury, Wilts   *M. E. Cunnington, 1933*
Yarton, Oxon   *Bradford, 1942a*
Yevering Bell, Northumberland   *Jobey, 1966a*

Abbreviations

Antiq. Journ.   Antiquaries Journal
Arch. Ael.⁴   Archaeologia Aeliana (fourth series)
Arch. Camb.   Archaeologia Cambrensis
Arch. Cant.   Archaeologia Cantiana
Arch. Journ.   Archaeological Journal
BAJ   Berkshire Archaeological Journal
B and H Arch.   Brighton and Hove Archaeologist
BBCS   Bulletin of the Board of Celtic Studies
BMQ   British Museum Quarterly
Cornish Arch.   Cornish Archaeology
Current Arch.   Current Archaeology
CW²   Cumberland and Westmorland Transactions
     (second series)
DAJ   Derbyshire Archaeological Journal
DES   Discovery and Excavation in Scotland
DMC   Devizes Museum Catalogue (see Cunnington
     & Goddard, 1934)
E. Herts. Arch. Soc. Trans.   East Hertfordshire
     Archaeological Society's Transactions
Glasgow Arch. Journ.   Glasgow Archaeological Journal
Inv. Arch. G.B.   Inventaria Archaeologica (Great
     Britain)
Jahrb. Röm.-Germ. Zentralmus. Mainz   Jahrbuch des
     Römisch-Germanischen Zentralmuseums Mainz
JBAA   Journal of the British Archaeological Association
JHS   Journal of Hellenic Studies
JRIC   Journal of the Royal Institution of Cornwall
JRS   Journal of Roman Studies
LAAA   Annals of Archaeology and Anthropology,
     Liverpool
Lincs AAS   Lincolnshire Architectural and
     Archaeological Society
NA   Norfolk Archaeology
Oxon.   Oxoniensia
PBUSS   Proceedings of the Bristol University
     Spelaeological Society
PCAS   Proceedings of the Cambridge Antiquarian
     Society
P. Cott. NHFC   Proceedings of the Cotteswold Natural
     History and Field Club
PDAES   Proceedings of the Devonshire Archaeological

Exploration Society
PDNHAS   Proceedings of the Dorset Natural History
     Archaeological Society
PHFC   Proceedings of the Hampshire Field Club and
     Archaeological Society
Phil. Trans. Royal Soc.   Philiological Transactions of
     the Royal Society
PIOWNHAS   Proceedings of the Isle of Wight
     Natural History and Archaeological Society
PPS   Proceedings of the Prehistoric Society
PPSEA   Proceedings of the Prehistoric Society of East
     Anglia
PSANHS   Proceedings of the Somerset Archaeological
     and Natural History Society
PSAS   Proceedings of the Society of Antiquaries of
     Scotland
Pubs. Cambs. Arch. Soc.   Publications of the
     Cambridge Archaeological Society
PWCFC   Proceedings of the West Cornwall Field
     Club
RCHM   Royal Commission on Historical
     Monuments
RCHM(S)   Royal Commission on Historical
     Monuments (Scotland)
Rec. of Bucks   Records of Buckinghamshire
Rep. Oxon. Arch. Soc.   Reports of the Oxfordshire
     Archaeological Society
SAC   Sussex Archaeological Collections
Scottish Arch. Forum   Scottish Archaeological Forum
Sy. AC   Surrey Archaeological Collections
TBAS   Transactions of the Birmingham
     Archaeological Society
TBGAS   Transactions of the Bristol and Gloucestershire
     Archaeological Society
TDA   Transactions of the Devon Association
TERAS   Transactions of the East Riding
     Archaeological Society
THSLC   Transactions of the Historic Society of
     Lancashire and Cheshire
TLAS   Transactions of the Leicestershire
     Archaeological Society

TNDFC   *Transactions of the Newbury and District*
  Field Club
Trans. S. Staffs AHS   *Transactions of the South*
  Staffordshire Archaeological and Historical Society
TWNFC   *Transactions of the Woolhope Naturalists'*

  Field Club
VCH   *Victoria County Histories*
WAM   *Wiltshire Archaeological Magazine*
YAJ   *Yorkshire Archaeological Journal*

Bibliography

The date quoted after the author's name is the year in which the paper was published. In some cases this does not correspond to the year for which the journal was issued. Volume numbers are all quoted in arabic figures.

Abercromby, J. (1912) *The Bronze Age Pottery of Great Britain and Ireland*, 2 vols (Oxford).

Akerman, J. Y., & Stone, S. (1857) 'An account of the investigation of some remarkable circular trenches and the discovery of an Ancient British cemetery at Standlake, Oxon'. *Archaeologia*, 37 (1857), 363–70.

Alcock, L. (1961) 'Castell Odo: an embanked settlement on Mynydd Ystum, near Aberdaron, Caernarvonshire'. *Arch. Camb.*, 109 (1960), 78–135.

(1965) 'Hillforts in Wales and the Marches'. *Antiquity*, 39 (1965), 184–95.

(1968) 'Excavations at South Cadbury Castle, 1967'. *Antiq. Journ.*, 48 (1968), 6–17.

(1969) 'Excavations at South Cadbury Castle, 1968'. *Antiq. Journ.*, 49 (1969), 30–40.

(1970) 'Excavations at South Cadbury Castle, 1969'. *Antiq. Journ.*, 50 (1970), 14–25.

Allen, D. F. (1944) 'The Belgic dynasties of Britain and their coins'. *Archaeologia*, 90 (1944), 1–46.

(1958) 'Belgic coins as illustrations of life in the Late Pre-Roman Iron Age of Britain'. *PPS*, 24 (1958), 43–63.

(1961a) 'The origins of coinage in Britain: a reappraisal'. In *Problems of the Iron Age in Southern Britain*, ed. Frere, S. S. (London), 97–308.

(1961b) 'A study of the Dobunnic coinage'. In *Bagendon – a Belgic Oppidum*, Clifford, E. M. (Cambridge), 75–149.

(1962) 'Celtic coins'. Ordnance Survey *Map of Southern Britain in the Iron Age*, 19–32.

(1963) *Sylloge of Coins of the British Isles: the Coins of the Coritani* (Oxford).

(1968a) 'Iron currency bars in Britain'. *PPS*, 33 (1967), 307–35.

(1968b) 'The chronology of Durotrigian coinage'. In Richmond, I. A., *Hod Hill* (London), vol. 2, 45–55.

(1970) 'The coins of the Iceni'. *Britannia*, 1 (1970), 1–33.

(1971) 'British potin coins: a review'. In *The Iron Age and its Hill-forts*, ed. Jesson, M., & Hill, D. (Southampton), 127–54.

Allen, J. R. (1896) 'The Trawsfynydd tankard'. *Arch. Camb.*, 13 (1896), 212–32.

Anthony, I. (1958) *The Iron Age Camp at Poston, Herefordshire* (the Woolhope Club).

Applebaum, E. S. (1951) 'Excavations at Wilbury Hill, an Iron Age hillfort near Letchworth, Hertfordshire 1933'. *Arch. Journ.*, 106 (1949), 12–45.

(1955) 'The agriculture of the British Early Iron Age as exemplified at Figheldean Down, Wiltshire'. *PPS*, 20 (1954), 103–14.

ApSimon, A. M. (1958) 'Notes on the Hammersmith type of La Tène I brooch'. *PBUSS*, 8 (1958), 164–8.

ApSimon, A. M., Rahtz, P. A., & Harris, L. G. (1958) 'The Iron Age A ditch and pottery at Pagan's Hill, Chew Stoke'. *PBUSS*, 8 (1958), 97–105.

Atkinson, R. J. C., & Piggott, S. (1955) 'The Torrs chamfrein'. *Archaeologia*, 96 (1955), 197–235.

Avery, M. (1968) 'Excavations at Meare East 1966'. *PSANHS*, 112 (1968), 21–39.

Avery, M., Sutton, J. E. G., & Banks, J. W. (1967) 'Rainsborough, Northants, England: excavations 1961–5'. *PPS*, 33 (1967), 207–306.

Bagshawe, T. W. (1928) 'Early Iron Age objects from Harpenden'. *Antiq. Journ.*, 8 (1928), 520–2.

Bailey, C. J. (1963) 'An Early Iron Age B hearth

site indicating salt working on the north shore of the Fleet at Wyke Regis'. *PDNHAS*, 84 (1962), 132–6.

Baker, F. T. (1960) 'The Iron Age salt industry in Lincolnshire'. *Lincs AAS*, 8 (1959–60), 26–34.

Balch, H. E. (1914) *Wookey Hole, its Caves and Cave Dwellers* (Oxford).

(1928) 'Excavations at Wookey Hole and other Mendip caves 1926–7'. *Antiq. Journ.*, 8 (1928), 193–209.

Baring-Gould, S. (1896) 'Third report of the Dartmoor Exploration Committee'. *TDA*, 28 (1896), 174–99.

(1902) (ed.) 'Eighth report of the Dartmoor Exploration Committee'. *TDA*, 34 (1902), 160–5.

Baring-Gould, S., Burnard, R., & Enys, J. D. (1899) 'Exploration of the stone camp on St David's Head'. *Arch. Camb.*, 16 (1899), 105–31.

Baring-Gould, S., Burnard, R., & Anderson, I. K. (1900) 'Exploration of Moel Trigarn'. *Arch. Camb.*, 17 (1900), 189–211.

Bates, C. S. (1871) 'A British cemetery near Plymouth'. *Archaeologia*, 40 (1871), 500.

Bellows, J. (1881) 'On some bronze and other articles found near Birdlip'. *TBGAS*, 5 (1880–1), 137–41.

Benson, G. C. (1953) 'Belgic occupation site at Gill's Cliff, Ventnor'. *PIOWNHAS*, 4 (1953), 303–11.

Benton, S. (1931) 'The excavation of the Sculptor's Cave, Covesea, Morayshire'. *PSAS*, 65 (1930–1), 177–216.

Bersu, G. (1940) 'Excavations at Little Woodbury, part I'. *PPS*, 6 (1940), 30–111.

Bersu, G., & Griffiths, W. E. (1949) 'Concentric circles at Llwyn-du-Bach, Peny-Groes, Caernarvonshire'. *Arch. Camb.*, 100 (1949), 173–206.

Biddle, M. (1966) 'Excavations at Winchester, 1965'. *Antiq. Journ.*, 46 (1966), 308–32.

(1967) 'Excavations at Winchester, 1966'. *Antiq. Journ.*, 47 (1967), 251–79.

(1968) 'Excavations at Winchester, 1967'. *Antiq. Journ.*, 48 (1968), 250–84.

Birchall, A. (1963) 'The Belgic problem: Aylesford revisited'. *BMQ*, 28 (1963), 21–9.

(1965) 'The Aylesford-Swarling culture: the problem of the Belgae reconsidered'. *PPS*, 31 (1965), 241–367.

Boon, G. C. (1954) 'A Greek vase from the Thames'. *JHS*, 74 (1954), 198.

(1969) 'Belgic and Roman Silchester: the excavations of 1954–8 with an excursus on the early history of Calleva'. *Archaeologia*, 102 (1969), 1–82.

Bowen, H. C. (1961) *Ancient Fields* (British Association for the Advancement of Science: undated).

(1969) 'The Celtic background'. In *The Roman Villa in Britain*, ed. Rivet, A. L. F. (London).

Bowen, H. C., & Fowler, P. J. (1966) 'Romano-British rural settlement in Dorset and Wiltshire'. In *Rural Settlement in Roman Britain*, ed. Thomas, A. C. (London), 43–67.

Boyden, J. R. (1957) 'Excavations at Hammer Wood, Iping, 1957'. *SAC*, 96 (1957), 149–63.

Bradford, J. S. P. (1940) 'The excavation of Cherbury Camp, 1939'. *Oxon.*, 5 (1940), 13–20.

(1942a) 'An Early Iron Age site at Allen's Pit, Dorchester'. *Oxon.*, 7 (1942), 36–60.

(1942b) 'An Early Iron Age settlement at Standlake, Oxon.' *Antiq. Journ.*, 22 (1942), 202–14.

(1942c) 'An Early Iron Age site at Blewburton Hill, Berks.' *BAJ*, 46 (1942), 97–104.

Bradford, J. S. P., & Goodchild, R. G. (1939) 'Excavations at Frilford, Berks., 1937–8'. *Oxon.*, 4 (1939), 1–70.

Bradley, R. (1969a) 'Excavations on Portsdown Hill, 1963–5'. *PHFC*, 24 (1967), 42–58.

(1969b) 'The South Oxfordshire Grim's Ditch and its significance'. *Oxon.*, 33 (1969), 1–13.

(1971) 'A field survey of the Chichester entrenchments'. In Cunliffe, B., *Excavations at Fishbourne* (London), vol. 1, 17–36.

Brailsford, J. W. (1948) 'Excavations at Little Woodbury, part II'. *PPS*, 14 (1948), 1–23.

(1949) 'Excavations at Little Woodbury, parts IV and V'. *PPS*, 15 (1949), 156–68.

(1958a) 'Early Iron Age "C" in Wessex'. *PPS*, 24 (1958), 101–19.

(1958b) 'A corrected restoration of the Belgic iron frame from Welwyn'. *Antiq. Journ.*, 38 (1958), 89–90.

(1971) 'The Sedgeford torc'. In *Prehistoric and Roman Studies*, ed. Sieveking, G. de G. (London), 16–19.

Brewster, T. C. M. (1963) *The Excavation of Staple Howe* (Scarborough).

(1971) 'The Garston Slack chariot burial, east Yorkshire'. *Antiquity*, 45 (1971), 289–2.

Briard, J. (1957) 'Le bronze de faciès Atlantique en Amorique'. *Congrès Préhistorique de France*, 15 (1956), 313–27.

(1965) *Les Dépôts bretons et l'âge du bronze atlantique* (Rennes).

Britton, D. (1960) 'The Isleham hoard, Cambridgeshire'. *Antiquity*, 34 (1960), 279–82.

(1971) 'The Heathery Burn cave revisited'. In *Prehistoric and Roman Studies*, ed. Sieveking, G. de G. (London), 20–37.

Brooks, R. T. (1964) 'The Rumps, St Minver: interim report on the 1963 excavations'.

Cornish Arch., 3 (1964), 26–33.

(1966) 'The Rumps: second interim report on the 1965 season'. *Cornish Arch.*, 5 (1966), 4–10.

(1968) 'The Rumps St Minver: third interim report, 1967 season'. *Cornish Arch.*, 7 (1968), 38–9.

Bugden, W. (1922) 'Hallstatt pottery from Eastbourne'. *Antiq. Journ.*, 2 (1922), 354–60.

Bulleid, A., & Gray, H. St G. (1911) *The Glastonbury Lake Village*, vol. 1 (Glastonbury Antiquarian Society).

(1917) *The Glastonbury Lake Village*, vol. 2 (Glastonbury Antiquarian Society).

(1948) *The Meare Lake Village*, vol 1 (Taunton).

(1953) *The Meare Lake Village*, vol. 2 (Taunton).

Burchell, J. P. T., & Frere, S. S. (1947) 'The occupation at Sandown Park, Esher, during the Stone Age, the Early Iron Age and the Anglo-Saxon period'. *Antiq. Journ.*, 27 (1947), 24–46.

Burgess, C. B. (1969a) 'Chronology and terminology in the British Bronze Age'. *Antiq. Journ.*, 49 (1969), 22–9.

(1969b) 'The Later Bronze Age in the British Isles and north-western France'. *Arch. Journ.*, 125 (1968), 1–45.

Burrow, E. J., Paine, A. E. W., Knowles, W. H., & Gray, J. W. (1925) 'Excavations on Leckhampton Hill, Cheltenham, during the summer of 1925'. *TBGAS*, 47 (1925), 81–112.

Burstow, G. P. (1958) 'A Late Bronze Age urnfield on Steyning Round Hill, Sussex'. *PPS*, 24 (1958), 158–64.

Burstow, G. P. & Holleyman, G. A. (1957) 'Late Bronze Age settlement on Itford Hill, Sussex'. *PPS*, 23 (1957), 167–212.

Bushe-Fox, J. P. (1915) *Excavations at Hengistbury Head, Hampshire, in 1911–12* (Oxford).

(1925) *Excavation of the Late-Celtic Urn Field at Swarling, Kent* (Oxford).

Calder, C. T. (1939) 'Excavations of Iron Age dwellings on the Calf of Eday in Orkney'. *PSAS*, 73 (1938–9), 167–85.

Calkin, J. B. (1949) 'The Isle of Purbeck in the Iron Age'. *PDNHAS*, 70 (1949), 29–59.

(1953) 'Kimmeridge coal-money'. *PDNHAS*, 75 (1953), 45–71.

(1964) 'The Bournemouth area in the Middle and Late Bronze Age, with the "Deverel-Rimbury" problem reconsidered'. *Arch. Journ.*, 119 (1962), 1–65.

Case, H. J. (1949) 'The Standlake Iron Age sword'. *Rep. Oxon. Arch. Soc.*, 87 (1949), 7–8.

Case, H. J., Bayne, N., Steele, S., Avery, G., & Sutermeister, H. (1966) 'Excavations at City Farm, Hanborough, Oxon.' *Oxon.*, 29–30 (1964/5), 1–88.

Chadwick, S., & Thompson, M. W. (1956) 'Note on an Iron Age habitation site near Battlesbury Camp, Warminster'. *WAM*, 56 (1956), 262–4.

Chatwin, P. B. (1930) 'Excavations on Corley Camp, near Coventry'. *TBAS*, 52 (1930), 282–7.

Childe, V. G. (1933) 'Excavations at Castle Law Fort, Midlothian'. *PSAS*, 67 (1932–3), 362–89.

(1935a) *The Prehistory of Scotland* (London).

(1935b) 'Excavation of the vitrified fort of Finavon, Angus'. *PSAS*, 69 (1934–5), 49–80.

(1941) 'The defences of Kaimes hillfort, Midlothian'. *PSAS*, 75 (1940–1), 43–54.

(1946) *Scotland Before the Scots* (London).

Childe, V. G., & Forde, C. D. (1932) 'Excavations in two Iron Age forts at Earn's Heugh, near Coldingham'. *PSAS*, 66 (1931–2), 152–83.

Childe, V. G., & Thorneycroft, W. (1938) 'The vitrified fort at Rahoy, Morvern, Argyll'. *PSAS*, 72 (1937–8), 23–43.

Christison, D. (1898) *Early Fortifications in Scotland* (Edinburgh).

(1900) 'The forts, camps and other fieldworks of Perth, Forfar and Kincardine'. *PSAS*, 34 (1899–1900), 74–6.

Christison, D., & Anderson, J. (1899) 'On the recently excavated fort on Castle Law, Abernethy, Perthshire'. *PSAS*, 33 (1898–9), 13–33.

Clark, J. G. D. (1936) 'The timber monument at Arminghall and its affinities'. *PPS*, 2 (1936), 16–51.

(1952) *Prehistoric Europe, the Economic Basis* (Cambridge).

Clark, J. G. D., & Fell, C. I. (1953) 'An Early Iron Age site at Micklemoor Hill, West Harling, Norfolk, and its pottery'. *PPS*, 19 (1953), 1–40.

Clarke, D. V. (1970) 'Bone dice and the Scottish Iron Age'. *PPS*, 36 (1970), 214–32.

Clarke, R. R. (1939) 'The Iron Age in Norfolk and Suffolk'. *Arch. Journ.*, 96 (1939), 1–113.

(1951a) 'A Celtic torc-terminal from North Creake, Norfolk'. *Arch. Journ.*, 106 (1949), 59–61.

(1951b) 'A hoard of metalwork of the Early Iron Age from Ringstead, Norfolk'. *PPS*, 17 (1951), 214–25.

(1955) 'The Early Iron Age treasure from Snettisham, Norfolk'. *PPS*, 20 (1954), 27–86.

(1960) *East Anglia* (London).

Clarke, R. R., & Apling, H. (1935) 'An Iron Age tumulus on Warborough Hill, Stiffkey, Norfolk'. *NA*, 25 (1935), 408–23.

Clarke, R. R., & Hawkes, C. F. C. (1955) 'An iron anthropoid sword from Shouldam, Norfolk, with related continental and British weapons'.

PPS, 21 (1955), 198–227.

Clay, R. C. C. (1924) 'An Early Iron Age site on Fifield Bavant Down'. *WAM*, 42 (1924), 457–96.

(1925) 'An inhabited site of La Tène I date on Swallowcliffe Down'. *WAM*, 43 (1925), 59–93.

(1927a) 'A Late Bronze Age urnfield at Pokesdown, Hants'. *Antiq. Journ.*, 7 (1927), 465–84.

(1927b) 'Supplementary report on the Early Iron Age village on Swallowcliffe Down'. *WAM*, 46 (1927), 540–7.

Clifford, E. M. (1934) 'An Early Iron Age site at Barnwood, Glos.' *TBGAS*, 56 (1934), 227–30.

(1961) *Bagendon – a Belgic Oppidum* (Cambridge).

Cocks, A. H. (1909) 'Prehistoric pit-dwellers at Ellesborough'. *Rec. of Bucks*, 9 (1909), 349–61.

Coles, J. M. (1959) 'Scottish swan's neck sunflower pins'. *PSAS*, 92 (1958–9), 1–9.

(1962a) 'Scottish Late Bronze Age metalwork: typology, distributions and chronology'. *PSAS*, 93 (1959–60), 16–134.

(1962b) 'European Bronze Age shields'. *PPS*, 28 (1962), 156–90.

Collins, A. E. P. (1947) 'Excavations on Blewburton Hill, 1947'. *BAJ*, 50 (1947), 4–29.

(1953) 'Excavations on Blewburton Hill, 1948 and 1949'. *BAJ*, 53 (1953), 21–64.

Collins, A. E. P., & F. J. (1959) 'Excavations on Blewburton Hill, 1953'. *BAJ*, 57 (1959), 52–73.

Collis, J. R. (1968) 'Excavations at Owslebury, Hants'. *Antiq. Journ.*, 48 (1968), 18–31.

(1971a) 'Functional and theoretical interpretations of British coinage'. *World Archaeology*, 3, 1 (1971), 71–84.

(1971b) 'Markets and money'. In *The Iron Age and its Hill-forts*, ed. Jesson, M., & Hill, D. (Southampton), 97–104.

Coombs, D. (1967) 'Mam Tor'. *DAJ*, 87 (1967), 158–9.

(1971) 'Mam Tor, a Bronze Age hillfort?' *Current Arch.*, 27 (July 1971), 100–2.

Corcoran, J. X. W. P. (1965) 'A bronze bucket in the Hunterian Museum, University of Glasgow'. *Antiq. Journ.*, 45 (1965), 12–17.

Corder, P., & Kirk, J. L. (1932) 'A Roman villa at Langton, near Malton, E. Yorkshire'. *Roman Malton and District*, report no. 4 (1932).

Corder, P., & Pryce, T. D. (1938) 'Belgic and other early pottery found at North Ferriby, Yorkshire'. *Antiq. Journ.*, 18 (1938), 262–77.

Cotton, M. A. (1955) 'British camps with timber-laced ramparts'. *Arch. Journ.*, 111 (1954), 26–105.

(1959) 'Cornish cliff castles'. *PWCFC*, 2 (1959), 113–21.

(1961a) 'The pre-Belgic Iron Age cultures of Gloucestershire'. In *Bagendon – a Belgic Oppidum*, Clifford, E. M. (Cambridge), 22–42.

(1961b) 'Observations on the classification of hillforts in southern England'. In *Problems of the Iron Age in Southern Britain*, ed. Frere, S. S. (London), 61–8.

(1962) 'Berkshire hillforts'. *BAJ*, 60 (1962), 30–52.

Cotton, M. A., & Frere, S. S. (1968) 'Ivinghoe Beacon, excavations 1963–5'. *Rec. of Bucks*, 18 (1968), 187–260.

Cowen, J. D. (1967) 'The Hallstatt sword of bronze: on the continent and in Britain'. *PPS*, 33 (1967), 377–444.

Cra'ster, M. D. (1961) 'The Aldwick Iron Age settlement, Barley, Hertfordshire'. *PCAS*, 54 (1961), 22–46.

(1969) 'New Addenbrooke's Iron Age site, Long Road, Cambridge'. *PCAS*, 62 (1969), 21–8.

Craw, J. H. (1924) 'On two bronze spoons from an Early Iron Age grave near Burnmouth, Berwickshire'. *PSAS*, 63 (1923–4), 143–160.

Crawford, O. G. S. (1921) 'The ancient settlements at Harlyn Bay'. *Antiq. Journ.*, 1 (1921), 283–99.

(1922) 'A prehistoric invasion of England'. *Antiq. Journ.*, 2 (1922), 27–35.

Crawford, O. G. S., & Keiller, A. (1928) *Wessex from the Air* (Oxford).

Crawford, O. G. S., & Wheeler, R. E. M. (1921) 'The Llynfawr and other hoards of the Bronze Age'. *Archaeologia*, 71 (1921), 133–40.

Cunliffe, B. (1961) 'Report on a Belgic and Roman site at the Causeway, Horndean, 1959'. *PHFC*, 22 (1961), 25–9.

(1964) *Winchester Excavations, 1949–1960*, vol. 1 (Winchester).

(1966) 'Stoke Clump, Hollingbury, and the Early pre-Roman Iron Age in Sussex'. *SAC*, 104 (1966), 109–20.

(1968a) 'Early pre-Roman Iron Age communities in eastern England'. *Antiq. Journ.*, 48 (1968), 175–91.

(1968b) 'Excavations at Eldon's Seat, Encombe, Dorset'. *PPS*, 34 (1968), 191–237.

(1970) 'A Bronze Age settlement at Chalton, Hants. (site 78)'. *Antiq. Journ.*, 50 (1970), 1–13.

(1971a) *Excavations at Fishbourne*: Vol. 1, *The Site* (London).

(1971b) 'Aspects of hill-forts and their cultural environments'. In *The Iron Age and its Hill-forts*, ed. Jesson, M., & Hill, D. (Southampton), 53–70.

Cunnington, E. (1884) 'On a hoard of bronze, iron and other objects found in Bulbury Camp, Dorset'. *Archaeologia*, 48 (1884), 115–20.

Cunnington, H. (1871) 'Oldbury Camp, Wilts'. *WAM*, 28 (1871), 277.

Cunnington, M. E. (1908) 'Oliver's Camp, Devizes'. *WAM*, 35 (1908), 408–44.

(1909) 'Notes of a Late Celtic rubbish heap near Oare'. *WAM*, 36 (1909), 125–39.

(1911) 'Knapp Hill Camp'. *WAM*, 37 (1911), 42–65.

(1923) *The Early Iron Age Inhabited Site at All Cannings Cross* (Devizes).

(1925) 'Figsbury Rings: an account of excavations in 1924'. *WAM*, 43 (1925), 48–58.

(1932a) 'Chisbury Camp'. *WAM*, 46 (1932), 4–7.

(1932b) 'The demolition of Chisenbury Trendle'. *WAM*, 46 (1932), 1–3.

(1932c) 'Was there a second Belgic invasion represented by bead-rim pottery?' *Antiq. Journ.*, 12 (1932), 27–34.

(1933) 'Excavations at Yarnbury Castle Camp. 1932'. *WAM*, 46 (1933), 198–213.

Cunnington, M. E., & B. H. (1913) 'Casterley Camp excavations'. *WAM*, 38 (1913), 53–105.

(1917) 'Lidbury Camp'. *WAM*, 40 (1917), 12–36.

Cunnington, M. E., & Goddard, E. H. (1934) *The Devizes Museum Catalogue*, Part II (Devizes).

Curle, A. O. (1910) 'Notice of some excavation on the fort occupying the summit of Bonchester Hill, parish of Hobkirk, Roxburghshire'. *PSAS*, 44 (1909–10), 225–36.

(1927) 'The development and antiquity of the Scottish brochs'. *Antiquity*, 1 (1927), 290–8.

Curwen, E. (1930) 'Lynchet burials near Lewes'. *SAC*, 71 (1930), 254–7.

Curwen, E., & E. C. (1927) 'Excavations in the Caburn, near Lewes'. *SAC*, 68 (1927), 1–56.

Curwen, E. & E. C., & Hawkes, C. F. C. (1931) 'Prehistoric remains from Kingston Buci'. *SAC*, 72 (1931), 185–217.

Curwen, E. C. (1929) 'Excavations in the Trundle, Goodwood, 1928'. *SAC*, 70 (1929), 33–85.

(1931) 'Excavations in the Trundle'. *SAC*, 72 (1931), 100–150.

(1932) 'Excavations at Hollingbury Camp, Sussex'. *Antiq. Journ.*, 12 (1932), 1–16.

(1933) 'Excavations on Thundersbarrow Hill, Sussex'. *Antiq. Journ.*, 13 (1933), 109–33.

(1934a) 'A prehistoric site in Kingley Vale, near Chichester'. *SAC*, (1934), 209–16.

(1934b) 'A Late Bronze Age farm and a Neolithic pit-dwelling on New Barn Down, Clapham, nr. Worthing'. *SAC*, 75 (1934), 137–70.

(1939) 'The Iron Age in Sussex'. *SAC*, 80 (1939), 214–16.

(1948) 'A bronze cauldron from Sompting, Sussex'. *Antiq. Journ.*, 28 (1948), 157–63.

(1954) *The Archaeology of Sussex*, 2nd edition (London).

Curwen, E. C., & Williamson, R. P. R. (1931) 'The date of Cissbury Camp'. *Antiq. Journ.* 11 (1931), 14–36.

Davies, H. (1936) 'The shale industries at Kimmeridge, Dorset'. *Arch. Journ.*, 93 (1936), 200–19.

Davies, J. A., & Phillips, C. W. (1929) 'The Percy Sladen Memorial Fund excavation at Bury Hill Camp, Winterbourne Down, Gloucestershire, 1926'. *PBUSS*, 3 (1929), 8–24.

Dehn, W. (1961) 'Zangentore an Spälkeltischen Oppida'. *Pamatky Archaeologickse*, 52, 2 (1961), 390.

Dehn, W., & Frey, O. H. (1962) 'Die absolute Chronologie der Hallstatt- und Frühlatenezeit Mitteleuropas auf Grund des Südimports'. *Atti VI° Cong. Int. Scienze Preist. e Protoist*, 1 (*Relazioni generali*), (1962), 197–208.

Dowden, W. A. (1957) 'Little Solisbury Hill Camp'. *PBUSS*, 8 (1957), 18–29.

(1962) 'Little Solisbury Hill Camp'. *PBUSS*, 9 (1962), 177–82.

Drew, C. D. (1935) 'A Late Bronze Age hoard from Lulworth, Dorset'. *Antiq. Journ.*, 15 (1935), 449–51.

Dryden, H. (1845) 'Roman and Romano-British remains at and near Shefford, Co. Beds.' *Pubs. Cambs Arch. Soc.*, 1 (1840–6), no. 8, 184.

Dudley, D. (1957) 'An excavation at Bodrifty, Mulfa Hill, near Penzance, Cornwall'. *Arch. Journ.*, 113 (1956), 1–32.

Dudley, D., & Jope, E. M. (1965) 'An Iron Age cist-burial with two brooches from Trevone, north Cornwall'. *Cornish Arch.*, 4 (1965), 18–23.

Dunning, G. C. (1931) 'Salmonsbury Camp, Gloucestershire'. *Antiquity*, 5 (1931), 489–91.

(1934) 'The swan's-neck and ring headed pin of the Early Iron Age in Britain'. *Arch. Journ.*, 91 (1934), 269–95.

Dunning, G. C., Hooley, W., & Tildesley, M. L. (1929) 'Excavation of an Early Iron Age village on Worthy Down, Winchester'. *PHFC*, 10 (1929), 178–92.

Dyer, J. F. (1961) 'Dray's Ditches, Bedfordshire, and Early Iron Age territorial boundaries in the eastern Chilterns'. *Antiq. Journ.*, 42 (1961), 44–62.

(1970) 'Ravensburgh Castle Excavations 1970'. (Duplicated: Putteridge Bury College of Education, Luton).

Dymond, C. W. (1902) *Worlebury, an Ancient Stronghold in the County of Somerset* (Bristol).

E. L. B. (1862) 'Bronze articles supposed to be spoons'. *Arch. Camb.*, 8 (1862), 208–19.

Ellis, F. (1900) 'An ancient bronze figure from Aust Cliff, Gloucestershire'. *TBGAS*, 23 (1900), 323–5.

Ellison, A., & Drewett, P. (1971) 'Pits and post-holes in the British Early Iron Age: some alternative explanations'. *PPS*, 37 (1971), 183–94.

Erith, F. H., & Longworth, I. (1960) 'A Bronze Age urnfield on Vinces Farm, Ardleigh, Essex'. *PPS*, 26 (1960), 178–92.

Evans, A. J. (1890) 'On a Late Celtic urnfield at Aylesford, Kent'. *Archaeologia*, 52 (1890), 369–74.

Falconer, J. P. E., & Adams, S. B. (1935) 'Recent finds at Solisbury Hill Camp, near Bath'. *PBUSS*, 4 (1935), 133–222.

Farrar, R. A. H. (1954) 'A Celtic burial with mirror-handle at West Bay near Bridport'. *PDNHAS*, 76 (1954), 90–4.

(1963) 'Note on prehistoric and Roman salt industry'. *PDNHAS*, 84 (1962), 137–44.

Feachem, R. W. (1958) 'The fortifications on Traprain Law'. *PSAS*, 89 (1955–6), 284–9.

(1961) 'Glenachan Rig Homestead, Cardon, Peeblesshire. *PSAS*, 92 (1958–9), 15–24.

(1962) 'The palisaded settlements at Harehope, Peeblesshire: excavations, 1960'. *PSAS*, 93 (1959–60), 174–91.

(1963) 'Unenclosed platform settlements'. *PSAS*, 94 (1960–1), 79–85.

(1966) 'The hill-forts of northern Britain'. In *The Iron Age of Northern Britain*, ed. Rivet, A. L. F. (Edinburgh), 59–88.

Fell, C. I. (1937) 'The Hunsbury hill-fort, Northants: a new survey of the material'. *Arch. Journ.*, 93 (1937), 57–100.

(1953) 'An Early Iron Age settlement at Linton, Cambridgeshire'. *PCAS*, 46 (1953), 31.

(1962) 'Shenbarrow Hill Camp, Stanton, Gloucestershire'. *TBGAS*, 80 (1962), 16–41.

Forde, Daryll C., Griffiths, W. E., Hogg, A. H. A., & Houlder, C. H. (1963) 'Excavations at Pen Dinas, Aberystwyth'. *Arch. Camb.*, 112 (1963), 125–53.

Forde-Johnston, J. (1964) 'Earl's Hill, Pontesbury, and related hill forts in England and Wales'. *Arch. Journ.* 119 (1962), 66–91.

Fowler, M. J. (1954) 'The typology of the brooches of the Iron Age in Wessex'. *Arch. Journ.*, 110 (1954), 88–105.

Fowler, P. J. (1967) 'The archaeology of Fyfield and Overton Downs, Wiltshire'. *WAM*, 62 (1967), 16–33.

(1970) 'Fieldwork and excavation in the Butcombe area, north Somerset'. *PBUSS*, 12, 2 (1970), 169–94.

Fowler, P. J., Musty, J. W. G., & Taylor, C. C. (1965) 'Some earthwork enclosures in Wiltshire'. *WAM*, 60 (1965), 52–74.

Fox, A. (1953) 'Hill-slope forts and related earthworks in south-west England and south Wales'. *Arch. Journ.*, 109 (1952), 1–22.

(1955) 'Celtic fields and farms on Dartmoor, in the light of recent excavations at Kestor'. *PPS*, 20 (1954), 87–102.

(1956) 'Teignmouth'. *TDA*, 88 (1956), 216–7.

(1961a) 'An Iron Age bowl from Rose Ash, north Devon'. *Antiq. Journ.*, 41 (1961), 186–98.

(1961b) 'South western hillforts'. In *Problems of the Iron Age in Southern Britain*, ed. Frere, S. S. (London), 35–60.

(1964) *South West England* (London).

Fox, A., Radford, R., Rogers, E. H., & Shorter, A. H. (1952) 'Report on the excavations at Milber Down, 1937–8'. *PDAES*, 4 (1952), 27–78.

Fox. C. F. (1923) *The Archaeology of the Cambridge Region* (Cambridge).

(1924) 'A settlement of the Early Iron Age at Abington Piggotts, Cambs, and its subsequent history as evidenced by objects preserved in the Piggott Collection'. *PPSEA*, 4 (1924), 211–33.

(1927) 'A la Tène I brooch from Wales: with notes on the typology and distribution of these brooches in Britain'. *Arch. Camb.*, 82 (1927), 67–112.

(1946) *A Find of the Early Iron Age from Llyn Cerrig-Bach, Anglesey* (Cardiff).

(1958) *Pattern and Purpose: a Survey of Early Celtic Art in Britain* (Cardiff).

Fox, C. F., & Hull, M. R. (1948) 'The incised ornament on the Celtic mirror from Colchester, Essex'. *Antiq. Journ.*, 28 (1948), 123–37.

Fox, C. F., & Hyde, H. A. (1939) 'A second cauldron and an iron sword from the Llyn Fawr hoard, Rhigos, Glamorganshire'. *Antiq. Journ.*, 19 (1939), 369–404.

Fox, C. F. & Wolseley, G. R. (1928) 'The Early Iron Age site at Findon Park'. *Antiq. Journ.*, 8 (1928), 449–60.

Frere, S. S. (1946) 'An Iron Age site at West Clandon, Surrey, and some aspects of Iron Age and Romano-British culture in the Wealden area'. *Arch. Journ.*, 101 (1946), 50–67.

(1954) 'Canterbury excavations, summer 1946, the Rose Lane sites'. *Arch. Cant.*, 68 (1954), 101–43.

(1961) *The Problems of the Iron Age in Southern Britain* (London).

(1967) *Britannia* (London).

Gardner, W. (1910) 'Pen-y-Corddyn, near Abergele'. *Arch. Camb.*, 10 (1910), 79–156.

Gardner, W., & Savory, H. N. (1964) *Dinorben: a Hillfort Occupied in Early Iron Age and Roman Times* (Cardiff).

Gelling, P. S. (1970) 'Excavations at Pilsdon Pen, 1969'. *PDNHAS*, 91 (1969), 177–8.

(1971) 'Excavation at Pilsdon Pen, 1970'. *PDNHAS*, 92 (1971), 126–7.

Giot, P. R. (1960) *Brittany* (London).

Godwin, H. (1941) 'Studies of the post-glacial history of British vegetation. VI. Correlations in the Somerset levels'. *New Phytologist*, 40 (1941), 108–32.

(1955) 'Studies of the post-glacial history of British vegetation. XIII. The Meare Pool region of the Somerset levels'. *Phil. Trans. Royal Soc.*, 239, B662 (1955), 161–90.

Gordon, A. S. R. (1941) 'The excavation of Gurnard's Head, an Iron Age cliff castle in western Cornwall'. *Arch. Journ.* 97 (1941), 96–111.

Gordon, M. (1969) 'Duns and forts – a note on some Iron Age monuments of the Atlantic province'. *Scottish Arch. Forum* (1969), 41–52.

Gray, H. St G. (1925) 'Excavations at Ham Hill, south Somerset (part 1)'. *PSANHS*, 70 (1925), 104–16.

(1926) 'Excavations at Ham Hill, south Somerset (part 2)'. *PSANHS*, 71 (1926), 57–76.

(1927) 'Excavations at Ham Hill, south Somerset (part 3)'. *PSANHS*, 72 (1927), 55–68.

(1930) 'Excavations at Kingsdown Camp, near Mells, Somerset'. *Archaeologia*, 80 (1930), 59–96.

(1933) 'Trial-excavations in the so-called "Danish camp" at Wareham, near Wells, Norfolk'. *Antiq. Journ.*, 13 (1933), 399–413.

(1940) 'Metal vessels found on Shapwick Heath, Somerset'. *PSANHS*, 85 (1939), 191–202.

Gray, J. W., & Brewer, G. W. S. (1904) 'Evidence of ancient occupation on Cleeve Hill, near Cheltenham'. *P.Cott. NHFC*, 15 (1904), 49–57.

Green, C. (1949) 'The Birdlip Early Iron Age burials: a review'. *PPS*, 15 (1949), 188–90.

Greenwell, W. (1877) *British Barrows* (Oxford).

(1906) 'Early Iron Age burials in Yorkshire'. *Archaeologia*, 60 (1906), 251–324.

Greenwell, W., & Gatty, R. A. (1910) 'The pit dwelling at Holderness'. *Man*, 10 (1910), no. 48.

Gresham, C. A. (1939) 'Spettisbury Rings, Dorset'. *Arch. Journ.*, 96 (1939), 114–31.

Griffiths, W. E., & Hogg, A. H. A. (1957) 'The hill-fort on Conway Mountain, Caernarvonshire'. *Arch. Camb.*, 105 (1956), 49–80.

Grimes, W. F. (1944) 'Excavations at Stanton Harcourt, Oxon., 1940'. *Oxon.*, 8–9 (1943–4), 19–63.

(1951) *The Prehistory of Wales* (Cardiff, 1951).

(1953) 'Art on British Iron Age pottery'. *PPS*, 18 (1953), 160–75.

(1961) 'Draughton, Heathrow and Colsterworth'. In *Problems of the Iron Age in Southern Britain*, ed. Frere, S. S. (London), 21–3.

Guthrie, A. (1969) 'Excavation of a settlement at Goldherring, Sancreed, 1958–61'. *Cornish Arch.*, 8 (1969), 5–39.

Hamilton, J. R. C. (1956) *Excavations at Jarlshof, Shetland* (HMSO, Edinburgh).

(1962) 'Brochs and broch builders'. In Wainwright, F. T., *The Northern Isles* (London), 53–90.

(1966) 'Forts, brochs and wheel-houses in northern Scotland'. In *The Iron Age in Northern Britain*, ed. Rivet, A. L. F. (Edinburgh), 111–30.

(1968) *Excavations at Clickhimin, Shetland* (HMSO, London).

Hamlin, A. (1968) 'Early Iron Age sites at Stanton Harcourt'. *Oxon.*, 31 (1966), 1–27.

Harden, D. B. (1942) 'Excavations in Smith's Pit II, Cassington, Oxon.' *Oxon.*, 7 (1942), 104–7.

(1950) 'Italic and Etruscan finds from Britain'. *Atti I Congr. Preist. e Protoist. Mediterr.* (Florence), 315–24.

Harding, D. W. (1968) 'The pottery from Kirtlington, and its implications for the chronology of the earliest Iron Age in the upper Thames region'. *Oxon.*, 31 (1966), 158–61.

Harding, D. W. & Blake, I. M. (1963) 'An Early Iron Age settlement in Dorset'. *Antiquity*, 37 (1963), 63–4.

Harding, J. M. (1964) 'Interim report on the excavation of a Late Bronze Age homestead in Weston Wood, Albury, Surrey'. *Sy. AC*, 61 (1964), 29–38.

Hardy, H. R., & Curwen, E. C. (1937) 'An Iron Age pottery site near Horsted Keynes'. *SAC*, 78 (1937), 252–65.

Hartley, B. R. (1957) 'The Wandlebury Iron Age hill fort, excavations of 1955–6'. *PCAS*, 50 (1957), 1–28.

Hastings, F. & Cunliffe, B. (1966) 'Excavation of an Iron Age farmstead at Hawk's Hill, Leatherhead'. *Sy. AC.*, 62 (1966), 1–43.

Hatt, J-J. (1960) Note in *Gallia*, xviii (1960), 245–6 Fig. 68.

Hawkes, C. F. C. (1931) 'Hill forts'. *Antiquity*, 5 (1931), 60–111.

(1935) 'The pottery from the sites on Plumpton Plain'. *PPS*, 1 (1935), 39–59.

(1936a) 'The excavations at Buckland Rings, Lymington, 1935'. *PHFC*, 13 (1936), 124–64.

(1936b) 'The Twyford Down village, the abandonment of St Catherine's Hill and the first settlement of Winchester'. *PHFC*, 13 (1936), 208–12.

(1939a) 'The Caburn pottery and its implications'. *SAC*, 80 (1939), 217–62.

(1939b) 'The pottery from Castle Hill,

Newhaven'. *SAC*, 80 (1939), 269–92.

(1939c) 'The excavations at Quarley Hill, 1938'. *PHFC*, 14 (1939), 136–94.

(1940a) 'The Marnian pottery and La Tène I brooch from Worth, Kent'. *Antiq. Journ.*, 20 (1940), 115–21.

(1940b) 'The excavations at Bury Hill, 1939'. *PHFC*, 14 (1940), 291–337.

(1940c) 'A site of the Late Bronze-Early Iron Age transition at Tottenhoe, Beds.' *Antiq. Journ.*, 20 (1940), 487–91.

(1948) 'Britons, Romans and Saxons round Salisbury and in Cranbourne Chase'. *Arch. Journ.*, 104 (1947), 27–81.

(1956) 'The British Iron Age: cultures, chronology and peoples'. *Cong. Int. Sciences Pré- et Proto-historiques, Actes de la IV Session* (Madrid 1954) (1956), 729–37.

(1959) 'The ABC of the British Iron Age'. *Antiquity*, 33 (1959), 170–81.

(1961) 'The western Third C culture and the Belgic Dobunni'. In *Bagendon – a Belgic Oppidum*, Clifford, E. M. (Cambridge), 43–74.

(1966) Appendix to Brooks, R. T., 'The Rumps, St Minver: second interim report on the 1965 season'. *Cornish Arch.*, 5 (1966), 9–10.

(1968) 'New thoughts on the Belgae'. *Antiquity*, 42 (1968), 6–16.

Hawkes, C. F. C., & Dunning, G. C. (1931) 'The Belgae of Gaul and Britain'. *Arch. Journ.*, 87 (1931), 150–335.

(1932) 'The second Belgic invasion'. *Antiq. Journ.*, 12 (1932), 411–30.

Hawkes, C. F. C., & Fell, C. I. (1945) 'The Early Iron Age settlement at Fengate, Peterborough'. *Arch. Journ.*, 100 (1945), 188–223.

Hawkes, C. F. C., & Hull, M. R. (1947) *Camulodunum* (Oxford).

Hawkes, C. F. C., Myres, J. N. L., & Stevens, C. G. (1930) *St Catherine's Hill, Winchester* (Winchester: reprinted from *PHFC* xi (1930)).

Hawkes, C. F. C., & Smith, M. A. (1947) 'On some buckets and cauldrons of the Bronze and Early Iron Ages'. *Antiq. Journ.*, 37 (1957), 131–98.

Hawkes, J. (1940) 'The excavations at Balksbury, 1939'. *PHFC*, 14 (1940), 338–45.

Hawkes, S. C. (1961) 'Longbridge Deverill, Cow Down, Wilts.' *PPS*, 27 (1961), 346–7.

(1964) *Some Belgic brooches from South Ferriby* (Hull Museum's Publications, no. 214).

(1970) 'Finds from two Middle Bronze Age pits at Winnall, Winchester, Hampshire'. *PHFC*, 26 (1969), 5–18.

Hawley, W. (1927) 'Further excavations on Park Brow'. *Archaeologia*, 76 (1927), 30–40.

Head, J. F., & Piggott, C. M. (1944) 'An Iron Age site at Bledlow, Bucks.' *Rec. of Bucks*, 14 (1944),

189–209.

Helbaek, H. (1953) 'Early crops in southern England'. *PPS*, 17 (1952), 194–233.

Hemp, W. J. (1928) 'A La Tène shield from Moel Hiraddug, Flintshire'. *Arch. Camb.* 83 (1928), 253–84.

Hencken, H. O'Neill (1932) *The Archaeology of Cornwall and Scilly* (London).

(1933) 'An excavation by H.M. Office of Works at Chysauster, Cornwall, 1931'. *Archaeologia*, 83 (1933), 237–84.

Hencken, T. C. (1938) 'The excavation of the Iron Age camp on Bredon Hill, Gloucestershire, 1935–37'. *Arch. Journ.*, 95 (1938), 1–111.

Henshall, A. S. (1950) 'Textiles and weaving appliances in prehistoric Britain'. *PPS*, 16 (1950), 130–62.

Hirst, F. C. (1936) 'Excavations at Porthmeor, Cornwall'. *JRIC*, 24 (1936), 1 *ff*

Hodson, F. R. (1960) 'Reflections on the "ABC of the British Iron Age" '. *Antiquity*, 34 (1960), 318–19.

(1962) 'Some pottery from Eastbourne, the "Marnians" and the pre-Roman Iron Age in southern England'. *PPS*, 28 (1962), 140–55.

(1964) 'Cultural groupings within the British pre-Roman Iron Age'. *PPS*, 30 (1964), 99–110.

(1968) 'The La Tène cemetery at Münsingen-am-Rain'. *Acta Bernensia*, 5.

(1971) 'Three Iron Age brooches from Hammersmith'. In *Prehistoric and Roman Studies*, ed. Sieveking, G. de G. (London), 50–6.

Hogg, A. H. A. (1942) 'Excavations in a native settlement at Ingram Hill, Northumberland'. *Arch. Ael.* 4, 20 (1942), 110–33.

(1956) 'Further excavations at Ingram Hill'. *Arch. Ael*, 4, 34 (1956), 150–60.

(1962) 'Garn Boduan and Tre'r Ceiri, excavations at two Caernarvonshire hill forts'. *Arch. Journ.*, 117 (1960), 1–39.

(1965) 'Early Iron Age Wales'. Chapter V in *Prehistoric and Early Wales*, ed. Foster, I. Ll., & Daniel, G. (London).

(1966) 'Native settlements in Wales'. In *Rural Settlement in Roman Britain*, ed. Thomas, A. C. (London), 28–38.

(1971) 'Some applications of surface fieldwork'. In *The Iron Age and its Hill-forts*, ed. Jesson, M., & Hill, D. (Southampton), 105–26.

Holleyman, G. A. (1937) 'Harrow Hill excavations, 1936'. *SAC*, 78 (1937), 230–52.

Holleyman, G. A., & Curwen, E.C. (1935) 'Late Bronze Age lynchet-settlements on Plumpton Plain, Sussex'. *PPS*, 1 (1935), 16–38.

Holmes, J., & Frend, W. H. C. 'A Belgic chieftain's grave on Hertford Heath'. *E. Herts. Arch. Soc. Trans.*, 14, part 1 (1959), 1–19.

Holmes, T. R. (1907) *Ancient Britain and the Invasions of Julius Caesar* (Oxford).

Jervise, A. (1863) 'An account of the excavation of the round or "bee-hive" shaped house and other underground chambers at West Grange of Conan, Forfarshire'. *PSAS*, 4 (1860–2), 492–9.

Jessup, R. F., & Cook, N. C. (1936) 'Excavations at Bigbury Camp, Harbledown'. *Arch. Cant.*, 48 (1936), 151–68.

Jobey, G. (1959) 'Excavations at a native settlement at Huckhoe, Northumberland'. *Arch. Ael.*[4], 37 (1959), 217–78.

(1962a) 'A note on scooped enclosures in Northumberland'. *Arch. Ael.*[4], 40 (1962), 47–58.

(1962b) 'An Iron Age homestead at West Brandon, Durham'. *Arch. Ael.*[4], 40 (1962), 1–34.

(1965) 'Hillforts and settlements in Northumberland'. *Arch. Ael.*[4], 43 (1965), 21–64.

(1966a) 'A field survey in Northumberland'. In *The Iron Age of Northern Britain*, ed. Rivet, A. L. F. (Edinburgh), 89–110.

(1966b) 'Homesteads and settlements of the frontier area'. In *Rural Settlement in Roman Britain*, ed. Thomas, A. C. (London), 1–14.

(1970) 'An Iron Age settlement and homestead at Burradon, Northumberland'. *Arch. Ael.*[4], 48 (1970), 51–95.

(1971) 'Early settlement and topography in the Border counties'. *Scottish Arch. Forum 1970* (Edinburgh), 73–84.

Jobey, G., & Tait, J. (1966) 'Excavations on palisaded settlements and cairnfields at Alnham, Northumberland'. *Arch. Ael.*[4], 44 (1966), 5–48.

Jones, G. D. B., & Thompson, F. H. (1965) 'Mam Tor'. *DAJ*, 85 (1965), 123–5.

Jope, E. M. (1961a) 'Daggers of the Early Iron Age in Britain'. *PPS*, 27 (1961), 307–43.

(1961b) 'The beginnings of La Tène ornamental style in the British Isles'. In *Problems of the Iron Age in Southern Britain*, ed. Frere, S. S. (London), 69–83.

(1971) 'The Witham shield'. In *Prehistoric and Roman Studies*, ed. Sieveking, G. de G. (London).

Kenyon, K. M. (1943) 'Excavations on the Wrekin, Shropshire, 1939'. *Arch. Journ.*, 99 (1942), 99–109.

(1950) 'Excavations at Breedon-on-the-Hill, 1946'. *TLAS*, 26 (1950), 17–82.

(1952) 'A survey of the evidence concerning the chronology and origins of Iron Age A in southern and Midland Britain'. *London Institute of Archaeology report*, 8, 29.

(1954) 'Excavations at Sutton Walls, Hereford-

shire, 1948–51'. *Arch. Journ.*, 110 (1954), 1–87.

Kimball, D. (1933) 'Cholesbury Camp'. *JBAA*, 34 (1933), 187.

King, D. G. (1961) 'Bury Wood Camp. Report on excavations, 1959'. *WAM*, 58 (1961), 40–7.

(1962) 'Bury Wood Camp. Report on excavations, 1960'. *WAM*, 58 (1962), 185–208.

(1967) 'Bury Wood Camp'. *WAM*, 62 (1967), 1–15.

Klein, W. G. (1928) 'Roman temple at Worth, Kent'. *Antiq. Journ.*, 8 (1928), 76–86.

Kossack, G. (1954) 'Pferdegeschirr aus Gräbern der älteren Hallstatt zeit Bayerns'. *Jahrb. Röm.-Germ. Zentralmus. Mainz*, 1 (1954), 111–78.

Laing, L. R. (1968) 'A Greek tin trade with Cornwall'. *Cornish Arch.*, 7 (1968), 15–23.

Langford, F. (1924) 'Third report on Read's Cavern'. *PBUSS*, 1 (1924), 135–43.

(1925) 'Fourth report on Read's Cavern'. *PBUSS*, 2 (1925), 51–5.

Langmaid, N. (1971) 'Norton Fitzwarren'. *Current Arch.*, 28 (Sept. 1971), 116–20.

Laver, P. G. (1927) 'The excavation of a tumulus at Lexden, Colchester'. *Archaeologia*, 76 (1926–7), 241–54.

Leaf, C. S. (1936) 'Two Bronze Age barrows at Chippenham, Cambridgeshire'. *PCAS*, 36 (1936), 134–55.

Leeds, E. T. (1927) 'Excavations at Chun Castle in Penwith, Cornwall'. *Archaeologia*, 76 (1927), 205–40.

(1931a) 'An Iron Age site near Radley, Berks.' *Antiq. Journ.*, 11 (1931), 399–404.

(1931b) 'Chastleton Camp, Oxfordshire, a hill fort of the Early Iron Age'. *Antiq. Journ.*, 11 (1931), 382–98.

(1933a) 'Torcs of the Early Iron Age in Britain'. *Antiq. Journ.*, 13 (1933), 466–7.

(1933b) *Celtic Ornament* (Oxford).

(1935) 'Recent Iron Age discoveries in Oxfordshire and north Berkshire'. *Antiq. Journ.*, 15 (1935), 30–41.

Lethbridge, T. C. (1953) 'Burial of an Iron Age warrior at Snailwell'. *PCAS*, 47 (1953), 25–37.

Liddell, D. M. (1930) 'Report on the excavations at Hembury Fort, Devon, 1930'. *PDAES*, 1 (1930), 40–63.

(1931) 'Report on the excavations at Hembury Fort, Devon. Second season 1931'. *PDAES*, 1 (1931), 90–120.

(1932) 'Report on the excavations at Hembury Fort. Third season 1932'. *PDAES*, 1 (1932), 162–90.

(1933) 'Excavations at Meon Hill'. *PHFC*, 12 (1933), 127–62.

(1935a) 'Report on the Hampshire Field Club's excavation at Meon Hill'. *PHFC*, 13 (1935), 7–54.

(1935b) 'Report on the excavations at Hembury Fort, 1934–5'. *PDAES*, 2 (1935), 135–70.

Longworth, I. H. (1968) 'A Bronze Age hoard from Portfield Farm, Whalley, Lancashire'. *BMQ*, 32, 1–2 (1968), 8–14.

Lowther, A. W. G. (1935) 'An Early Iron Age oven at St Martha's Hill, near Guildford'. *Sy. AC*, 43 (1935), 113–14.

(1947) 'Caesar's Camp, Wimbledon, Surrey, the excavation of 1937'. *Arch. Journ.*, 102 (1947), 15–20.

(1949) 'Iron Age pottery from St. George's Hill Camp, Weybridge'. *Sy. AC*, 41 (1949), 144–6.

MacGregor, M. (1962) 'The Early Iron Age metalwork from Stanwick, N. R. Yorks, England'. *PPS*, 28 (1962), 17–56.

MacGregor, M., & Simpson, D. D. A. (1963) 'A group of iron objects from Barbury Castle, Wilts'. *WAM*, 58 (1963), 394–402.

MacKie, E. (1965a) 'The origin and development of the broch and wheelhouse building cultures of the Scottish Iron Age'. *PPS*, 31 (1965), 93–146.

(1965b) 'Brochs and the Hebridean Iron Age'. *Antiquity*, 39 (1965), 266–78.

(1965c) 'A dwelling site of the Earlier Iron Age at Balevullin, Tiree, excavated in 1912 by A. Henderson Bishop'. *PSAS*, 96 (1962–3), 155–83.

(1969) 'Radiocarbon dates and the Scottish Iron Age'. *Antiquity*, 43 (1969), 15–26.

Manby, T. G. (1963) (Note on Clotherholm sword) *YAJ*, 41 (1963), 15–17.

Mariën, M.-E. (1958) *Trouvailles du Champ d'Urnes et des tombelles hallstattiennes de Court-Saint-Etienne* (Brussels).

Maryon, H. (1944) 'The Bawsey torc'. *Antiq. Journ.*, 24 (1944), 149–51.

May, J. (1964–9) 'Dragonby' (duplicated annual interim reports: University of Nottingham).

(1965–9) 'Ancaster' (duplicated interim reports on each season's digging: University of Nottingham, Dept. of Classics).

(1970) 'Dragonby – an interim report on excavations on an Iron Age and Romano-British site near Scunthorpe, Lincolnshire, 1964–9'. *Antiq. Journ.* 50 (1970), 222–245.

Megaw, J. V. S. (1971) 'A group of Later Iron Age collars or neck rings from western Britain'. In *Prehistoric and Roman Studies*, ed. Sieveking, G. de G. (London), 145–55.

Megaw, J. V. S., Thomas, A. D., & Wailes, B. (1961) 'The Bronze Age settlement at Gwithian, Cornwall, preliminary report'. *PWCFC*, 2, 5 (1961), 200.

Miles, H., & T. J. (1969) 'Settlement sites of the Late pre-Roman Iron Age in the Somerset levels'. *PSANHS*, 113 (1968/9), 17–55.

Money, J. H. (1941) 'An interim report on excavations at High Rocks, Tunbridge Wells, 1940'. *SAC*, 82 (1941), 104–9.

(1960) 'Excavations of High Rocks, Tunbridge Wells, 1954–56'. *SAC*, 98 (1960), 173–222.

(1968) 'Excavations in the Iron Age hill-fort at High Rocks, near Tunbridge Wells, 1957–61'. *SAC*, 106 (1968), 158–205.

Mortimer, J. R. (1869) 'Notice of the opening of an Anglo-Saxon grave, at Grimthorpe, Yorkshire'. *Reliquary*, 9 (1869), 180–2.

(1895) 'The opening of six mounds at Scarborough, near Beverley'. *TERAS*, 3 (1895), 21–3.

(1905) *Forty Years' Researches in British and Saxon Burial Mounds of East Yorkshire* (London).

(1911) 'Dane's Graves'. *TERAS*, 18 (1911), 30–52.

Munro, R. (1882) *Ancient Scottish Lake Dwellings* (Edinburgh).

Musson, C. (1970) 'Breiddin 1969' (duplicated: University of South Wales and Monmouthshire, Dept of Archaeology, Cardiff).

Myres, J. N. L. (1937) 'A prehistoric and Roman site on Mount Farm, Dorchester'. *Oxon.*, 2 (1937), 12–40.

Nash-Williams, V. E. (1933a) 'A Late bronze hoard from Cardiff'. *Antiq. Journ.*, 13 (1933), 299–300.

(1933b) 'An Early Iron Age hill fort at Llanmelin, near Caerwent, Monmouthshire'. *Arch. Camb.*, 88 (1933), 237–315.

(1939) 'An Early Iron Age coastal camp at Sudbrook, near the Severn Tunnel, Monmouthshire'. *Arch. Camb.*, 94 (1939), 42–79.

Neish, J., & Stuart, J. (1860) 'Reference notes to plan and views of ancient remains on the summit of the Laws, Forfarshire'. *PSAS*, 3 (1857–60), 440–54.

Nenquin, J. (1961) *Salt, a Study in Economic Prehistory* (Brugge).

Newcomb, R. M. (1968) 'Geographical location analysis and Iron Age settlement in West Penwith'. *Cornish Arch.*, 7 (1968), 5–13.

(1970) 'The spatial distribution of hill-forts in West Penwith'. *Cornish Arch.*, 9 (1970), 47–52.

O'Neil, B. H. St J. (1934) 'Excavation at Titterstone Clee Hill Camp, Shropshire, 1932'. *Antiq. Journ.*, 14 (1934), 13–32.

(1937) 'Excavations at Breiddin Hill Camp, Montgomeryshire, 1933–35'. *Arch. Camb.*, 92 (1937), 86–128.

(1942) 'Excavations at Ffridd Faldwyn Camp, Montgomeryshire, 1937–39'. *Arch. Camb.*, 97 (1942), 1–57.

Owles, E. J. (1969) 'The Ipswich gold torcs'. *Antiquity*, 43 (1969), 208–11.

(1971) 'The sixth Ipswich torc'. *Antiquity*, 45 (1971), 294–6.

Painter, K. S. (1971) 'An Iron Age gold-alloy torc from Glascote, Tamworth, Staffordshire'. *Trans. S. Staffs. AHS*, 11 (1970), 1–6.

Palmer, L. S. (1922) 'The Keltic cavern'. *PBUSS*, 1 (1922), 9–20.

(1923) 'Second report on the Keltic cavern'. *PBUSS*, 1 (1923), 87–91.

Parson, W. J., & Curwen, E. C. (1933) 'An agricultural settlement on Charleston Brow, near Firle Beacon'. *SAC*, 74 (1933), 164–80.

Peacock, D. P. S. (1968) 'A petrological study of certain Iron Age pottery from western England'. *PPS*, 34 (1968), 414–27.

(1969) 'A contribution to the study of Glastonbury ware from south-western Britain'. *Antiq. Journ.* 49 (1969), 41–61.

(1971) 'Roman amphorae in pre-Roman Britain'. In *The Iron Age and its Hill-forts*, ed. Jesson, M., & Hill, D. (Southampton), 161–88.

Peake, H. (1922) *The Bronze Age and the Celtic World* (London).

Peake, H., Coghlan, H., & Hawkes, C. F. C. (1932) 'Early Iron Age remains on Boxford Common, Berks'. *TNDFC*, 6 (1931), 136–50.

(1933) 'Further excavations on Boxford Common'. *TNDFC*, 6 (1933), 211–17.

Perry, B. T. (1966) 'Some recent discoveries in Hampshire'. In *Rural Settlement in Roman Britain*, ed. Thomas, A. C. (London), 39–42.

(1970) 'Iron Age enclosures and settlements on the Hampshire chalklands'. *Arch. Journ.*, 126 (1969), 29–43.

Philips, J. T. (1960) 'An Iron Age site at Driffield, East Riding, Yorks'. *YAJ*, 40 (1959–62), 183–91.

Piggott, C. M. (1938a) 'A Middle Bronze Age barrow and Deverel-Rimbury urnfield, at Latch Farm, Christchurch, Hampshire'. *PPS*, 4 (1938), 169–87.

(1938b) 'The Iron Age pottery from Theale'. *TNDFC*, 8 (1938), 52–62.

(1940) 'Report on the pottery from Winklebury Camp, Hants'. *PHFC*, 15 (1940), 56–7.

(1942) 'Five Late Bronze Age enclosures in north Wiltshire'. *PPS*, 8 (1942), 48–61.

(1946) 'Late Bronze Age razors of the British Isles'. *PPS*, 12 (1946), 121–41.

(1950) 'The excavations at Hownam Rings, Roxburghshire 1948'. *PSAS*, 82 (1947–8), 193–224.

(1951) 'The Iron Age settlement at Hayhope Knowe, Roxburghshire: excavations, 1949'. *PSAS*, 83 (1948–9), 45–67.

(1952) 'The excavations at Bonchester Hill, 1950'. *PSAS*, 82 (1949–50), 113–37.

(1953) 'An Iron Age barrow in the New Forest'. *Antiq. Journ.*, 33 (1953), 14–21.

(1955) 'Milton Loch Crannog I: a native house of the second century A.D. in Kirkcudbrightshire'. *PSAS*, 87 (1952–3), 134–52.

Piggott, C. M., & Seaby, W. A. (1937) 'Early Iron Age site at Southcote, Reading'. *PPS*, 3 (1937), 43–57.

Piggott, S. (1927) 'Early Iron Age rubbish pits at Knighton Hill, Berks.' *Antiq. Journ.*, 7 (1927), 517.

(1931) 'Ladle Hill – an unfinished hill-fort'. *Antiquity*, 5 (1931), 474–85.

(1950) 'Swords and scabbards of the British Early Iron Age'. *PPS*, 16 (1950), 1–28.

(1951) 'Excavations in the broch and hillfort of Torwoodlee, Selkirkshire, 1950'. *PSAS*, 85 (1950–1), 92–117.

(1955) 'A Late Bronze Age hoard from Peeblesshire'. *PSAS*, 87 (1952–3), 175–86.

(1956) Introduction in RCHM(S), *Roxburghshire* I, 15.

(1959) 'The carnyx in Early Iron Age Britain'. *Antiq. Journ.*, 39 (1959), 19–32.

(1960) 'Excavations at Braidwood fort, Midlothian'. *PSAS*, 91 (1957–8), 61–77.

(1966) 'A scheme for the Scottish Iron Age'. In *The Iron Age in Northern Britain*, ed. Rivet, A. L. F. (Edinburgh), 1–16.

Piggott, S., & C. M. (1940) 'Excavations at Ram's Hill, Uffington, Berks.' *Antiq. Journ.* 20 (1940), 465–80.

(1954) 'Excavations at Castle Law, Glencorse, and at Craig's Quarry, Dirleton, 1948–9'. *PSAS*, 86 (1951–2), 191–5.

Pitt-Rivers, A. H. L. F. (1881) 'Excavations at Mount Caburn Camp, near Lewes'. *Archaeologia*, 46 (1881), 423–95.

(1887) *Excavations in Cranbourne Chase*, vol. 1 (privately printed, London).

(1888) *Excavations in Cranbourne Chase*, vol. 2 (privately printed, London).

(1892) *Excavations in Cranbourne Chase*, vol. 3 (privately printed, London).

(1898) *Excavations at Cranbourne Chase*, vol. 4 (privately printed, London).

Powell, T. G. E. (1950) 'The Late Bronze Age hoard from Welby, Leicestershire'. *Arch. Journ.*, 105 (1948), 27–40.

(1963) 'Excavations at Skelmore Heads near Ulverston'. *CW*[2], 63 (1963), 1–30.

Preston, J. P., & Hawkes, C. F. C. (1933) 'Three Late Bronze Age barrows on the Cloven Way'. *Antiq. Journ.*, 13 (1933), 414–54.

Radford, C. A. R. (1951) 'Report on the excavations at Castle Dore'. *JRIC*, (N. S.) 1 (1951), 1–119.

(1952) 'Prehistoric settlements on Dartmoor and the Cornish Moors'. *PPS*, 18 (1952), 55–84.

(1955) 'The tribes of southern Britain'. *PPS*, 20 (1954), 1–26.

Raistrick, A. (1938) 'Prehistoric cultivations at Grassington, West Yorkshire'. *YAJ*, 33 (1936–8), 166–74.

(1939) 'Iron Age settlements in West Yorkshire'. *YAJ*, 34 (1939), 115–50.

Ratcliffe-Densham, H. B. A. & M. M. (1953) 'A Celtic farm on Blackpatch'. *SAC*, 91 (1953), 69–83.

(1961) 'An anomalous earthwork of the Late Bronze Age, on Cock Hill'. *SAC*, 99 (1961), 78–101.

Rhatz, P. A. (1969) 'Cannington hillfort 1963'. *PSANHS*, 113 (1968–9), 56–68.

Rhatz, P. A., & ApSimon, A. M. (1962) 'Excavations at Shearplace Hill, Sydling St Nicholas, Dorset, England'. *PPS*, 28 (1962), 289–328.

Rhatz, P. A., & Brown, J. C. (1959) 'Blaise Castle Hill, Bristol, 1957'. *PBUSS*, 8 (1959), 147–71.

Richardson, K. M. (1940) 'Excavations at Poundbury, Dorchester, Dorset, 1939'. *Antiq. Journ.*, 20 (1940), 429–48.

(1951) 'The excavation of an Iron Age village on Boscombe Down West'. *WAM*, 54 (1951), 123–68.

Richardson, K. M., & Young, A. (1951) 'An Iron Age A site on the Chilterns'. *Antiq. Journ.* 31 (1951), 132–48.

Richmond, I. A. (1968) *Hod Hill*, vol. 2: *Excavations carried out between 1951 and 1958* (London).

Riehm, K. (1961) 'Prehistoric salt boiling'. *Antiquity*, 35 (1961), 181–91.

Riley, D. N. (1947) 'A Late Bronze Age and Iron Age site on Standlake Downs, Oxon.' *Oxon.*, 11–12 (1946–7), 27–43.

Ritchie, A. (1970) 'Palisaded sites in northern Britain: their context and affinities'. *Scottish Arch. Forum* (Glasgow), 48–67.

Rivet, A. L. F. (1961) 'Some of the problems of hill-forts'. In *Problems of the Iron Age in Southern Britain*, ed. Frere, S. S. (London), 29–34.

Rutter, J. G., & Duke, G. (1958) *Excavations at Crossgates near Scarborough, 1947–56* (Scarborough).

Sandars, N. K. (1957) *Bronze Age Cultures in France* (Cambridge).

Saunders, A. (1961) 'Excavations at Castle Gotha, St Austell, Cornwall'. *PWCFC*, 2, 5 (1961), 216–20.

Savory, N. H. (1937) 'An Early Iron Age site at Long Wittenham, Berks.' *Oxon.*, 2 (1937), 1–11.

(1939) 'The Early Iron Age'. *VCH Oxon.*, 1, 251–61.

(1948) 'The sword-bearers'. *PPS*, 14 (1948), 155–76.

(1954) 'The Excavation of an Early Iron Age fortified settlement on Mynydd Bychan, Llysworney (Glam.), 1949–50, part I'. *Arch. Camb.* 103 (1954), 85–108.

(1956) 'The excavation of an Early Iron Age fortified settlement on Mynydd Bychan, Llysworney, Glam., 1949–50, part II'. *Arch. Camb.*, 104 (1955), 14–51.

(1958) 'The Late Bronze Age in Wales: some new discoveries and new interpretations'. *Arch. Camb.*, 107 (1958), 3–63.

(1961) 'Excavations at Dinas Emrys, Beddglent, Caernarvonshire, 1954–56'. *Arch. Camb.*, 109 (1960), 13–77.

(1964) 'The Tal-y-Llyn hoard'. *Antiquity*, 38 (1964), 18–31.

(1971) 'A Welsh Bronze Age hillfort'. *Antiquity*, 45 (1971), 251–261.

Scott, L. (1947) 'The problem of the brochs'. *PPS*, (1944), 1–36.

(1948) 'Gallo-British colonies: the aisled round-house culture in the north'. *PPS*, 14 (1948), 46–125.

Sheppard, T. (1907) 'Note on a British chariot-burial at Hunmanby in East Yorkshire'. *YAJ*, 19 (1907), 482–8.

(1938) 'Excavations at Eastburn, East Yorkshire'. *YAJ*, 34 (1938), 35–47.

(1941) 'The Parc-y-Meirch hoard, St George Parish, Denbighshire'. *Arch. Camb.*, 96 (1941), 1–10.

Simmons, I. G. (1970) 'Environment and early Man on Dartmoor'. *PPS*, 35 (1969), 203–219.

Simpson, D. D. A. (1969) 'Excavations at Kaimes hillfort, Midlothian, 1964–8'. *Glasgow Arch. Journ.*, N.S. 1 (1969), 7–28.

Simpson, W. G. (1966) 'Romano-British settlement on the Welland Gravels'. In *Rural Settlement in Roman Britain*, ed. Thomas, A. C. (London), 15–25.

Smith, C. R. (1852) *Collectanea Antiqua*, vol. 2 (1852).

Smith, M. A. (1959) 'Some Somerset hoards and their place in the Bronze Age of southern Britain'. *PPS*, 25 (1959), 144–87.

Smith, R. A. (1908) 'Romano-British remains at Cobham'. *Sy. AC.*, 21 (1908), 192–203.

(1909a) 'A hoard of metal found at Santon Downham, Suffolk'. *PCAS*, 13 (1909), 146–63.

(1909b) 'Romano-British remains at Cobham'. *Sy. AC*, 22 (1909), 137–55.

(1912) 'On Late-Celtic antiquities discovered at Welwyn, Herts.' *Archaeologia*, 63 (1911–12), 1–30.

(1925) *A Guide to the Antiquities of the Early Iron Age of Central and Western Europe* (British Museum, London).

(1926) 'Two early British bronze bowls'. *Antiq. Journ.*, 6 (1926), 276–83.

(1927) 'Park Brow, the finds and foreign parallels'. *Archaeologia*, 76 (1927), 14–29.

(1928) 'Pre-Roman remains at Scarborough'. *Archaeologia*, 77 (1928), 179–200.

(1934) 'Scarborough and Hallstatt'. *Antiq. Journ.*, 14 (1934), 301–2.

Spratling, M. (1966) 'The date of the Tal-y-Llyn hoard'. *Antiquity*, 40 (1966), 229–30.

Stanford, S. C. (1966–71) Duplicated interim reports on the annual excavations on Midsummer Hill camp, Eastnor, Herefordshire.

(1967) 'Croft Ambrey hillfort'. *TWNFC*, 39 (1967), 31–9.

(1971a) 'Credenhill Camp, Herefordshire: an Iron Age hill-fort capital'. *Arch. Journ.*, 127 (1971), 82–129.

(1971b) 'Invention, adoption and imposition – the evidence of the hill-forts'. In *The Iron Age and its Hill-forts*, ed. Jesson, M., & Hill, D. (Southampton), 41–52.

Stead, I. M. (1965) *The La Tène cultures of Eastern Yorkshire* (York).

(1967) 'A La Tène III burial at Welwyn Garden City'. *Archaeologia*, 101 (1967), 1–62.

(1968) 'An Iron Age hill-fort at Grimthorpe, Yorkshire, England'. *PPS*, 34 (1968), 148–90.

(1969) 'Verulamium, 1966–8'. *Antiquity*, 43 (March 1969), 45–52.

(1970) 'Excavations in Blagden Copse, Hurstbourne Tarrant, Hampshire, 1961'. *PHFC*, 23 (1968), 81–9.

(1971) 'The reconstruction of Iron Age buckets from Aylesford and Baldock'. In *Prehistoric and Roman Studies*, ed. Sieveking, G. de G. (London), 250–82.

Steer, K. A. (1958) 'The Early Iron Age homestead at West Plean'. *PSAS*, 89 (1955–6), 227–51.

Stevens, F. (1934) 'The Highfield pit dwellings, Fisherton, Salisbury'. *WAM*, 46 (1934), 579–624.

Stevenson, R. B. K. (1949) 'Braidwood fort, Midlothian: the exploration of two huts'. *PSAS*, 83 (1948–9), 1–11.

Stone, J. F. S. (1935) 'Three "Peterborough" dwelling pits and a doubly-stockaded Early Iron Age ditch at Winterbourne Dauntsey'. *WAM*, 46 (1935), 445–53.

(1936) 'An enclosure on Boscombe Down East'. *WAM*, 47 (1936), 466–89.

(1941) 'The Deverel-Rimbury settlement on Thorney Down, Winterbourne Gunner, South Wiltshire'. *PPS*, 7 (1941), 114–33.

Stuart, J. (1871) 'Notes on wooden structures in the Moss of Whiteburn, on the estate of Spottiswoode, Berwickshire'. *PSAS*, 8 (1868–9), 16–20.

Stuart, J. D. M., & Birbeck, J. M. (1936) 'A Celtic village on Twyford Down'. *PHFC*, 13 (1936), 118–207.

Sutton, J. E. G. (1968) 'Iron Age hill-forts and some other earthenworks in Oxfordshire'. *Oxon.*, 31 (1966), 28–42.

Swinnerton, H. H. (1932) 'The prehistoric pottery sites of the Lincolnshire coast'. *Antiq. Journ.*, 12 (1932), 239–53.

Tebbutt, C. F. (1932) 'Early Iron Age settlement on Jack's Hill, Great Wymondley, Herts.' *PPSEA*, 6 (1932), 371–74.

Thomas, A. C. (1964) 'Minor sites in the Gwithian area (Iron Age to recent times)'. *Cornish Arch.*, 3 (1964), 37–62.

(1966) 'The character and origins of Roman Dumnonia'. In *Rural Settlement in Roman Britain*, ed. Thomas, A. C. (London), 74–98.

Thomas, W. G., & Walker, R. F. (1959) 'Excavations at Trelissey'. *BBCS*, 18.3 (1959), 295–303.

Threipland, L. M. (1957) 'An excavation at St Mawgan-in-Pydar, north Cornwall'. *Arch. Journ.*, 113 (1956), 33–81.

Toms, H. S. (1914) 'Notes on a survey of Hollingbury Camp'. *B and H. Archaeologist*, 1 (1914), 12.

Tratman, E. K. (1931) 'Final report on the excavation at Read's Cavern'. *PBUSS*, 4 (1931), 8–10.

(1970) 'The Glastonbury Lake Village: a reconsideration'. *PBUSS*, 12 (1970), 143–67.

Tylecote, R. F. (1962) *Metallurgy in Archaeology* (London).

Varley, W. J. (1935) 'Maiden Castle, Bickerton. Preliminary excavations, 1935'. *LAAA*, 22, 1–2 (1935), 97–110.

(1936) 'Further excavations at Maiden Castle, Bickerton, 1935'. *LAAA*, 23, 3–4 (1936), 110–12.

(1939) *Report of the first year's excavations, 1939. Castle Hill, Almondbury* (excavation Committee's pamphlet).

(1950a) 'Excavations of the castle ditch, Eddisbury, 1935–1938'. *THSLC*, 102 (1950), 1–68.

(1950b) 'The hillforts of the Welsh Marches'. *Arch. Journ.*, 105 (1948), 41–66.

Wacher, J. S. (1964) 'Excavations at Breedon-on-the hill, Leicestershire, 1957'. *Antiq. Journ.*, 44 (1964), 122–42.

(1968) 'Poxwell 1968, Interim Report' (duplicated).

Wainwright, G. J. (1967a) *Coygan Camp* (Cambrian Archaeological Association, 1967).

(1967b) 'The excavation of an Iron Age hillfort on Bathampton Down, Somerset'. *TBGAS*, 86

(1967), 42–59.

(1968) 'The excavation of a Durotrigian farmstead near Tollard Royal in Cranbourne Chase, southern England'. *PPS*, 34 (1968), 102–47.

(1969), 'Walesland Rath'. *Current Arch.*, 12 (Jan. 1969), 4–7.

(1970) 'The excavations of Balksbury Camp, Andover, Hants'. *PHFC*, 26 (1969), 21–55.

Wainwright, G. J. and Longworth, I. H. (1969) 'The excavation of a group of round barrows on Ampleforth Moor, Yorkshire'. *YAJ*, 42 (1969), 283–94.

Ward, T. (1907) 'Roman remains at Cwmbrwyn, Carmarthenshire'. *Arch. Camb.*, 24 (1907), 175–212.

Ward-Perkins, J. B. (1938) 'An Early Iron Age site at Crayford, Kent'. *PPS*, 4 (1938), 151–68.

(1939) 'Iron Age metal horse bits in the British Isles'. *PPS*, 5 (1939), 173.

(1940) 'Two early lynch pins from Kings Langley, Herts., and from Teddington, Stratford on Avon'. *Antiq. Journ.*, 20 (1940), 358–67.

(1944) 'Excavations on the Iron Age hill fort of Oldbury, near Ightham, Kent'. *Archaeologia*, 90 (1944), 127–76.

Waterman, D. M., Kent, B. W., & Stickland, H. J. (1954) 'Two inland sites with Iron Age A pottery in the West Riding of Yorkshire'. *YAJ*, 38 (1952–5), 383–97.

Way, A. (1869) 'Notices of certain bronze relics of a peculiar type assigned to the Late Celtic period'. *Arch. Journ.*, 26 (1869), 52–83.

W.B. (1938) 'Iron Age settlements in Penigent Gill'. *YAJ*, 34 (1938), 413–19.

Wedlake, W. J. (1958) *Excavations at Camerton, Somerset* (Camerton Excavation Club, 1958).

Wheeler, R. E. M. (1929) 'Old England, Brentford'. *Antiquity*, 3 (1929), 20–32.

(1935) 'The excavation of Maiden Castle, Dorset. First interim report'. *Antiq. Journ.*, 15 (1935), 265–75.

(1936) 'The excavation of Maiden Castle, Dorset. Second interim report'. *Antiq. Journ.*, 16 (1936), 265–83.

(1937) 'The excavation of Maiden Castle, Dorset. Third interim report'. *Antiq. Journ.*, 17 (1937), 261–82.

(1943) *Maiden Castle, Dorset* (Oxford).

(1953) 'An Early Iron Age "beach-head" at Lulworth, Dorset'. *Antiq. Journ.*, 33 (1953), 1–13.

(1954) *The Stanwick Fortifications* (London).

Wheeler, R. E. M. & T.V. (1932) *Report on the excavation of Prehistoric, Roman and post-Roman site in Lydney Park, Gloucestershire* (Oxford).

(1936) *Verulamium: a Belgic and two Roman cities* (London).

Wheeler, R. E. M., & Richardson, K. M. (1957) *Hillforts of Northern France* (London).

White, G. M. (1934) 'Prehistoric remains from Selsey Bill'. *Antiq. Journ.*, 14 (1934), 40–52.

Whitley, M. (1943) 'Excavations at Chalbury Camp, Dorset, 1939'. *Antiq. Journ.*, 23 (1943), 98–121.

Williams, A. (1939a) 'Prehistoric and Roman pottery in the Museum of the Royal Institution of South Wales, Swansea'. *Arch. Camb.*, 94 (1939), 21–9.

(1939b) 'Excavations at the Knave promontory fort Rhossili, Glamorgan'. *Arch. Camb.*, 94 (1939), 210–19.

(1940) 'The excavation of Bishopston Valley promontory fort, Glamorgan'. *Arch. Camb.* (1940), 9–19.

(1941) 'The excavation of the High Penard promontory fort, Glamorgan'. *Arch. Camb.*, 96 (1941), 23–30.

(1947) 'Excavations at Langford Downs, Oxon. (near Lechlade) in 1943'. *Oxon.*, 11–12 (1946–7), 44–64.

(1951a) 'Excavations at Allard's Quarry, Marnhull, Dorset'. *PDNHAS*, 72 (1951), 20–75.

(1951b) 'Excavations at Board Mill, Stanton Harcourt, Oxon., 1944'. *Oxon.*, 16 (1951), 5–22.

Williams, J. (1777) *An Account of Some Remarkable Ancient Ruins, Lately Discovered in the Highlands And Northern parts of Scotland* (Edinburgh).

Williams-Freeman, J. P. (1915) *An Introduction to Field Archaeology as Illustrated by Hampshire* (London).

Willis, L., & Rogers, E. H. (1951) 'Dainton earth works'. *PDAES*, 4, 4 (1951), 79–101.

Wilson, A. E. (1938) 'Excavations in the ramparts and gateway of the Caburn, August–October 1937'. *SAC* 79 (1938), 169–94.

(1939) 'Excavations at the Caburn, 1938'. *SAC*, 80 (1939), 193–213.

(1940) 'Report on the excavations at Highdown Hill, Sussex, August 1939'. *SAC*, 81 (1940), 173–204.

(1950) 'Excavations on Highdown Hill, 1947'. *SAC*, 89 (1950), 163–78.

(1954) 'Sussex on the eve of the Roman Conquest'. *SAC*, 93 (1954), 59–77.

Woodruff, C. H. (1904) 'Further discoveries of Late Celtic and Romano-British interments at Walmer'. *Arch. Cant.*, 26 (1904), 9–23.

Worsfold, F. H. (1943) 'A report on the Late Bronze Age site excavated at Minnis Bay, Birchington, Kent, 1938–1940'. *PPS*, 9 (1943), 28.

Worth, R. H. (1935) 'Dartmoor Exploration Committee, twelfth report'. *TDA*, 67 (1935),

115-30.

(1943) 'The prehistoric rounds of Dartmoor'. *TDA*, 75 (1943), 273-302.

Young, A. (1955) 'An aisled farmhouse at Allasdale, Isle of Barra'. *PSAS*, 87 (1952-3), 80-105.

(1964) 'Brochs and duns'. *PSAS*, 95 (1961-2), 171-98.

Young, A., & Richardson, K. M. (1955) 'Report on the excavations at Blackbury Castle'. *PDAES*, 5 (1955), 43-67.

Index

The following plates are grouped in subject matter and are not necessarily shown in numerical sequence.

1   Hambledon Hill, Dorset. Platforms for huts and the lines of earlier defences can clearly be seen within the enclosed area (pp. 247, 250)

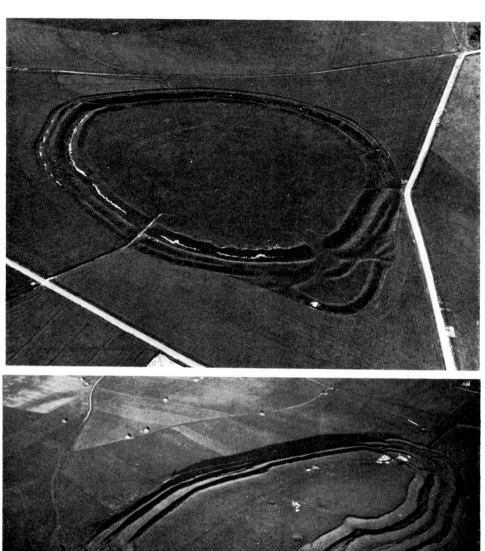

2a (above) Yarnbury, Wilts. The earlier defended enclosure can be seen within the line of the outer defences (pp. 246–7)
2b (below) Maiden Castle, Dorset, showing the complex outworks of the western entrance (pp. 246–7)

3a (above)   The hillfort of Finavon, Angus (p. 237)
3b (below)   A multiple-enclosure fort at Castle an Dinas, St Columb Major,
Cornwall (pp. 186–8)

4   Section across the rampart and ditch of the hillfort at Danebury, Hants (pp. 238–47)

5   The east entrance of the hillfort at Danebury, Hants. The photograph is taken from the position of the latest gate looking outward along the long corridor approach (pp. 238–47)

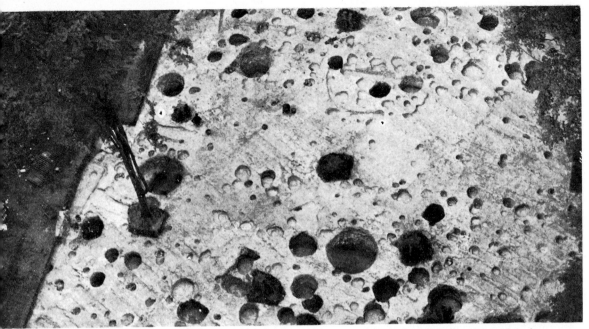

6 Area excavation inside the hillfort of Danebury, Hants, showing streets, the post-holes of timber buildings and storage pits (p. 256)

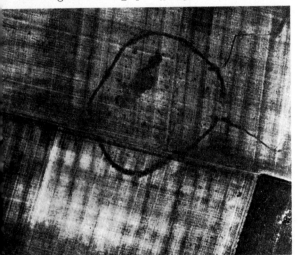

7a Vertical air view of Little Woodbury, Wilts, before excavation (pp. 155–7)

7b The Durotrigian farmstead on Berwick Down, Tollard Royal, Wilts (pp. 160–1)

8 The settlement enclosure and adjacent field system on Farley Mount, Hants (p. 171)

9a Jarlshof, Shetland. The houses of the Bronze and Iron Age settlements (pp. 216–17)

9b Jarlshof, Shetland. The aisled roundhouse and wheelhouse (p. 222)

10a Jarlshof, Shetland. The interior of the wheelhouse (p. 222)

10b The broch of Gurness, Orkney (pp. 219–22)

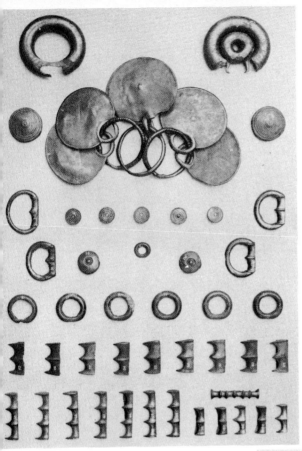

12   Part of the hoard of seventh-century metalwork from Parc-y-Meirch, Denbigh (pp. 133–6) (scale: approx. $\frac{2}{5}$)

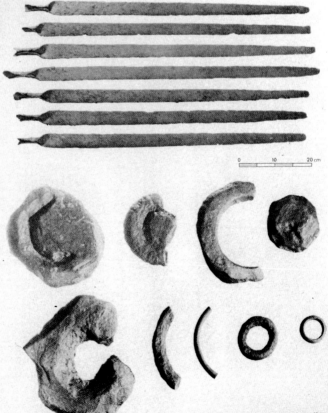

13a   Iron sword-shaped currency bars from a hoard found at Danebury, Hants (p. 172)

13b Stages in the manufacture of a Kimmeridge shale armlet shown by the debris found in the settlement at Eldon's Seat (Encombe), Dorset (pp. 276–7)

11 Bronze cauldron from Llyn Fawr, Glam (pp. 136–8)
(maximum diameter: 52 cm)

14 Bronze dagger sheath from Minster Ditch, Oxford (p. 280) (actual length of sheath: 35 cm)

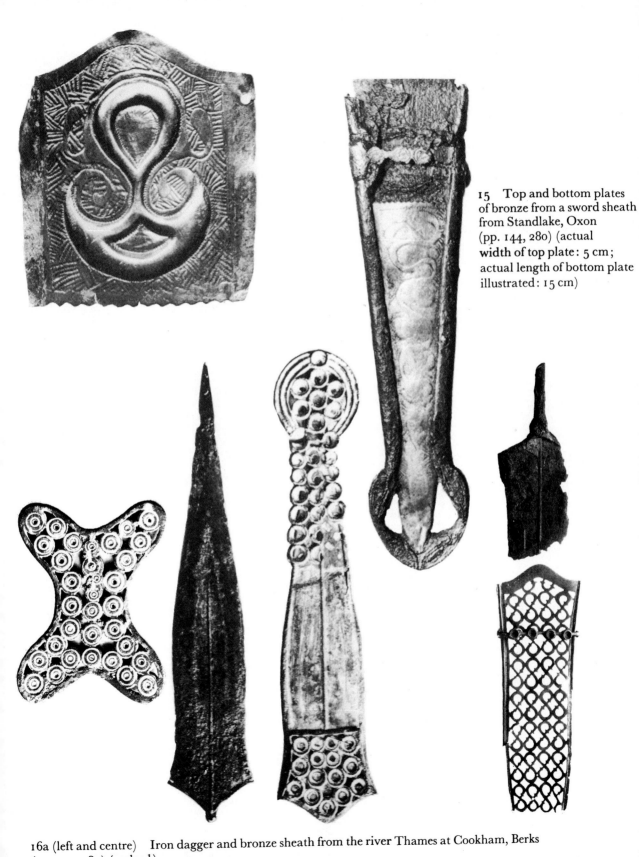

15 Top and bottom plates of bronze from a sword sheath from Standlake, Oxon (pp. 144, 280) (actual **width of top plate: 5 cm;** actual length of bottom plate illustrated: 15 cm)

16a (left and centre) Iron dagger and bronze sheath from the river Thames at Cookham, Berks (pp. 142, 280) (scale: ½)
16b (right) Iron dagger and bronze sheath from the river Thames at Hammersmith (pp. 142, 280) (scale: ³⁄₇)

17a   Iron dagger and
bronze-bound wooden sheath
from the river Thames at
Mortlake, Surrey (pp. 142, 280)
(actual length: 33 cm)

17b   Iron dagger and bronze-bound
wooden sheath from the river Thames at
Mortlake, Surrey (pp. 142, 280) (actual
length of dagger blade: 32 cm)

18   Top of the bronze dagger sheath from Wisbech,
Cambs (p. 280) (actual length: 12·7 cm)

19a Bronze shield
boss from the river
Thames at
Wandsworth (p. 280)
(actual length: 36 cm)

19b Bronze shield from
the river Witham in
Lincolnshire (p. 280)
(actual length: 1·12 m)

20 Detail of incised and repoussé decoration
on a circular bronze shield boss from the river
Thames at Wandsworth (p. 280) (overall
diameter of boss: 32·5 cm)

21 Bronze helmet from the river Thames at Waterloo Bridge
(pp. 282–3) (actual size: 20·5 cm in diameter at base)

22a Bronze fibula of La Tène I type
from Danebury, Hants (p. 144)
(actual length: 4·6 cm)

24   Gold torcs from the Ipswich hoard (pp. 283–4) (various scales but approx. 18·5 cm in maximum diameter)

25a, b   Gold torcs from the Ipswich hoard
(p. 283); c, terminal of a gold torc from
Sedgeford, Norfolk (pp. 283–4)

23   Iron fire-dog from Capel Garmon, Denbigh

22b   Bronze Iberian style figurine
from Aust, Glos (p. 147)
(actual height: 14·6 cm)

26a (right)   Reconstruction of the bronze-bound bucket from Aylesford, Kent (p. 79) (scale: approx. ½)
26b (left)   Reconstruction of the bronze-bound bucket from Great Chesterford, Essex (p. 79)
(scale: approx. ½)

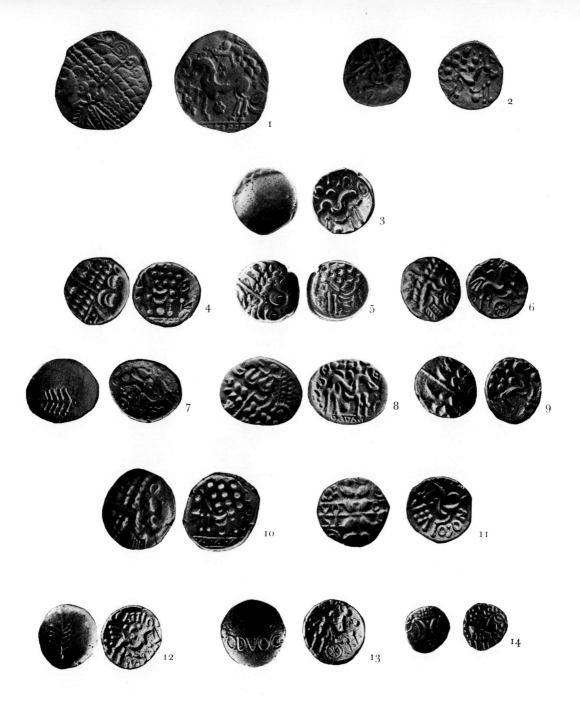

27 Coins: 1 Gallo-Belgic A (gold); 2 Gallo-Belgic C (gold); 3 Gallo-Belgic E (gold);
4 British A (gold); 5 British B (gold); 6 British Q (gold); 7 British R (gold); 8 British H (gold);
9 British I (gold); 10 Durotriges, Class A (silver); 11 Coritani, Volisios Dumnocoveros (gold);
12 Dobunni, Catti (gold); 13 Dobunni, Bodvoc (gold); 14 Iceni, Anted (silver) (all full size)

28 Coins: 1 Commius (gold); 2 Tincommius (gold); 3 Tincommius (gold); 4 Verica (gold); 5 Verica (gold); 6 Tasciovanus, Verulamium mint (gold); 7 Tasciovanus, Camulodunum mint (gold); 8 Cunobelin (gold); 9 Cunobelin (bronze); 10 Epaticcus (gold); 11 Epaticcus (silver); 12 Dubnovellaunus, Essex type (gold); 13 Dubnovellaunus, Kent type (silver) (all full size)